Praise for *Don't Thank Me for*

"This gripping and carefully documented record of the US wars in Indochina, interlaced with vivid and tragic personal experiences, provides a unique and invaluable perspective on some of the most awful crimes of the postwar years."

    NOAM CHOMSKY, Professor Emeritus MIT, Linguist, Public Intellectual and Author of dozens of books on US foreign policy

"S. Brian Willson's new book is a must read. Brian writes like no one I have ever read. Brian speaks like no one I have ever heard. He is a truth-teller on the highest level This book not only reveals the horrors the United States did to the people of Viet Nam, it also covers the insane and barbarous history of US wars all over the world, including the genocide against the Native Americans and the holocaust of the Africans who were stolen against their will and brought to this country to be used as slaves. Read this book and tell others to read it as well."

    CYNTHIA McKINNEY, Former US Congresswoman from Georgia and presidential candidate for the Green Party in 2008

"S. Brian Willson has a way of synthesizing information that gets right to the heart of the matter, deepening our understanding of the culturally embedded myths that perpetuate our nation's violent behavior. By providing the historical context for our involvement in Viet Nam, Willson pulls back a curtain on US imperialism that cannot easily be closed again."

    MARTIN SHEEN

"Our country badly needs more truth telling. Brian Willson tells the truth about the Vietnam War and about the sordid US history of lies, war and empire: and he writes as one who courageously put his body on the line for these truths. A MUST READ for all of us. The alternative is ever more dangerous perpetual wars."

    DANIEL ELLSBERG, Author, *The Pentagon Papers* and *The Doomsday Machine: Confessions of a Nuclear War Planner*

"Few people really understood the terror imposed upon innocent people by the US policies and Vietnam, Cambodia, Laos and Central America. Brian Willson, a lawyer and a scholar did and does. Not only has he given his body for his beliefs but he has penned an extremely important book complete with insights and history that make it imperative reading for every American citizen. I highly recommend it."

    HELEN CALDICOTT

" Unless the truth about a war is told over and over again, lies about that war will take over. There is no more powerful way to keep truth in the picture than through the personal account of someone who was there and who has studied what put him there as a moral responsibility. Brian Willson is driven by the goal of preventing repetition of some of the worst crimes the earth has seen, by preventing their recasting as noble humanitarian efforts. If you know anyone who has been through US schools or seen US movies, get him or her this book as an antidote."

    DAVID SWANSON, Author, *War Is A Lie*

"Brian Willson's book and his continuing opposition to the racist nature of the US war against Viet Nam, Laos and Cambodia was correct when he first spoke out, just as it is these many years later. When congressional members of the time and liberals alike describe the war as "a mistake", they consciously mask the racism, the xenophobia, and the exceptionalism that was then and is now at the root of the self-serving justification for America's wars without end."

    LOUIS WOLF, Co-founder and Research Director of *CovertAction Quarterly*, now *CovertAction Magazine*

"S. Brian Willson's *Don't Thank Me for My Service* is a timely reminder of the US anti-communist hysteria and terrible devastation of the Vietnam War. In an era of repeated wars and imperial projects, Willson's book serves as a lamplight from where we have emerged and the absolute necessity of continued resistance."

    PETER PHILLIPS Ph.D., Professor Political Sociology, Sonoma State University

"Brian Willson is one of my personal heroes, a genuine American "exception" to the rule of racism, militarism, and occupation that has characterized this country's history for too long. His recital of that history is more necessary than ever, as the United States enters yet another year of an endless "war against terror." An entire generation of Americans has now grown up in the shadow of that war; I hope many of them will read this book and borrow a bit of Brian's courage."

    REBECCA GORDON, Author, *Letters From Nicaragua, American Nuremberg,* and *Mainstreaming Torture*

"This new book by Brian Willson, like his others, is a must read for anyone who cares about social justice and human rights. Willson does not mince words, but the truth is absolutely essential if we are to put a stop to the US killing machine."

    ROXANNE DUNBAR-ORTIZ, Author, *An Indigenous Peoples' History of the United States*

"Don't Thank Me for My Service tells the Truth about the US war in Vietnam and American history. Don't Thank Me is of the same genre as Howard Zinn's "Peoples History of the US" and should be read by every American who cares about this country and the future of the world. Future generations will thank Brian for writing this book which helps us learn the Truth about our history and inspires us to find the courage to change our country's way of relating to the rest of the world before it is too late."

    DAVID HARTSOUGH, Author, *Waging Peace: Global Adventures of a Lifelong Activist* and Director of Peaceworkers, San Francisco

"I cannot emphasize enough how important this work is to contribute to the true history of the US Empire that is being scrubbed and sanitized for our "protection." If parents and teachers made sure the young people in the US understood the true nature of the deeply ingrained violence that the US is steeped in, then, perhaps, it could finally end. Brian has long been my "go-to guy" for such truth from a very real and compassionate basis."

    CINDY SHEEHAN, Peace, Social Justice, and Alternative Media Activist

"Brian Willson, a patriot and a hero, helps us to understand the unspeakable truth: Our prime business as a nation is the arms business and war. The so-called defense system is the world's largest employer. We have sown death and destruction world wide at the expense of health care, education and infrastructure. The result is a polity with the world's worst distributive justice.... In the wake of WW II we have killed some 25 million people, mostly noncombatants.... As a military officer, lawyer, scholar and activist Brian Willson has identified a pathetic reality. Sadly, US students have also experienced the horror of military-industrial/NRA governance. Together with Brian Willson and the international peace movement they will replace the military triumphalism in our culture with the abolition of war."

    BLASE BONPANE, Ph.D., Director, Office of the Americas

"...one of the most important books I have ever read. Vietnam Veteran S. Brian Willson tells the horrible truth, not only about the illegal, immoral and genocidal US war in Vietnam, but he also reveals the insane violence and killing that this country has perpetrated on millions of poor people all over the world. Only a very small percentage of people in this country understand what Brian is saying. Hopefully, more people will read this book and come to understand the unbelievable crimes against humanity our country has committed since it was first founded."

    FRANK DORREL, Associate Producer of *Paying the Price for Peace: The Story of S. Brian Willson* and Producer of *What I've Learned About US Foreign Policy*

Don't Thank Me for My Service

My Viet Nam Awakening to the Long History of US Lies

by S. Brian Willson

Clarity Press, Inc.

© S. Brian Willson
ISBN: 978-0-9998747-3-8
EBOOK ISBN: 978-0-9998747-4-5

Editor: Becky Luening
Cover design: R. Jordan Santos
Cover photo: Ellen Shub. Viet Nam veteran John David Borgman burns his US Marine captain's uniform at the Pentagon during anti-nuclear protest, Washington, DC, April 1980.

ALL RIGHTS RESERVED: Except for purposes of review, this book may not be copied or stored in any information retrieval system, in whole or in part, without permission in writing from the publishers.

Library of Congress Cataloguing-in-Publication Data:

Names: Willson, S. Brian, 1941– author.
Title: Don't thank me for my service : my Viet Nam awakening to the long history of US lies / by S. Brian Willson.
Description: Atlanta, GA : Clarity Press, Inc., 2018. | Includes bibliographical references and index.
Identifiers: LCCN 2018016868 (print) | LCCN 2018017763 (ebook) | ISBN 9780999874745 | ISBN 9780999874738
Subjects: LCSH: Vietnam War, 1961-1975--United States. | United States--Military policy--Moral and ethical aspects. | United States--Foreign relations--Moral and ethical aspects. | United States--Politics and government--Moral and ethical aspects. | Political culture--United States--History.
Classification: LCC DS558 (ebook) | LCC DS558 .W54 2018 (print) | DDC 959.704/30973--dc23
LC record available at https://lccn.loc.gov/2018016868

Clarity Press, Inc.
2625 Piedmont Rd. NE
Atlanta, GA 30324
http://www.claritypress.com

*To the children and veterans living at the
Viet Nam Friendship Village in Van Canh, Hanoi:
May they be comforted and healed in some
measure from the egregious impacts of war.*

"If we do not speak of it, others will surely rewrite the script. Each of the body bags, all of the mass graves will be reopened and their contents abracadabraed into a noble cause."
—George Swiers, *Vietnam Reconsidered*

Table of Contents

Don't Thank Me for My Service ix

A Snapshot of Viet Nam "Service" xiii

Chapter One: Historical Context 1

Chapter Two: Cold War Hysteria 29

Chapter Three: Criminal Intent 73

Chapter Four: Chronicle of Barbarism 123

Chapter Five: Chemical Warfare 167

Chapter Six: Upheaval and Resistance at Home 185

Chapter Seven: Upheaval and Resistance among Active Duty Military 259

Chapter Eight: The Lasting Toll of War 291

Chapter Nine: My Story 307

Appendix I: Overt and Covert US Interventions Around the World, by the Numbers 341

Appendix II: Casualties and Destruction in Southeast Asia 344

Acknowledgments 354

About the Author 355

Index 357

The author stands in front of a counter mortar radar unit,
Binh Thuy Air Base, Spring 1969.

Don't Thank Me For My Service

*"Who controls the past controls the future.
Who controls the present controls the past."*
—George Orwell, *1984*

ON MAY 25, 2012, President Barack Obama announced a fiftieth anniversary commemoration of the American war in Viet Nam, to be rolled out over thirteen years with a sixty-five million dollar budget approved by Congress:

> As we observe the fiftieth anniversary of the Vietnam War, we reflect with solemn reverence upon the valor of a generation that served with honor. We pay tribute to the more than three million servicemen and women who left their families to serve bravely, a world away.... They pushed through jungles and rice paddies, heat and monsoon, fighting heroically to protect the ideals we hold dear as Americans. Through more than a decade of combat, over air, land, and sea, these proud Americans upheld the highest traditions of our armed forces.[1]

The "ideals we hold dear as Americans" apparently do not include taking responsibility for our actions. Pentagon staff, overseeing what is popularly referred to as the "Vietnam War Commemoration", readily acknowledge that issues like chemical warfare (Agent Orange), post-traumatic stress disorder, and the antiwar movement that developed in response to the war—both within the military and the society in general—"don't even remotely fall into what we do," because "this agency doesn't deal with those particular issues." What the staff do promise is educational resources for high school students and teachers and "high quality educational content for classroom use based on best practices of pedagogy."[2] Despite this claim, the Pentagon's curriculum as described doesn't appear to offer many opportunities for critical thinking. The commemoration's official website, www.vietnamwar50th.com, stresses an intent "to honor and pay tribute" to those who

---

[1] See https://www.federalregister.gov/articles/2012/06/01/2012-13514/commemoration-of-the-50th-anniversary-of-the-vietnam-war. See also the official web site at http://www.vietnamwar50th.com/;
The White House, For Immediate Release, May 25, 2012: Presidential Proclamation—Commemoration of the 50th Anniversary of the Vietnam War: NOW, THEREFORE, I, BARACK OBAMA President of the United States of America . . . do hereby proclaim May 28, 2012, through November 11, 2025, as the Commemoration of the 50th Anniversary of the Vietnam War. I call upon Federal, State, and local officials to honor our Vietnam veterans, our fallen, our wounded, those unaccounted for, our former prisoners of war, their families, and all who served with appropriate programs, ceremonies, and activities.

[2] Emily Green, "Ghosts of Agent Orange," *Street Roots*, May 9, 2014.

made contributions during the war and to promote commemorative events to honor and thank Viet Nam veterans and their families.

In George Orwell's novel, *1984*,[3] the Ministry of Truth rearranges facts and rewrites history. On the face of the building in which it is housed are engraved these slogans: *War Is Peace; Freedom Is Slavery; Ignorance Is Strength*. Language is one of the most important tools of the totalitarian state. If all citizens accept the lies that the ruling party imposes—if all records tell the same tale—then the lie passes into history and becomes truth. All that is needed is an unending series of victories over our own memory. *Reality control,* this is called: in Orwell's Newspeak, *doublethink* is the official state language. The Ministry of Truth's task is to alter the past to suit the present. In my observation, the DOD's Vietnam War Commemoration aims to do just that. Celebrating the heroics of past war in a contextual vacuum is part of grooming yet another generation of heroes to step up for our nation's future wars.

Rather than conduct an honest evaluation that would uncover the most important lessons from the US intervention in Viet Nam—lessons that in my mind might reasonably teach us to do away with war—the Department of Defense (DOD) has chosen to promote an *ex-post facto* justification of the war that denies consciousness of the terrible destruction and damage done to the Vietnamese people and land. Nor does this official commemoration discuss the war's lasting egregious impact on US American service members and their families—from loss of life and physical disability and illness to the transmission of birth defects to the veterans' progeny. It does not mention the millions of Vietnamese, including women and children, captured and tortured and killed during the war. There is no representation of American soldiers who heroically resisted the American War in Viet Nam nor tribute paid to voices and postwar reconciliation activities of many thoughtful veterans.

The most significant facts and lessons of the US intervention—its utter lawlessness, in committing the Nuremberg crime of unprovoked aggression (considered the ultimate crime against peace); the volume and magnitude of atrocities and war crimes committed on the ground and from the air; the systematic crimes against humanity—will never be mentioned in official commemoration materials. This is unfortunate, because these crimes were paid for by US citizens, and we would do well to understand our complicity in the murder, with impunity, of as many as six million Southeast Asians.

Myths persist: that the antiwar movement somehow prevented a clear-cut US military victory in Viet Nam, and that the antiwar movement dishonored the nation's returning veterans. The truth is that from the very beginning, the US possessed absolutely no legal or moral authority whatsoever to wage war against the Vietnamese and their neighbors; talk of seeking victory under such circumstances does nothing but perpetuate imperial barbarism. In fact, it is the US government, with the assistance of the media, that abused US soldiers, airmen, sailors, and marines by lying about the origins and causes of the conflict, that sent its youth to kill and be killed in a grotesquely illegal war, and that ignored their psychological, physical, and social needs when they first returned home.

---

3 George Orwell, *1984: A Novel* (New York: Harcourt Brace & Co., 1949).

Upon hearing about the DOD's thirteen-year commemoration, members of the national organization Veterans For Peace (VFP) came together to organize a "Viet Nam: Full Disclosure" campaign,[4] an effort to speak what is unspeakable about the American war in Vietnam and to keep alive the antiwar perspective on the war. This VFP truth-telling campaign is a clear alternative to the official Vietnam War Commemoration that seeks to sanitize and mythologize the US conflict in order to legitimize the continuing pattern of imperial and destructive wars.

After my initial anger about Obama's May 2012 proclamation subsided, I realized this fiftieth anniversary "commemoration" provides all Americans with an opportunity to share our true experiential and historical accounts of the war, and that presenting my own perspective could serve as an antidote to the flimsy revisionist history. Thus was I provoked to write this book—my personal contribution to the Viet Nam Full Disclosure campaign initiated by Veterans For Peace—my own attempt to convey a full disclosure of the history, conduct, and damages of the thirty-year war waged by the United States of America against the peoples of Southeast Asia.

* * *

Thousands of books have been written about the US war against Viet Nam expressing various perspectives—some supporting, some opposing, and others attempting neutrality; covering history, combat experiences, war memoirs, and military and political analysis. Drawing from many references, this book is a radical alternative to any official history authored by the US government or traditional academia. It offers detailed chronologies of US history, especially the history of the US war in Viet Nam, interspersed with contextual analysis and personal anecdotes.

In this book, I begin by locating myself in the American War, presenting a brief snapshot of my experience as an Air Force Security Officer in Viet Nam, in 1969.

---

4 Veterans For Peace Vietnam Full Disclosure Campaign has produced a marvelous website: http://vietnamfulldisclosure.org.

From the Veterans For Peace (VFP) website, http://veteransforpeace.org: "Veterans For Peace is a global organization of Military Veterans and allies whose collective efforts are to build a culture of peace by using our experiences and lifting our voices. We inform the public of the true causes of war and the enormous costs of wars, with an obligation to heal the wounds of wars. Our network is comprised of over 140 chapters worldwide whose work includes: educating the public, advocating for a dismantling of the war economy, providing services that assist veterans and victims of war, and most significantly, working to end all wars." VFP Contact: 1404 North Broadway, St Louis, MO 63102; (314) 725-6005; vfp@veteransforpeace.org.

VFP Statement of Purpose: We, having dutifully served our nation, do hereby affirm our greater responsibility to serve the cause of world peace. To this end we will work, with others
- To increase public awareness of the costs of war
- To restrain our government from intervening, overtly and covertly, in the internal affairs of other nations
- To end the arms race and to reduce and eventually eliminate nuclear weapons
- To seek justice for veterans and victims of war
- To abolish war as an instrument of national policy.
- To achieve these goals, members of Veterans For Peace pledge to use non-violent means and to maintain an organization that is both democratic and open with the understanding that all members are trusted to act in the best interests of the group for the larger purpose of world peace.

Chapter One, Historical Context, locates the war in context and explores the origins of the values, themes, and behavior of what we have come to call *US America*.

In Chapter Two, Cold War Hysteria, I describe the heavy influence of Cold War propaganda and the rhetoric of fear that drove US foreign policies in the decades leading up to our involvement in Viet Nam.

Chapter Three, Criminal Intent, tracks early actions taken by the US to prevent the Vietnamese people from achieving genuine autonomy.

Chapter Four, Chronicle of Barbarism, covers the official overt invasion and brutal occupation of Viet Nam, Laos, and Cambodia by the United States Military beginning in 1965, with all of its massacres and unspeakable genocidal behavior, until the peace agreement was signed in 1973.

Chapter Five, Chemical Warfare, covers the US Military's use of chemicals in Southeast Asia, including its liberal application of Agent Orange all over South Viet Nam.

In Chapter Six, Upheaval and Resistance at Home, I gather stories and statistics related to the vigorous anti-war and related people's movements of those times, and draw some connections between those movements.

Chapter Seven, Upheaval and Resistance among Active Duty Military, focuses on the widespread resistance mounted from within the ranks, in every branch of the US Military.

Chapter Eight, The Lasting Toll of War, describes just a few of the war's long-term effects on the Vietnamese people and their environment as well as the US soldiers who came home from the war, and offers examples of its sociopolitical ripple effects.

Finally, in Chapter Nine, My Story, I give a fuller recounting of my own military experiences, especially the five months in Viet Nam that led to a life-changing epiphany and new identity that would radically reshape my future.

At the end of the book I have included two appendices. Appendix I identifies sources for tallying hundreds of US overt, and thousands of covert, interventions since 1798. Appendix II is a summary of human casualties and destruction of infrastructure caused by the US-American war in Southeast Asia.

Extensive footnoting throughout makes it easier for the reader to identify sources, and offers occasional side notes and author commentaries.

A Snapshot of Viet Nam "Service"

"Death is our business and business is good."
—Slogan painted on US helicopter,
Mekong Delta, Viet Nam, 1969

"We have met the enemy and he is us."
—Pogo, in comic strip drawn by Walt Kelly, 1970

Excerpt from the Diary of an Air Force Security Commander

Monday, April 14, 1969. It's a hot and humid mid-morning in the Mekong Delta. I am very nervous as I drive my military jeep from Binh Thuy airbase to the ferry landing at Can Tho City with one passenger, a South Vietnamese Lieutenant named "Bo." Bo is directing me to the site of a supposedly fresh bombing, which I have reluctantly agreed to assess to determine whether it is a success. The traffic is crazy as usual with military and civilian vehicles, and motorcycles and motorbikes zig zagging while magically missing each other. I need to be alert just to stay the course. We wait in the traffic for the next ferry with a line of military and civilian vehicles, Shell and Esso fuel trucks, dump trucks, motorcycles, and dozens and dozens of pedestrians. Though the ferry is rather large, I think about 200 feet long, one often has to wait for a second ferry. Finally we make it onto the ferry. After crossing the one-and-a-half-mile wide, fast-moving Bassac River, the ferry lands at the north riverbank village of Binh Minh in southern Vinh Long Province.

After disembarking, we merge into a line of busy military traffic driving north on Highway 4. Within two or three kilometers, Bo directs me to turn left onto a narrow, one-lane, rough dirt road elevated above rice paddies visible on each side, with people working in them. This is not unusual. All roads in the delta sooner or later run into one of the many hundreds of waterways or canals along which any number of small fishing and farming villages dot the landscape.

Somewhere in this vicinity, apparently, a bombing target that has been hit. The lieutenant is very fluent in English, but we barely talk. I see smoke rising from several locations, a familiar sight that can be indicative of farming or military activities. Helicopters fly overhead—another routine sight. An elderly woman walks by, carrying buckets on each side of a yoke balanced on her neck and supported by her arms. I imagine she is probably so used to war that she simply continues to carry out routine chores. I see other people walking here and there, and young boys, several of whom are walking water buffalo along the way. Nothing unusual, but as I continue driving slowly on the rutted path, my anxiety is rising as a wave of intense fear moves through me. Bo carries an M-16, but he assures

The author poses with his immediate superior, Captain Joel,
Tan Son Nhut Air Base, April 19, 1969.

I had just completed a meeting with our squadron intelligence officers examining 7th Air Force maps and bombing data in efforts to determine whether official reports identified casualties as "VC" enemy, or as civilians of inhabited villages, as my personal observations had revealed. We jointly concluded that "VC" units that were identified as having been annihilated in bombings were in fact inhabited villages where virtually all the residents were murdered from the air from low-flying bombers. Joel asked that a polaroid photo be taken of us. On the back of the photo he inscribed the words, "Pacifist and Warrior." This is the first day of my life's journey as a conscious anti-war human being.

The author stands in front of a portion of his Combat Security Police Section,
Phan Rang Air Base, Viet Nam, June 1969. [Photo: USAF]

xiv

me there is no danger at this time of day. I have only a .38 sidearm stowed under my driver's seat.

As the jeep approaches a tall grassy area on the left side of the road, we find ourselves suddenly close to a couple of columns of dark smoke and I notice a strong, acrid smell. The lieutenant directs me to park. *Shit! What the fuck am I getting into now,* I ask myself? I step out of the jeep and accompany Bo on a short path that leads through the tall grass into a clearing. There I confront a massive scene of utter destruction. Immediately to my right, a water buffalo lies on its right side, bellowing shrilly in pain. I notice it has a piece of skull missing and a huge, three-foot-long gash in its belly and I feel a sudden urge to vomit. When I turn the other way, I see countless human bodies scattered across the ground, some grouped together in bunches amidst the smoke from what appears to be the burning vestiges of small thatched homes. I watch a small girl attempt to get up with the aid of a stick, then fall down, crying in pain. *Jesus Christ, this place really was bombed within the hour. And I'm supposed to assess the success, or not, of this bombing? Fuck! It's been totally destroyed*

For a moment, I stagger around aimlessly, in shock. I place a handkerchief over my mouth and nose to block out the awful smells—a combination of acrid burning flesh and chemicals: lingering air droplets of napalm, and what I surmise is the residue of exploded bombs. I gag and cough up a bit of bile. Then I find I can walk no further because there are bodies lying at my feet. I look down at the open eyes of what appears to be a young woman. She is clutching three very young, blackened and bloodied children, probably hers. Looking closer, I realize she has no eyelids and that they were probably burned off by napalm. I find myself captivated, intoxicated almost, by her open eyes. *Is she alive? Her face is partially melted. Oh, my God! Oh my God! Jesus Christ! I want to lift her into my arms. It's like she's my sister or something.*[5] I am shaking, overwhelmed with tears as I gag out more vomit. I knew in an instant that we are all connected, a truth that had up to then eluded me in my well-conditioned, protected Western mind.

Another thought comes to me, clear as a lightning bolt: *This war is a fucking, evil lie! Shit! Fuck! My family is lying all around me!*

I don't know what I am doing, or what to do. I am nearly numb, fueled by adrenaline but moving as if on automatic pilot. I gather sufficient composure to stand upright and try to assess the magnitude of the scene. I roughly estimate over a hundred bodies, perhaps as many as one hundred fifty, lying in an area the size of a small baseball field. I recognize the bodies as mostly young women and small children and a few elderly. These villagers were struck quickly with little chance to flee, hit first I believe with 500- or 750-pound bombs followed by napalm bombs as evidenced by their charred skin. At least half the bodies are motionless and silent, apparently already dead. The others are just barely alive; some are moaning. They will probably die soon if not provided emergency medical attention.

I see no weapons. These are farmers and fishing villagers. Besides their simple tools, I believe they are unarmed and undefended. These villagers were completely vulnerable

---

5 I think of this woman so often, looking into her eyes, I have given her a name, "Mai Ly," a rearrangement of the letters from "My Lai," made famous by the US Army massacre in March 1968.

to the A-37s that dropped the bombs. South Vietnamese pilots flying at less than 300 feet could easily see their human targets—a turkey shoot. *So many bodies ripped apart by shrapnel and charred by napalm. And, so, so many small children! Jesus, fucking Christ!*

I burst out crying and begin gagging again. My body is still trembling when Bo, the lieutenant walking on my right, startles me with a question, "What is your problem?" He is obviously pleased with the "success" of the bombing, and I can only guess how he can justify killing dozens of small children, young mothers, and grandparents—more dead Communists? *Communists?! Jesus Christ, the war is one massive, fucking lie. I can't believe I am part of it.*

I wipe the snot from my nose but miss the saliva that slips out of my mouth as I instinctively respond to his question: "I just witnessed the death of my family." As soon as I speak these words, I think, *Where did that come from?* But it rings true. At that moment I feel more related to these dead Vietnamese villagers than to anyone involved in the military establishment I am part of. *I pulled no triggers. I dropped no bombs. But I am part of a massive murder machine. I just can't fucking believe it!*

Suddenly, the Vietnamese lieutenant says we must leave before more time elapses. It's just a few minutes after high noon. Although some of the bombing victims are still alive, we simply ignore them. My cheeks feel extra hot, my face is flushed with tears, and my body continues to tremble as I climb back into the jeep with Bo and begin the drive back down the narrow dirt lane to Highway 4. I feel sick to my stomach. After a kilometer or so, I pull over because my hands shake so much I have a hard time steering. I tell Bo I don't think I can drive, but he seems not at all sympathetic and directs me to continue. After a series of deep breaths I continue driving. I turn onto Highway 4, and head south in slow moving traffic of military and agricultural trucks. Bo and I arrive at Binh Minh and wait for the next ferry in a kind of nervous silence. I am distraught. There is so much traffic we have to wait for a second ferry. Psychically, we are in two very different worlds. Finally we fit on the next ferry, soon landing in Can Tho. As I drive the five miles to Binh Thuy, I again face the need to attentively veer in and out of busy traffic that seems ruleless. But once more I pull over because I am shaking terribly, and my hands have difficulty controlling the steering wheel. Bo is very upset, but I am experiencing some kind of trauma shock. After a series of deep breaths, I am able to resume driving, slowly.

There has been virtually no conversation between us on the drive back to Binh Thuy, but as we pass the US Army's 29th Evacuation Hospital just east of the base, I burst out in tears. "Shouldn't we stop and seek emergency medical assistance to aid those still alive in that village"? Bo vigorously shakes his head. "No, we need to get back." He is adamant. I argue emotionally that we should stop. But I feel weak, both mentally and physically, and I do not stop the jeep. Soon we are on Binh Thuy airbase where in a few hours I will be back on duty as the lieutenant night security commander. *Oh, my god! Jesus, help me! Fuck!* Suicide begins to come to my mind. I take a nap.[6]

—S. Brian Willson, 6/10/15

---

[6] The particular day in Viet Nam described above is extracted from Chapter Nine, "My Story," pp. 323–326.

Chapter One
Historical Context

"Nobody talks about them. . . .
It never happened. Nothing ever happened.
Even while it was happening it wasn't happening.
It didn't matter. It was of no interest."
—Harold Pinter, Nobel Prize–winning British Playwright

Introduction

In my study of US American history, I uncovered a unifying theme: Prosperity for a few (generally White Eurocentric males), through expansion at any cost, to preserve the "exceptional" American Way of Life (AWOL). This end has been structurally guided and facilitated by our nation's founding documents, including the US Constitution. In effect, the US was founded as a White male supremacy state, and the course set at the beginning has never been reversed, though in the 1960s multiple aligned social movements came very close to accomplishing a radical social revolution.

A quick review of the empirical record reveals at least 560 overt military interventions by the US into dozens of countries since 1798, a staggering 390 since the end of World War II, and thousands of covert interventions since 1947 (Appendix I). This reality overwhelms any rhetoric about the United States being committed to equal justice under law, or being a beacon of freedom and democracy for the rest of the world.

These interventions have assured *de facto* subsidies for American "interests," i.e., money/profits from global markets regulated on our terms, cheap or free labor, and access to raw materials. Millions of people around the globe have been murdered with total impunity as a result of our interventions; the pattern illustrates what Noam Chomsky calls the "Fifth Freedom"—the freedom to rob and exploit. This freedom is fiercely protected with use of force and violence when a country or movement chooses to protect the domestic needs of its own members and citizens aspiring for democratization, better living standards, and expansion of human rights and opportunities.[1] Such Indigenous and sovereign goals are perceived as threatening to the US's easy access to the human and material resources required to assure continuation of the insatiably consumptive AWOL.

The people of Viet Nam possessed a most natural and understandable desire for autonomy and independence from Western control. But Vietnamese sovereignty was a serious threat to US plans for global hegemony on its selfish terms, i.e., obedience to corporate,

---

[1] Noam Chomsky, *Turning the Tide: US Intervention in Central America and the Struggle for Peace* (Boston: South End Press, 1985), 43–50.

exploitive capitalism. A Vietnamese victory had the potential to empower the other eighty percent of the world's peoples yearning for liberation after five hundred years of brutal impoverishment by the Eurocentric twenty percent. Therefore, in the geostrategic Western psyche, independence for Viet Nam was seen as a deadly virus that had to be stopped at any cost.

The US-waged war in Viet Nam was not an aberration, as I initially hoped. In fact it is but one of hundreds of examples in a long pattern of brutal exploitation of other peoples and their resources in order to fuel the American Way of Life.

The Presence of the Past

History repeats itself when we refuse to embrace its troubling lessons, its demonstrative patterns. If the history is ugly, it only gets uglier with each repetition. Sages of history have articulated this pattern:

> *"The past never leaves us and the future is already here."*
> —Lewis Mumford, *The Myth of the Machine*

> *"Wherever Western man went, slavery, land robbery, lawlessness, culture-wrecking, and the outright extermination of both wild beasts and tame men went with him."*
> —Lewis Mumford, *The Myth of the Machine*

> *"The West has ravaged the world for five hundred years, under the flag of master-slave theory which in our finest hour of hypocrisy was called 'the white man's burden'... What sets the West apart is its persistence to stop at nothing."*
> —Hans Koning, *Columbus*

> *"Those who do not remember the past are condemned to repeat it."*
> —George Santayana, *The Life of Reason*

Rupert Sheldrake, a controversial parapsychologist, biochemist, and visionary, describes an interesting theory similar to psychologist Carl Jung's collective unconsciousness,[2] or concept of a group mind, a kind of inherited collective memory. Sheldrake suggests a process by which the past becomes present through what he calls "morphic fields." A morphic unit is any form or organization such as an atom, cell, social group, pattern of behavior, or even a galaxy. These units possess fields that organize around characteristic structure and activity patterns. The fields are in turn shaped and stabilized by "morphic resonance," which incorporates causal influences from previous structures of activity, then transmits them through both space and time. The memory within the morphic fields is cumulative and thus the past is always present.[3]

---

2 Carl G. Jung, *Man and His Symbols* (New York: Anchor Press, 1964), 107.
3 Rupert Sheldrake, *The Presence of the Past* (New York: Vintage Books, 1989), 371.

Carl Jung discussed defensive societal mechanisms of "projecting one's shadow"[4] onto others to avoid acknowledging disturbing qualities within oneself. He described a "psychology of war" in which "everything which our own nation does is good, everything which the other nations do is wicked. The center of all that is mean and vile is always to be found several miles behind the enemy's lines."[5] Thus, the collective shadow of US imperialism blinds us from "seeing" our own chronic pattern of arrogant, aggressive global behavior. And so it is repeated over and over, preserved by our phony sense of "exceptionalism." Any willingness to honestly critique harms done by that behavior is blocked at every turn.

Understanding historical events and the patterns that emerge from them is terribly important as a precondition for building a better today and tomorrow. Otherwise, we live at the mercy of previously embedded, dysfunctional behaviors.

A Note about Impunity

As noted above, cultural historians, philosophers, psychologists, essayists, and scientists caution us to seriously understand the past and its patterns. Sigmund Freud declared that in psychic life, nothing of what has been formed in the past ever disappears. Everything that has occurred is preserved in one way or another and, in fact, reappears under either favorable or unfavorable circumstances. When impunity dominates history, justice as a permanent value in the history of humans ceases to exist. This psychopathology produces a sickness in the soul—of the individual, as well as of a nation—where nothing is real. Everything becomes pretend, the lies told over and over in many different forms throughout time.[6]

Impunity produces severe disturbances within the individual and collective psyche, manifesting in behavioral psychopathologies of huge magnitude, such as wars. Think of a spoiled child who has never been taught boundaries or been held to account for harmful behavior. Collective as well as individual narcissism can lead to extreme antisocial conduct. Security is experienced through individuality, and rigid adherence to individual and national economic privatization, but not social justice. Identity is achieved partly through possessions. The *acquisitive* habit settles into the inner life, preempting an authentic *inquisitive* and social mind. A social compact is destroyed in deference to privatization, creating anomie. Life is commodified. Disparity between the Haves and Have-Nots becomes extreme; today the process by which this is accomplished is called *neoliberal economics*. History is negated, successfully concealing past traumas such as unspeakable genocides and deceitfully based wars.[7]

---

4 Jung, 93.

5 June Singer, *Boundaries of the Soul: The Practice of Jung's Psychology* (New York: Anchor Books, 1994), 176–177, citing Jung's 1928 studies.

6 S. Brian Willson, "The Pretend Society," http://www.brianwillson.com/the-pretend-society/.

7 B. Paz Rojas, "Impunity and the Inner History of Life," *Social Justice: A Journal of Crime, Conflict and World Order*, 26(4), 1999.

How many US citizens know of the crimes our country systematically commits throughout the world, crimes that are constant, remorseless, and fully documented? British playwright and Nobel Prize recipient Harold Pinter sadly commented: "Nobody talks about them. . . . It never happened. Nothing ever happened. Even while it was happening it wasn't happening. It didn't matter. It was of no interest."[8] Without historical context, there is little capacity to critique the veracity of contemporary policies and rhetoric. So, it is believed, the US just couldn't be involved in patterns of criminal interventions; our origins just couldn't be built on dispossession and genocide. "That is not the American way." But the fact is that it *is* the American way. We simply don't know about it and don't want to know about it. Impunity has erased memory.

Now let us look at the historical, religious, and intellectual origins of the United States.

The Doctrine of Christian Discovery: Conquest Rationalized

In 1095, over nine hundred years ago, Pope Urban II launched the Crusades with issuance of an edict, *Papal Bull Terra Nullius* (empty land, or land belonging to no one), to restore Christian access to holy places in and near Jerusalem that were at that time occupied by Muslims. The edict was later used in international law to describe territory that has never been subject to the sovereignty of any "state." Sovereignty over such territory, that is *terra nullius*, could be acquired through invasion and/or occupation, "legitimizing" the claim by European monarchs of a right to land "discovered" in *non*-Christian areas.[9]

By the time the Italian explorer Cristoforo Columbo set sail in 1492 under the Spanish flag, seeking westward trade routes to the East Indies for purposes of colonization, the Doctrine of Christian Discovery was well established. Upon "discovering" land, though it turned out to be the West Indies (Hispaniola), rather than the East Indies, Columbus celebrated and took possession of the "new" territory. Upon encountering human beings, he wrote in his log that "they do not bear arms," in fact "are totally unskilled in arms" as they "willingly traded everything they owned." Further, he noted that they "would make fine servants" and "could easily be made Christians. . . . With fifty men we could subjugate them all and make them do whatever we want."[10]

Thus, extraordinarily gruesome Eurocentric values were introduced into the New World. Bartolomé de Las Casas, a Spanish priest who arrived in Hispaniola in 1502 and became known as the "Apostle of the Indians," was shocked to witness the unspeakable punishments being inflicted on the peaceful Indigenous inhabitants. He spelled out the Spaniards' behavior: vicious search for wealth with "dreadful . . . unlimited close-fisted avarice" and their commitment of "such inhumanities and barbarisms . . . as no age can parallel" in "a continuous recreational slaughter . . . cruelty never before seen, nor heard

---

8 Harold Pinter, *Various Voices: Prose, Poetry, Politics, 1948–1998* (New York: Grove Press, 1998, 237.

9 Wikipedia, "Terra Nullius": http://en.wikipedia.org/wiki/Terra_nullius; Grace Li Xiu Woo, "Decolonization and Canada's 'Idle No More' Movement," *Arctic Review on Law and Politics*, Vol. 4, No. 2, 2013, 181–206: http://site.uit.no/arcticreview/files/2014/10/Decolonization-and-Canadas-Idle-No-More-Movement.pdf.

10 Hans Koning, *Columbus: His Enterprise . . . Exploding the Myth* (New York: Monthly Review Press, 1991), 51–53.

of, nor read of." He identified routine murder, rape, theft, kidnapping, vandalism, child molestation, acts of cruelty, torture, humiliation, dismemberment, and beheading.[11] The Indigenous, he said, possessed no vocabulary to even describe such bestiality.

By 1542, fifty years after Columbus's arrival, the original Indigenous population of the Taino (Arawak), estimated at 8 million, had been decimated to a mere 200. Causes of death for these millions included mutilations (e.g., arms cut off) for not producing (virtually nonexistent) gold quotas, being hunted down and eaten by dogs, being shot with muskets, gouged by swords, hanged or burned to death, as well as European-borne diseases. Within another decade or two, the Taino were genetically extinct.[12] This genocide foretold an ominous future for the world.

Our Forbears

The European settlers who invaded the New World—traders, soldiers, farmers, and townspeople—introduced a "modern," radically different structural basis of society organized to pursue economic relations geared to laws of the commercial market, including codification of law protecting private title to land demarcated with fences and boundaries. This was in dramatic contrast to the traditional Indigenous societies which were guided by social relationships and adhered to laws of nature within ancestral hunting grounds. Concepts of "ownership" and private property simply did not exist.[13] European agricultural practices geared for large commercial production and export forced more sustainable native subsistence economies to either assimilate or be eliminated altogether.[14]

The first English settlers, whether identified as Pilgrims or Puritans, used a variety of different words in replicating the concept of *Terra Nullius* in the "New World," including "unpeopled," used by Plymouth Pilgrim leader William Bradford,[15] "empty land," used by Mayflower organizer and separatist Robert Cushman,[16] and "vacant land," used by Pilgrim soldier Myles Standish.[17] "Unused" was a common settler term,[18] as was "waste land";[19] "uninhabited" was the description used by the English Parliament;[20] "empty dwellings"

---

11 Bartolomé de las Casas, *A Short Account of the Destruction of the Indies*, 1552, as cited in Barry Lopez, *The Rediscovery of North America* (Lexington, KY: The University Press of Kentucky, 1990), 1–9.

12 Kirkpatrick Sale, *The Conquest of Paradise: Christopher Columbus and the Columbian Legacy* (New York: Alfred A. Knopf, 1990), 155–161.

13 Tim Ingold, ed., *Companion Encyclopedia of Anthropology* (London, UK: Routledge, 2002), 947.

14 Arlene Hirschfelder and Martha Kreipe de Montano, *The Native American Almanac: A Portrait of Native America Today* (New York: Prentice Hall, 1993), 1.

15 Richard Drinnon, *Facing West: The Metaphysics of Indian-Hating and Empire Building* (Minneapolis: University of Minnesota Press, 1980), 49.

16 John Frederick Martin, *Profits in the Wilderness: Entrepreneurship and the Founding of New England Towns in the Seventeenth Century* (Chapel Hill: North Carolina Press, 1981), 117.

17 Ward Churchill, *A Little Matter of Genocide: Holocaust and Denial in the Americas 1492 to the Present* (San Francisco: City Light Books, 1997), 170.

18 William Cronon, *Changes in the Land: Indians, Colonists, and the Ecology of New England*, Revised (New York: Hill and Wang, 2003) 24–53.

19 William Strachey, *History and Travel into Virginia Britannia* (London: Printed for Hakluyt Society, 1849.

20 Stuart Banner, *How the Indians Lost Their Land: Law and Power on the Frontier* (Cambridge: Harvard University Press, 2005), 116.

occupied by "brutes" was the description by the soon-to-be governor of the Massachusetts Bay Colony, Puritan John Winthrop;[21] and another was "empty wilderness."[22]

The first permanent settlements, established by English invaders in Jamestown, Virginia in 1607, and subsequently in Plymouth, Massachusetts in 1620, did not seek to do business or trade with "savages." The settlers were *employees* sponsored by private, for-profit commercial corporate enterprises funded by English venture capitalists, i.e., investors who sought to establish a foothold in the exploitive colonies of the New World. Two interrelated stockholding companies of merchants—from London and Plymouth, England, respectively—were granted land rights by the Crown, which had claimed much of the New World's Atlantic seaboard. Often nothing more than indentured servants, these settler-employees were expected to maximize New World "opportunities" by doing the grunt work of planting and harvesting crops, then sending the products back to England to satisfy stockholder/investor needs for quick profits.[23]

The Massachusetts Bay Colony, a commercial stock company owned by the London merchants, sought to create a Bible Commonwealth under its first governor, lawyer John Winthrop. Interested in the redemption or "purification" of the world, the Puritans believed they were "God's chosen people." Their firmly held convictions claim divine underpinnings of US American Exceptionalism: "*[W]e shall find that the God of Israel is among us. . . . For we must consider that we shall be as a city upon a hill. The eyes of all people are upon us. . . .*"[24]

Legal Origins of the USA

EXPANSION OF PRIVATE PROPERTY, NOT HUMAN LIBERTY

It is instructive to examine the Eurocentric values that underlie the US Constitution, as it is these values that have shaped the structural direction of our culture. The Constitution itself, despite the added Bill of Rights, is primarily designed to protect *private* property and *commercial* enterprises (commodities) at the expense of human liberty and the Commons—the interrelationship of people, plants, and animals with their landscapes of water bodies and coasts, estuaries, forests, hills, grasses and soils, terrains and atmosphere, that belong to all. Even the Fifth and Fourteenth Amendments include language assuring protection of property: In the Fifth, "no person shall be . . . denied life, liberty, or property, without due process of law"; in the Fourteenth, "nor shall any state deprive any person of life, liberty, or property, without due process of law."

In 1938, US Supreme Court Justice Hugo Black stated: "Of the cases in this court in which the Fourteenth Amendment was applied during its first fifty years after its adoption, less than one half of one percent invoked it in protection of the Negro race, and more than

---

21 *Winthrop Papers*, 1629, 2:140–141.

22 Cronon, 51–57.

23 Richard B. Morris and Jeffrey B. Morris, eds., *Encyclopedia of American History*, Bicentennial Edition. New York: Harper & Row, 1976), 31; Charles C. Mann, "America, Found & Lost," *National Geographic* (May 2007), 52.

24 Page Smith, *A New Age Now Begins*, Vol. I (New York: McGraw-Hill Book Co., 1976), 19–20.

fifty percent asked that its benefits be extended to corporations."[25] This is not surprising. The US society is built on material prosperity (commodities) derived from a number of subsidies:

- *free land* (nature considered as property) forcefully stolen from the Indigenous peoples who had inhabited these lands for millennia, insidiously enabling profitable and extensive Eurocentric settlements;
- *free chattel* (humans considered as property) to perform grueling labor, Africans forcefully stolen from millennia-old tribal communities, in addition to enslaved indigenous and indentured European servants, insidiously enabling profitable Eurocentric agriculture; and
- *cheap and stolen ("free") raw materials* (nature considered as property) derived from a long, entrenched pattern of brutal global imperialism, especially in the twentieth century. Each of the three subsidies has resulted in millions of human beings being killed with impunity.

The United States as a culture is like a spoiled child who has never been held to account for egregious crimes (i.e. genocides) committed as an adolescent, and inevitably developed increasingly disturbing, psychopathic behavior as an adult. Genocide is a form of economic "externality," providing lucrative benefits to the criminals in charge while detrimentally affecting others, who obviously did not choose to incur that cost.

This pattern of forcefully stealing the fundamental ingredients of community—land, labor, and material resources—while killing millions with impunity, understandably has shaped our national attitudes, values, and behavior, favoring a commodity society while preempting one based on universal principles that cherish nature and symbiotic social relationships. Evident in our early European ancestors, these materialist values later manifested in the politics of the so-called enlightened "Founding Fathers" and the Constitution they authored, and continue to guide us today.

Cultural analysts such as Lewis Mumford have described how unchecked "power punctuates the entire history of mankind with outbursts of collective paranoia and tribal delusions of grandeur mingled with malevolent suspicions, murderous hatreds, and atrociously inhumane acts."[26] Mumford again:

> A personal over-concentration of power as an end in itself is suspect to the psychologist as an attempt to conceal inferiority, impotence, and anxiety. When this inferiority is combined with defensive inordinate ambitions, uncontrolled hostility and suspicion, and a loss of any sense of the subject's own limitation, "delusions of grandeur" result, which is the typical syndrome of paranoia, one of the most difficult psychological states to exorcise.[27]

---

25 Thom Hartmann, *Unequal Protection: The Rise of Corporate Dominance and the Theft of Human Rights* (Emmaus, PA: Rodale, 2002), 157.

26 Lewis Mumford, *The Myth of the Machine: Technics and Human Development* (1966; New York: Harcourt, Brace & World, Inc., 1967), 204.

27 Mumford, 1967, 218.

This diagnosis fits the United States to a "T."

Essentially, it is property—in the form of stolen land, slave labor, and raw materials—that serves as the foundation for our national identity, along with the attendant desire for material prosperity that we hold so dear. This is illustrated in an examination of the participants at the founding Constitutional Convention in Philadelphia, May 25 to September 17, 1787, and the final document they authored. A convention held entirely in enforced secrecy during its 116-day duration, it is noteworthy that many of the fifty-five participating White men, including most of our propertied Founding Fathers, such as George Washington, Benjamin Franklin, Patrick Henry, and Thomas Jefferson, were early speculators/investors in hundreds of thousands of acres of land in association with at least ten major land companies. They expected to profit from their many private land holdings, much of it acquired from the Indians, in illegal defiance of the Proclamation of 1763 which had strictly prohibited colonial expansion and settlements west of a line parallel to the Appalachian Mountains, beyond which lands were to be reserved for Indians only.[28] From 1763 to the Revolution, settlers and investors in land were increasingly at odds with the British Crown, which seemed more interested in maintaining peace with the Indians than serving the expansionist desires of the European colonists.[29]

More than half of the selected delegates to the Convention were educated lawyers. The remaining were planters, merchants, physicians, and college professors. Not one member represented, in his immediate personal economic interests, the small farming or mechanic classes.[30] Most believed their property rights were adversely affected by the relatively "weak" Articles of Confederation government and thus were highly economically motivated to reconstruct the system.[31]

Less than halfway through the secret Constitutional deliberations, on July 13, 1787, the existing Continental Congress II of the Confederation (Congress I, 1775–1781; Congress II, 1781–1789) adopted its greatest achievement: The Northwest Ordinance. This ordinance more honestly revealed the objective of the European invaders, even before creation of a new government, to expand their control over additional territory, enabling extension of "civilization" into the "uncivilized frontier" north of the Ohio River that had been occupied "safely" by the Indigenous as their ancestral lands. Ignoring all Indigenous rights, in 1788 alone, 18,000 settlers immediately moved into this expanded Ohio territory, a region that would eventually become the states of Ohio, Indiana, Illinois, Michigan, Wisconsin, and Minnesota.[32]

James Madison, the principal architect of the Constitution, argued during Convention debates that "landowners ought to have a share in the government . . . so constituted

---

28 Anthony F. C. Wallace, *Jefferson and the Indians: The Tragic Fate of the First Americans* (Cambridge, MA: Harvard University Press, 1999), 36–49.

29 Wallace, 40.

30 Charles Beard, *An Economic Interpretation of the Constitution of the United States* (New York: The MacMillan Company, 1913, 1943), 149–151.

31 Beard, 1913, 73.

32 Hirschfelder and de Montano, 9; Wallace, 161–166; Morris and Morris, 139.

as to protect the minority of the opulent against the majority."[33] The final document articulated a strong national government, assuring that westward expansion by White Europeans would be protected from Indian resistance by a national army. "Opening" of western lands for "development" would dramatically enhance their value, financially benefitting land speculators including many of the delegates. Under protection of the new Constitution, throughout the 1790s, the majority of landless men in Virginia had already safely moved west of the Appalachians, and by 1820, the trans-Appalachian population had grown from about 350,000 to more than two million.[34]

Only 39 men, or 70 percent, of the Convention's original 55 attendees, signed the document, and many of those were slaveholders. In the end, it was adopted by just 13 states by a vote of fewer than 2,000 carefully selected male delegates.[35]

Founding Father John Jay held a vision that "the people who own the country ought to govern it."[36] This referred, of course, to those who owned land, slaves, and commercial enterprises. Jay believed that the upper classes "were the better kind of people," those "who are orderly and industrious, who are content with their situation and not uneasy in their circumstances."[37] Jay himself was from a family of wealthy merchants and government officials in New York City, and served as a member of the First and Second Continental Congresses, including a term as president. He was chief justice of the first Supreme Court from 1789 to 1795.

Certainly, it is true that the Founders possessed what they regarded as noble visions. Thomas Jefferson's vision was the creation of an "empire for liberty."[38] Jefferson believed that territorial expansion without war could actually be accomplished through economic and peaceable means of coercion. He believed that expanding control over lands and seas was important for liberating commerce to achieve prosperity for the new country even if it required going beyond the authority of the new Constitution.[39] President Jefferson's purchase of the Louisiana Territory from France in 1803 was certainly accomplished without Constitutional authority.

US historian William Appleman Williams aptly described US America in the title of his book, *Empire as a Way of Life*.[40] Like Jefferson's "empire for liberty," James Madison's

---

33 *Notes of the Secret Debates of the Federal Convention of 1787*, Taken by the Late Hon Robert Yates, Chief Justice of the State of New York, & One of the Delegates from That State to the Said Convention (Yale Law School, Lillian Goldman Library, The Avalon Project: Documents in Law, History and Diplomacy, accessed Oct 28, 2012).

34 Robert A. Dahl, *How Democratic is the American Constitution* (New Haven: Yale University Press, 2001), 25.

35 Dahl, 2.

36 Jerry Fresia, *Toward an American Revolution: Exposing the Constitution and other Illusions* (Boston: South End Press, 1988), 32.

37 Fresia, 32.

38 Williams, 1980, 59.

39 Robert W. Tucker and David C. Hendrickson, *Empire of Liberty: The Statecraft of Thomas Jefferson* (New York: Oxford University Press, 1990), ix, 25–32, 157–171.

40 Williams, 1980.

vision was imperial expansion, what he called "imperial republicanism."[41] The engine of the new nation was to be an increasingly expansive mercantile system, an idea at odds with any desire for democracy.[42] In fact, concern for preserving property rights (wealth) and fear of popular sentiment (democracy) was a large influence in the final content of the Constitution.

George Washington, in his second presidential term, declared that emergence of "democratic societies" severely threatened the peace of the new republic. Shocked over the emerging dissent over his tax policy, he proclaimed that democratic societies were nothing but "self-created bodies, forming themselves into permanent censors" operating "under the shade of night" who expressed "absurd" and "arrogant" attacks on the acts of Congress whose members, as representatives of the people, have "undergone the most deliberate and solemn discussion by the representatives of the people, chosen for the express purpose and bringing with them from the different parts of the Union the sense of their constituents, . . . to form *their will* into laws for the government of the whole"[43] [italics in original]. Thus, as a political-economic document, the Constitution reveals a genuine fear and distrust of the political tendencies of common people, i.e., "factions," or what Madison described in *Federalist Paper #10* (November 22, 1787) as the dangers of an "unjust and interested majority," i.e., the large number of unpropertied citizens.

Thus our Founding Fathers reflected an extraordinary anti-majoritarian, explicitly anti-democratic bias.[44] This explains the Constitutional theme of preserving private property and commercial enterprises, controlled by a small minority, ultimately at the expense of human freedom and the health of the Commons.[45]

It is important to recognize that the Constitution was never submitted to the public for ratification. Since no direct popular vote was even attempted, it is impossible to know what the popular sentiment was. A considerable proportion of the adult white male population was prohibited from participating in the election of the delegates to the separate ratifying state conventions due to property qualifications for voting. Historian Charles A. Beard conjectures that of the estimated 160,000 who voted in the election of delegates for the various state conventions, not more than 100,000 favored adoption of the Constitution.[46] And of course, women, enslaved Africans, the original Indigenous inhabitants, un-propertied white adult males, and white males under 21 had no vote at all. The 1790 Census counted a total United States population of 3.93 million persons: 3.2 million free and nearly 700,000 African slaves. But of the 3.2 million "free" persons, the vast majority were prohibited from voting. So, in effect, the approximately 100,000 propertied white males who favored adoption comprised but two-and-a-half percent of the population.

---

41 Williams, 1980, 20, 60.
42 Williams, 1980, 20.
43 Charles Beard, *Economic Origins of Jeffersonian Democracy* (New York: The MacMillan Company, 1915, 1943), 258–260.
44 Fresia, 78; Dahl, 29, 33.
45 Fresia, 25–95.
46 Beard, 1913, 250.

So it cannot be said that the Constitution was "an expression of the clear and deliberate will of the whole people" nor of a majority of the adult males, nor at the outside, of one-fifth of them, nor, indeed, of white people.[47] In essence, debtors, the poor and uninfluential, the overwhelming majority of all human beings living in the 13 states of the Union at the time were either opposed to the Constitution or were not allowed to register a formal, legal opinion.

No less than 85 articles and essays, a collection of documents known as the *Federalist Papers*, were written in 1787–1788 to urge ratification of the newly drafted US Constitution. The authors were Alexander Hamilton, James Madison, and John Jay. Aristocratic Hamilton possessed such contempt for commoners he declared that "the people are a 'great beast' that must be tamed... rebellious and independent farmers had to be taught, sometimes by force, that the ideals of the revolutionary pamphlets were not to be taken too seriously."[48]

Madison's *Federalist #10* stressed an equally low opinion of popular sentiment: "The influence of factious leaders may kindle a flame within their particular States, but will be unable to spread a general conflagration through the other States. . . . A rage for paper money, for an abolition of debts, for an equal division of property, or for any other improper or wicked project, will be less apt to pervade the whole body of the Union than a particular member of it. . . . The most common and durable source of factions has been the various and unequal distribution of property."

As noble as the effort to create a Bill of Rights for the people and the decades-long expansion of the voting franchise were, the power of private property in the structure of corporations has led to severe erosion of the principles of social and personal justice and preservation of the Commons. The granting of Constitutional rights to corporations as "persons" as a matter of law, an extraordinarily absurd principle, has fundamentally preempted rights of citizen-persons, rights already tenuous due to the historical patterns of oligarchy, i.e. concentration of power in the hands of a wealthy minority of propertied people.

In the 1700s, corporations were limited to operating with *municipal* charters of limited duration for the purpose of carrying out prescribed *public* functions. In the 1800s, however, the corporation morphed into a non-expiring entity that performs *business* functions organized to pursue *private* ends for *individual* gain. As a result, entrepreneurial and commerce groups have won a disproportionate share of wealth and power in the USA.[49]

In his 1911 *Devil's Dictionary*, Ambrose Bierce defined a corporation as an "ingenious device for obtaining individual profit without individual responsibility." This truth summarizes a trend over the past 200 years whereby legal systems have been changed to

---

47 Beard, 1913, 250–251.

48 Noam Chomsky, *Profit over People* (New York: Seven Stories Press, 1999), 46; Eric Foner, *Tom Paine and Revolutionary America* (New York: Oxford University Press, 1976), 190, as cited in Fresia, 3, 231n6. It is interesting to note that Hamilton, Madison and Jay were relatively young men at the time of the writing of these articles—30, 36 and 42 years old, respectively.

49 Morton J. Horowitz, *The Transformation of American Law, 1780–1860* (New York: Oxford University Press, 1992), xvi.

limit legal liabilities of corporations while giving those same corporations the rights and protections of individual citizens.[50]

The US Supreme Court held in the 1819 *Dartmouth College Case* that a corporate charter was a *private* contract, and therefore regulation of state charters for corporations must be compatible with the Commerce Clause of the Constitution. Over the next several decades, political and economic power was radically shifted from *pre*commercial and *anti*development common law values, to *merchant-friendly, entrepreneurial* values that subordinated natural laws and customs to concentrate disproportionate economic gain for *individuals* or *corporations*. As legal power was shifted from workers, farmers, and local consumers to the mostly white men of commerce and industry, the law no longer served as a paternalistic protector in the moral sense of the community at large, but rather as a device to facilitate individual and corporate achievement of economic and political power.[51]

Thus, US history reveals the strong will of Capital intentionally encouraging legal redistribution of wealth upward, working against the weakest groups in the increasingly stratified political-economic structure of the Republic itself.[52] The roots of this attitude can be found in the Constitution, and are especially evident in the Commerce Clause.

The infamous 1886 Supreme Court ruling, *Santa Clara County v. Southern Pacific Railroad*, in which a clerk's summary note misinterpreted the justices' decision, further advanced the notion of corporations as persons.

Throughout the twentieth century, more than a dozen subsequent Supreme Court decisions have broadened the rights of corporations as persons, granting them protection under the First, Fourth, Fifth, Sixth, and Seventh Amendments. The 2010 *Citizens United v. Federal Election Commission* ruled that limits on any independent corporation's political expenditures are unconstitutional as a matter of law. Thus, the long trend of private power (money/wealth) having undue influence over the public political process is more deeply entrenched than ever, such that lawmaking itself is conducted by the bribed, selected agents of the most powerful corporations.

Meanwhile, the principle of private property protection within the United States has increasingly been extended to the rest of the world, often by economic intimidation if not brute force. Woodrow Wilson, who opposed extra-continental expansion *prior* to the Spanish-American War, changed his mind soon after. In 1907, while president of Princeton University (six years before being elected president of the United States), Wilson wrote:

> Since trade ignores national boundaries and the manufacturer insists on having the world as a market, the flag of his nation must follow him, and the doors of the nations which are closed against him must be

---

50 George Draffan for POCLAD/Program on Corporations, Law and Democracy, *The Elite Consensus: When Corporations Wield the Constitution* (New York: Apex Press, 2003), v, xi.
51 Horowitz, 253.
52 Horowitz, 254.

battered down. Concessions obtained by financiers must be safeguarded by ministers of state, even if the sovereignty of unwilling nations be outraged in the process. Colonies must be obtained or planted, in order that no useful corner of the world may be overlooked or left unused.[53]

During Wilson's two terms as president, 1913–1921, he saw fit to safeguard US interests by sending US Marines into Nicaragua (1912–1925); Mexico (1913–1919); Haiti (1914–1934); Dominican Republic (1914, 1916–1924); China (1916, 1917, 1920); Cuba (1917–1933); Soviet Russia (1918–1920); Panama (1918–1920); Honduras (1919); Dalmatia, a historical region of Croatia (1919); Turkey (1919); and Guatemala (1920).[54] Wilson also initiated air power for the first time in US history with use of aerial bombing, aerial combat, and aerial reconnaissance support of ground troops in Mexico, 1913–1914[55] and again in Haiti, 1919.[56]

As historian Albert K. Weinberg observed in his exhaustive study, *Manifest Destiny*, "The very peoples who had drunk most deeply of the new humanitarian nationalism succumbed most readily to the expansionist intoxication which led into the age of imperialism."[57]

A Nation Built on Three Genocides

First Genocide: Systematic Elimination of Indigenous Inhabitants and Theft of their Land

Massachusetts Bay Colony Governor John Winthrop's 1630 proclamation that "we shall be as a city upon a hill," of course, was meant to describe a city ruled exclusively by White Eurocentric males. The American Way of Life, from the beginning, was blessed by God, giving its rulers the supreme justification for doing whatever it took to maintain that way, including eliminating the ancient inhabitants who resided in "America" before White man's arrival. Maintaining the US American way has inevitably required warring with others, beginning as early as 1637, when Governor Winthrop ordered his Puritan assistant, John Endicott, and Puritan military commander, John Mason, to eliminate the Pequot Indians in Connecticut.

John Mason set about "to cut off the remembrance of [the Pequot] from the Earth."[58] On May 26, 1637, he torched a major Pequot settlement on the Mystic River, where today sits a major US Navy submarine base. In a little more than an hour, the entire village

---

53 Sidney Lens, *The Forging of the American Empire: From the Revolution to Vietnam: A History of US Imperialism* (Chicago: Haymarket Books, 1971), 195.

54 Richard F. Grimmett, *Instances of Use of United States Armed Forces Abroad, 1798–2008* (Washington, DC: Congressional Research Service, 2009).

55 "Up From Kitty Hawk: A Chronology of Aerospace Power since 1903," *Air Force Magazine* (December 2003); Daniel L. Haulman, *One Hundred Years of Flight: USAF Chronology of Significant Air and Space Events, 1903–2002* (Maxwell AFB, AL: Air University Press, 2003), 11; Jerry K. Sweeney, ed., *A Handbook of American Military History: From the Revolutionary War to the Present* (Boulder, CO: Westview Press,1996), 110, 115.

56 Patrick Bellegarde-Smith, *Haiti: The Breached Citadel* (Boulder, CO: Westview Press, 1990), 80.

57 Albert K. Weinberg, *Manifest Destiny* (Chicago: Quadrangle Paperbacks, 1935, 1963), 11.

58 Drinnon, 55.

of 80 houses was destroyed and six to seven hundred of its inhabitants—men, women, and children—burned to death.[59] Known as the Pequot War, the Puritans' assault on the Pequot began in 1634 and was one of the first of hundreds of wars between European settlers and Native Americans. It was the Puritans' first decisive answer to the question of whether Native Americans were authentic human beings. They were not. Very few Pequots survived the four-year "war."

From the beginning, European settlers of the New World organized irregular armed units to viciously attack and murder unarmed innocents (a.k.a. civilians)—Indigenous women, children, and elderly—using unlimited violent means, including outright massacres and the burning of towns and food stocks. The first two centuries of British colonization, the 1600s to 1800s, produced several generations of experienced "Indian fighters" (early version of "rangers"). Settlers, mostly farmers by trade, they waged battles totally independent of any formal military organization.[60]

When Columbus invaded the New World, there were as many as eighteen million indigenous inhabitants living north of the Rio Grande, in perhaps six hundred autonomous tribal cultures speaking as many as two thousand languages.[61] Systematic elimination by starvation, disease, murder, and utter hopelessness/suicide of over ninety-eight percent of the millions of Indigenous inhabitants caused their numbers to plummet to 250 thousand by 1900, enabled the conquering Europeans to develop vast amounts of land stolen with impunity.[62] This genocide, engineered by the "superior" Eurocentric invaders in the name of "progress," possessed all the components of the subsequent burning of villages and uprooting of natives we find throughout US war history, including in the Philippines, Korea, Viet Nam, and beyond.[63]

The Viet Nam war was one of many ugly, barbaric wars waged by our nation in the twentieth century justified with espousal of the outrageous "domino theory," concocted during the Cold War. Violent wars to fight the Communist bogeyman, however, are merely a modern version of the historical genocidal violence driven by dread of the pan-Indian movements that date from before the Pequots and Narragansetts of New England. If one group of "natives" is allowed to exist free of Western market control, what is to stop others from liberating themselves—from rising up, one after another, to throw off

---

59 Alan Axelrod, *Chronicle of the Indian Wars from Colonial Times to Wounded Knee* (New York: Prentice-Hall General reference, 1993), 14–22; Drinnon, 55, 33–61]; Arlene Hirschfelder, *Native Americans: A History in Pictures* (New York: Dorling Kindersley Publishing, 2000), 33; Kenneth C. Davis, *Don't Know Much About History: Everything You Need to Know about American History But Never Learned* (New York: Avon Books, 1990), 34.

60 Roxanne Dunbar-Ortiz, *An Indigenous Peoples' History of the United States* (Boston: Beacon Press, 2014), 58–60.

61 Howard Zinn, *A People's History of the United States* (New York: HarperPerennial, 1980), 18; David E. Stannard, *American Holocaust: The Conquest of the New World* (New York: Oxford University Press, 1992), 261–268; Russell Thornton, *American Indian Holocaust and Survival: A Population History Since 1492* (Norman, Oklahoma: University of Oklahoma Press, 1987), 22–25; Hirschfelder and de Montano, 83; Hirschfelder, 10.

62 Thornton, 30; Stannard, 267–278.

63 Zinn, 1980, 131.

their "association of the philanthropic, the pious and the profitable" called colonialism?[64] Vertically oriented hierarchical power, whether monarchial, dictatorial, or "democratic," has historically tended toward various forms of tyranny when entrenched government invariably becomes threatened by the genuine power of people seeking self-determination and the chance to practice true democracy.[65]

The perceived threat to the US posed by organized people power is often described as a "virus" that can spread. Stopping this virus remains a rationale in arguments for US interventions. Zbigniew Brzezinski, former National Security Advisor to President Jimmy Carter, described the critical importance for US America to "manage" Eurasia. In *The Grand Chessboard* (1997), he identifies "three grand imperatives of imperial geostrategy": (1) to "prevent collusion and maintain security dependence among the vassals," (2) "keep tributaries pliant and protected," and (3) "keep the barbarians from coming together." He suggests: "The United States may have to determine how to cope with regional coalitions that seek to push America out of Eurasia, thereby threatening American status as a global power."[66]

PRESENCE OF THE PAST *TODAY*—INDIGENOUS GENOCIDE

The last big massacre of Indigenous Americans after a long line of wars against the Indians took place at Wounded Knee on December 29, 1890, on the Lakota (Sioux) Pine Ridge Indian Reservation in South Dakota. The Lakota, exhausted from decades of forceful separation from their ancestral territories and suffering high death rates, were increasingly participating in the Ghost Dance, which held that if certain rituals were sincerely performed, the Whites would vanish and the buffalo and other dead relatives would be re-born. But the US troops of the Seventh Cavalry claimed the Ghost Dance was a sign of insubordination to Whites and used it as an excuse to murder 300 unarmed Lakota, including many women and children, after they were hopelessly surrounded. The dead were buried on New Year's Day, 1891.

From the perspective of its perpetrators, the massacre at Wounded Knee was likely revenge for the earlier defeat of Seventh Cavalry regiment led by General Custer that was wiped out at Little Big Horn 14 years earlier on June 25, 1876. Discovery of gold in the Black Hills of South Dakota in 1874 made the land increasingly valuable, attracting an influx of thousands of White settlers and making Custer's intended clearing efforts critically important.[67]

After defeating the collective Indian cultures, the challenge of the White masters was to either assimilate or digest the survivors. One strategy involved kidnapping, as Indian children were often forcibly removed from their parents and enrolled in "boarding schools," residential Indian schools that more closely resembled military training. These

---

64 Drinnon, 404.

65 Etienne De La Boetie, *The Politics of Obedience: The Discourse of Voluntary Servitude*, trans. Harry Kurz (Montreal, Canada: Black Rose Books, 1997; original @1553), 58–59.

66 Zbigniew Brzezinski, *The Grand Chessboard: American Primacy and Its Geostrategic Imperatives* (New York: Basic Books, 1997), 31, 40, 55.

67 Dunbar-Ortiz, 145–157.

schools still existed as late as the 1980s. At any one time about half of all Native American children attended them.[68]

The architect of the US Indian boarding school system was Captain Richard Pratt, a veteran of the Civil War who had been involved in violent campaigns to eliminate the Plains Indians. Pratt's "educational" goal was to rid the Indians of their dress, their language, and their collective way of thinking. In fact, Pratt claimed that the noble objective was "to kill the Indian, save the man."[69] Indians speaking their native language were severely punished with physical beatings and humiliation, because English was considered the only civilized way to converse. Cruelly enforced civilization, however, amounts to *deracement*, and de facto extinction, in effect, cultural collapse. Half the children did not survive the experience, dying either from the unhealthy European diet, or during an escape, or from suicide. The survivors experienced alcoholism, suicide, loneliness, and deep trauma. The resulting cultural disintegration amounted to genocide.[70]

Today, the Pine Ridge Reservation has anywhere from 28,000 to 40,000 inhabitants and is the eighth largest reservation in the US. Life is bleak. Even though sale of liquor is prohibited on the reservation, the rate of alcoholism is estimated to be as high as 80 percent. Average male life expectancy is 48, the lowest in the Western hemisphere outside of Haiti. The overwhelming majority of reservation inhabitants are unemployed: 49 percent live below the official poverty level, but the rate is 61 percent for children under 18. The infant mortality rate is five times the US national average. Teen suicide is 159 percent of the national average. As late as 2012, more than 60 percent of the dwellings lack electricity or running water.[71]

Second Genocide: Slavery of Africans and Theft of Their Labor

It is estimated that Africa lost fifty to sixty million human beings to death and slavery during the nearly four hundred years of the transatlantic slave trade. It has been calculated that only ten to fifteen million survived the kidnapping process and the subsequent long, forced march of hundreds of miles to the African coast, during which the captives were chained to one another. If that wasn't savage enough, they were forced to endure the transport of six to ten weeks on one of 54,000 separate slave voyages, five thousand miles across the ocean. Called floating coffins, each ship held anywhere from 250 to 600 Africans.[72] The trans-Atlantic slave trade is the largest known forced intercontinental movement of human beings in history.[73] In the worst cases, the slaves were crammed into

---

68 Ward Churchill, *Kill the Indian, Save the Man: The Genocidal Impact of American Residential Schools* (San Francisco: City Lights Books, 2004), 13; Hirschfelder and de Montano, 95–96.

69 Churchill, 2004, 14; Arlene Hirschfelder, *Native Americans: A History in Pictures* (New York: Dorling Kindersley Publishing, 2000), 128–129.

70 Churchill, 2004, 8–12; Julian Berger, *The Gaia Atlas of First Peoples* (New York: Anchor Books, 1990), 122–123.

71 Chris Hedges and Joe Sacco, *Days of Destruction, Days of Revolt* (New York: Nation Books, 2012), 2–17.

72 Zinn, 1980, 28–29; "The Story of Africa," BBC World Service web site: http://bbc.co.uk/worldservice/specials/1624_story_of_africa; George Francis Dow, *Slave Ships and Slaving* (New York: Dover Publications, 1970), xxvi–xxxv; Peter M. Bergman, *The Chronological History of the Negro in America* (New York: Harper & Row Publishers, 1969), 1–2.

73 http://www.academia.edu/5551320/Motivations_and_Impacts_of_Atlantic_Slave_Trade

horizontal compartments no larger than six feet by one foot by two and a half feet, but often smaller, or in holding pens where they were chained to each other by the neck and by the legs for many days at a time.[74] The conditions on the trans-Atlantic voyages were so horrible that as many as twenty to thirty percent of captives died before reaching the Americas, due to dysentery, smallpox, suffocation in cramped quarters, or, if rebellious, being shot or tortured by sailors and thrown overboard.[75] Some slaves, when momentarily free of their chains for exercise or washing, jumped overboard rather than continue to suffer unspeakable misery.

Oloudah Equiano, the first known enslaved African to record the grueling conditions he witnessed, declared he "had never seen among any people such instances of brutal cruelty,"[76] echoing de Las Casas' description of Columbus's treatment of the West Indians. Alexander Falconbridge, a slave ship surgeon who later became governor of a British colony for freed slaves in Sierra Leone, described how sickened he felt when witnessing the floor of slave quarters "so covered with blood and mucus that it resembled a slaughterhouse."[77]

Every African kidnapped from his or her ancient tribal community was seized in deference to intense pressures of the "iron hand of commerce."[78] Western civilization developed as a capitalist enterprise that could only be economically profitable by using free labor. Colonists proclaimed that slaves were the strength of the Western World and that their settlements "cannot subsist without supplies of them." Planters in the colonies and merchants in England demanded that the English Parliament support the slave trade, and at their behest the moral standard of a whole people was lowered for the sake of material advantage. The English knew that the slave trade was indispensable to "healthy" British economics.[79] Because slavery was so indispensable for the success of capitalist enterprises and the risks in the trade were large, investors in the slave trade insisted that each "legal" slave merchant be covered by underwriters who would make good for any "property" lost during the voyage.[80]

Thus, millions of African people suffered the most unspeakable barbarities in ways that no White person can imagine, even to this day, committed by the hands of privileged European men who enjoyed the impunity that comes with elevated social status. This capitalist-enforced savagery enabled development exploiting the resources on stolen Indigenous lands.

---

74 "The Story of Africa," BBC World Service; Zinn, 1980, 29; Vincent Virga with Alan Brinkley, *Eyes of the Nation: A Visual History of the United States* (New York: Alfred A. Knopf, 1997), 73.
75 "The Story of Africa," BBC World Service; DuBois, 5; Zinn, 28–29; Dow, xxvi-xxxv.
76 "The Story of Africa," BBC World Service.
77 "The Story of Africa," BBC World Service.
78 Dow, xxii.
79 Bergman, 1–2; W.E.B. DuBois, *The Suppression of the African Slave Trade to the United States of America, 1638–1870* (Williamstown, Massachusetts: Corner House Publishers, 1970), 4, 194.
80 Dow, xxxv.

Presence of the Past *Today*—Genocide of Slavery

The idea of *race*, that physical and mental traits are linked, is one of the most dangerous myths of our time. And, as observed by Ashley Montagu, myths are mostly immune from rational discourse.[81]

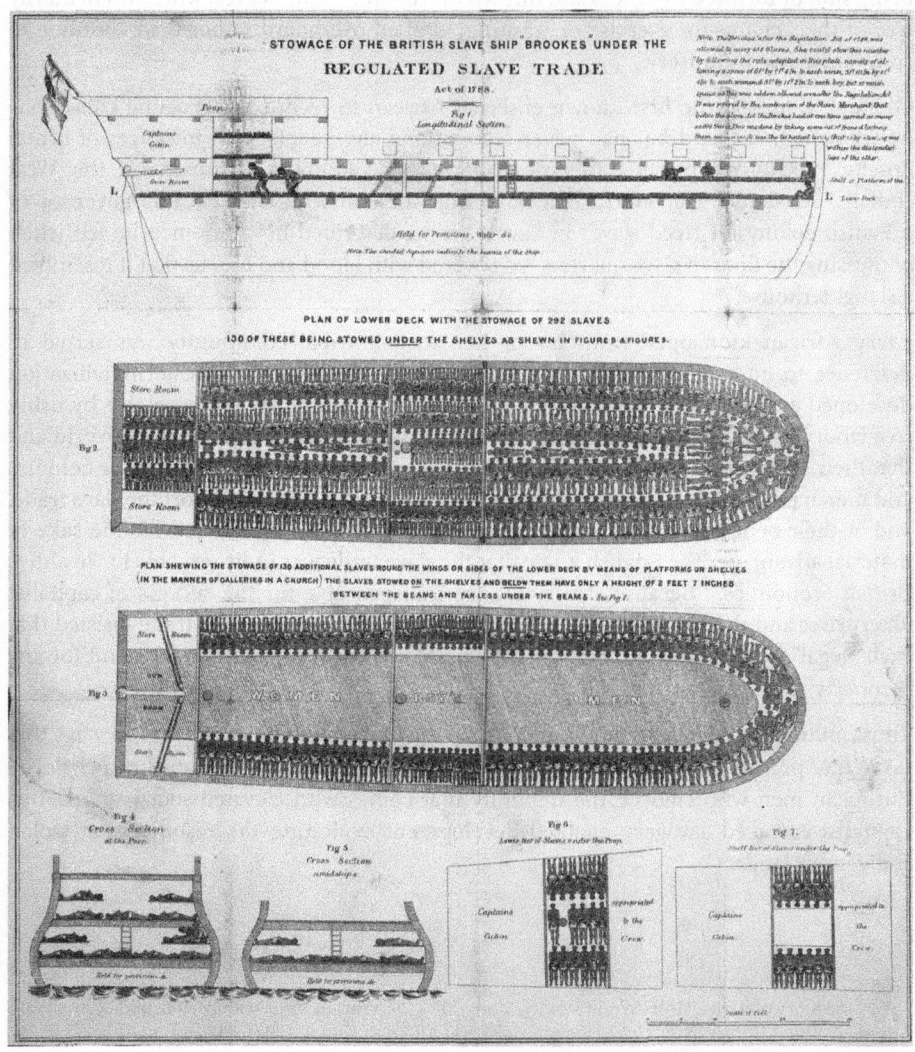

Slave ship poster illustrating stowage of the British slave ship *Brookes* under the regulated Slave Trade Act 1788.

---

81 Ashley Montagu, *Man's Most Dangerous Myth: The Fallacy of Race*, 5th ed. (New York: Oxford University Press, 1974).

Racial prejudice in the fifty United States is strongly correlated to income inequality because of the way political power has historically discriminated against lower status and weaker groups, generation after generation. Greater inequality and class differences are the most significant and common causes of stress that underlie personal and social illness.[82] Racial segregation mandated by law began in the post-Civil War Reconstruction period. Jim Crow laws were ostensibly overturned by the Civil Rights Act of 1964, and the Voting Rights Act of 1965, though policies and attitudes deeply rooted in White prejudice against African Americans remain virulent to this day, enabling grotesque disparities especially in the way Black Americans are treated within the criminal injustice system.

Lynchings: Between 1882 and 1968, a documented 4,742 Black Americans were lynched in the US, twenty-six percent for no alleged crime whatsoever. One lynching occurred every week on average. At least as many African Americans were victims of what amounted to *legal* lynchings (shootings by Whites deemed "self-defense," speedy trials and quick convictions by all-White juries, speedy "legal" police street executions, etc.), as well as privately orchestrated murders or collective rural murders called "nigger hunts."[83]

Between *known* vigilante lynchings, "legal" lynchings, privately arranged murders, and collective "nigger hunts," it is believed that at least ten thousand Black Americans were murdered in this eighty-six-year period of US American history. In much of the United States, virtually all Black people lived in constant fear.

Official Executions: Not surprisingly, statistics reveal that African Americans are disproportionately killed by the state. Between 1930 and 2005, a total of 4,805 persons were legally executed in the US. Although the 1930 US Census lists the total population as 90 percent White and 10 percent non-White, and the 2005 Census lists the total population as 67 percent White (non-Hispanic) and 33 percent non-White, of those executed, 52.5 percent, or 2,524, were non-White. The race of victims of the crimes committed (or allegedly committed) by all those executed since 1976 is predominantly White (80.6 percent as opposed to 19.4 percent non-White).[84]

Imprisonment: On an average day, more than 2.5 million US citizens are housed under lock and key. The United States of America has more than nine thousand jails and prisons, and boasts the highest per-capita detention rate in the world: 800 prisoners for every 100 thousand people (the world's average is 146). That's right: The US, with but 4.6 percent of the world's population, holds a quarter of the world's prisoners. Sixty-five percent of these

---

82 Richard Wilkinson, *The Impact of Inequality* (New York: The New Press, 2005).

83 James Allen, Hilton Als, John Lewis, and Leon F. Litwack, *Without Sanctuary: Lynching Photography in America* (Santa Fe, New Mexico: Twin Palms Publishers, 2000), 12, 37 (n. 37); Wendy Koch, "Senate Moves to Apologize for Injustice," *USA TODAY*, June 13, 2005. "An estimated 4,500 to 5,000 Americans were killed by lynching, most of them black men in the South ... lynchings often were public spectacles, some attended by civic leaders, and happened in all mainland US states except four in New England."

84 Death Penalty Information Center, (DPIC), Washington, DC, *Facts about the Death Penalty*, January 19, 2005; US Department of Justice, Bureau of Justice Statistics, *Capital Punishment*, 2002; *Death Row USA*, Spring 2004, NAACP Legal Defense and Education Fund, New York, NY; http://www.census.gov/population/pop-profile/dynamic/RACEHO.pdf.

prisoners are non-White, even though in 2013 the non-White population as a whole was thirty-seven percent.[85]

Disparity in incarceration between African and White Americans is dramatic in the extreme.[86]

Per capita detention rates (PCDR)*	
All Blacks (African Americans)	2,526
All Whites	376
Black males only	4,834
White males only	681
Black males 25–29	12,809
White males 25–29	1,607

*prisoners per 100,000 population within each group

Clearly, Blacks are arrested and imprisoned at disproportionate rates. African Americans are more than six times as likely as Whites to be sentenced to prison for *identical* crimes. For example, people of all races use and sell illegal drugs at very similar rates. White youth are known to use cocaine at seven times the rate of Black students, yet in a number of states, African Americans make up eighty to ninety percent of all drug offenders sent to prison.[87]

Racially unjust incarceration rates are rooted in history. Persistent racism following the Civil War manifested partly in "vagrancy" laws that allowed police to sweep African American men off the streets with virtually no due process, and then rent them out as convict labor. This, of course, dramatically increased the number of Black prisoners.[88]

Contemporary Racism as Toxic as Ever: The deep rage expressed in more than 150 citizen actions across the US in October 2014 after a grand jury refused to indict a White police officer for an August 2014 shooting of an unarmed Black male teen in Ferguson, Missouri, transcended anger over what happened in this particular case. Reminding us just how toxic racism is, the miscarriage of justice revealed a broken system of racial injustice passing for an authentic US American criminal justice system. Multiple recent events illustrate just how differently Whites and Blacks are treated by law enforcement in this country: Blacks are killed with impunity.

On the street, killings by police are widespread and apparently on the rise. Some reports have disclosed as many as 1,700 police killings from May 2013 to November 2014.[89] If,

---

85 Bureau of Justice, *Corrections Statistics;* Federal Bureau of Prisons, *Quick facts;* Bureau of Justice Statistics, *Census of State and Federal Correctional Facilities;* Bureau of Justice Statistics, *Census of Jails;* Bureau of Justice Statistics, *Jails in Indian Country;* US Department of Justice, Office of Justice and Delinquency Prevention, *Juvenile Residential Facility Census.*

86 http://www.prisonpolicy.org/prisonindex.shtml.

87 Michelle Alexander, *The New Jim Crow: Mass Incarceration in the Age of Colorblindness* (New York: The New Press, 2012), 98, 99, 118.

88 "Just the Facts: A Nation Built on the Back of Slavery and racism," *Yes!*, Summer 2015, 25–27.

89 Nadia Prupis, "While FBI Finds Police Killings on the Rise, Real Number of Killings Remains Unknown," Nadia Prupis, Commondreams, http://www.commondreams.org/news/2014/11/13/while-fbi-finds-police-killings-rise-real-number-killings-remains-unknown

in fact, 1,700 have been killed by police in the eighteen months between May 2013 and October 2014, that means three civilians are killed *every* day, the vast majority most likely Black men. Three different sources disclose over 1,100 civilians killed by US police in 2015, over three a day, half of them Nonwhite.[90]

The online public interest journal *ProPublica* found in October 2014 that young Black men are twenty-one times more likely to be killed by police than young White men.[91] The murder of young unarmed black men has been persistent throughout US history. The average of one lynching a week occurring for almost a century under Jim Crow is echoed by current rates of one Black person (most often young males) killed every thirty-six hours by police in the US. Whether lynched by rope or summarily executed by bullets, extrajudicial killings of those perceived as "different" are an ugly manifestation of White supremacy in which dehumanizing attitudes fueled by fear and hate inevitably manifest in violence. The existing unjust order is further preserved and maintained by denial.[92]

Greenwood, a 36-block section of Tulsa, Oklahoma—at the time the wealthiest African-American community in the US—was completely destroyed on May 31–June 1, 1921. A white mob attacked residents and businesses, on the ground and by air. It was one of the worst incidents of racial violence in the history of the United States. [*Wikipedia*, "Tulsa race riot," accessed August 7, 2018: https://en.wikipedia.org/wiki/Tulsa_race_riot.]

Third Genocide: Global Imperial Plunder

The genocides described above, against Indigenous peoples and Africans, guaranteed the conquest of the continental lands of the United States, and expansion assuring prosperity. The tone was set for the third genocide: plunder of expanding frontiers around the world in the twentieth century.

---

90 http://killedbypolice.net/ (1204); http://www.theguardian.com/us-news/ng-interactive/2015/jun/01/the-counted-police-killings-us-database (1139); http://mappingpoliceviolence.org/2015/ (1152)

91 Nadia Prupis, "While FBI Finds Police Killings on the Rise, Real Number of Killings Remains Unknown—FBI report finds police killings highest in 20 years, but critics say agency's figures fail to provide real scope of police killings," *Common Dreams*, Thursday, November 13, 2014.

92 Mike King, "The Political Fight for a Cure: The Cancer of Police Violence," *CounterPunch*, November 22, 2012.

Appendix I chronicles 560 US military interventions since 1798 in dozens of countries to protect US "interests," i.e., to protect US investments or access to resources perceived as necessary to maintain lucrative profits for US corporations and to meet the demand of the highly consumptive US lifestyles. Millions have been killed, maimed, and displaced in these interventions. Although illegal under international law and treaties, these crimes have been and continue to be committed with impunity.

Our national historic pattern of global intervention intensified around the time of President William McKinley in the late 1890s. By that time, the entire continent had been militarily wrested from the original rightful Indigenous inhabitants, and US agriculture and manufacturing enterprises were producing surpluses in excess of domestic demand. Continued profit desperately needed expanding markets, and the McKinley Administration was only too willing to do its part to preserve the religion of "prosperity." No matter what the pretext, the intent of almost all US military interventions can inevitably be tied to gobbling up resources, increasing markets, and exploiting labor, for the sake of corporate profits. US military interventions dramatically increased in the world over the next hundred years, prompting some observers to label the 1900s the American Century.[93]

In 1947, coinciding with the advent of the Cold War, the Central Intelligence Agency (CIA) was created, leading to the launch of thousands of illegal covert interventions in more than a hundred countries. Dark, plausibly deniable, destabilizing actions conducted by the agency continue to this day, all secret, all rationalized to preserve—again—what our political leaders in concert with their corporate partners describe as "US interests," i.e., to assure control of raw materials and expansion of markets.

John Stockwell, a former CIA operative in Angola and Viet Nam, concluded that at least twenty million people were killed during the Cold War, in what he has called the Third World War, making it the second or third bloodiest war in all of human history.[94] When the Church Committee Report on CIA activities was published in 1976, its chair, US Senator Frank Church (D-ID), stated that he had identified nine hundred major and three thousand minor covert operations that took place from 1961 to 1974.[95] In 1990, Stockwell extrapolated that the CIA likely had initiated and overseen about three thousand major and over ten thousand minor covert operations up to that time, with millions of people murdered in the process.[96]

Nobody really knows just how many people were killed, maimed, and displaced in the "American Century" due to US policies alone but conservative English military historian

---

93 Harold Evans, *The American Century* (New York: Alfred A. Knopf, 1998), a theme echoed in a 1941 essay, "The American Century" by *Time*'s Tom Luce.

94 John Stockwell, "The CIA and the Gulf War," a speech, February 20, 1991, Louden Nelson Community Center, Santa Cruz, CA.

95 J. Prados, *President's Secret Wars: CIA and Pentagon Covert Operations from World War II through the Persian Gulf* (Chicago: Elephant, Ivan R. Dee, 1996), 336.

96 John Stockwell, *The Praetorian Guard: The US Role in the New World Order* (Cambridge, MA: South End Press, 1991), 70; John Stockwell, *The United States In Search of Enemies: A Selected 'National Security' Reading List*, rev. (self-published, June 1987).

John Keegan estimates fifty million killed by various wars since 1945.[97] Essayist and novelist John Ralston Saul reported that statistics reveal a total seventy-five million war-related deaths between 1960 and the mid-1990s alone.[98]

Electrical and nuclear engineer Arjun Makhijani argued that nuclear weapons have not in fact produced peace; that the Cold War engaged in by the US and USSR was in fact a series of local proxy *hot wars* with the US generally supporting the Haves and the USSR the Have Nots. These "low intensity conflicts" killed millions in the Third World, and the violence continues today as the disparity between rich and poor continues to grow.[99] Now we are all threatened as the US wages war of wholesale terror against reactionary retail terror, which can threaten to go nuclear at any time. It is clear that the "terrorism" we claim to fight against is a direct result of 50 years of the First World's continuing refusal to address the structurally unjust global playing field.

Presence of the past today—Global genocide

John Locke defined *empire* as a way of life that takes wealth and freedom away from others to provide for one's own welfare, pleasure, and power.[100] Empire has been the national way of life from our nation's very origins.

The total area of the original thirteen states was nearly 900 thousand square miles of what had been North American Indigenous territory. Westward expansion by the US was first justified by the Monroe Doctrine, which asserted that the American continents "are henceforth not to be considered as subjects for future colonization by any European powers . . . [and] any attempt on their part to extend their system to any portion of this hemisphere" would be considered "as dangerous to our peace and safety." The worldview of the white settlers leading cross-continental expansion can be understood by the doctrine of Manifest Destiny. John L. O'Sullivan, editor of the *Democratic Review*, a periodical published between 1837 and 1859, declared in a July 1845 issue that it is "our manifest destiny to over spread the continent allotted by Providence for the development of our yearly multiplying millions."[101] This expansion spread with ferocity into Indian territories throughout the 19th century.

In the 1904 Roosevelt Corollary, President Theodore Roosevelt expanded the Monroe Doctrine from one of prohibiting intervention by European powers to one of authorized intervention *by the US* outside its own borders: "Chronic wrongdoing, or an impotence which results in a general loosening of the ties of civilized society, may in America, as elsewhere, ultimately require intervention by some civilized nation, and in the Western Hemisphere the adherence of the United States to the Monroe Doctrine may force the United States, however reluctantly, in flagrant cases of such wrong doing or impotence, to the exercise of an international police power."[102]

---

97 John Keegan, *A History of Warfare* (Toronto: Vintage, 1994), 56.
98 John Ralston Saul, *The Unconscious Civilization* (New York: The Free Press, 1997), 11.
99 "Nuclear Targeting: The First 60 Years," *Bulletin of the Atomic Scientists, 59*(3), 2003.
100 Williams, 1980, 26.
101 John O'Sullivan, "Annexation," *United States Magazine and Democratic Review 17*, no.1 (July-Aug. 1845).
102 Morris and Morris, 350.

The imperial pattern established in the 1600s, first on the continent, now global, has become empire as a *way of life*.[103] Today, the Pentagon pursues no less than full-spectrum dominance over global air space, atmospheric space, sea space, ground space (territory), cyberspace, and our inner mind space.[104] In addition to waging drone and missile wars against a number of nations and conducting active ground war operations as deemed "necessary," the US secretly deploys elite US Special Forces into *at least* 134 countries around the globe to assure overseas power projection in Asia, Africa, and Latin America, and elsewhere, under authority of the Special Operations Command (SOCOM).[105]

As recently as December 2014, the US House of Representatives, by a vote of 411 to 10, passed Resolution 758: "Strongly condemning the actions of the Russian Federation, under President Vladimir Putin, which has carried out a policy of aggression against neighboring countries aimed at political and economic domination." Like the pot calling the kettle black, this is consistent with US history preserving its identity through demonizing others as the "enemy." This attitude pre-empts any honest analysis, whether in Congress or among the electorate. US media, owned by the same interests that own our political "leadership," works to convince the US American people to support war-like policies toward the *evil du jour*, in this case Russia and its president.

Phony "Exceptionalism"

Because the self-image of the United States has been built on collective *denial* of the painful realities of the dispossession of others—Indigenous inhabitants in the Americas, Africans, and Third World peoples—fantasy politics in the US has become a way of life.[106] Our collective fantasy is consistently reinforced by virtually all our education, entertainment, political discourse, religious sermonizing, sports, etc. Most of us have been emotionally and intellectually programmed in the perpetuation of the heroic myths of our origins, and the consequential feelings of righteousness that have led us into war after war. Some might say the wool has been pulled over our eyes. However, I assert that the wool was in our eyes to begin with, and remains in our eyes, not over them. We continue to be a pretend society.

The crimes underlying our founding and expansion, our "original sins," continue to contaminate the soul of US America. The third genocide is ongoing, perpetuated by our extravagant materialist values. Since systematic injustices are never talked about, let alone seriously addressed, people in our culture blissfully live in ignorance or denial of our nature as violent plunderers. Our thinking and behavior are marked by severe distortions based on our unshakable belief in our *exceptionalism*. A quest for truth is one of the first

---

103 Williams, 1980.

104 Bruce Gagnon, "The Pentagon's Strategy for World Domination: Full Spectrum Dominance, from Asia to Africa," *Global Research*, August 25, 2014, http://www.globalresearch.ca/the-pentagons-strategy-for-world-domination-full-spectrum-dominancew-from-asia-to-africa/5397514.

105 Nick Turse, Truthdig.com, January 16, 2014, Tom Dispatch, "The Special Ops Surge In 134 Countries": http://www.truthdig.com/report/item/the_special_ops_surge_in_134_countries_20140116/

106 Michael A. Milburn and Sheree D. Conrad, *The Politics of Denial* (Cambridge, MA: The MIT Press, 1996), 3.

steps toward change. Understanding history helps clarify the *why* of our interventions, including Viet Nam. Recovery of our humanity is at stake.

I grew up believing that the United States is the greatest country in the history of the world, endowed by our Creator to bring prosperity to the impoverished and Christianity to the heathen. Believing this mythology led me (and millions of others) to obey orders to go to war in Viet Nam. In retrospect, the American war in Viet Nam seems incredibly, tragically absurd—and worse, criminal. It is no wonder that for many of us, the myth of US America was utterly collapsed by our experience in the war.

The "Wild West" of the new world that European invaders set out to conquer doesn't exist anymore, or perhaps it is everywhere, as imperialist projects continue seeking new frontiers, working feverishly to assure one regimented, homogenous worldwide culture, a culture that in fact leads to spiritual death. "Winning the west" has come to represent Capitalism's insidious winning of the world, with *globalization of materialism*. As a result, all of us humans, and much of the remainder of life on this planet, are endangered.[107]

US American Identity and Demonization of the "Other"

Demonizing others has served to rationalize war after war from the very beginning. In 1776, in the Declaration of Independence, Thomas Jefferson described the original Native Americans as "merciless Indian Savages." Their legitimacy as an autonomous peoples was not even considered. The predominant attitude from the outset was that they had to be either eliminated or assimilated. Expansion of the American territory for profits could not be stopped.[108]

In 1779, the Continental Congress ordered Supreme Commanding General George Washington to destroy the native Iroquois nations in upstate New York. The Iroquois, considered the most advanced Indian federation in the New World at that time, were desperately defending the preservation of their agricultural practices on sacred ancestral lands, which were being threatened by encroaching European settlers. Four of the six Iroquois nations had allied themselves with the British, who were protecting their sovereignty. The invading and occupying settlers, aggressively seeking land,[109] formed a Continental Army to assure their successful occupation of these "empty" lands. They believed, as Winthrop had earlier prophesized, they were God's chosen people with the eyes of all people watching them as they conquered the New World.[110]

On May 31, 1779, General Washington dutifully obeyed and ordered Major General John Sullivan to train and equip his forty-five hundred soldiers to battle these "merciless Indian Savages." Making up his contingent was more than one-quarter of the Continental Army

---

107 Drinnon, 465.

108 Manifest Destiny became an intrinsic part of the US *Weltanshauung* (a German word for world view). One demonized enemy after another continued to be created as necessary to expand AWOL, and the trend continues to this day—*evil de jure*. The result is global empire.

109 Lucrative subsidies of stolen land were what made our early nation's economy profitable, subsequently secured by the subsidy of free labor. Without these subsidies, the settlers could not have succeeded.

110 Page Smith, 19-20.

soldiers at the time. In preparing for the campaign, on July 4, 1779, Sullivan's officers offered a toast, "Civilization or death to all American savages." The campaign would be the largest Revolutionary War battle of 1779.[111]

Washington's orders:[112]

> The Expedition you are appointed to command is to be directed against the hostile tribes of the Six Nations of Indians, with their associates and adherents. The immediate objects are the total destruction and devastation of their settlements, and the capture of as many prisoners of every age and sex as possible. It will be essential to ruin their crops now in the ground and prevent their planting more.
>
> I would recommend, that some post in the center of the Indian Country, should be occupied with all expedition, with a sufficient quantity of provisions whence parties should be detached to lay waste all the settlements around, with instructions to do it in the most effectual manner, that the country may not be merely overrun, but destroyed.
>
> But you will not by any means listen to any overture of peace before the total ruinment of their settlements is effected. Our future security will be in their inability to injure us and in the terror with which the severity of the chastisement they receive will inspire them.

Note that Washington's words reveal, explicitly and implicitly, these original and ongoing US military operating principles:

1. Total war/genocide—civilians and combatants alike considered legitimate targets; tactics to include destruction of food and crops; occupation; cultural genocide
2. Preventing [not wanting] peace[113]

---

111 Ray Raphael, *Founding Myths: Stories That Hide Our Patriotic Past* (New York: The New Press, 2004), 229.

112 John C. Fitzpatrick, ed., *Writings of George Washington* (Washington: Government Printing Office, 1936), XV, 189–193; Drinnon, 331.

113 The US has a long pattern of preventing, not wanting peace. In November 1951, there was a temporary cessation of shooting in Korea the day after an agreement on a cease-fire line. Washington experienced near hysterical fear as the US and Syngman Rhee feared Korean peace would be the political end of them. And Secretary of State Dulles feared that peace would severely interfere with a plan to build the old axis powers, including now Japan, for a new anti-Soviet crusade. Commander of US forces in Korea, General Van Fleet, confirmed this when making a public speech in 1952: "Korea has been a blessing. There had to be a Korea either here or some place in the world" [I.F. Stone, *The Hidden History of the Korean War, 1950–1951* (New York: Monthly Review Press, 1952), 345–348].

In May 1986, US Cabinet-level officials were alarmed that the Sandinista government in Nicaragua had agreed to sign a peace plan ending the US Contra war. Washington portrayed the plan as unacceptable "while denouncing the Sandinistas for refusing to negotiate." One US official was reported to have said "there was a peace scare." [*New York Times*, August 6, 1987, article by Joel Brinkley]. *New York Times* columnist Anthony Lewis said of the Reagan administration: "They want war. That is the policy. . . . As Mr. Wright [Speaker of the House] said, they 'are scared to death that peace will break out'" [*New York Times*, November 19, 1987].

3. Aggression—sold as national security
4. Terror—scorched earth
5. Revenge—criminalization of victims' self-defense

A terrorist, scorched-earth campaign ordered and sanctioned by the Continental Congress, the Sullivan campaign was nothing short of a massacre of a civilian population. It ranks with Sherman's horrendous March to the Sea in 1864 and US search-and-destroy missions ordered during the Viet Nam war. Forty well-established Seneca towns were totally destroyed, with the dwellings looted and torched, cornfields and fruit orchards burned. Where women and children were discovered, they were slaughtered. Within one month of the September 1779 assault, the Iroquois agricultural domain had been destroyed. As a nation they never fully recovered.[114]

Since 1798, the US has overtly participated in at least 560 military interventions in other countries against demonized "enemies." Between 1775 and 1902, US Continental and regular army units engaged in over 9,000 distinct battles and skirmishes with the enemy, many fought against indigenous peoples. Following the Civil War, US Navy ships made thousands of military port calls in Asia, Latin America, and the Caribbean[115] and were involved in as many as fifteen hundred hostile episodes[116] while capturing some four thousand vessels.[117] By the early 1900s, the US had surpassed the mighty British with the most powerful navy in the world.[118] And since World War II, the US has covertly intervened thousands of times in over a hundred countries while bombing thirty of them (see Appendix I). All have been illegal interventions, in contravention of international law, usually justified with noble sounding rhetoric about protecting US Americans from communism or terrorism or some evil dictator.

---

114 Raphael, 235–238; Smith, 1172–1173.

115 Benjamin R. Beede, ed., *The War of 1898 and US Interventions 1898–1934: An Encyclopedia* (New York: Garland Publishing, 1994), 679–681, 683, 692–695. Between 1869 and 1897, US sent warships into Latin American ports a nearly unbelievable 5,980 times (average 206 US warship calls to Latin America ports per year, or about one every other day for 29 years). See: S. S. Roberts, "An Indicator of Informal Empire: Patterns of US Navy Cruising on Overseas Stations, 1869–1897" (Alexandria, Virginia: Center for Naval Analysis, Alexandria, VA), cited in Williams, 1980, 122.

From the mid-19th century into the 20th century, the US military had conquered all lands and original inhabitants to the western edge of its continent, stolen half of Mexico, invaded Korea, annexed Hawaii, conquered the Philippines, Puerto Rico, and Cuba. As it pushed south, by 1930, Washington had sent military gunboats into Latin American ports over 6,000 times, in addition to having invaded Cuba and Mexico again, Guatemala, Honduras, and taken Panama from Columbia, fought protracted wars in the Dominican Republic, Nicaragua, and Haiti, all enabling US corporations and financial houses to dominate the economies of most of Mexico, the Caribbean, Central America, and much of South America. See Greg Grandin, *Empire's Workshop: Latin America, the United States, and the Rise of the New Imperialism.* New York: Metropolitan Books, 2006), 3.

116 Robert W. Nesser, *Statistical and Chronological History of the United States Navy, 1775–1907*, Vol II. New York: MacMillan, 1909), 24–281.

117 Nesser, 284–471; Wright, 687; Drinnon, 461–467.

118 "Power At Sea: A Naval Power Dataset, 1865–2011," http://myweb.fsu.edu/bbc09/Crisher-Souva%20-%20Power%20At%20Sea%20v2.0%20full.pdf.

But the real reasons for going to war are never entirely hidden. Long ago it became clear that any perceived threat to US material progress was to be considered an enemy to US America's grand expansionist destiny. In 1935, President Franklin Roosevelt reminded us: "Foreign markets must be regained. There is no other way if we would avoid painful economic dislocation, social readjustments and unemployment."[119]

The US-initiated war against the Vietnamese, Laotian, and Cambodian peoples, 1945–1975, dramatically illustrates the unspeakable brutality embedded in the "American" ethos, i.e., forceful dispossession of others, with full impunity. US soldiers employed in Viet Nam were trained to despise and dehumanize the "enemy" and used the same derogatory terms that had been used in previous conflicts with Asian peoples, i.e. gook, dink, slope, etc.[120] My own commander in Viet Nam called the Vietnamese "vermin."

Mimicking Jefferson's dehumanization of the enemy, William Westmoreland, then–US Commanding General in Viet Nam, confidently proclaimed in 1974, "The Oriental doesn't put the same high price on life as does a Westerner . . . Life is cheap in the Orient."[121] Likewise, in talking about Iraq, President George W. Bush said, "We're dealing with an enemy that has no conscience . . . We value life and human dignity. They don't care about life and dignity."[122]

So, we are led to believe, Native Americans, Orientals, and Arabs, at least, just do not value life as much as we US Americans do. It is comforting to know that we can murder them at will and not feel remorse. I do wonder, though, when this delusion will become as fatal to our nation, as it has for the many US military veterans who have suffered such terrible cognitive dissonance and moral injury that they committed suicide. More Viet Nam veterans have killed themselves than were killed in combat, and we see the trend repeating itself among US veterans returning from multiple tours in Iraq and Afghanistan.

What other countries can match our incredible pattern of imperial intervention? The truth is, few would want to. But have we any right to complain when others begin following our example? When George W. Bush claimed terrorists were simply jealous of our "freedom," perhaps he was onto something.

Essentially, being at war against sanctioned enemies forms the core of US American identity, driven by this mythological notion of US American exceptionalism. It is tragic that the US prides itself on such a negative identity of hateful opposition to enemies, real or imagined. Our country's very origins—resting in forceful dispossession of others masked by a noble sounding story—in effect is a kind of wool *in* our eyes that prevents us from seeing the truth and ensures we stay in a very comfortable place called *denial*.

---

[119] William Appleman Williams, *The Contours of American History* (Cleveland: The World Publishing Co., 1961), 455.
[120] Drinnon, 461–467.
[121] Peter Davis, Viet Nam documentary film, *Hearts and Minds*, 1974.
[122] Derrick Z. Jackson, "The Westmoreland Mind-Set," *The Boston Globe*, July 20, 2005.

Chapter Two
Cold War Hysteria

*"We are willing to help people
who believe the way we do."*
—Dean Acheson, Truman's Secretary of State, 1947

Introduction

I cannot stress enough the overwhelming toxic spell that Cold War propaganda cast on the minds of three generations, including some of the most intelligent people, and its influence continues today. Relentless Cold War rhetoric accomplished a near total indoctrination of our entire US culture. Religious institutions, academic and educational institutions from kindergarten through graduate school, professional associations, political associations from local to national, the scientific community, economic system, entertainment industry from radio and TV to Hollywood and sports, fraternal organizations, boy scouts, etc.—all systematically were complicit in and cooperated to preserve unquestioning belief in the unique nobility of the US American system while instilling rabid, paranoid fear of "enemies"—in our midst as well as "out there"—in order to rationalize otherwise pathologically inexplicable behavior around the world as well as at home. The atrocities committed in the name of defeating communist bogeymen are nearly beyond belief. Our cultural schooling is so pervasive as to generate a universally compelling mythology powerful enough to conceal its own contradictions.

Forty years of fanatical "good *us* versus evil *them*" leads directly from the 1917 Russian Revolution to Korea and Viet Nam. Our cultural corruption was so complete we proudly utilized B-52s blessed by God-fearing chaplains flying five miles high to bomb unarmed, mostly Buddhist peasants living nine thousand miles across the Pacific.[1] It is very difficult to recognize in ourselves what would be considered criminally insane behavior if carried out by others.

Having been born on July 4, 1941, I was a proudly patriotic baby of the World War II generation. I attended Baptist Sunday school and adult church with my parents and brother every week, without fail, and we regularly read passages from the Bible before breakfast. We were law-abiding citizens and my father, too old for military service, never missed a day of work. My mother was a homemaker. I thanked God regularly for being born in the United States of America, the greatest country in the history of the world

---

1 Alex Carey, *Taking the Risk Out of Democracy: Corporate Propaganda Versus Freedom and Liberty* (Chicago: University of Illinois Press, 1997), 136; Photograph of pilots standing in prayer with caption, "A Prayer, A Takeoff and the B-52 Strike Is On: A Job To Do," *Life* Magazine, November 12, 1965, 36.

blessed by our Creator to bring prosperity to the impoverished and Christianity to the heathen. Like my dad, I believed that as long as J. Edgar Hoover was head of the FBI, our democratic Christian freedoms were most certainly secure from our enemies. The propaganda I grew up with about US America was nothing short of spectacular, virtually all of it unchallenged by anyone I knew. It was part of my very fiber.

The Role of Propaganda in Managing Public Opinion

> *"WAR IS PEACE.*
> *FREEDOM IS SLAVERY.*
> *IGNORANCE IS STRENGTH."*
>
> —from George Orwell's *1984*: Official doublethink party slogans inscribed at the entrance of the Ministry of Truth in the fictional Oceania

Our propaganda system works very skillfully to mold public opinion toward supporting, and securing obedience to, demands of the power system. Using carefully crafted visual images, sophisticated rhetoric, and sometimes force, propaganda works astoundingly well in shaping ideology. It is amazingly effective in convincing a nation's youth to follow superiors' orders to kill complete strangers in foreign lands while being at high risk of being killed and maimed themselves. The call of "patriotic duty" certainly succeeded in getting me, a law student, to become, despite growing questions about the war, a participant in what I later understood to be a mindless murder machine.

In following orders to Viet Nam, I ignored my growing conscience and took my place as a cog in the machine, not wanting to be different or considered disloyal.

I wonder when and how modern humans might liberate our minds from colonization from the overwhelming cultural power of ideology that constantly and craftily uses advertising and propaganda to convince us to do something we would not entertain on our own. Such obedience serves to distract us from our genuine, archetypal humanity rooted in empathy, cooperation, mutual respect, and a sense of fairness.

Let's look at propaganda history and at its utilization in United States politics.

Noted US American journalist Walter Lippman, a Harvard graduate and founder in 1913 of *The New Republic*, a liberal magazine, served as an intelligence officer in World War I before becoming an adviser to President Wilson after the war. In 1922, he wrote his classic *Public Opinion*, arguing that the average person was incapable of seeing the world clearly, or understanding it, and therefore not equipped to make serious decisions or engage in rational discourse. "Democracy," Lippman argued, required a supra-governmental body of detached professionals to analyze data and conduct the national enterprise.[2] The key for Lippman was the "manufacture of consent" using techniques aimed at marshalling mass support behind specific executive policies.[3]

---

2 Walter Lippman, *Public Opinion* (1922; New York: Free Press, 1997).
3 Lippman, 158.

Edward Bernays, an Austrian-American Jew, nephew of Sigmund Freud, was heavily influenced by Lippman. He served as a foot soldier for Wilson's Committee on Public Information (CPI) in 1917–18, headed by liberal newspaperman George Creel. CPI was one of the first intensive government propaganda campaigns designed to garner public support for war. Bernays' pioneering books, *Crystallizing Public Opinion* (1923), and *Propaganda* (1928), described how the "masses" in modern society pose an increasing threat to the customary interests of order, echoing Alexander Hamilton's discounting opinions of the "average man."[4] Bernays' very first words in *Propaganda* declare: "The conscious and intelligent manipulation of the organized habits and opinions of the masses is an important element in democratic society. Those who manipulate this unseen mechanism of society constitute an invisible government which is the true ruling power of our country."[5]

Elite entitlement and hierarchy, Bernays argued, were inevitably the result of historical events that had imposed extra stress on "the higher strata of society." He saw multiple press/informational outlets and public schools as a steam engine that had the power to rob the power of kings and transfer it to the common person. He believed that such unwanted challenges from the grassroots mandated government efforts to shape and direct public opinion to assure preservation of order.[6] In a 1947 essay, "The Engineering of Consent," Bernays conveyed ideas similar to Lippman's "manufacture of consent."[7] Ironically, Jewish Bernays' earlier writings served to inspire Nazi propaganda minister Joseph Goebbels.[8] Bernays grasped that propaganda easily seduces even those whom it most horrifies and harms, connoting a tragic chapter in the evolutionary history of the human psyche.[9]

French sociologist Gabriel Tarde concluded more than a hundred years ago that public discourse is shaped by expanding media structures, *standardizing* human thought and perception.[10] In modern times we continue to experience the colonization of our minds due to a combination of corporate-owned mass media, think tanks funded by and in cahoots with big-monied interests, sophisticated public relations firms crafting redundant language and images to indoctrinate the viewer/listener/reader with the values of corporate capitalism, and an education system designed to produce obedient citizens and compliant workers.[11]

---

4 Edward Bernays, *Crystallizing Public Opinion* (New York: Boni and Liveright, 1923; Edward Bernays, *Propaganada* (New York: H. Liveright, 1928).

5 Bernays, 1928, 1.

6 Stuart Ewen, *PR! A Social History of Spin* (New York: Basic Books, 1996), 4.

7 *The ANNALS of the American Academy of Political and Social Science*, March 1947, 250, 113–120.

8 Ewen, 4.

9 Mark Crispin Miller, introduction to Edward Bernays, *Propaganda* (originally published 1928; Brooklyn: Ig Publishing, 2005), 30.

10 Ewen, 69, 418n10 & 11.

11 Draffan, 2003, 8; Anthony Pratkanis and Eliot Aronson, *Age of Propaganda: The Everyday Use and Abuse of Persuasion* (New York: W.H. Freeman and Co., 1992).

Meanwhile, wars easily continue,[12] facilitated by deceit and lies,[13] elaborate propaganda mind-control systems[14] that permeate our education institutions[15] and Hollywood,[16] and are promoted by the concentrated monopoly of corporate mass media.[17] Our collective minds are systematically colonized to accept the unacceptable.

Presidents and Politicians: Products and Practitioners of Propaganda

Presidents are, of course, excellent liars and pretenders, playing youth off as cannon fodder when force is needed to preserve economic and political power. When World War I began in 1914, President Woodrow Wilson's sympathies increasingly lay with the British and the US banks that were funding the allied war effort, even as he publicly proclaimed US neutrality.[18] However, he recognized that the great majority of Americans wanted no part of the fighting in Europe, and in 1916 he successfully sought re-election on the appealing slogan, "He Kept Us out of War."[19] Soon after his second inauguration, however, Wilson asked Congress for a declaration of war, which was approved in April 1917, although six senators and 50 members of the House of Representatives had the wit or wisdom to vote against it. Wilson promised this would be "the war to end all wars" as he was under pressure to bail out desperate US bankers such as J.P. Morgan who had been bankrolling the British war effort against Germany.

To convince a reluctant, isolationist public to become enthusiastic about the war, Wilson created a national propaganda office, the Committee on Public Information (CPI) (see above), which used all forms of media—newspapers, magazines, posters, still photographs, radio, telegraph, cable and movies—to broadcast its message. George Creel recruited seventy-five thousand "Four Minute Men" to travel the country publicly proclaiming the nobility of the war and need for a national conscription to face the belligerent Germans. Each spoke for four minutes, calculated to be an ideal length based

---

12 Norman Soloman, *War Made Easy: How Presidents and Pundits Keep Spinning Us to Death* (Hoboken, NJ: Wiley & Sons, 2005).

13 David Model, *Lying for Empire: How to Commit War Crimes with a Straight Face* (Monroe, ME: Common Courage Press, 2005); Sheldon Rampton and John Stauber, *Weapons of Mass Deception: The Uses of Propaganda in Bush's War on Iraq* (New York: Jeremy P. Tarcher/Penguin, 2003); John R. MacArthur, *Second Front: Censorship and Propaganda in the Gulf War* (Berkeley, CA: University of California Press, 1992).

14 Christopher Simpson, *Science of Coercion: Communication Research & Psychological Warfare 1945-1960* (New York: Oxford University Press, 1994); Herbert I. Schiller, *The Mind Managers* (Boston: Beacon Press, 1973).

15 John Taylor Gatto, *Dumbing Us Down: The Hidden Curriculum of Compulsory Schooling* (Vancouver, Canada, New Society, 1992); Ivan Illich, *Deschooling Society* (New York: Harper & Row, 1971).

16 Carl Boggs and Tom Pollard, *The Hollywood War Machine: US Militarism and Popular Culture* (Boulder, CO: Paradigm Publishers, 2007).

17 Ben H. Bagdikian, *The Media Monopoly* (Boston: Beacon Press, 2000).

18 Charles Callan Tansill, *America Goes To War* (Boston: Little, Brown and Company, 1938), 16, 67–70; Charles A. Beard and Mary R. Beard, *America in Midpassage*, Vol 1 (New York: The MacMillan Company, 1939), 414–415; Harry Elmer Barnes, *The Genesis of the World War* (New York: Alfred A. Knopf, 1927), 590–653; Thomas Fleming, *The Illusion of Victory: America In World War I* (New York: Basic Books, 2004), 47, 68–70.

19 Evans, 147.

on average human attention span. By the end of the war, CPI recruits had made more than seven-and-a-half million speeches to 314 million people in 5,200 communities. They traveled to Latin America as well as Europe.[20] The campaign was so successful it later inspired Adolf Hitler's propaganda techniques on a grand scale. Joseph Goebbels, Germany's propaganda minister, studied CPI's efforts and took great instruction from Creel's committee.[21]

After the gruesomeness of World War I, US Americans felt betrayed and resolved to never again make the same mistake. Yet just two decades later, President Franklin Roosevelt began the maneuvers by which the nation would once again be plunged into the European cauldron, despite his declared platform of neutrality toward the war. Unsuccessful in his naval provocations of the Germans in the Atlantic, he eventually pushed the imperial Japanese to the wall with a series of hostile economic-warfare measures and impossible ultimatums. Roosevelt knew of the attack on Pearl Harbor in advance, historians say, and indeed had intentionally provoked it.[22]

Even though the Soviet military force was to become the most critical in the Allied defeat of the Nazis in World War II, deep fear of the Bolsheviks had motivated US America's wealthy class, with the complicity of the US government, to support the rise of Nazi Germany from the early 1930s into the war years, because these capitalists trusted the capitalist Nazis to serve as a block to the threat of socialism. Elite power brokers included leaders of Wall Street and wealthy "barons" such as the Rockefellers and Andrew Mellon, and corporations such as Ford Motor, IBM, General Motors, General Electric, Standard Oil, Texaco, ITT, International Harvester, Chase Manhattan Bank, the House of Morgan banking dynasty, DuPont, United Aircraft, etc.[23] The same economic forces that helped build up Germany in pre-war years stood to make huge profits from the impending war.

Knowing these realities, Franklin Roosevelt nonetheless campaigned for re-election with the promise, in 1940: "I have said this before, but I shall say it again and again: Your boys are not going to be sent into any foreign wars."[24] Roosevelt was lying when he made this declaration, as he had lied before. Yet many, many Americans trusted Roosevelt with their lives. During the war more than 400,000 US Americans paid the ultimate price.

---

20 George Creel, *How We Advertised America* (New York: Harper & Brothers, 1920); *Complete Report of the Chairman of the Committee on Public Information: 1917:1918:1919* (Washington, DC, Government Printing Office, 1920).

21 Pratkanis, 8; Leonard Doob, "Goebbels' Principles of Propaganda," *Public Opinion Quarterly* 14 (1950), 419–442, cited in Dan D. Nimmo and Chevelle Newsome, *Political Commentators in the United States in the 20th Century: A Bio-Critical Sourcebook* (Westport, CT: Greenwood, 1997); Alan Axelrod, *Selling the Great War* (New York: Macmillan, 2009), 218–219.

22 Charles A. Beard, *President Roosevelt and the Coming of the War 1941: A Study in Appearances and Realities* (New Haven: Yale University Press, 1948), 519; Robert B. Stinnett, *Day of Deceit: The Truth about FDR and Pearl Harbor* (New York: The Free Press, 2000), 177–188; Zezima, 82–85; Charles Callan Tansill, *Back Door to War: The Roosevelt Foreign Policy 1933–1941* (Chicago: Henry Regnery Company, 1952).

23 Charles Higham, *Trading With the Enemy: The Nazi-American Money Plot 1933–1949* (New York: Delacorte Press, 1983); Michael Zezima, *Saving Private Power: The Hidden History of 'The Good War'* (New York: Soft Skull Press, 2000), 26–50.

24 Robert Goralski, *World War II Almanac: 1931–1945* (New York: Bonanza Books, 1981), 137].

Since World War II, nine presidents, Truman to Obama, have lied to the people to justify hundreds of military interventions, while covering up thousands of covert intrusions.[25] Propaganda rules supreme.

Atomic Bombings

The dropping of atomic bombs on Japan was surely one of the cruelest acts in human history. Although the reason given for the bombings was that it would shorten the war and save American lives, the US knew the Japanese were already defeated and earnestly seeking terms for surrender. Truman and his advisors knew the war was, for all intents and purposes, over. In any case, means for ending the conflict peacefully certainly existed. Instead, US political leaders calculated that using the bomb against Japan would strengthen their post-war hand against the Soviet Union.[26] The bomb seemed a sure ticket to force the Soviets to withdraw from Eastern Europe, to consent to US economic and political plans for the region, and to impress upon the whole world the need to accept the US capitalist vision.[27] Even as Truman realized the war had already been won, he saw the Russians as a dangerous ideological threat that needed to be stopped, and began to shift from military to political imagery. In anticipation of the July 16, 1945 test of the new weapon at the Alamogordo Test Range in New Mexico, seen as assuring post-war control, he proclaimed, "I'll certainly have a hammer on those boys."[28]

The bomb dropped on Hiroshima did not target the city's military base, an important one, but was aimed instead at the center of the city, taking great toll on the civilian population.[29] Truman, however, reported that the Hiroshima bombing was targeted to "avoid... the killing of civilians."[30] Counter to Truman's words, the US Strategic Bombing Survey officially reported that "Hiroshima and Nagasaki were chosen as targets because of their concentration of activities and population."[31]

Just four months before the atomic bombings of Japan, Secretary of War Henry L. Stimson had stated his belief that the Soviet Union's demands in Eastern Europe were motivated by

---

25 RE: Presidents Truman through George W. Bush, see David Model, *Lying for Empire: How to Commit War Crimes with a Straight Face* (Monroe, ME: Common Courage Press, 2005); RE: Obama, see: Center for Media Democracy's John Stauber, "How Obama Took over the Peace Movement," http://www.prwatch.org/node/8297; Peter Phillips, "Barack Obama Administration Continues US Military Dominance," http://www.projectcensored.org/articles/story/http-wwwprojectcensoredorg-articles-story-barack-obama-administration-c/; "'Our President Is Deceiving the American Public': Pentagon Papers Whistleblower on President Obama and the Wars in Afghanistan and Iraq," http://www.democracynow.org/2010/3/30/our_president_is_deceiving_the_american; "Obama's speech on Afghanistan: A compendium of lies," December 3, 2009, http://www.wsws.org/en/articles/2009/12/pers-d03.html.

26 Gar Alperovitz, *The Decision to Use the Atom Bomb* (New York: Vintage Books, 1996), 3–7; Gar Alperovitz, *Atomic Diplomacy: Hiroshima & Potsdam, The Use of the Atomic Bomb and the American Confrontation with Soviet Power*, expanded and updated edition (New York: Penguin Books, 1985), 5. The August 14 Japanese surrender had been anticipated *before* the atomic bombings.

27 Alperovitz, 1985, 282–283, 289–290.

28 Robert Jay Lifton and Greg Mitchell, *Hiroshima In America: Fifty Years of Denial* (New York: G.P. Putnam's Sons, 1995), 160.

29 Lifton and Mitchell, 1995, 5.

30 Alperovitz, 1996, 521.

31 Zinn, 1980, 415.

concerns for security rather than goals of world conquest. Stimson nonetheless became influenced by US Ambassador to the Soviet Union W. Averell Harriman into taking a strong anti-Soviet position, rather than one of cautionary diplomacy,[32] agreeing to use the bomb as a "diplomatic weapon" to "browbeat the Russians."[33] Historian Kenneth C. Davis speculated the motive for the bombing was to cut off the possibility of Russia's having any control in East Asia.

Playwright and historian Charles L. Mee, Jr., described the psychological impact of the bombs on Stalin, who knew the US use of the "doomsday machine" was not militarily necessary. "It was this last chilling fact that doubtless made the greatest impression on the Russians," writes Mee. Author, historian, and broadcaster Studs Terkel declared the bomb was dropped "so little Harry could show Molotov and Stalin we've got the cards . . . we've got something and they'd better behave themselves in Europe. . . . The evidence is overwhelming. And yet you tell that to 99 percent of Americans and they'll spit in your eye."

It is unspeakable to think that the Japanese were so cruelly used as a pawn in the US battle against the Communist threat represented by the Soviet Union. Again, the key to the public's support for such abominable acts can be found in institutionalized racism and propaganda that served to whip up fear and dehumanization of "the other."

In February 1942, two months after Pearl Harbor, President Roosevelt had issued Executive Order 9066, forcing the relocation to inland concentration camps of all persons of Japanese ancestry, ostensibly to prevent espionage. The US had a prototype—a long record of militarily pushing native Indigenous people westward, then forcibly removing them to reservations, i.e., concentration camps where they could be "civilized." Roosevelt's order resulted in the tragically unfair incarceration of 117 thousand Japanese, nearly two-thirds of whom were native-born US citizens, in some sixty concentration camps of different types scattered about the country in twenty-one US states. The same racist hatred of "the Japs" that made it morally and politically acceptable to imprison thousands without due process at home, was used to excuse the annihilation of hundreds of thousands by bombing them in their native homeland in order to scare the Soviets.[34] This is another reminder how easily US Americans are frightened into exchanging their "ideals" for "security."

---

32 Godfrey Hodgspn, *The Colonel: The Life and Wars of Henry Stimson, 1867–1950* (New York: Alfred A. Knopf, 1990), 342–366.

33 This and the speculations mentioned in the following paragraph are all found in Michael Zezima, *Saving Private Power: The Hidden History of the 'The Good War'* (New York: Soft Skull Press, 2000), 127–128.

34 *wikipedia*, Internment of Japanese Americans: http://en.wikipedia.org/wiki/Internment_of_Japanese_Americans#Facilities; Documents and Photographs from the National Archives Related to Japanese Relocation during World War II: http://www.archives.gov/education/lessons/japanese-relocation/; Michi Weglyn, *Years of Infamy: The Untold Story of America's Concentration Camps* (New York: William Morrow and Co., 1976). Richard Drinnon, *Keeper of Concentration Camps: Dillon S. Myer and American Racism* (Berkeley: University of California Press, 1987), 29–159. Psychological implications in some camps were comparable to schizophrenic symptoms observed by psychologist Bruno Bettelheim in the Nazi camps, and their totalitarian nature intending severe indoctrination emulated Soviet brainwashing [Drinnon, 1987, 157, 285].

Post-Bomb

For many US Americans, fear of Communism took the assault on reason to an extreme. Even the FBI was not perceived as a sufficient protector. My father, along with thousands of others, was an early member, in the late 1950s, of the right-wing John Birch Society, a Christian organization so rabidly anti-communist their publication "Public Opinion" famously preached that communists ate their babies. This periodical regularly sat on the coffee table next to my father's chair.[35]

Though this was an extreme position, liberals were also fearful of "Communism" in the Cold War, using tamer rhetoric even as they supported repressive domestic policies against thousands of dissenters, including enforced loyalty oaths for public servants who simply raised mild questions. Massive mind-control techniques were so successful the majority of US Americans became convinced that their daily existence was threatened by a nation—the Soviet Union—that had lost one sixth of its population and virtually all of its industrial and agricultural capacity in fighting the Nazis.

It is amazing indeed, but no less amazing is the fact that I and several million other young men, and a few thousand women, so easily followed orders of authority figures to travel 9,000 miles wearing government-issued uniforms with backpacks and deadly weapons in order to kill "Communists" in a small country called Viet Nam. In hindsight, this strikes me not only as astounding and absurd, but grotesquely criminal. Most of us had never met a Vietnamese person, knew no Vietnamese history, and could not even locate the country on a world map. Our societal training was to obey and not to question the wisdom of our political leaders, a masterful triumph of propaganda that can slip into tyranny.

That this phenomenon of popular robotic-like obedience to vertical, patriarchal authority is not new does not make it any less absurd. Hierarchy emerged with the advent of "civilization" some 6,000 years ago and coincides with 14,600 major wars since,[36] fought with obedient young men against other obedient young men, all strangers to each other. Urban "civilization" has produced patterns of systematic violence and warfare previously unknown,[37] what social commentator Andrew Bard Schmookler calls its "original sin."[38] Joseph Conrad, in his 1899 novel *Heart of Darkness*, captured this ugly side of humans, depicting how "civilization" covers over the harsh realities of the cruel exploitation upon which it is built.[39]

---

35 I heard the same rap in 1986 when I interviewed captured CIA-trained and Reagan-funded Contra terrorists who had been striving to overthrow the Nicaraguan Sandinista government. They acknowledged that their US trainers taught them that the Sandinistas ate their own children.

36 James Hillman, *A Terrible Love of War* (New York: The Penguin Press, 2004), 17.

37 Ashley Montagu, *The Nature of Human Aggression* (Oxford: Oxford University Press, 1976), 43–53, 59–60; Ashley Montagu, ed., *Learning Non-Aggression: The Experience of Non-Literate Societies* (Oxford: Oxford University Press, 1978); Jean Guilaine and Jean Zammit, *The Origin of War: Violence in Prehistory*, trans. Melanie Hersey (2001; Malden, MA: Blackwell Publishing, 2005).

38 Andrew B. Schmookler, *Out of Weakness: Healing the Wounds That Drive Us to War* (New York: Bantam Books, 1988), 303.

39 *Heart of Darkness*, written by Polish-born English novelist Joseph Conrad, was originally published in 1899 as a three-part series in U.K's *Blackwood's* Magazine. It is considered one of the most-read works

Knowing this long history helps me understand not only Cold War mania, but also the deep historical and psychological forces of conditioning that continue to lead our nation into war. It also helps explain how I, as an individual, could so willingly obey, virtually without question, the state's directives to participate in killing impoverished strangers in a far-off land. Our fathers, and people in authority, certainly would not lead us astray, I thought. But betray us they did, even as they tragically betrayed themselves. Cultural historian Lewis Mumford described how easily authority systems can morph into collective states of paranoia and delusions of grandeur, one of the most difficult psychological disorders to treat.[40]

It is amazing and ironic how much we in the United States cower in fear and terror behind all our missiles and bombs. But of course a country with but a small percentage of the world's population that consumes at least one-fourth of the world's resources, must constantly defend its history of theft of land, labor, and resources from others who just might want only their fair share.

So our healing as a nation depends on our removing the wool that remains in our eyes—that we seek to understand and grapple with these forces, these lies that continually drive us to war and violence. We must strive to unravel the pretend US America—its skewed origin stories, its false mythologies, and its phony sense of "exceptionalism"—in an honest pursuit of "liberty and justice for all." Only when we cleanse the wool from our eyes will we finally be able to see with our hearts as well as our heads. This recovery of authentic humanity remains an essential quest in my own journey. It seems that our collective survival as a species depends upon just such an evolutionary awakening.

Cold War Origins and the Pathological Fear of Communism

The Cold War is generally considered to have begun sometime between the end of WWII and President Truman's declaration of the Truman Doctrine on March 12, 1947. In that speech, Truman characterized the Greek Civil War as part of a global struggle "between alternative ways of life." He stated that a "Communist" victory in Greece would result in the countries of Europe, the Middle East, Africa, and Asia falling like dominoes.[41]

---

of the last hundred years, largely an autobiographical description of Conrad's six-month journey in 1890 into the "Congo Free State," at the time being plundered by Belgium. In fact the story could apply to almost any place in the world where European nations, later the United States, plundered peoples for profits and material privileges without acknowledging the terrible, ugly consequences. Francis Ford Coppola's 1979 movie *Apocalypse Now* translates the "Heart of Darkness" to Viet Nam and Cambodia. Adam Hochschild's *King Leopold's Ghost* [New York: A Mariner Book, 1999] describes the diabolical exploitation of the Congo Free State by King Leopold II of Belgian between 1885 and 1908. Estimates of murdered Congolese in this period run as high as 13 million. Please don't read this as if this is something that the United States or other European nations would not do, or have not done. Indeed the US and Europe are founded on these practices, all under the cover of "civilization."

40 Mumford, 1967, 204, 218.

41 Edward Pessen, *Losing Our Souls: The American Experience in the Cold War* (Chicago: Ivan R. Dee, 1993), 50, 67.

However, origins of the Cold War can be traced back to the November 7, 1917, Russian revolution.[42] Prior to 1917, Russia was a semi-colonial possession of European capital that had settled into a typical Third World pattern, supplying raw materials to industrial countries while primarily developing itself with foreign capital and watching its debt escalate as a result. But a radical break came with the Bolshevik takeover in October-November 1917, which "extricated Russia from the Western-dominated periphery." This was unacceptable to the capitalist West.[43]

During Russia's 1918-1920 civil war, a number of the allied nations and Japan invaded Russia in efforts to crush socialism. Winston Churchill, England's Minister for War and Air (1919-1921), sought desperately "to strangle at its birth" the Bolshevik state.[44] Eleven Western nations and Japan, determined to nip the revolution in the bud, formed expeditionary forces that invaded Russia in 1918 with nearly nine hundred thousand troops in three regions: Archangel in northern Russia, including five thousand US troops; the Odessa region and Crimea in Southern Russia; and Vladivostok in eastern Russia, including seven thousand US troops who remained there until 1920. US casualties during the occupation in northern Russia reached 2,845. The State Department told Congress: "All these operations were to offset effects of the Bolshevik revolution in Russia."[45]

This US intervention into Russia occurred on President Wilson's orders without a Congressional declaration of war. It also occurred during peace negotiations that had gotten underway on January 4, 1919 in Versailles, France, to formally end the First World War. The Versailles Treaty was signed June 28, 1919, by Germany and Britain, France, Italy, and Russia, but not by the US.[46]

The intervention into Russia illustrates how terrified the US and the West were of the ideological alternative to capitalism that the Bolsheviks represented. "High level US planning documents identify the primary threat as 'radical and nationalistic regimes' that are responsive to popular pressures for 'immediate improvement in the low living standards of the masses' and development for domestic needs, tendencies that conflict with the demand for a 'political and economic climate conducive to private investment,' with adequate repatriation of profits and 'protection of our raw materials.'"[47]

In essence, the Soviet Union was considered a gigantic "rotten apple," a "challenge . . . to the very survival of the capitalist order." As Europe was beginning to self-destruct, the US

---

42 "Bolsheviki Seize State Buildings, Defying Kerensky," *New York Times*, November 7, 1917.
43 Noam Chomsky, *Year 501: The Conquest Continues* (Boston: South End Press, 1993), 66-67.
44 Zezima, 26-27.
45 Martin Gilbert, *The First World War: A Complete History* (New York: Henry Holt, 1994), 515-516; D. F. Fleming, *The Cold War and Its Origins, 1917-1920*, Vol I (Garden City, NJ: Doubleday, 1961), 16-35; Howard Zinn, *The Twentieth Century: A People's History* (New York: Perennial Library/Harper & Row, 1984), 110-111; David S. Foglesong, *America's Secret War Against Bolshevism: US Intervention in the Russian Civil War, 1917-1920* (Chapel Hill, NC: University of North Carolina Press, 1995), 2-9, 272-273.
46 Charles A. Beard and Mary R. Beard, *A Basic History of the United States* (New York: Doubleday, Doran & Co., 1944), 436; Versailles is 10 miles outside of Paris.
47 Noam Chomsky, "The Face of Colonialism a Century Later" (*PeaceWork*, July/August 1998), 19.

was for the first time becoming a decisive world influence. The Bolshevik revolution, i.e., Communism, was seen as a global enemy that had to be crushed.[48]

The Russian Revolution was the historical factor leading to the US Red Scare that lasted from late World War I to the 1930s.[49] Repression justified by the scare was exerted everywhere, both inside and outside our borders.

Attorney General Alexander Mitchell Palmer, a Quaker, declared that Communism was "eating its way into the homes of the American workman" and that Socialists were responsible for most of the country's social problems.[50] The crackdown on dissent accelerated significantly after the end of the war. Congress in 1919 refused to seat Socialist representative Victor L. Berger from Wisconsin because of his views condemning US entrance into the war. A number of other Socialists who had been elected were barred from taking various public offices. With strong support from Congress and the public, in 1919 Attorney General Palmer systematically clamped down on political dissent.[51]

Palmer and J. Edgar Hoover (head of the new "anti-radical division" of the Bureau of Investigation) amassed on index cards somewhere between 150,000[52] to 200,000[53] names of people suspected of radical activities such as questioning the war and/or articulating a challenge to capitalist economic structures. They used these collected names to conduct a series of raids in bowling alleys, pool halls, cafes, and other places believed to be "radical" hangouts.[54] During the first major raid, which took place in multiple cities on November 7, 1919, the second anniversary of the Russian Revolution, 650 people were arrested on suspicion of radicalism. The vast majority just happened to be at the wrong place at the wrong time during the sweeps.[55] Of the people arrested, 249 were deported[56] to Russia.[57] On January 2, 1920, a second massive raid culminated in arrests of an estimated 4,000[58] to 10,000 suspects[59] in thirty-three cities[60] in twenty-three states,[61] and led to 3,000

---

48 Chomsky, 1993, 67; Chomsky, 1992, 37.

49 "Senate Orders Reds Here Investigated; Directs Overman Committee to Turn the Light on American Bolshevism. Mass of Evidence at Hand—Walsh, Borah, and Others Attack Congressmen Who Attended a Soviet Meeting," *New York Times*, February 05, 1919.

50 Peter Knight, ed., *Conspiracy Theories in American History: An Encyclopedia* (Santa Barbara, CA: ABC-CLIO, 2003), 7.

51 Robert Justin Goldstein, *Political Repression in Modern America* (Cambridge, NY: Schenkman, 1978), 154–157; Geoffrey Stone, *Perilous Times: Free Speech in Wartime from the Sedition Act of 1798 to the War on Terrorism* (New York: W.W. Norton, 2004), 220–224.

52 Curt Gentry, *J. Edgar Hoover: The Man and the Secrets* (New York: W.W. Norton, 1991), 79.

53 Stone, 223.

54 Goldstein, 156–155.

55 Stone, 223; Goldstein, 156.

56 Stone, 223.

57 Goldstein 154–158.

58 Stone, 223.

59 Goldstein, 156.

60 Stone, 223.

61 Roy Talbert, Jr., *Negative Intelligence: The Army and the American Left, 1917–1941* (Jackson: University Press of Mississippi, 1991), 175.

deportations.[62] By 1921, the amassed list of suspects grew to 450,000[63] as the fanatical fear of Reds continued to sweep the nation.

Palmer's Justice Department conducted the majority of arrests without legal warrants. A group of distinguished lawyers and law professors, including Felix Frankfurter and Roscoe Pound, published a *Report upon the Illegal Practices of the United States Department of Justice* that thoroughly documented the fact that the department had ordered wholesale arrests of suspected "radicals" without legal authorization, that it had unlawfully held them incommunicado, and that agent provocateurs had actively participated in unlawful entrapment. Palmer responded by saying, "I apologize for nothing that the Department of Justice has done in this matter. I glory in it."[64] Palmer publicly described those arrested as "alien filth" possessing "sly and crafty eyes . . . lopsided faces, sloping brows, and misshapen features," which sheltered "cupidity, cruelty, insanity and crime."[65]

This history is important as it foreshadows a culture of fanatical fear of Communism that led to increasingly repressive policies during World War II, the Truman and Eisenhower years of the Cold War, and the Viet Nam war. Fear of terrorism has justified further repression in post-9/11 wars against "Islamists," and against so-called anarchists in the 2000s.

Nonetheless, at the same time the Red Scare was instilling fear in the US public, the March 1932 issue of Henry Luce's *Fortune* Magazine couldn't resist touting the capitalist business advantages of trading with the Soviet Union. Its readership included executives of the business community who were already doing millions of dollars worth of business with the "Reds." Tapping into profits from both import and export markets in the Soviet Union were companies such as RCA, Ford Motor Co, Westinghouse, Caterpillar Tractor, John Deere, General Electric, American Express, Macy's, Marshall Field, Standard Oil, and US Steel.[66]

Opposition to WWI mounted from the Left, for example from labor leader Eugene Debs and his associates, and was cruelly crushed, and its ideas of peace and justice reviled, as the Russian Revolution was publicly declared, over and over, to be a direct threat to the US. Repression of the entire Left, which continued for many years after the war, included purging of Leftist influence in the trade union movement, a phenomenon that would be repeated after the Second World War. The "consensus" on foreign policy in the 1950s Cold War period had its earlier counterpart in a "consensus" on domestic policy in the 1920s.[67]

---

62 Stone, 224.
63 Gentry, 79.
64 Stone, 225.
65 Goldstein, 158.
66 Michael Barson and Steven Heller, *Red Scared! The Commie Menace in Propaganda and Popular Culture* (San Francisco: Chronicle Books, 2001), 26.
67 Douglas F. Doud, *The Twisted Dream: Capitalist Development in the United States since 1776* (Cambridge, MA: Winthrop Publishers, 1977), 296.

Accusations of creeping Bolshevism to the south of the US-Mexican border intensified in January 1927 when President Calvin Coolidge's Secretary of State, Franklin B. Kellogg, accused Mexico's President Calles of "seeking to establish in Nicaragua a Bolshevist regime."[68] US troops had already been dispatched to Nicaragua in 1926 "to protect interests of the United States"[69] as fears escalated that the hundred-year-old Monroe Doctrine was threatened by the Reds of Russia.

Origins of US Office of Strategic Services (OSS)

June 26, 1939. President Franklin Roosevelt orders the FBI, the War Department's Military Intelligence Division (MID), and Office of Naval Intelligence (ONI) to investigate "all espionage, counterespionage, and sabotage matters." Soon "subversive activities" are added to the order, mandating the kind of information law enforcement agencies are to promptly report to the FBI. This comes to be called the "Interdepartmental Intelligence Conference."[70]

September 5, 1939. President Roosevelt declares US neutrality four days after Germany invades Poland.

June 5, 1940. President Roosevelt orders responsibility for counterintelligence investigations involving civilians within the US and its territories to be placed under authority of J. Edgar Hoover.[71]

July 11, 1941. Five months before the Japanese attack on Pearl Harbor, Roosevelt establishes the Office of the Coordinator of [War] Information (COI) to gather and interpret domestic and worldwide intelligence on "black" propaganda, guerrilla warfare, espionage, sabotage, and "un-American" subversive activities. World War I hero and Wall Street lawyer William "Wild Bill" Donovan is named as director, much to the displeasure of J. Edgar Hoover, who is jealous of Donovan's new powers and sees them as impinging on his reign over domestic intelligence activities as head of the FBI.[72]

June 13, 1942. A section of the COI is renamed the Office of Strategic Services (OSS) and headed by Donovan, who envisions the new office as an international secret service for the US to meet challenges posed first by the Nazis and subsequently by Communist forces. The OSS will be staffed by young "calculatingly reckless" officers possessing "disciplined daring," "trained for aggressive action."[73]

---

68 Richard V. Houlahan, "Kellogg Offers Evidence of Red Plots in Nicaragua and Aid from Calles; Moscow Directly Accused," *New York Times*, January 13, 1927.

69 Grimmett, 10.

70 Gentry, 210–211; Thomas F. Troy, *Wild Bill and Intrepid: Donovan, Stephenson, and the Origins of the CIA* (New Haven, CT: Yale University Press, 1996), 36, 95.

71 Talbert, 258.

72 Troy, 19, 132; Thomas Fleming, *The New Dealers' War: F. D. R. and the War within World War II* (New York: Basic Books, 2001), 131; Gentry, 266.

73 R. Harris Smith, *OSS: The Secret History of America's First Central Intelligence Agency* (Berkeley, CA: University of California Press, 1972), 1–35; Troy, 132.

The other section of the COI, the propaganda arm, becomes the Office of War Information (OWI) and is headed up by experienced radio newsman Elmer Davis. With enthusiasm rivaling George Creel's elaborate World War I Committee on Public Information, the COI commences to stir feelings of national solidarity whereby various business interests are given tools to practice an ideological propaganda campaign incorporating patriotism as part of their bottom line. The interrelationship between government and industry is encouraged. W.J. Wier of Chicago's prestigious advertising and public relations agency, Lord and Thomas, links war victory and consumption in a post-war society as a victory for capitalism,[74] boasting that with OWI, "we sit with the greatest force for moving mass psychology that the world has ever seen" and that "nothing that Goebbels has can hold a candle to it. . . . We can explain why the American way of life—with its bathtubs and pop-up toasters and electric refrigerators and radios and insulated homes—is worth sacrificing anything and everything not only to preserve but to take forward in a future more glorious than ever."[75]

July 1944. At the Democratic presidential convention, President Franklin Roosevelt, seeking an unprecedented fourth term, refuses to back his Vice President Henry Wallace, very popular with rank-and-file voters, and the last ardent proponent of the New Deal, in favor of relatively unknown US Senator Harry Truman from Missouri. The war, not the New Deal, had saved the second Roosevelt administration, and the capitalist system, i.e., big-monied interests, vehemently oppose the popular Wallace, who is perceived as too far left and overly friendly with labor.[76] (In truth, Wallace was not a Socialist and did not support the Communists, but he vociferously advocated for a "people's capitalism" and sought peaceful co-existence with the Soviets.[77])

November 1944. The Roosevelt-Truman team wins the presidential election. To placate Wallace, Roosevelt names him Secretary of Commerce.

---

74 Paul M. Haridakis, Barbara S. Hugenberg, and Stanley T. Wearden, *War and the Media: Essays on News Reporting, Propaganda and Popular Culture* (Jefferson, NC: McFarland, 2009), 106–107; Ewen, 341.

75 Ewen, 341, 443n6, citing W. J. Wier, "Opportunity!" *Printers' Ink*, 199 (October 1942), 13. For a modern assessment of the media, see Edward S. Herman and Noam Chomsky, *Manufacturing Consent: The Political Economy of the Mass Media* (New York: Pantheon Books, 1988, 2002).

76 http://en.wikipedia.org/wiki/1944_Democratic_National_Convention; D. D. Guttenplan, *American Radical: The Life and Times of I.F. Stone* (Farrar, Straus and Giroux, 2009), 191, 219.

77 David Caute, *The Great Fear: The Anti-Communist Purge under Truman and Eisenhower* (New York: Simon and Schuster, 1978), 31.

October 1, 1945. The OSS is abolished under Truman. The State and War Departments salvage some of their components and, in 1946, they become the Central Intelligence Group, a short-lived entity that is replaced in 1947 by the Central Intelligence Agency.[78]

Cold War Revival Following World War II

On January 3, 1945, the House Un-American Activities Committee (HUAC) was established as a standing committee. The only permanent investigating committee in the House, it possessed widespread subpoena powers and was charged with investigating the character and objectives of "un-American" propaganda activities, foreign or domestic. HUAC replaced the Dies Committee that was established in 1938 to investigate Nazi, Fascist, Communist, and other organizations deemed "un-American" in character. The popular Dies Committee had succeeded the Fish Committee, which in 1931 issued a report describing connections between Communism, "aliens," Blacks, and free love. The Fish Committee had succeeded the Overman Committee of 1918–19, which was charged to investigate German and Bolshevik suspects in the US.[79] Other western democracies had credible Socialist or Communist parties; such an intense watch on domestic organizations and their branding as "radical" was peculiar to the US at the time.

The establishment of HUAC marked the beginning of intense revival of anti-Communist fervor in the United States. Between 1946 and 1954, Congress would conduct no fewer than 135 Communism-related investigations.[80] Early bomb tests were swiftly followed by the atomic bombing of Japan by the US, and selective prosecution of war crimes at Nuremberg—events marking the end of the Second World War, also witnessed the beginnings of the new Cold War.

COLD WAR REVIVAL

February 4–11, 1945. Roosevelt, Churchill, and Stalin attend the Yalta Conference, held in Crimea, a peninsula south of the Ukrainian mainland. Knowing Germany is on the verge of surrender, they pledge to bring war criminals to trial. Stalin surprisingly agrees to intervene in Asia's war region—China and Korea—ninety days following the date of Germany's expected surrender.

April 12, 1945. Roosevelt dies and is immediately replaced by Vice President Harry Truman.

April 1945. New President Harry Truman's Secretary of War, Henry L. Stimson, tells a conference of US leaders that the Soviet Union's demands in Eastern Europe are motivated by concerns for Soviet security, not by any goals of

---

78 Troy, 132.
79 Caute, 88–89; Morris and Morris, 424, 453.
80 Marty Jezer, *The Dark Ages: Life in the United States 1945–1960* (Boston: South End Press, 1982), 81, 91; Caute, 85.

world conquest. Hawkish John Foster Dulles, Admiral William D. Leahy, General Lucius Clay, State Department official Robert Murphy, Charles E. Bohlen, and a key aide of prominent financier Bernard Baruch all agree that security concerns, not ideology, dictate the Soviets' pragmatic policies.[81]

May 2, 1945. Five days before Germany's surrender, Truman appoints US Supreme Court Justice Robert H. Jackson to be the chief US prosecutor at the planned trials of Nazi war criminals to be held in Nuremberg, Germany.

July 16, 1945. The first nuclear explosion is conducted at the White Sands Missile Range, part of the Alamogordo Test Range located 30 miles southeast of Socorro, New Mexico, in what is known as the *Journada del Muerto* (Journey of Death) desert. The test is named *Trinity*.

July 17–August 2, 1945. The Potsdam Conference, a meeting of the world's leaders regarding the end of WWII and post-war strategies, is held in Potsdam in occupied Germany, the start date pushed back from the original schedule by Truman, so that the US might boast of a successful test of its "cosmic" bomb.

August 6, 1945. The US drops an atomic bomb on Hiroshima, Japan, population 350,000, instantly killing 100,000 and fatally injuring 50,000. Many thousands more die in subsequent years from radiation sickness, though the total number of casualties remains uncertain.[82]

August 8, 1945. The four major victorious Allies in World War II—the US, the USSR, the UK, and France—sign an executive agreement, the *London Agreement and Charter*, providing that the *major* war criminals, whose offenses had no particular geographical location, will be tried by an International Military Tribunal (IMT) at Nuremberg, Germany, under three major categories: Crimes against Peace, Crimes against Humanity, and Crimes against the Laws of War.

August 8, 1945. As promised at Yalta, Stalin sends Soviet troops into Manchuria and Korea, exactly ninety days after Germany's surrender.

August 9, 1945. The US drops a plutonium bomb on Nagasaki, population 270,000, instantly killing as many as 100,000, only 250 of them Japanese military personnel. Thousands more die in subsequent years from radiation sickness. Like Hiroshima, in its rationale for dropping the bomb, US military officers cite Nagasaki as a military city.[83]

August 14, 1945. The Japanese formally announce the surrender that was anticipated for weeks before the dropping of the atomic bombs.

---

81 Daniel Yergen, *Shattered Peace: The Origins of the Cold War* (New York: Penguin Books, 1977, 1990), 80–82; Pessen, 63.

82 Lifton and Mitchell, xvii; *http://atomicbombmuseum.org/3_health.shtml; http://www.rerf.or.jp/general/qa_e/qa1.html*.

83 http://www.rerf.or.jp/general/qa_e/qa1.html; http://atomicbombmuseum.org/3_health.shtml/; Lifton, 27, 163.

> November 20, 1945–October 1, 1946. The first Nuremberg trials are conducted. Twenty-four major Nazis are tried. Twelve are sentenced to death, seven imprisoned for lengthy terms, three acquitted, and, for two, charges are dismissed.
>
> December 1946–April 1949. Twelve subsequent trials of military and industrial officials are held at Nuremberg.
>
> December 11, 1946. The General Assembly of the United Nations affirms the principles of international law recognized by the Charter of the Nuremberg Tribunal and the Judgment of the Tribunal.[84]

The Nuremberg Principles

US Supreme Court Justice Robert H. Jackson, loaned by President Truman to be one of the four prosecutors at Nuremberg, stated, "For the first time, four of the most powerful nations have agreed not only upon the principle of liability for war crimes of persecution, but also upon the principle of individual responsibility for *the crime of attacking international peace*" [*italics* added by author]. A total of seven Nuremberg Principles were set forth in the agreement.

The Declaration of the Judgment of the International Military Tribunal at Nuremberg concluded, "To initiate a war of aggression is the *supreme international crime*, differing only from other war crimes in that it contains within itself the accumulated evil of the whole" [*italics* added by author].

In addition to the problem of a tribunal dispensing victors' justice, it ignored the crimes of the Allies, prosecuting only crimes of the Axis. In a stunning example of a grotesque double standard, the tribunal simply excluded all crimes from the air. German bombings of Rotterdam in Holland and Coventry in England were small compared with the British and US bombings of German cities.[85] The number of civilians murdered by Allied bombings in Germany and Japan far exceeded the bombing casualties of the Axis. If this seems shocking, even more shocking is the fact that the signing of the London Agreement and Charter on August 8 was sandwiched between the dropping on August 6, of the "Little Boy" atomic bomb on Hiroshima, and the dropping on August 9 of the "Fat Man" plutonium bomb on Nagasaki, making a mockery of the very international law that Nuremberg was presuming to enforce. The exception of aerial bombardment as a war crime only assured the continuance of global lawlessness.[86]

Just as disturbing as the double standard applied to war crimes, however, is the fact that, at the same time that major Nazis politicians, military officials and industrialists were being tried for their crimes, the US was making deals with a number of members of Hitler's

---

84 Ironically, this affirmation occurred only eight days before the Vietnamese were forced into war against the French, who were violating Nuremberg by their insistence on continued colonial occupation of Indochina.

85 Zinn, 1980, 412.

86 F.J.P. Veale, *Advance to Barbarism: How the Reversion to Barbarism in Warfare and War-Trials Menaces Our Future* (Appleton, WI: C.C. Nelson Publishing Co., 1953), xvi,138, 297.

Soviet-savvy intelligence network. Headed by General Reinhard Gehlen, its members became key participants in carrying out US OSS operations, and that of its successor, the CIA.[87] Furthermore, in a secret 1945 program authorized by President Truman called "Operation Paperclip," a number of hardcore Nazi Party and SS men—scientists, engineers and technicians—were welcomed into the US to work on biological and chemical warfare, rocket and missile technology. More than 750 of these German specialists became key players for the new US Cold War military-industrial-communications complex[88] in its war against the Soviet Union.

The fact is, US involvement in World War II rejuvenated US capitalism, a goal the New Deal had failed to accomplish. Corporate profits skyrocketed, going from $6.4 billion in 1940 to $10.8 billion in 1944. The gross national product (GNP) was $90 billion dollars in 1940, and by 1944, it had reached $200 billion. Corporate profits were the highest in history. All established social groups materially benefitted as prosperity returned throughout the country. Consumer income increased from $75 billion in 1940 to $150 billion dollars in 1944, as the materialism of the American Way of Life dramatically increased. By war's end, US America was on its way to entrenched global hegemony, and its possession and willingness to use the bomb boosted its arrogance and confidence that it was invincible.[89]

Post-WWII Cold War: First Stop, Korea[90]

Korea is where the Cold War first arrived. At the conclusion of World War II, the Soviet Union and the United States jointly occupied previously undivided Korea in order to expel the defeated Japanese, who had effectively ruled the entire peninsula since 1905. On August 11, 1945, three days prior to Japan's formal surrender, Truman unilaterally created a temporary demarcation line separating the Russian and US forces approximately along the 38th parallel, surprisingly with the assent of Stalin. This line was not intended to create two separate countries but merely to be a temporary division as they awaited unifying elections. A Korean war was inconceivable before Truman's arbitrary decision to divide Korea, made from the comfort of his air-conditioned White House in Washington, DC. But because of that division, the Korean Peninsula has not been at peace since; more than seventy years later, millions of families are still divided by the fortified, fenced demilitarized zone (DMZ).[91]

---

87 Zepezauer, 6–7; Zezima, 155–157; Christopher Simpson, *Blowback: The First Full Account of America's Recruitment of Nazis, and its Disastrous Effect on our Domestic and Foreign Policy* (New York: Weidenfeld & Nicolson, 1988), 40–65.

88 Zezima, 159–61; Simpson, 36–39.

89 Zinn, 1980, 416; Lawrence S. Wittner, *Rebels Against War: The American Peace Movement, 1941–1960* (New York: Columbia University Press, 1969), 111–112.

90 This section is an excerpt of a longer essay published on the author's website: http://www.brianwillson.com/history-of-u-s-sabotage-of-korean-peace-and-reunification/.

91 Bruce Cumings, *Korea's Place in the Sun: A Modern History* (New York: W.W. Norton, 1997), 238.

With the defeat of Japan, the people of Korea were confident they would now be able to build their own society, resuming control over their sovereignty. At this moment in their lives, the Korean people could not have imagined that they were about to become victims of an even more tragic and cruel injustice, this time inflicted upon them by a Western nation, the United States of America, rather than by one of their historic Asian nemeses.

On August 15, 1945, the day after the Japanese surrender, the Korean people, the majority of whom were seriously impoverished, openly celebrated their liberation after 40 years of miserable Japanese occupation. Ironically, on the same day and unbeknown to most Koreans, the US proclaimed establishment of "legal" occupational control over the south, though US troops wouldn't land until September 8. Confident of their ability to regain control of their own country, Koreans had immediately formed the Committee for the Preparation of Korean Independence (CKPI). By August 28, all Korean provinces on the entire peninsula had established local peoples' democratic committees. On September 6, delegates from throughout Korea, both north and south of the artificially imposed demarcation line, despite the new US occupation orders, gathered in Seoul to create the Korean People's Republic (KPR). Two days later, Koreans were shocked to face masses of incoming US troops. Coincidentally, the Koreans' announcement of their unified independence came only four days after Ho Chi Minh's declaration of a unified independence for all of Viet Nam.

Rather than allow one unifying election for all of Korea, as the Cold War developed, both major powers insisted that reunification of north and south be carried out according to their respective ideological biases. The US supported an extremely repressive ruler in the South, Methodist Syngman Rhee, who was flown on General Douglas MacArthur's personal plane from his home in the US in mid-October 1945 to serve as its surrogate anti-Communist leader in a primarily Confucian society.[92] The US occupied the southern portion of the Peninsula from 1945 to 1948, and kept a smaller number of troops there after 1948. The North was led by guerrilla fighter Kim Il Sung, a fiercely independent man greatly vilified by the West but generally supported by the Soviet Union. Russian troops had all left by 1948.

The two sides of Korea, led by Kim Il Sung in the north and the US-financed and US-armed Syngman Rhee in the south, increasingly clashed as their military forces moved back and forth across the 38th parallel after 1948. US Embassy and military documents show that between January 1949 and June 25, 1950, the South Korean Army (ROKA) mounted over 2,000 armed attacks into the north.[93]

In an August 2, 1949 memo, US military advisor Captain James H. Hausman briefed US General William L. Roberts, chief of the US Military Government Korea, that "with very few exceptions... all attacks on South Korea have been reprisals, and almost all incidents have been agitated by SKSF [South Korean Security Forces]." Subsequently, Roberts admitted publicly that the South was largely responsible for the fighting that summer.

---

[92] Bruce Cumings, *The Korean War: A History* (New York: Modern Library, 2011), 106.
[93] Channing Liem, *The Korean War: An Unanswered Question* (Albany, NY: Committee for a New Korea Policy, 1992), 41.

This is corroborated in an August 26, 1949 Memorandum of Conversation signed by Gregory Henderson, Third Secretary to the US Embassy in Seoul, reporting the comments of Colonel Min Ki Sik, Assistant Commandant of the Korean School of Arms who at the time was a recent graduate of the US Army Infantry School, Fort Benning, Georgia: "One hears that the Army never attacks North Korea and is always getting attacked. This is not true. Mostly our Army is doing the attacking first and we attack harder. Our troops feel stronger."[94]

Quelling popular self-determination aspirations (democracy) around the world was critical for the assurance of US global hegemony after World War II. As will be seen, Secretary of State Dean Acheson and chief State Department planner Kennan knew that successful suppression of Korea's popular movement for democracy was essential to achieving the United States' post-war containment policy.[95] The success of the revolution in next-door China on October 1, 1949, greatly accelerated US anxieties and contributed to extra support for the tyrannical but anti-Communist Rhee.

A vigorous pro-democracy reunification movement was met with brutal repression. In the spring of 1950, South Korea had 60,000 political prisoners, and by September 1950, 100,000 people had been murdered by the state without any trial whatsoever.[96] Such repression by the US-supported Rhee regime was seen as justified, accepted by most US Americans because of the deep fear of Communists, which often manifested in strikingly racist terms. By 1949, Truman's Attorney General J. Howard McGrath described Communists as "rodents" and said that Koreans were subhuman. Such racist and ethnocentric attitudes have prevailed throughout US history, always at the ready to describe the next evil *du jour*.[97] Public pronouncements made by Rhee throughout 1949 and early 1950 consistently spoke of intentions to attack the North. "If we have to settle this thing by war, we will do all the fighting needed."[98]

Exactly what happened on June 25, 1950, when the "hot" war broke out, remains unclear, but the fighting on that day is considered by some scholars to have been escalation of the ongoing war of national independence against US imperial intervention originally provoked by Truman's August 1945 decision to impose an arbitrary 38th-parallel dividing line.[99] Guerrilla war had already been raging within parts of the south between Koreans who, like the vast majority, desired distinct independence from outsiders, and the small minority of Koreans collaborating with US American and Rhee imperial occupation forces.

---

94 Also see Martin Hart-Landsberg, *Korea Division, Reunification, & US Foreign Policy* (New York: Monthly Review Press, 1998), 89, 117.
95 Bruce Cumings, *Korea's Place in the Sun: A Modern History* (New York: W.W. Norton & Co., 1997), 246.
96 Hart-Landsberg, 124.
97 Bruce Cumings, *The Origins of the Korean War: The Roaring of the Cataract 1947–1950*, Vol II (Princeton, NJ: Princeton University Press, 1990), 691.
98 "Rhee Predicts Force to End Korean Rift," *Washington Evening Star*, October 31, 1949; "Korean Army Set For War," *The Washington Post*, November 1, 1949.
99 George Katsiaficas, *Asia's Unknown Uprisings: South Korean Social Movements in the 20th Century*, Vol. 1 (Oakland, CA: PM Press, 2012), 114.

Systematic, brutal repression by Rhee's security forces against identified, and imagined, dissenters, well protected by US military presence, is illustrated by the struggle that took place in 1948 on the Korean island of Jeju, in which a US-organized and Korean-implemented scorched earth campaign resulted in as many as 80,000 of the island's 300,000 residents being murdered, with another 40,000 forced to flee in boats.[100] US officers considered Jeju a "Red island" and had no respect for the lives of its residents, seen as no more than "ignorant, uneducated farmers and fishermen."[101]

The United Nations wasn't any more neutral in 1950 than it is today. The Security Council's June 27, 1950 resolution to defend South Korea was based on little accurate information, and it was clear there was no interest in acquiring such information, as the United States exerted great pressure on the other members to get its way. The Soviet Union was absent, its boycott of the UN due to the latter's refusal to seat Communist China in place of Taiwan, and Yugoslavia's request that North Korea be invited to present its perspective were dismissed out of hand.[102] The fact that token military forces from 16 other countries were to become militarily involved in one way or another, technically enabled the war to be fought by United Nations forces. But it was to be an American show, a fact finalized on July 7 with a UN resolution that, in effect, made the United Nations' forces subject to US General Douglas MacArthur without making MacArthur subject to the UN.[103]

Korea was the forerunner for everything subsequently experienced in Viet Nam: (1) US support of a corrupt, tyrannical ruler imported into the country by the US itself; (2) regular atrocities and mass slaughter of civilians ordered or sanctioned by the US military; (3) imprisonment and torture of those opposed to the US and its puppet; (4) assassinations of "dissidents"; (5) cities and many agricultural areas bombed to total destruction; (6) careful management of war news; (7) consistent sabotaging of peace talks throughout the war's duration; and (8) systematic use of napalm.

Reports of numerous atrocities committed during the Korean War by US ground and air forces, suppressed during the war, resurfaced in 1999 when eyewitness accounts emerged from Korean survivors as well as American military veterans who had been ordered to kill large numbers of civilians in 1950.[104] Declassified US Air Force documents disclosed compliance with orders to bomb fleeing civilians. In one case some 2,000 Korean civilians were forced into an open mountain area near Yongdong and slaughtered from the air. In other cases hundreds of civilian refugees were blown up as they fled across bridges or machine-gunned as they sought protection under viaducts. A Korea Truth Commission

---

100 Cumings, 1997, 221; Cumings, 2011, 121; Katsiaficus, 93–96.

101 Cumings, 1990, 254.

102 I. F. Stone, *The Hidden History of the Korean War, 1950–1951* (New York: Monthly Review Press, 1952), 47–48.

103 When Miguel d'Escoto Brockman, Maryknoll priest and former Nicaraguan foreign minister, served as president of the United Nations General Assembly in 2008 and 2009, he concluded that the UN was a failure due to the ability of powerful members like the United States to "defend and apply the law of the jungle that might makes right." Seeing that its structure and culture rendered authentic reform and innovation improbable, he called the UN a fraud and said it was beyond reform [*Democracy Now!*, April 26, 2010].

104 Charles J. Hanley, Sang-Hun Choe, and Martha Mendoza, *The Bridge at No Gun Ri* (New York: Henry Holt and Co., 2001).

Seoul Firing Squad, April 14, 1950 [Photo: National Archives]

Accompanying memorandum to this and similar photos, dated April 26, 1950:

> Photo shows a normal execution as carried out quite frequently in South Korea, the victims being called confessed Communists, convicted for subversive activities against the government of Republic of Korea. Execution was by military police under supervision of Provost Marshal of the Korean Army. Observers at execution included approximately two hundred (200) Korean Army personnel and a half dozen US American Army officers, including the Army Attache. Pictures were taken by Mr. Donald Nichols, OSI District #8. US officers reported that the "victims were singing the Communist song and giving cheers for the leaders of North Korea when the firing squad opened fire. They faced the squad with a sullen attitude and died bravely."

in the 2000s discovered more than 1,200 massacre sites where atrocities were said to have been committed by US forces or South Korean forces under direction of US officers.[105]

On November 5, 1950, General MacArthur ordered Major General Emmett O'Donnell, Jr., commander of the Far Eastern Air Forces (FEAF) "to destroy every means of communication and every installation, factory, city, and village" from the border with Manchuria south toward the battle lines above the DMZ. O'Donnell was authorized to use incendiary munitions and was "expected to burn all the cities to the ground."[106] In the month of November 1950 alone, 3,300 tons of napalm were dropped on North Korea's population centers.[107]

---

105 Katsiafacas, 117.

106 Robert Frank Futrell, *The United States Air Force in Korea 1950–53* (Washington, DC: Office of Air Force History, 1983), 221.

107 Yuki Tanaka and Marilyn B. Young, eds., *Bombing Civilians: A Twentieth-Century History* (New York: The New Press, 2009), 158].

US bombing, over the 37 months of the war, destroyed all of the North's 70-plus cities, and many cities in the South as well. FEAF dropped a total of 386,037 tons of conventional bombs, 32,357 tons of napalm, 313,600 rockets, and 55,797 smoke rockets, and expended 166,853,100 rounds of machine-gun ammunition. It claimed to have destroyed 976 aircraft, 1,327 tanks, 86,920 vehicles, 963 locomotives, 10,407 railroad cars, 1,153 bridges, 118,231 buildings, 65 tunnels, and 563 barges and boats, among other targets, while killing nearly 185,000 enemy troops. The price for FEAF was high, as it lost nearly 2,000 aircraft, suffering 1,841 casualties, mostly of air crews.[108] Total bombing tonnage, 1950-53, from over one million sorties was 700,000.[109]

US General Curtis LeMay, commander of the 1,008 bomber crews of the Strategic Air Command (SAC), was authorized to bomb with incendiaries virtually all urban and rural village areas during the war. Many dams and dikes were destroyed wiping out rice crops. Saturation bombing and scorched earth policies were commonly used throughout the war. By the end of the war, LeMay was proud of the number of casualties caused, concluding that "we killed off—what?—twenty percent of the population of North Korea."[110] In truth, the figure may be higher, as much as a staggering one-third of its nine million pre-war population. LeMay boasted further, that "over a period of about three years or so . . . we burned down *every* town in North Korea and South Korea, too."[111] (Italics added by author). At one point, the bombing had pulverized most targets to such small fragments that the number of daily bombers was reduced to 25 sorties a day.[112]

An estimated 4 to 5 million Koreans and Chinese were killed during the US hot war.[113] The number of Koreans murdered in the US-supported Rhee campaign of terror between 1945 and 1950 adds another million or so to the death toll.[114] The brutal war in defense of the Syngman Rhee regime, a capitalist model being carefully fostered by the US, was not fought for the benefit of most Koreans, who earnestly sought an undivided peninsula. Separate US State Department, CIA, and Joint Army-Navy Intelligence reports indicate an overwhelming percentage of Koreans wanted a democratic, grass-roots independent Socialist society, not a capitalist society dependent on and answerable to Western powers.[115]

---

108 Futrell, 692.

109 Raphael Littauer and Norman Uphoff, eds., *The Air War in Indochina*, rev. ed. (Boston, MA: Beacon Press, 1972), 209.

110 Richard Rhodes, "The General and World War III," *The New Yorker*, June 19, 1995, 53.

111 Cumings, 1997, 293, 298.

112 Tanaka and Young, 262n17.

113 Jon Halliday and Bruce Cumings, *Korea: The Unknown War* (New York: Pantheon Books, 1988), 200; Hart-Landsberg, 133; *Third World Guide: 86-87* (New York: Grove Press, 1986), 169.

114 Lee Wha Rang, *Wanted: Justice for the Victims of the Holocausts in Korea (April 15, 1998)*: www.kimsoft.com/1997/kr-holo.htm; Gregory Henderson, *Korea: Politics of the Vortex* (Cambridge, MA: Harvard University Press, 1968), 167; Hugh Deane, *The Korean War: 1945-1953* (San Francisco: China Books, 1999), 96; Cumings, 1990, 721, 770; Alan Winnington and Wilfred Burchett, *Plain Perfidy: The Plot to Wreck Korean Peace* (London, UK: The Britain-China Friendship Association, 1954), 167-168.

115 Hart-Landsberg, 175; Cumings, 1997, 193-194, 202-203.

Despite US policy makers' and politicians' knowledge of this passionate Korean desire for independence, US support for the repressive Rhee continued. An armistice was signed on July 27, 1953, that ended the hot war in a stalemate, much to the frustration of the US. But, to this date, there has been no peace treaty signed and officially the US is still at war with North Korea. The continued division of a once homogenous Korea and the devastation wrought by the war remains one of the twentieth century's most unaddressed crimes.

South Korea's Syngman Rhee was merely the first in a series of Asian dictators backed by the US after World War II. Many others would soon follow: Chiang Kai Shek and his son in Taiwan; Ferdinand Marcos in the Philippines; Ngo Dinh Diem, General Nguyen Cao Ky, and General Nguyen Van Thieu in South Viet Nam; General Lon Nol in Cambodia; General Suharto in Indonesia, and a foursome of generals in Thailand.[116]

Churchill's Iron Curtain Speech

Nine months after his failed bid for re-election as Britain's prime minister, Winston Churchill visited President Truman in Missouri, where on March 5, 1946 he gave his now famous Iron Curtain speech at Westminister College: "From Stettin in the Baltic to Trieste in the Adriatic, an iron curtain has descended across the Continent." This historical moment, with its introduction of this powerful metaphor, sealed the entrenchment of the Cold War, and further promotion of a post-war Anglo-American alliance that would be intensely hostile to the Soviet Union, despite the fact that the Soviets had substantially assured allied military victory over the Nazis in World War II.[117]

On September 10, 1946, Truman's Secretary of Commerce, Henry Wallace, warned in a speech made at Madison Square Garden in New York that "to make Britain the key to our foreign policy would be the height of folly." He feared that "British imperialist policy in the Near East alone, combined with Russian retaliation, would lead the United States straight to war." Wallace's expressed distaste for US involvement with Britain and Europe was popular across the political spectrum. He clearly opposed the emerging Cold War foreign policy. With monied interests becoming ever more anxious about Wallace, Truman demanded that the Commerce Secretary refrain from talking about foreign policy issues. The last of FDR's twelve New Deal appointees, Wallace refused and was asked to resign on September 20. Using his next position as editor of *The New Republic*, Wallace continued to harshly critique Truman's foreign policy, which he believed was leading the US toward war.[118]

The firing of Wallace represented the final triumph of the bipartisan monied oligarchy that had emerged from the earlier Progressive Movement and the New Deal. The oligarchy

---

116 Chalmers Johnson, *Blowback: The Costs and Consequences of American Empire* (New York: Metropolitan Books, 2000), 26.

117 D. D. Guttenplan, *American Radical: The Life and Times of I. F. Stone* (New York: Farrar, Strauss and Giroux, 2009), 219; Iron Curtain, Wikipedia: http://en.wikipedia.org/wiki/Iron_Curtain.

118 Guttenplan, 220; Henry A. Wallace, Wikipedia, http://en.wikipedia.org/wiki/Henry_A._Wallace#Secretary_of_Commerce.

was composed of four major groups: (1) leaders of the three major corporate components of the economy—labor, agriculture, and finance; (2) sophisticated professional politicians (a "syndicalist oligarchy"); (3) academic and religious liberals known as "ameliorative capitalists"; and (4) permanent government servants and the military establishment.[119] In the making for 50 years, these oligarchic powers were intent on global expansion that unfortunately meant increasing exploitation of other peoples. Expansion into new overseas territories was very lucrative, and assured the continued prosperous triumph of US American capitalism.

When the question emerged whether the US society could define itself without recourse to dominating others around the world, the Cold War answered with a resounding No! The US was bound and determined to be an empire, like the British.

Cold War Signposts

March 12, 1947. President Truman addresses a joint session of Congress to request authorization for a program of economic and military aid to Greece and Turkey because "the free peoples of the world look to us for support in maintaining their freedoms" from "attempted subjugation by armed minorities or outside pressure."[120]

March 22, 1947. Truman issues Executive Order 9835, creating the domestic Federal Employee Loyalty Program, to search out any "infiltration of disloyal persons" into the US government. The program affects 2.5 million government employees.[121] Initiation of loyalty oaths creates a great "wave of hysteria" about Communism that lasts for two decades, in spite of the fact the Executive Order itself was intended to allay such a wave.[122]

April 16, 1947. Financier and philanthropist Bernard Baruch, in an address to the South Carolina legislature, declares, "Let us not be deceived—today we are in the midst of a Cold War." The term took hold.[123]

April 23, 1947. The US Senate formally endorses the Truman Doctrine.

May 20, 1947. A military mission is created in Turkey as a bulwark against supposed foreign aggression.[124]

---

119 Williams, 1961, 469–478.

120 Guttenplan, 225.

121 Felix Greene, *The Enemy: What Every American Should Know About Imperialism* (New York: Random House, 1970), 233; Caute, 155.

122 Zinn, 1980, 420. With Truman, as with other authority figures who possess at their disposal the concentrated power to be discretionarily applied against people depending on their politics, it was not so much a matter of what was done as *who* was doing it to whom and who was making capital out of it [Caute, 28]. Any assumption that US citizens were loyal was destroyed. Paranoia reigned as US Americans' trust for each disintegrated. The second US Red Scare set off by Truman's domestic loyalty initiative continued for decades, to a greater or lesser degree, until the fall of the Berlin Wall in November 1989 and the collapse of the Soviet Union in December 1991.

123 Barson and Heller, 56.

124 Morris and Morris, 467.

May 23, 1947. The US intervenes in the bloody Greek civil war (1946–1949), taking the side of the neo-fascists against the Greek Left who had fought so courageously against the Nazis.[125]

June 5, 1947. Secretary of State George E. Marshall announces a comprehensive recovery program for Europe that comes to be known as The Marshall Plan.

The Truman Doctrine Ushers in a National Security State

Truman's March 12, 1947 containment speech, often described as the formal declaration of the Cold War between the Free World and the forces of Communism, helped entrench the idea that whatever occurs in the entire world is the specific business of the United States. Expressing fear of an international Communist threat and marking the beginning of US containment policy, his appeal to Congress officially launched the first of thousands of US covert and overt interventions around the world. Despite Truman's focus on Greece and Turkey in this speech, internal documents reveal that South Korea was as important, if not more important, in terms of needing to be contained.[126] This was made clear in 1949, when both Secretary of State Acheson and the head of State's policy planning, George Kennan, concluded that successful suppression by Syngman Rhee of a Korean people's independence movement would be a key litmus test of the US's emerging policy of global containment of Communism. The Korean people's tenacious desire for independence was an "internal threat" that could easily become contagious to other restive populations. The whole world was watching.[127]

Henry Wallace's prediction that the Truman Doctrine would usher in a repressive century of fear came true.[128] Wallace denounced the increasing persecution of radicals at home, and said that "the men who speak of reigns of terror in Europe are fast introducing a reign of terror here at home,"[129] echoing the principle of "shadow projection" articulated by psychologist Carl Jung. The radical journalist I. F. Stone, like Wallace, understood that the manufactured Red Scare at home enabled imperial policies abroad to be conducted with a minimum of effective dissent, would weaken the Left, stifle critical dialogue, foster development of a lucrative military industrial complex, and bring to power those who sought to terminate the New Deal.

The Loyalty Program successfully stifled effective free speech for decades.[130] It became increasingly difficult to secure sponsors for any content deemed to have a radical edge, whether for print or broadcast. Because of this inability to get corporate advertising, only information and perspectives that were acceptable to the fear-driven population

---

125 William Blum, *Killing Hope: US Military and CIA Intervention since World War II* (Monroe, Maine: Common Courage Press, 1995), 37–38.
126 Cumings, 2011, 112.
127 Cumings, 1997, 246.
128 http://en.wikipedia.org/wiki/Henry_A._Wallace#Secretary_of_Commerce.
129 David Caute, *The Great Fear: The Anti-Communist Purge Under Truman and Eisenhower* (New York: Simon and Schuster, 1978), 31.
130 Myra MacPherson, *All Governments Lie! The Life and Times of Rebel Journalist I. F. Stone* (New York: Scribner, 2006), 247.

were available, including those in government, business, and academia. The result was an increasingly dumbed-down public, as fanciful and deceptive propaganda served as a substitute for facts that might stimulate broad public discussion of the issues. Bereft of any honest history or critical analysis, few intellectuals regularly opposed the fanatical anti-Communist crusade, and even many on the Left to this day remain ignorant of the lessons of the past while often lacking an imaginary vision of a socially reconstructed society.[131]

The glories of post–World War II US were proudly proclaimed by magazine magnate Henry Luce, publisher of *Life, Time, Fortune*, and *Sports Illustrated*. Luce had written an editorial in the February 17, 1941 issue of *Life* magazine titled "The American Century," and in another *Time* Magazine editorial, he bragged that "God had founded America as a global beacon of freedom,"[132] echoing Puritan Winthrop's proclamation, more than three hundred years earlier, that, "we shall be as a city upon a hill. The eyes of all people are upon us." It was all good.

The European Recovery Program (ERP) announced by Secretary of State George E. Marshall on June 5, 1947 was to be a comprehensive recovery program for Europe through the Economic Cooperation Administration (ECA). The Marshall Plan, as it came to be known, dovetailed nicely with the Truman Doctrine as the economic part of the US containment policy authored by the State Department's George Kennan. Under this plan, in April 1948, Congress authorized $17 billion in grants and loans to 16 Western European nations, including Greece and Turkey, for various investment projects, seeking as well private investment in Europe.[133] The Soviet Union declined aid, choosing not to become dependent upon US financing.[134]

Over seventy percent of these funds were explicitly to be spent for US-made goods and resources and thereby served as a mechanism for expansion of US exports. The program was sold to Congress and the public as a gesture of kindness and as a means of "rolling back the tide of Communism," but the US used this opportunity to virtually ram American-controlled oil down the throats of Europe, replacing coal as their primary energy resource. "Without the Marshall Plan American oil business in Europe would already have been shot to pieces," explains historian Douglas Doud, since it effectively "blocked projects for European crude oil production and helped American oil companies to gain control of Europe's refineries."[135]

From initial aid to Greece and Turkey, it was but a short jump to aid Western Europe with the ERP. Future Secretary of State John Foster Dulles and his brother Allen Dulles, former OSS officer and future director of the CIA, were in the forefront of those who pushed for European reconstruction along with creation of an intelligence network to replace the

---

131 Jezer, 102–106.
132 Greene, 1970, 332.
133 Morris and Morris, 468–469.
134 Richard B. Morris and Graham W. Irwin, *Harper Encyclopedia of the Modern World* (New York: Harper and Row, 1970), 586.
135 Doud, 235–236, n28.

OSS.[136] The ERP was the first sustained foreign assistance program ever funded by the US that was largely aimed at containment of the Soviet Union, which effectively meant subversion of the very popular indigenous Communist and Socialist parties.[137]

Among ERP projects was a secret money-laundering scheme whereby untraceable cash devoted to secret CIA operations was channeled through its newly created benign-sounding Office of Policy Coordination (OPC), under the direction of former OSS operative Frank Wisner. The CIA essentially used these funds to commit political warfare, with initial efforts focused on defeating popular Leftist and Communist electoral candidates in France and Italy through "useful" propaganda, dirty tricks, and lucrative payoffs. It supplied money to create secret paramilitary teams of former Gestapo officers and Corsican gangs to break unions and their strikes, burn party offices, beat up party members (sometimes killing them), and employ psychological warfare teams to assure destruction of the Communist Party by any means necessary. This was called Operation Gladio.[138] It created false fronts to disguise its intentions and to hide CIA operatives. It also worked closely with the American Federation of Labor (AFL), which already was operating its own secret networks in Europe to promote anti-Communist labor leaders. Its aim was to destabilize Communist and Socialist movements in Italy, France, and elsewhere, and it was prepared to subvert any electoral victories identified as "Communist," including those in Leftist unions.[139]

Creation of the CIA and the Religion of National Security

On July 26, 1947, President Truman signed into law the National Security Act, combining the army, navy, and air force into a single national military establishment under a Secretary of Defense with cabinet status. The act (ironically and dishonestly) replaced the Department of War and Secretary of War with the Department of Defense and Secretary of Defense.[140] The act also established a National Security Council (NSC) and under it, the Central Intelligence Agency (CIA) to correlate and evaluate intelligence matters. This effectively began the replacement of the republic with a national security state, setting in motion a pattern of imperial global interventions that has continued to this day.[141]

A year later, on June 18, 1948, President Truman signed National Security Directive 10/2 (NSC 10/2) in which covert operations were specifically, and broadly, defined. The CIA, directly answerable to the president through the NSC, was given primary responsibility

---

136 Peter Grose, *Gentleman Spy: The Life of Allen Dulles* (New York: Houghton Mifflin Co., 1994), 272.

137 Noam Chomsky, *Deterring Democracy* (New York: Hill and Wang, 1992), 47.

138 Mark Zepezauer, *The CIA's Greatest Hits* (Tuscon: Odonian Press, 1994), 8–9 ("Operation Gladio"); Michael Zezima, *Saving Private Power: The Hidden History of 'The Good War'* (New York: Soft Skull Press, 2000), 154.

139 John Prados, *Safe for Democracy: The Secret Wars of the CIA* (Chicago: Ivan R. Dee, 2006), 37, 93; Tim Weiner, *Legacy of Ashes: The History of the CIA* (New York: Doubleday, 2007), 28–29; William Blum, *Rogue State: A Guide to the World's Only Superpower* (Monroe, Maine: Common Courage Press, 2000), 127–128; Zepezauer, 6–9; Alfred W. McCoy, *The Politics of Heroin: CIA Complicity in the Global Drug Trade* (Chicago: Lawrence Hill Books, 1991), 56–60.

140 Throughout the remainder of this book, references to the US Department of Defense will read "Department of Defense/War," to more accurately reflect the role of the department.

141 Pessen, 19–20; Gore Vidal, *The Last Empire, Essays 1992–2000* (New York: Doubleday, 2001), 315, 215.

for carrying out covert actions, "from time to time," as directed by the NSC. There was an important stipulation, however, that the "the US government [be able to] plausibly disclaim any responsibility for them."[142] This vaguely worded authority has been used *thousands* of times for justification to carry out (or attempt to carry out) covert actions ranging from assassinations, overthrow of governments, paramilitary operations, concerted self-serving propaganda campaigns, manipulative interference in free elections, and economic destabilization—i.e., to intervene anywhere and whenever the US chooses.

An essentially Calvinist society, riding high following its victory over the Axis, believed ever more in its Manifest Destiny to decide how the rest of humanity would live. "We expected that most of the world would make itself over in our image," wrote historian D. F. Fleming.[143] When that failed, and as the nation witnessed more than 40 post-WWII Third World revolutions representing half the world's population struggling to free themselves from centuries of Western colonialism, the US American psyche seemed to twist and snap,[144] making the USA ever more dangerous in the world. Since the creation of the CIA in 1947–48, US American presidents have possessed the authority to subvert any government, political movement, or cultural group that it doesn't like. And it has done so.

On February 24, 1948, George Kennan, head planner in the State Department, authored the following refreshing, though brutally honest, internal memo.[145]

> We have about 50 percent of the world's wealth, but only 6.3 percent of its population.... Our real task ... is to devise a pattern of relationships which will permit us to maintain this position of disparity without positive detriment to our national security.... We should cease to talk about ... unreal objectives such as human rights, the raising of the living standards, and democratization.... [W]e are going to have to deal in straight power concepts.

Americans grow up believing in our exceptionalism. We are insulated psychologically and intellectually from the rest of the world, just as the oceans on our east and west have insulated our country geographically. In the United States, the mythology of the "American Way of Life"—that anyone who follows a certain formula would be guaranteed a comfortable material life—has, at least until recently, worked out for much of the White male citizenry. There's a hidden reason for our comfort quotient, however, that becomes visible when we are able to look beyond our borders. Today's statistics are a little different from Kennan's 1948 data, but the disparity is still extreme: 4.6 percent of the world's population own close to 30 percent of the wealth. The global disparity continues to reflect our geopolitical policies. We are dependent upon successfully exploiting others in order to satisfy our own need for "prosperity."

---

142 National Security Council Directive on Office of Special Projects. National Archives and Records Administration, Records of the National Security Council, NSC 10/2, June 18, 1948.

143 Jezer, 36.

144 Wasserman, 170.

145 "Policy Planning Study 23: Review of Current Trends in US Foreign Policy," February 24, 1948, *Foreign Relations of the United States*, vol 1 (Washington, DC: GPO, 1948; declassified in 1975), 509–529.

Less than a month after Kennan issued his memo, on March 15, 1948, Texas Congressman Lyndon Baines Johnson delivered a speech on the floor of the US House of Representatives in which he said: "No matter what else we have of offensive or defensive weapons, without superior air power America is a bound and throttled giant, impotent and easy prey to any yellow dwarf with a pocket knife."[146] LBJ's macho intent to use advanced weaponry to overcome vulnerability not only assumed the right to intervene in the affairs of Asia, but, by being couched in incredibly racist language, sent a message that the inferiority of "yellow" people was reason enough for intervening.

As stated earlier, the US perceived Viet Nam's popular revolution as a serious threat to free markets in Southeast Asia. Laos and all of Southeast Asia came to be at the mercy of the US, economically. It is worth noting that those who created and operated the OSS and its successor, the CIA, were White Anglo-Saxon Protestant graduates of "proper" Ivy League schools who reflected the deep biases and racist attitudes of their Eurocentric ancestors. This, of course, significantly biased US foreign policies, generally pre-empting a genuine understanding of other cultures, especially the values that are most cherished by peoples from other than Eurocentric orientations.[147]

On November 24, 1948, National Security Council Document 20/4, "US Objectives with Respect to the USSR to Counter Soviet Threats to US Security," mandated reducing "the power and influence of the USSR to limits which no longer constituted a threat to world peace, national independence and stability in the world family of nations," and that "any surviving Bolshevik" regime should not be able to control sufficient military resources to threaten any other regime. The buildup of US power was to create divisions among the peoples of the Soviet Union and "bring about change in the conduct" of the USSR.[148]

The Soviets detonated their first atomic bomb on August 29, 1949, increasing US anxiety about a new arms race.[149] Fear among the US public was fanned by repeated announcements of a "missile gap" and "bomber gap" and a "conventional-forces gap," which, as it turned out, were pure fictions, but helped in the national campaign to sell civil defense as well as spurring millions of families to build home fall-out shelters. And it seemed that most US Americans believed that God sided with those who possessed the mightiest military. Despite assurances of God being on our side, studies revealed that US children had notably increased levels of anxiety and paranoia.[150]

After many years of fighting, the Chinese Communist Revolution prevailed against Chiang Kai-shek's US-backed, rightwing Kuomintang forces, and on October 1, 1949, Communist leaders declared the creation of the Chinese People's Republic. The US had

---

146 Noam Chomsky, *American Power and the New Mandarins: Historical and Political Essays* (New York: Vintage Books, 1969), 248, citing March 15, 1948 Congressional Record.
147 Victor Marchetti and John D. Marks, *The CIA and the Cult of Intelligence* (New York: Alfred A. Knopf, 1974), 278.
148 "US Objectives with Respect to the USSR to Counter Soviet Threats to US Security," *Foreign Relations of the United States*, Vol. 1 (Washington, DC: Government Printing Office, Department of State, 1948), 663–669.
149 Barson and Heller, 58.
150 Seymour Melman, *Our Depleted Society* (New York: A Delta Book, 1965), 164, 157, 170.

been covertly aiding the Kuomintang forces with special forces, military aid, and air support for years. The triumph of Mao Tse-Tung stunned US conservatives as much as the success of the earlier 1917 Bolshevik revolution. International Communism was the new "Army of Devils" (a term used by Cotton Mather to describe the Salem witches), and the "evil threat" was very convenient in at least temporarily solving the country's economic dilemma.[151] In 1950, *US News & World Report* said that "so long as war is a threat; so long as every alarm can step up spending, lending for defense at home and aid abroad; the Cold War is almost a guarantee against a bad depression."[152]

It was on February 9, 1950 that the most well-known (and shameful) anti-Communist, Joseph McCarthy, junior senator from Wisconsin, gave his famous speech in Wheeling, West Virginia, in which he falsely claimed to possess the names of 205 known Communists working in the US State Department, which he said was "thoroughly infested with Communists."[153]

NSC 68: The US, Not the Soviets, Possessed a Global Monolithic Plan

On April 14, 1950, President Truman approved a comprehensive National Security Council study known as NSC 68 (1949–1950). The most fundamental document of the US Cold War, its recommendations began to be implemented on the eve of our hot war in Korea. NSC 68 asserted that the US had the unique right and responsibility to impose our chosen "order among nations" so that "our free society can flourish. . . . Our policy and action . . . must be such to foster a fundamental change in the nature of the Soviet system" and "foster the seeds of destruction within the Soviet system" that will "hasten" its "decay." It added, "The Soviet Union, unlike previous aspirants to hegemony, is animated by a new fanatic faith, antithetical to our own, and seeks to impose its absolute authority over the rest of the world." The foundation of the strategy was "fomenting and supporting unrest and revolt in selected satellite countries" with a view "to reduce the power and influence of the Kremlin inside the Soviet Union." Any less global imperial policy would have "drastic effects on our belief in ourselves and in *our way of life*." The US ability to act had apocalyptic ramifications: either *"fulfillment or destruction not only of this Republic but of civilization."* NSC 68 concluded that "the assault on free institutions is world-wide" and "imposes on us, in our own interests, the responsibility of *world leadership*" such that we must seek "to foster a world environment in which the *American system* can survive and flourish." "Any measures, covert or overt, violent or nonviolent" will be called upon as necessary for "frustrating the Kremlin design," which included "overt psychological warfare" as well as various kinds of "economic warfare." Utmost care "must be taken to

---

151 Harvey Wasserman, *America Born & Reborn* (New York: Collier Books/Macmillan, 1983), 167.

152 Seymour Melman, "Limits of Military Power: Economic and Other," Vol 11, No. 1, Summer 1986, *International Security*, 72–87.

153 Pessen, 152–153; My own father earnestly kept a written record of people within the US government whom McCarthy regularly identified as members of the Communist Party.

avoid permanently impairing our economy and the fundamental values and institutions inherent in *our way of life*."[154] [Italics added.]

NSC 68 went on to claim that even "if there were no Soviet Union we would face the great problem of the free society . . . of reconciling order, security . . . with the requirement of freedom." The subsequent Korean War was the first time the CIA operated in a hot war. Its arguments became the foundation for tripling the "Defense" budget, stationing troops in Europe, and significantly boosting US conventional and nuclear weapons systems, thus further escalating the arms race.[155]

NSC 68 reveals this incredible irony: Throughout the Cold War years, we were taught to fear the evil Soviets, while our government spent literally trillions of dollars *defending our real monolithic plan from their fictional one*. Further, the Cold War and its consequent expensive arms race only ensured preservation of an obsessively consumptive Western way of life that is literally destroying life on the planet as we face eco catastrophe due to global warming. Industrial civilization is an intense heat engine.

Staggering Soviet Losses in WWII Ignored by the West

The US government *knew* that the Soviet Union was so devastated from the war that it had no capacity or will to imagine or carry out a monolithic plan to control the West. Yet, post-World War II hostility toward the Soviet Union resumed anti-Bolshevik and anti-Communist hatred that had begun in 1917–1918. This, despite the fact, as mentioned earlier in this chapter, that the Soviet armies essentially were responsible for the final defeat of the Nazis in World War II, a war in which the Soviets suffered incredible losses. A 1994 study published by the Russian Academy of Science estimated USSR casualties at 26.6 million, or 13.5 percent, of its pre WWII war population of 196.7 million.[156]

Before their defeat in 1945, the Nazis had leveled or crippled 15 large Soviet cities, more than 1,700 towns, 70,000 villages, and nearly 100,000 collective farms, while devastating most of its factories, railroads, highways, bridges, and electric power stations.[157] In contrast, the US suffered fewer than 420,000 deaths, or only three-tenths of a percent of its population, and did not lose any infrastructure.

US Naval Intelligence reported in January 1946 that the USSR was "exhausted . . . not expected to take any action during the next five years which might develop into hostilities with Anglo-Americans." Its policies were determined to be defensive in nature, designed only "to establish a Soviet Monroe Doctrine for the area under her shadow, primarily

---

154 National Security Memorandum No. 68 (NSC-68) on "United States Objectives and Programs for National Security" written by a Joint State-Defense Department Committee, under the supervision of Paul Nitze, Director of the Policy Planning Staff, in April 14, 1950, pursuant to the President's Directive of January 31, 1950.

155 John Lewis Gaddis, *We Know Now: Rethinking Cold War History* (New York: Oxford University Press, 1998), 84, 109.

156 Michael Ellman and S. Maksudov, "Soviet Deaths in the Great Patriotic War: A Note," *Europe-Asia Studies*, Vol. 46, No. 4, 1994, 671–680.

157 Wasserman, 168; Walter LaFeber, *America, Russia, and the Cold war, 1945–1971* (New York: John Wiley and Sons, 1972), 14.

and urgently for security."[158] Honest historians, academicians, and political leaders knew the basis of Stalin's insistence on having friendly neighbors and secure borders on its west flank. Unlike the US, the Soviet Union had no oceans to protect it from external aggression. In 1812, Napoleonic France invaded Russia through Germany. Imperial Japan invaded Siberia in 1906. Germany invaded Russia in 1914 and again in 1941. And Poland invaded Russia in 1920 over an old territorial dispute and new ideological fears of Bolshevism. Thus, Russia's Western border had been invaded at least four times in recent history.[159]

George Kennan, architect of the US containment policy, ultimately concluded that "the image of a Stalinist Russia poised and yearning to attack the West was largely a fiction of the Western imagination." He reminded US Americans that the Russian people believed profoundly in "decency, honesty, kindness, and loyalty in the relations between individuals, in fact that the Russians are human beings after all."[160]

But the fiction of the Soviet threat provoked George Orwell in 1948 to write his prophetic *1984* that described control by a privileged party elite persecuting individual thought through a tyrannical system epitomized by "Big Brother Is Watching You." Such Big Brother activity was justified in order to protect "the greater good." Official deception, secret surveillance, manipulation of the past by a totalitarian/authoritarian state, and use of black-white doublethink were its hallmarks. The imagined monolithic, monstrous enemy served, and continues to serve, to ensure support of grandiose military expenditures by a terrorized, fearful American population.[161]

After World War II, an incredible switch occurred in popular US ideology, when Americans suddenly were obliged to accept that former war allies, Russia and China, were now considered enemies, while former enemies Germany and Japan were allies. What remained consistent was US America's need for a perceived alien menace, a demonized enemy "out there," enabling us to continue ignoring our own dark shadows.[162]

The Growing Subversive Threat at Home and Abroad

In September 1947, the House Committee on Un-American Activities (HUAC) subpoenaed 79 Hollywood screenwriters, directors, and actors, claiming without substantiation that they had injected Communist propaganda into their films. Ten appeared before the committee but refused to cooperate. They were convicted of contempt of Congress and sentenced to a year in prison. Blacklisted, they became known as the Hollywood Ten.[163] One of these, screenwriter and novelist Dalton Trumbo, in

---

158 Lawrence Wittner, *Cold War America* (New York: Praeger, 1974), 9; Pessen, 63; Wasserman, 168.
159 Jezer, 23.
160 Wittner, 52; Wasserman, 169; Fleming, 538.
161 Wasserman, 169.
162 Lawrence S. Wittner, *Rebels against War: The American Peace Movement, 1941–1960* (New York: Columbia University Press, 1969), 106–107.
163 *Wikipedia*, "Hollywood Blacklist" https://en.wikipedia.org/wiki/Hollywood_blacklist#The_Hollywood_Ten; Patrick McGilligan and Paul Buhle, *Tender Comrades: A Backstory of the Hollywood Blacklist* (Minneapolis: University of Minnesota Press, 2012).

1939 had written the famous and poignant, extraordinary antiwar novel, *Johnny Got His Gun*.[164] Friendly witnesses before the committee, claiming pro-Soviet bias of Hollywood films made during World War II, included film studio heads Jack Warner of Warner Brothers and Louis B. Mayer of MGM, and Russian-born ideologue and dogmatist Ayn Rand (Russian name, Alisa Zinovyevna Rosenbaum), author of the 1943 best-seller, *The Fountainhead*.[165]

A June 1950 publication titled *Red Channels: The Report of Communist Influence in Radio and Television* listed the names of 151 "subversive entertainers," 130 organizations, and 17 publications with suspicious ties to Communism. This blacklist of radio and television personalities accomplished what HUAC had done to movie stars and directors: it destroyed their livelihoods and careers.[166] *Red Channels* was an outgrowth of a weekly newsletter, *Facts to Combat Communism, Counterattack*, distributed to 4,000 subscribers in the business and corporate world beginning in 1947, which included names of so-called "subversives" going back to the 1930s. The newsletter also publicized other witch-hunting groups' efforts, such as the American Legion National Americanism Committee, which in 1948 began publishing its own newsletter, *Summary of Trends and Developments Exposing the Communist Conspiracy*.[167]

In 1950, after the "loss" of China to Communism in 1949, the thought of similarly "losing" Korea truly terrified the US elite, who needed the resources, markets, and labor of Asia to assure their long-term prosperity. The viability of a westernized Japan was required as part of the plan to secure easy access to Asian markets and resources. After Korea, Viet Nam, Laos and Cambodia would become the next big victims of the United States' monolithic plan to impose a capitalist model around the world, under the cover that "monolithic" Soviet Communism was an enemy that threatened civilization itself—a classic example of shadow projection that mirrored the pathological nature of the US's own foreign policy. The phrase, *our objectives*, so often used in US policy discussions and documents, meant, in effect, construction of an international order "harmonious with our fundamental national purposes," i.e., a "world environment in which only *the American system* can survive and flourish."[168]

As the US perceived the Chinese "loss" to be a severe threat to free markets in Southeast Asia, the agricultural country of Laos, with two million people living in an area about twice the size of Pennsylvania, emerged as having immense strategic significance. General Donovan, who had been in charge of the US WWII OSS (1942–1946) and later helped

---

164 *Wikipedia*, "Johnny Got His Gun"; https://en.wikipedia.org/wiki/Johnny_Got_His_Gun; *Wikipedia*, "Dalton Trumbo"; https://en.wikipedia.org/wiki/Dalton_Trumbo; Dalton Trumbo, *Johnny Got His Gun* (Philadelphia: J.B. Lippincott, 1939).

165 History Matters, The US Survey Course on the Web: http://historymatters.gmu.edu/d/6442 - three "friendly" witnesses claimed certain films during World War II portrayed a pro-Soviet bias: studio heads Jack L. Warner of Warner Bros. and Louis B. Mayer of M-G-M, and Russian-born novelist and philosopher Ayn Rand.

166 Barson and Heller, 88; Jezer, 100–101.

167 Jezer, 100, citing Merle Miller, *The Judges and the Judged* (New York: Doubleday, 1952), 81–84); *Red Channels: The Report of Communist Influence in Radio and Television* (New York: Counterattack, 1950).

168 See especially Williams, 1980, 189–190.

create the CIA in summer 1947, became ambassador to Thailand in August 1953. Once settled, he arranged for an old OSS sidekick from Thailand, Major James Thompson, to move into next-door Laos to create an espionage network linked with local opium-growing tribesmen, including the Hmong in northeast Thailand.[169]

From 1949 to 1959, its "containment of communism" policy cost the United States over $65 billion. Of all the nations receiving aid from the US during this period, none received more than Laos.[170]

Meanwhile, decades' worth of US anti-Communist propaganda and the public's "Pavlovian" reaction to the word "communism" were proving persuasive in Central American affairs as well. In 1950, Edward Bernays (see p. 31) began a contractual relationship with the nervous United Fruit Company, as Guatemala's democratically elected government was discussing the need for land reform. United Fruit had owned most of Guatemala since 1901. Bernays coordinated an intense public relations campaign blaming the expropriation of Guatemalan lands in 1953 on the establishment of a "Communist beachhead" in the Western Hemisphere.[171] President Eisenhower and the CIA naturally took up United Fruit's cause, declaring to the public that a Soviet beachhead was rapidly unfolding in Guatemala. In August 1953, Eisenhower gave his approval to begin planning the overthrow of Guatemala's popular, democratically elected President Jacabo Arbenz.[172]

The 1954 US Ambassador to Guatemala, John Peurifoy, dutifully took orders from Secretary of State John Foster Dulles and his brother Allen Dulles at the CIA. He initiated an urgent public relations campaign, built on Bernays' propaganda efforts, with the message that it was necessary "to prevent Guatemala from falling into the lap of international communism" and that we "cannot permit a Soviet Republic to be established between Texas and the Panama Canal."[173] Peurifoy was so determined to rid Guatemala of the popular Arbenz that he identified a long list of leaders he wanted shot.[174] In June 1954,

---

169 Wilfred Burchett, "Pawn and Patriots: The US Fight for Laos," in *Laos: War and Revolution,* ed. Nina S. Adams and Alfred W. McCoy Adams and McCoy, 283–284 (New York: Harper Colophon Books, 1970).

170 Norman Cousins and Alfred McCoy, "Living It Up in Laos," Chapter 16 in Adams and McCoy, eds., *Laos: War and Revolution* (New York: Harper Colophon, 1970), 340.

171 Stephen Schlesinger and Stephen Kinzer, *Bitter Fruit: The Untold Story of the American Coup in Guatemala* (Garden City, NJ: Anchor Books, 1983), 79, 82–89; Edward Bernays, *Biography of an Idea: Memoirs of Public Relations Counsel Edward L. Bernays* (New York: Simon & Schuster, 1965), 744–775; Jonathan L. Fried, Marvin E., Deborah T. Levenson, and Nancy Peckenham, *Guatemala: In Rebellion: Unfinished History* (New York: Grove Press, 1983), 67.

172 Schlesinger and Kinzer, 1983, 108; Nick Cullather, *Secret History: The CIA's Classified Account of Its Operations in Guatemala 1952-1954* (Stanford, CA: Stanford University Press, 1999), 26.
Note: It is interesting how this refrain is repeated over time. In the mid-1980s, President Ronald Reagan similarly claimed a Soviet beachhead was being created in Nicaragua, posing a serious threat to US national security. Reagan was making an all-out effort to convince the US American people and Congress to contribute millions of dollars to overthrow the "cancer" of a Communist, terrorist Sandinista revolutionary government in Nicaragua [Bernard Weintraub, "Reagan Condemns Nicaragua in Plea for Aid to Rebels," *New York Times*, March 17, 1986]. In fact, the 1980s Nicaragua government was the result of a 1979 popular overthrow of a brutal dictator, a US-supported puppet who for more than four decades had protected a corporate playground for North American financial interests at the expense of the Nicaraguan people.

173 Schlesinger and Kinzer, 140.

174 Schlesinger and Kinzer, 207.

the CIA's aptly named Project Success was successful in overthrowing Arbenz, whose only crime had been to use eminent domain to distribute unused United Fruit land to that country's impoverished landless, paying United Fruit the land value it had claimed on tax returns.[175] But these efforts by Arbenz at "the first true agrarian reform of Central America" were seen by the US as a very dangerous precedent.[176] As secret machinations began to enact the overthrow, Secretary of State Dulles deceitfully explained, "The situation is being cured by the Guatemalans themselves."[177]

It's worth noting that both Dulles brothers had histories of investments in United Fruit. Foster had served as the company's lawyer while Allen served on its board of directors.[178] The unspeakable cost to the country of Guatemala is that it has never recovered its people's democracy since that 1954 US coup, and at least 200,000 Guatemalans have been murdered and displaced as a result.[179]

In September 1954, three months after Arbenz was ousted, Peurifoy was rewarded with an appointment as ambassador to Thailand, replacing Donovan. In retrospect, Peurifoy's involvement in the 1954 overthrow of Arbenz in Guatemala foreshadowed the horrible plight that was in store for Laos and the rest of Southeast Asia.

The disturbing Cold War pattern of CIA-engineered overthrows of legitimately elected heads of state began in Iran, one year before Donovan became ambassador to Thailand. John Foster Dulles had expressed his intent to rid Iran of its popular democratically elected Prime Minister Mohammad Mossadegh. Immediately upon taking office in 1951, Mossadegh had instituted nationalization of that country's oil, owned since 1908 by the British Anglo-Persian Company, later the Anglo-Iranian Oil Company, a pillar of the British economy. Allen Dulles used his top CIA Middle East operative, Kermit "Kim" Roosevelt, Jr., grandson of Theodore Roosevelt and distant cousin of Franklin, to engineer the toppling of Mossadegh, with the help of British MI6 intelligence, in August 1953, code-named Operation Ajax.[180]

It was a unique situation under newly elected President Dwight Eisenhower, who had campaigned to end the war in Korea, that a pair of privileged siblings, both graduates of Princeton University and George Washington University law school, would oversee *both* the overt and covert sides of US war-making policy in the 1950s. They worked in near harmony for a number of years pursuing the common goals of making the world safe for US capitalism that began with overthrowing Iran's Mossadegh.

---

175 Schlesinger and Kinzer, 76.

176 Piero Gleijeses, *Shattered Hope: The Guatemalan Revolution and the United States, 1944–1954* (Princeton, NJ: Princeton University Press, 1991), 3.

177 Melman, 166. Note: The overthrow of Arbenz occurred in the very same month that the US was installing its illegal Saigon Military Mission to begin covert operations in Viet Nam in efforts to preserve Western control after defeat of the French. The Saigon Military Mission operated in secret defiance of the July 1954 Geneva Peace Accords that concluded the French-Indochina War.

178 Walter La Feber, *Inevitable Revolutions: The United States in Central America*, 2nd ed. (New York: W.W. Norton, 1993), 120–121.

179 Blum, 2000, 130–131.

180 Blum, 1995, 64–72.

Iran shared a long border with the Soviet Union. The possibility of Iran falling to communism, becoming a "second China," was terrifying to US political and economic leaders who feared the loss of future oil supplies. Operation Ajax took place less than a month after the Korean Armistice, and a month before the allocation of another $785 million for the French in Viet Nam.[181] After the coup, in 1954 the Anglo-Iranian Oil Company was rechristened as British Petroleum (BP), restored to foreign ownership with the US and British sharing the majority 80 percent. The coup also restored the deposed Shah to power with the secret support of the CIA, initiating one of the world's most repressive regimes with the notorious Iranian secret police, SAVAK (*Sāzemān-e Ettelāāt va Amniyat-e Keshvar*/Organization of Intelligence and National Security). SAVAK, jointly created by the CIA and Israel, routinely used torture to quell any dissent. Finally an Iranian people's revolution ousted the horrible Shah in January 1979, a devastating blow to US interests[182] for which the Iranians have never been forgiven.

The US overthrow of the democratically elected Mossadegh in 1953 led to more than 60 years of Iranian hatred and distrust of the US. And, along with the US-protected apartheid regime of Israel, it continues as a major contributing factor to the hostility still seething between the US and the Middle East, and the war of US terror against the world.

Any curtailment of US investments and expected profits—*anywhere*—was deemed (and remains) totally unacceptable, in this view. US meddling in other countries served as a blueprint for controlling events in Southeast Asia. The US chose to hurriedly build up Thailand's infrastructure to serve as a protected major base from which to launch clandestine air and ground operations into Laos and North Viet Nam.[183]

Using fear of Communism as rationale, the US was involved in a litany of international crimes: the overthrow or disruption of governments on several continents, a number of assassinations or their attempt on political leaders and dissidents, collaboration with despicable repressive regimes, employment of Nazi war criminals as Pentagon scientists or CIA operatives, the grotesque invasions and occupations of Korea and Viet Nam, and interventions with "low-intensity" warfare in dozens of countries that have murdered/maimed/displaced millions of people, while stockpiling nuclear weapons threatening all-out war.

In the process, however, the US has lost its industrial competitiveness, while its independent free press has been mostly eviscerated. The Great Fear, combined with ongoing, concerted efforts to keep the American public in the dark, managed to produce a large degree of public apathy and added to the tragic public acquiescence in regard to US atrocities committed in Korea, Viet Nam, Iran, Guatemala, Iran, Chile, among many countries. Moral callousness has become a collective malady.[184]

---

181 Kevin Dougherty and Jason Stewart, *The Timeline of the Vietnam War: The Ultimate Guide to this Divisive Conflict in American History* (San Diego, CA: Thunder Bay Press, 2008), 23.

182 William Blum, 2000, 51, 130; Stephen Kinzer, *All the Shah's Men: An American Coup and the Roots of Middle East Terror* (Hoboken, NJ: John Wiley & Sons, 2003), 1–6; Blum, 1995, 64–72.

183 Adams and McCoy, 283–284.

184 Pessen, 200–220; in general, see Caute, 1978.

In his annual State of the Union message to Congress on January 6, 1941, Franklin D. Roosevelt urged a reluctant public to support intervention in the European War on behalf of Great Britain. He spoke of Four Freedoms—freedom from fear, freedom from want, freedom of speech, freedom of religion—sacred to US America. In 1985, historian Noam Chomsky identified an additional, fifth fundamental freedom, far more important than the other four: freedom to rob and exploit others. When the Fifth Freedom, to expand profits and power at others' expense, is threatened, the US quickly justifies righteous use of force, no matter how diabolical. The Marines invade, and the planes begin to bomb.[185]

The Cold War witnessed more than 390 military interventions in dozens of countries, including Southeast Asia, as the US pressured the majority of the world's people, through thousands of covert interventions in dozens of countries, to "cry uncle," thereby assuring US prosperity.[186] How many dead people in the Third World does it take to extract each barrel of oil to guarantee our Western comforts?

The U-2 Affair: A Pivotal Cold War Crisis

News of the Soviets' successful test of an intercontinental ballistic missile (ICBM) on August 26, 1957 was reported as giving the "Communists" an edge in the missile race. Thus was US anxiety raised about what the Russians might do as part of their (fictional) monolithic plan to take over the globe. On October 4, 1957, the Soviet Union sent US Americans into shock when they launched the first satellite to successfully orbit the earth. On December 17, the US successfully launched its own ICBM, among other efforts to keep up with the Russians.

On May 1, 1960, two weeks before a planned summit in Paris between Soviet Premier Nikita Khrushchev and President Dwight Eisenhower, a secret US reconnaissance spy plane was shot down by a Soviet surface-to-air missile. The pilot, Gary Powers, parachuted to safety near Sverdlovsk in the central Ural Mountains of the Soviet Union, where he was captured. He had been halfway on his scheduled 13-hour, 4,000-mile flight from a U-2 base in Peshawar, Pakistan, to Bodo, Norway. His mission was filming military targets over the Ural Mountains.

The exposure of an American spying operation, a pivotal moment during the tense Cold War, greatly embarrassed Eisenhower and he initially claimed it was a "weather observation" plane. But Powers, caught red-handed, admitted he was taking pictures of Soviet airfields for the purpose of identifying types of aircraft and missiles, missile testing

---

185 Chomsky, 1985, 47.
186 Total post-WWII interventions: (1) Congressional Research Service/CRS, *Instances of Use of United States Armed Forces Abroad, 1798–2008*. Washington, DC: CRS Report for Congress, February 2, 2009: 163 interventions post-WWII to 2008); (2) B. M. Blechman and S. S. Kaplan, *Force without War: US Armed Forces as a Political Instrument*, Appendix B (Washington, DC: The Brookings Institution, 1978): 196 additional uses of US armed forces "as a political instrument" January 1, 1946–December 31, 1975; (3) J. M. Collins, *America's Small Wars: Lessons for the Future* (Washington: US Brassey's, 1991), Figure 4 on page 14 lists 60 "Foremost US Low Intensity Conflicts from 1899 to 1990" revealing 37 not already included in the CRS or Blechman data. Thus, from these sources one can identify over 390 interventions since World War II up to 2008.

and training sites, special weapons storage, submarine production, atomic weapons production, and aircraft deployment patterns. Shortly after the U-2 was shot down, Lincoln White, a State Department spokesperson, declared with a straight face "There was absolutely no—no—no deliberate attempt to violate Soviet airspace. There never has been."[187] Eisenhower, who had ordered each of the flights himself, knowing the Cold War diplomatic risks involved, was the first US president to publicly confess that he lied to the public. But the Paris summit was scuttled when Eisenhower refused to apologize and Khrushchev walked out. By that time, thanks to the intelligence successfully gathered by the U-2, the US knew there was no missile or bomber gap even as it continued to claim there was.

U-2 planes were designed to fly 500 mph at 70,000 feet with a range of 6,400 miles. The U-2 spy plane program was a joint venture between the CIA, Air Force, and Lockheed Corporation, which manufactured about 48 of the planes in the 1950s.[188] At 70,000 feet (more than 13 miles), A U-2's surveillance equipment could photograph a Soviet general's license plate number. The development and deployment of these planes was considered one of the greatest intelligence achievements in history and a secret victory for the CIA. The two major U-2 bases were located in Atsugi, Japan, and Adana (Incirlik), Turkey, with other U-2 staging bases in Pakistan, West Germany, and Norway. More than 200 U-2 flights were made over the Asian mainland between 1956 and 1960. Twenty-four of those were over the Soviet Union, where they identified 20,000 targets. Besides the shoot-down of Power's plane, a number of other U-2s were shot down, one over Cuba on October 27, 1962, during the missile crisis, and at least four over China in the 1960s and 1970s. As a result of the shoot-downs, satellites substantially began to replace U-2s for surveillance. In August 1960, Eisenhower secretly created the National Reconnaissance Office (NRO) to begin gathering intelligence from outer space.[189]

The Cuban Revolution: US Shocked, Cold War Deepened

As the US increasingly embroiled itself in efforts to thwart "Communism" in distant Southeast Asia, it was shocked as well as infuriated when popular revolutionaries, 9,000 miles to its west, triumphantly marched into Havana, Cuba, on January 1, 1959. Located just 90 miles to the south, these "Communists" were a lot closer to home.

The Cuban Revolution ended 60 years of US colonization and exploitation. The island nation had served as a fantastic playground for the rich while imposing a miserable cesspool on the multitudes of poor in Cuba. It had served as a virtual colony of the United States, providing a profitable venue for numerous investments as well as a protected and lucrative center for organized crime in the Western Hemisphere. By the early 1950s, US-supported, iron-fisted dictator Batista had suspended all political liberties. Utterly

---

187 David Wise, *The Politics of Lying: Government Deception, Secrecy, and Power* (New York: Vintage Books, 1973), 49.

188 M. Todd Hunter, "Secret Tragedy Becomes National Memorial," *DAV Magazine*, July/August 2015.

189 In general, Michael R. Beschloss, *May Day: Eisenhower, Khrushchev and the U-2 Affair* (New York: Harper & Row Publishers, 1986), 5, 156, 361, 365, 368, 391, 395; Seymour Melman, 39, 166; fas.org/sgp/crs/intel/RL30727.pdf.

corrupt, his government enforced an ever-widening gap between the poor multitudes and the very few rich. The US government was almost the sole support for Batista's army and police, furnishing all their tanks, planes, bombs, and ammunition, and US citizens controlled most of the utilities, banks, hotels, industries, trains, sugar and tobacco plantations, mining, and other business interests. As many as 20,000 discontented Cubans were murdered by Batista's security forces in the 1950s alone.[190]

Relieved to finally be freed from decades of repression and socioeconomic misery, the overwhelming majority of Cuban people immediately began celebrating when Fidel Castro and his forces finally overthrew US-supported dictator Fulgencio Batista on January 1, 1959. In contrast, Cubans whose lucrative commercial and financial interests had been aligned with and protected by Batista fled to the United States.

A year later, January 18, 1960, the CIA under Eisenhower set up a special task force, Branch 4 of the Western Hemisphere Division, to plan the overthrow of Fidel Castro. The task force was composed primarily of veterans from the 1954 overthrow of President Arbenz in Guatemala.[191]

In 1961, the US broke diplomatic relations with Cuba and set about to sabotage the revolution. The record of demonic US efforts to destabilize and overthrow the Cuban government since 1959 to the present is nothing short of staggering. When John F. Kennedy was inaugurated as president on January 20, 1961, he inherited from Eisenhower both Viet Nam and the soon-to-be Cuban Bay of Pigs political and military disaster.[192]

On April 17, 1961, the CIA-planned-and-funded invasion of Cuba, at its southern Bay of Pigs, utilizing 1,400 expat Cuban mercenaries, was overwhelmingly defeated by Castro-led Cuban forces. The CIA "employed" private aircraft and ships to carry out the actual invasion, which was to be supported by unmarked US Navy jets. The decision by Eisenhower and Kennedy to wage a secret war against Cuba was, of course, grotesquely illegal, and made totally independently of the US Congress. By organizing the invasion of Cuba, the US government knowingly violated US neutrality laws. Secretary of State Dean Rusk in April declared, with a straight face, "The American people are entitled to know whether we are intervening in Cuba or intend to do so in the future. The answer to that question is no." When the truth was revealed that it was a CIA operation, many US politicians and members of the public were both humiliated and furious.

A fundamentalist Cold Warrior, Kennedy concluded that, due to the Communist threat existing everywhere, "our frontiers today are on every continent." He declared that this reality imposed on the US "obligations which stretch ten thousand miles across the Pacific, and three and four thousand miles across the Atlantic, and thousands of miles to the

---

190 Eduardo del Rio (pen name Rius), *Cuba for Beginners: An Illustrated Guide for Americans (and their Government) to Socialist Cuba*. (New York: Pathfinder Press, 1986), 67, 77; Jose Alvarez, *Cuban Agriculture before 1959: The Political & Economic Situations*, EDIS document FE479, a publication of the Department of Food and Resource Economics, Florida Cooperative Extension Service, UF/IFAS. Gainesville, FL: University of Florida Press, 2004.

191 Noam Chomsky, *Understanding Power*, Ch. 5, n 29); first training base established in Panama, Peter Wyden, *Bay of Pigs* (New York: Simon and Schuster, 1980), 19.

192 Melman, 158, 160, 163, 166.

South. Only the United States—and we are only six percent of the world's population—bears this kind of burden."[193] Kennedy conveniently chose not to acknowledge what was of most importance: gaining control of a disproportionate percentage of the world's resources needed to sustain the US way of life, in the psychopathic spirit of imperial document NSC 68.

THE MISSILE CRISIS AND PRELIMINARY EVENTS

April 13, 1961. Kennedy declares to a group of newspaper publishers that "our way of life is under attack" from Communists.[194]

August 15, 1961. East German authorities begin building a wall to permanently block free access between East and West Berlin, further aggravating the Cold War and fueling US containment as well as roll-back, a policy aimed at eliminating Communist threats through regime change. [The Berlin Wall would stand until Nov. 9, 1989, two years before the dissolution of the USSR.]

November 1, 1961. Richard Goodwin, White House Specialist on Latin America, advises in a memo to the president that his attorney general, Robert Kennedy, would be the best coordinator of a revived plan, Operation Mongoose, to overthrow Castro.[195]

November 8, 1961. A CIA document is prepared: *Types of Covert Action Against the Castro Regime.*[196]

November 30, 1961. Determined to rid Cuba of Castro and the Socialist revolution in order to repossess the island for American interests, John Kennedy authorizes the launching of Operation Mongoose, shifting responsibility from the CIA to the military, while keeping the CIA intrinsically involved. Kennedy appoints Edward Lansdale, an Air Force brigadier general, as the project's chief of operations.[197] The group assigned to oversee Mongoose includes National Security Adviser McGeorge Bundy, Deputy Under Secretary of State Alexis Johnson, Under Secretary of Defense/War Roswell Gilpatric, new CIA Director John McCone, and Joint Chief of Staff head General Lyman Lemnitzer, with Robert Kennedy and General Maxwell Taylor named co-chairs. Within a few weeks, William K. Harvey is placed in charge of CIA's Task Force W, the actual unit that will carry out Mongoose, a force that employs 400 people combined at CIA headquarters in Washington, DC, and in the Miami field CIA Station.[198]

---

193 Williams, 1980, 198–199.
194 Walton, 55.
195 Jane Franklin, *Cuba and the United States*, Melbourne, Australia: Ocean Press, 1997), 45.
196 Jon Elliston, *Psywar on Cuba: The Declassified History of US Anti-Castro Propaganda* (Melbourne, Australia: Ocean Press, 1999), 72–73.
197 Elliston, 74; Bamford, *Body of Secrets*, 79.
198 J. Franklin, 1997, 45–46.

January 3, 1962. The US State Department issues a white paper that describes Cuba as a Soviet satellite. On the same day, in a diplomatic note to the US government, Cuba protests commission by the US of 119 violations of its territory, 76 by planes flying out of the US Naval Base at Guantanamo alone.[199]

February 3, 1962. President Kennedy announces a total embargo of trade with Cuba, to formally commence on February 7.[200] The blockade is equivalent to an act of war.

February 20, 1962. Lansdale presents a 26-page, top-secret timetable for carrying out the overthrow of the Cuban government in October 1962. The Pentagon prepares contingency plans for a military invasion of Cuba using as many as 100,000 troops. The plan includes using CIA agents and operatives to: commit a variety of sabotage actions; implement massive propaganda operations including radio broadcasts; use the OAS, NATO, and United Nations for international support; and request that Jacqueline Kennedy visit Cuban children refugees in Florida with US Information Agency coverage—with guerrilla actions to commence inside Cuba in August and September.[201]

March 13, 1962. A memorandum to the Secretary of Defense/War, with the subject line "Justification for US Military Intervention in Cuba," signed by Lyman Lemnitzer, Chairman, Joint Chiefs of Staff, describes a "false flag" plan codenamed Operation Northwoods.[202] As requested by Lansdale, the top-secret memo discloses plans to covertly engineer various pretexts for justifying a US invasion of Cuba. Part of Operation Mongoose, the proposals include staged assassinations of Cubans living in the United States, a faked "Communist Cuban terror campaign in the Miami area, in other Florida cities and in Washington," including "sinking a boatload of Cuban refugees (real or simulated)," a faked Cuban air force attack on a civilian jetliner, and a concocted "Remember the Maine"-type incident that involved blowing up a US ship in Cuban waters and then blaming the incident on Cuban sabotage.[203]

October 6, 1962. Admiral Robert L. Dennison, chief of the Atlantic Forces, receives a memo from Defense Secretary Robert McNamara ordering the Joint Chiefs of Staff to start putting into effect OPLAN 314 and OPLAN 316, contingency plans for invading Cuba.[204]

---

199 J. Franklin, 1997, 47.
200 J. Franklin, 1997, 48–49.
201 Elliston.
202 National Security Archives, http://www.gwu.edu/~nsarchiv/news/20010430/doc1.pdf; James Bamford, *Body of Secrets*, pp. 82–91.
203 Bamford, 82–91.
204 J. Franklin, 1997, 56.

October 15, 1962. US analysis of U-2 photos of Cuba taken on October 14 indicates Soviet construction of intermediate-range nuclear missiles on the island.[205]

October 16–29, 1962. The US-Soviet-Cuba missile crisis preempts Kennedy's secret Project Cuba invasion plan. This further angers Cuban exiles and the mafia operating out of Florida, the major CIA instruments for overthrow of Castro, who are still furious over the failed Bay of Pigs invasion a year earlier—a failure blamed on President Kennedy for his refusal to provide air support during the invasion. (Their knowledge of secret plans to overthrow the Cuban government gives them undue influence in Washington.)

October 27, 1962. A U-2 spy plane is shot down over Cuba, killing the US pilot.[206] On the same day, President Kennedy sends a letter to Nikita Khrushchev with a proposal that the Soviet Union immediately withdraw its missiles from Cuba. In exchange, the US will end its naval blockade and issue a pledge not to invade Cuba. [Just as important, Attorney General Robert Kennedy agrees privately with Soviet Ambassador Anatoly F. Dobrynin that the US will withdraw its Jupiter missiles from Turkey.[207]] Kennedy's pledge to Khrushchev to not invade Cuba crushes Cuban exiles' dreams and enrages them further.

October 30, 1962. In a final completion of the saga, all sabotage activities of Operation Mongoose are ordered halted, though three six-man teams remain clandestinely deployed inside Cuba.[208]

Psychological Impact of Cuban Missile Crisis

Occurring in the context of the Cold War, the terrifying events known as the Cuban Missile Crisis brought the world to the brink of a nuclear war, and in so doing caused a loss of confidence among many in the US who were increasingly emotionally exhausted from the government's obsession with security. Severe psychological repercussions included a sense of powerlessness and frustration. Individuals possessed no avenue for meaningful opposition to government policies that could choose life or death for all of us. The almost total reduction of decision-making power by the Congress in regards to foreign policy and war revealed the almost total political incompetence of our supposedly democratic system of governance. After all, under the Constitution, the Congress possesses sole responsibility with respect to "the common defense and general welfare." The Cold War demands for ever more political conformity produced a national identity crisis due to the cognitive dissonance between our textbook teachings of democratic civics and the country's actual oligarchic behavior.

---

205 J. Franklin, 1997, 57.
206 J. Franklin, 1997, 59.
207 J. Franklin, 1997, 59.
208 J. Franklin, 1997, 60.

The Cuban Missile Crisis undoubtedly woke up many US citizens to the importance of acting to avert nuclear war, and helped breathe new life into the citizen activism that flowered in the 1960s in response to the grotesque criminality and barbarity of the Viet Nam war. As people finally recognized and claimed their own significant power, not only in the antiwar movement, but in fighting for civil rights, free speech, and the rights of women, workers, and people of all colors, US democracy experienced a rebirth.

Widespread democratic "people power" terrified the system, however, and in response, power brokers went into high gear, imposing what has become a 45-year reactionary tactic to assure an impotent democracy. The reinstitution of a general feeling of powerlessness among the masses has led to both dehumanization of the population and increasing accommodation to a narrower and narrower point of view, with very constricted political debate. Thus, the political dynamic moves farther and farther to the right.

Political leaders on both sides of the aisle continue to use the rhetoric of fear. The Cold War, having thawed, seemingly morphed into an endless War on Terror, but is making a big comeback, with a resurgence of fear-mongering in the US toward North Korea, China, and Putin's Russia. Whether of communism, terrorism, or fanatical islam, fear is used to feed and grow a military industrial machine that so overwhelms national politics that there are no authentic policy alternatives short of reliance on military systems of power, both at home and abroad.

Chapter Three
Criminal Intent

*"To be radical is to go to the root of the matter.
For man, however, the root is man himself."*[1]
—Karl Marx

Introduction

The history and nature of US involvement and intervention into Southeast Asia presents a well-documented case study of the extent to which our country will go to defeat social revolutions. To recognize our relentless criminal imposition of an industrialized model of "civilized" development on local, subsistence economies, a model too often accomplished through brutal warfare, requires a willingness to grasp the grotesque perversion in the extreme of our US American policy, which is rooted in fundamentalist Christianity. What has eluded our Western minds is that our model of development only leads to a modernized version of poverty where never-ending consumption produces class exaggeration, selfishness, and social instability, all in the name of progress.

Former US Secretary of War Robert McNamara, in his memoir, *In Retrospect*[2] in 1995, and in a sequel published in 1999, *Argument Without End*,[3] acknowledged the terrible mistake and wrongness of the Vietnam war, and said he hoped we would learn the lessons so such tragedy need not be repeated in the future. But despite his earnestness in analyzing the tragedy and explaining why we went so wrong, he misses the underlying cause of the war and the roots of its immorality—an historical imperial arrogance that justifies our country's intervention in the affairs of others. I daresay the vast majority of Vietnamese innately understand why the US war was wrong and why they had to fight to the end for self-determination, to preserve their hard-won independence and autonomy. But such simple desires are hard to grasp for the Western mind that is so deeply steeped in "exceptionalism," the belief in its own superiority. The idea that we have a divine right or duty to manipulate others for their own salvation is a grotesque perversion of what we call democracy, and certainly of what we teach about our so-called Christian values.

United States Relations 1945–1967 (The Pentagon Papers) is an official, formerly secret, history of US involvement in Viet Nam contained in 47 volumes and 7,000 pages published by the Pentagon. This history reveals a conscious effort to deceive the US

---

[1] It goes without saying that "man" and "himself" includes "woman" and "herself" as well.
[2] Robert S. McNamara, *In Retrospect: The Tragedy and Lessons of Vietnam* (New York: Times Books, 1995).
[3] Robert S. McNamara, James Blight, Robert K. Brigham, Thomas J. Biersteker, and Col. Herbert Schandler, *Argument Without End: In Search of Answers to the Vietnam Tragedy* (New York: Public Affairs, 1999).

audience from the very beginning of our involvement immediately after World War II to the conduct of that involvement for more than twenty years. The behavior of the United States government is so brutal and savage, it is difficult to comprehend. The question of the morality of the war, however, is never raised. Interestingly, the Papers were requested by Secretary McNamara and were meant to be a thorough history of the US involvement. They provide voluminous evidence that the US was the aggressor and had first propped up the French in their last-gasp effort to hold onto their colony, and then steered the defeated French away from any successful negotiations that would acknowledge Vietnamese rights to self-determination. The US saw Indochina as a problem, the only acceptable solution to which was total US military victory in association with our own created and funded right-wing South Vietnamese surrogates. Deceit and lies were important to assure manipulation of the US American people.[4] The papers even disclose use of the pretext of "humanitarian" intervention at a time in 1961 when serious flooding in the Mekong Delta raised the possibility that flood relief could be a justification "for moving in US military personnel for humanitarian purposes with subsequent retention."[5]

US American "Manifest Destiny," a phrase first coined in 1845, persists in defeating determined efforts for independence and autonomy in the developing world. As a people we have not been able to purge ourselves of our arrogant attitude that we must control the world's resources, a sickness that makes us insensitive to the needs of other people and cultures, clouding our vision, making it difficult to see and think clearly. As a result, we are an ignorant, dangerous people. Our sense of privilege severely prevents our own maturation and capacity for living within our means, and developing relationships with other peoples based upon mutual respect and a shared desire for the health and well being of all.

Historical Interest in Southeast Asia

It is highly probable that the first colonial settlers living in New England reached what is today's Viet Nam when sailing as international pirates during the North American extension (King William's War) of the War of the Grand Alliance (1689–1697), in which Britain, Holland, Spain, Portugal, Sweden, and the Holy Roman Empire acted in alliance against French expansion. That war reached Asia when English, French, and Dutch colonial governors and merchants quickly took up the struggle against French commercial rivals operating in their Asian domain.

The North America extension of the war witnessed conflict between French and English settlers and their respective Indian allies in colonial New England. The pirates returned from the Far East with gold, silver, and other exotic wealth to the eastern coast of "America," trading wares from Boston to Charleston, South Carolina. In time the Eurocentric mindset coordinated exploitation of resources, labor, and markets on a global scale. The early American settlers had initiated trade with China and Southeastern Asia while still members of the British Empire. This experience strengthened the colonies' desire for

---

4 See page 252, note 295, for citations to the *Pentagon Papers*.
5 Pentagon Papers, Beacon/Gravel Edition, Vol II, 85.

independence from Britain.⁶ Early colonial ideology integrated economics (commerce) with Christianity and prosperity, giving birth to a class of acquisitive Christian capitalist entrepreneurs.⁷

William Gilpin, a wealthy Quaker, in 1846 held up the virtues of US American ambitions in Asia, when he prophesied, "[T]he untransacted destiny of the American people is to subdue the continent—to rush over this vast field to the Pacific Ocean—to animate the many hundred millions of its people, and to cheer them upward. . . ."⁸ The term "Manifest Destiny," coined just the year before, was already being envisioned to include Asia.

In 1849, US Senator Thomas Hart Benton (D-MO, 1820–1850) gave a speech urging trade and "rich commerce" with Eastern Asia to "realize the grand idea of Columbus" carrying "wealth and dominion with it."⁹

In 1857, Dr. Peter Parker, a missionary serving in China, formally urged the US State Department to take possession of Formosa, for the benefit of "enterprising fellow-citizens." This is an early example of the direct connections that often existed between missionaries and the government, and missionaries' secular appreciation of imperial commercial policies.¹⁰ In the twentieth century, one of the largest US missionary organizations, Wycliffe Bible Translators, worked closely with the US government and one of US America's most powerful families (the Rockefellers) to conquer the vast Amazon region by using religion to tranquilize the Indigenous, thereby clearing a pathway to profitable commercial development.¹¹

By the 1890s, the European invaders had completely conquered the Indigenous lands within the continental United States. The last of the major battles by the US Army occurred in December 1890 with the massacre of Lakota at Wounded Knee in the newly created state of South Dakota, just as the country was experiencing one of its periodic depressions when domestic agriculture and manufacturing had produced surpluses the domestic market could not absorb. Suddenly there was no more frontier left to develop—except across the oceans and into Latin America and Asia. The emergent corporate capitalism desperately needed new profitable markets that could only be found overseas. Asia was becoming increasingly important as we scrambled to compete with Russia and European nations who were also scrambling for markets.

---

6 William Appleman Williams, Thomas McCormick, Lloyd Gardener, and Walter LaFeber, eds., *America in Vietnam: A Documented History* (Garden City, NJ: Anchor Books/Doubleday, 1985), 3–5; in general, William Appleman Williams, *The Tragedy of American Diplomacy* (New York: W.W. Norton, 1972).

7 R.H. Tawney, *Religion and the Rise of Capitalism* (New York: Harcourt, Brace and Co., 1926).

8 Williams, 1985, 12, citing William Gilpin, *Mission of the North American People, Geographical, Social, and Political* [Philadelphia, PA: J.B. Lippincott & Co., 1874), 130.

9 Williams, 1985, 11

10 Williams, 1985, 10–11.

11 Gerard Colby with Charlotte Dennett, *Thy Will Be Done, The Conquest of the Amazon: Nelson Rockefeller and Evangelism in the Age of Oil* (New York: HarperCollins, 1995).

Mass burial of Native Americans at Wounded Knee, 1890:
Who are the "savages"?

Even before being elected president in 1898, William McKinley had declared, "We want a foreign market for our surplus products."[12] In 1898, Indiana Senator Albert Beveridge repeated the increasingly popular sentiment:

> American factories are making more than the American people can use; American soil is producing more than they can consume. Fate has written our policy for us; the trade of the world must and shall be ours. . . . We will cover the ocean with our merchant marine. We will build a navy to the measure of our greatness.[13]

As the US State Department explained in 1898, "the enlargement of foreign consumption of the products of our mills and workshops has, therefore, become a serious problem of statesmanship as well as of commerce."[14] Echoing growing political pressure for intervention to protect US investments, Massachusetts Senator Henry Cabot Lodge declared, "where the flag once goes up it must never come down."[15] Senator Lodge's grandson, Henry Cabot Lodge, Jr., later became US Ambassador to South Viet Nam under both Presidents Kennedy and Johnson.

In April 1898, McKinley received his Congressional declaration of war on Spain that would soon bring into the US orbit the Philippines, Cuba, Guam, and Puerto Rico. The President confessed he had asked God for light and guidance as to whether to take the

---

12 Zinn, 292.
13 Zinn, 292.
14 Zinn, 292.
15 Sidney Lens, *The Forging of the American Empire, From the Revolution to Vietnam: A History of US Imperialism* (London: Pluto Press, 2003), 175–178

Philippines and he received a message that it was incumbent upon the Americans "to educate the Filipinos, and uplift and civilize and Christianize them."[15] Expansion into Asian markets coincident to this intervention into the Philippines was diplomatically disguised as US "Open Door Policy," which purported to be about establishing "perfect equality of treatment for commerce."[17] Three policy "Notes" written by US Secretary of State John Hay identified "spheres of influence," and established rules for enterprising, imperial European competitor nations that might engage in "open" trade and economic activity with China, greater Asia, and elsewhere.[18] The *Open Door Notes*, combined with Spanish American war conquests, introduced a triumph of corporation capitalism[19] that would eventually usher in "the American Century" proclaimed by *Time*'s Henry Luce in 1941.[20] More than 100 years later, the United States' so-called "pivot to Asia" seems a modern version of McKinley's Open Door Policy, with the same goals of remaining competitive and dominant militarily and economically with Asian markets and powers.[21]

In 1939, with Rockefeller Foundation funding, the Council on Foreign Relations, a prestigious ruling group of business leaders, academics, government planners, nonprofits and media elite founded in 1921 and the most influential US private policy planning group at that time, created the influential *War and Peace Studies Project*, designed to safeguard US interests in a post-WWII world. After FDR's re-election in November 1940, their studies focused on Far East policy, stressing the need to maintain unquestioned world power, especially in Southeast Asia. The council sought to limit exercise of sovereignty by any foreign nation(s) that might constitute a threat to US access to territories and markets in order to satisfy the insatiable demands of US prosperity and security—our "national interests." US interests in Southeast Asia were both economic—a source of critical raw materials and new markets—and strategic—securing safe access to air and sea routes.

The idea of a "Grand Area" was dreamed up in 1941 by the Council on Foreign Relations, it posited a world economy that would be led by the US once Germany was finally defeated. This was consistent with the "spheres of influence" argued for earlier in the *Open Door Notes*, intended to protect US American private enterprise, initially in Asia, but ultimately around the world.[22]

Simply speaking, it was now felt and contended that the Western Hemisphere failed to provide sufficient resources to satisfy the needs of the US American people (and the avarice of corporate interests). The advancement of our culture is entirely dependent upon consuming more than our fair share of the world's resources, at the expense of other peoples and the earth's ecosystem. Others' needs for resources are deferred to ensure our

---

16 Zinn, 305–306.
17 Williams, 1969, 443.
18 Williams, 1985, 20–22.
19 Williams, 1969, 443.
20 Williams, 1985, 22–27.
21 Richard Bush III, "The Response of China's Neighbors to the US 'Pivot' to Asia" (January 31, 2012), *Brookings Institute*.
22 Laurence H. Shoup and William Minter, *Imperial Brain Trust: The Council on Foreign Relations and United States Foreign Policy* (New York: Monthly Review Press, 1970), 223–253; Noam Chomsky, *Deterring Democracy* (New York: Hill and Wang, 1992), 45–49.

own comfortable "American Way of Life." Tin, natural rubber, bauxite, iron ore, quinine, kapok, coconut products, palm oil, tungsten, chromium, rice, and reserves of oil—then as now, the raw materials found in the Pacific region were perceived as essential. The US, which now has 4.5 percent of the world's population, consumes at least 25 percent of the world's resources (a conservative estimate). As a resource-defined nation, the US is now almost totally dependent upon imports from abroad, and Asia is considered as important in satisfying these needs as Latin America and Africa. Welcome to empire as a way of life![23]

Southeast Asia: Colonial Context, Cultural History

Despite its 250-year experience exploiting markets and resources in Southeast Asia, the US knows virtually nothing about the local history of the peoples who live there—their culture, values and aspirations.

In the mid-1960s, Viet Nam's population was about 34 million; 18 million north of the temporary dividing line of the Seventeenth parallel, and 16 million to the south. Historically the country is composed of over fifty distinct ethnic groups including Vietnamese, Thai/Lao and Hmong tribes, smaller groups of mountain people (generically referred to by the French as Montagnards), Malayo-Polynesian and Mon-Khmer-speaking groups, Cambodians, and Chinese.[24] But, of course, the US knew only that the region possessed readily accessible geostrategic resources and other interests that promised great potential for increasing US commercial profits.

What the French and the Americans who occupied Viet Nam had to learn the hard way was that they were engaged in a struggle that, for the Vietnamese people, occurred in the context of 4,000 years of relentless and heroic resistance to outside invading forces.[25]

Historically, Viet Nam had close ties to China. In 111 BC, its territory was annexed by China, and it was governed as a Chinese province and imbued with Confucian social and political values for more than a thousand years. The Vietnamese adopted a hierarchical system of mandarin bureaucracy, as a result. Despite this heavy influence, the Vietnamese remained substantially distinct ethnically, and grew to deeply resent China's political domination. In 939 AD they revolted and announced independence from China. Over the centuries, Viet Nam effectively repelled repeated Chinese attempts at subjugation, and even today the Vietnamese regularly celebrate their heroic overthrow of the Chinese invaders.[26]

From the seventeenth century into the nineteenth, the European nations of England, France, the Netherlands, and Portugal competed for commercial resources and religious converts in Viet Nam. However, by 1802 the Vietnamese were at relative peace and they

---

23 US American Historian William Appleman Williams' 1980 book is devoted to describing this concept. Its title: *Empire as a Way of Life: An Essay on the Causes and Character of America's Present Predicament Along with a Few Thoughts About an Alternative.*

24 George McTurnan Kahin and John W. Lewis, *The United States in Vietnam* (New York: Delta, 1967), 3–7.

25 Kahin and Lewis, 420.

26 Kahin and Lewis, 3–5.

united their northern (Tonkin), central (Annam), and southern (Cochin) regions into one independent nation.[27] French Catholic missionaries, who had followed European traders into Southeast Asia in the 1500s, were met with fierce Indigenous resistance when attempting to evangelize the locals in the mid-nineteenth century. The French used this provocation to dispatch French military forces to protect not only the missionaries but increasingly valuable resources.[28]

In 1857, the French attacked what is present-day Danang. They captured Saigon in 1859, and by 1867 had conquered the southernmost part of the country and claimed Cochin China as a colony of France. In 1883, the French conquered the remainder of the Vietnamese state and took over Annam (central) and Tonkin (north) as protectorates. The Vietnamese mandarins subsequently divided into two groups: the collaborators and the resisters. In 1887, the French merged the three regions of Viet Nam with Cambodia to form a union that was joined by Laos in 1893 and came to be called French Indochina. The capital of the French colony, initially in Saigon, was moved to Hanoi in 1902, then to Dalat in 1939, then back to Hanoi in 1945.[29]

Some 100,000 Vietnamese soldiers and workers were sent to France in 1915 during World War I to aid in the war against Germany. The social and political ideas these Vietnamese came into contact with were inconsistent with those of the colonial mandarin system, and when they returned home many joined the Vietnamese nationalist movement to rid themselves of French rule. Efforts to achieve even small reforms through the French colonial administration were met with frustration and failure, and drove the movement for independence.[30]

The Vietnamese People Once Again Resist

During the 1920s, the major underground nationalist organization was the Viet Nam Quoc Dan Dang (VNQDD/Vietnamese Nationalist Party). Its main objective was the overthrow of French rule and establishment of a republican government. In early 1930, the VNQDD led a revolt in hopes of creating uprisings throughout the country. The French quickly put down the rebellion and effectively destroyed the VNQDD.[31]

Subsequently, the major underground organizing against the French was undertaken by Communist organizations united as the Indochinese Communist Party, by Nguyen Ai Quoc, or Ho Chi Minh, along with other future leaders Pham Van Dong, Vo Nguyen Giap, and Truong Chinh. On July 1, 1940, after the German invasion and occupation, a French collaborative puppet government was formed in Vichy, France. On September 22, 1940, Japanese forces attacked northern portions of Viet Nam, and the Tonkin region was surrendered by the French to the Japanese, allied with Germany as one of the Axis powers.

---

27 Marvin E. Gettleman, Jane Franklin, Marilyn B. Young, and H. Bruce Franklin, eds., *Vietnam and America: A Documented History* (New York: Grove, 1995), 3.
28 Kahin and Lewis, 5–8.
29 Kahin and Lewis, 5–11; *Wikipedia*, French Indochina: http://en.wikipedia.org/wiki/French_Indochina.
30 Kahin and Lewis, 5–11.
31 Kahin and Lewis, 11.

The Japanese occupiers, recognizing French Vichy sovereignty in Viet Nam, ordered an end to all resistance. Shortly thereafter, in November 1940, a large Vietnamese peasant revolt erupted against the French *and* Japanese in My Tho–Dinh Tuong Province and Ben Tre–Kien Hoa Province, both in the Mekong Delta.[32]

In this way, World War II events undermined the French colonial structure in Indochina. Japanese occupation was accomplished with the French now cooperating in administrative and security functions along with their cooperative Vietnamese elites. Now there were two occupiers, one working for the other, interestingly, but both working against the wishes of the Vietnamese people. Although the French administrative machinery was left intact, by December 1941 Viet Nam was for the most part a colony of Japan.

Under these conditions, the fusion of nationalism and communism dramatically increased as Ho Chi Minh secured significant backing from increasing numbers of non-Communist nationalists in efforts to resist both the French and the Japanese. It was in this context also that a cooperative relationship was later established between US OSS officers and the Vietnamese toward the end of World War II.

On February 8, 1941, Ho Chi Minh returned to Viet Nam from exile to assume direct leadership of the Vietnamese revolution. For nearly a century, French colonialism in Indochina "had been one of the worst possible examples of peonage, disregard for human rights, and French cupidity" in which "the Vietnamese had been cruelly exploited, brutally maltreated, and generally used as French chattel." These are the words of former US Army Colonel Archimedes L. A. Patti, who as an OSS officer worked closely with Ho Chi Minh and Viet Minh units during critical times in May through September 1945.[33] The OSS had supported Viet Minh forces in struggles against the Japanese near the end of World War II by providing them with 5,000 weapons, ammunition, and training. In turn, Viet Minh networks provided intelligence on Japanese military activities prior to the Japanese surrender and helped rescue downed US pilots in the vast rural regions of Southeast Asia.[34]

That May, Indochinese Communist Party members met in southern China near the border with Tonkin and agreed to disband in favor of a new organizational form. The Viet Nam Independence League, or Viet Minh, short for *Viet Nam Doc Lap Dong Minh*, was a broader coalition appealing politically and nationally to increasing numbers of non-Communist adherents. The Viet Minh, a united front organization chaired by Ho Chi Minh, represented the collaboration of all nationalists in coming together to fight against both the occupying Japanese and French, under the guerilla leadership of Vo Nguyen Giap.[35]

---

32 Wilfred Burchett, *Vietnam: Inside Story of the Guerilla War* (New York: International, 1965, 1968), 228–229.

33 Archimedes L. A. Patti, *Why Viet Nam? Prelude to America's Albatross* (Berkeley: University of California Press, 1980), 43–71; 83–87; 96–102; 125–129; 189–203; 366–374.

34 Ralph W. McGehee, *Deadly Deceits: My 25 Years in the CIA* (New York: Sheridan Square, 1983), 130; and in general, Patti.

35 Bowman, 14–15.

The Viet Minh were the only strong force opposing the Japanese. They so impressed the OSS team that the US officers convinced Viet Minh leaders that the US would back their struggle for independence, an idea that had already been suggested by President Roosevelt's promise in the Atlantic Charter to support the self-determination of all peoples.[36]

The Atlantic Charter: The Promise of Anti-Colonial Rhetoric

The Atlantic Charter was a joint statement of principles issued by British Prime Minister Winston Churchill and US President Franklin Roosevelt on August 14, 1941. Neither a formal alliance nor legally binding, it reiterated some of the anti-colonial rhetoric offered in 1919 by Wilson's Fourteen Points, one of which, Point 5, called for "an absolutely impartial adjustment of all colonial claims, based on the principle that the interests of the population must have equal weight with the equitable claims of government." The Charter, prepared at secret meetings on board the US Cruiser *Augusta* and the British Battleship *Prince of Wales* in Argentia Bay off Newfoundland, included:

    1. renunciation of territorial or other aggrandizement;

    2. opposition to territorial changes contrary to wishes of people immediately concerned;

    3. *support of the right of peoples to choose their own government* [*italics* added];

    4. support, with due respect for existing obligations, for the easing of restrictions on trade, and access to raw materials on equal terms;

    5. support for cooperative efforts to improve the economic position and social security of the peoples of the world;

    6. the right to freedom from want and fear;

    7. freedom of the seas; and

    8. disarmament of aggressor nations pending establishment of a permanent peace structure.[37]

On September 24, 1941, the Atlantic Charter was endorsed by fifteen anti-axis nations, including the Soviet Union.[38]

The principles espoused in the charter gave hope and encouragement to independence movements such as were playing out in Viet Nam, driven by a people unified in their passion for ridding their country of French colonialists and Japanese invaders.

---

    36 Kahin and Lewis, 17–18; Ellen J. Hammer, *The Struggle for Indochina* (Stanford, CA: Stanford University Press, 1954), 130–151; Donald Lancaster, *The Emancipation of French Indochina* (London, UK: Oxford University Press, 1961), 143; Bernard B. Fall, *The Two Vietnams* (New York: Praeger, 1964), 100–101.
    37 Morris and Morris, 436.
    38 Morris and Morris, 436.

Strategic Importance of Southeast Asia Articulated

By the beginning of FDR's third term as president in 1941, Henry L. Stimson (Secretary of War), Sumner Welles (Undersecretary of State), President Roosevelt, and Cordell Hull (Secretary of State), all of them members of the Council on Foreign Relations, had accepted the council's conclusion on the strategic importance of Southeast Asia.[39]

FDR quickly imposed a trade embargo that undermined resource-dependent Japan, which possessed imperial ambitions to compete with the US for greater control of Asia's resources. With an intention to anger Japan, Roosevelt ordered a blockade of the oil and scrap metal Japan needed for its war efforts, much of which had been supplied by the US up until then. Some historians see this policy as a preface to FDR's plan to deliberately provoke Japan to attack Pearl Harbor in order to justify entrance into the war. It is well documented that the US had intercepted Japanese secret messages as early as August 1941, that FDR had foreknowledge of the attack, and that efforts to reveal FDR's plan were intentionally thwarted. US political leaders saw this as the only way to get the US public to support going to war and risking US lives and military equipment. When FDR met with his war cabinet on November 25, 1941, twelve days before the actual attack on Pearl Harbor, Secretary of War Henry L. Stimson later explained, "we realized that in order to have the full support of the American people it was desirable to make sure the Japanese [fired the first shot] so that there should remain no doubt in anyone's mind as to who were the aggressors."[40]

In examining the central figures in US government decision-making related to Southeast Asia, it appears the Council on Foreign Relations and the economic class it represented were clearly in control. Council members included all the presidents, the long-term secretaries of state, presidential advisers, and a number of other important players.[41] In effect, it was a continuation of the oligarchic plutocracy that was there at the founding of US "civilization."

During the period between 1940 and 1963, the Council on Foreign Relations devoted an extraordinary amount of attention to Southeast Asia, creating at least five study and discussion groups, emphasizing the area as an economic and strategic prize because of its numerous raw materials, abundant food production, large population with corresponding markets, and critical air and sea communication/trade routes.[42]

On January 24, 1944, Roosevelt submitted a memo to Secretary of State Cordell Hull that included these words: "Indo-China should *not* go back to France but . . . it should be administered by an international trusteeship. France has had the country—thirty million inhabitants for nearly one hundred years, and the people are worse off than they were at the beginning."[43]

---

39 Laurence H. Shoup and William Minter, *Imperial Brain Trust: The Council on Foreign Relations and United States Foreign Policy* (New York: Monthly Review Press, 1970), 233.
40 See note 22, p. 33.
41 Shoup and Minter, 245–248.
42 Shoup and Minter, 232.
43 Williams, 1985, 30.

A policy paper issued by new president Harry Truman's State Department on June 22, 1945 revealed his administration's priority of supporting France and European interests over any concern for self-determination of colonial peoples, ignoring the promises pledged in the August 1941 Atlantic Charter.[44]

The Charter forming the United Nations was signed by 51 nations, including the United States, on June 26, 1945. Article 2.3 of the UN Charter requires all parties to settle disputes by peaceful means. Article 2.4 stipulates that all members shall refrain from threat or use of force in international relations.

Post–World War II Vietnamese struggles were complicated by arrangements made by the Allies at the July 17–August 2, 1945 Potsdam Conference. The much-criticized arrangements stipulated that Chiang Kai-shek's nationalist Chinese troops would reoccupy Viet Nam north of the 16th Parallel and British forces would take over south of the parallel. Under Potsdam, the mandate of the British and Chinese forces was *limited* to "the round-up and disarming of the Japanese, and the recovery of Allied Prisoners of War and Internees" as approved on July 24 by Truman.[45] Similarly, on August 11, Truman arbitrarily divided Korea at the 38th Parallel, a division from which that country has never recovered.

US Support of France's Attempt at Re-colonization of Viet Nam

US policy in Viet Nam, according to Noam Chomsky, was in effect, "a conscious application of principles of imperial planning that formed part of a consensus established long before the specific period, the 1960s, to which attention is generally restricted."[46] A chronological review of historical events predating the official beginning date of the US war in Vietnam bears out Chomsky's observation.

On August 11, 1945, learning that Japan was about to surrender, the Vietnamese began to prepare an insurrection to seize Hanoi from the Japanese. By late August, Viet Minh forces seized control of towns and villages in Annam and Tonkin. On August 29, Ho Chi Minh formed his first provisional government and on September 2, the day Japan formally signed its surrender, he proclaimed Vietnamese independence—the Democratic Republic of Viet Nam (DRV)—before 400,000 supporters. Had the Truman Administration supported Vietnamese independence rather than supporting French re-colonization, all of the bloodshed and tragedy to follow would have been averted.[47]

August 30, 1945, Ho Chi Minh sent his first cable to President Truman, requesting support for Vietnamese independence based partly on principles enunciated in the 1941 Atlantic Charter. Ho Chi Minh had, 26 years earlier in 1919, attempted to petition President Wilson at Versailles on the basis of Wilson's Fourteen Points. Between August 30, 1945,

---

44 George McTurnan Kahin, *Intervention: How America Became Involved in Vietnam* (New York: Alfred A. Knopf, 1986), 5–6.

45 Patti, 455–456.

46 Noam Chomsky, *Towards a New Cold War* (New York: Pantheon, 1982), 101.

47 Fredrik Logevall, *Embers of War: The Fall of an Empire and the Making of America's Vietnam* (New York: Random House, 2012), 92–109.

and February 1946, Ho sent a total of eight messages to Truman asking for help.[48] All went unanswered.

One of Ho's letters described the humanitarian reasons for support, citing that two million Vietnamese had died of starvation during the winter of 1944 and spring of 1945 when the French seized and stored all available rice until it rotted. Compounding this crisis, flooding of three-fourths of cultivated land in the summer-autumn 1945 was followed by a severe drought, causing five-sixths loss of normal harvest. Still there was no response from the Truman administration.[49]

When, on September 2, 1945, Ho Chi Minh appeared in Hanoi's Ba Dinh Square to announce Viet Nam's independence, thereby abolishing the monarchy of Bao Dai and ending eighty years of colonial administration, at least four US OSS agents were present as invited guests—civilian Robert H. Knapp, US Army Captain Ramon Grelecki, US Army Captain Roger P. Bernique, and US Army Colonel Archimedes L.A. Patti.[50] Despite this historic reciprocal support relationship between the OSS and the Viet Minh forged in common struggle against the Japanese at the end of World War II, the Truman administration chose to support the French over the Vietnamese.

With US weapons provided by Truman and augmented by British troops, the French military began an all-out assault on Saigon on September 22, in a post-WWII effort to reclaim its colony.[51] By December, when French troops stormed further south into the Mekong Delta, including Can Tho City, they were driving US tanks. Truman had earlier approved a British request to transfer 800 Lend-Lease jeeps and trucks over to the French.[52] The tragic fact is that less than a year after Franklin Roosevelt's statement that Indochina should *not* go back to France, Truman had effected a 180-degree policy shift.

Lt. Colonel A. Peter Dewey, an OSS officer, was the first US American to die in Viet Nam. Dewey was allegedly shot by the Viet Minh while driving an unmarked jeep near the Saigon airport on September 26, 1945. His body was never recovered.[53]

On October 5, 1945, Dean Acheson, Truman's Acting Secretary of State, sent this telegram to the US Charge d'affaires in China: "US has no thought of opposing the reestablishment of French control in Indochina and no official statement by US Government has questioned even by implication French sovereignty over Indochina."[54]

---

48 Patti, 380–381, 454–455; Gettleman et al., 1995, 35, 46–47; The unwillingness or downright refusal to honor agreements and rhetorical commitments to justice under law is an entrenched US pattern as witnessed from the history of US American Indian appeals to the US government for peace and recognition.

49 Zinn, 1980, 461.

50 Patti, 248–253.

51 Gettleman et al., 1995, 34.

52 Gettleman et al., 1995, 34, 39; Neil Sheehan, *A Bright Shining Lie* (New York: Random House, 1988), 152; Patti, 380; Kahin, 1986, 8; Marilyn B. Young, *The Vietnam Wars: 1945–1990* (New York: HarperPerennial, 1991), 22, 29; H. Bruce Franklin, *Vietnam & Other American Fantasies* (Amherst: University of Massachusetts Press, 2000), 50.

53 Nancy Zaroulis and Gerald Sullivan, *Who Spoke Up? American Protest Against the War in Vietnam, 1963–1975* (New York: Holt, Rinehart and Winston, 1984), 13; Patti, 320–210.

54 Young, 1991, 12.

Then, on October 21, 1945, less than seven weeks after Viet Nam's declaration of independence six months after Roosevelt's death and in the first months of Truman's presidency, a US *Department of State Bulletin* written by John Carter Vincent, one of the State Department's top experts on Asia, declared, "with regard to the situation in French Indochina, this government does not question French sovereignty in that area." The liberals were simply not prepared to support revolutionary struggles/change in the East Indies, and Carter Vincent stated, "it is our policy to encourage and facilitate the reestablishment of American business in China."[55]

Over the course of two months, October and November of 1945, at least eight and possibly a dozen US troop ships that had been taking US troops home from the war received new orders interrupting that mission to transport 13,000 US-armed French troops and Foreign Legionnaires from France to Viet Nam in a re-colonization attempt. The enlisted US crew, members of the US Merchant Marine, organized angry protests and sent a cablegram to President Harry Truman with this message:

> We, the unlicensed personnel [i.e., non-officers] of the *S.S. Winchester Victory*, vigorously protest the use of this and other American vessels for carrying foreign combat troops to foreign soil for the purpose of engaging in hostilities to further the imperialist policies of foreign governments when there are American troops waiting to come home. Request immediate congressional investigation of this matter.

As if this wasn't enough, upon arriving in Viet Nam, the crew were shocked to be saluted by Japanese soldiers recently rearmed by the British to suppress the Vietnamese.[56]

Thus, within two months of Japan's surrender: first, US ships were carrying French forces back to Viet Nam, and second, Washington then provided France with credit to purchase 75 troop transport ships from the United States. Soon the US was directly supplying France with a quantity of modern weaponry, including Lend-Lease military equipment that could be used in Viet Nam.[57]

Post–World War II, US Cold War behaviors reveal a great deal about the nature of the US national psyche as expressed in arrogant political and vicious military policies. Unrestrained terror was in store for its many victims around the world as a grossly exaggerated fear of communism—not just a national, but a Western paranoia—allowed a fury of violence to be unleashed on Third World peoples. The US in particular, and the West in general, under the cloud of their own fear of communism, were simply not willing to accept, or even try to understand, these or other peoples' authentic desire for national self-determination, to recognize that these democracy movements, striving for independence from Western colonial forces, were as legitimate, or even moreso, as the movement that had led to US independence from British rule.

---

55 Williams, 1985, 38–39.
56 H. Bruce Franklin, 2000, 50; Christian G. Appy, *Patriots: The Vietnam War Remembered from All Sides* (New York: Viking, 2003), 37.
57 Kahin, 1986, 7–8.

On March 6, 1946, Ho Chi Minh signed an agreement with France that recognized the Democratic Republic of Viet Nam (DRV) as a free state within the as yet unformed Indochinese Federation and the French Union. This agreement allowed the French to safely introduce 15,000 troops into northern Viet Nam to replace the departing Chinese occupation forces. However, it also stipulated that 3,000 of those troops would be withdrawn, in each of the five years following, until by the end of 1951 *all* French troops would be removed.[58]

French bombardment of Haiphong in October 1946[59] understandably deepened tensions between the French and Vietnamese such that a two-day battle broke out between the French Navy and the Viet Minh in the Port of Haiphong on November 20, provoking the Paris government to cable its generals in Viet Nam to "teach those insolent Annamites a lesson." On November 23, the French ordered the Viet Minh to withdraw all their troops within two hours, but the order was ignored by the Vietnamese. Supported by offshore naval batteries from the cruiser *Suffren*, the French then attacked the Chinese quarters in the port city, and the resulting 25,000 casualties included 6,000 dead.[60]

On December 19, 1946, the Viet Minh attacked the French in Hanoi, ignoring the warning to disarm, ushering in the bloody guerrilla war that would become known as the French Indochina War (1946–1954). At this point the vast majority of Vietnamese, no matter their political differences, rallied together to defeat the French.[61]

In a secret policy statement dated September 27, 1948, the US State Department explicitly told France that US arms were "available for reshipment to Indochina or for releasing stocks from reserves to be forwarded to Indochina."[62]

In February 1950, the US and Great Britain extended *de jure* recognition to the regime of French puppet Bao Dai in South Viet Nam.[63]

National Security Council Document 64 (NSC 64), approved by President Truman on March 27, 1950, the original basis for the "domino theory," stipulated that "all practicable measures be taken to prevent further Communist expansion in Southeast Asia" to prevent a "grave hazard."[64] Holding the line in Southeast Asia was critical to US security interests, according to this document. Any movement for autonomy or independence from Western economic systems was considered a virus, to be eliminated at any cost.

---

58 Gettleman et al., 1995, 47–48; Bowman, 16.
59 Zinn, 1980, 461.
60 Patti, 383.
61 Patti, 383; Harry G. Summers, Jr., *Historical Atlas of the Vietnam War* (Boston: Houghton Mifflin Company, 1995), 16; Bowman, 16.
62 Kahin, 1986, 8.
63 Bowman, 33.
64 Patti, 389, 403.

On April 14, 1950, the same day NSC 68 was secretly approved, Secretary of War/Defense Louis Johnson sent a top-secret letter to Secretary of State Acheson summarizing the US Joint Chiefs of Staff's recommendations, called for in NSC 64 and issued in February 1950: "To undertake a determination of all practicable United States measures to protect its security in Indochina and to prevent the expansion of Communist aggression in that area." Section 2 (a-g) of the letter (below)[65] offers a concise answer to the ongoing quandary of why the US was in Viet Nam.

2. The mainland states of Southeast Asia also are at present of critical strategic importance to the United States because:

   a. They are the major sources of certain strategic materials required for the completion of United States stock-pile projects;

   b. The area is a crossroad of communications;

   c. Southeast Asia is a vital segment in the line of containment of communism stretching from Japan southward and around to the Indian Peninsula. The security of the three major non-Communist base areas in this quarter of the world—Japan, India, and Australia—depends in a large measure on the denial of Southeast Asia to the Communists. If Southeast Asia is lost, these three base areas will tend to be isolated from one another;

   d. The fall of Indochina would undoubtedly lead to the fall of the other mainland states of Southeast Asia. Their fall would:

      (1) Require changing the Philippines and Indonesia from supporting positions in the Asian offshore island chain to front-line bases for the defense of the Western Hemisphere. It would also call for a review of the strategic deployment of United States forces in the Far East; and

      (2) Bring about almost immediately a dangerous condition with respect to the internal security of the Philippines, Malaya, and Indonesia, and would contribute to their probable eventual fall to the Communists.

   e. The fall of Southeast Asia would result in the virtually complete denial to the United States of the Pacific littoral of Asia. Southeast Asian mainland areas are important in the conduct of operations to contain Communist expansion;

---

65 Department of State, *Foreign Relations of the United States, 1950*, VI, 780–785, cited in Williams, 1985, 111–113.

  f. Communist control of this area would alleviate considerably the food problem of China and would make available to the USSR important strategic materials. In this connection, Soviet control of all the major components of Asia's war potential might become a decisive factor affecting the balance of power between the United States and the USSR. "A Soviet position of dominance over Asia, Western Europe, or both, would constitute a major threat to United States security"; and

  g. A Soviet position of dominance over the Far East would also threaten the United States position in Japan since that country could thereby be denied its Asian markets, sources of food and other raw materials. The feasibility of retention by the United States of its Asian offshore island bases could thus be jeopardized.

In early May, Secretary of State Acheson agreed to provide arms assistance to the French Associated States of Indochina.[66]

On June 27, 1950, the Korean "hot" war broke out, and by June 30 Truman began sending thousands of ground troops and air personnel to launch an incessant bombing campaign in that country. But, even while the US military was heavily involved in attempting to control Korea, its *direct* involvement in Viet Nam began on July 26, 1950, when President Truman sent $15 million in military aid to the French forces.[67] About a week later, on August 3, a 35-member US Military Assistance Advisory Group (MAAG) arrived in Viet Nam, to train French soldiers in the use of US equipment in efforts to defeat the Viet Minh.[68]

Once US soldiers began actively assisting the French combat troops, MAAG quickly grew to 350 members. Based in Saigon, the group was also responsible for administering and overseeing US aid in Viet Nam. From 1950 to 1954, the US provided more than $3 billion in aid to the French ($26 billion in 2015 dollars). This included a $4 million-a-year retainer paid to Viet Nam Emperor Bao Dai, which he invested in Swiss banks and foreign real estate.[69] On September 7, 1951, the US signed an agreement with Saigon for direct aid to South Viet Nam.[70]

In 1952, when at least 54 US C-47 transport aircraft were "lent" to France for use in Indochina, they came with 28 US Air Force mechanics to service them. Four French fighter squadrons were maintained only because the US provided "attrition aircraft" to replace F-6Fs and F-8Fs when these wore out. This explicit, direct supply of US war material to the French in Indochina developed during the Truman administration was justified under the Mutual Defense Assistance Program.[71]

---

66 Bowman, 33.
67 Dougherty and Stewart, 19.
68 Bowman, 34.
69 Douglas Valentine, *The Phoenix Program* (Lincoln, NE: iUniverse, 2000), 24.
70 Bowman, 34.
71 Kahin, 1986, 37.

In July 1953, when the French were becoming nervous about a possible defeat in Southeast Asia, Secretary of State Dulles strongly urged the French not to seek a negotiated end to the war, and promised more military aid from the United States. Dulles reiterated the critical value of Viet Nam as a source of raw materials as well as its geo-strategic importance in Southeast Asia.[72] On August 4, 1953, President Eisenhower justified giving military help to France along the same lines—because "our security, our power and ability to get certain things we need from the riches of Indochina territory and from Southwest Asia" were at stake.[73]

In September 1953, with US encouragement, France chose to make one final effort to recoup from a series of military defeats at the hands of the Viet Minh, whose forces had grown to an estimated 290,000. France had lost all domestic political support for its Indochina military war but nonetheless wanted one more chance to succeed, hoping to protect its vast investments in coal, cement, and heavy industry in the north, its rubber and other plantations in the south, and its 6,500 French business reps and technicians in Hanoi.[74] Called the Navarre Plan, after General Henri Navarre, commander-in-chief of French Union forces in Indochina, the new French campaign drew on 517,000 men. Only 80,000 were French, and 20,000 of these were from the French Foreign Legion (half of whom had served in Nazi armies); 48,000 came from France's North African colonies, including Senegal; and 369,000 were Indochinese (the majority Vietnamese).[75] Of the French combat battalions in Indochina, 84 were in Tonkin (northern Viet Nam), 65 in Annam (central), and 42 in Cochin (southern), with 12 in Cambodia and 62 in Laos.[76]

After the French announcement of the Navarre Plan, and less than three months after the active war in Korea ended with the signing an armistice on July 27, former World War II naval officer and then–vice-president Richard Nixon made a fall field trip to northern Viet Nam to help bolster French Union forces, who were facing increasing chances of defeat. Dressed in battle fatigues and helmet, Nixon stressed to French officers and Vietnamese conscripts that they had full US support. Indeed, the US by that time was paying 80 percent of France's war costs and supplying 200 military advisers, 1,400 tanks, 340 planes, 350 patrol boats, 240,000 small-arms ammunition, and 15 million bullets.[77] Nixon sought to persuade the French *not* to negotiate with the Viet Minh, believing that, should the French leave, Viet Nam and its neighbors "would fall like husks before the Communist hurricane."[78]

---

72 Gabriel Kolko, "The United States in Vietnam 1944–66: Origins and Objectives of an Intervention," in Ken Coates, Peter Limqueco and Peter Weiss, eds., *Prevent the Crime of Silence: Reports from the Sessions of the International War Crimes Tribunal, Founded by Bertram Russell* (London, UK: Allen Lane The Penguin Press, 1971), 88–90.

73 Greene, 1970, 108.

74 Michael MacLear, *Vietnam: The Ten Thousand Day War* (London, UK: Thames Methuen, 1981), 66.

75 Kahin and Lewis, 36; Kahin, 1986, 39.

76 Kahin, 1986, 39.

77 MacLear, 50.

78 Anthony Summers, *The Arrogance of Power: The Secret World of Richard Nixon* (New York: Viking, 2000), 165.

The US supported the Navarre Plan with an influx of forty B-26 bombers, while dispatching an additional two hundred US Air Force technicians dressed in civilian clothes. Congress appropriated $785 million to finance this last burst of effort by the Navarre offensive. The US had, by this time, also provided 300,000 small arms and machine guns.[79]

As the French neared inevitable defeat in early 1954, Vice-President Nixon only increased his public opposition to the convening of an Indochina peace conference, explaining again that South Viet Nam would be the first in a line of dominoes to fall, leading to Communist takeover of Asia.[80] He was willing to stick his neck out to thwart any peace conference. In April, during a "not for attribution" speech to the American Society of Newspaper Editors, Nixon concluded: "If to avoid further Communist expansion in Asia and Indochina, we must take the risk now of putting our boys in, I think the Executive has to take the politically unpopular decision and do it."[81] His remark foreshadowed a future US executive decision to send troops to Viet Nam. One month later the French were soundly defeated even as the US was preparing contingency plans for covert intervention to replace the French as the country's Western colonizer.

The *idea* of the US Saigon Military Mission (SMM) was born in a January 1954 Washington policy meeting at which attendees anxiously contemplated the impending French defeat, which would finally take place at Dien Bien Phu four months later. Secretary of State John Foster Dulles and his brother Allen Dulles chose to send US Air Force Colonel Edward Geary Lansdale to Viet Nam to "develop quickly a way to keep Viet Nam from going Communist." Lansdale, who had been a San Francisco advertising executive prior to World War II, was credited with the put-down of the Communist "Huk" rebellion in the Philippines, and became founder and chief of the CIA's part in the SMM.[82]

Dated January 16, 1954, National Security Council Document 5405 (NSC 5405), "US Objectives and Courses of Action with Respect to Southeast Asia," concluded that the loss of territory, especially of Malaysia and Indonesia, could result in economic and political pressures on Japan that would make it more vulnerable to communism, and thereby hinder Japan's rise as an economic power in Asia with sufficient markets in neighboring states, a keystone of the US strategic position in the western Pacific.[83]

On March 12, 1954, two months before the defeat at Dien Bien Phu, the Joint Chiefs of Staff in Washington issued a memorandum concluding that "current intelligence" suggested that any "settlement based on *free* elections would be attended by almost certain loss of the Associated States of Indochina to Communist control."[84] President Eisenhower admitted it was common knowledge that presidential elections, if held in 1954, would

---

79 Zinn, 1980, 462.
80 A. J. Langguth, *Our Vietnam: The War, 1954–1975* (New York: Simon & Schuster, 2000), Chapter 1.
81 I. F. Stone, *Polemics and Prophesies 1967–1970* (New York: Vintage Books, 1972), 383; Barbara W. Tuchman, *The March of Folly: From Troy to Vietnam* (New York: Alfred A. Knopf, 1984), 261–262.
82 Young, 1991, 44.
83 Noam Chomsky, *Rethinking Camelot* (Boston: South End, 1993), 40; Kahin, 1986, 31.
84 *The Pentagon Papers*, Gravel Edition, Volume 1, Document 23, Memorandum for the Secretary of Defense by the Joint Chiefs of Staff, "Preparation of Department of Defense Views Regarding Negotiations on Indochina for the Forthcoming Geneva Conference," 12 March 1954, 448–451.

result in possibly 80 percent of the population voting for Ho Chi Minh rather than the unpopular Emperor Bao Dai.[85]

Anticipating the defeat of the French at Dien Bien Phu, Arthur Radford, chair of the US Joint Chiefs of Staff, on March 20 proposed nuclear strikes against the Viet Minh, but settled for one massive air strike supported by back-up air strikes, paratrooper drops, and the mining of Haiphong Harbor. Five days later, with its approval of the Radford plan, the NSC made clear its decision that the US would have to replace France in efforts to defeat the Vietnamese independence movement.[86] On April 5, 1954, the NSC continued to contemplate nuclear intervention to rescue France at Dien Bien Phu. NSC plans stipulated: "Nuclear weapons will be available for use as required by the tactical situation and as approved by the President."[87]

In April, the prospect of war with Viet Nam began to be floated publicly. The April 4, 1954, *US News & World Report* carried an article, "Why US Risks War for Indochina: It's the Key to Control of All Asia." At an April 7, 1954 press conference, President Eisenhower, in answering the question, "What is the strategic importance of Indochina?" mentioned production of materials such as tin and tungsten and rubber. He expressed concern for hundreds of millions of human beings who would pass under a Communist dictatorship "inimical to the free world," plus "broader considerations that might follow what you would call the 'falling domino' principle . . . the loss of Indochina, of Burma, of Thailand, of the Peninsula, and Indonesia following . . . [multiplying] the disadvantages that you would suffer through loss of materials, sources of materials, but [also] . . . millions and millions of people." Eisenhower further explained: the Communist threat "turns the so-called island defensive chain of Japan, Formosa, of the Philippines and to the southward; it moves in to threaten Australia and New Zealand. It takes away, in its economic aspects, that region that Japan must have as a trading area or Japan, in turn, will have only one place in the world to go—that is, toward the Communist areas in order to live. So, the possible consequences of the loss are just incalculable to the free world."[88]

Eisenhower and his Secretary of State John Foster Dulles not only wanted to acquire Indochina's resources, which included oil and iron ore, "the cheapest way that we can." Dulles constantly stressed the strategic value of the entire area due because of its possession of major navy and air bases.[89] By the end of the Eisenhower presidency, the number of US military advisors in Viet Nam had grown from 200 to 700, hoping to accomplish with manpower what the billions in military aid to France had not—defeat of the Vietnamese independence movement.[90]

---

85 Dwight Eisenhower, *Mandate for Change, 1953–1956: The White House Years* (Garden City, NY: Doubleday, 1963), 372.
86 Bowman, 35.
87 H. Bruce Franklin, 2000, 156.
88 Williams, 1985, Chapter 36, "Counting the Dominoes," 156–157, citing its source as United States Government, *Public Papers of the Presidents of the United States: Dwight Eisenhower, 1954* (Washington, 1958), 381–390.
89 Greene, 1970, 108.
90 Gabriel Kolko, *Anatomy of a War: Vietnam, the United States, and the Modern Historical Experience* (New York: The New Press, 1985), 81.

In a decisive battle at Dien Bien Phu, 20,000 French forces were defeated by 50,000 Vietnamese Viet Minh on May 7, 1954. General Vo Nguyen Giap, the North Vietnamese architect of the assault, had spent two months preparing the attack. The Viet Minh supply line stretched 500 miles, and close to 20,000 Vietnamese labored for three months to rebuild and widen the supply roads in order to accommodate hundreds of artillery pieces and 800 Russian-built supply trucks. The French suffered 7,000 casualties, and their remaining 13,000 troops were taken prisoner. The Vietnamese were elated, even though they suffered heavy casualties themselves—nearly 25,000.[91]

The very next day, May 8, 1954, delegations from nine countries assembled in Geneva to start negotiations for ending the war in Viet Nam and achieving a larger settlement in greater Indochina. The French Indochina War had dragged on from December 19, 1946 to May 7, 1954, or 2,695 days; nearly 8 years. It had cost France $10 billion.[92] One source estimates a million Vietnamese died in the war.[93] Another source indicates that, in addition to 95,000 French soldiers killed, including 50,000 from France's African, Arab, and Caribbean colonies, the Vietnamese suffered 1.3 million casualties, including one million civilians.[94]

Explicit Instruction from the US: *Do Not* Sign Geneva Agreements

The US did not support the Final Declaration, due to fears of an independent Viet Nam united under Communist Ho Chi Minh, who was most certain to win the national election.[95] Secretary of State John Foster Dulles walked out of the conference because of his disagreement with the majority on democratic elections unifying the north and the south of the country. The US determination that no unifying elections would be held in Viet Nam ignited a subsequent US war against 45 million people that took as many as six million lives.[96]

The Vietnamese government, headed by French puppet, Emperor Bao Dai, denounced the Geneva Agreement's requirement of unifying elections. In a classic case of deceit, on July 21, 1954, US "observer" Walter Bedell Smith, Allen Dulles' predecessor as director of the CIA, issued a tepid oral declaration that the US "will refrain from the threat or the use of force to disturb" the Geneva Agreements and "views any renewal of the aggression in violation of the aforesaid agreements with grave concern and as seriously threatening international peace and security." He was careful to say that the US supported the *concept* of free elections supervised by the UN, even as the US refused to sign the agreements.[97]

---

91 Dougherty and Stewart, 30–32.
92 Bernard Fall, *Hell in a Very Small Place: The Siege of Dien Bien Phu* (Philadelphia, PA: Lippincott, 1967), vii-viii.
93 Bernard Fall, *Last Reflections on a War* (Garden City, NY: Doubleday, 1967), 224.
94 Lorraine Glennon, ed., *Our Times: The Illustrated History of the 20th Century* (Atlanta: Turner Publishing,1995), 400.
95 Kahin and Lewis, 1967, 60–61; Noam Chomsky, *American Power & the New Mandarins* (New York: Vintage Books, 1969), 281; Kolko in Coates, "Prevent the Crime of Silence," 1971, 95.
96 John Pilger, *The New Rulers of the World* (London, UK: Verso, 2002), 103.
97 Williams, 1985, 168–170; Bowman, 37–38; Patti, 441–443.

After John Foster Dulles, with the full support of President Eisenhower, issued express instructions to US officials not to sign the Geneva Agreements, the US immediately formulated a new post–Geneva Viet Nam policy that rested on repudiating two key political features of the Geneva Agreements: that the line separating the two zones at the Seventeenth Parallel "should not in any way be interpreted as constituting a political or territorial boundary," and the reunification elections. A new mutual security pact was concretized via creation of the Southeast Asia Treaty Organization (SEATO). More important, the US quietly assumed the role of the French who had been forced to leave Viet Nam, assuring payments to the Vietnamese civil servants and soldiers who had been French collaborators. The US provided training and advisers to the former French-officered Vietnamese military component of the French Expeditionary forces, now a 234,000 Vietnamese National Army.[98] Bao Dai initially remained the head of state of Viet Nam, his reign now restricted to the territory south of the Seventeenth Parallel. Thus the US moved quickly to preserve (South) Viet Nam as a Western client state separate from Communist control.[99]

On August 20, 1954, one month after the Geneva Agreements, the US effectively disassociated itself from the Geneva Agreements. National Security Council memorandum NSC 5492/2 provided a "legal" framework that justified the Eisenhower administration's campaign to support a non-Communist government in the South, and to engage in ongoing harassment against the North while becoming the new principal supplier of financial and military aid to the fictional Republic of Viet Nam (RVN, i.e., South Viet Nam). The purported policy justification was to prevent the "loss" in northern Viet Nam from spreading elsewhere in Southeast Asia and the southwest Pacific.[100]

US-initiated, Clandestine Destabilization

The deceit commenced even before the signing of the Geneva Agreements. On June 1, 1954, the Saigon Military Mission (SMM) under Eisenhower quietly entered South Viet Nam, three weeks after the defeat of the French, but seven weeks *prior* to the signing of the Geneva Agreements, with the intention of assisting Western-friendly collaborative Vietnamese in conducting covert, unconventional warfare and paramilitary operations in Viet Minh-controlled areas. Under the leadership of SMM chief Edward Lansdale, covert combat, disinformation, sabotage, assassination, psychological warfare (psywar), and other tactics were coordinated and implemented *immediately* throughout Viet Nam, all in violation of the subsequent Geneva Agreements and thus all, from the moment the agreements were signed, explicitly illegal.[101]

France finally relinquished legal control of Viet Nam on June 4, 1954, giving Viet Nam its independence.[102] On June 18, 1954, Bao Dai, the last emperor of the Nguyen Dynasty

---

98 MacLear, 64.
99 Kahin, 1986, 70–71.
100 Kahin and Lewis, 61.
101 Cecil B. Currey, *Edward Lansdale: The Unquiet American*. Washington, DC: Brassey's (1998), 139–155; Gettleman et al., 1995, 81–92.
102 Cincinnatus, *Self-Destruction: The Disintegration and Decay of the United States Army during the*

of Viet Nam, now enjoying life in exile as a wealthy playboy in his French estate on the Mediterranean Sea, played a key role in selecting the premier for the newly formed South Vietnamese government. Fifty-four-year-old Ngo Dinh Diem was a Vietnamese aristocrat from a Roman Catholic mandarin family that had dutifully served the French-controlled, imperial court at Hue, in central Viet Nam. For four years before being selected as premier, Diem had resided at Maryknoll Catholic Order headquarters in New York State under the auspices of conservative Cardinal Francis Joseph Spellman. The new ruler would oversee a country that was still largely Buddhist.[103]

Diem arrived in Viet Nam to begin preparing for his rule on June 26, less than a month before the signing of the Geneva Agreements officially concluding the war.[104] The agreements would *stipulate* unifying elections be held two years hence, with, in the meantime, no introduction of arms or troops to de-stabilize any part of Viet Nam. But in fact, the US was already making sure there would be no elections.

Meanwhile, at about the same time, in early July Ngo Dinh Diem formally took office as premier of Viet Nam and Ho Chi Minh renamed the Viet Minh the North Vietnamese People's Army (NVPA).[105]

On July 20, 1954, the Geneva Agreement on the Cessation of Hostilities in Viet Nam was signed by General Ta Quang Buu for the Viet Minh and General Henri Delteil for France, officially ending the French Indochina War and hostilities in Viet Nam, Laos, and Cambodia. The next day, a second document, Final Declaration of the Geneva Conference, promised general support from Britain, France, Laos, China, the Soviet Union, Cambodia, and the Democratic Republic of Viet Nam, but was never signed. In sum, the agreement and the declaration stated that: (1) Viet Nam would be provisionally partitioned at the Seventeenth Parallel pending nationwide elections mandated and scheduled for July 20, 1956; (2) there were to be no military bases, re-armaments, or troop movements north or south of the Seventeenth Parallel pending the elections; and (3) an International Control Commission composed of representatives of India, Poland, and Canada would supervise implementation of agreements.[106]

On September 8, 1954, the US's NSC 5492/2, proposed Southeast Asia Collective Defense Treaty, was officially signed in Manila, Philippines, creating the Southeast Asia Treaty Organization, or SEATO. Signing onto the treaty, also known as the Manila Pact, were the US, Britain, France, Australia, New Zealand, Philippines, Thailand, and Pakistan. The more powerful *neutral* nations in the area, India, Burma (now Myanmar), and Indonesia, refused to join;[107] this was especially troubling for the US because of Burma and Indonesia's strategic geo-political location and abundant resources of oil, rubber, tin, and iron ore.[108]

Vietnam Era (New York: W.W. Norton, 1981), 30.
   103 Gettleman et al., 1995, 116–117; Kahin and Lewis, 66; Bowman, 37; Cincinnatus, 30.
   104 Stanley Karnow, *Vietnam: A History* (New York: Penguin, 1984), 678.
   105 Cincinnatus, 30.
   106 Kahin and Lewis, 1967, 348–376.
   107 Young, 1991, 46.
   108 Kahin, 1986, 31.

This NSC memorandum suggested that the treaty was intended to furnish a legal basis for the US "to order an attack on Communist China in the event it commits armed aggression which endangers the peace, safety and vital interests of the United States," and allowed US support to a "legitimate local government [i.e., South Viet Nam] which requires assistance to defeat local Communist subversion or rebellion not constituting armed attack." It even allowed the US the *"freedom to use nuclear weapons"* if necessary. The political and "legal" rationale for subsequent and full US intervention in Viet Nam was quickly taking shape.[109]

US administrations have never seriously considered themselves bound by the law. NSC 5429/2 is a good example. The use of force in the absence of armed attack, as recommended in this very important document, was in clear and explicit violation of law (the UN Charter, other treaties, and the US Constitution).[110]

Early in Lansdale's clandestine Viet Nam service, he headed a team of agents that carried out undercover operations against North Viet Nam. The team turned in a vivid report of its actions shortly before pulling out of Hanoi after Dien Bien Phu. The team's October 1954 report, later included among the Pentagon Papers, described its activities:

> [S]pent the last days of Hanoi in contaminating the oil supply of the bus company for a gradual wreckage of engines in the buses, [and] in taking actions for delayed sabotage of the railroad. The team had a bad moment when contaminating the oil. . . . They had to work quickly at night in an enclosed storage room. Fumes from the contaminant came close to knocking them out. Dizzy and weak-kneed, they masked their faces with handkerchiefs and completed the job.[111]

Landsdale's efforts in Viet Nam in the 1950s were sufficiently notorious to be immortalized in two novels: *The Ugly American* (1958) by William Lederer and Eugene Burdick, and *The Quiet American* (1955) by Graham Greene.

The political leaders in the Democratic Republic of Viet Nam (DRV) in Hanoi in February 1955 proposed establishing normal relations between the two temporary zones in preparation for the mandated July 1956 elections. However, by this time Diem was repressing and eliminating internal opposition of every political persuasion in the southern zone[112] and was cooperating with the US to thwart the elections. Meanwhile, US support was increasingly militarized. On February 12, the first 300 US advisors arrived to take over the training of the South Viet Nam Armed Forces.[113]

---

109 Gareth Porter, ed., *Vietnam: A History in Documents* (New York: New American Library, 1981), 164–166, as cited in Gettleman et al., 1995, 50.
110 Noam Chomsky, "A Special Supplement: Vietnam: How Government Became Wolves," *New York Review of Books*, 18(11), June 15, 1972.
111 Eric Pace, "Edward Lansdale Dies at 79; Adviser on Guerrilla Warfare," *New York Times* obituary, February 24, 1987.
112 Kolko, in Coates, "Prevent the Crime of Silence," 1971, 96–97.
113 Patti, 462; Cincinnatus, 30.

On July 16, 1955, one year before the mandated elections were to take place, Diem, with US support, announced the rejection of the Geneva reunification elections, and that fall, he declared South Viet Nam an independent republic, with himself as president.[114]

The so-called independent nation of the Republic of Viet Nam was "officially" created on October 26, 1955 with political, military, and financial support from the US. Diem was president, prime minister, defense minister, and supreme commander of the armed forces, all in one. The new sham government was immediately recognized by the US, France, Great Britain, Australia, New Zealand, Italy, Japan, Thailand, and South Korea.[115] Within a year of Diem's return to Saigon, the CIA had managed to cajole, lure, and terrify nearly a million northern Vietnamese, mostly Catholics, to relocate to the south to form Diem's essential constituency. President Eisenhower's CIA moved many of them via its airline, Civil Air Transport, and on US Navy ships. The assisted migration included 110,000 Vietnamese soldiers who had fought with the French Union Forces against their own countrymen and women, and civilian officials who had worked for the French-controlled administration.[116] Thanks to the clandestine support of the US, the Catholic oligarch had plenty of police, army, and administrators, and now Catholic constituents, to maintain rule in the primarily Buddhist culture.

All these machinations point to the fact that this was not an authentic civil war, but merely one orchestrated by the US to ensure that self-determination would not prevail in Viet Nam. Tragically, the US concentrated all its efforts to preserve traditional colonialism[117] when the vast majority of Vietnamese wanted independence.

In the months leading up to the mandated elections, the South Vietnamese government under Diem reiterated its refusal to honor the Geneva Agreements. In violation of the Agreements, the US sent 350 additional military men to Saigon under the pretext of recovering and redistributing military equipment abandoned by the French. This clearly and defiantly raised the number of US forces in South Viet Nam above the limit of 342 mandated in the Geneva Agreements. When the deadline set for nationwide elections passed, Diem's intransigence served to convince many Vietnamese that they would likely have to resort to insurgency to achieve their dream of independence.[118]

In June of 1956, Assistant Secretary of State Walter S. Robertson, who had accompanied Dulles to a meeting with Diem in March, attacked the Geneva Agreements while lauding Diem's earlier rigged elections for being "free," and reiterated the US commitment to support "a friendly non-Communist government in Viet Nam." The intention was to

---

114 Kolko, in Coates, "Prevent the Crime of Silence," 1971, 97–98.
115 Bowman, 43.
116 McGehee, 132, 133; Kahin and Lewis, 75.
117 Kolko, in Coates, "Prevent the Crime of Silence," 1971, 77.
118 Richard W. Stewart, *Deepening Involvement, 1945–1965* (Washington, DC: Center of Military History, United States Army, 1963), 20.

"diminish and eventually eradicate Communist subversion and influence" while helping to sustain Diem's internal security forces.[119]

In 1957, the US Air Force took over from the departing French the task of training South Vietnamese Air Force pilots. The first six Skyraider attack aircraft were delivered in early September 1959; 25 more arrived in early 1960.[120]

By the end of 1958, Diem had incarcerated an estimated 40,000 Vietnamese political prisoners, but by 1961 his regime held as many as 160,000 political prisoners. And by 1959, Diem had 450,000 men in his army, supporting a repressive regime that had already murdered at least 16,600 political dissidents.[121]

In 1958, the US established the practice of designating *precleared* zones of attack as *free areas* for jettisoning unexpended aircraft ordnance.[122] This is believed to be the origin of the idea of *specified strike* zones, which became the pervasive *free-fire zones* of the 1960s—ultimately 75 percent of the area of South Viet Nam would be a free-fire zone.[123]

The first "uprising" of resistance against Diem, on January 17, 1960, was concentrated in three districts in Ben Tre (Kien Hoa) Province in the Mekong Delta, and was led by Nguyen Thi Dinh, a remarkable woman who later became deputy commander of the armed forces for the National Front for the Liberation of South Viet Nam (commonly known as the National Liberation Front, or NLF). A second uprising, in September 1960, greatly expanded the territory controlled by the resistance within that province.[124]

As the Vietnamese resistance forces stepped up their insurgency, Eisenhower increased the number of US military advisors in Viet Nam. By May 7, 1960, the number of advisors had climbed to 685.[125]

In December 1960, the NLF was formed at a congress in the south attended by representatives from a dozen political parties and religious groups, including remnants of the Cao Dai, Hoa Hao, and Binh Xuyen. In effect, this was a rebirth of the Viet Minh.[126] The Diem regime labeled the NLF *Viet Cong*, a pejorative formed by contraction of *Viet Nam Cong San* (Vietnamese Communists).[127]

---

119 "United States Policy with Respect to Vietnam," Address by the Assistant Secretary of State for Far Eastern Affairs, Walter S. Robertson, Washington, June 1, 1956, delivered to the American Friends of Vietnam at the Willard Hotel in Washington, DC. http://www.mtholyoke.edu/acad/intrel/willard.htm, accessed January 3, 2016.

120 John Morrocco, ed., *The Vietnam Experience: Thunder from Above, Air War, 1941–1968* (Boston, MA: Boston Publishing Company, 1984), 10–11.

121 Kolko, in Coates, "Prevent the Crime of Silence," 1971, 99–100.

122 Edward Doyle and Stephen Weiss, eds., *A Collision of Cultures* (Boston: Boston Publishing, 1984), 139.

123 Stockholm International Peace Research Institute (SIPRI), *Ecological Consequences of the Second Indochina War* (Stockholm, Sweden: SIPRI, 1976), 13.

124 Kahin, 1986, 112.

125 *The Pentagon Papers*, Gravel Edition, Volume 2, Chapter 6, "The Advisory Build-Up, 1961–1967" (Boston: Beacon Press, 1971), Chronology: February 27, 1960, Msg, Saigon to State 2525: MAAG, Viet Nam, increasing MAAG advisors from 342 to 685.

126 Bowman, 49–50.

127 Bowman, 49–50.

Early Military Buildup in Southeast Asia under Kennedy

Early in 1961, President Kennedy approved a secret counterinsurgency plan for Viet Nam and Laos that included covert actions while calling for government "reform" and military restructuring as a basis for expanded US assistance.[128] CIA operations with Hmong guerrillas had been going on under Eisenhower since 1959 as part of a regional intelligence-gathering effort to thwart Viet Minh activities in Viet Nam.[129]

Concerned about the "Communist problem," Kennedy declared, "We cannot and will not accept any visible humiliation over Laos." That spring, he transformed the group of US military advisers already stationed in Laos, who had been wearing civilian clothes, into a military assistance and advisory group that would dress in uniforms while accompanying Laotian troops.[130]

Early in March 1961, President Kennedy sought to reinvigorate infiltration efforts of the CIA's Project Tiger into North Viet Nam by use of small South Vietnamese ground units, frogmen, and the preferred method: air-dropping commandos. One of the pilots who headed up the secret dropping of CIA-trained commandos was future RVN premier and vice-president Nguyen Cao Ky, the VNAF commanding officer at Tan Son Nhut. From 1961 to 1963, virtually all of the small teams dropped into the north were captured or killed without leaving a trace, though a few were put on show trials in Hanoi. By 1963, nearly 200 commandos had been lost. The US military took over this mission from the CIA, and over the next several years 450 more South Vietnamese commandos were lost. The mission was essentially a failure because, from the beginning of the program, North Viet Nam had infiltrated the planning and knew when and where the drops were to be made.[131]

John F. Kennedy and Viet Nam: 1961

Chronology

March 23, 1961. After a US C-47 intelligence-gathering plane is shot down over the Plain of Jars in Laos, President Kennedy urges that all US reconnaissance planes be identified with Laotian markings.[132]

April 28, 1961. Speaking to the press, President Kennedy declares: "Today no war has been declared—and however fierce the struggle may be, it may never be declared in the traditional fashion. Our way of life is under attack. Those who make themselves our enemy are advancing around the globe. The survival of our friends is in danger."[133]

---

128 "Memorandum for the President," November 11, 1961, in *The Pentagon Papers* (Gravel ed.), 2: 114); the invasion of Cuba was also planned at the same time.

129 McCoy, 305.

130 Arthur M. Schlesinger, Jr., *A Thousand Days: John F. Kennedy in the White House* (Boston: Houghton Mifflin Co., 1965), 332, 336).

131 John Prados, *Lost Crusader: The Secret Wars of CIA Director William Colby* (Oxford: Oxford University Press, 2003), 75–81; John Prados, *Safe for Democracy: The Secret Wars of the CIA* (Chicago: Ivan R. Dee, 2006), 340.

132 Dougherty and Stewart, 37.

133 Richard J. Walton, *Cold War and Counterrevolution: The Foreign Policy of John F. Kennedy* (Baltimore, MD: Penguin Books, 1972), 54–55.

May 11, 1961. President Kennedy sends 400 special forces (Green Berets) and 100 military advisers to South Viet Nam.[134]

May 22, 1961. In an interview published in the highly regarded British newspaper, *The Guardian,* Ho Chi Minh warns, "Your American imperialism spends so much money to keep Ngo Dinh Diem in power. . . . In history, when people are oppressed too hard, they make a revolution. Our people in the South are oppressed too hard by Diem. So Diem will fall, as did Chiang Kai-shek and Syngman Rhee and Batista. . . . All the money America spends on Diem is lost money."[135]

May 31, 1961. On his way to Vienna to meet with Soviet leader Nikita Khrushchev, Kennedy stops in Paris to visit with former French president Charles de Gaulle. De Gaulle warns Kennedy not to get embroiled in Viet Nam, predicting, "you will, step by step, be sucked into a bottomless military and political quagmire despite the losses and expenditures that you may squander."[136]

June 16, 1961. Following a meeting with South Vietnamese envoy Nguyen Dinh Thuan, President Kennedy authorizes direct training and *combat supervision* (author's emphasis) to South Vietnamese troops. A month later Kennedy increases Lansdale's CIA clandestine warfare "Observation Group" from 340 to 805 men, and shifts the group's focus to North Viet Nam.[137]

November 30, 1961. President Kennedy personally approves, in principle, the start of Operation Ranch Hand.[138]

Chemical Warfare: Operation Ranch Hand

The British were the first to use chemical anti-plant agents in modern warfare. Their use of these agents against guerrillas in Malaya during the 1950s was dwarfed, however, by the US use of chemical agents in Indochina, which went on for a full decade, beginning with test spraying in 1961.[139] Intentional poisoning of the environment was a major component of US strategy and tactics in Vietnam, Laos, and Cambodia. It was systematically carried out for over ten years and targeted vast areas of countryside. Many scholars and environmentalists have used the term *ecocide* in describing the US chemical warfare campaign in Southeast Asia.[140]

---

134 Morris and Morris, 498; Bowman, 51; Dougherty and Stewart, 38.
135 David Armstrong, *A Trumpet of Arms: Alternative Media in America* (Boston: South End Press, 1981), 96.
136 Walton, 171.
137 Bowman, 51.
138 National Security Action Memorandum (NSAM-115), "Defoliant Operations in Vietnam," November 30, 1961.
139 SIPRI, 24.
140 SIPRI, 1.

A number of types of herbicide were applied by US forces in Viet Nam, each identified by a color painted in a four-inch band around the 55-gallon drum that contained the chemical. The major chemical agents employed by the US were Agent Orange (forests), Agent White (forests) and Agent Blue (rice crops). Lesser-used chemicals were Agents Pink, Green, and Purple.[141]

The US initiation of small experiments with aerial application of herbicides in Viet Nam sparked debate within the Air Force, as some officials feared the USAF could be accused of chemical warfare. However, *civilians* within the Pentagon convinced President Kennedy that attacks on food crops were important for the war effort.[142]

Initially, the Air Force's chemical warfare of spraying and defoliation was code-named "Operation Hades." But someone determined Hades was not PR-friendly—Hades being the god of the underworld where the dead reside—so the name was changed to Operation Ranch Hand.[143] The overall herbicide program also involved other branches of the military using hand sprayers, spray trucks, helicopters and boats to apply chemical agents, generally in smaller quantities than sprayed by the US Air Force and its South Vietnamese counterpart. This supplementary herbicide operation was code-named Operation Trail Dust.[144]

Yale University botany professor Arthur Galston has stated that the use of Agent Orange as a defoliant and herbicide in Viet Nam was the most extensive and most damaging of chemical warfare campaigns in the history of the world. But Agent Orange was just the beginning of terrors rained down on Viet Nam and its neighbors.

Napalm

Napalm, deemed to be the most "effective" weapon in the South Vietnamese Air Force's arsenal, is a petroleum-based substance mixed with a thickening agent into a gel that burns continuously and sticks to anything it touches. Napalm was delivered to Viet Nam in canister drums. The term is derived from the two words *naphthene* and *palmitate*, as it is obtained from the salts of aluminum, palmitic or other fatty acids, and naphthenic acids. These acids have a viscous consistency which, when mixed with gasoline, results in an incendiary jelly.

Napalm burns at two thousand degrees Fahrenheit. The high-temperature fire deoxygenates the air, causing asphyxiation while generating large quantities of carbon monoxide gas. It was the main ingredient of the incendiary bombs first used by the US against Japan in 1945. A more advanced formula was subsequently developed and used by the US in the Korean War and by the French in Indochina and Algeria.

---

141 SIPRI, 25–26.

142 Gabriel Kolko, *Anatomy of a War: Vietnam, the United States, and the Modern Historical Experience* (New York: Pantheon, 1985), 144.

143 Gettleman et al., 1995, 464.

144 Stellman et al., 681–687.

A newer, "superior" napalm product developed and manufactured by Dow Chemical during the American war in Viet Nam used synthetic plastic, or polystyrene, in place of soap jelly. *Supernapalm,* or *napalm B* as it was called, contained 50 percent polystyrene, 25 percent benzene, and 25 percent gasoline.

One napalm bomb could ignite, with fire and raging flames, a surface area about the size of a football field—about an acre.[145] The US dropped nearly 375,000 tons of the new "improved" napalm in Viet Nam, using it on a daily basis. This compares to 14,000 tons used against Japan in World War II and 32,357 tons dropped on Korea. In the case of the latter, almost every city, town, and village in North Korea was incinerated, and vast areas of the country were turned into scorched earth wastelands.[146] An article in the February 10, 1969, edition of *Business Week* termed the chemical "the fiery essence of all that is horrible about the war in Vietnam."

Anti-Personnel Chemicals—CS Gas

Although often referred to as a gas, 2-chlorobenzalmalononitrile, commonly known as CS, is a solid dispersed as an ultra-fine powder (aerosol) with military applications for seriously disabling unprotected personnel. Exposure causes tearing, sneezing, and irritation of the upper respiratory tract. Little information has been released about the expenditures of CS in Southeast Asia, but it is known that the US did procure nine million tons during the war years.[147]

Secret Counterinsurgency Plan Approved by Kennedy

After the ill-fated CIA invasion of the Bay of Pigs in Cuba in April 1961, a humiliated President Kennedy reasserted his military credibility by approving a secret counterinsurgency plan for Viet Nam and Laos. Deciding to escalate covert actions and US military assistance to a "reformed" government, Kennedy approved sending an additional 100 US advisers, exceeding the agreed-upon 685-man limit of the United States Military Mission. Then, in May 1961, 400 Green Berets were sent with additional logistic support to step up covert warfare.[148]

On September 21, 1961, the US Army's 5th Special Forces Group (airborne) was activated and took charge of all Special Forces operations in Viet Nam.[149] Little by little, US counterinsurgency efforts were growing into something more resembling open warfare.

---

145 John Morrocco, ed., *The Vietnam Experience: Thunder from Above, Air War, 1941–1968* (Boston: Boston Publishing Co., 1984), 20; Gilbert Dreyfus, *Liberation,* Dec. 1967/Jan. 1968, "Napalm: What It Is, What It Does," 63–66.

146 Sven Lindqvist, *A History of Bombing* (New York: The New Press, 2000), 162–163; H. Bruce Franklin, 74; Robert Frank Futrell, *The United States Air Force in Korea 1950–53* (Washington, DC: Office of Air Force History, 1983), 692.

147 SIPRI, 53–54.

148 Richard J. Walton, *Cold War and Counter-Revolution: The Foreign Policy of John F. Kennedy,* (Baltimore, MD: Penguin Books, Inc., 1972), 169; 169; Morris and Morris, 498; Bowman 51; Dougherty and Stewart, 38.

149 Dougherty and Stewart, 39.

In October 1961, the US State Department issued a white paper, "A Threat to the Peace: North Vietnam's Effort to Conquer South Vietnam," to which Under Secretary of State George Ball responded, "The guerrillas . . . are poorly trained and equipped and are not motivated by deep conviction. Rather, they are merely unsophisticated villagers or peasants who have been conscripted by terror or treachery."[150] A US intelligence report dated October 5 estimated 80 to 90 percent of the Viet Cong in South Viet Nam had been recruited locally and did not depend upon supplies from the North.[151]

At a National Security Council (NSC) meeting held on October 11, President Kennedy was briefed by the Joint Chiefs of Staff that 40,000 US troops could clean up "the Viet Cong threat, and another 120,000 could cope with possible North Vietnamese or Chinese intervention."[152] Lyman Lemnitzer, Chair of the Joint Chiefs, addressed a memo to General Maxwell Taylor outlining US military plans, titled, "Counterinsurgency Operations in South Vietnam, begin 12 October 1961, conducted/coordinated by US Army."[153]

Heavy pressure for escalation continued to be applied at the White House. Returning from an October 18–24, 1961 assessment mission, presidential aides Maxwell Taylor and Walt Rostow informed Kennedy, "If Viet Nam goes, it will be exceedingly difficult to hold Southeast Asia."[154] In response, on October 24, President Kennedy sent additional military advisers and US helicopter units to South Viet Nam "to prevent a Communist takeover of Viet Nam."[155]

On November 10, 1961, US Special Forces medical specialists were sent to Viet Nam to provide assistance to the Montagnard tribes in the central highlands,[156] and two days later, US F-101 reconnaissance jets began monitoring remote guerrilla units in South Viet Nam.[157] A month later, December 11, 1961, the first US helicopter units arrived in South Viet Nam aboard the carrier *USS Core*. This contingent included 33 helicopters and 400 air and ground crewmen to operate and maintain them. Their assignment was to airlift South Vietnamese Army troops into combat.[158]

Bombing Begins

Beginning in mid-December 1961, US-piloted air operations over Viet Nam were authorized to launch combat missions as long as a Vietnamese crewmember was aboard.[159] The code name for this US "advisory" effort in support of the South Vietnamese Air Force (SVNAF) was Operation Farm Gate. Because the 1954 Geneva Agreement prohibited

---

150 Gettleman et al., 1995, 154–155.
151 Dougherty and Stewart, 40.
152 Bowman, 53.
153 *The Pentagon Papers*, Gravel Edition, Volume 2, 650–651; CM-390-61.
154 Dougherty and Stewart, 40.
155 Dougherty and Stewart, 40.
156 Dougherty and Stewart, 40.
157 Dougherty and Stewart, 40.
158 Kahin, 1986, 139; Dougherty and Stewart, 41.
159 Dougherty and Stewart, 144–146.

introduction of combat bombers and forces into Indochina, the T-28s trainers and B-26 and SC-47 bombers were designated as reconnaissance planes, even though they were actually bomber aircraft intended for illegal operations.[160]

USAF Major Richard Secord, who would later be promoted to Major General, was one of the members of the 1st Commando Wing flying Farm Gate missions in Viet Nam in 1961. He piloted more than 200 secret combat missions in T-28 fighter-bombers bearing the markings of the South Vietnamese Air Force. One of the Vietnamese pilots he met during this assignment was Nguyen Cao Ky.[161] The T-28, the early mainstay of the Air Commando Fighter Force, was well designed for counterintelligence (COIN) missions. Originally a trainer, it was later modified to serve as a fighter-bomber.

On December 20, 1961, the *New York Times* reported about 2,000 uniformed US troops and specialists in addition to advisers were "operating in battle areas with South Vietnamese forces" and were authorized to fire back if fired upon.[162] Kennedy authorized attacks against Viet Nam in late 1961.[163] On December 23, 1961, UH-1 Huey helicopters from the 57th Transportation Company and the 8th Transportation Company participated in Operation Chopper, the first air mobile combat action in Viet Nam.[164] And by the end of 1961, the US Military Assistance Advisory Group numbered 2,100, almost three times the level authorized by the Geneva Agreements of 1954. Despite all this evidence to the contrary, on January 15, 1962, President Kennedy proclaimed at a press conference that there were no Americans engaged in fighting in Viet Nam.[165]

Reports issued from Viet Nam in early 1962 hint at the conduct and horrors of the war to come. A US Farm Gate B-26 bombing operation carried out on January 21, 1962 in *Cambodia*, rather than on the Vietnamese side of the border, was later described in a report by Roger Hilsman, Kennedy's director of intelligence in the State Department, then–assistant Secretary of State for the Far East, as the result of a US senior adviser having committed a "tragic error in map-reading." The consequences: Instead of strafing a cluster of Vietnamese huts near the border, the bombs landed on a Cambodian village

---

160 Bowman, 54; Dougherty and Stewart, 41; The bad faith and forked tongue of US White men again is revealed—a long pattern from our origins—as taught to us by Native Americans.

161 Richard Secord, *wikipedia*, http://en.wikipedia.org/wiki/Richard_Secord; Warner, 192; Chomsky, 1988, 106 n20, cites an article by Fox Butterfield in the March 7, 1987, *Economist*, "The Road From Laos to Nicaragua," describing Richard Secord's history of being "secretly attached to the C.I.A. mission in Laos running the clandestine war against the North Vietnamese." Chomsky adds that, in reality, the bombing was against the *peasants* of northern Laos, "though the well-documented facts are inadmissible." Chomsky also cites an article by Butterfield in the December 6, 1986 *New York Times*, "The White House Crisis: The Fate of the Hostages; Ex-General Provided Arms Channel."

162 Bowman, 54; Dougherty and Stewart, 41.

163 *The Pentagon Papers: The Defense Department History of United States Decision-making on Vietnam*, Senator Gravel Edition, Boston: Beacon, 1972, Vol. II, 656–658, 677; William Conrad Gibbons, ed., *The US Government and the Vietnam War: Executive and Legislative Roles and Relationships*, Part II (1961–1964), (Princeton, NJ: Princeton University Press, 1986), 70–71. For early press coverage of these attacks, which elicited little protest in the US for several years, see for example, A.P., "US Pilots Aiding Combat In Vietnam," *New York Times*, March 10, 1962.

164 Dougherty and Stewart, 41.

165 Dougherty and Stewart, 42.

just over the border, killing and wounding a number of villagers and school children.[166] The first US helicopter to be shot down in Viet Nam by the Viet Cong/NLF, on February 4, 1962, was one of 15 choppers ferrying troops in an attack against the village of Hong My in the Mekong Delta.[167]

On February 6, 1962, President Kennedy created the Military Assistance Command Viet Nam (MACV) under command of General Paul Harkins, to replace MAAG-Viet Nam. US military forces in Viet Nam by this time numbered around 3,200.[168] The US Air Force had already flown hundreds of combat missions, often with the accompaniment of low-ranking Vietnamese enlisted men for the sake of appearances.[169] The MACV identified nine written rules of engagement and issued a card to each soldier listing them.[170] By March, US military forces were actively engaged in combat.[171]

By the end of 1962, there were 11,300 US military personnel in South Viet Nam, including twenty-nine special forces detachments.[172] The first Australian military force also arrived in 1962, composed of thirty men trained in jungle warfare.[173]

Sample News Stories Emanating from Viet Nam in 1962

February 11, 1962. The first Operation Farm Gate casualties, nine US and South Vietnamese crewmembers are killed when their plane crashes seventy miles north of Saigon.[174]

April 22, 1962. Twenty-nine US helicopters are employed in airlifting six hundred South Vietnamese troops into a battle in the Mekong Delta.[175]

May 11, 1962. After traveling to Viet Nam, Secretary of War/Defense reports "we are winning the war."[176]

October 15, 1962. News reports of US helicopter crewmen initiating combat against the Viet Cong are denied by US officials.[177]

---

166 Chomsky, 1993, 53.
167 Bowman, 55; Dougherty and Stewart, 43.
168 Bowman, 54.
169 Chomsky, 1993, 51.
170 Terrence Maitland and Peter McInerney, *The Vietnam Experience: A Contagion of War* (Boston, MA: Boston Publishing Company, 1983), 17.
171 Kolko, in Coates, "Prevent the Crime of Silence," 1971, 107.
172 Bowman, 57.
173 Philip Caputo, *10,000 Days of Thunder* (New York: Atheneum Books, 2005), 36.
174 Dougherty and Stewart, 43; Bowman 55.
175 Dougherty and Stewart, 44.
176 Dougherty and Stewart, 45.
177 Dougherty and Stewart, 47.

Officers sitting in front of Intelligence wall maps at 823rd Combat Security Police Squadron headquarters, 7th Air Force, Tan Son Nhut Air Base, Saigon, noting "VC enemy" activity, and "targets," April 19, 1969.

Inventing Bombing Targets

Early bombing planners invented targets from Tan Son Nhut Air Base, so as to keep the growing number of planes busy.

Late in 1961, the US Air Force 2nd Air Division at Tan Son Nhut in Viet Nam (which became the 7th Air Force on April 1, 1966) formed what amounted to a hybrid Vietnamese-American air force with the SVNAF. The Joint Air Operations Center at Tan Son Nhut, which oversaw fighter-bomber missions throughout South Viet Nam, was staffed and in fact run by US officers. General "Buck" Anthis, 2nd Air Division commander, was responsible for all US Air Force operations in Viet Nam and Thailand. Known as Mr. COIN (Counterintelligence) AIR, he stubbornly refused to believe the advisers who regularly informed him that US bombs were murdering countless civilians and driving them into the ranks of the Viet Cong.[178]

On February 27, 1962, two South Vietnamese pilots flying US AD-6 fighter planes bombed the presidential palace in Saigon, leading President Diem to believe that his main enemies were within the South Vietnamese military.[179]

By mid-1962, the CIA was busy in Viet Nam conducting intelligence and sabotage operations against the north and counter-terror (i.e., US-organized terror) missions in the south.[180]

---

178 Sheehan, 112–114.
179 Dougherty and Stewart, 43.
180 Chomsky, 1993, 51.

Early Signs of Entrenchment

On April 9, 1962, two US soldiers were killed in a Viet Cong ambush while on a combat mission with South Vietnamese troops.[181]

On January 2–3, 1963, the Battle of Ap Bac (Tan Phu Village, Cai Lay District, My Tho Province, in central Mekong Delta, 12 miles west of My Tho City, nearly 40 miles south of Saigon, and 45 miles north of Binh Thuy) drew public attention to Viet Nam as 2,000 to 3,000 ARVN troops from its 7th Division, supported by US advisors, armored personnel carriers (APCs), and helicopters, suffered their first major defeat when they were overpowered by 200–300 members of the Viet Cong (NLF's People's Liberation Armed Forces/PLAF).[182] Three of the 50 US advisers were killed and seven others wounded. Of the 15 US helicopters that supported the ARVN operation, five were shot down, and nine of the other 10 were severely damaged.[183]

The Viet Cong victory at Ap Bac dramatically upset the US/ARVN pacification program in the Delta (pacification being a euphemism for elimination of anyone suspected of belonging to or supporting the Viet Cong). An early sign that the South Vietnamese Army was no match for the Viet Cong, the defeat in effect revealed that helicopters and tanks were not sufficient to guarantee military successes over the Vietnamese, who possessed an intense will and a long tradition of defeating foreign invaders.

But the US had no idea of the depth of aggrieved peoples' determination and will to fight for a righteous cause such as their own freedom. Ignoring the obvious lesson of Ap Bac, the US continued business as usual, and on April 11, 1963, MACV was granted its request for one hundred US troops from the 25th Infantry Division to serve as door gunners on US helicopters.[184]

On August 30, 1963, two US pilots were killed when their helicopter was shot down by Viet Cong near Tay Ninh.[185]

Strategic Hamlets: Internment Camps for Vietnamese Villagers

On March 12, 1962, President Diem had initiated forced relocation of villagers into *strategic hamlets*,[186] in effect concentration camps, a pacification policy fully endorsed by the US.[187] The forced relocations were particularly extensive in the Mekong Delta,[188] and provoked massive discontent in the countryside as traditional villages were completely

---

181 Dougherty and Stewart, 44.

182 Patti, 464; Dougherty and Stewart, 50; Wilfred G, Burchett, *Vietnam: Inside Story of the Guerilla War* (New York: International Publishers, 1965), 85–88.

183 Morrocco, 18; "America's Advisory War in Vietnam, 1962-64: A G.I.'s Combat Chronology," *VFW Magazine*, August 2011, www.vfw.org; David Halberstam, "Vietnamese Reds Win Major Clash; Inflict 100 Casualties in Fighting Larger Force," *New York Times*, January 4, 1963.

184 Dougherty and Stewart, 53.

185 Dougherty and Stewart, 55.

186 Dougherty and Stewart, 44.

187 Kolko, in Coates, "Prevent the Crime of Silence," 1971, 101–102.

188 Sheehan, 309.

uprooted. Viet Nam's indigenous peasants understandably resisted and deeply resented being forcibly removed from their socially cohesive communities, where ties to the land had developed over hundreds of years.[189]

Tampering with village autonomy in this way indicated serious ignorance on the part of Catholic, Western-thinking Diem as well as his early US military advisors, who sought to clear out the sea of peasants they perceived as the enemy. In Viet Nam the system of clearing the villages directly impacted nearly 95 percent of the population, and any governmental authority imposed from above stopped at the village gate.[190] Some US military officials knew of this principle, but their voices were ignored. A student at the US Army War College wrote: "The only governmental structure that consistently has claimed the loyalty and support of the people in Viet Nam is the village. It is the central fact in the life of every Vietnamese."[191]

Laos, Cambodia, Thailand

On May 15, 1962, President Kennedy sent 5,000 Marines and 50 jet fighters to Thailand in response to the popular Pathet Lao (Lao Nation) campaign in Laos.[192] The Pathet Lao had tried to effect social change peacefully through the electoral process in a coalition government. The US refused to honor that sovereign process, and consequently the Pathet Lao chose the alternative of strategic armed struggle. The US was determined to "save" Laos from communism and "neutralism," and the CIA had been involved as early as the mid-1950s in doing so, orchestrating coups in 1958, 1959, and 1960. The CIA created the *Armée Clandestine,* working clandestinely with the US Army in the mid-1950s as it organized Hmong hill tribespeople (also known as "Meo," considered a derogatory term).[193] Green Berets crossed into Laos from South Viet Nam every day on combat missions.[194]

On July 23, 1962, the International Agreement on the Neutrality of Laos was signed in Geneva between fourteen states and Laos, among them Burma, Cambodia, Thailand, Republic of Viet Nam (South), the Democratic Republic of Viet Nam (North) and the United States. The fourteen nations pledged to respect Laotian neutrality, to refrain from interference—direct or indirect—in the internal affairs of Laos, and to refrain from drawing Laos into military alliance or to establish military bases in Laotian territory. The Laotian government pledged to promulgate constitutionally its commitments with the force of law.[195] It is obvious that the Laos neutrality agreement did not in any way interfere with the conduct of the US war waged against North Viet Nam, Cambodia, and Laos.

---

189 Kahin and Lewis, 140.
190 Cincinnatus, 24.
191 Cincinnatus, 223 n4.
192 Harry G. Summers, Jr., *The Vietnam War Almanac* (Novato, CA: Presidio Press, 1999), 31.
193 Blum, 1995, 141–142; Blum, 2000, 136.
194 Warner, 254.
195 Bowman, 56.

Laos, the only landlocked country in Indochina, is mountainous and covered with rain forests. The Mekong River flows through Laos from north to south, and the country's boundary is contiguous with North and part of South Viet Nam. It was, therefore in a strategic position in the US war against North Viet Nam.

The OSS had begun alliances with international drug dealers as early as 1943 to facilitate our invasion of Italy through Sicily, and the CIA continued in post-WWII years to protect a number of drug lords, such as the Corsican syndicates funding covert anti-Communist activities in Europe and, increasingly, allied traffickers in Southeast Asia.[196] The CIA's secret alliance with the Hmong hill tribes in Laos against the revolutionary Pathet Lao, who were sympathetic with the North Vietnamese, was intensified by the fact that the Hmong were the country's leading opium growers and aligned with local political and business leaders who supplied the growing heroin markets, especially among large numbers of US troops.

Thailand: Sanctuary for US Operations against Laos and Viet Nam

Thailand benefitted immensely from US American financial aid between 1950 and 1975 while supporting the US war against North Viet Nam and the Pathet Lao in Laos. Approximately 650 million in US dollars was given in economic aid, the majority earmarked for counter-insurgency activities. Additionally, the US granted $940 million to the Thai military. On top of this, the US provided an additional $760 million to support Thai mercenary troops in Viet Nam. And the US funded the construction and renovation of its older airbases to the tune of $250 million. US military personnel, stationed permanently or temporarily in the country, pumped in another $850 million. Thailand was the second largest recipient of US aid in Southeast Asia after Viet Nam.[197]

The five major US airbases built in Thailand in the 1950s by US Strategic Air Command (SAC) include Udorn and Nakhom Phanom, the center for coordinating secret bombings and clandestine activities and directing air commandos on the border with Laos. By 1968 there were about 200 CIA operatives in Laos, where clandestine military operations had begun in 1961.[198] Nakhon Phanom, along the western banks of the Mekong River, had been a sleepy town of a few thousand people and a few shops around a central square before it was forced to be a military town servicing thousands of troops and covert operators.[199]

---

196 Alfred W. McCoy, *The Politics of Heroin: CIA Complicity in the Global Drug Trade* (Brooklyn, NY: Lawrence Hill Books, 1991), 31–38.

197 Arne Kislenko, "A Not So Silent Partner: Thailand's Role in Covert Operations, Counter-Insurgency, and the Wars in Indochina," *The Journal of Conflict Studies*, 24(1), Summer 2004.

198 Warner, 1996, 255; Herman and Chomsky, 254.

199 Warner, 1996, 162.

AIR AMERICA, USAID, AND HEROIN | The CIA employed one of its key assets—semi-private Air America, with over 200 aircraft of different sizes—to move drugs to South Viet Nam to feed the huge demand of US soldiers, as well as airlifting South Vietnamese special forces from secret bases in South Viet Nam and Thailand into Laos, Cambodia, and North Viet Nam. The heroin followed the GIs home in the 1970s, and captured one-third of the US drug market. In 1973, the Pentagon reported that 35 percent of all Army enlisted men who had served in South Viet Nam had tried heroin and 20 percent became addicted during their tour of duty.[200] By 1967, facilitation of the opium trade was substantially improved when the CIA, working under cover of the US Agency for International Development (USAID), funded General Vang Pao to form his own private airline, Xieng Khouang Air Transport, to carry "relief" supplies of opium and heroin to Vientiane. As a Hmong officer, Pao commanded the CIA's secret army from 1960–1975.[201] The administrator of USAID admitted in 1970 that the agency's involvement in Laos (and Southeast Asia in general) was not routine, but he believed it to be in the national interest.[202]

Large-scale Bombing of Laos

On May 7, 1964, Souvanna Phouma in Laos announced a shotgun formation of a new (right-wing) Royal Lao government, blessed by the US, ending the tripartite coalition government and making the 1962 Geneva Agreements for Laos, in effect, null and void. The Lao government and its CIA-funded Hmong army were a small, corrupt elite that included generals supplying opium to soldiers in Viet Nam. Eventually 12,000 US advisers were involved in Laos, including 1,200 Green Berets.[203] By early 1964, the popular Pathet Lao had begun occupying the Plain of Jars, a place whose communities had lived in peace for 700 years. By mid-May the US had begun flying reconnaissance missions over Laos and bombing the main bases of the popular Pathet Lao with high explosives and napalm. These missions hit the Plain of Jars, the provincial city of Sam Neua, and lower Laos. US tactical air forces were also actively supporting ground operations against the Pathet Lao.[204] By the end of May 1964, Thailand formally granted base facilities for US planes to enjoy "privileged sanctuaries" from which to bomb the Pathet Lao. It is worth noting that in all the years of their war in Indochina, the French never used bombs.[205] Beginning

---

200 Melman, 158; Kolko, 1985, 363; in general, McCoy.
201 McCoy, 318.
202 Adams and McCoy, 407–408.
203 Adams and McCoy, 445.
204 Wilfred G. Burchett, *The Second Indochina War: Cambodia and Laos* (New York: International Publishers, 1970), 163–64; Bowman, 70, 79; June 1969, Jacques Decornoy published in *Le Monde* a series of articles revealing secret bombings since 1964 of Pathet Lao zones in the Plain of Jars, Laos.
205 Chris Bishop, ed., *Vietnam War Diary, 1964–1975* (London, UK: Chartwell Books), 10; Adams and McCoy, xvi–xviii, 231, 458.

Lao villagers gathered at the mouth of a cave, waiting out a bombing assault.

in 1964, Laos was bombed more intensively than Viet Nam; over time, its territory and people became the most protracted and extensive bombing targets in history. On June 13, 1969, Souvanna Phouma, the premier of Laos, acknowledged publicly that US planes were regularly carrying out bombing raids in Laos.[206] Despite attempts at systematic population removal through ground operations and heavy bombing, over one-third of the population remained in areas controlled by the Pathet Lao. In fact, it was estimated that half the population, including most young men and women, joined the revolutionary Pathet Lao, which possessed a large popular base.[207] An area larger than the state of New York, containing over one million people, was carpet-bombed. In effect, the Plain of Jars became a free-fire zone and nearly all villages and towns were destroyed, with large numbers of civilians killed, estimated by war's end at 350,000.[208]

B-52s and F-4s dropped at will 500-pound bombs, napalm, and anti-personnel bombs ("pineapple" bombs throwing out hundreds of "bombies"—pellets that could not destroy structures but deeply pierced flesh, entering in a zig-zag pattern difficult to remove even if a surgeon was nearby). Thousands of attack sorties were flown against the Plain of Jars. From May 1964 through September 1969 alone, over 75,000 tons of bombs were dropped there, killing and wounding tens of thousands, driving virtually everyone underground and leveling the entire above-ground society. The US goal was to eliminate everything—all homes, lands, and villages—in order to destroy the real enemy, social revolution. The bombing was so intense by 1969 that farming was impossible.[209]

---

206 "This Day in History," https://thisdayinusmilhist.wordpress.com/2005/06/13/june-13/.
207 Adams and McCoy, xvi-xviii, 231, 234.
208 Herman and Chomsky, 260.
209 Zinn, 1980, 472; in general, see Fred Branfman, *Voices from the Plain of Jars* (New York: Harper Colophon Books, 1972); Adams and McCoy, 379.

Diem's Repression of Vietnamese Buddhists

Enforcing a ban on the multicolored Buddhist flag, South Vietnamese troops and police fired upon 20,000 Buddhists, who had gathered to celebrate the 2527th birthday of the Buddha, in the city of Hue on May 8, 1963, killing nine. The attack served to increase and intensify protests by Buddhists against Diem's repression.[210] Although Buddhists formed at least 70 percent of the population, and Catholics less than 10 percent,[211] the Diem regime insisted on treating Buddhists as the enemy.[212] Buddhist demonstrations continued through August.

At noon on June 11, 1963, a 66-year-old Buddhist monk named Thich Quang Duc immolated himself on a Saigon street corner during a large Buddhist demonstration against Diem's repressive government. Madame Nhu, the wife of Diem's brother, Ngo Dinh Nhu, in a speech, referred to Duc and other Buddhist monks' suicide burnings as "barbeques" and offered to supply the matches.[213] As Diem was a bachelor, Madame Nhu, who lived in the Presidential Palace with her husband, was considered South Viet Nam's First Lady. Self-immolation had no precedent in Vietnamese history but reflected the intolerable gap between morality and the gruesome reality of the US-supported Diem regime.[214]

Diem continued to pursue pro-Catholic policies that antagonized Buddhist groups. Two months later, on August 21, South Vietnamese troops loyal to Diem raided a number of Buddhist temples and sanctuaries around the country, beating and killing several monks.[215] President Kennedy denounced the attacks. Buddhist groups continued to stage increasingly intense protests that included additional instances of self-immolation. On October 5, 1963, another monk self-immolated (the sixth such event that year).[216]

> ### President Kennedy Reverses Policy, Plans to Withdraw
>
> **May 6, 1963.** At a high-level Pacific Command meeting in Hawaii, Secretary of War/Defense Robert McNamara orders concrete plans drawn up for withdrawing 1,000 US troops from Viet Nam by the year's end, as directed by the president. President Kennedy issues National Security Action Memorandum 239 (NSAM 239), ordering his national security team to also pursue a nuclear test ban treaty and begin planning for a general, and then a complete, disarmament.[217]

---

210 "7 Reported Dead in Riots Over South Vietnam Order," *New York Times*, May 10, 1963, 12; Bowman, 59.

211 Bowman, 59.

212 Dougherty and Stewart, 53.

213 Bowman, 60.

214 Frances FitzGerald, *Fire in the Lake: The Vietnamese and the Americans in Vietnam* (Boston: Little Brown and Co, 1972), 133.

215 Dougherty and Stewart, 54.

216 UPI, *The Vietnam War: An Almanac*, 61; Leo J. Daugherty and George Louis Mattson, *Nam: A Photographic History* (New York: Metro Books, 2001), 33.

217 James W. Douglass, *JFK and the Unspeakable: Why He Died & Why It Matters* (Maryknoll, NY: Orbis

June 10, 1963. In a commencement address delivered at American University in Washington, DC, President Kennedy says, "I also believe that we must re-examine our own attitudes—as individuals and as a Nation—for our attitude is as essential as theirs [the USSR's]." In this speech, Kennedy reveals that he has experienced a conversion from Cold War warrior to serious advocate for peace with the USSR.[218]

August 29, 1963. A cable from US Ambassador Henry Cabot Lodge, Jr., to Secretary of State Dean Rusk reveals plots to overthrow the Diem government—the president along with his brother, head of Diem's hated security forces.[219]

September 20, 1963. In an address to the United Nations, President Kennedy urges the Limited Test Ban Treaty as a lever for a permanent peace in the world. Kennedy approves US diplomat William Attwood to initiate a secret dialogue with Castro to pursue normalization of relations.[220]

September 30, 1963. Not able to trust his own State Department, President Kennedy opens a secret channel of communications with Khrushchev via Press Secretary Pierre Salinger and a Washington-based member of the Soviet secret police.[221]

October 11, 1963. President Kennedy issues a secret—and as it turns out, his last—memo, NSAM 263, ordering the beginning of US withdrawal of 1,000 US troops from Vietnam by the end of the year, as a first step in a large troop withdrawal to be substantially completed by the end of 1965.[222] The withdrawal is vigorously opposed by both the State and War/Defense Departments and the CIA.

November 1-2, 1963. A US-supported military coup topples the government of South Viet Nam, assassinating Diem and his brother. Nhu's hated security forces surrender while conspiring Vietnamese generals seize strategic points in and around Saigon. (Later it is revealed that the brothers were murdered by South Vietnamese army officers.[223]) In the countryside, peasants immediately demolish the hated strategic hamlets built by Diem with the support of the US.[224] The coup and assassination mark the end of the myth of an independent South Viet Nam, and in effect, begin the overt Americanization of the war.

Books, 2008), xxxv.
  218 Douglass, 2008, xxvi.
  219 Gettleman et al., 1995, 225, 227.
  220 Douglass, 2008, xxvii.
  221 Douglass, 2008, xxviii.
  222 Douglass, 2008, 93–94; Peter Dale Scott, *Deep Politics and the Death of JFK* (Berkeley: University of California Press, 1993), 24.
  223 Gettleman et al., 1995, 225.
  224 Bowman, 62.

November 15, 1963. A US military official in Saigon announces that a thousand US military personnel will begin withdrawing on December 3.[225]

November 22, 1963. President Kennedy is assassinated and Lyndon B. Johnson takes over the presidency.

President Johnson Immediately Reverses Kennedy's Plans

On November 26, 1963, four days after being sworn into office, President Lyndon Baines Johnson issued NSAM 273, initiating a plan for covert military attacks on North Viet Nam with "estimates of such factors as (a) resulting damage to NVN, (b) the plausibility of denial, (c) possible North Vietnamese retaliation." These plans, as well as covert military operations within Laos, were covert and kept secret from the US people. Thus, the first phase of Kennedy's withdrawal of troops from Viet Nam and his larger strategy for world peace, in concert with Khrushchev's commitment, was ignored. In fact, it was reversed.[226] Johnson in effect had paved the way for "Americanizing" the war.[227]

In June 1964, the first New Zealand force entered Viet Nam at the request of the US as an administrative unit assisting the South Vietnamese government. In 1967 New Zealand combat units entered the country.[228]

Bombing of North Viet Nam Begins with a Pretext

Even as the US decided to seriously escalate with enormous amounts of military arms and troops, entrenching ever more deeply the strategic and political assumptions underpinning the conflict in Viet Nam, it was determined not to repeat the frustrating stalemate of the earlier Korean War. It needed a pretext for a formal, expanded war. That pretext was the Tonkin Gulf incident later documented by *The Pentagon Papers* that described provocative covert US air missions against North Viet Nam preceding the Tonkin Gulf incidents by several months.[229]

In January 1964, air operations using Special Forces ("Air America") in Southeast Asia were taken over from the CIA by the MACV. Commanded by an Army colonel, the Special Operations Group (SOG), formed in Saigon in January to implement OPLAN

---

225 Bowman, 63.

226 Douglas, 2008, 93–94.

227 Gettleman, et al., 241–248; Bowman, 64–65; NSAM 273: (1) covert attacks against the DRV financed and organized by the US but executed by mercenaries and Saigon forces; (2) appointment of a new US commander to prepare for enlargement of bases and eventual influx of large numbers of US combat troops; (3) overt attacks on the North in expected "retaliation" for military responses to the covert attacks; (4) gradual shift from "retaliatory" attacks to sustained US air attacks on the North; (5) deployment of US troops, first to defend US air bases, then to control the countryside. Part of this plan was to orchestrate a rationale for legislation/resolution from Congress granting military *carte blanche* (full discretionary power) authority to wage war.

228 Caputo, 36.

229 Peter Dale Scott, *Drugs, Oil, and War: The United States in Afghanistan, Colombia, and Indochina* (Blue Ridge Summit, PA: Rowman and Littlefield, 2003), 168, 175, 180); Scott cited "Report to Assistant Secretary of State Bundy," November 7, 1964, *New York Times*, 37.

34A, was composed of Army Green Berets, Navy SEALS, and air commandos. Within months its name changed to Studies and Operations Group, thereby retaining the same acronym, SOG.[230]

Early in February 1964, only three months after the coup against Diem, President Johnson revised NSAM 273 and launched OPLAN 34A from Paradise Island off the coast of DaNang, initiating bombing raids against North Viet Nam with T-28s. In April, Thai and Air America pilots, flying old US American fighter planes, directed attacks against the Pathet Lao and the Ho Chi Minh Trail inside Laos. With US-paid mercenaries, the US conducted covert ground and air sabotage missions inside North Viet Nam in addition to sea attacks along the north coast.[231] These SOG operations, elaborate in their execution, in effect helped provoke the subsequent Tonkin Gulf incident, revealing the eagerness of US officials to escalate the war. It was an elaborate plan prepared by USMC Major General Victor Krulak, Special Assistant for Counterinsurgency and Special Activities of the Joint Chiefs of Staff included U-2 spy flights as well as plans to kidnap North Vietnamese for intelligence gathering, and aerial photographic reconnaissance to support bombing raids.[232]

Quite separately, and predating OPLAN and SOG by two years, the US had been conducting special operations patrols from Navy Destroyers. Code-named DESOTO, the patrols utilized signals equipment to gather key intelligence on North Viet Nam's coastal defenses and warning radar. From February through August 1964, the intelligence gathering destroyers *USS Craig* and *USS Maddox* patrolled Viet Nam's northern coasts, noting radar and defensive responses to the OPLAN 34A's constant probing and attacking.[233]

Walt Rostow, Senior White House Specialist on Southeast Asia, and a principal architect of the counterinsurgency doctrine, was one of the main voices arguing for bombing North Viet Nam. In a letter dated February 13, 1964, he urged President Johnson to prepare a Congressional resolution, to be submitted at an opportune moment, that would grant authority to wage war—the equivalent of authorizing virtually unlimited war without end against the Vietnamese. In a few months, this proposal was to become the essence of the Gulf of Tonkin Resolution.[234]

Throughout 1964, ARVN desertion rates increased, and draft dodging was common. In response, US CIA Director John McCone suggested that "two or possibly three divisions" from Chiang Kai-shek's army on Taiwan be sent to the southern tip of the Mekong Delta "in order to give impetus and support to the hard-pressed ARVN effort in the area."[235]

---

230 John L. Plaster, *SOG: The Secret Wars of America's Commandos in Vietnam* (New York: Simon & Shuster, 1997), 23–24, 28, 31, 59, 74–75; Scott, 2003, 183n57; Bowman, 64–65.

231 FitzGerald, 264; Bowman, 67, 69, 70; Blum, 1995, 141–142; Scott, 2003, 175.

232 Gettleman et al., 1995, 240; Valentine, 53; Bowman, 64–67; Scott, 2003, 168, 175, 180.

233 *Wikipedia*, DESOTO patrol: http://en.wikipedia.org/wiki/DESOTO_patrol; FitzGerald, 264–265; Bowman, 67, 69, 70; Blum, 1995, 142–143.

234 Bowman, 68; Gettleman et al., 1995, 240; Zinn, 1980, 467.

235 Kahin, 1986, 207.

During March 1964, US Republican presidential aspirant Barry Goldwater advocated "carrying the war to North Vietnam. Ten years ago," he said, "we should have bombed North Vietnam, destroyed the only access they had to North Vietnam, with no risk to our lives." The previous day, he had mused aloud to students how, ten years before, "we might have dropped a low-yield atom bomb on North Vietnam to defoliate the trees."[236]

On March 18, 1964, the *New York Times* reported that Assistant Secretary of State Thomas C. Mann had briefed US diplomats that the United States "would no longer seek to punish military juntas for overthrowing democratic regimes." Mann deemed "rightist and military" dictatorships acceptable, providing that their program included "the protection of $9 billion in US investments in Latin America" and a concerted "opposition to communism."[237] This sentiment had dominated US policy for some time, but now it was being honestly expressed. Mann's words echoed State Department George Kennan's February 24, 1948 policy statement in which he talked about letting go of concerns about human rights in order to "deal in straight power concepts" (see p. 57).

On March 20, 1964, when South Vietnamese ground and air operations attacked the Cambodian village of Chantrea, one of two observer planes carrying US military advisers was shot down.[238]

On April 9–12, 1964, four US advisers were killed during fighting in the Mekong Delta in which ARVN losses amounted to over 50. During one mortar barrage, a US helicopter base was forced to evacuate.[239] In 1964, the US continued to accuse the North Vietnamese of arming the Viet Cong, when in fact the major supplier of weapons for their forces was the US itself: An estimated 125,000 light weapons were lost to the Viet Cong between 1962 and 1964.[240]

On May 20, 1964, the first Marine ground combat unit—Marine Advisory Team One, with 30 communications personnel and 76 infantrymen—arrived in Viet Nam at DaNang.[241]

On May 24, 1964, during an interview, presidential candidate Goldwater again proposed using low-yield atomic bombs in North Viet Nam to defoliate forests and to bomb bridges, roads, and railroad lines bringing supplies from China.[242]

President Johnson's Doubts in 1964

Six months into his presidency, Johnson asked US Democratic Senator Richard Russell from Georgia, Chair of the Senate Committee on Armed Services, "What do you think of this Vietnam thing?" Russell answered: "It's the damn worst mess I ever saw, and I don't like to brag. I never have been right many times in my life. But I knew that we were going

---

236 Theodore H. White, *The Making of a President 1964* (New York: Atheneum, 1965), 106.
237 Greene, 1970, 192–193, 194n10 citing the *New York Times,* March 19, 1964.
238 Bowman, 70.
239 Bishop, 10; Bowman, 71.
240 Melman, 164–165.
241 *VFW,* August 2011.
242 Bowman, 75; White, 311.

to get into this sort of mess when we went in there."²⁴³ To which Johnson replied: "That's the way that I've been feeling for six months." Later that day, Johnson told his national security adviser, McGeorge Bundy: "I don't think it's worth fighting for, and I don't think that we can get out. It just the biggest damn mess I ever saw." Bundy replied: "It is. It's an awful mess." Johnson then said, "It's damned easy to get in a war, but it's gonna be awfully hard to extricate yourself if you get in."²⁴⁴

At this point, in May 1964, there were fewer than 16,000 Americans in Viet Nam. But Johnson, like all presidents, did not want a foreign policy aggression to be lost on his watch. Only two months later, the Gulf of Tonkin Resolution gave the president authority to take "all necessary measures" to defend South Viet Nam.

In June 1964, General William Westmoreland replaced General Paul Harkins as MACV commander of the 16,000 US "advisers" on Viet Nam soil. President Johnson ordered experienced CIA analyst William Bundy, Assistant Secretary of State for the Far East and brother of McGeorge Bundy, to write a war resolution to be sent to Congress when the right moment arose, an idea earlier proposed by Johnson aide, Walt Rostow.²⁴⁵

Nguyen Cao Ky, the commander of the South Vietnamese Air Force, announced on July 21, 1964, with his usual arrogance, that it was prepared to bomb North Viet Nam at any time: "We are ready. We could go this afternoon. I cannot assure that all of North Vietnam would be destroyed, but Hanoi would certainly be destroyed."²⁴⁶ The bellicose comments uttered were similar to those of another US puppet, South Korea's Syngman Rhee. Fifteen years earlier, in 1949, itching to attack the portion of Korea north of the US-imposed 38th Parallel with his US-equipped military, Rhee had boasted that "when we have to settle this thing by war, we will do all the fighting. We are not asking our friends to do our fighting for us. . . . We can't live much longer this way."²⁴⁷ Simultaneously, Rhee's defense minister had bragged that his army was ready and waiting to invade North Korea.²⁴⁸

A couple of days after Ky's announcement, General Nguyen Khanh, then–South Vietnamese Premier, urged a rally of 100,000 people in Saigon to get ready for "liberating their native land." At that rally, Nguyen Cao Ky described sabotage missions inside North Vietnam and reported that Vietnamese pilots were being readied for large-scale attacks from the air. Ky also declared that the sabotage teams had already entered North Vietnam by air, sea, and land at intervals dating back to at least 1961.²⁴⁹

---

243 George McGovern, "Discovering Greatness in Lyndon Johnson," *New York Times*, December 5, 1999].

244 US Department of State, *Foreign Relations of the United States, 1964–68*, Volume XXVII, Mainland Southeast Asia: Regional Affairs, Washington, DC, Document Number 53, Telephone Conversation between President Johnson and the President's Special Assistant for National Security Affairs (Bundy).

245 Tim Weiner, *Legacy of Ashes: The History of the CIA* (New York: Doubleday, 2007), 243.

246 Kahin and Lewis, 154.

247 "Rhee Predicts Force to End Korean Rift," AP Seoul, *Washington Evening Star*, October 31, 1949.

248 "Korean Army Set for War," AP Tokyo, *The Washington Post*, November 1, 1949.

249 Gettleman et al., 1995, 240; Peter Grose, "Sabotage Raids on North Confirmed by Saigon Aide," *New York Times*, July 23, 1964.

Gulf of Tonkin

In the early morning hours of July 31, 1964, the SOG dispatched an OPLAN 34A Navy SEAL team with 20 South Vietnamese Marines in a raid intended to knock out North Vietnamese radar installations on the islands of Hon Me and Hon Nieu, just a few miles off the coast of Viet Nam in the Gulf of Tonkin, 200 miles north of the DMZ. The nearby *USS Maddox,* patrolling about eight miles off the coast, was monitoring the North Vietnamese electronic defenses and radar operations as part of its routine DESOTO intelligence-gathering missions.[250]

On August 1, the *Maddox* maneuvered to within a few miles of each of the two islands in the Gulf.[251] The next day, OPLAN 34A covert offensive raids continued on coastal defenses of North Viet Nam. Meanwhile the *Maddox* continued to monitor electronic defenses in the vicinity and detected three North Viet Nam PT boats approaching, the latter defending the North's political sovereignty against foreign invaders. The commander of the *Maddox* requested help from a nearby destroyer, *USS Turner Joy,* and fighter jets from the aircraft carrier, *USS Ticonderoga.* Shortly after 3:00 pm, the *Maddox* fired three times at the PT boats. These shots were never reported nor acknowledged by the Pentagon or the White House, which instead insisted the North shot first. The *Maddox* was still firing when four Navy jets blasted the North's patrol boats, killing four Vietnamese sailors while heavily damaging two of the boats. The *Maddox* sustained only one bullet hole.[252] On August 3, President Johnson sent his first diplomatic note to Hanoi warning of "grave consequences" for any "further unprovoked military action," at the same moment that another OPLAN 34A mission was sabotaging a radar station on the island of Hon Matt.[253]

During a storm on the night of August 4, the captains of the two US destroyers, the commanders of the Seventh Fleet, and officials at the Pentagon received an urgent alert from onshore signals intelligence (SIGNIT) operators that three North Vietnamese patrol boats were returning. In Washington, McNamara called the president. At 10:00 pm in the Gulf of Tonkin—10:00 am in Washington—the US destroyers sent a message they were under attack. The radar and sonar operators on the *Maddox* and *Turner Joy* reported seeing ghostly blotches in the night, and the destroyers opened fire. The 2005 declassified NSA report described how "the two destroyers gyrated wildly in the dark waters of the Gulf of Tonkin, the *Turner Joy* firing over 300 rounds madly" as both ships took furious evasive maneuvers. "It was this high-speed gyrating by the American warships through the waters that created all the additional sonar reports of more torpedoes." In fact they had been firing at their own shadows. The only definite target that the *Maddox* fired at that night turned out to be the *Turner Joy,* which was saved from destruction when the *Maddox* main gun overseer refused to execute the direct order to fire. No damage was

---

250 Gettleman et al., 1995, 249; Valentine, 53; James William Gibson, *The Perfect War: The War We Couldn't Lose and How We Did* (New York: Vintage Books, 1988), 89.

251 Gettleman et al., 1995, 249.

252 Weiner, 2007, 240–241; Gettleman et al., 249; John Prados, *Vietnam: The History of an Unwinnable War, 1945–1975* (Lawrence, KS: University Press of Kansas, 2009), 93–95.

253 Weiner, 241; Gettleman et al., 1995, 250.

inflicted on any US ship or plane.[254] Nevertheless, Ray Cline, Deputy CIA Director of Intelligence at the time, said, "It was just what Johnson was looking for." The President immediately ordered US air strikes against North Vietnamese naval bases.[255]

Herrick of the *Maddox* immediately cabled Washington: "ENTIRE ACTION LEAVES MANY DOUBTS." The doubts quickly vanished as the NSA told both Johnson and McNamara that it had intercepted a North Vietnamese Navy communiqué that read, "SACRIFICED TWO SHIPS AND ALL THE REST ARE OKAY." However, no SIGNIT listener found any such communiqué. Upon closer review, the message actually said, "WE SACRIFICED TWO COMRADES BUT ALL ARE BRAVE." The message had been composed at the moment the *Maddox* and *Turner Joy* opened fire on August 4; it was *not* about what happened that night but rather about the August 2 incident, two nights earlier. The NSA buried this very important discovery, and everyone remained silent, since the US bombing was now on. The smoking gun wouldn't be revealed until November 2005, when the NSA issued a detailed declassified confession of what really happened.[256]

In this detailed confession, the NSA admitted that "the overwhelming body of reports, if used, would have told the story that no attack had happened. So a conscious effort ensued to demonstrate that the attack occurred . . . to make the SIGNIT fit the claim of what happened during the evening of 4 August in the Gulf of Tonkin." The intelligence, the NSA concluded, "was deliberately skewed to support the notion that there had been an attack," as US intelligence officers "rationalized the contradictory evidence away." Johnson had been ready for at least two months to bomb North Viet Nam. But four years after the fact, Lyndon Johnson himself said, "Those stupid sailors were just shooting at flying fish."[257]

President Johnson went on national TV on August 4, 1964, at 11:30 pm, 13 hours after the supposed attack, and informed the public that retaliatory action was already under way: "Air action is now in execution against gunboats and certain supporting facilities in North Viet Nam which have been used in these hostile operations."[258] The Johnson-McNamara conversation, which was recorded by Johnson in the White House, shows readiness and eagerness to escalate, even on suspect intelligence, knowing the signals of August 4 were mistaken but welcoming them as justification for a Congressional blank check for unlimited, timeless aggressive war against the Communists in Viet Nam.

On August 7, 1964, seventeen days before the Democratic convention in Atlantic City, New Jersey, Congress passed the Gulf of Tonkin Resolution by a stunning vote of 416-0 in the House, and 88-2 in the Senate. Only two Senators, Wayne Morse (D-OR) and Ernest Gruening (D-AK), voted no. A virtual declaration of war, the resolution granted

---

254 Gettleman et al., 1995, 250.

255 Weiner, 241; Kahin and Lewis, 155–160.

256 Weiner, 241–242.

257 Weiner, 242–243; Weiner, on page 608, cites Robert J. Hanyok, "Skunks, Bogies, Silent Hounds, and the Flying Fish: The Gulf of Tonkin Mystery, August 2–4, 1964," *Cryptologic Quarterly*, Vol. 19, No. 4/Vol 20, No. 1, Winter 2000/Spring 2001, declassified November 2005. The *Quarterly* is an official and highly classified publication of the NSA.

258 Kahin and Lewis, 158.

the President authority to "take all necessary measures to repel any armed attack against the forces of the United States and to prevent further aggression" and "take all necessary steps" to assist any member or protocol state of the Southeast Asia Collective Defense Treaty.[259] In fact, the resolution was an astute political move that deprived Johnson's principal opponent in the upcoming election, hawkish Goldwater, the chance to make Viet Nam a campaign issue.

Johnson was angry enough at Wayne Morse that he asked the FBI to investigate his supporters in Oregon.[260] By 1966, as several senators, including William Fulbright and Robert Kennedy, joined Morse and Gruening in their criticism of the war, Johnson ordered the FBI's J. Edgar Hoover to monitor their public remarks for a point-by-point comparison with the "Communist Party line." Johnson shared with Hoover the opinion that Fulbright and Morse were "definitely under control of the Soviet Embassy."[261] Throughout the war, the FBI agreed with the assumptions of Presidents Johnson and Nixon that domestic opposition to the war was somehow enabled by financial support from outside, foreign governments, especially Communist ones. This thinking is an example of what psychologist Carl Jung called "the Shadow," where someone projects onto others the darkness from within the self. The CIA had been providing aid for years to anti-government groups in Eastern Europe and elsewhere, so it was logical to the US executive branch that other governments might be working to undermine the US.[262]

Johnson Lied Himself into the Presidency

President Johnson, running for election in November 1964, promised multiple times that fall that he would not send military troops to Viet Nam:[263]

September 25: "We don't want our American boys to do the fighting for Asian boys."

September 29: "We are not going north and we are not going south; we are going to try to get them to save their own freedom with their own men."[264]

October 21: "We are not about to send American boys nine or ten thousand miles from home to do what Asian boys ought to be doing themselves."

The fact is, however, Johnson already had 16,000 US military advisors in South Viet Nam, as he continued to launch provocative, invasive attacks against North Viet Nam with covert actions from the sea, and clandestine commando infiltrators from the air and ground. Bombing in the South had commenced in late 1961 under Kennedy. Now, with the Gulf of Tonkin Resolution, Johnson had the authority to use US military forces any way he saw fit, including bombing the North.

---

[259] *Joint Resolution of Congress, H.J. RES 1145, August 7, 1964* (Gulf of Tonkin Resolution).
[260] Evans, 531.
[261] Gentry, 605.
[262] Betty Medsger, *The Burglary: The Discovery of J. Edgar Hoover's Secret FBI* (New York: Alfred A. Knopf, 2014), 366.
[263] Gettleman et al., 1995, 241.
[264] But, on October 14, 1964, Johnson authorized US aircraft to fly with Laotian planes further deepening US involvement in a wider war. [Bishop, 12].

In national elections held on November 3, 1964, Johnson won the presidential election in a landslide, garnering 61.1 percent of the vote. But Goldwater's hawkish policy prevailed. As noted above, Johnson had been conducting secret military escalations against North Viet Nam long before his November election victory. Johnson apparently secretly admired both Goldwater's "war on crime" strategy and his promotion of dramatic escalation of the war in Southeast Asia. In March 1965, Johnson announced crime as a domestic enemy and launched his own war on crime—on the same day that he ordered the Marines to openly invade Viet Nam.[265] As history has disclosed, Goldwater's conservative platform also laid the foundation for Ronald Reagan's "revolution" less than two decades later.

Operation Rolling Thunder

In 1965, as Johnson began a major military build-up in Viet Nam, Robert Taber published *The War of the Flea*, a book about revolutionary and counterrevolutionary warfare, in which he concluded: "There is only one means of defeating an insurgent people who will not surrender, and that is extermination. There is only one way to control a territory that harbors resistance, and that is to turn it into a desert. Where these means cannot, for whatever reason, be used, the war is lost."[266]

Early 1965 witnessed a fundamental policy change to waging unlimited war against the South, i.e., bombing South Vietnam at more than triple the intensity of the bombing in North Vietnam. The vigorous assault culminated on March 2, 1965 with Johnson's launch of Operation Rolling Thunder, one of the most intensive bombing campaigns in world history, a sustained daily assault that continued, with occasional suspensions, until Johnson called for a temporary halt on October 31, 1968.[267] From 1965 through 1969 (one year into the Nixon presidency), the Pentagon reported the quantity of ordnance expended in Indochina to be four and half million tons by *aerial bombardment alone,* or over seventy tons of bombs for every square mile of Viet Nam, both North and South. This was equivalent to about five hundred pounds for *each man, woman, and child* in Viet Nam.[268] Other estimates have concluded that, south of the DMZ alone, by the end of the war a thousand pounds of explosives (one-half ton) had been expended for each individual there.[269]

---

265 See *Niagara Falls Gazette*, Monday, March 8, 1965 that showed three separate headlines on its front page: (1) AP, "Marines Set Up Guard At Viet Nam Air Base"; (2) UPI, "Troopers Smash Negroes' March; 67 Are Injured "; and (3) AP, "Johnson Charts Battle On Crime."

266 Robert Taber, *The War of the Flea: A Study of Guerrilla Warfare, Theory and Practice* (New York: Citadel Press, 1965), 11.

267 Bowman, 105–107.

268 Ken Coates, Peter Limqueco, and Peter Weiss, eds., *Prevent the Crime of Silence: Reports from the Sessions of the International War Crimes Tribunal, Founded by Bertram Russell* (London, UK: Allen Lane/The Penguin Press, 1971), 11.

269 Gettleman et al., 1995, 5.

As noted Viet Nam war historian Bernard Fall pointed out, "What changed the character of the Vietnam war was *not* the decision to bomb North Vietnam; *not* the decision to use American ground troops in South Vietnam; but the decision to wage *unlimited* aerial warfare inside the country at the price of literally pounding the place to bits" [author's italics].[270] *The Pentagon Papers* makes little mention of this history. Artillery bombardments may have been even more damaging than the unprecedented amount of bombing from the air. Parts of a secret "Viet Cong Motivation and Morale" study, introduced by McNamara into congressional testimony in January 1966, indicated that artillery bombardment seemed more effective than air attack in getting villagers "to move where they will be safe from such attacks, . . . regardless of their attitude toward the Government of Viet Nam."[271]

USAF Chief of Staff Curtis LeMay "repeatedly told President Johnson that if his squadrons were allowed to conduct an all-out bombing campaign against North Vietnam, he could bomb the country 'back to the Stone Age.'"[272] "My solution to the problem," he said, "would be to tell them frankly that they've got to draw in their horns and stop their aggression, or we're going to bomb them back into the Stone Age. And we would shove them back into the Stone Age with Air power or Naval power—not with ground forces."[273] In 1965, the year his book was published, LeMay wrote an article published in *National Geographic*, "United States Air Force—Power for Peace."[274] In an interview two years after the publication of his book, General LeMay said, "I never said we should bomb them back to the Stone Age. I said we had the capability to do it. I wanted to save lives on both sides"[275]—another fine example of doublethink.[276]

---

270 John Tirman, *The Deaths of Others: The Fate of Civilians in America's Wars* (New York: Oxford University Press, 2011), 167.

271 Noam Chomsky and E. S. Herman, *The Washington Connection and Third World Fascism: The Political Economy Of Human Rights*, Volume I (Boston: South End Press, 1979), 302–303.

272 Caputo, 40.

273 General Curtis E. LeMay, *Mission with LeMay: My Story* (Garden City, NY: Doubleday, 1965), 565.

274 Curtis LeMay, "United States Air Force—Power for Peace," *National Geographic*, February 1965.

275 *The Washington Post*, October 4, 1968, A8.

276 George Orwell, *Nineteen Eight Four. A Novel* (New York: Harcourt, Brace & Co., 1949). In the novel, doublethink is a propaganda technique employed by the Ministry of Truth of Oceania, whose three slogans are inscribed at its entrance: "WAR IS PEACE," "FREEDOM IS SLAVERY," "IGNORANCE IS STRENGTH."

January–February 1965 Highlights

January 13, 1965. Two US aircraft are shot down over Laos.[277]

January 20, 1965. Johnson is inaugurated as president, the fourth to direct US military involvement in Southeast Asia.

February 7, 1965. National Liberation Front forces simultaneously attack the US helicopter base at Camp Halloway and the barracks of US advisers at Pleiku in the central highlands, killing 8 soldiers and wounding 126; destroying 10 aircraft and damaging 125 others.[278] Johnson orders retaliatory bombings, code-named Operation Flaming Dart, carried out on a North Vietnamese army camp February 7–8.[279]

February 10, 1965. The NLF blows up US military barracks at Qui Nhon, 75 miles east of Pleiku.[280] The blast kills 9 Americans and injures 126, and destroys multiple aircraft.

February 10, 1965. While on a return trip from Saigon, McGeorge Bundy, Special Assistant to Johnson for National Security Affairs, writes in a memo that "without new US action ... [a Viet Nam defeat] appears inevitable."[281]

February 13, 1965. Johnson announces a massive bombing campaign over North Viet Nam called Operation Rolling Thunder, justified as retaliation for increased North Vietnamese raids on US installations.

February 27, 1965. The US State Department issues a fourteen-thousand-word white paper, *Aggression From the North: the Record of North Vietnam's Campaign to Conquer South Vietnam*,[282] which *de facto* establishes a justification for a "legal" US war.[283]

---

277 Bishop, 14.
278 Dougherty and Stewart, 76; Bowman, 104.
279 Dougherty and Stewart, 76; Summers, 1999, 33.
280 Bowman, 105.
281 Michael Beschloss, *Reaching for Glory: Lyndon Johnson's Secret White House Tapes, 1964–1965* (New York: Touchtone, 2001), 175.
282 US Department of State, *Publication 7839, Far Eastern Series 130* (Washington, DC, February 1965).
283 Gettleman et al., 1995, 255–268; Bowman, 106–107.

Chapter Four
Chronicle of Barbarism

> "I doubt if Americans will ever be able to comprehend the depravity represented by the United States' actions in Viet Nam. . . . a pattern of gradually escalating contempt for Asian life and dignity and a resulting scale of death and destruction that stuns the imagination and legitimizes —nay requires—use of the term genocide."
> —David Dellinger, 1968[1]

Introduction

This section chronicles some of the more notable massacres and campaigns, as well as significant political events associated with the timeline of the war, beginning with the US Marine landing at Da Nang in 1965.

Viet Nam was part of a pattern of the US actively opposing popular governments and movements in pursuit of its own selfish interests. The same year US ground troops openly invaded Viet Nam, a shorter covert war was occurring 800 miles to its southeast in the Dominican Republic, a nation of less than 4 million people.

On April 28–30, 1965, on Johnson's orders, 23,000 Marines and army paratroopers invaded the Dominican Republic to suppress a popular uprising organized to re-install the country's first democratically elected president, liberal but anti-Communist Juan Bosch. In February 1963, Bosch had become the first democratically elected president of the Dominican Republic since 1924, advocating a liberal program of land reform, low-rent housing, and modest nationalization of key service businesses.[2] His social ideas were perceived by the US, as usual, as a threat to US investor interests. With the encouragement of the US, the Dominican military had overthrown Bosch in September 1963. However, 19 months later, the 1965 popular rebellion demanded his re-instatement. The US troops ensured that Bosch was not to be re-instated nor to be re-elected in the 1966 elections, the latter won by Joaquin Balaguer, a strongman who then ruled the 8 million people in a ruthless manner for over 22 years.[3]

---

1 Commentary by Dave Dellinger, "War Crimes Tribunal: Unmasking Genocide," *Liberation*, December 1967/ January 1968, reporting on his participation as a member of the Bertrand Russell War Crimes Tribunal held in Roskilde, Denmark, Nov. 20–Dec. 1, 1967.

2 Blum, 2000, 139–140.

3 Blum, 1995, 175–184; Sarah Kershaw, "Joaquin Balaguer, 95, Dies; Dominated Dominican Life," *New York Times*, July 15, 2002, http://nytimes.com/2002/07/15.world/joaquin-balageur-95-ies-dominated-dominican-life.html, accessed October 25, 2014.

The US occupation of the Dominican Republic in the 1960s is significant because it shows the pattern of US intention to thwart popular sovereignty in developing nations. US involvement in SE Asia was just one of many such interventions around the world. This intervention into the Dominican Republic, which lasted until September 1966, was the fifth time in the 20th century the US had invaded and occupied the country. The four others, in 1903, 1904, 1914, and 1916–1924, were also purportedly to "protect American interests."[4] Seven months after the US Marines invaded Viet Nam, a massive overthrow was carried out in Indonesia, beginning in October 1965 (see sidebar).

President Johnson escalated the war against the Vietnamese by ordering US Marines to land in Viet Nam on March 8, 1965, the same day he delivered his war-against-crime message to the Eighty-ninth Congress. In this speech, "Crime, Its Prevalence, and Measures of Prevention," he identified crime as a domestic enemy. In actuality, that war was being waged mainly against inner-city poor African American males; at the same time, White racists and the KKK enjoyed the complicity of the government's southern FBI agents in their attacks on both Blacks and Whites participating in the Civil Rights struggles.

The following chronology reveals how the escalation of the war in Viet Nam and its increasingly barbaric methods revealed to more and more US Americans the immorality of their country's foreign policy. A deep, widespread revulsion eventually built to a kind of collective rage that served as a tipping point and one of the forces that finally brought the war to an end.

Chronology of Barbarism

March 8, 1965. US ground troops are delivered onto the beaches at Da Nang, the first openly acknowledged invasion of the war. The 3rd Battalion of the 9th Marine Regiment and 1st Battalion of the 3rd Marine Regiment from the Third Marine Division (3,500 troops) are ostensibly there to defend the US military base being used in the air war. Joining the 23,000 US military personnel/advisers already in place, the US Marines are greeted by sightseers, prostitutes, and four US Army soldiers (a greeting staged twice in order to capture the "correct" propaganda images for the public back home).[5]

March 9, 1965. President Johnson authorizes the use of napalm.

March 14, 1965. US and South Vietnamese aircraft use napalm over North Viet Nam for the first time.[6]

Spring 1965. The US-supported and funded Ky government decrees neutralism a capital offense, prohibiting "all moves which weaken the national anti-Communist effort and are harmful to the anti-Communist struggle of the people and the Armed Forces," among other behaviors.[7]

---

4 Grimmett.
5 Personal communication, David Scott, ex-US Marine who was part of the March 8, 1965 landing force.
6 Bowman, 108; Bishop, 18.
7 Staughton Lynd and Thomas Hayden, *The Other Side* (New York: New American Library, 1967), 225.

INDONESIA MASSACRE: CIA-FACILITATED, PRECURSOR TO PHOENIX | As part of its efforts to eradicate Communists from strategic Asian nations, the US enthusiastically supported General Suharto and his US-trained and US-armed army's overthrow of neutralist President Sukarno of Indonesia, who was perceived as being friendly with Communists. An earlier US coup attempted against Sukarno in 1958 had failed miserably, despite intelligence provided by U-2 reconnaissance flights, so in this 1965 coup, General Suharto finally offered the US the opportunity it was seeking.[8]

The US Embassy and the CIA station in Jakarta systematically compiled comprehensive lists of "Communist" operatives and provided their names to Suharto's death squads, which led to 500,000 to 1,000,000 murders that wiped out the Indonesian Communist Party.[9] Historian William Blum cites the March 12, 1966 *New York Times*, which described the Indonesian purge as "one of the most savage mass slaughters of modern political history." Historian Peter Dale Scott asserts that this systematic reign of terror by death squads in Indonesia in 1965 served as the model for the subsequent Phoenix program in Viet Nam[10] (see below). It was also the model for subsequent US-funded terror campaigns designed to overthrow Socialist Salvador Allende in Chile in 1973 and death squads in El Salvador and Guatemala in the 1980s that destroyed popular uprisings by restive impoverished peasants seeking basic justice after decades of egregious oligarchic repression.[11]

Indonesia, with its fertile soils, wealth of natural resources, and strategic location, was certainly an important area to control in the minds of US political leaders. As noted earlier in this book, Richard Nixon, while still a private citizen, in a 1965 speech presented in Asia, argued in favor of bombing North Viet Nam to protect the "immense mineral potential" of Indonesia, which he later referred to as "by far the greatest prize in the southeast Asian area."[12]

---

8 Weiner, 142; Beschloss, 151.

9 Ralph McGehee, *Deadly Deceits: My 25 Years in the CIA* (New York: Sheridan Square, 1983), 57; Blum, 1995, 193–194.

10 Peter Dale Scott, "The United States and the Overthrow of Sukarno, 1965–1967," *Pacific Affairs*, 58, Summer 1985.

11 Parry, 10–11.

12 Cited in Peter Dale Scott, "Exporting Military-Economic Development: America and the Overthrow of Sukarno," in Malcolm Caldwell (ed.), *Ten Years' Military Terror in Indonesia* (Nottingham, UK: The Spokesman Journal of the Bertrand Russell Peace Foundation, 1975), 241.

April 7, 1965. Johnson gives a major Viet Nam address at Johns Hopkins University in response to growing antiwar protests on campus. The speech is the first major example of the political impact of campus demonstrations.[13]

April 11, 1965. During a national TV address, Johnson quotes Deuteronomy from the Old Testament, proclaiming, "We will not be defeated. We will not grow tired. We will not withdraw, either openly or under the cloak of a meaningless agreement."[14]

April 26, 1965. McNamara says, with a straight face, "Each target is chosen after a careful review of reconnaissance photographs to ensure that it is isolated and apart from urban populations."[15] His assertion does not match up with a *Washington Post* report that US pilots are "given a square marked on a map and told to hit every hamlet within the area. The pilots know they are sometimes bombing women and children."[16]

July 1, 1965. Viet Cong forces attack the US airbase at Da Nang with mortar support. Three aircraft are destroyed and three others damaged; the assault kills one USAF airman and wounds three Marines.[17]

July 2, 1965. Johnson consults with former President Eisenhower about the dangers of military escalation in Viet Nam. The US death toll stands at 446, and Johnson is worried about the probability of increased casualty numbers. More troubling is the apparent instability of the South Vietnamese government. A junta led by Nguyen Cao Ky is the ninth to seize power in Saigon since Diem's assassination in November of 1963.[18]

July 8, 1965. US Ambassador to Viet Nam Maxwell Taylor is replaced by Henry Cabot Lodge, Jr.[19]

July 28, 1965. Johnson announces shipment of 44 additional combat battalions to Viet Nam, increasing the US presence to 125,000 troops. Monthly draft calls increase to 35,000 per month.[20]

August 5, 1965. CBS airs a report by Morley Safer (*CBS Evening News with Walter Cronkite*) showing Marines in Cam Ne burning villagers' thatched roofs with Zippo lighters. Concluding with critical commentary on the treatment of the villagers, the story generates an angry reaction from Johnson who, convinced that Safer must be a Communist, orders a security check on the reporter. Informed that Safer isn't a Communist, just a Canadian, the president comments, "Well, I knew he wasn't an American."

---

13 Bowman, 111.
14 Roger Neville Williams, *The New Exiles: American War Resister's In Canada* (New York: Liveright Publishers, 1971), 12.
15 Felix Greene, *Vietnam! Vietnam!* (Palo Alto, CA: Fulton Publishing Company, 1966), 101.
16 Doyle and Weiss, 139.
17 Bowman, 119.
18 Weiner, 252.
19 Dougherty and Stewart, 83.
20 Dougherty and Stewart, 83.

August 6, 1965. *Time* magazine reports that US "Marines have begun to kill prisoners" in Viet Nam. [Coincidentally the twentieth anniversary of the US atomic bombing of Hiroshima.]

August 23, 1965. Viet Cong mortars the US airbase at Bien Hoa, damaging 49 aircraft.[21]

September 15, 1965. US bombs hit a kindergarten in the provincial town of Nam Dinh, south of Hanoi. The words above the entrance, translated into English: "Make our children healthy." A cooperative workers' house in the center of the provincial capital is also hit and destroyed sometime during a rash of US bombing raids, July 29, August 2, August 4, and September 15, 1965, two of which take place at night.[22]

September 16, 1965. B-52 bombers hit their first "targets" in the Mekong Delta.[23]

October 4, 1965. Secret bombing of Cambodia begins.[24]

October 9, 1965. In the *National Guardian*, Wilfred Burchett writes, "during August and September there has been systematic bombing of irrigation dams and flood control dikes in an attempt to produce famine and even disastrous flooding of the Red River, which could cost literally millions of lives."[25]

October 18, 1965. *Newsweek* reports the US Air Force flew at least 26,858 sorties against Viet Nam in a *single week*.[26]

October 26, 1965. The New York City Council votes to officially designate a "Support American Viet Nam Effort Day" by a vote of 28-to-2.

October 29, 1965. Civilian presidential aspirant Richard Nixon writes a letter, published in the *New York Times*, in response to an early 1965 Boston antiwar demonstration, in which he declares: "victory for the Viet Cong . . . would mean ultimately the destruction of freedom of speech for all men for all time not only in Asia but in the United States as well."[27]

---

21 Dougherty and Stewart, 84.

22 Greene, 1966, 100–101.

23 Bishop, 30.

24 This is three and a half years prior to the subsequent secret carpet bombings launched by President Nixon that began March 18, 1969. From October 4, 1965 to August 15, 1973, the United States dropped far more ordnance on Cambodia than was previously believed: 2,756,941 tons, dropped in 230,516 sorties on 113,716 sites. Just over 10 percent of this bombing was indiscriminate, with 3,580 of the sites listed as having "unknown" targets and another 8,238 sites having no target listed at all. Civilian casualties in Cambodia drove an enraged populace into the arms of an insurgency that had enjoyed relatively little support until the bombing began, setting in motion the expansion of the Viet Nam war deeper into Cambodia, a coup d'état in 1970, the rapid rise of the Khmer Rouge, and ultimately the Cambodian genocide [Owen and Kiernan, http://japanfocus.org/products/details/2420].

25 Armstrong, 99.

26 Greene, 1966, 158.

27 Greene, 1970, 236. In retrospect, Nixon's statement seems quite mad, considering the fact that all the Vietnamese wanted was self-determination free of imperial outsiders.

October 30, 1965. Twenty-five thousand people turn out for a New York City demonstration in support of the Viet Nam war, led by five recipients of the Congressional Medal of Honor.[28]

December 11, 1965. US engineers begin expanding military facilities in Thailand.[29]

January 1, 1966. US Senator Strom Thurmond states that nuclear weapons should be used if necessary to gain victory in Viet Nam.[30]

February 23, 1966. The US mission in Saigon discloses that 90,000 South Vietnamese soldiers deserted in 1965, almost 14 percent of ARVN troop strength, twice the number of 1964 desertions. In contrast, the US estimates that fewer than 20,000 Viet Cong defected during the previous year.[31]

March 9, 1966. The State Department issues a 52-page document arguing US intervention in Viet Nam is legally justified under international law, the UN Charter, and the US Constitution.[32]

March 16, 1966. Reporting on his recent visit to Viet Nam, US Rep. Clement Zablocki (D-WI) asserts that for every Viet Cong guerrilla killed in recent search-and-destroy missions, six civilians have been killed.[33]

January 18, 1966. In a flagrant disregard for civilians, a memo drafted by Assistant Secretary of Defense/War John McNaughton suggests destroying locks and dams as a tactic to create mass starvation.[34]

March 19, 1966. South Korea sends 20,000 additional troops to Viet Nam to join the 21,000 Korean troops already there.[35] Known for being fierce fighters, the Koreans are essentially mercenaries, paid by the US for their support.

Early 1966. McNamara argues that to achieve peace with the North Vietnamese, US military strength will need to be increased. He recommends calling up 235,000 men in the US Reserve and National Guard and increasing regular armed forces by approximately 375,000. The latter will necessitate expanding the draft and extending tours of men already on active duty. By mid-1966, these measures will produce approximately 600,000 additional men.[36]

---

28 Bowman, 128.
29 Bowman, 131.
30 Bowman, 132.
31 Bowman, 136.
32 Bowman, 136.
33 Bowman, 137.
34 *The Pentagon Papers*, Gravel Edition, Volume 4, Chapter I, "The Air War in North Vietnam, 1965–1968," pp. 1–276 (Boston: Beacon Press, 1971).
35 Bowman, 137.
36 Kahin, 1986, 364. Note: Though McNamara's recommendations were tempered a bit by Johnson, I was caught up in this increased draft rate and received my draft notice in March 1966 during my fourth semester of law school.

THE HO CHI MINH TRAIL: B-52s VERSUS BICYCLES, SHOVELS, AND THE RESILIENT DETERMINATION OF THE VIETNAMESE PEOPLE | The Ho Chi Minh Trail was an elaborate system of roads, depots, and rest areas that facilitated movement of military materiel and associated supplies from North Viet Nam to the North Vietnamese Army (NVA) and Viet Cong (VC) fighters in various areas of South Viet Nam. A lifeline for all those Vietnamese fighting to defend their country from US invasion and occupation, the trail laced in and out of Laos along the two countries' joint border.

In 1963, the Ho Chi Minh Trail was more than six hundred miles long.[37] In addition to the thousands of people carrying up to ten thousand tons of supplies a week (by trucks after the trail was subsequently widened), units of fighters worked their way south on draft animals, bicycles, and on foot, many preparing for coordinated combat operations. In early 1964, the trail was still so narrow it was only passable by bicycle or pack animals, including occasional elephants. The trail was paved heading south to the Mu Gia Pass about 70 miles north of the demilitarized zone (DMZ), where it passed into Laos, but the remaining southward trail for several years early on in the war was passable only to walkers, animals, and bicycles.

Bicycles, a most appropriate technology the Vietnamese called *steel horses*, rolled around the clock to keep the trail open despite incessant high-tech US bombings. Bicycles—modified with extra suspension, stronger frames, widened handlebars fitted with pallets, and rear carriers—were the most durable and consistent carriers of supplies. Each one could carry 300–400 pounds, compared to the maximum of a walker's 80 pounds. An exceptional bicycle could carry a ton per week.[38]

Villagers living along the trail worked day and night with shovels and human spirit to keep it open, and were usually able to repair it within a few hours of each bombing. The Vietnamese who toiled day and night moving supplies or repairing the trail faced many hazards—not only exposure to constant bombing and toxic herbicides, but malaria and severe weather. Many thousands were killed and maimed.

continued...

---

37 Caputo, 38.

38 John Prados, *The Blood Road: The Ho Chi Minh Trail and the Vietnam War* (New York: John Wiley & Sons, 1999), 2, 27, 85, 372–378; *Wikipedia*, Ho Chi Minh Trail: http://en.wikipedia.org/wiki/Ho_Chi_Minh_trail; Jim Fitzpatrick, *The Bicycle in Wartime: An Illustrated History* (Kilcoy, Queensland, Australia: Star Hill, 2011), "The Bicycle in Vietnam," 175–204.

> By 1970, the Ho Chi Minh Trail extended 12,000 miles connecting five main roads and twenty-nine branch roads with many smaller pathways, cutoffs and bypasses. Between 1964 and 1972, fighter-bombers flew 426,000 sorties against areas of lower Laos, with B-52s adding at least 30,000 more. The 1.7 million tons of bombs dropped on the lower trail were the equivalent of more than a dozen Hiroshimas. The men and women working on the trail regularly defused thousands of unexploded bombs, destroyed thousands of magnetic bombs and anti-personnel mines, while taking 1,196 prisoners from downed US aircrews and members of infiltrating commando ground units, and from the ill-fated US and South Vietnamese 1971 invasion of Laos, code-named *Lam Son 719* (Dewey Canyon II). The total volume of materials moved down the trail in 1974 was twenty-two times what had been moved in 1966.[39] Much of the chemical warfare waged by US and allied forces targeted the trail, heavily spraying the triple canopy forest with defoliants in order to uncover the human activity, providing clearer targets for their bombers.

April 12, 1966. US B-52s begin bombing the Ho Chi Minh Trail.[40]

April 20, 1966. McNamara reports to the Senate Foreign Relations Committee that the US is preparing to drop 638,000 tons of bombs on Viet Nam—half the total used by the US against Nazi forces in Europe and Africa in all of World War II.[41]

May 11, 1966. President Johnson declares, "We have used our power in Vietnam with great restraint."[42]

May 12, 1966. It is revealed the US is spending $7 million *every day* on mortar and artillery shells, and bullets for machine guns and rifles.[43]

August 1966. Twenty US soldiers are killed when one of their own planes mistakenly bombs them with napalm. Meanwhile, US aid continues to flow to Viet Nam at the rate of a billion dollars a month—some 40 percent of it into the pockets of the Vietnamese elite.[44] Johnson finds it increasingly difficult to

---

39 Prados, 1999, 372–378. Prados notes that Vietnamese records produced in the 1990s revealed 1,777,072 tons of supplies were moved down the main trail during the years 1965–1975. This averaged 487 tons a day to supply a dozen regular North Vietnamese divisions (as many as 180,000 troops) plus as many as 600,000 Viet Cong. In contrast, since each US soldier required 50 pounds a day of supplies, during the peak US troop strength (late 1968–early 1969), the US daily requirement was 13,700 tons a day to supply 543,000 troops. Thus, on average US troops required 28 times the amount of supplies to remain operational than the NVA and Viet Cong. Comparison of the amount of supplies needed to service the two sides shows that superiority in numbers does not necessarily equate to superiority of strategy nor lead to "success" of a military mission.

40 *Wikipedia,* Ho Chi Minh trail: http://en.wikipedia.org/wiki/Ho_Chi_Minh_trail

41 Greene, 1966, 158.

42 Greene, 1966, 158.

43 Greene, 1966, 158.

44 Glennon, 484.

maintain the rationale for his war policy as the number and intensity of war critics increases. During a private conversation with reporters, when asked to explain why we are still in Viet Nam, Johnson loses his temper and suddenly unzips his fly, pulls out his penis, and declares, "This is why!"[45]

October 5, 1966. McNamara tells President Johnson, "We're going to just snow the place under with bombs, and I'm doing it purposely to make them cry 'Stop.'"[46] US troops are given permission to use tear gas in operations in Viet Nam.[47]

October 31–November 1, 1966. Johnson remarks before US troops stationed in Korea: "There are three billion people in the world and we have only 200 million of them. We are outnumbered 15 to one. If might did make right, they would sweep over the United States and take what we have. We have what they want."[48]

November 2, 1966. Speaking before a civic meeting in Anchorage, Alaska on his way back from Viet Nam, Johnson says: "If we are going to have visits from any aggressors or any enemies, I would rather have that aggression take place out 10,000 miles from here than take place here in Anchorage."[49]

January 8, 1967. Thirty thousand US and ARVN troops are launched in Operation Cedar Falls, an ambitious effort to eliminate Viet Cong strongholds in the Iron Triangle 20 miles north of Saigon in Bing Duong Province near the border with Cambodia. US forces bomb all the villages and spray the rice crops and jungles with deadly herbicides in preparation for a blitzkrieg. The infantry, accompanied by tanks and huge bulldozers called Rome Plows, attempt to eradicate "enemy" webs of bunkers and tunnels, while forcing 7,000 peasants to resettle elsewhere, leaving behind their ancestral lands and most of their possessions and farm animals. This disruption of villages is an early effort to deny the Viet Cong support and supplies.[50]

January 26, 1967. At the conclusion of Operation Cedar Falls, commander Major General William DuPuy proclaims it "a blow from which the VC in this area may never recover." Typical of US Americans, DuPuy has little knowledge of Vietnamese history and culture, let alone the tenacity of the Viet Cong, who quickly return and resume control of the area.[51]

---

45 Robert Dallek, *Flawed Giant: Lyndon Johnson and His Times, 1961–1973* (New York: Oxford University Press, 1998), 491.

46 "New LBJ White House Tapes Released . . . Through End of 1966," *American-Statesman*, November 18, 2006].

47 Bishop, 32.

48 Chomsky, 1969, 249.

49 The American Presidency Project: americanpresidency.org, Lyndon B. Johnson; Noam Chomsky, *The Essential Chomsky* (New York: The New Press, 2008), 226.

50 Caputo, 42.

51 Caputo, 42.

The Phoenix Program[52]

As early as 1962, the CIA had created, in Viet Nam, so-called counter-terror (CT) teams, hunter-killer teams made up of 5 to 20 well trained and aggressive men. Some CT members were disillusioned former Viet Cong, tasked to collect intelligence and apprehend suspected Viet Cong leaders. CT teams were similar in structure to domestic "Special Weapons And Tactics" or SWAT teams created in the late 1960s in the US.[53] The CIA's comprehensive program for eradicating "Communists" in Indonesia, developed in 1965 (see sidebar, p. 125), served as a blueprint for the US Military's Phoenix program, phoenix being the English translation for the Vietnamese word *Phung Hoang*, a colorful mythical bird that has the ability to fly anywhere. In 1966, the Vietnamese CTs took on the more benign name of provincial reconnaissance units (PRUs).[54]

In 1967, the CIA transferred several of its "pacification" elements to what became Civil Operations and Revolutionary Development Support, or CORDS. That May, CIA officer Robert Komer, working directly with national security adviser Walt Rostow in the Johnson White House, arrived in Saigon as head of CORDS with full ambassadorial rank, answering only to MACV Commander Westmoreland and US Ambassador Ellsworth Bunker.[55] Believing in the success of Cedar Falls (see p. 131) in supposedly eradicating the local population of the Iron Triangle, MACV became excited about the prospects of forced urbanization as a way to deny peasant support to the North Vietnamese and Viet Cong. Komer strategized that the process of "degrading" the enemy could be accelerated by reducing its population base with an aggressive pacification program.[56] Komer was nicknamed "Blowtorch" for the passion he brought to pacification programs.[57]

CORDS integrated civilian and military efforts at all levels in a single chain of command as CIA strength in Viet Nam peaked at more than 700 staff.[58] CORDS created the Intelligence Coordination and Exploitation (ICEX) group to coordinate central intelligence for CIA agents, US civilian and military personnel, and the Saigon military-intelligence-police network, developing especially detailed computerized biographical information on anyone suspected of being in the Viet Cong Infrastructure (VCI).[59] As Vietnamese were designated Viet Cong targets in village-by-village assessments, the secret Vietnamese police and the PRUs became *the* active death squads terrorizing the VCI.[60] It was not

---

52 In Greek folklore, Phoenix is a centuries long-lived bird that cyclically burns to death, then arises from its own ashes.
53 Valentine, 45.
54 Prados, 2003, 186.
55 Valentine, 127.
56 Karnow, 439.
57 Chomsky, 1979, 308.
58 Dougherty and Stewart, 102; Prados, 2003, 186.
59 Prados, 2003, 188; Valentine, 131.
60 Prados, 2003, 195–197.

unusual for US operatives in the Phoenix program to give orders to "take out a village" and "take no prisoners ... all the people are Communist sympathizers."[61]

In 1966, when McNamara asked the CIA to create a technique by which to measure trends in pacification, Komer had devised a hamlet evaluation system (HES) by which every hamlet in the country could be graded for both "security" and "development." How many peasants were under control of the South Vietnamese government? How many had moved from the debit to credit side of the anti-Communist camp? US military advisers assigned to 222 of South Viet Nam's 242 districts used worksheets to evaluate "progress." In the fall of 1967, General Westmoreland was sufficiently gratified that 75 percent of the population (12 million South Vietnamese) was pacified. He believed the "cross-over point" had been reached, meaning that US and ARVN troops were killing the enemy faster than they could be replaced, and concluded that attrition was working.[62] Westmoreland had estimated from his data a total of 285,000 NLF and North Vietnamese troops fighting in the South. But the CIA separately counted the number of enemy at between 500,000 and 600,000. If accurate, the higher CIA figures proved that progress in fact had not been made. It appeared that the NLF was recruiting people from numerous local communities in the South, not from the North. For comparison, the number of military forces from US American, South Vietnamese, Korean, Thai, Filipino, and Australian armies combined totaled 1,300,000.[63]

ICEX quickly morphed into the White House–supported Operation Phoenix assassination program, and Komer was replaced with William Colby of the CIA. Phoenix succeeded in "neutralizing" some 84,000 members of the VCI with 21,000 killed according to some reports. The South Vietnamese government later claimed that 40,994 suspected civilians were killed (murdered) under Phoenix, from its inception in August 1968 to the middle of 1971.[64]

A quota system rewarded those credited with neutralizing VCI—$11,000 for a live VCI and half that for a dead one. Success was measured by body counts and the number of captured civil detainees, who were all listed as VCI, even though most were women and children. Detainees were regularly brutalized, and torture was standard policy of both US and South Vietnamese government interrogators. Ex-prisoners claimed that more than 90 percent of arrestees were tortured. The South Vietnamese police had a favorite saying: "If they are innocent, beat them until they become guilty."[65] A November 5, 1971 United Press International (UPI) report published in *Le Monde* quoted a US adviser saying that local officials in the Delta killed outright 80 percent of captured "suspects."[66]

---

61 John Doe, "Phoenix Program," found in Harold V. Hall and Leighton C. Whitaker, eds., *Collective Violence: Effective Strategies For Assessing and Intervening in Fatal Group and Institutional Aggression* (New York: CRC Press, 1999), 633–642.
62 Young, 1991, 213–214; Gibson, 305–311.
63 Young, 1991, 214.
64 Chomsky, 1979, 323–324; McGehee, 141.
65 Chomsky, 1979, 325.
66 Chomsky, 1979, 327.

Chronology of Barbarism Continued

November 17, 1967. Following an optimistic White House briefing with General Westmoreland, Ambassador Bunker, and Komer, Johnson tells the American television audience, "We are inflicting greater losses than we're taking.... We are making progress."[67]

November 22, 1967. A *New York Times* article titled "Westmoreland Says Ranks of Vietcong Thin Steadily," quotes the general: "The enemy's hopes are bankrupt," "[his forces are] declining at a steady rate," and "he can fight his large forces only at the edge of his sanctuaries [in other countries]," so now "[the war's end] begins to come into view" as "[the South Vietnamese army] will take charge of the final mopping up of the Vietcong."[68]

November 29, 1967. An emotional McNamara announces his plan to resign as Defense/War Secretary during a press briefing, stating, "Mr. President . . . I cannot find words to express what lies in my heart today. . . ." Behind closed doors, he has begun to regularly express doubts about Johnson's war strategy, angering the president. McNamara joins a growing list of Johnson's top aides who have resigned over the war, including Bill Moyers, McGeorge Bundy, and George Ball.[69]

December 23, 1967. Upon returning from his second visit to Viet Nam, Johnson declares, "all the challenges have been met. The enemy is not beaten, but he knows that he has met his master in the field." Made just five weeks before the TET offensive, this would be Johnson's final trip to Viet Nam.[70]

December 23, 1967. *National Guardian* journalist Wilfred Burchett, who had spent much time accompanying the Viet Cong, claims the NLF are taking the initiative in the war, planning a major offensive, and "able to mount simultaneous attacks on widely separated objectives in divisional strength."[71] The contrast between claims made by US military and political leaders and major US media, and Burchett's insider reporting could not have been more dramatic.

December 31, 1967. Invitations to the US Embassy's New Year's Eve party in Saigon read: "Come see the light at the end of the tunnel."[72]

December 31, 1967. US military troops in Viet Nam number 485,600.[73]

---

67 ABC-TV News coverage of President Johnson Press Conference, November 17, 1967.
68 H. Bruce Franklin, 2000, 92.
69 http://www.historyplace.com/unitedstates/vietnam/index-1965.html, *The History Place*, "The Vietnam War: The Jungle War, 1965–1968"
70 http://www.historyplace.com/unitedstates/vietnam/index-1965.html
71 H. B. Franklin, 2000, 93.
72 Jonathan Neale, *The American War: Vietnam 1960–1975* (London, UK: Bookmarks, 2001), 92.
73 Summers, 1999, 44.

January 24, 1968. Robert Komer proclaims at a Saigon press conference: "We begin '68 in a better position than we have ever been before, but we've still got problems of bureaucratic inefficiency." In the same press conference, he says, "Let me say briefly I don't see how we can fail to do somewhat better in 1968 than we've done in 1967."[74]

January 26, 1968. Westmoreland's optimistic year-end report reaches officials in Washington just four days before the start of the TET offensive:[75]

> "The year [1967] ended with the enemy increasingly resorting to desperation tactics in attempting to achieve military/psychological victory; and he has experienced only failure in these attempts. . . . The enemy lost control of large sectors of the population . . . In many areas the enemy has been driven away from the population centers; in others he has been compelled to disperse and evade contact, thus nullifying much of his potential . . . The friendly picture gives rise to optimism for increased successes in 1968."

The Tet Offensive

It was Vietnamese civilians who bore the brunt of devastation as their villages were systematically destroyed along with the village life essential to Vietnamese culture. Prior to 1968, there were already 800,000 refugees in the south. By 1972 the number would grow to five million out of a total population of 18 million.[76] (Another source identifies 10 million southern refugees in 1972 out of a total population of 19 million, citing reports of the US Senate.[77])

Late in January 1968, a large sign in both English and Vietnamese was erected at the entrance of the US Navy base next to the Binh Thuy airbase. The English words: "*Wishes Our Vietnamese Friends A Happy New Year & A Successful TET.*" Tet is short for Tết Nguyên Đán, the traditional Vietnamese celebration of Lunar New Year. Little did they know what was about to happen!

With the launch of the Tet Offensive, the optimism of Westmoreland, Johnson, et al., proved to be a lie, even though the NLF fighting units suffered tremendous losses from which they would never fully recover.

Tet 1968 saw an offensive campaign that continued from the opening salvo January 30–31 until mid-March, leading to deepening embitterment of US attitudes toward

---

[74] Dennis Bloodworth, *An Eye for the Dragon: Southeast Asia Observed, 1954–1970* (New York: Farrar, Straus and Giroux, 1970), 314.

[75] From Westmoreland year-end report, as cited in *The Pentagon Papers* (Gravel ed.), Vol. IV, 538, 539; Dave Richard Palmer, *Summons of the Trumpet* (New York: Presidio Press, 1995), 263.

[76] Cincinnatus, 24, 233, 99.

[77] Gettleman et al., 1995, 5.

the Vietnamese, and contributing to increased atrocities and murders of civilians. As historian Wilfred Burchett tells it:[78]

> [The NLF forces carried out an action] unparalleled in military history, launching a surprise attack along a front of over 700 miles, in many cases seizing and occupying, at least temporarily, virtually every important town from the 17th parallel down to the Ca Mau peninsula in the deep south of the Mekong Delta. Eleven out of 14 major air bases were attacked, 30 airfields in all, including a number occupied long enough to destroy all planes and helicopters.

Tet 1968 was, in effect, a massive popular movement that coordinated about 84,000 NLF and NVA troops in mounting simultaneous assaults on:[79]

- five of the six largest cities in the country;
- 36 of the 44 provincial capitals;
- 64 of the 242 district towns;
- 50 hamlets;
- Cholon, the sprawling Chinese section in Saigon;
- the heavily fortified US Embassy in Saigon;
- the imperial city of Hue.

Thirteen of the sixteen provincial capitals of the Mekong Delta and many of the district capitals were initially attacked.[80] As many as 200,000 prisoners were freed, making up in numbers for war casualties.[81]

CHRONOLOGY OF BARBARISM CONTINUED

February 7, 1968. For many hours, Air Force Major Chester L. Brown circles above the city of Ben Tre (pop. 140,000) in Kien Hoa Province directing air and artillery fire onto the homes and businesses below, until it is pulverized. Eighty-five percent of the city is destroyed over three days of attacks. "It became necessary to destroy the town in order to save it," Brown later tells the press.[82]

February 10, 1968. Journalist Wilfred Burchett's headline in the *National Guardian*: "Vietnam: The Lies Crumble."[83] The invincibility of the US has been punctured.

February 27, 1968. CBS evening news anchor Walter Cronkite, in a special report entitled "Who, What, When, Where, Why?" provides editorial observations

---

[78] Wilfred G. Burchett, *Vietnam: Inside Story of the Guerrilla War* (New York: International Publishers, 1968), v.
[79] Summers, 1995, 130–131.
[80] Young, 1991, 220.
[81] H. B. Franklin, 2000, 95.
[82] Griffiths, 120–121.
[83] H. B. Franklin, 2000, 96.

based on his recent trip to Viet Nam, where he observed the Tet Offensive. At the end of the broadcast, Cronkite says, "For it seems now more certain than ever that the bloody experience of Vietnam is to end in a stalemate." LBJ is quoted as saying, after watching Cronkite's broadcast, "That's it. If I've lost Cronkite, I've lost middle America."[84]

March 4, 1968. New US Secretary of Defense/War Vance Clifford recommends that Operation Phoenix be pursued more vigorously in closer liaison with US intelligence and military planners.[85]

March 31, 1968. President Johnson announces he will not seek nor accept nomination for another term as president, throwing the US political scene into a wild scramble. As the antiwar movement in the US builds in momentum, Johnson is overwhelmed by the fact that US military success in Vietnam looks ever more doubtful, and is determined not to be the first president to lose a war.

The My Lai Massacre and its Elaborate Coverup

On March 16, 1968, in the hamlet of My Lai in Son My Village, Quang Ngai Province, members of I Corps[86]—more than 100 soldiers of C Company ("Charlie"), 1st Battalion, 20th Infantry, 11th Infantry Brigade, Americal Division—massacred 504 unarmed civilians without a single shot ever fired against company soldiers.[87] (As will be illustrated in the next chapter, extreme acts of violence were being perpetrated at home as well as in Viet Nam. Less than three weeks later, on April 4, 1968, Martin Luther King Jr., would be assassinated in Memphis, Tennessee.)

News of the My Lai Massacre reached Europeans much sooner than the US American public. On May 16, 1968, exactly two months after the atrocity, details were published in the French publication *Sud Vietnam en Lutte*, and in *Bulletin du Vietnam*, a publication of the North Vietnamese delegation to the Paris Peace talks. However, the story was not picked up in the US press. The massacre, mostly of children and women, was immediately covered up and not reported publicly in the US press until November 13, 1969.

---

84 "Walter Cronkite: The Most Trusted Man." *Columbia Journalism Review,* Nov-Dec 2001, v40 i4, 64(1); Don Arnold, "Other Campus Life," The Touchstone, 9(5), Nov./Dec. 1999.

85 Chomsky and Herman, 323, citing *The Pentagon Papers*. Interestingly, on the same date, March 4, 1968, one month to the day before Martin Luther King, Jr.'s assassination, Hoover issued a memo identifying FBI goals in a counter-intelligence program targeting "Black Nationalist Hate-Groups":

"1. Prevent the coalition of militant black nationalist groups ... [which] might be the first step toward a real 'Mau Mau' in America, the beginning of a true black revolution; 2. Prevent the rise of a messiah who could unify and electrify the militant black nationalist movement.... King could be a very real contender for this position should he abandon his supposed 'obedience' to 'white, liberal doctrines' (nonviolence) and embrace black nationalism...."

86 The US military command divided South Viet Nam into four tactical zones, or military geographical regions, namely I Corps (northern), II Corps (central), III Corps (Saigon and proximal areas to) and IV Corps (southern/Mekong Delta).

87 Seymour Hersh, *My Lai 4: A Report on the Massacre and its Aftermath* (New York: Random House, 1970), 44–60; William Thomas Allison, *My Lai: An American Atrocity in the Vietnam War* (Baltimore: Johns Hopkins University Press, 2012), 33, 36, 41, 43, 74, 97, 107.

The author in front of statue at the My Lai Massacre war vestige site near Quang Ngai, Viet Nam, during a April 2016 visit. [Photo: Becky Luening]

Ex-combat Americal infantryman Ron Ridenhour gathered information about the incident at My Lai by interviewing Americal comrades who had participated in the massacre. It was Ridenhour's March 1969 report, which he forwarded to the Army inspector general, that led to the official investigation.[88]

---

88 Hersh, 1970, 104.

The author, seated next to the names of 504 Vietnamese civilians who were massacred at My Lai on March 16, 1968, by American forces. April 2016. [Photo: Mike Hastie]

Finally, on November 24, 1969, Lt. General W. R. Peers was directed by the secretary of the Army to review "possible suppression or withholding of information by persons involved in the incident" at My Lai. After more than 26,000 pages worth of testimony was gathered from 403 witnesses, Peers' inquiry recommended charges be brought against 28 officers and two noncommissioned officers involved in a cover-up of the massacre. The Peers report concluded that the brigade commander, Colonel Oran Henderson, and the commanding officer, Lt. Colonel Frank Barker, had substantial knowledge of the war crime but did nothing about it. Meanwhile, in a separate investigation by the Army's Criminal Investigation Division, it was concluded that 33 of the 105 members of Charlie Company participated in the massacre, and that 28 officers helped cover it up. They discovered enough evidence to charge 30 soldiers with the crimes of murder, rape, sodomy, and mutilation. Seventeen of the men had left the Army, so charges against them were dropped.[89] In the end, charges were brought against 13 men, but only six cases were ever tried—even though in some cases the evidence was overwhelming, and some of the defendants admitted killing the civilians.

---

89 Hersh, 1970, 171–180.

In the end, only one man was found guilty. Lieutenant William Calley was convicted of premeditated murder of 104 villagers at My Lai.[90] Calley was immediately sentenced to life imprisonment at Leavenworth Penitentiary, but, due to the political nature of the crime and the trial, he only served three and a half years in house arrest at his quarters at Fort Benning, Georgia, before being pardoned by President Nixon in 1974.

Henderson, who had been charged with the My Lai cover-up, told reporters in 1971, "Every unit of brigade size has its My Lai hidden someplace."[91]

Colin Powell's Peripheral Role in the Coverup

Major Colin Powell returned to Viet Nam on July 27, 1968, for his second tour as chief of operations for the commander of the Americal division. He became privy to a letter written by specialist fourth class Tom Glen sent to Creighton Abrams, commander of all US forces in Viet Nam, accusing the Americal division of routine brutality against civilians. In his letter, which had been forwarded to Americal headquarters, Glen wrote, "Far beyond merely dismissing the Vietnamese as 'slopes' or 'gooks,' in both deed and thought, too many American soldiers seem to discount their very humanity; and with this attitude inflict upon the Vietnamese citizenry humiliations, both psychological and physical, that can have only a debilitating effect." Glen contended that many Vietnamese were fleeing from Americans who "for mere pleasure, fire indiscriminately into Vietnamese homes and without provocation or justification shoot at the people themselves." Gratuitous cruelty was also being inflicted on Viet Cong suspects, Glen reported. Glen had heard secondhand about the My Lai massacre, which he concluded was just one part of the abusive pattern that had become routine in the division.

The letter's disturbing allegations were not well received at Americal headquarters. Powell reviewed Glen's letter but chose not to question Glen or assign anyone else to do so. Powell accepted at face value a claim from Glen's superior officer that Glen did not know what he was talking about. In Powell's response, dated December 13, 1968, he simply asserted that US soldiers were taught to treat Vietnamese courteously and respectfully, noting that Americal troops had all gone through an hour-long course on how to treat prisoners of war under the Geneva Conventions. Powell concluded, "relations between Americal soldiers and the Vietnamese people are excellent." In other words, he reported exactly what his superiors wanted to hear.[92]

Colin Powell's peripheral role in the My Lai cover-up did not slow his climb up the Army's ladder. In his best-selling memoir, *My American Journey,* Powell never mentioned the fact that he ignored Army Specialist Tom Glen's complaint of routine soldier brutality toward civilians.[93] Powell pleaded ignorance about My Lai, which had predated his arrival at the Americal. Powell retired from the US Army at the rank of four-star general and then

---

90 Steven Mintz and Sara McNeil (2013). *The My Lai Massacre: Report of the Department of the Army Review* (1970). Digital History: http://www.digitalhistory.uh.edu/disp_textbook.cfm?smtID=3&psid=1171.

91 Zinn, 1980, 181.

92 For all facts related in this and preceding paragraph: Robert Parry and Norman Solomon, "Behind Colin Powell's Legend," *The Consortium,* 1996: https://consortiumnews.com/archive/colin3.html

93 Colin Powell, *My American Journey* (New York: Ballantine Books, 1996).

became National Security Advisor to President Reagan, chair of the Joint Chiefs of Staff during the first Gulf massacre, and Secretary of State under President Bush II.

My Lai Heroes:
Hugh Thompson, Lawrence Colburn, Glenn Andreotta

Many additional civilians, beyond the staggering number of 504, would certainly have been murdered at My Lai had it not been for the principled actions of one US helicopter crew: pilot Hugh Thompson and door gunners Lawrence Colburn and Glenn Andreotta. Observing the terrible scene from above, Thompson set his helicopter down near an irrigation ditch full of bodies. When Thompson asked the soldiers on the ground to help the civilians, some of whom were still alive, some soldiers responded by suggesting they should shoot them out of their misery. Stunned, Thompson reluctantly got back in his helicopter and began to lift off. He flew around, wondering what to do. He and his gunners then observed elderly adults and children running for shelter, being chased by soldiers. "We thought they had about 30 seconds before they'd die," recalled Colburn. Thompson proceeded to land his chopper between the troops and the civilians, jumped out and confronted an officer, and asked for assistance in escorting the civilians out of the shelter. The officer responded he would get them out with a hand grenade. Furious, Thompson announced he would take the civilians out, turned to Colburn and Andreotta and ordered them to shoot any Americans who fired. "Glenn and I were staring at each other, dumbfounded," said Colburn. The ground soldiers waited and watched, but there were no further shootings. Andreotta died shortly thereafter in combat operations.[94]

At the eventual trial, the eyewitness testimony of Thompson and Colburn proved crucial. But instead of thanking them, the two heroes were vilified in the American press. Many saw Calley as a scapegoat for regrettable but inevitable civilian casualties. "Rallies for Calley" were held all over the country. Jimmy Carter, then governor of Georgia, urged citizens to leave car headlights on to show support for Calley. Thompson, who got nasty letters and death threats, remembered thinking: "Has everyone gone mad?" He feared he would be court-martialed for his command to Colburn and Andreotta to fire if necessary on fellow US soldiers.[95]

But Thompson was not court-martialed, and he and Colburn lived in relative quiet until 1989 when a documentary on My Lai was aired on television. David Egan, a Clemson University professor, campaigned to have Thompson and his team awarded the coveted Soldier's Medal. However, it wasn't until March 6, 1998, after much internal squabbling among Pentagon officials fearing a new rash of bad publicity, and facing increased pressure from reporters, that Thompson and Colburn received their well-deserved medals at a ceremony at the Vietnam Veterans Memorial Wall in Washington, DC.[96]

---

94 Neil Boyce, "Hugh Thompson, Reviled, Then Honored for His Actions at My Lai," *US News & World Report*, August 20, 2001.
95 Boyce.
96 Boyce.

Tiger Force Massacres

Tiger Force was founded by Major David Hackworth in November 1965 to "out-guerrilla the guerrillas." A 45-man reconnaissance platoon of the 1st Battalion, 327th Infantry, 101st Airborne Division, it operated in small teams, often groups of twos and threes wearing camouflage and carrying enough rations and supplies to last several weeks. Only 45 men were accepted in the Tigers after being tested for experience and proficiency in combat; the soldier's willingness to kill had to be demonstrated.

In spring 1967, Tiger Force operations throughout the Quang Ngai Province territory in I Corp consisted of a series of wanton atrocities: burning homes to the ground, destroying rice crops and cattle, tying up, then torturing countless civilians before murdering them. They brutally cut off ears, slit throats. After their onslaught, 70 to 80 percent of all homes and their occupants had been wiped out, from inland to the South China Sea. Survivors were herded into deplorable refugee camps.

By late summer, the death squad unit had moved into Quang Tin Province to the north, where it continued atrocity after atrocity. And on and on it went. Estimates of civilian casualties in the path of Tiger Force rampages were as high as 50,000 per year.[97]

South Korean Massacres

From September 1965 to March 1973, the South Korean Marine Corps (ROKMC) 2nd (Blue Dragon) Brigade, Capital (Tiger) Division, and 9th (White Horse) Division, operated with US Marines and the US Army's Americal Division (23rd Infantry Division), marauding II Corp's coastal provinces, from the cities of Qui Nhon in the north to Phan Rang in the south. South Korean *mercenary* forces, numbering 50,000 at any one time, were paid 100 percent by the US.[98] They committed a series of My Lai–scale massacres with aggregate murders running into the thousands. Quakers documented at least 12 separate massacres of 100 or more civilians, and dozens of other massacres of 20 or more unarmed civilians plus countless individual murders, robberies, rapes, tortures, and destruction of land and personal property.[99]

Bob Kerrey's Massacre

Lieutenant Bob Kerrey's SEAL unit committed an atrocity in which as many as 24 villagers were murdered, at least half of them women and children. The incident took place in Thang Phong Village, Kien Hoa Province in the Delta, 50 miles east of Binh Thuy. Kerrey's unit first came to this village on February 13, 1969, to look for the senior Viet Cong leader in

---

97 Nick Turse, *Kill Anything That Moves* (New York: Metropolitan Books, 2013), 135–143; Sheehan, 686–687; in general, see Michael Sallah and Mitch Weiss, *Tiger Force* (New York: Back Bay Books, 2006).

98 August 21–22, 1969, President Nixon met with South Korean dictator/President Park Chung Hee in San Francisco where Nixon praised South Korea for having more fighting men (i.e., US paid mercenaries) in Viet Nam than any other country other than the US and South Viet Nam. He announced intention to provide an additional $250 million to maintain South Korea's 50,000-man Tiger Division.

99 Chomsky and Herman, 321; Summers, 1995, 154.

SYSTEMATIC MURDER, SYSTEMATIC LIES | In 2009, Lt. William Calley, in a talk before members of the Kiwanis Club of Greater Columbus, Georgia, publicly apologized for his participation in the My Lai massacre. "There is not a day that goes by that I do not feel remorse for what happened that day in My Lai," Calley confessed. His voice started to break when he added, "I feel remorse for the Vietnamese who were killed, for their families, for the American soldiers involved and their families. I am very sorry." He reiterated that he was merely following the orders of his superior officers, which was the truth.[100]

Mass murder of unarmed civilians proved to be a direct and predictable consequence of US military "pacification," manifesting in such tactics as "search and destroy" (*scorched earth*) and "free-fire zones." Operation Wheeler Wallawa, in 1967–1968, claimed 10,000 killed (including those at My Lai on March 16, 1968); though most were civilians, they were "counted" as VC. Operation Speedy Express (1968–1969) killed nearly 11,000, the vast majority of them civilians; probably very few authentic guerrillas.[101] *Newsweek* reporters in-country declared mass killings were "a matter of policy."[102]

Though exceptional in its scale of destruction and mass murder for a specific ground operation, versus the destruction caused by massive numbers of bombings, the My Lai massacre "reflected the patterns and psychology of brutalization at the heart of US military operations in Viet Nam." A further tragedy is that the massacre has nearly disappeared from collective American memory. Very few young people today even recognize the name.[103]

While the US sought to stifle active dissent in the military and domestically, using repressive tactics as well as illegal covert operations, it was overtly, systematically committing mass murder in Southeast Asia under the pretexts provided by systematic lies—noble-sounding rhetoric.

the area, known as the *village secretary*. Former SEAL squad member Gerhard Klann told *60 Minutes II* (May 1, 2001) and the *New York Times* (April 29, 2001) that on February 25, the Vietnamese civilians were herded into a group and massacred, an account denied by Kerrey. But Klann's account was virtually the same as that of a surviving Vietnamese eyewitness. At the time, the surrounding area was part of Operation Speedy Express,

---

100 Dick McMichael, "William Calley Apologizes for My Lai Massacre," *Ledger-Enquirer*, August 21, 2009.

101 Noam Chomsky and E. S. Herman, *The Washington Connection and Third World Fascism: The Political Economy Of Human Rights—Volume I* (Boston: South End Press, 1979) 313-321; Kevin Buckley, "Pacification's Deadly Price," *Newsweek*, June 19, 1972, 42–43.

102 John Marciano, *The American War in Vietnam: Crime or Commemoration?* (New York: Monthly Review Press, 2016), 128.

103 Christian Appy, *Working-Class War* (Chapel Hill, NC: University of North Carolina Press, 1993), 277.

which, in turn, was part of the expanded Acceleration Pacification Campaign (APC) that was so important for ensuring that "Vietnamization" would equate to a winnable war. Of course, Speedy Express was designed to eliminate the entrenched Viet Cong (i.e., the Vietnamese people who resided there); in that sense it was, in effect, part of the Phoenix elimination program.

Thang Phong, lying near the South China Sea, is in Kien Hoa Province. US military planners considered nearly everyone in the province a member of the NLF, i.e., an evil Communist. Therefore the CIA's Phoenix assassination campaign and Operation Speedy Express both operated on the premise that all Vietnamese in Kien Hoa (regardless of age or sex) were active members or supporters of the VC. That no distinction was made between combatants and noncombatants, was typical in the war, especially as time wore on.

When Dan Rather, on *60 Minutes II*, asked why his after-action report asserted that his squad killed 14 Viet Cong, Kerrey responded, "We would not have separated out and mentioned them as women and children. We just didn't—sex, age, nothing would have been reported in that fashion. We considered everyone in that area to be VC. And that's how we would report it."

During a second interview with Rather on *60 Minutes II*, "Memories of a Massacre" (May 1, 2001), Kerrey commented on the shootings of February 25, 1969, at Thanh Phong: "To describe it [the attack] as an atrocity, I would say, is pretty close to being right, because that's how I felt it."[104] His part in the massacre continued to haunt the former US Senator. Controversy in the US and especially Viet Nam surrounding Kerrey's appointment as chairman of the board of trustees of Fulbright University Vietnam, when the school was created under President Barak Obama in 2016, led to his eventual removal.

Operation Speedy Express

Operation Speedy Express' 1969 massacres, committed in IV Corp's Mekong Delta (see above), were very similar to the US Army Tiger Force massacres committed in I Corps: Sweeps, disappearances, interrogations, detentions, tortures, and assassinations were freely conducted by the US Army's 9th Infantry Division with little oversight. The focus seemed to be the systematic *destruction of village life*: bombing villages, defoliating crops, forcing peasants off their land, day-and-night artillery barrages—in this game, nothing was considered out of bounds.

Speedy Express, launched in December 1968 by the 9th Division immediately after Nixon's election but before he officially took office on January 20, 1969, was the last major US military campaign in the Mekong Delta in preparation for Vietnamization. Its commander, General Julian Ewell, was known as "the Butcher of the Delta,[105] and "Bloody."[106] Speedy Express troops were ordered to produce high body counts and Ewell promised that any officers who did not achieve high body counts wouldn't be with the

---

104 Gregory L. Vistica, *The Education of Lieutenant Kerrey* (New York: St. Martin's Press, 2003), 240; Gregory L. Vistica, "What Happened in Thanh Phong," *New York Times Magazine*, April 29, 2001.
105 Appy, 2003, 323.
106 Emerson, 154.

9th Division for very long.[107] Ewell was famous for telling his troops to "get a hundred a day, every day,"[108] and awarding a *Sat Cong* ("kill Viet Cong") badge to any soldier who personally killed a VC.[109] The 9th Division committed seven battalions (8,000 troops) utilizing 50 artillery pieces and 50 heavily armed helicopters (outfitted with rockets and mini-guns) to carry out search-and-destroy and scorched-earth operations.

Machine-gunning civilians was sometimes described as *squirrel hunting*. Speedy Express was declared a success in May 1969 after a 182-day murder rampage in which they reported 10,899 "enemy" casualties (average of 60 murders/day), but the accompanying number of small arms captured (only 748, an average of 4 weapons/day) was embarrassingly small. The US claimed only 40 KIA of its own along with 312 WIA. The 9th conducted 3,381 tactical air strikes, including numerous bombings with napalm, high explosive bombs, anti-personnel bombs, B-52 Arc Light bombs, and rockets. Artillery shellings occurred around the clock while armed helicopters roamed night and day, shooting anyone in sight. It was reported that in many villages the US troops "destroyed *every* house with artillery, air strikes, or by burning them down with cigarette lighters."[110]

[From my own experience witnessing the immediate aftermath of bombings of inhabited villages in nearby Vinh Long Province, I would say the only explanation for the high casualty rates with the low number of weapons found in Speedy Express is that the murdered were innocent civilians, and accumulating body counts was official policy. A dead Vietnamese was a Viet Cong.] Other historians have drawn similar conclusions.[111] This was the nature of the US war in Viet Nam: atrocity after atrocity, amounting to genocide.

Westmoreland: Naïve or Criminal?

General Westmoreland had to have been keenly aware of the hundreds of atrocities, even as he attempted to bury reports about them. A policy of genocide was never formally identified as such. In a speech presented at the Waldorf Astoria Hotel in New York in April 1967, Westmoreland said, "the end is not in sight.... We will have to grind him down. In effect we are fighting a war of attrition. The only alternative is a war of annihilation"[112] (in other words, genocide). But as some military observers assessed, attrition was not a strategy but a belief in using blood and brute force rather than brains. The US continued relying on unrivaled firepower and mobility, as if fighting a conventional war against Soviet troops in Europe. Westmoreland was infatuated with casualty graphs, products of search-and-destroy methods totally inappropriate in a revolutionary guerrilla war where the Vietnamese accepted casualties in order to achieve their political aim of independence. Blood and firepower simply alienated most Vietnamese.[113]

---

107 David H. Hackworth, *About Face* (New York: Simon & Schuster, 1989), 668, 677.
108 Emerson, 154.
109 Doyle and Weiss, 147.
110 Kevin Buckley, "Pacification's Deadly Price," *Newsweek*, June 19, 1972, 42–43.
111 Buckley, 42; Chomsky and Herman, 1979, 314–315.
112 Cincinnatus, 73.
113 Cincinnatus, 73.

News reports, books, and first-hand accounts from veterans and journalists about US war crimes were mounting. In 1968, Clergy and Laymen Concerned About Vietnam (CALCAV) commissioned a study that documented thousands of acts of grotesque US conduct and compared the behavior with established laws of war binding on the US government.[114]

A number of studies were published in 1970: Edward Herman documented numerous atrocities in a book titled *Atrocities in Vietnam*;[115] retired General Telford Taylor documented the US crimes of Nuremberg proportions in his study, *Nuremberg and Vietnam*;[116] and another study, *War Crimes and the American Conscience*, edited by Erwin Knoll,[117] continued to describe the clear pattern of US criminality. In 1971, international law expert Richard Falk, historical scholar Gabriel Kolko, and psychiatrist Robert Jay Lifton collaborated on the book, *Crimes of War: A Legal, Political-Documentary, and Psychological Inquiry into the Responsibility of Leaders, Citizens, and Soldiers for Criminal Acts in Wars*.[118]

Westmoreland was either naively ignorant of, or criminally complicit in, extensive corruption at many levels. He perpetuated deceit with his practiced denial of damning facts about the extent of morale issues, racism, and desertion rates during his reign as commander of US military operations in Viet Nam, 1964–1968. Additionally, the stench of corruption of hundreds of officers and civilians, both Vietnamese and US, was rampant as personal profit and career enhancement often preempted diligent duty. The corruption included, of course, the CIA, which was not only directly involved in the drug trade to finance portions of the war, but even protected Vietnamese officials' poppy fields, flying their heroin out of the country on Air America planes.[119]

Military PX noncommissioned officer (NCO) club scandals involved employees stealing goods for quick and easy profit. Items like kerosene, sheet metal, oil, gasoline engines, claymore mines, hand grenades, rifles, and bags of cement were sometimes sold to the Viet Cong in a lucrative black market. The "stench of corruption" was indeed extremely foul.[120]

Major General Carl C. Turner, former provost general of the US Army, was sentenced to three years in prison for obtaining guns under false pretenses through enlisted men's and NCO's clubs. A sergeant major of the Army was accused of receiving illicit profits from the military NCO club system and using Westmoreland's successor General Creighton

---

114 Seymour Melman, *In the Name of America* (Annandale, VA: Turnpike Press for the Clergy and Laymen Concerned About Vietnam, 1968).

115 Edward S. Herman, *Atrocities in Vietnam: Myths and Realities* (Philadelphia, PA: Pilgrim Press, 1970).

116 Telford Taylor, *Nuremberg and Vietnam: An American Tragedy* (Chicago: Quadrangle Books, 1970).

117 Erwin Knoll, ed., *War Crimes and the American Conscience* (New York: Holt, Rinehart and Winston, 1970).

118 Richard A. Falk, Gabriel Kolko and Robert Jay Lifton, eds., *Crimes of War: A Legal, Political-Documentary, and Psychological Inquiry into the Responsibility of Leaders, Citizens, and Soldiers for Criminal Acts in Wars* (New York: Random House, 1971).

119 Cincinnatus, 67–69.

120 Cincinnatus, 68–69.

Abrams' personal airplane to haul crates of whiskey in and out of Viet Nam. A number of other sergeants were also implicated in a scheme that included widespread bribes, kickbacks, extortion, and extreme negligence.[121]

US policy was, in fact, accomplished with genocidal intent. I discovered this at Binh Thuy when I was exposed up close to the deliberate bombing of nearby inhabited farming villages. Atrocities were regularly committed on the ground as well as from the air. As others have stated, US American military policy did not make atrocities by individual soldiers inevitable, but it certainly made it inevitable that US American forces as a whole would kill (murder) many civilians.[122] The Marine lieutenant colonel in charge of the Combined Action Program in Viet Nam's I Corps described their "pacification" program thus: "We had conspired with the government of South Vietnam to literally destroy the hopes, aspirations and emotional stability of thirteen thousand human beings.... This was not and is not war, it is genocide." He attempted unsuccessfully to influence his superiors and policy makers that this kind of behavior was counterproductive in revolutionary warfare.[123]

Nguyen Cao Ky

On April 7, 1968, the *Washington Post* reported a March 1968 conversation with Nguyen Cao Ky, the newly elected vice-president of South Vietnam in the corrupt 1967 elections:[124]

> In most of the cases, the men who have been elected in South Vietnam are not the men that people want; they do not represent the people. The people voted for them because someone told them to vote. Our last elections were ... useful to elect a regime which is wrong and corrupted and weak and would fall immediately with a revolution.... I recognize the evil where the evil is, and I say that laws must be changed, because what we now have are laws that defend the rich. We need new laws to defend the poor.

Ky had also made it known that, even as he was rabidly anti-Communist, he possessed more regard for Ho Chi Minh than for any "foreigners." Hatred for US Americans had also been harbored by former President Diem and his brother Nhu. Nhu had made it clear that he wanted all the material aid he could get from the Americans—"their money, arms, and equipment but not them." Shortly before his and his brother's murders on November 2, 1963 by ARVN soldiers in a CIA-backed coup, Nhu was reported to have said that the Americans "have done everything to push me into the arms of Ho Chi Minh." The brothers were also said to have held secret meetings with intermediaries pursuing

---

121 Cincinnatus, 150.
122 Appy, 1993, 201.
123 Cincinnatus, 226n29.
124 Don Luce and John Sommer, *Viet Nam: The Unheard Voices* (Ithaca, NY: Cornell University Press, 1969), 63.

collaboration with the North to end the increasingly violent war before it got worse.[125] During a 1977 interview with BBC Radio, Ky admitted that the US made all the decisions and only informed the South Viet Nam government later, that Ho Chi Minh was a true leader; and that "we" were "not nationalists but puppets and lackeys of America."[126]

US Delusion and Vietnamization

July 1968. In an article titled "The Bases of Accommodation," published in the periodical *Foreign Affairs,* Samuel Huntington explains how the rural revolution in Viet Nam is being undermined by the destruction of its social base, accomplished through "forced-draft urbanization and modernization" to "produce a massive migration from countryside to city." The article describes what is essentially systematic murder and the physical destruction of a defenseless rural society.[127]

August 1, 1968. General George S. Brown becomes commander of 7th Air Force in Southeast Asia and begins overseeing the process called "Vietnamization" of the air war even before Nixon is elected president. When US American ground strength begins to be reduced in 1969, 7th Air Force will be counted upon to bring the heavy support needed by the ARVN as South Vietnamese forces assume more and more of the ground combat role. The 7th Air Force's official headquarters are at Tan Son Nhut, Saigon, but much of its operations are directed from secret Southeast Asia headquarters located primarily at Nakhon Phanom, in northern Thailand.[128]

August 5–8, 1968. The Republican convention in Miami Beach nominates Richard Nixon for president. The candidate promises "to bring an honorable end to the war in Vietnam."

October 1968. Operation Sealord begins. In the largest combined naval operation of the entire war, over 1,200 US and South Vietnamese Navy gunboats and warships target NVA supply lines extending from Cambodia into the Mekong Delta. NVA supply camps in the Delta and along other waterways are successfully disrupted during the two-year operation.

October 1968. CIA agent Ralph McGehee arrives in Saigon, joining the more than 700 CIA employees already scattered throughout Saigon and upcountry. McGehee learns early on that "the US [is] supporting Thieu's tiny oligarchy against a population largely organized, committed, and dedicated

---

125 Bloodworth, 269–270.

126 Michael Charlton Interview with Nguyen Cao Ky, "Many Reasons Why," BBC Radio 3, November 19, 1977 (printed version: "Nguyen Cao Ky: 'What South Vietnam Needs is a Man like Ho,'" *The Listener* 24, November 1977: http://just.nicepeople.free.fr/Nguyen_Cao_Ky_interview.pdf).

127 Noam Chomsky, *Towards a New Cold War* (The New Press, 1982, 2003), 231.

128 Fred Branfman, *Voices From the Plain of Jars: Life Under an Air War* (New York: Harper Colophon Books, 1972), 5 n2, 16 n14; Nina S. Adams and Alfred W. McCoy (eds.), *Laos: War and Revolution* (New York: Harper Colophon Books, 1970), 238.

to a Communist victory."[129] In contrast to the optimistic reports of MACV, CORDS and Phoenix, McGehee sees a stubborn refusal on the US side to grasp the total corruption of the South Vietnamese government and the fact that the vast majority of the Vietnamese people are fighting *against* the US forces and *for* the NLF. Further, he states that in the history of US–South Vietnamese efforts, there has not been one clear-cut case of a high-ranking Viet Cong agent being identified and apprehended. (In his memoir, McGehee later cites a November 1969 report placing the number of Viet Cong agents in the South Vietnamese army and government in the neighborhood of 30,000.) His reports are never accurately quoted by Washington politicians. Exasperation and the sense of betrayal he feels from top intelligence officials bring him to the point of contemplating suicide, and to the conclusion that US intelligence has little to do with reality.[130]

October 3, 1968. Presidential candidate George Wallace introduces General Curtis LeMay as his running mate. In his impromptu speech, LeMay says, "We seem to have a phobia about nuclear weapons.... The smart thing to do when you're in war ... [is] get in it with both feet and get it over with as soon as you can ... use the force that's necessary.... Maybe use a little more to make sure it's enough to stop the fighting as soon as possible.... I think there are many times when it should be most efficient to *use nuclear weapons*."[131]

October 31, 1968. On the eve of the US presidential elections, President Johnson announces a halt to Operation Rolling Thunder, the longest sustained strategic air bombardment in history, in the hope of restarting the peace talks and enhancing Democratic candidate Hubert Humphrey's chances for victory.

November 1, 1968. Four-party negotiations commence in Paris, this time including representatives of the NLF as well as the South Vietnamese government.[132]

November 1, 1968. CORDS Director William Colby replaces Komer and escalates coordination of all pacification efforts, launching the Acceleration Pacification Campaign (APC) with the objective of expanding government control over 1,200 villages controlled by the Viet Cong. APC will become the centerpiece of Nixon and Kissinger's "Vietnamization" policy, in which responsibility for the counterinsurgency is ostensibly passed to the Republic of Viet Nam. The Vietnamese component, called *Le Loi* (pacification program), includes assassination and torture as well as civic building programs, all taught and sanctioned by US forces. The United States has

---

129 McGehee, 125–126.

130 McGehee, 147–157.

131 Jules Witcover, *The Making of an Ink-Stained Wretch: Half a Century Pounding the Political Beat* (Johns Hopkins University Press, 2005), 125.

132 Clark Dougan and Stephen Weiss, *The Vietnam Experience: Nineteen Sixty-Eight* (Boston: Boston Publishing, 1983), 180.

high hopes for the program, believing the VC to be on the defensive after being badly drained by the Tet Offensive. The US emphasis on torture and assassination are in blatant defiance of the 1949 Geneva Convention, ratified by the US in 1955, which expressly prohibited torture of prisoners in war. Before Komer departs in November 1968, he establishes an expectation for Phoenix to "neutralize" 3,000 VCI *every month*, and beefs up the APC with CIA assassination squads, with former counter-terror or CT teams now termed provincial reconnaissance units (PRUs).[133]

In addition to ending the war in Viet Nam, Nixon promised to restore law and order to the nation's cities at home, which were being torn apart by riots and crime. Both major party candidates supported the war with their own brand of rhetorical gobbledygook. Mass murder of Southeast Asians continued unabated, along with the deaths and maimings of many more US soldiers.

According to Christopher Hitchens, author of *The Trial of Henry Kissinger*,[134] Henry Kissinger's serial crimes began in the fall of 1968 near the end of the tight presidential race. At the Paris Peace negotiations begun on May 13, 1968, the Johnson administration was on the brink of a critical breakthrough to ending the war in Viet Nam. But Nixon had set out to sabotage the talks as early as mid-September, in conspiracy with Kissinger, who had become a trusted "back channel" secret source within the US negotiating team. In effect, secret promises from the Republicans of special favors, should they win the election, were made to the South Vietnamese in exchange for scuttling the talks. Nixon calculated that thwarting the negotiations might finish off Humphrey's Peace Plank campaign. By distancing himself from "Johnson's war," Humphrey had managed to pull within just two points of Nixon in the polls.

In his biography of Henry Kissinger, *The Price of Power*,[135] Seymour Hersh wrote, "If word of a possible agreement leaked out, the [South Vietnamese] government might be tempted by the Republicans to stall the negotiations or find other ways to make it impossible to reach agreement before the election." The leak arrived, and Nixon put this secret and vital information to immediate use: Through the back channels, he urged Saigon's ruling clique to resist the settlement being negotiated at Paris. On November 1, Johnson ordered a bombing halt—a gesture that signaled the breakthrough—but he had already been checkmated behind the scenes. The South Vietnamese regime of Nguyen Van Thieu, Christopher Hitchens commented, made Johnson "look a fool by boycotting the peace talks the very next day." This may have tipped the election to Nixon.

Nixon's informant, Henry Kissinger, was considered a trusted ally of Johnson emissary W. Averell Harriman, leader of the Paris talks. The result of his treachery, writes Hitchens, was "four more years of an unwinnable and undeclared and murderous war, which was

---

133 Sheehan, 732.
134 Christopher Hitchens, *The Trial of Henry Kissinger* (London: Verso, 2001), 6–13.
135 Seymour Hersh, *The Price of Power* (New York: Summit Books, 1983), 17.

OPERATION ROLLING THUNDER | Throughout this three-and-a-half-year bombing campaign, the US hammered North Viet Nam with 304,000 tactical sorties carried out by US Navy and Air Force fighter-bombers, in addition to 2,380 B-52 sorties. Despite dropping 643,000 tons of bombs on North Viet Nam, the equivalent of 500 tons or a million pounds per day, the campaign had little actual success in halting the flow of soldiers and supplies into the South or in damaging the enemy's morale. In fact, it was a colossal failure, as the North Vietnamese patriotically rallied around their leaders in response to the onslaught,[136] in which many towns south of Hanoi were completely leveled. The US estimated 182,000 North Vietnamese civilians perished as a result of the relentless bombing campaign. On the other side, North Viet Nam's sophisticated, Soviet-supplied air defense system downed more than 900 US Rolling Thunder aircraft; 818 US pilots wound up dead or missing, and hundreds more were taken captive.[137]

The degree of destruction and death inflicted by Rolling Thunder can be grasped by examining the case study of the provincial capital of Ha Tinh, located 250 miles south of Hanoi, 150 miles north of the DMZ. Between 1965 and 1968, the province of 800,000 people was bombed nearly 26,000 times. On the first days of Rolling Thunder, US forces simultaneously bombed the municipal hospital, filled with 170 patients and staff, and the Ha Tinh secondary school, where 750 students and teachers were present.

Total disregard for civilian life was displayed in the leveling of five smaller cities in North Viet Nam with populations numbering between 10,000 and 30,000—Phy Ly, Ninh Binh, Thanh Hoa, Vinh, and Ha Tinh—while the North's third largest city, Nam Dinh, population 90,000, was severely damaged. Another 18 populated communities were also obliterated.[138] McNamara, differing sharply with the Joint Chiefs of Staff over the so-called success of Rolling Thunder, testified before the Senate Armed Services Committee in 1967 that the bombing had not significantly reduced infiltration from the North, and that no bombing strategy was likely to be any more successful.[139] The US Government Accounting Office (GAO) calculated that in 1967 alone, the US spent an average of $9.60 on Rolling Thunder for every $1.00 worth of damage inflicted.[140]

---

136 Yuki Tanaka and Marilyn B. Young, eds., *Bombing Civilians: A Twentieth-Century History* (New York: The New Press, 2009), 163–164.

137 Tim Page, *Another Vietnam: Pictures of the War from the Other Side* (Washington, DC: National Geographic, 2002), 23.

138 Maclear, 334–335.

139 Prados, 2009, 208.

140 Caputo, 40.

to spread before it burned out, and was to end on the same terms and conditions as had been on the table in the fall of 1968."[141]

The war still stirred patriotic excitement in some. On the occasion of Christmas 1968, Colonel George S. Patton, III, son of the famous World War II Patton, sent Christmas cards, "From Colonel and Mrs. George S. Patton III—Peace on Earth," enclosing color photographs of dismembered Viet Cong fighters stacked in a pile.[142]

But the general public was tiring of the war and the toll it was taking. US military forces numbered 536,100 in Viet Nam at the end of December 1968. By that time, 30,610 American soldiers had been killed since the beginning of the US war.[143] Since the level of antiwar dissent seemed directly proportional to the level of US casualties and fatalities, Nixon set out to reduce those losses, which were occurring predominantly in the ground war, by transferring responsibility for the ground war to the South Vietnamese. At the same time, an increased bombing campaign would provide cover during the transition. The political intention ostensibly was to eventually create a South Vietnamese army powerful enough to be able to defend itself with financial support and military supplies from the US.

Upon his inauguration on January 20, 1969, Nixon became the fifth US president in 20 years to deal with the question of American involvement in Viet Nam (Truman, Eisenhower, Kennedy, and Johnson before him). He appointed Henry Cabot Lodge, Jr., as chief United States negotiator at the Paris Peace talks, replacing Harriman. Nixon's new Secretary of Defense/War, Melvin Laird, visited Viet Nam from March 6–11, 1969 and once more in later March, to quick-start what would become known as Nixon's Vietnamization program. As Nixon's adviser on national security affairs, Kissinger continued to be influential in the war's execution. (In 1973, he took on the additional role of Secretary of State, replacing William P. Rogers.)

According to notes from a March 28, 1969, National Security Council (NSC) meeting, the South Vietnamese military improvement was substantial, and the US was in fact close to "de-Americanizing" the war. It was at this meeting that Secretary of Defense/War Melvin Laird spoke up and suggested a better term might be "Vietnamizing" the war. Thus *Vietnamization* was born and became a very handy term for describing the transfer of responsibility. On January 30, the *New York Times* had called upon the US to initiate troop withdrawals, and on March 21 the paper said it was time to begin withdrawals.[144]

---

141 Greg Goldin, "Henry: Portrait of a Serial Killer," *LA Weekly*, Art & Books, April 25, 2001. Note: This 1968 November election surprise is similar to the surprise twelve years later in October 1980 when behind-the-scenes jockeying calculated a delayed release of the 52 US hostages held at the US Iranian embassy after the November 1979 Iranian Revolution. This delay seems to have assured Ronald Reagan's victory over incumbent President Jimmy Carter. On Inauguration Day January 20, 1981, the hostages were released only minutes after Reagan's noon swearing-in [Gary Sick, *October Surprise: America's Hostages in Iran and the Election of Ronald Reagan* (New York: Times Books, 1991), 192–193].

142 Hersh, 1970, 9; Kevin P. Buckley, "General Abram Deserves a Better War," *New York Times Magazine*, October 5, 1969.

143 Summers, 1999, 48.

144 Henry Kissinger, *White House Years* (Boston: Little, Brown and Company, 1979), 271–2, 294.

The Illegal War Continues Under a New Commander in Chief

Nixon's war plan entailed reducing domestic dissent by ending the draft and beginning withdrawal of US troops, while intensifying the air war to help facilitate the process of Vietnamization. Decreases in numbers of US troops were offset by dramatic increases in equipment, planes, and pilots for the SVNAF, and additional mechanization, troops, and firepower for the ARVN. In effect, Vietnamization intensified the war. This is how it looked:

- Invasion of Laos, code-named "Dewey Canyon I," commencing two days after Nixon took office (January 22 to March 1969).

- Incessant (secret) bombing of Cambodia beginning March 18, 1969 (58 days after Nixon took office; 10 days after this author arrived in country). This particular bombing campaign did not end until 1973.

- Increasing amounts of equipment, planes, and pilots for the SVNAF, and more equipment and firepower for ARVN ground units, beginning spring 1969.

- Invasion of Cambodia, May–June 1970.

- Second invasion of Laos, "Dewey Canyon II," February–April 1971.

- Intensification of the Phoenix Program, meaning increased numbers of South Vietnamese citizens being rounded up, tortured, murdered.

- Huge increases in numbers of armed South Vietnamese in the ARVN whose job it was, along with air power, to systematically increase body counts in ever-expanding free-fire zones.

- Increased US bombing in South as well as North Viet Nam.

As Vietnamization took effect, the US goal remained the same—to systematically and dramatically increase body counts in expanded *free-fire zones* as designated by US military planners. Euphemistically called *pacification,* wholesale slaughter of civilians became the norm in efforts to produce the massive body counts that had become the indicia for success or failure in the US war. In effect it was a policy of extermination, as so much of Viet Nam was eventually considered part of a free-fire zone, in which everyone was considered "enemy" and could be killed at will. Thus, it was a policy of genocide.

Dewey Canyon I and the Secret Invasion of Laos

January 22, 1969. Two days after his inauguration, Nixon commences a secret operation, code-named Dewey Canyon I, that extends the Viet Nam war into neighboring Laos. The invasion, orchestrated from Thau Thien Province in northern portions of South Viet Nam along the Laotian border, continues into March.

January 1969. Over 4 million South Vietnamese, nearly a quarter of the population, experience one or more air strikes within 1.8 miles of their hamlet.[145]

February 22-23, 1969. In a second Tet Offensive, Saigon and approximately seventy other cities are hit with rockets and mortars, causing 245 US American casualties.[146] [This during the last two weeks of this author's speeded-up USAF ranger training, which concluded the first week of March, 1969.]

March 8, 1969. US Marines enter Laos in support of South Vietnamese troops.[147] [This is the very same day this author arrived at Binh Thuy Air Base in the Mekong Delta.]

Note: Two years later, in describing their role in the invasion of Laos during "Winter Soldier Investigations" of US war crimes held by Vietnam Veterans Against the War (VVAW) in Detroit, Michigan (Jan. 3–Feb. 1, 1971), five US Marines claimed that an entire regiment of the 3rd Marines had penetrated several miles into that neutral nation, conducting combat maneuvers along Highway 922 and beyond, and "suffered dozens of casualties in fierce fighting." They further charged that the US military refused to medevac out the wounded and dead to prevent the press from discovering the secret operation.[148]

Bombing of Cambodia

On March 18, 1969, President Nixon ordered secret B-52 bombings of Cambodia, dubbed Operation Breakfast, following the advice of his National Security Advisor Henry Kissinger, which detailed specific targets.[149] The Ho Chi Minh Trail was especially heavily targeted with bombings extending into southern Laos,[150] demonstrating the expansive nature of the war. The US dropped thousands of sensors along the trail to detect movement of vehicles and troops. Data was sent to super IBM-360 computers at

---

145 Kolko, 1985, 200.
146 Bowman, 221.
147 Bowman, 223.
148 Gerald Nicosia, *Home to War* (New York: Crown Publishers, 2001), 88–89.
149 Hersh, 1983, 121–122.
150 Hersh, 1983, 55n.

Nakhon Phanom, Thailand, which in turn guided B-52 bombing missions.[151] Subsequent Cambodian bombings nicknamed *Dinner, Snacks,* and *Dessert,* combined with *Operation Breakfast,* were referred to as the *Menu* bombings.

A veteran who participated in the campaign, later testified, "The technicians who program the computer perform no act of war, for the man who places the sensor does not see it operate. The man who plots the strike never sees the plane that conducts it. The pilot, navigator, and bombardier do not see the bombs hit. The damage assessor is not in the plane, and all the others who helped mount the raid never participated in it at all."[152]

It is precisely the nature of modern, high-tech war that mass murder "takes on a corporate character, where every participant has limited [or zero] liability. The total effect, however, is a thousand times more pernicious."[153] This was the point of Hannah Arendt's classic essay, *Eichmann in Jerusalem,* in which she described Eichmann, the coordinator of deportation of Jews to the death camps, as "terribly and terrifying normal, neither perverted nor sadistic, a normality much more terrifying than all the atrocities put together."[154]

By March 1969, the total level of bombardment reached 130,000 tons a month, the equivalent of nearly two Hiroshimas, in South Viet Nam and Laos alone[155]. Designed to weaken base camps and supply lines in Cambodia, in the first 14 months, March 1969 through April 1970, a total of 3,630 flights over Cambodia dropped 110,000 tons of bombs.[156]

Cambodia, starting in the southeast fishhook region that protrudes into Viet Nam's Bình Long and Tây Ninh provinces, was also intensively defoliated, starting on March 18, 1969, in areas heavily populated by numerous small villages and inhabited by employees and families of the French Memot rubber plantation. The defoliation of Cambodia has never been admitted, but is revealed in the book, *The Chemical Scythe: Lessons of 2,4,5-T and Dioxin.*[157]

In two heavy bombing days, April 24-25, 1969, a hundred B-52s based in Thailand and Guam dropped 3,000 *tons* of bombs along the Cambodian border 70 miles northwest of Saigon.[158]

The bombing of Cambodia did not end until summer 1973. These secret carpet bombings were preceded by earlier bombings launched over Cambodia on October 4, 1965, three

---

151 Warner, 254–255.

152 Kim McQuaid, *The Anxious Years: America in the Vietnam-Watergate Era* (New York: Basic Books, Inc., 1989), 77.

153 Lewes, 4.

154 Arendt, 276.

155 Noam Chomsky, "After Pinkville," in *Prevent the Crime of Silence,* ed. Ken Coates, Peter Limqueco, and Peter Weiss, 32 (London: Allen Lane the Penguin Press, 1971).

156 Bowman, 223.

157 E. W. Pfeiffer, "Secret Defoliation in Vietnam," review of book by Alistair Hay [*The Chemical Scythe: Lessons of 2,4,5-T and Dioxin* (New York: Plenum Publishing, 1982)], *Covert Action Information Bulletin,* 18 (Winter 1983), 58–59.

158 Bishop, 146.

and a half years earlier. From that point in time to August 15, 1973, the United States dropped a phenomenal amount of explosives on Cambodia: 2,756,941 tons in 230,516 sorties on 113,716 sites.[159]

No Intention of Ending the War

When, on May 8, 1969, the NLF submitted its ten-point peace plan at the Paris talks, it was virtually ignored by the United States.

On May 19, 1969, Nixon launched a public campaign to marshal public opinion for the "prompt release of all American prisoners of war," the vast majority of whom were unrecovered flight crews shot down over North Viet Nam, Laos, Cambodia, China, or the ocean. Thus, a domestically divisive political issue was created by linking prisoners of war (POW) with the missing in action (MIA) a deliberate move to manipulate support of grieving families, then a grieving nation, which would rather not face the history of the US having committed the supreme international crime of invading Southeast Asia, and its conduct in a 30-year war, committing one war crime after another while perpetuating crimes against humanity.

Texas billionaire right-winger Ross Perot was placed in charge of building the necessary mass support. Nixon's intention was to end the war with the hope that the failing South Vietnamese puppet government would remain intact after the US retreat. Part of the strategy required sabotaging the Paris Peace talks and one way to do that was to create an issue that could *not* be resolved—attempting to forever link POW with MIA. Unlike in all previous wars where there was only one category, Prisoners of War, US negotiators demanded that every single body be accounted for. Linking the two categories together as POW/MIA, served to imply the Vietnamese were using our prisoners as pawns in a diplomatic game with the attacking US forces despite the fact that there were, and remain, nearly 300,000 Vietnamese missing in action for which the US government showed no concern whatsoever.[160] This issue effectively stalemated the Paris talks for nearly four years.

Despite the noises he had made during his campaign about ending the war, Nixon did not embrace peace when it was offered. In a speech delivered on November 3, 1969, President Nixon denied the existence of any initiatives for a settlement by both the South and the North Vietnamese, and made it clear he had no intention of withdrawing our military support for the South or of broadening the Saigon regime to include the North or the NLF.[161]

---

159 Owen and Kiernan, http://japanfocus.org/products/details/2420.
160 Franklin, 2000, 173–201; "Inhuman Stance on Prisoners," *New York Times* editorial, May 29, 1969.
161 Chomsky, in Coates, Limqueco and Weiss, 50.

Invasion of Cambodia

An invasion of Cambodia ordered by President Nixon on April 30, 1970 involved 8,000 US and as many ARVN troops conducting 13 major ground operations within 19 miles of the Cambodia–South Viet Nam border. The invasion was a real test for Vietnamization. Both American and South Vietnamese high commands had long wanted to strike at the border base areas which were situated about 35 miles from Saigon. During May, the joint forces carried out search-and-destroy operations in a dozen base areas adjoining the II, III, and IV Corps areas of South Viet Nam; all US ground troops were gone from Cambodia by June 1.

A US-Vietnamese naval task force commanded by Rear Admiral Herbert S. Matthews, Deputy Commander Naval Forces Viet Nam, simultaneously swept up the Mekong River to open a supply line to Cambodia's besieged capital, Phnom Penh as ARVN units continued to range the base areas. The invasion had little immediate impact on conditions in I Corps. During the invasion, US jets flew 26 missions over Cambodia.

The 1970 invasion of Cambodia was the first such operation for the ARVN, and that spring the desertion rate rose from its normal level of 8,000 per month to 12,000. After the 1971 ARVN Laos operation, codenamed Dewey Canyon II, which was a disaster, it was questionable how many battalions remained combat effective.[162] The Cambodia and Laos invasions took an emotional toll on US soldiers as well, played out partly in an explosive heroin epidemic.[163] [The one soldier this author met years later who had taken part in the invasion of Cambodia died of alcoholism at the age of 38 on the sidewalk of a southwestern US city.]

Dewey Canyon II, the Second Invasion of Laos

January 29, 1971. Dewey Canyon II, code name for the second secret invasion of Laos, commences with the prepatory movement of 9,000 troops from the US 1st Brigade, 5th Infantry Division, to Khe Sanh, near the Laotian border, to back up some 20,000 ARVN troops in Operation "Lam Son 719." The ARVN forces are preparing to invade Laos with US air support including 2,600 helicopters, supposedly without US ground forces or advisers. The largest contingent committed to a military operation during the war, the ARVN troops comprise a significant counterpart of the forces involved in the May–June 1970 invasion of Cambodia, another major test of the effectiveness of Vietnamization. Dewey Canyon II is intended to knock out Laotian base areas believed to be critical to North Vietnamese war efforts.[164]

February 8, 1971. The actual invasion begins, utilizing top ARVN officers that have been trained and tutored by US military and civilian officials for as many as 15 years, both in Viet Nam and in the US.

---

162 FitzGerald, 418.
163 Wells, 456.
164 Bowman, 276–279.

April 6, 1971. The seven-week operation ends miserably with a gruesome tally: Over 100 US helicopters destroyed, 608 seriously damaged; 5 fixed-wing aircraft shot down; about a dozen South Vietnamese helicopters destroyed or damaged beyond repair; more than two-thirds of their armored vehicles destroyed. ARVN force casualties number nearly half their 20,000 troops. US casualties number 1,400, with at least 215 killed, including 72 pilots and crew. Dewey Canyon II is deemed a colossal failure, exposing the South Vietnamese military as grossly incompetent.[165]

April 7, 1971. In a nationally televised address the day after the conclusion of the invasion of Laos flubbed by "Lam Son 719," which should have signaled the failure of Vietnamization, Nixon declares, "Tonight I can report that Vietnamization has succeeded."[166]

May 8, 1972. President Nixon announces that North Viet Nam's major supply harbor in Haiphong has been sealed off, with planes dropping mines in and around the port of Haiphong as well as smaller ports.[167]

May 10, 1972. Code-named Linebacker I, bombing of North Viet Nam is ordered by President Nixon in response to the NVA's Easter offensive.

June 1972. For three days, US fighter-bombers fly 52 sorties around the clock against Hongai, a coal-mining and fishing town on Ha Long Bay in the Gulf of Tonkin that had been bombed on and off for six years.

December 18–29, 1972. During Linebacker II bombings of North Viet Nam, also known as the Christmas Bombings, 40,000 tons of bombs are dropped over densely populated areas stretching from Hanoi to Haiphong.[168]

> **TWIN DETERRENTS: FEAR AND PUBLIC OPINION** | The mining of Haiphong Harbor is one of four specific actions taken or contemplated by the US during the war that many scholars and pundits believed might provoke Moscow or Peking to enter the war. The other three actions were a ground invasion of North Viet Nam (never carried out), serious contemplation of the use of nuclear weapons, and the destruction of dikes in the Red River Delta (several were destroyed). Over time, it became clear that two basic factors limiting US aggression in Southeast Asia were public opinion and fear of provoking the Soviet Union or China.[169]

---

165 Richard Pyle and Horst Faas, *Lost over Laos* (Cambridge, MA: Da Capo Press, 2003), 148n2.
166 Summers, 1995, 172.
167 Bowman, 309–310.
168 *The Vietnam War: An Almanac*, 333.
169 Fred Halstead, *Out Now! A Participant's Account of the Movement in the United States Against the Vietnam War* (New York: Pathfinder, 1978, 2006), 773.

> **CLUSTER BOMBS** | Hongai, near Haiphong, was the target for the US Military's early experimentation with pellet bombs, an early prototype of cluster bombs, which are notorious for discharging hundreds of fragments, many shaped in the form of plastic darts. The most common cluster bombs, tested in Laos, sent out as many as 160 canisters (bomblets) each, when they exploded. The unexploded "bombies" continue to kill and maim 20,000 people a year in Laos. Merely a sideshow to Viet Nam during the war, the small country never posed the slightest threat to the US.[170] In 2016, Barack Obama became the first US President to travel to Laos, at which time he declared that the US had a moral obligation to help cleanup 80 million unexploded cluster bombs (of 270 million dropped), allocating $90 million for that purpose.[171] Laos, per capita, is the most heavily bombed country in history.[172]

Funding of Vietnamese Prisons and Torture by US Agency for International Development (USAID)

CIA torture experiments of the 1950s and early 1960s became the basis for new methods of torture disseminated through the Office of Public Safety (OPS) program of the US Agency for International Development's (USAID), which at that time was involved in training police forces in Asia and Latin America as part of an anti-communist offensive. The first OPS program to train foreign police was established in 1955 in Sukarno's Indonesia, and was quickly integrated into CIA operations. In the same year, the CIA contracted with Michigan State University to run covert training programs for Diem's police in South Viet Nam. AID's expanded OPS programs—a conduit for CIA training of police, jailers, and torturers ("interrogators")—were not limited to Southeast Asia. An insidious cover for CIA counter-insurgency, the OPS trained over a million police officials in forty-seven countries in torture and "interrogation" techniques developed by the CIA.[173]

Thus, in Viet Nam, there was a direct link between the US and brutal jailers, torturers, and murderers, first under Diem, then with all his successors, including Ky and Thieu. CIA counter-terror (CT) teams were set up as early as 1962 as specially trained counter-guerrilla teams, who used techniques of terror—assassination, physical abuses, kidnappings, rape, and intimidation—of those Vietnamese believed to be in the Viet

---

170 John Pilger, *The New Rulers of the World* (London, UK: Verso, 2002), 100–101.
171 Rebecca Wright, "'My friends were afraid of me': What 80 million unexploded US bombs did to Laos," *CNN*, September 6, 2016: http://www.cnn.com/2016/09/05/asia/united-states-laos-secret-war/index.html.
172 Christina Lin, "US apologizes to Laos over cluster bombs, then sells them to pound Yemen," *Asia Times*, September 8, 2016: http://atimes.com/2016/09/us-cluster-bombs-obama-apologizes-to-laos-sells-more-to-pound-yemen/.
173 Alfred McCoy, *A Question of Torture: CIA Interrogation, from the Cold War to the War on Terror* (New York: Henry Holt and Company, 2006), 10–11, 61; Michael McClintock, *Instruments of Statecraft: US Guerrilla Warfare, Counter-Insurgency, Counter-Terrorism 1940–1990* (New York: Pantheon Books, 1992), 181, 188–190; *The Wikileaks Files: The World According to US Empire* (London: Verso, 2015), 101, 484.

Cong Infrastructure (VCI). In essence these CT teams were death squads using evidence that more than not proved to be unsubstantiated gossip. The CT teams later became the CIA-trained province reconnaissance units (PRUs), which brought suspects to one of the many provincial interrogation centers (PICs), such as at Can Tho, usually under CIA oversight, where interrogators virtually always tortured the detainees, including use of electric shock and sadistic beatings, summarily executing many of them without trial or due process. Women prisoners were regularly raped before being murdered.[174]

The National Interrogation Center (NIC) in Saigon served as the Central Intelligence Organization (CIO) headquarters first created by Diem. There the CIA coordinated civilian, police, and military intelligence. Several hundred prisoners were held in NIC at any one time. Each provincial capital possessed a PIC, but larger regional interrogation centers were built first, each holding 200–300 prisoners. The French earlier had built a 500 capacity regional jail in Can Tho where 2,000 crowded prisoners slept nude on concrete slabs.[175]

By early 1966, there was no more space in the prisons of South Viet Nam's government for "communist offenders." As more and more people were being captured by PRUs and placed in PICs, jails, and detention camps, a large percentage of lesser prisoners were necessarily squeezed out. In fall 1967, the forty-two provincial jails where most VCI suspects were imprisoned had a capacity of 14,000. There were four national prisons: Con Son Prison held about 3,550 VCI members (of 10,000 total held at Con Son); Chi Hoa Prison in Saigon held over 4,000; Tan Hiep Prison outside Bien Hoa held nearly 1,000; and Thu Duc in Binh Thuan Province held about 675 VCI, all women. Approximately 35,000 POWs were held in six MACV camps scattered around South Viet Nam. VC and NVA prisoners fell under US supervision while ARVN camps held ARVN deserters and war criminals.[176] These prisons collectively held nearly 60,000 prisoners. In 1968, a Saigon newspaper estimated there were about 100,000 people in South Viet Nam prisons, many held in horrid conditions.[177] After the war, International Red Cross records revealed that at the height of the war, there had been 65,000 to 70,000 people held in South Vietnamese prison camps where they often had been beaten and tortured, often under the oversight, and even participation, of US advisers.[178]

By 1968, a number of US Army Green Berets worked under the direction of the CIA.[179] And the CIA's Phoenix assassination program that was in full swing by late 1968 used Green Berets (and Navy Seals) as part of the systematic rounding up, detaining, interrogating/torturing, and murdering of VCI suspects. A Green Beret captain admitted that Green Berets participated in "hundreds" of summary executions in South Viet Nam.[180]

---

174 McCoy, 2006, 61–65.
175 Luce and Sommer, 157.
176 Douglas Valentine, *The Phoenix Program* (Lincoln, NE: iUniverse, 2000), 152.
177 Luce and Sommer, 157.
178 Howard Zinn, *A People's History of the United States* (New York: HarperPerennial, 1980, 1990), 468–469.
179 McClintock, 181.
180 McCoy, 66.

It will never be known how many Vietnamese were tortured or murdered because of USAID-funded police and jailer training, prison building, and "pacification" programs[181] through institutions like Michigan State University[182] and Southern Illinois University.[183] The building of gulag-style prisons and torture chambers in Viet Nam was greatly facilitated by AID's OPS, CIA's convenient cover. OPS also trained and equipped Viet Nam's police and prison guards for interrogating and torturing political prisoners, mostly Buddhist students and monks, such as those imprisoned in large numbers at Con Son Island where the infamous "tiger cages" were hidden with the knowledge of US officials and under a US-funded Directorate of Corrections.[184]

Con Son Island prison was located in the South China Sea, 110 miles southeast of the tip of the Mekong Delta. The Con Son Island tiger cages, essentially medieval-style dungeons where so-called hard-core VCI were imprisoned by US and South Vietnamese officials, were exposed in July 1970. Don Luce, who had previously directed International Voluntary Services (IVS) in Viet Nam, heard of the tiger cages from the Vietnamese, and was able to lead a Congressional delegation there in 1970.

Ninety percent of the funds used by the Saigon government came from the US. Frank Walton, head of the Public Safety Directorate under the wing of the US-created Civil Operations and Rural Development Support (CORDS), had resisted the request for a visit to Con Son, but the Congressional team persisted. Walton anxiously accompanied Don Luce and the two Congressmen, Augustus Hawkins (D-CA) and William Anderson (D-TN), and Congressional aide Tom Harkin (later a US Senator from Iowa). Prison warden Colonel Nguyen Van Le worked under Randolph Berkeley, chief of the Corrections and Detention Division of the Public Safety Directorate. Colonel Nguyen Van Le declared the prisoners as "very bad people" as "they will not salute the flag. They will not even salute the American flag."[185]

Small stone compartments, 5 feet wide by 9 feet long, held 3 beaten prisoners each in cells funded mostly by the US.[186] Prisoners were bolted to the floor, handcuffed to a bar or rod, or put in leg irons with the chain around a bar. Legs shackled for months and years at a time were ruined, causing partial or complete paralysis. Above each cell was a wooden bucket of lime, which was flung down on the prisoners through large openings in the roofs of the cells, making it difficult to breathe. Prisoners could only crawl on their hands and knees even when unbolted from the floor. Prisoners told of regular thirst, hunger, beatings. Food was small amounts of rice with sand and pebbles mixed in. Buddhist monks and nuns were the majority of prisoners. Crowded women prisoners ranged in age from 15 to 70, pleading for water, as they could hardly move.[187]

---

181 Gloria Emerson, *Winners and Losers* (New York: Harcourt Brace Jovanovich, 1972/1976), 308.
182 Emerson, 279–284.
183 Emerson, 302–308.
184 Valentine, 348–349; FitzGerald, 366.
185 Emerson, 345.
186 Emerson, 344; Valentine, 348–349
187 Emerson, 344–345.

Torture was routine in all the PICs: rape, gang rape, rape using eels, snakes, hard objects, rape followed by murder, electric shock (the "Bell Telephone Hour") through wires attached to genitals or the tongue, "the water treatment," the "airplane" in which a prisoner's arms were tied behind the back and a rope looped over a hook on the ceiling so the prisoner was suspended while being beaten, beatings with rubber hoses and whips, use of police dogs to maul prisoners.[188] At one PIC, a physician working with the American Friends Service Committee in Quang Ngai province reported treating "political prisoners" who had been terribly tortured with the knowledge of both Vietnamese and US officials, who were conducting a lucrative extortion racket at the center.[189]

It is important to stress that all these tortures occurred with the knowledge of US officials, and sometimes with their participation.[190] With all this systematized torture, the PICs were nonetheless faulted for producing poor information—and then only information on low-level members of the VCI.[191]

Randolph Berkeley, of the USAID Public Safety Directorate, joked that the Vietnamese warden was well liked, that he played soccer with some of the prisoners.... Yet prisoners had scars on their heads, had missing fingers and were regularly urinated on by guards. US authorities denied all the allegations.[192] One US official claimed that the "bulk of the inmates are either hard-core Communist defenders or they are serious professional criminals" who were "reasonably well-treated and that they looked in reasonably good health."[193]

A Phoenix legal adviser believed that William Colby, the CIA official overseeing the Phoenix "pacification" program, had concealed existence of the brutal Con Son Island prison. After Don Luce and his delegation exposed Con Son, the prisoners were transferred to a nearby island location in barbed wire cells called "cow cages," which by some assessments were worse.[194] The same Phoenix adviser who was sickened by Con Son said, "The responsibility for all this is on the Americans who pushed the program.... The Province Security Committees did whatever the hell they wanted and the pressure our 'neutralization' quotas put on them meant they had to sentence so many people a month regardless. And God, if you ever saw those prisons."[195] By 1972, Phoenix reported neutralizing 81,740 VCI, including murdering 26,369 of them.[196]

In February 1971, Luce, who had been kicked out of Viet Nam after his exposure of the tiger cages, disclosed that the construction consortium of Raymond, Morrison, Knudson-Brown, Root and Jones (RMK-BRJ) had a contract with the US Department of Navy to

---

188 Valentine, 85.
189 FitzGerald, 367.
190 Valentine, 78–85.
191 Valentine, 85; McGehee, 156; Harold Ford, *CIA and the Vietnam Policymakers: Three Episodes 1962–1968* (Washington, DC: Center for the Study of Intelligence, Central Intelligence Agency, 1998), 129.
192 Emerson, 343–346.
193 FitzGerald, 474n10, citing the *New York Times*, July 17, 1970.
194 Valentine, 349.
195 Valentine, 349.
196 McCoy, 2006, 68.

build new "isolation" cells at Con Son to replace the tiger cages.[197] RMK-BRJ, called The Vietnam Builders, was a consortium of private contractors who in 1964-65 had been awarded lucrative "no-bid" (no open bidding or competitive process) contracts to build the US military infrastructure throughout South Viet Nam.[198]

Peace Treaty and the War's End

January 27, 1973. Henry Kissinger for the US, and Le Duc Tho, chief negotiator for North Viet Nam, finally sign *The Paris Peace Accords, Ending the War and Restoring Peace in Vietnam*, the war-ending peace treaty, in Paris.

January 27, 1973. The same day the peace treaty is signed with Viet Nam, US Secretary of Defense/War Melvin Laird announces the end of the military draft, though the law remains on the books in case of "emergencies."[199]

January 28, 1973. The Viet Nam cease-fire commences at 0800 hours, Saigon time (1900 hours, January 27, Eastern Standard Time). Although the cease-fire will not last, the war is on its way to being over.

July 31, 1973. Congress votes to end all bombing in Indochina and to ban any future military moves in that area without prior congressional approval.

April 29-30, 1975. The largest helicopter evacuation on record removes the last US Americans from Saigon, including US Ambassador Graham Martin. In 19 hours, 81 helicopters carry more than 1,000 US Americans and nearly 6,000 Vietnamese to aircraft carriers waiting offshore. Thousands more Vietnamese collaborators and sympathizers are left behind.

April 30, 1975. North Vietnamese forces roll into Saigon as the US-equipped, trained, and paid South Viet Nam forces surrender.[200]

---

197 Emerson, 348.
198 James M. Carter, "War Profiting From Vietnam to Iraq," *CounterPunch*, December 11, 2003.
199 Bowman, 337-338.
200 Bowman, 345.

Major Characteristics of War

One factor that permeates all war-making is the need of policymakers to be personally credible. Immense effort is exerted to preserve public perception of the nobility of war while ignoring virtually all its costs. As losing a war is an unthinkable threat to one's very manhood, we see politicians willing to sacrifice everything to avoid the humiliation, embarrassment and stigma of personal failure and defeat. Thus, it can be argued that our nation's thirty-year, grinding, lawless, immoral war against Southeast Asian peoples was needlessly perpetuated to preserve the egos of mostly white male members of the capitalist politico-military-industrial cabal whose immense power and obscene obsession with private riches places them at a safe remove from reality. The heavy consequences of their actions are unspeakable, and unspoken of in the annals of human history.[201]

Telford Taylor, US chief counsel at the Nuremberg trials of Nazi war criminals in 1946 (who supported the US intervention in Southeast Asia until 1965), finally posed this question:

> How could it ever have been thought that air strikes, free-fire zones and a mass uprooting and removal of the rural population were the way to win "the allegiance of the South Vietnamese"? . . . And so . . . the anti-aggression spirit of Nuremberg and the United Nations Charter is invoked to justify our venture in Viet Nam, where we have smashed the country to bits, and will not even take the trouble to clean up the blood and rubble. . . . Somehow we failed, ourselves, to learn the lessons we undertook to teach at Nuremberg.[202]

[Perhaps the reason we failed to learn the lessons offered by Nuremberg is that, as one of the victors, the horrible war crimes *our side* committed in World War II—firebombing of Dresden and Tokyo, the nuclear devastation of Hiroshima and Nagasaki—were never acknowledged as such, much less brought to trial or punished. And of course, to admit that what happened in Viet Nam *was* a criminal operation would be to give up our notion of the USA as a legitimate, deserving Superpower and our belief in the incorruptible Goodness of our nation. Sadly, the war in Viet Nam was not an aberration but part of a pattern that has been with us since our nation's founding. It shares three major characteristics, identified below, with nearly every other US military intervention, before or since—policies that essentially originated with the White European settlers who eliminated millions of Indigenous occupants and stole their land.]

Criminalization of Self-defense

Contrary to international law, the US view is that self-defense against US-initiated, pre-emptive, aggression is considered a crime against the US, to be punished with ever more violent aggression. Disobedience to the American Way—any failure to comply with our

---

201 See Fredrik Logevall, *Choosing War: The Lost Chance for Peace and the Escalation of War in Vietnam* (Berkeley: University of California Press, 1999).
202 Telford Taylor, *Nuremberg and Vietnam: An American Tragedy* (New York: Bantam, 1971), 206–207.

wishes and whims—is simply prohibited. When the US attacks, invades, and occupies another land or country—virtually always in violation of international law—those who resist or are uncooperative are considered criminals or illegal combatants, subject to capture, torture ("interrogation"), and imprisonment in secret dungeons such as Bagram, Afghanistan, or Guantanamo, Cuba, with no due process whatsoever.

Policy-dictated Terror, Atrocity

In Viet Nam the policy of atrocity was *intentional*. The historic record shows systematic, brutal application of terrorist tactics employed from the air and on the ground against the Vietnamese people. Indeed, war *is* terrorism, on a grand scale!

It could be argued that the chaos, violence and senselessness of war breeds atrocious, terrorist behavior, as there are plenty of examples of such in US wars previous to Viet Nam. In the Civil War, Union commanders executed Confederate fighters on the spot, burned towns to the ground, and threatened civilians with retaliation if they were perceived to be involved in resistance. US brutality and torture against Filipinos during the Spanish-American War was systematic, as were pre-World War II Marine occupations of Haiti, Nicaragua, and the Dominican Republic. Atrocities were committed on both sides during WWII. In Korea, intense US racism made it routine to torture, mutilate, and murder enemy soldiers as well as many civilians.[1]

Genocide, Ethnic Cleansing, Total Destruction

The US War policy of atrocity upon atrocity amounted to genocide. Article II of The Convention on the Prevention and Punishment of the Crime of Genocide, signed in 1948, defines the crime of genocide as having two essential elements: (1) the *mental* element—the "*intent to destroy*, in whole or in part, a national, ethnical, racial or religious group, as such," and (2) the "*physical* element which includes *any* of five acts described in sections a, b, c, d and e: (a) killing members of the group; (b) causing serious bodily or mental harm to members of the group; (c) deliberately inflicting on the group conditions of life calculated to bring about its physical destruction in whole or in part; (d) imposing measures intended to prevent births within the group; (e) forcibly transferring children of the group to another group" (italics added by author).

Even while the war was being waged, it was clear to many Vietnamese that US policy was *intent on* destroying or deracinating an entire people. In 1967, Ton That Thien, managing editor of the *Vietnam Guardian*, astutely described the only way to US American "victory" in Viet Nam: "You can win if you keep killing for a generation. You simply exterminate all the Vietnamese—the way you killed the Indians in America."[2]

The US used a strategy of attrition when it could not achieve surrender by bombing, search and destroy, or scorched earth. *Everyone* in Viet Nam was seen as the enemy—all Vietnamese fair game for murder. US "military logic" led to no other conclusion.[3]

---

1 Doyle and Weiss, 150.
2 Chomsky, 1969, 239.
3 FitzGerald, 375.

The *de facto* destruction of an entire society (village, land culture, family)—social death—was similar to the US military campaign waged against Indigenous Americans. The attitude seemed to be, the only good Vietnamese was a dead one.

By early 1967, the US thought it had sufficient troops in-country to "atrit" the "enemy." Troops on the ground helped locate numerous "targets" for subsequent bombings, with massive firepower intended to destroy the enemy's humanpower. The civilian toll was enormous.[4] Troops increasingly plundered both rural areas and population centers with the intention of destroying the fabric of historic Vietnamese rural life.[5] According to Seymour Hersh's report on the My Lai incident, "It was standard operating procedure to *eliminate* the enemy's *shelter* and *food* supply"[6] (italics added by author). Reporter and author Bernard B. Fall had concluded in 1967 that Viet Nam as a cultural and historic identity was being "threatened with extinction" as the country was "battered into a moonscape," dying under the "largest military machine ever unleashed on an area of this size."[7]

---

4 Kolko, 1985, 179–180.
5 Young, 1991, 162–164.
6 Hersh, 1970, 175.
7 Fall, *Last Reflections* (1967), 33–34, 47.

CHAPTER FIVE
Chemical Warfare

"We pretended there was no problem with Agent Orange after Vietnam and later the Pentagon recanted, after untold suffering by veterans."

—Jim McDermott, US Representative (D-WA)

Left: Ranch Hand UC-123 clearing a roadside in central South Vietnam in 1966. Note the aircraft's very low altitude. [Photo: US Air Force] Right: At the War Remnants Museum in Ho Chi Minh City, Viet Nam, in March 2016, author stands in front of stark photo depicting deforestation caused by some of the chemicals applied in South Viet Nam by US forces during the American war. [Photo: Mike Hastie]

Introduction

US chemical warfare in Southeast Asia, heavily concentrated in South Viet Nam, encapsulated nearly every criminal dimension of the war. It is a classic example of the US Military's lavish use of "advanced" technology to subdue the very people they were purportedly there to help. Pursuing an unidentifiable enemy in effect negated any practicable distinction between civilians and enemies, so at some point the decision was made to obliterate them all indiscriminately.[1]

As mentioned in the preceding chapter, it was under President John F. Kennedy's watch that in Viet Nam, the United States launched its most egregious chemical warfare

---

1 Edgar Lederer, "Report of the Sub-Committee on Chemical Warfare in Vietnam," cited in John Duffet, ed., *Against the Crime of Silence: Proceedings of the Russell International War Crimes Tribunal* (New York: O'Hare Books, 1968), 338–364.

experiment in history. The following chronology outlines the early development of the US military's chemical spraying program.

Chemical Spraying Program—Early Development

May–October 1959. The first large-scale US military defoliation experiment is conducted at Camp Drum, New York, utilizing a spray system in the application of Agent Purple[2] that will be the model for future application of chemicals in Viet Nam.[3]

August 10, 1961. In the first defoliation test mission carried out in Viet Nam, a South Vietnamese Air Force (SVNAF) H-34 helicopter, equipped with a liquid insecticide spraying apparatus, disperses the chemical Dinoxol alongside a road north of Kontum in the Central Highlands.[4]

August 24, 1961. The first fixed-wing spray mission, flown by an SVNAF C-47, disperses Dinoxol over a four-kilometer stretch of Route 13, about 80 kilometers north of Saigon near the village of Chon Thanh, a target personally selected by South Vietnamese President Diem.[5]

September 23, 1961. A joint State-Defense message, calling for emergency action in support of the Diem government, suggests including chemicals for a defoliation program on a list of items to be delivered without delay.[6]

September 29, 1961. In a meeting with an American delegation, President Diem and his advisors ask for immediate assistance in destroying crops in Viet Cong strongholds before they can be harvested.[7]

November 7, 1961. Defense Secretary McNamara sends a memorandum to the Chairman of the Joint Chiefs of Staff and the Secretary of the Air Force directing the Air Force "to provide, on a priority basis, the required aircraft, personnel, and chemicals" to attack fast-maturing Viet Cong crops.[8]

November 11, 1961. A National Security Council (NSC) decision authorizes "aircraft, personnel and chemical defoliants" to be dispatched to Viet Nam "to kill Viet Cong food crops and defoliate selected border and jungle areas,

---

2 In these tests, Agent Purple, a 50:30:20 mixture of the n-butyl ester of 2,4-D, and the n-butyl and isobutyl esters of 2,4,5-T, was found to be most effective on broadleaf plants, and 145,000 of the agent was reportedly applied in Vietnam from 1962–1964, but because of its volatility, it was replaced by Agent Orange in 1965. [US Institute of Medicine, Committee to Review the Health Effects in Vietnam Veterans of Exposure to Herbicides, *Veterans and Agent Orange Health Effects of Herbicides Used in Vietnam* (Washington, DC: National Academies Press, 1994).]

3 Jeanne Mager Stellman et al., "The Extent and Patterns of Usage of Agent Orange and Other Herbicides in Vietnam," *Nature* 422, April 17, 2003, 681–687.

4 H. Lindsey Arison, III, "The Herbicidal Warfare Program in Vietnam, 1961–1971: Operations Trail Dust/Ranch Hand," Vietnam Veterans of America, http://www.utvet.com/agentorange2.html.

5 Arison.

6 Arison.

7 Arison.

8 Arison.

to assist in uncovering enemy hideout and transit areas."[9] Crops believed to be available to the Viet Cong are intentionally, systematically poisoned to ensure "resources control," and the inevitable destruction of villages and resulting deaths of residents is callously described as "collateral damage."[10]

November 30, 1961. President Kennedy personally approves, in principle, the start of Operation Ranch Hand.[11]

December 15, 1961. The first large supply of chemicals ships out of Oakland, California, on the *S.S. Sooner State*: 111,000 gallons of Agent Purple and 49,000 gallons of Agent Pink. A second shipment later in the month contains an additional 17,000 gallons of Agent Purple and 31,000 gallons of Agent Pink.[12] Agent Green herbicides and 15,000 pounds of cacodylic acid are already in storage in Saigon, having been sent for use in a rice crop destruction operation, in which President Kennedy's approval came too late in the season. The Department of Defense/War (DOD) procures additional chemicals for use in the defoliation of Viet Cong base areas, border regions, and transportation routes on an expedited basis.[13]

January 12, 1962. The first official Operation Ranch Hand chemical defoliation mission is launched with C-123s.[14] The Ranch Hand motto: *"Only We Can Prevent Forests."*[15]

Operation Ranch Hand

Between August 10, 1961 and October 31, 1971, more than 21 million gallons of herbicides were applied to vast areas of South Viet Nam. The chemical spray directly affected as many as 4.8 million Vietnamese, distributed among 3,181 villages located in or near spraying operation target areas,[16] as well as thousands of volunteers and regular army troops working and moving along the Ho Chi Minh Trail.

By December 1965, Operation Ranch Hand missions had begun to successfully defoliate major reinforcement and supply routes through Laos near the Ho Chi Minh Trail, but the herbicides applied were not limited to defoliants. Agent Blue, for example, of which one component was cacodylic acid, a crystalline substance containing arsenic, was designed with food crops in mind.[17] Standard operating procedure for US forces in Viet Nam was to destroy both villagers' homes *and* their food supplies.[18] News of the chemical warfare

---

9 Kahin, 1986, 140, 478n47.

10 Cincinnatus, 42, 228n47.

11 National Security Action Memorandum (NSAM-115), "Defoliant Operations in Vietnam," November 30, 1961.

12 Arison.

13 Arison.

14 Bowman, 54; Dougherty and Stewart, 42.

15 Young, 1991, 82; Gettleman et al., 1995, 465.

16 "Scientists Boost Estimate of Agent Orange Used in Vietnam," *USA Today*, April 16, 2003.

17 Stellman et al., 681–687.

18 Hersh, 1970, 175.

raised serious ethical concerns among the scientific community. In a December 21, 1965 article titled "US Spray Destroys Rice in Vietcong Territory," the *New York Times* reported that twenty-nine US scientists were urging President Johnson to prohibit the use of chemical and biological weapons by US military in Viet Nam.

Twenty herbicide-spraying missions in Vinh Long Province alone, just north of Binh Thuy and Can Tho, near my 1969 duty area, contaminated much of the rice crop that provided basic sustenance for thirty inhabited villages, within an area of approximately 180 square miles (115,200 acres). Little did we know at the time the lethal effects of these chemicals sprayed in Vietnam's air, water, and soil would come back to haunt us.

In addition to targeted spraying missions, former Ranch Hand pilots reported 26,000 aborted operations in which 260,000 gallons of the herbicide were simply dumped on the landscape. Some dumping was ruled "accidental," as when engine failures required pilots to lighten their load at the expense of whatever lay below. Chemical dumping was reported over populated areas as well as bodies of water. A further impetus for the practice was a US military regulation that required all spray aircraft to return to base *empty*.[19]

Not content with chemical defoliation, in 1966 the military sought to destroy large areas of forest and jungle by fire. Project Rose began with B-52s dropping incendiaries on already defoliated forests. Chemical companies and the government conveniently concealed the fact that burning the already defoliated trees dramatically increased the toxicity of the dioxins and caused them to be more widely dispersed through the air.[20]

Collusion of Chemical Companies

The Pentagon signed lucrative contracts with seven different US chemical companies, worth a total of 57 million dollars combined,[21] to produce a variety of defoliants, including Agent Orange: Dow Chemical (Midland, Michigan); Hercules Inc. (Wilmington, Deleware); Monsanto (St. Louis, Missouri); Diamond Alkali (Dallas, Texas); Uniroyal Inc. (Middlebury, Connecticut); Thompson Chemical (Newark, New Jersey); and Thompson-Hayward Agriculture and Nutrition (Kansas City, Missouri).[22]

In 1964 , Dow Chemical, the biggest US producer of these herbicides, experienced an incident at its 2-4-5-T manufacturing plant in Midland, Michigan, in which exposure to the herbicide resulted in over 50 workers developing chloracne, a serious skin disease. The director of Dow's Midland Division, Dr. Benjamin Holder, reported a number of symptoms related to chemical exposure, including fatigue, lassitude (weariness), depression, blackheads (prevalent on the face, neck, and back), and weight loss. Heavy

---

19 Cathy Scott-Clark and Adrian Levy, "Spectre Orange," *The Guardian*, March 28, 2003; Philip Jones Griffiths, *Agent Orange: "Collateral Damage"* (London, UK: Trolley Ltd, 2003), 166; http://www.theguardian.com/world/2003/mar/29/usa.adrianlevy.

20 Griffiths,, 166.

21 Scott-Clark and Levy.

22 Monsanto, Agent Orange, Dioxins and Plan Colombia, http://www.sourcewatch.org/index.php/Monsanto,_Agent_Orange,_Dioxins_and_Plan_Colombia; Fred Wilcox, *Waiting for an Army to Die* (New York: Seven Stories Press, 1989/2011), 107.

exposure to the herbicide, Dr. Holder said, could lead to internal organ damage and nervous system disorders.[23] That same year, Dow hired a University of Pennsylvania dermatologist to test dioxin on 70 prisoners at Holmesburg Prison in Philadelphia. When administered increased doses of dioxin, eighty of the prisoners developed chloracne.[24]

Dioxin is a by-product of the manufacture of Agent Orange, in which two chemicals, 2-4-D and 2-4-5-T, are combined. It is a hundred times more potent than the next most potent chemical, benzidine, and 100,000,000 times more potent than vinyl chloride.[25] In South Vietnam, the herbicide Agent Orange was applied at an average concentration 13 times the rate recommended by the US Department of Agriculture for domestic use. The EPA has confirmed dioxin is 3,000,000 times more carcinogenic than DDT.[26]

In an internal memo circulated February 22, 1965, Dow summoned a meeting of thirteen executives to discuss the suspected hazards of dioxin in 2-4-5-T.[27] On March 19, 1965, Dow invited officials from Monsanto, Diamond Alkali, Hooker Chemical, and Hercules to come to its Midland headquarters to discuss the health problems associated with finding "highly toxic impurities" in 2-4-5-T and related substances.[28] Dow hoped that other herbicide makers would institute "self-imposed controls" on dioxin production, before the government and other outsiders discovered the problem that might curtail production and interfere with their lucrative profits.

On June 24, 1965, Dow's chief toxicologist, Dr. D. K. Rowe, wrote to Dow's Canadian manager describing the dangers of dioxin and the implications for Dow: "As you well know, we had a serious situation in our operating plants because of contamination of 2-4-5-trichlorophenol with impurities, the most active of which is 2-3-7-8-tetrachlorodibenzdioxin. The material is exceptionally toxic: it has a tremendous potential for producing chloracne and serious injury."[29] A postscript to the letter: "Under no circumstances may this letter be reproduced, shown or sent to anyone outside Dow."[30]

A toxicologist from competitor Hercules noted that Dow was concerned the government might learn of its study showing that dioxin caused severe liver damage in rabbits. This fact, if it became public, could severely deleteriously impact the entire herbicide industry. So these concerns were kept quiet as the US government and its military, and the chemical companies themselves, offered a united front to the public about the military necessity of chemical defoliation in conducting the war in Viet Nam, and continued to assert that the chemicals posed no danger to humans.[31]

---

23 Doyle, 61, 81–90.
24 Doyle, 89.
25 "Dioxin Reportedly Worst Cancer Causer," *The Boston Globe*, July 24, 1983.
26 Stanford Biology Study Group, "The Destruction of Indochina," *Bulletin of the Atomic Scientists* 27(5) (May 1971), 36–40; Griffiths, 173.
27 Griffiths, 164.
28 Max Blumenthal, "Files Show Dioxin Makers Knew of Hazards," *New York Times*, July 6, 1983, p. 1.
29 Doyle, 84–86.
30 Griffiths, 165.
31 Griffiths, 165.

A serious shortage of defoliants in 1967 led Johnson to issue an order that military demand for 2,4,5-T (one of the main components of Agent Orange along with 2,4-D) was to be fully met. Subsequently, the Pentagon intensified its defoliation of Vietnamese jungles and increased the dosage of herbicides used, calling upon the chemical companies to escalate production. The escalated production process, which called for faster "cooking" at higher temperatures, in turn caused elevated levels of the highly toxic byproduct dioxin. A 2003 research study, published in *Nature*, found that the quantity of dioxin in herbicides sprayed in Viet Nam was more than double the estimates given previously by US government sources.[32]

As noted above, the intensification of chemical spraying at this time was not just to deny cover to the enemy via defoliation, but also to reduce the Viet Cong to starvation in what was termed the "food denial program." The blue agent was intentionally designed for this purpose. Ironically, 1967 was the year of the UN Freedom from Hunger Campaign[33].

In 1968, as the American Association for the Advancement of Science (AAAS) informed the State and War/Defense Departments of its concerns with use of Agent Orange in Viet Nam, the military strategists were acknowledging that the chemical spraying possessed "little military" value. But the program continued. In late 1969, Bionetics Research Laboratories reported that dioxin, even at the lowest dose given, causes cleft palates, missing and deformed eyes, cystic kidneys, and enlarged livers, as well as deaths and still births, in laboratory animals. Despite this research, the spraying continued until 1970, along with the public representations of its validity as a military strategy and the claim of no detriments to human health. By that time, however, the Deputy Secretary of Defense/War and the Surgeon General had banned dioxin for domestic use, and soon thereafter spraying in Viet Nam was officially terminated.[34]

Criminal Implications

The Vietnamese have claimed for years the severe health and environmental effects of wartime herbicide spraying. New research points to the criminal implications of the widespread and indiscriminate application of toxic chemicals, confirming that the US Government not only illicitly used these weapons of mass destruction, but also stymied any independent assessment of the impact of their deployment, while ignoring hard evidence of the death and the suffering of those exposed, including US soldiers, and long-term damages to Vietnam and her people. The policy was one of evasion and deception.[35]

It took the intervention by a former commander of the US Navy in Viet Nam, Admiral Elmo Zumwalt, for the government finally to admit that it had been aware of the potential dangers of the chemicals used in Viet Nam from the start of Ranch Hand. Zumwalt's

---

32 David Perlman, "Seeing red over Agent Orange: US understated use of dioxin during Vietnam, researcher says," *SFGate*, April 1, 2003 (accessed Jan. 29, 2016): http://www.sfgate.com/news/article/Seeing-red-over-Agent-Orange-U-S-understated-2621172.php

33 Duffett, 349–350.

34 Griffiths, 167–169; Wilcox, *Scorched Earth*, 2011, 202–203.

35 Scott-Clark and Levy.

son, a swift boat commander, contracted two forms of cancer that he believed were caused by his exposure to Agent Orange. In 1988, Zumwalt compiled data in a classified report that he presented to the Veterans Administration, linking Agent Orange to 28 life-threatening conditions, including bone cancer, skin cancer, and brain cancer—in fact, almost every cancer known to man—in addition to chronic skin disorders, birth defects, gastrointestinal diseases, and neurological defects.[36]

Zumwalt also uncovered irrefutable evidence that the US military had dispensed "Agent Orange in concentrations 6 to 25 times the suggested rate" and that "4.2 million US soldiers could have made transient or significant contact with the herbicides because of Operation Ranch Hand." This figure is twice the official estimate of the number of US veterans who may have been contaminated with Tetrachlorodibenzo-p-doxin (TCCD).[37]

Zumwalt obtained a 1988 letter written to Congress by Dr. James Clary, the military scientist who designed the spray tanks for Ranch Hand, in which the doctor admitted: "When we initiated the herbicide program in the 1960s, we were aware of the potential for damage due to dioxin contamination in the herbicide. We were even aware that the military formulation had a higher dioxin concentration than the civilian version, due to the lower cost and speed of manufacture. However, because the material was to be used on the enemy, none of us were overly concerned."[38]

Veterans' Lawsuit

By 1984, thousands of sick veterans came together as plaintiffs in a class action lawsuit initially filed in 1978 against the herbicide manufacturers. The veterans sought 44 billion dollars in damages for a long list of medical problems, including severe skin rashes, nervous disorders, dizziness, chronic coughing, impotence, liver and kidney disease, cancers, and birth defects in offspring. They had been systematically ignored and humiliated by a Veterans Administration (VA) that refused to acknowledge their health issues were connected to chemical poisoning in Viet Nam. More than 25 years after the end of the war, the VA finally recognized and began offering compensation for 14 illnesses, plus spina bifida birth defects in offspring of Viet Nam veterans, as presumptively caused by exposure to Agent Orange or other herbicides during military service.[39]

In early 1984, I was hired by the Massachusetts Commissioner of Veterans Services to direct the Western Massachusetts Agent Orange Information Office. I interviewed hundreds of veterans to assess patterns of deleterious health effects, as well as birth defects in their offspring, that might be consequences of toxic poisoning related to the veteran's proximity to herbicide spraying. I coordinated a number of community forums in the state where veterans and their families could express their growing concerns about specific health problems and deformities cropping up in their children.

---

36 Scott-Clark and Levy.
37 Scott-Clark and Levy.
38 Scott-Clark and Levy; Griffiths, 2003, 165.
39 Veterans' Diseases Associated with Agent Orange, http://www.publichealth.va.gov/exposures/agentorange/conditions/, accessed May 6, 2015.

I testified in 1984 before US Federal District Court with presiding Judge Jack B. Weinstein in Brooklyn, New York, as a formal representative of Governor Michael Dukakis, on behalf of the overwhelming majority of Massachusetts Viet Nam veterans who had registered their firm opposition to any settlement with the chemical companies. Veterans felt a trial where all the facts could come out was most important, win or lose. There was no question in the plaintiffs' minds that they, indeed, had evidence to prove the chemical companies had knowledge about the dangers of dioxin they had chosen not to

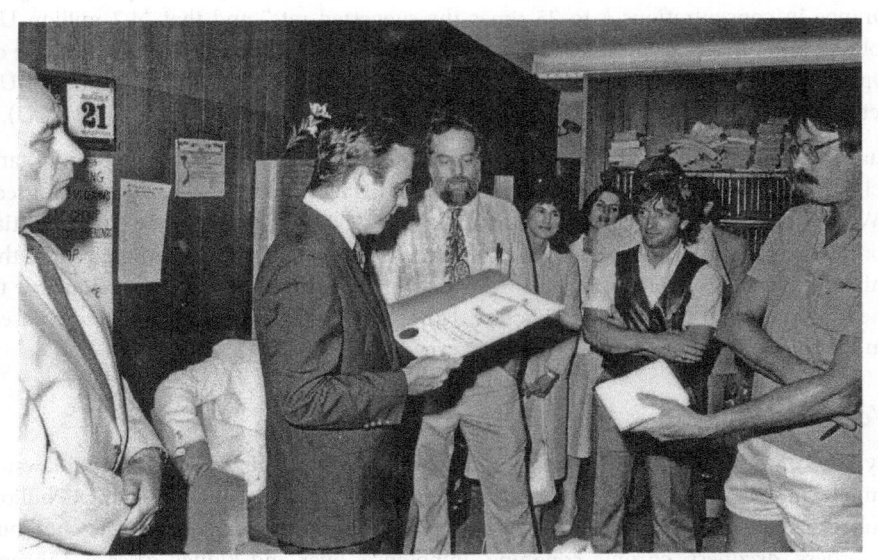

On August 12, 1985, a certificate from the Commonwealth of Massachusetts, signed by Governor Michael S. Dukakis, was awarded to the author for "Humanitarian Service above and beyond normal expectations to your fellow Vietnam Veterans." As coordinator of the Vietnam Veterans Outreach Center in Greenfield, Massachusetts, that service included interviewing and testifying on behalf of fellow veterans in a lawsuit brought against Agent Orange chemical manufacturers. In the photo, Dukakis' Secretary of Human Services, Phil Johnston, presents the award to the author (center), while Commissioner Halachis looks on at left.

share with the government or the public. The chemical companies argued that they were "just following orders" from the US military when they manufactured batches of Agent Orange with as much as 15,000 times more dioxin than the 2-4-5-T sold for domestic use. The companies filed various motions over a period of years in efforts to obstruct the possibility of any trial.[40]

The deleterious health effects on humans of exposure to dioxin, the major ingredient of Agent Orange, was known as early as 1957.[41] During preliminary fact-gathering in preparation for the veterans' lawsuit, it was revealed that the chemical companies, and

---

40 Wilcox, 1989/2011, 108.
41 "Jim Hopkins," *Hustler,* October 1981; Jack Doyle, *Trespass against Us* (Monroe, ME: Common Courage Press, 2004), 81–83.

some US authorities, indeed had *clearly* known about the serious health effects of Agent Orange by 1965, and probably long before that, and that they had deliberately hidden evidence of dioxin-related medical problems. This fact was subsequently buried after the forced settlement, but occasionally an investigative reporter like Jon Dillingham rediscovers this tragic trail of deceit.[42]

When, in 1984, the judge forced a settlement of 180 million dollars rather than allowing a trial, it caused intense anger and deep disappointment among Viet Nam veterans, who again felt sold out and betrayed by their government. A public trial would have shown the world what happens to human beings who are exposed to deadly chemicals like dioxin. But instead of honoring their commitment to veterans, a number of VA doctors at the time insisted on calling them crazy or malingerers, said they were feigning illnesses and filing false claims to secure disability payments.

The forced settlement was in fact a great victory for the chemical companies. The 180 million dollars turned out to be chump change compared to the magnitude of harm done and immensity of the continuing health impacts. By 1997, as the number of veterans exhibiting symptoms of chemical exposure continued to mount, the Agent Orange settlement fund was exhausted.[43]

Personal Exposure

According to official USAF computer data on Operation Ranch Hand, eight percent of the application occurred in the Delta's IV Corps area where I served, in March through August 1969. Having been the night security commander at Binh Thuy Air Base, I was aware of hand spraying of herbicides in addition to several aerial spraying missions around the base perimeter, though at the time I had no knowledge of any health concerns. There were few trees in the immediate vicinity of our airbase, but it was to our security advantage to minimize any vertical vegetation such as the tall elephant grass that concealed enemy encroachers. In addition, thousands of waterways and canals in the delta, including several surrounding Binh Thuy, would certainly have been contaminated from spraying.

The more I learned about the Agent Orange class action lawsuit in my work with the Agent Orange Information Project in Massachusetts in 1984, the more concerned I became about my own possible exposure. I made a formal inquiry to the US Army's Agent Orange Task Force in Washington asking for available records of herbicide spraying in the region of my military service in 1969. In the meantime, I discovered the HERBS Tapes, a log of aerial herbicide applications maintained by the Chemical Operations Division, US MACV. The computerized data tabulated herbicide mission activity for *each* aerial mission between July 1965 and February 1971, including: type of herbicide and number of gallons sprayed; number of aircraft; coordinates of each mission flight path; province in which the mission

---

[42] Jon Dillingham, "Vietnam Chemical Companies, US Authorities Knew the Dangers of Agent Orange," *Global Research*, August 10, 2009: http://www.globalresearch.ca/vietnam-chemical-companies-us-authorities-knew-the-dangers-of-agent-orange/14720.

[43] Doyle, 72–78; Wilcox, *Scorched Earth*, (2011), 63–64.

flew; purpose of the mission (defoliation or crop destruction); and number of aborts. Flight paths were identified in coordinates utilizing the Universal Transverse Mercator (UTM) system, a rectangular grid ruled off in 100,000-meter subgrids. The information was subsequently mapped utilizing the UTM system.[44]

In June 1984, I received this reply from Richard S. Christian, Director Environmental Support Group, Department of the Army: "Our research at this time indicates your unit was not in close proximity to areas of high herbicide usage." However, by then I had carefully examined *The Vietnam Map Book* which used the information from the HERBS Tapes to plot on easy-to-read maps all the US Air Force aerial spray missions based on the UTM system, though it did not include spraying by the Navy or the Marines, or manual perimeter spraying. I learned that from January 15, 1969 to July 2, 1969, around the time of my presence there, there were more than 60 aerial spraying missions of Agent Orange, Agent White, and Agent Blue in the areas in southern Vinh Long and northern Phong Dinh Provinces around Binh Thuy, which included the towns of Can Tho, Vinh Long, and Sa Dec. On five separate dates—February 4 (109 acres), February 11 (264 acres), March 13 (165 acres), April 21 (180 acres), and June 14, 1969 (200 acres)—spraying had occurred *immediately adjacent* to the rectangular perimeter of Binh Thuy airbase, an accumulative 918 acres of toxic spraying.[45]

Vietnamese Victims' Lawsuit

In 2004, lawyers representing a number of Vietnamese victims of Agent Orange poisoning filed a class action lawsuit again charging the chemical companies with war crimes. The chemical companies argued that the US does not have to "heed the rules of civil conduct that can have no application in the theater of war" and "owes no duty in tort to enemy combatants or even to noncombatants in a war zone."[46] Not surprisingly, the next year, federal district judge Weinstein, the same judge who had forced a settlement in the 1994 veterans lawsuit, dismissed the case.[47]

The Vietnamese victims appealed, but in another heartless decision, in 2007, the Court of Appeals ruled against them. The Second Circuit Court upheld Weinstein's ruling, concluding that, although the herbicides contained dioxin, a known poison, they were not intended for use on human beings, and therefore could not be considered chemical weapons, and thus their use was not a violation of international law.[48] On appeal, the Supreme Court refused on March 2, 2009, to reconsider the case.

---

44 Clark Smith and Don Watkins, *The Vietnam Map Book: A Self Help Guide to Herbicide Exposure* (Berkeley, CA: Agent Orange Veteran's Advisory Committee, November 1981), Winter Soldier Archive, 200 Center St., Box 1251, Berkeley, CA 94704.

45 Note: *The Chicago Tribune* has on its website an interactive map for viewing defoliant spraying missions in Viet Nam by date and location: http://www.chicagotribune.com/chi-091204-agentorange-map-htmlstory.html.

46 Wilcox, *Scorched Earth*, 2011, 104.

47 William Glaberson, "Agent Orange Case for Millions of Vietnamese Is Dismissed," *New York Times*, March 10, 2005; http://www.nytimes.com/2005/03/10/nyregion/10cnd-oran.html?_r=0.

48 February 22, 2008 decision, Second Circuit Court of Appeals, RE: *Vietnamese Association of Victims of Agent Orange v. Dow Chemical Co.*

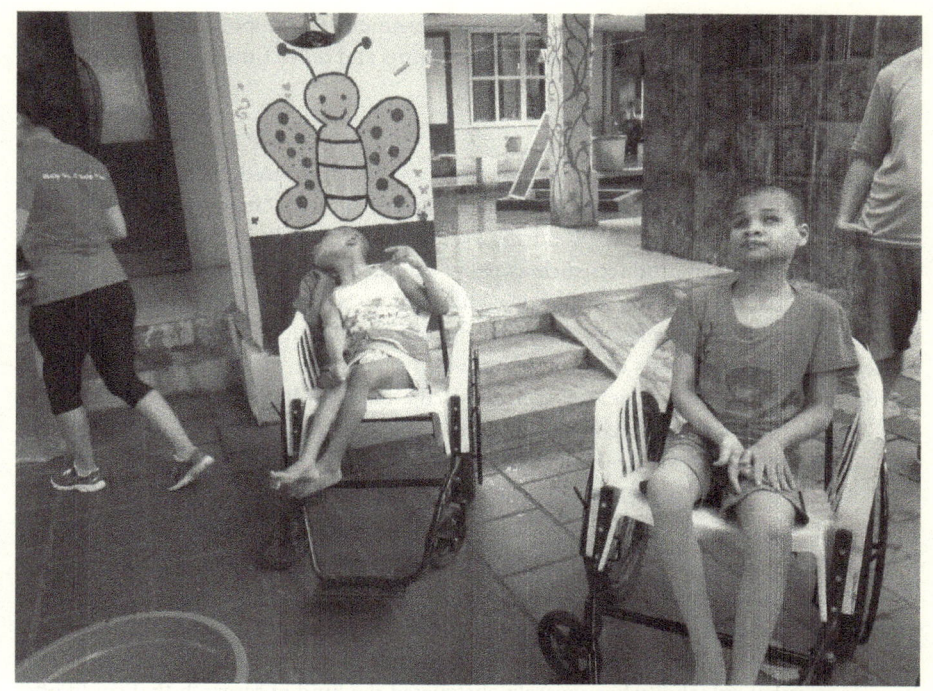

Due to extensive spraying of chemical agents on the Vietnamese landscape by American forces during the war, children continue to be born with debilitating disabilities. This photo was taken in April 2016 at an orphanage in Ba Vi, west of Ha Noi, just one of many such institutions in Viet Nam. [Photo: Becky Luening]

Who knows how many Agent Orange victims there really are? The numbers continue to grow. Dioxin causes genetic damage passed on from one generation to another; the chemical is still present in "hot spots" and continues to poison people in Viet Nam. Several million Vietnamese continue to suffer, 650,000 of them children, as do hundreds of thousands of US American and allied war veterans and their offspring. Vietnamese officials and community workers estimate they need at least a thousand new community centers, often called Peace Villages, to accommodate the staggering number of children suffering the disastrous after effects of the US chemical war. Currently Viet Nam has a dozen such villages. One of them, the Vietnam Friendship Village in Hanoi, was founded by my friend and fellow faster in the 1986 Veterans Fast for Life, Viet Nam veteran George Mizo, who returned to Viet Nam in 1988 on a mission of healing and reconciliation.[49]

In 1991, the US Congress passed the Agent Orange Act, directing the Academy of Sciences to conduct comprehensive studies of the health effects of exposure to herbicides in Viet Nam. This started a process of identifying a number of diseases and health diagnoses for the purposes of determining eligibility for VA benefits for US veterans, but there would be no restitution for the Vietnamese. The Vietnam Agent Orange Relief and Responsibility Campaign (VAORRC), an initiative of US veterans and allies, lobbies

---

[49] Scott-Clark and Levy; Robert Dreyfuss, "Apocalypse Still," *Mother Jones* (Jan.–Feb. 2000), http://www.motherjones.com/politics/2000/01/apocalypse-still; Wilcox, *Scorched Earth*, 2011, 102.

for legislation that would compel the US government to honor its moral and legal responsibility to compensate the Vietnamese victims and *all* victims, of Agent Orange.[50]

A Poisoned Environment

Essentially, dioxin is an unavoidable byproduct of chlorine-based chemical production processes. In past decades, chemical companies came up with creative, marketable uses for chlorine such as for poison gas during World War I. Chlorine is present in hundreds of normal commercial products such as paper products, medicines, disinfectants, water purification, paints, virtually all plastics, children's toys, dairy carton liners and other food packaging. It is now present *everywhere* in our environment. The tiniest amount can cause damage since it tends to weaken immune systems. The most serious health effect, in addition to causing a variety of cancers, is the embryonic damage as dioxin blocks and distorts hormones, thereby causing fetal deformities. Dioxin is one of the most perilous threats to our species. We have created a Faustian bargain living in a synthetic environment that severely poisons us as we enjoy its conveniences.[51]

Being the epicenter of dioxin/Agent Orange destruction, Viet Nam provides us the ultimate lab for examining clues to its horrific progression. For scientists, it poses a perfect control study where ethnically identical people are geographically separated into two groups: those who were in the North during the war and were not sprayed; and those who were exposed by being in the South. The tenacious resistance of the US to acknowledging its own criminal culpability has severely obstructed the kind of research that could offer targeted treatment for victims of chemical warfare in the US as well as Viet Nam. Such research would no doubt uncover overwhelming evidence of its lethality, which (in a sane world) should compel our species to radically shift from dependence upon poisonous industrial processes to more organic and sustainable technologies, and to integrate our lifestyles with principles that will assure life for "the Seventh Generation."[52]

Ironically, Monsanto, the company that manufactured huge amounts of Agent Orange for this massive wartime experiment, now staffs profitable offices in both Hanoi and Ho Chi Minh City, as Viet Nam becomes ever more dependent on "modern" chemical agriculture. Monsanto is the world's leader in genetically modified seeds that by design require heavy use of chemical herbicides.[53] The question arises whether the heavy application of agricultural chemicals pushed by this company and others might be responsible for some of the many health issues attributed to Agent Orange in Viet Nam.

Monsanto benefits from a close relationship with the US government: Like other multinational companies, it is able to easily find tax loopholes, while effectively authoring self-serving regulations; it funds academic research at public universities to aid in promoting its latest products; Monsanto board members and senior staff benefit from a continuous "revolving door" with government and universities, while maintaining close

---

50 http://www.vn-agentorange.org/.
51 Griffiths, 172–174.
52 Griffiths, 174.
53 http://www.monsanto.com/whoweare/pages/vietnam.aspx.

relationships with former and contemporary US government figures, such as regulators with the Environmental Agency (EPA) and Food and Drug Administration (FDA), and with other industry leaders, including war-industrial giant Lockheed. Board members have included former US Representatives and Senators, White House Aides, Secretaries of Defense/War, Agriculture, Commerce, and Supreme Court Justices.[54]

Agent Orange in Okinawa, Japan[55]

Because Okinawa, Japan was the Pentagon's top support base for the war in Viet Nam, many toxic substance were stored, sprayed, buried and dumped on the island. Many barrels of defoliants passed through Okinawa on the way to Johnston Island for final disposal. Agent Orange and other chemical toxins were also sprayed to kill vegetation around US military base roads, runways and radar sites in Okinawa. Containers of chemicals were routinely buried underneath bases or dumped into surrounding waters. In 2005, the Pentagon acknowledged three areas of large-scale contamination and four dumpsites at Camp Kinser, in the city of Urasoe (population 114,000).

In Nago, another city on Okinawa, use of defoliants was discovered to have contaminated seaweed and clams. Nago was also the location for Pentagon testing of biological weapons in the early 1960s. The city is located near Henoko Bay, where the US is currently attempting to build an offshore military base, a project that is being passionately resisted in daily protests by locals who wish to preserve the natural features of their pristine bay.

A number of barrels, bearing insignia of the Dow Chemical Company, one of the Agent Orange manufacturers, have also been unearthed on Kadena Air Force Base in Okinawa City. Kadena Air Base was the Pentagon's busiest Okinawa installation during the Viet Nam war. As with Viet Nam, the US Government has fought claims of harm caused by these chemicals in Japan. To make matters worse, the US-Japan Status of Forces Agreement relieves Washington of all costs of remediating land returned to public usage.

---

54 "Monsanto: A Corporate Profile," 2013, *Food & Water Watch*, http://documents.foodandwaterwatch.org/doc/MonsantoReport.pdf#_ga=1.246453316.1795590104.1365015785; "Partially Debunked: List of Monsanto Employees in Government," https://www.metabunk.org/threads/partially-debunked-list-of-monsanto-employees-in-government.3664/

55 Kimberly Hughes, "Determined citizens are working to uncover 'one of the best kept secrets of the Cold War era,'" November 18, 2014, *The Diplomat*; http://thediplomat.com/2014/11/agent-orange-in-okinawa/; Jon Mitchell, "Agent Orange Dioxin, Toxic Dumps at Okinawa US Military Base," Global Research, October 7, 2015, http://www.globalresearch.ca/agent-orange-dioxin-toxic-dumps-at-okinawa-us-military-base/5480266, reprinted from *The Asia-Pacific Journal*, Vol. 13, Issue. 39, No. 1, October 5, 2015.

Evidence of US Use of Germ and Chemical Warfare in Korea[56]

On a trip to South Korea in 2001, I investigated eye-witness reports of survivors from South Cholla Province who remembered seeing, in 1952, aerial spraying of a white cloud or mist from light planes on rugged, 3,900-foot Mudung Mountain. They said that humans exposed to the spray immediately developed signs of sickness, including dark skin discoloration. Most of the people present at that time—local villagers, temporary refugees, and guerrillas in hiding—died shortly after exposure.

I had recently become aware of documented evidence of germ warfare employed by the United States in North Korea and China in early 1952, but these claims about germ warfare in the South were new to me.

Throughout its brief history, the US has developed and demonstrated a number of high-tech tools in going to war against those it chooses to demonize as its enemy. Its toolbox includes methods for depriving civilians of food and water in order to induce surrender or capitulation. Historically, we know that the United States intentionally used germs in military campaigns. For example, in the nineteenth century the US Army deliberately used smallpox-contaminated blankets to eliminate thousands of Indigenous Americans, especially in the Central Plains region. British General Jeffrey Amherst had earlier used this same tactic against Chief Pontiac and his Indigenous forces in the summer of 1763 in what is now western Pennsylvania, at the conclusion of what we call the French and Indian War. Chief Pontiac had sided with the French and in so doing had stirred the ire of Amherst, who responded with orders to "extirpate" the Indigenous, who one of his colonels called vermin, with smallpox-infected blankets and handkerchiefs.[57]

The US formalized its own germ and chemical warfare program with creation in 1943 of the Biological Warfare Laboratories at US Army Camp Detrick in Frederick, Maryland. Following defeat of the Japanese in 1945, the US War Department's Chemical Warfare Service (later the Chemical Corps) continued the bacteriological warfare program. The Far East Command Medical Section created its Unit 406 Medical General Laboratory for such purposes in 1946 near Atsugi air base in Yokohama, Japan. Later it added branches in Tokyo and Kyoto.

In 1946, the US chose to grant immunity from war crimes prosecution to Japanese scientists who had been involved in germ warfare in return for their cooperation in sharing their advanced knowledge of biological warfare with the US, rather than with the Soviet Union. US scientists examined nearly three dozen Japanese reports and hundreds of pages of autopsy reports, and conducted numerous interviews with the Japanese scientists. The briefings included ways of inducing, as well as learning the effects of, hemorrhagic fever.

---

56 Much of the information on the history of US use of biological warfare in Korea and China is the result of the lengthy, exhaustive study by two Canadian professors at York University: Stephen Endicott and Edward Hagerman, *The United States and Biological Warfare: Secrets From the Early Cold War and Korea* (Bloomington, Indiana: Indiana University Press, 1998).

57 "Jeffrey Amherst and Smallpox Blankets: Lord Jeffrey Amherst's letters discussing germ warfare against American Indians", http://www.umass.edu/legal/derrico/amherst/lord_jeff.html#1.

By the time the "hot" war started in Korea, the US biological weapons system was up and running. Prior to June 25, 1950, commonly cited as the starting date for the war, the Ad Hoc Committee on Chemical, Biological, and Radiological Warfare recommended construction of a new biological warfare production facility, implementation of field tests of biological warfare agents and munitions, and expansion of biological warfare research. By the fall of 1950, advanced testing had begun at Dugway Proving Grounds in Utah, and a production facility was constructed at Pine Bluff Arsenal in Arkansas. By July 1951, the US was testing anti-animal biological agents at Eglin Air Force Base in Florida.

Also, at the time the Korean War broke out, the Far East Command's Medical Unit 406 included departments of epidemiology, bacteriology, entomology, and viral and rickettsial diseases. Unit 406 scientists were already working on hemorrhagic fever in 1951 before Korea's first fatal case of the unusual disease was reported in April 1951. The monthly technical report of Unit 406 for August 1951 stated: "New activities relate to studies of a disease heretofore considered Leptospirosis, but resembling that described by Japanese as Epidemic Hemorrhagic Fever." That part of the report was preceded by noting that "Work of a classified nature, for security reasons, is reported elsewhere" (which has never been identified). This report was issued just prior to the timeframe given by the eyewitnesses who reported seeing aerial spraying of "white powder" in South Cholla Province (September-October 1951).

In October 1951, the US Joint Chiefs of Staff (JCS) hand-delivered a secret order to General Mathew B. Ridgeway, then commander of all UN forces, to start germ warfare on a limited experimental scale in Korea. Two months later, US Secretary of Defense Robert A. Lovett ordered that "actual readiness be achieved in the earliest practicable time" for offensive use of biological weapons. The First Marine Air Wing operating under the direction of the Fifth Air Force carried out the secret missions. The US had a number of CIA operatives in North Korea and China collecting data on the effectiveness of the germ warfare program. If uncovered, the US was to fall back on the fact that it had not ratified the 1925 Geneva Protocol on biological warfare, and had not participated in the 1907 Hague Convention that outlawed chemical weapons.

During the Korean War, the US was shocked by the fact that a large percentage of its Korean POWs had collaborated in some way with their captors. In contrast, very few North Korean and Chinese prisoners collaborated with their UN captors, even though they were subjected to more brutality and violence.[58] At least thirty-six captured US air crew, including a number of officers, issued confessions admitting their participation in biological warfare. Though many of the US POWs, once released, recanted under threat of courts martial, many, surprisingly, did not. An exhaustive study conducted by the US Army concluded that neither "brainwashing" nor physical abuse were causes of the high degree of collaboration. Instead, the cause was attributed to poor cultural orientation that failed to offer insight and maturity to understand political and cultural contexts.[59]

---

58 S. Brian Willson, "History of US Sabotage of Korean Peace and Reunification," September 1, 2001: http://www.brianwillson.com/history-of-u-s-sabotage-of-korean-peace-and-reunification/.

59 Endicott and Hagerman, 156–164; Eugene Kinkead, *In Every War But One* (New York: WW Norton & Co., 1959), 16–19.

Because of the widespread collaboration by US soldiers and airmen in Korea, the CIA in 1953 formally launched a secret, insidious mind-control program called MKUltra under orders of CIA director Allen Welsh Dulles. It sought to develop mind-controlling drugs for use in the Cold War in response to alleged Soviet, Chinese, and North Korean use of mind-control techniques on US prisoners of war in Korea.[60] It was assumed the "Communists" had used similar "special" techniques to extract sensitive information, when in fact, as the US study disclosed, the airmen's behavior was primarily due to immaturity and poor training. Poor training in this context could very well mean a failure of US indoctrination and military conditioning, which just didn't hold up in the face of the realities they experienced in Korea, and the men's own natural moral response.

It is also worth noting that Unit 406's addition of the 8003 Far East Medical Research Laboratory to its resources, in 1952, coincided with the US Air Force's crash program to develop and unleash biological weapons. The Air Force had already been planning a covert biological warfare capability with its Far Eastern air wing.

The *Commission of International Association of Democratic Lawyers—Report On US Crimes In Korea* (March 31, 1952) concluded that the US used both germ ("deliberate dispersion of flies and other insects artificially infected with bacteria...with the intention of spreading death and disease") and chemical ("use of poison gas bombs and other chemical substances") warfare against both civilians and combatants in North Korea. Established at the September 1951 Berlin Congress of the Association, the Commission consisted of eight lawyers, one each from Austria, Italy, Great Britain, France, China, Belgium, Brazil, and Poland. The Association had been prompted by a *Report of the Committee of the Women's International Democratic Federation in Korea, May 16-27, 1951*, an international commission of 22 women from 18 countries (including Canada and 7 Western European nations) that found systematic war crimes, by a number of means, were being committed by US forces and South Korean forces under the command of the US, though it did not specifically discuss use of bacteriological or chemical weapons.

China convened its own international study, and its *Report of the International Scientific Commission for the Investigation of the Facts Concerning Bacteriological Warfare in Korea and China*, issued in Peking in 1952, found significant use by the US of germ warfare. Of course, the US denied the various allegations and accusations of its use of biological and chemical warfare, and does so to this day. However, we now have the benefit of the exhaustive, 20-year study, thanks to Stephen Endicott and Edward Hagerman.[61] Carefully researched, their report concludes that the United States experimented with and deployed biological weapons during the Korean War, and that the US government lied, both to Congress and the US public, in saying that its biological warfare program was purely defensive (for retaliation only). A large and sophisticated offensive biological weapons

---

60 Wikipedia, MKUltra; Department of Energy, Advisory Committee on Human Radiation Experiments Report (ACHRE Report), Chapter 3, "Supreme Court Dissents Invoke the Nuremberg Code: CIA and DOD Human Subjects Research Scandals," *Advisory Committee on Human Radiation Experiments Final Report*, https://ehss.energy.gov/ohre/roadmap/achre/chap3_4.html.

61 Endicott and Hagerman.

system had been developed in the post-World War II years, and was used in North Korea. However, their study does not identify any use of germ warfare in South Korea.

The Mudung Mountain Site: Hemorraghic Fever?

At the time of the Korean War, the US had three types of gases in its inventory of chemical weapons—Phosgene, Mustard and Sarin. The symptoms described at Mudung Mountain seem to rule out gas, however, they do suggest the possibility of a kind of hemorrhagic fever.[62] And we know that the US was experimenting with inducing hemorrhagic fever, among other biological warfare tactics. Spraying from airplanes was one of the methods used for dispensing the agents. The program was shrouded in secrecy then, as now.

Use of Germ and Chemical Warfare by the US, Post-Korea[63]

When President Nixon was in office (1969–1974), the US waged bacteriological warfare against Cuba. First, Nixon directed that clouds be seeded over non-agricultural areas to induce torrential downpours and flooding, while attempting to prevent rains over cane and other agricultural areas to induce drought. Then the CIA introduced African Swine Fever, the first outbreak of the disease in the Western hemisphere in the twentieth century, forcing Cubans to slaughter 500,000 pigs, a major source of protein for the island. Under President Ronald Reagan and Vice President George H. W. Bush, there were new outbreaks of African Swine Fever, and two outbreaks of hemorrhagic dengue. It was the first eruption of hemorrhagic dengue in generations in Latin America.

Furthermore, the US has thwarted the international community in its recent efforts to adopt a new Geneva Protocol that would set up a stringent enforcement regime for carrying out on-site inspections at military and bio-tech locations to assure compliance with the 1972 Biological and Toxin Weapons Convention (BWC) banning germ and toxin weapons. The US signed the BWC, but took three years to ratify it. In 1975, the US Senate finally ratified both the 1925 Geneva Protocol (for the Prohibition of the Use in War of Asphyxiating, Poisonous or Other Gases, and of Bacteriological Methods of Warfare) and the BWC. After all that, the convention has been criticized for being relatively weak.

Drawing Conclusions

At the time of the Korean War, the US government possessed an active, offensive biological warfare program incorporating the Japanese biological warfare experiments conducted in Manchuria in the 1930s and 1940s. These experiments included the inducement of lethal hemorrhagic fevers, along with testing of many poisoning agents. Though the operations were top secret, it is known that the US used biological warfare in North Korea

---

62 *Textbook of Military Medicine: Medical Aspects of Chemical and Biological Warfare* (Washington, DC: Office of the Surgeon General, US Department of the Army, 1997).

63 Bill Schaap, "US Biological Warfare: The 1981 Cuba Dengue Epidemic," *Covert Action,* No. 17 (Summer 1982), 28–31; William Blum, *Killing Hope: US Military and CIA Interventions Since World War II* (Monroe, Maine: Common Courage Press, 1995), 188–189; William Blum, *Rogue State: A Guide to the World's Only Superpower* (Monroe, Maine: Common Courage Press, 2000), 108–111.

and portions of China in early 1952, possibly in late 1951. Thus, the evidence suggests the possibility that similar "experiments" with disabling biological poisons were being carried out in remote regions in South Korea around the same time. Such use would be further evidence of US willingness to use any instrument in war, no matter how diabolical or illegal.

Agent Orange in Korea[64]

The Department of Defense (DoD) acknowledges that, in 1968-69, 59,000 gallons combined of three highly toxic chemicals—Agent Orange, Agent Blue, and Monuron— were sprayed over 21,000 acres along Korea's 151-mile-long, 350-yard-wide demilitarized zone (DMZ). The VA has confirmed US soldiers' exposure to Agent Orange from April 1968 through July 1969, as the military defoliated the fields of fire between the front-line defensive positions and the south-barrier fence.

The herbicides were applied through hand spraying and distribution of pelletized herbicides. The effects of spraying were sometimes observed as far as 200 meters down wind.[65] Citing declassified DoD documents, Korean officials fear thousands of its soldiers were exposed, with as many as 30,000 suffering from illnesses related to their exposure.[66]

Though the DoD claims only Republic of Korea troops were involved in the actual spraying of Agent Orange in Korea, it has come to light that some of the 40,000 US troops in areas near the spraying may have been exposed.

In May 2011, three former US soldiers admitted dumping hundreds of barrels of chemical substances, including Agent Orange, at Camp Carroll in South Korea in 1978.[67] More recent evidence has disclosed application of chemical defoliants by US helicopters and other aircraft as early as the mid-1950s.[68]

---

64 "Agent Orange sprayed over DMZ in 1968-69", *Korea Herald*, June 3, 2011; John L. Davis, "Agent Orange Defoliated Korea's DMZ", *VFW Magazine*, Vol. 87, No. 6, February 2000; Leonard J. Selfon, "Agent Orange Presumptive List Expanded," *The VVA Veteran*, Mar.-Apr. 2003; Franklin Fisher, "Study finds high pollution levels at most US bases in S. Korea," *Stars and Stripes*, Pacific edition, February 11, 2006.

65 Selfon.

66 Davis.

67 Gwyn Kirk and Christine Ahn, "Agent Orange in Korea: Whistleblowers have unearthed the widespread use of Agent Orange by the US military in Korea," *Foreign Policy in Focus*, July 7, 2011.

68 Kwon Tae-ho, "USFK sprayed defoliant from 1955 to 1995, new testimony suggests," *The Hankyoreh*, May 31, 2011.

Chapter Six
Upheaval and Resistance at Home

*"We live in a culture of death—and
it is up to us to resist it."*
—Daniel Berrigan[1]

Introduction

The emergence in the 1960s of a dynamic democratic movement was largely an eruption of citizens' active and angry responses to both the ongoing war in Southeast Asia and the historical ravages of racism and Jim Crow here at home, combining a vigorous free speech movement, women's movement, with empowerment of African Americans, Chicanos, and Native Americans—broad-based popular democracy appeared to be breaking out in the United States of America. It was as exciting to vast swaths of the citizenry as it was terrifying to the oligarchic power brokers, who saw this broad-based movement as a threat to the traditional political and economic powers of corporate capitalism that had reigned for much of our country's history.

A creeping public awareness of the barbarity of the war erupted forcefully in 1968–69, strengthening the emerging domestic, veteran, and GI resistance movements that had already developed in response to the war. Already the Civil Rights movement was emerging as a major domestic force, and to many the war against the Vietnamese and the segregation of African Americans were seen as racist and interrelated.[2]

It is critical to remember that this incredible domestic resistance that arose in the 1960s and 1970s in response to the war was grounded in and intertwined with social justice struggles at home. For example, in September 1963, long before earning a reputation as a leader in the antiwar student movement, Students for a Democratic Society (SDS) formed the Economic Research and Action Project (ERAP) to organize unemployed white youths to go "into the ghetto" in northern cities.[3]

The incredible irony was lost on me at the time, but the US was essentially conducting three wars simultaneously at the time of the US Marine invasion of DaNang. This fact helps in understanding the rage so many people, including young students, were feeling

---

1 *Waging Nonviolence*, May 9, 2014, interview with Ken Butigan.
2 Muhammad Ali explained it perfectly in 1966 when he refused induction into the Army: "My conscience won't let me go shoot my brother, or some darker people, or some poor hungry people in the mud for big powerful America. And shoot them for what? They never called me nigger, they never lynched me, they didn't put no dogs on me, they didn't rob me of my nationality, rape and kill my mother and father. ... Shoot them for what? How can I shoot them poor people? Just take me to jail."
3 Kirkpatrick Sale, *SDS* (New York: Random House, 1973), 95–96.

in the 1960s—rage fueled by double standards exhibited by the US government at home and abroad. The three wars were neatly captured on one newspaper's front page—the March 8, 1965, edition of the *Niagara Falls Gazette:*

> (AP) **Marines Set up Guard at Viet Nam Air Base: Danang, Viet Nam**—The US Marines landed by sea and air in South Viet Nam today to strengthen the defense of the key Danang air base against attack by the Communist Viet Cong. [Additional headlines on the front page related to the emerging US war against Viet Nam: "Hanoi Says Six Planes Raid Village"; "Clash with Viet Reds Is Possible" (in which it was stated that the arrival of the Marines "could lead to the first ground fighting between US combat units and Communist guerrillas in the war"); and "Rebel Troops Attack Camp."]

> (UPI) **Troopers Smash Negroes' March; 67 Are Injured: Selma, Ala**—State troopers and deputies on horseback, under orders from Governor George Wallace to stop a "freedom" march to the state capital, Sunday tear-gassed 600 Negroes and set them reeling and bleeding under the lashes of clubs, bull whips and ropes. At least 67 Negroes were injured in the melee, including integration leader John Lewis who suffered a possible skull fracture. The hospitals reported . . . 17 Negroes were hospitalized with broken arms and legs, head injuries, hysteria and other injuries. . . . The place where officers intercepted the negroes near Edward Pettus Bridge resembled a battle scene, with abandoned bedrolls and clothing lying mingled with spent teargas shells. . . .

> (AP) **Johnson Charts Battle on Crime**—President Johnson asked Congress today to ban mail-order firearms, tighten controls over drugs, and strengthen safety in the streets as part of an attack on crime as a national problem. . . . Various bills will be submitted to carry out the idea. . . .

History provides a dynamic template for guiding what can happen when the people are viscerally motivated, and act collectively in various ways, in response to systemic injustice. As the war dragged on, many military veterans became active in the antiwar movement in ways that substantially boosted the civilian protests. In response, US officials acted to neutralize individuals considered as enemies. Whether far away in Viet Nam or among neighbors and fellow citizens at home, anyone who seriously criticized unjust government policies was suspect.

CIVIL RIGHTS STRUGGLE: JIM CROW | Eighty years of Jim Crow had, in addition to shutting out African Americans from all public services, terrorized thousands who were brutally apprehended, tortured, then murdered at public lynching spectacles. Submerged rage sooner or later seeks expression, not necessarily or even predictably neatly.

Between 1882 and 1968, at least 4,742 Black Americans were lynched in the US. This does not include the often-used method of publicly burning people alive. Though the incidence of lynchings had declined by the late 1940s, between 1947 and 1968, 27 Blacks were lynched. Many more African Americans were victims of the equivalent of *legal* lynching (excessively speedy trials, all-White juries, rapid "legal" executions), privately orchestrated murders other than by lynching, and collective rural murders called "nigger hunts." Evidence suggests that the vast majority of lynchings were for *trivial* offenses, if, in fact, any offense had been committed at all. A southern critic of lynching observed that when the Black victim has "offended that intangible something called racial superiority," White men lynch much more readily, protecting themselves from what they deem threatening, out-of-control "pests." What alarmed southern Whites during reconstruction was not evidence of Black failure or criminality but evidence of Black success, assertion, independence, advancement, even engagement in very profitable businesses. Civil rights activist and former NAACP director Walter White concluded, "lynching is much more an expression of Southern fear of Negro *progress* than of negro crime."[4]

Thus, in addition to *known* vigilante lynchings, thousands more Black Americans were figuratively lynched in this 80-year period of US American history. The reality was that virtually every Black citizen/resident living during this period experienced *terror* on a regular basis when being confronted by a White person, not knowing whether he or she would be the next victim of being tortured, mutilated, and lynched.

More disturbing perhaps was the fact that the lynchers and their supporters, "ordinary" people, not so different from ourselves, decent folks from good families, lacked any ethical qualms about their actions.[5] This troubling phenomenon is described in Philip Zimbardo's *The Lucifer Effect*,[6] a study of the psychology of evil that reveals a complex interplay of powerful dispositional, situational, and systemic forces that impact the psychic processes of inner transformation when good or

---

4 Allen et al., 12, 25, 26, 29, 30, 34.

5 Allen et al., 34.

6 Philip Zimbardo, *The Lucifer Effect: Understanding How Good People Turn Evil* (New York: Random House, 2008).

> ordinary people do bad or evil things. Zimbardo identifies "heroes" who do the "right" thing and suggests that any of us ordinary folks could as easily become heroes as perpetrators of evil depending on the impacts of various "situational" forces. He concludes that every person is a hero in waiting to be counted on to do the right thing when the moment of decision arrives, by discovering the reservoir of our hidden strengths and virtues.
>
> Profiling and demonization (projections onto others) are common defense mechanisms that play devious tricks on the mind, while enabling avoidance of one's own shadows and fears. Demonizing conveniently justifies the most unspeakable acts taken against the "other," no matter who the other may be. Jews were once called "vermin." Now many Jewish people call Palestinians "vermin."[7] In Viet Nam, my commander on occasion called the Vietnamese (and me, as well) "vermin." Racism is a most terrible sickness of the human mind. And it was this ugly reality that authentically motivated the deeper empathic dimensions of many of those persons participating in the civil rights and antiwar movement of the 1960s.

Resistance Grows with Buildup of War

In 1960–61, demonization of the Vietnamese began in earnest while the US continued building up its military presence in Viet Nam. As the nation proceeded down its warpath, US Americans, reading reports of US military activity in Viet Nam, began to register alarm about another emerging war in Asia. While there weren't many protests at this time, this chronology reflects the political context in which the antiwar movement emerged and grew.

Early Organizing and Resistance as War Builds

January 1, 1960. The Student League for Industrial Democracy (SLID) is reorganized under a new name, Students for a Democratic Society (SDS), with University of Michigan graduate and student activist Robert Alan Haber elected as its first president.[8]

February 1, 1960. Four Black students from North Carolina A&T College protest lunch-counter segregation at the local Woolworth five-and-dime store. The sit-in prompts the first of the widespread student protests against racial segregation critical to the Civil Rights movement of the 1960s.[9]

---

7 Liat Weingart, "The Wrath of the Jews," http://www.alternet.org/story/20745/the_wrath_of_the_jews.

8 *Wikipedia*, Student League for Industrial Democracy, http://en.wikipedia.org/wiki/Student_League_for_Industrial_Democracy_(1946–59), accessed May 7, 2015; Dan Berger, *Outlaws of America* (Oakland: AK Press, 2006), 319.

9 DeBenedetti, 41.

April 15, 1960. Southern Christian Leadership Conference (SCLC) director Ella Baker convenes a meeting of 200 student activists at her alma mater, Shaw University, in Raleigh, North Carolina, to build upon the activism inspired by the lunch-counter sit-ins that began in Greensboro, North Carolina and Nashville, Tennessee, in direct confrontation to racial segregation. At this meeting the Student Nonviolent Coordinating Committee (SNCC) is formed.[10]

December 20, 1961. The *New York Times* reports that about 2,000 uniformed US troops and specialists in addition to advisers are "operating in battle areas with South Vietnamese forces," and are authorized to fire back if fired upon.[11]

December 29, 1961. Forty-five students and activists from around the country meet in Ann Arbor, Michigan to discuss the future of SDS.[12]

March 10, 1962. The *New York Times* publishes an Associated Press report: "US Pilots Aiding Combat in Vietnam."

May 11, 1962. US Secretary of Defense/War Robert McNamara makes the first of many trips to Viet Nam to meet with Ngo Dinh Diem, the US-puppet prime minister of the fictionally created South Vietnamese government. After 48 hours in country, McNamara concludes: "We are winning the war."[13]

May 30, 1962. Some 5,000 US troops are stationed in Viet Nam.

June 1962. At an SDS convention at the United Auto Workers FDR Camp in Port Huron, Michigan, delegates draft their first official manifesto. Growing out of a draft statement prepared by Tom Hayden, a University of Michigan student and founding member of SDS, the Port Huron Statement, as it comes to be known, articulates a political philosophy of participatory democracy and political activism that will have widespread impact on the 1960s generation, especially within the civil rights and antiwar movements. The concluding paragraph:[14]

> We believe that the universities are an overlooked seat of influence [in pursuit of social change]. . . . [Our agenda] will involve national efforts at university reform by an alliance of students and faculty. They must wrest control of the educational process from the administrative bureaucracy. They must make fraternal and functional contact with allies in labor, civil rights, and other liberal forces outside the campus. They must import major public issues into the

---

10 DeBenedetti, 42; Peter M. Bergman, *The Chronological History of the Negro in America* (New York: Harper & Row, 1969), 569.
11 Bowman, 54; Dougherty and Stewart, 41.
12 James Miller, *"Democracy in the Streets" From Port Huron to the Siege of Chicago* (New York: Simon and Schuster, 1987), 76.
13 Bowman, 56.
14 Halstead, 38–41; Zaroulis and Sullivan, 29–30.

curriculum—research and teaching on problems of war and peace is an outstanding example. They must make debate and controversy, not dull pedantic cant, the common style for educational life. They must consciously build a base for their assault upon the loci of power.

December 31, 1962. More than 11,000 US advisory and support personnel are operating in Viet Nam, including 29 Special Forces detachments.[15]

October 21, 1962. David Halberstam, a journalist for the *New York Times*, writes that "Americans and Vietnamese march together, fight together, and die together,"[16] contradicting the official line that US troops are not involved in any fighting.

April 14, 1963. Easter Peace Walks—beginning at three locations (downtown Philadelphia, Ossining, New York, and Storrs, Connecticut) and converging at the United Nations in New York—are organized to condemn the US war brewing against the Vietnamese. Shortly before Easter 1963, Bertrand Russell, a key figure in the British Campaign for Nuclear Disarmament, issues a statement declaring that the US war in Viet Nam is a war of annihilation.[17]

May 2, 1964. The first major student demonstrations against the Viet Nam war take place. In New York City, as many as 1,000 students march through Times Square to the United Nations to protest US intervention in Viet Nam. On the same day, more than 700 students and young people march through San Francisco, and smaller demonstrations take place in Boston, Massachusetts, Madison, Wisconsin and Seattle, Washington.[18] The slogan "We Won't Go" becomes popular.[19]

August 7, 1964. The Gulf of Tonkin Resolution grants President Johnson authority to wage virtually unlimited war against the Vietnamese.[20]

September 30, 1964. Students and faculty organize a 10-hour sit-in against the war in Sproul Hall at the University of California at Berkeley[21] Student activists, many recently returned from a summer of civil rights activities in the South, conflict with the university over the right to use school facilities for political advocacy. Out of debates, protests, sit-ins, and other activities taking place on campus from October to December 1964, the Free Speech Movement arises under the informal leadership of student Mario Savio, and is later recognized as the first of many student protest movements of the 1960s and early 1970s.

---

15 Bowman, 57.
16 Greene, 1966, 38.
17 Halstead, 33–34.
18 Halsted, 36–37; "Students Protest US Aid in Vietnam," *New York Times*, May 3, 1964.
19 Zinn, 1980, 476.
20 Joint Resolution of Congress, H.J. RES 1145, August 7, 1964.
21 Bishop, 12.

1965. SNCC is the first group outside the traditional antiwar movement to endorse draft resistance, urging African Americans to resist the draft and refuse to fight for a White America that would order young Black Americans to "kill other Colored people." By this time, SNCC has become one of the most important radical organizations confronting racial segregation in the South through civil disobedience and voter registration.

April 17, 1965. SNCC is a supporter, in conjunction with SDS, of the April 17, 1965 March on Washington against the US war in Viet Nam.[22]

January 6, 1966. SNCC releases the following Statement on Vietnam:[23]

> **SNCC STATEMENT ON VIETNAM** | The Student Nonviolent Coordinating Committee has a right and a responsibility to dissent with United States foreign policy on any issue when it sees fit. The Student Nonviolent Coordinating Committee now states its opposition to the United States' involvement in Vietnam on these grounds:
>
> We believe the United States government has been deceptive in its claims of concern for the freedom of the Vietnamese people, just as the government has been deceptive in claiming concern for the freedom of colored people in other countries as [sic] the Dominican Republic, the Congo, South Africa, Rhodesia, and in the United States itself.
>
> We, the Student Nonviolent Coordinating Committee, have been involved in the black peoples' struggle for liberation and self-determination in this country for the past five years. Our work, particularly in the South, has taught us that the United States government has never guaranteed the freedom of oppressed citizens, and is not yet truly determined to end the rule of terror and oppression within its own borders.
>
> We ourselves have often been victims of violence and confinement executed by United States governmental officials. We recall the numerous persons who have been murdered in the South because of their efforts to secure their civil and human rights, and whose murderers have been allowed to escape penalty for their crimes.
>
> The murder of Samuel Young in Tuskegee, Alabama, is no different than the murder of peasants in Vietnam, for both Young and the Vietnamese sought, and are seeking, to secure the rights guaranteed them by law. In each case, the United States government bears a great part of the responsibility for these deaths.
>
> Samuel Young was murdered because United States law is not being enforced. Vietnamese are murdered because the United States is pursuing

---

22 Halstead, 306; Wells, 70; DeBenedetti, 120; Berger, 34.

23 Civil Rights Movement Veterans website, http://www.crmvet.org/docs/snccviet.htm, accessed June 23, 2016.

an aggressive policy in violation of international law. The United States is no respecter of persons or law when such persons or laws run counter to its needs or desires.

We recall the indifference, suspicion and outright hostility with which our reports of violence have been met in the past by government officials.

We know that for the most part, elections in this country, in the North as well as the South, are not free. We have seen that the 1965 Voting Rights Act and the 1964 Civil Rights Act have not yet been implemented with full federal power and sincerity.

We question, then, the ability and even the desire of the United States government to guarantee free elections abroad. We maintain that our country's cry of "preserve freedom in the world" is a hypocritical mask, behind which it squashes liberation movements which are not bound, and refuse to be bound, by the expediencies of United States cold war policies.

We are in sympathy with, and support, the men in this country who are unwilling to respond to a military draft which would compel them to contribute their lives to United States aggression in Vietnam in the name of the "freedom" we find so false in this country.

We recoil with horror at the inconsistency of a supposedly "free" society where responsibility to freedom is equated with the responsibility to lend oneself to military aggression. We take note of the fact that 16% of the draftees from this country are Negroes called on to stifle the liberation of Vietnam, to preserve a "democracy" which does not exist for them at home.

We ask, where is the draft for the freedom fight in the United States?

We therefore encourage those Americans who prefer to use their energy in building democratic forms within this country. We believe that work in the civil rights movement and with other human relations organizations is a valid alternative to the draft. We urge all Americans to seek this alternative, knowing full well that it may cost them their lives—as painfully as in Vietnam.

Civil Rights Struggle

Medgar Evers

On June 12, 1963, just hours after President Kennedy's nationally televised civil rights speech, Medgar Evers, 37, NAACP field secretary, World War II veteran of the battle at Normandy, and father of three children, was shot while exiting his car in his own driveway in Jackson, Mississippi, and died soon thereafter at a nearby hospital. He had just returned from a meeting with NAACP attorneys, and was carrying t-shirts reading "Jim Crow Must Go." The son of a poor farmer, as a child Evers had walked three miles every day to attend a small segregated school.

The bullet from a 1917 Enfield World War I rifle struck Evers from the back and ripped through his heart. He staggered 30 feet before collapsing. He was taken to the local Jackson hospital where at first he was refused medical care because of his skin color. When aid was finally reluctantly given, it was too late. Evers' assassin was Mississippi KKK leader Byron de la Beckwith, a salesman from Greenwood, Mississippi, who had also served in World War II at the Battle of Guadalcanal and Battle of Tarawa.[24] Beckwith was acquitted due to hung juries in 1964 trials, but was eventually tried again and convicted of first-degree murder in 1994. He was sentenced to life imprisonment and died in prison in 2001 at the age of 80.[25]

Birmingham Church Bombing

During a Sunday morning service on September 15, 1963, with 200 attendees present, the Ku Klux Klan bombed the three-story Birmingham, Alabama 16th Street Baptist Church, a venue that had been a rallying point for civil rights activities. Four young Black girls were murdered in the blast (Addie Mae Collins, 14; Denise McNair, 11; Carole Robertson, 14; and Cynthia Wesley, 14) and more than 20 other attendees were injured. A witness identified KKK member Robert Edward Chambliss, a 59-year-old truck driver, as one of the men who placed multiple sticks of dynamite underneath the church. Chambliss was subsequently fined $100 and sentenced to six months in jail for possession of dynamite.[26]

Chambliss, who joined the Klan at age 20, had firebombed houses of black families throughout the 1940s to the 1960s. This bombing was the third in 11 days following a federal court order mandating integration of Alabama's schools. By 1963, homemade bombs had been exploded so often in Birmingham's African American homes and churches that the city was nicknamed *Bombingham*.[27]

Two other African Americans were killed that Sunday, September 15. Birmingham police shot 16-year-old Johnny Robinson when he refused to follow orders to stop stoning cars, and two White punks shot and killed 13-year-old Virgil Ware as he rode his bicycle in a north Birmingham suburb.[28]

In 1971, when Alabama Attorney General Bill Baxley requested copies of the original FBI files on the Birmingham church bombing, he discovered that J. Edgar Hoover had refused to reveal names of the four suspects to the prosecution. The four were Robert Chambliss; 33-year-old Thomas E. Blanton, Jr., who many years later was arrested while clerking at

---

24 Berger, 321; *Wikipedia*, Byron de la Beckwith, http://www.google.com/search?q=Byron+de+la+Beckwith&hl=en&gbv=2&oq=&gs_l=.
25 *Wikipedia*, Byron de la Beckwith.
26 John Herbers, "Birmingham Klansman Guilty in Dynamite Case; Two Other Defendants Face Trial Today—Dr. King Gives City an Ultimatum on Jobs," *New York Times*, October 9, 1963.
27 http://www.history.com/topics/black-history/birmingham-church-bombing
28 http://www.nydailynews.com/news/justice-story/justice-story-birmingham-church-bombing-article-1.1441568

a Wal-Mart store; 45-year-old truck driver Herman Cash; and 33-year-old truck driver Bobby Frank Cherry, a Marine veteran and demolition expert.[29]

When the first trial of the church bombing finally took place in 1977, 14 years after the bombing, Chambliss, aged 73, was convicted and sentenced to life imprisonment. He died in prison in 1985.[30] Blanton wasn't tried until 2001 when he was found guilty at age 62 of four counts of murder and sentenced to life in prison with possibility of parole.[31] Cash died in 1994 without having been charged.[32] Cherry was convicted in 2002 and sentenced to life in prison where he died in 2004.[33]

VIOLENCE ESCALATES IN THE SOUTH

November 22, 1963. President Kennedy is assassinated in Dallas, Texas.

December 23, 1963. Two days before Christmas, one month after the assassination and four months after the large civil rights march on Washington, DC, a nine-hour conference is held at FBI headquarters in Washington to discuss "neutralizing" Martin Luther King. No less than 21 proposals are presented and discussed, raising the possibility of "using" ministers, "disgruntled" acquaintances, "aggressive" newsmen, "colored" agents, Dr. King's housekeeper, and even Dr. King's wife and "a good looking female plant in King's office." The Bureau was to take a "discreet approach" in developing information about Dr. King for use "at an opportune time in a counterintelligence move to *discredit* him." It was generally agreed that the Bureau should make use of "all available investigative techniques coupled with meticulous planning, boldness, and ingenuity, tempered only with good judgment," but that "discretion must not reach the point of timidity." The discussion was described by one of Hoover's assistants as an analysis of the avenues aimed at *neutralizing* King, who was perceived not only as an effective Negro leader, but also a Communist.[34]

June 21, 1964. Three civil rights workers—James Earl Chaney, a 21-year-old African American born and raised in Meridian, Mississippi; Andrew Goodman, a 20-year-old Queens College student; and Michael Mickey Schwerner, a 24-year-old New York City social worker—are murdered by

---

29 Wikipedia, 16th Street Baptist Church Bombing, http://en.wikipedia.org/wiki/16th_Street_Baptist_Church_bombing; Mike Clary, "Birmingham's Painful Past Reopened: Crime: Ex-Klansmen Face Trial in '63 Bombing of Black Church. Four Girls Died," *Los Angeles Times*, April 14, 2001.

30 "Robert E. Chambliss, Figure in '63 Bombing," *New York Times* obituary, October 30, 1985.

31 "Former Klansman Faces Prison in 1963 Killings," *The Vindicator*, Youngstown, OH, May 2, 2001.

32 Kevin Sack, "As Church Bombing Trial Begins in Birmingham, the City's Past Is Very Much Present," *New York Times*, April 25, 2001.

33 Michelle O'Donnell, "Bobby Frank Cherry, 74, Klansman in Bombing, Dies," *New York Times*, November 19, 2004.

34 William F. Pepper, *An Act of State: The Execution of Martin Luther King* (London, UK: Verso, 2003), 11; Final Report of the Select Committee to Study Governmental Operations with Respect to Intelligence Activities of the United States Senate, 94th Congress, 2nd Session, 1978, Book II, April 26 (legislative day, April 14), 1976.

gunshot in Philadelphia, Mississippi. Their disappearance remains a mystery until their bodies are discovered 44 days later in an earthen dam not far from where they were last seen. The three had just started work registering African American voters as part of the Freedom Summer campaign. The murderers and conspirators in the case include members of the KKK, the Neshoba County Sheriff's Office, and members of Philadelphia's small-town police department. Consistent with J. Edgar Hoover's hostility toward civil rights workers, the FBI was uncooperative in the murder investigation.[35]

February 18, 1965. Jimmy Lee Jackson, 26, a civil rights activist, is shot in the stomach by an Alabama state trooper as police violently break up a peaceful nighttime march in Marion, Mississippi, a small town near Selma. The march is in protest of the arrest of James Orange, a field secretary of the Southern Christian Leadership Conference (SCLC). Marion city officials turn off the streetlights, enabling the local and state police to attack the marchers with clubs while firing their weapons in darkness. Jackson is protecting his mother from police clubs when he is shot, and is taken 50 miles to Selma's Good Samaritan Hospital.

February 21, 1965. Malcolm X, 39, is assassinated at the Audubon Ballroom in Harlem by members of the Nation of Islam as he prepares to speak to the assembled crowd on the need for Blacks and Whites to coexist peaceably.

February 26, 1965. Jimmy Lee Jackson dies in the hospital.

March 7, 1965. Jackson's death is the catalyst for a Selma-to-Montgomery march. The extreme violence unleashed upon marchers by White police is broadcast on national television and the violent events are documented by a number of photographers and journalists.[36]

August 11–16, 1965. A routine traffic stop in South Central Los Angeles provides the spark that lights the fire of seething rage known as the Watts Riots. The six-day riots leave 34 dead and over 1,000 injured, nearly 4,000 arrested, and an estimated $100 million in property destruction.[37]

October 1966. Huey Newton and Bobby Seale form the Black Panther Party at Merritt Community College in Oakland, California, where they are both enrolled as students.[38] The Black Panthers will later be deemed by the Weathermen to be the vanguard of the Black liberation movement.[39]

---

35 *Wikipedia*, Mississippi Civil Rights Workers' Murders, http://en.wikipedia.org/wiki/Mississippi_civil_rights_workers'_murders; Faith S. Holsaert, Martha Prescod, Norman Noonan, Judy Richardson, Betty Graham Robinson, Jean Smith Young, and Dorothy M. Zellner, eds., *Hands on the Freedom Plow: Personal Accounts by Women in SNCC* (Urbana, IL: University of Illinois Press, 2010), 562; Robert Cooney and Helen Michalowski, *The Power of the People: Active Nonviolence in the United States* (Philadelphia: New Society Publishers 1987), 169–171.

36 Jimmie Lee Jackson Biography, http://www.biography.com/people/jimmie-lee-jackson-21402111#synopsis

37 "1,000 Riot in L.A.; Police and Motorists Attacked Routine Arrest of 3 Sparks Watts Melee; 8 Blocks Sealed Off," *Los Angeles Times*, Aug 12, 1965.

38 Berger, 322.

39 Wells, 304.

August 25, 1967. The FBI launches a counterintelligence program specifically targeting the Black Panther Party, intended to "expose, disrupt, misdirect, discredit or otherwise neutralize the activities of black nationalists."[40]

February 7, 1968. In the aftermath of escalated tensions after students are refused entry to the only bowling alley in town on the basis of race, police fire on Black student demonstrators at South Carolina State College in Orangeburg, killing three and wounding thirty-three.[41]

March 4, 1968. Exactly one month before King's assassination, FBI Director J. Edgar Hoover issues a memo identifying FBI goals in a counter-intelligence program against *Black Nationalist Hate-Groups*:

1. Prevent the coalition of militant black nationalist groups . . . [which] might be the first step toward a real 'Mau Mau' in America, the beginning of a true black revolution.

2. Prevent the rise of a messiah who could unify and electrify the militant black nationalist movement. . . . King could be a very real contender for this position should he abandon his supposed 'obedience' to 'white, liberal doctrines' (nonviolence) and embrace black nationalism. . . ."[42]

Immolations in Protest of the War

At the height of the war, Vietnamese were dying at the average rate of 1,700 per day in what most of them experienced as a war of independence. It was as simple as that: The Vietnamese people wanted to be free of colonial powers telling them how to live, think, and shop. Imagine being murdered for wanting to be free. Sensitive US Americans could imagine the horror being experienced by Vietnamese people, wrought by the "democratic" US government's murderous policies, and some took drastic action to try to stop the violence.

Though the US war in Viet Nam was no aberration, many US citizens became increasingly morally troubled as the truth came out about US *excesses* in the conduct of the war. The use of high-tech weaponry created extra angst. The immorality of the war became blatantly evident as it progressed, with:

- pervasive use of massive *undirected* fire called "harassment and interdiction" (H&I);
- creation of "free-fire zones" (i.e., genocide zones) covering 75 percent of South Viet Nam;
- frequent use of artillery to replace ground operations in *populated* areas;
- the most massive bombing campaign in human history;

---

40 Berger, 322.
41 Berger, 323.
42 Trager, 1015; Churchill and Vander Wall, 108–110. This memo illustrates the obsession the FBI, and especially Hoover, had with King, which had become evident more than four years earlier, in a proposal advanced on December 23, 1963 to discredit and neutralize King. Note that Hoover's 1968 memo comes just 12 days before the My Lai Massacre: As the US sought to restrain dissent at home, it was committing mass murders overseas under pretext of diabolical lies.

- a massive application of chemical warfare as never before—napalm, phosphorous, tear gas, and a variety of toxic herbicides;
- obsession with *body counts* (massive numbers of murders) as an index of war progress;
- "pacification" by means of removal or killing virtually everyone in the countryside; and
- the literal collapse of the US Armed Forces in magnitude and concentrated focus as never before.[43]

It is difficult to find adequate vocabulary to convey the nature of our own bestiality, except perhaps the words Jefferson used in demonizing the Indians: "merciless savages." A few brave souls, in both Viet Nam and in the United States, chose to sacrifice their own lives in protest.

The first immolation during the war in protest of the Diem regime's brutal repression, imprisonment, and murder of Buddhists occurred on June 11, 1963, when Buddhist monk Thich Quang Duc doused himself on fire on a Saigon street. His act set in motion other immolations that would take place in both Viet Nam and the United States as the war progressed. On the seventh anniversary of this event, June 11, 1970, another Buddhist monk immolated himself at a Saigon pagoda.[44] Visitors to Viet Nam can see memorials to some of the Buddhist monks who sacrificed themselves, for example at the Thien Mu Pagoda in Hue, and the Chua Long Son in Nha Trang.

Alice Herz

March 16, 1965: Alice Herz, an 82-year-old retired professor of German-Jewish ancestry, was the first known person in the United States to self-immolate in angst over the barbaric war the US was waging against the Vietnamese. After fleeing Nazi Germany, Herz had spent time in a French internment camp before coming to the United States in 1942. At the time of her death she was a retired professor, a member of the Detroit, Michigan Unitarian Universalist church, a Quaker, and member of the Women's International League for Peace and Freedom (WILPF). Before immolating herself she distributed a testament to friends and to the public in which she shared her grief about the war and explained that her motivation derived from acts of self-immolation of Buddhist Vietnamese monks and nuns. She also confided her frustration over the ineffectiveness of all the accepted US protest methods, such as marching, street protesting, and writing of countless articles and letters.[45] After setting herself on fire on a Detroit street corner next to Wayne State University, Alice Herz died in a hospital on March 26, ten days later.[46]

---

43 Colonel Robert D. Heinl, Jr., "The Collapse of the Armed Forces," *Armed Forces Journal*, June 7, 1971, 30–37, in Gettleman et al., 1995, 326–335; FitzGerald, 375–376.

44 FitzGerald, 420.

45 *Wikipedia*, Alice Herz: http://en.wikipedia.org/wiki/Alice_Herz; Her leaflet addressed to the American People, described how US Presidents "have deceived and misguided you. . . . Through hatred and fear, deliberately whipped up during the last twenty years" creating an "Arsenal of Destruction—unlimited . . . Awake and Take Action Before It Is Too Late . . . To make myself heard I have chosen the flaming death of the Buddhists on the Wayne State University Campus of Detroit" [Shingo Shibata, *Phoenix: Letters and Documents of Alice Herz: The Thought and Practice of a Modern-day Martyr* (Amsterdam: B.R. Gruner Publishing Co., 1976), 2–3].

46 Zaroulis and Sullivan, 1–5; DeBenedetti, 107.

NORMAN MORRISON

November 2, 1965: Quaker pacifist Norman Morrison, executive director of the Stony Run Friends Meeting Society in Baltimore, Maryland, was a graduate of Chautauqua Central High School in New York, my alma mater; and the first Eagle Scout I knew. Norman was 31 years old and the father of three when he drove from his Baltimore home to the Pentagon parking lot where he poured a combustible fluid on himself and then lit himself on fire. Shortly before his death, he sent a note to his wife, Anne: "For weeks even months I have been praying only that I be shown what I must do. This morning with no warning I was shown. . . . Know that I love thee but must act for the children of the priest's village."[47]

Norman Morrison was seen as a hero in North Viet Nam, where his act was commemorated with a postage stamp issued in 1965.

Morrison had agonized over the US criminal war for months and was distressed by the lack of public outrage, especially from Quakers. On the morning of November 2, as he prepared a lecture for an upcoming class, he wrote: "Quakers seek to begin with life, not with theory. . . . The life is mightier than the book that reports it."

Over lunch, Norman and Anne had discussed the latest issue of *I. F. Stone's Weekly*, which had reprinted a letter, published in *Paris Match*, written by a Catholic priest who barely survived US bombings: "I have seen my faithful burned up. I have seen the bodies of women and children blown to bits. I have seen all my village razed."[48] After lunch, Anne went to school to pick up their 6-year-old son Ben and 5-year-old daughter Christina, while Norman stayed with their daughter, Emily, who was nine days shy of her first birthday. With no evident premeditation or discussion, Norman drove to the Pentagon with baby Emily. At about 5:20 p.m., within 40 feet of the window of Secretary of Defense/War Robert McNamara, Norman safely placed Emily aside before dousing himself. Within a few minutes, Norman was dead, the second US American to immolate in protest of the war.[49]

On December 23, 1965, *New York Times* published an AP wire photo of this Hanoi-issued postage stamp with the caption: "Hanoi Stamp: *Washington Post* said this stamp was on sale in the North Vietnam capital. It has a picture of Norman R. Morrison, who committed suicide by burning himself outside the Pentagon to protest the United States' policies in Vietnam."

---

[47] Sallie B. King, "They Who Burned Themselves for Peace: Quaker and Buddhist Self-Immolators during the Vietnam War," *Buddhist-Christian Studies Annual*, 2000, 127; Anne Morrison Welsh, *Held in the Light: Norman Morrison's Sacrifice for Peace and His Family's Journey of Healing* (Maryknoll, NY: Orbis Books, 2008), 36; "Colleagues Stunned By Quaker's Self-Immolation; Tactic 'Unprecedented' In the Society," *New York Times*, November 4, 1965; Sean Devine, Playwright, *Re: Union* (Winnipeg, Manitoba, Canada: Scirocco Drama, 2013), a compelling play about Norman Morrison.

[48] Jean Larteguy, "A Priest Tells How Our Bombers Razed His Church and Killed His People," from *Paris-Match*, October 2, 1965, reprinted in *I.F. Stone's Weekly*, November 1, 1965, 3.

[49] In general, see Welsh's *Held in the Light*. Note: Anne Morrison Welsh is Morrison's widow, remarried.

More Immolations

By the end of the war, at least 76 Vietnamese monks and nuns had immolated themselves in the space of seven years, the first being Quang Duc on June 11, 1963. These self-immolations, carried out in protest of the war, were seen as sacrifice rather than suicide. Several occurred during the 1966 protest against the corrupt Nguyen Cao Ky.[50]

In the US, nine different individuals set themselves on fire in protest of the war in Viet Nam.[51] In chronological order, the seven others who immolated themselves following Alice Herz and Norman Morrison were:

Roger LaPorte's self-sacrifice is memorialized in an Vietnamese exhibit, at the Hoa Lo Prison museum in Hanoi, on antiwar activism abroad during the US American War in Viet Nam.

November 9, 1965: Roger LaPorte, 21, a Catholic worker, on the Dag Hammarskjold UN Plaza, New York City;

August 19, 1967: J. D. Copping, Navy veteran, on a city street in Panorama, California;

October 12, 1967: Hiroko Hayashi, 36, a Japanese-American Buddhist, on a San Diego, California street;

October 15, 1967: Florence Beaumont, 55, a housewife and mother of two, in a neighborhood of La Puente, in greater Los Angeles, California;

December 4, 1967: Erik Thoen, 27, a Zen Buddhist, in a Sunnyside, California field;

March 19, 1968: Ronald Brazee, 16, a high school honor student, near his Auburn, New York home (Ronald died in a hospital on April 27);

May 10, 1970: George Winne, Jr., 23, son of a navy captain, former ROTC student, student of history at San Diego State University, in Revelle Plaza on the UCSD campus.

There were a few others who attempted self-immolation, but failed in the process.[52] All were seemingly regular folks, sensitive individuals who experienced a flame inside, ignited by their connections as human beings with the Vietnamese.

---

50 Robert J. Topmiller, "Buddhism in Vietnam, Most Venerable Thich Quang Duc," quangduc.com/English/vnbuddhism/013quangduc.html; Robert Topmiller, email to author, October 14, 2006.

51 Nancy Zaroulis and Gerald Sullivan, *Who Spoke Up? American Protest against the War in Vietnam, 1963–1975* (New York: Holt, Rinehart and Winston, 1984), 1–5; Charles DeBenedetti, *An American Ordeal: The Antiwar Movement of the Vietnam Era* (Syracuse, NY: Syracuse University Press, 1990), 107, 129–30, 186, 194, 280.

52 Zaroulis and Sullivan, 3n.

Civil Rights Struggle: Selma, 1965

On March 25, 1965, less than three weeks after infamous Bloody Sunday, Viola Liuzzo, a 39-year-old member of the same Detroit Unitarian Universalist church as Alice Herz, was murdered as she drove civil rights activists from Selma, Alabama back to the Montgomery airport after their participation in the Selma-to-Montgomery civil rights marches. She was assassinated with two bullets to the head as one Black civil rights activist sat next to her in the passenger seat. The marches that commenced on March 7, inspired by the murder of Jimmy Lee Jackson (see above), continued to demand voting rights for African Americans and an end to systematic police brutality. At the successful conclusion of the last march, begun March 21 in Selma and arriving in Montgomery on March 25, 25,000 people celebrated at a rally under protection of federalized National Guardsmen.

Liuzzo, a housewife and mother of five, married to a labor activist, had traveled from Detroit to Selma on March 16 after watching on TV the events of March 7, when nearly 600 marchers, led by civil rights leaders Hosea Williams and John Lewis, attempted to walk the 54 miles from Selma to the state capitol in Montgomery. Dallas County and Selma Sheriff Jim Clark had recruited, deputized, and armed a large posse made up of as many as 200 local KKK rednecks, who, supplemented by heavily armed and mounted state police, mercilessly gassed and beat the marchers. Dubbed "Bloody Sunday," more than 60 African Americans were injured in the police attack that day, and 17 of those required hospitalization. One of the injured was future Congressperson John Lewis, who suffered a fractured skull.

Upon her arrival in Selma on March 16, Liuzzo immediately began helping with logistics for the hundreds of marchers who continued throughout that month to walk from Selma to Montgomery despite the dangers involved. She was aware that a week before her arrival, three white Unitarian Universalist ministers who had joined the march— Rev. Orloff Miller, 33, and Rev. James Reeb, 38, from Boston, and Rev. Clark Olsen, 31, from Berkeley—had been attacked and beaten by members of the KKK after dining in an integrated restaurant. The merciless clubbing of 38-year-old Rev. James Reeb from Boston caused severe brain injuries. When the Selma public hospital refused to treat Reeb, he was taken two hours away to the Birmingham University Hospital, where he died two days later on March 11.[53] After Reeb had been severely beaten, one tenth of all Unitarian Universalist clergy, or about 200, had responded to Martin Luther King's call to all clergy to come to Selma to support the equal rights struggle. One of those was Rev. Richard Leonard from the Community Unitarian Church in New York who later wrote about those intense days in Selma.[54]

---

53 Accounts of the Selma to Montgomery marches: Cooney and Michalowski, 170–173, with photo; Holsaert et al., 447–451, 468–472, 562–564; David J. Garrow, *Bearing the Cross: Martin Luther King, Jr., and the Southern Christian Leadership Conference* (New York: Vintage Books, 1988), 358–430.

54 Richard D. Leonard, *Call to Selma: Eighteen Days of Witness* (Boston: Skinner House Books, 2002). It is the only hour-by-hour account of the famous march written by one of the 300 marchers from Selma to Montgomery.

One of the Klansman involved in the orchestration of Liuzzo's murder was an adrenaline junkie and known thug who had been an FBI informant since 1960. He had acknowledged participating in beatings and arson attacks on the 1961 Freedom Riders for having the audacity to test the constitutionality of newly ordered integrated facilities in interstate commerce. He had observed FBI agents filming the beatings while Hoover asserted his agency had no intention of protecting civil rights workers.[55]

After Liuzzo's assassination, the FBI feared that they might be held accountable for their informant's role in the murder. Prior to the shooting, the undercover agent had called his associates to inform them that he and other Klansman were on their way to Montgomery to implement their plan for violence. The FBI quickly launched a cover-up campaign to conceal the fact that an FBI informant was involved.[56] Hoover sought to discredit Liuzzo, insinuating that she was a drug addict and sexually promiscuous. Testing, however, revealed no traces of drugs in Liuzzo's system, nor evidence of any recent sex. The FBI's smear campaign was finally uncovered in 1978 through documents obtained under the Freedom of Information Act.[57]

The extreme violence of the events of March 1965 in Alabama appeared to provoke national leaders into finally taking legislative action. A few days after Rev. Reeb was clubbed to death and John Lewis had his skull fractured, President Johnson summoned a nighttime session of Congress to introduce the draft of his Voting Rights Act, at which time he acknowledged, "the real hero of this struggle is the American Negro."[58] The final draft was introduced in Congress on March 17, 1965, in response to Selma's Bloody Sunday. On August 6, 1965, Johnson signed the act into law; it prohibited discrimination in voting.

Antiwar Movement

1965

March 24–25, 1965. University of Michigan at Ann Arbor faculty and students, including members of SDS, initiate the first all-night Viet Nam teach-ins. Over 3,000 students participate in the first event.[59] They contact faculty and students on dozens of other campuses, urging them to organize their own teach-ins, and thirty-five other universities follow suit.

April 17, 1965. A coalition of SDS and SNCC members organize the largest antiwar protest held up until that time in Washington, DC. Organizers expect 2,000, but actual marchers number between 20,000 and 25,000, about

---

55 Michael Friedly and David Gallen, *Martin Luther King, Jr.: The FBI File* (New York: Carroll & Graf, 1993), 64; Cooney and Michalowski, 162–165.
56 Stanton, 52–55.
57 Gentry, 585–586.
58 Guttenplan, 397.
59 Halstead, 62–65; "Professors Hold Vietnam Protest; 3 Bomb Threats Disrupt 'Teach-in' at Michigan U.," *New York Times*, March 25, 1965.

the same as the number of US soldiers serving in Viet Nam at the time.[60] The march establishes a close activist working relationship between SDS, the most radical of antiwar student groups, and SNCC, the militant group of mostly young Black people doing the most courageous anti-segregation work in the South.[61]

May 5, 1965. Several hundred UC Berkeley students march on the Berkeley draft board and present the staff with a black coffin. Forty of the assembled students burn their draft cards. Along with the war in Viet Nam, students protest the April 28 invasion of the Dominican Republic[62] (the fifth US invasion of the island in the twentieth century; US occupation forces would remain until September 1966.)

May 12, 1965. The California Senate's Byrne Committee releases a report calling the Berkeley campus a Communist haven. California gubernatorial candidate Ronald Reagan announces that, if elected, he will appoint former CIA Director John McCone to investigate the Berkeley campus unrest.[63]

May 21, 1965. One of the greatest teach-ins begins at the University of California at Berkeley. No less than 30,000 persons participate in the event, called *Viet Nam Day*. Notable speaker Norman Mailer condemns US air power, declaring, "America is coterminous with the mafia." He demands a cessation of "pulverizing people whose faces we have never seen," while deploring the choice of US Americans to be "the most advanced monsters of civilization, pulverizing instinct with our detonations, our State Department experts in their little bow ties, and our bombs," and calls Lyndon Johnson "a bully with an Air Force."[64] Mailer draws a parallel between Viet Nam and the Dominican Republic, pointing out the US racism in both invasions. Punctuating his speech with *"Hot DAMN, Viet Nam!"*, a phrase that many listeners latch onto for use in similar future confrontations.

May 23, 1965. Just after midnight on the second day of the UC Berkeley teach-in, several hundred participants, led by members of the Young Socialist Alliance, march to the Berkeley draft board, hang Lyndon Johnson in effigy, and burn 19 draft cards.[65]

---

60 Halstead, 56, 306; "15,000 White House Pickets Denounce Vietnam War; Students Picket at White House," *New York Times*, April 18, 1965.

61 David Gilbert, *No Surrender* (Montreal, Canada: Abraham Guillen Press, 2004), 247.

62 "Students at UC March on Draft Board," *Los Angeles Times*, May 6, 1965.

63 "Changes Weighed by Coast Regents: Board Gets 2 Reports Based on Campus Disorders," *New York Times*, May 22, 1965; "Students at UC March on Draft Board," *Los Angeles Times*, May 22, 1965.

64 Halstead, 72, 80. In an interview with columnist Seumas Milne published by *The Guardian* on November 6, 2009, Noam Chomsky declared that US administrations were guided by a "godfather principle, straight out of the mafia: that defiance cannot be tolerated. It's a major feature of state policy." [http://www.theguardian.com/world/2009/nov/07/noam-chomsky-us-foreign-policy]

65 W. J. Rorabaugh, *Berkeley at War: The 1960s* (New York: Oxford University Press, 1989), 92.

June 16, 1965. A planned antiwar march on the Pentagon turns into a five-hour teach-in on the Pentagon steps and inside. In two days, more than 50,000 leaflets are distributed without interference at the entrances and inside the building.[66]

July 28, 1965. The McComb Mississippi Vietnam Position, first circulated as a leaflet in McComb, Mississippi, is printed in the Mississippi Freedom Democratic Party (MFDP) McComb branch newsletter. The first known civil rights movement antiwar protest, the leaflet is circulated several years before Martin Luther King, Jr.'s public opposition to the war, in response to the death in Viet Nam combat of a 23-year-old civil rights activist named John D. Shaw.[67]

> *Here are five reasons why Negroes should not be in any war fighting for America:*
>
> 1. *No Mississippi Negroes should be fighting in Vietnam for the White Man's freedom, until all the Negro people are free in Mississippi.*
>
> 2. *Negro boys should not honor the draft here in Mississippi. Mothers should encourage their sons not to go. We will gain respect and dignity as a race only by forcing the US Government and the Mississippi Government to come with guns, dogs and trucks to take our sons away to fight and be killed protecting Mississippi, Alabama, Georgia, and Louisiana.*
>
> 3. *No one has a right to ask us to risk our lives and kill other Colored People in Santo Domingo and Vietnam, so that the White American can get richer.*
>
> 4. *We will be looked upon as traitors by all the Colored People of the world if the Negro people continue to fight and die without a cause.*
>
> 5. *Last week a white soldier from New Jersey was discharged from the Army because he refused to fight in Vietnam; he went on a hunger strike. Negro boys can do the same thing. We can write and ask our sons if they know what they are fighting for. If he answers "Freedom," tell him that's what we are fighting for here in Mississippi. And if he says Democracy, tell him the truth — we don't know anything about Communism, Socialism, and all that, but we do know that Negroes have caught hell right here under this American Democracy.*

---

66 *New York Times*, June 17, 1965.

67 Mississippi Freedom Democratic Party, "The War on Vietnam: A McComb, Mississippi, Protest" in *Black Protest: History, Documents, and Analyses, 1619 to the Present*, ed. Joanne Grant, 415–416 (Greenwich, CT: Fawcett, 1968, 1974). Also see: http://www.crmvet.org/docs/mccombv.htm (accessed 6/23/16).

August 1965. Several hundred people organized by the Vietnam Day Committee (VDC) try on several occasions to block troop trains by standing on the Santa Fe Railroad tracks in West Berkeley and Emeryville, California. Conservative Alameda County Supervisor Joseph Bort comments, "The manner in which these people protest is tantamount to treason." UC Berkeley faculty are sharply divided in their opinions regarding the tactics.[68]

August 13, 1965. A counterculture newspaper, *The Berkeley Barb*, begins publication. The paper is founded by Max Scherr to chronicle and encourage the antiwar movement. Scherr, a middle-aged radical who had previously owned the Steppenwolf Bar in Berkeley, would serve as editor and publisher of the *Barb* until the mid-1970s.[69]

August 24, 1965. John Seltz of Berkeley, California, stands holding a red flag in front of a US troop train as it leaves the train station, jumping clear of the tracks only at the last minute.[70] [Some train engineers' "solution" to the many sit-ins and blocking actions that took place on railroad tracks, in protest of the Santa Fe-run troop trains that passed through Berkeley on their way to Emeryville in the mid-to-late 1960s, was to open the front steam conduit and spray steam all around, forcing people off the tracks.[71]]

October 7, 1965. A UC Berkeley faculty group of about 40, calling itself "The Faculty Peace Committee," addresses a crowd of about 600 in Sproul Plaza on the Berkeley campus, urging President Johnson to stop the bombing in North Viet Nam.[72]

October 15–16, 1965. Large antiwar demonstrations take place throughout the US and the world. At a demonstration in front of the Army Induction Center on Whitehall Street in Manhattan, 22-year-old Catholic Worker David J. Miller publicly burns his draft card, the first person to do so since Johnson's August 30 signing of the bill that made such action a felony.[73]

---

68 Rorabaugh, 94; "Demonstrators Try to Stop Troop Train on Coast; Deputies and Policemen Lead Carrier Past Crowd of 200 Protesting Vietnam Policy," *New York Times*, August 7, 1965.

69 Armstrong, 115; *Wikipedia*: Berkeley Barb, http://en.wikipedia.org/wiki/Berkeley_Barb.

70 Daugherty and Mattson, 77.

71 During the 1960s, the most violent harassment of protestors on the West Coast occurred at Concord, California Naval Weapons Station and its associated Port Chicago terminal. The Pentagon's major West Coast arsenal, this was the place from which most weapons, including napalm and white phosphorous, were being shipped to Viet Nam. Former US Attorney for the Northern District of California, Cecil Poole, reported that in one incident protestors placed a tree log on the tracks. [Carole Hick, Interviewer, "Troubles at the Concord Naval Weapons Station," *Northern California US District Court Oral History Series: Civil Rights, Law, and the Federal Courts: The Life of Cecil Poole, 1914–1997* (The Bancroft Library, University of California, Berkeley, 1993).] The protestors were present 24 hours a day, but after vigilante attacks began occurring at night, including rape, protestors decided to be present only during daylight hours. At least one participant's car was set on fire, and subjection to taunts or flying bottles thrown by passersby was common. [Franklin Zahn, *Deserter from Violence: Experiments with Gandhi's Truth* (New York: Philosophical Library, 1984), 259–260.]

72 "Berkeley Faculty Warned on Politics," *New York Times*, November 8, 1965.

73 Zaroulis and Sullivan, 56–57; Cooney and Michalowski, 186.

October 15, 1965. The UC Berkeley Vietnam Day Committee's campus teach-in is followed by a march on the Oakland Army induction center:[74] Some 15,000 demonstrators leave the campus in the evening and march toward Oakland. Marchers include children, grandmothers, and a busload of Ken Kesey's Merry Pranksters as well as college and high school students. The march is unpermitted, as Oakland and Berkeley city authorities had refused a parade permit. As marchers approach Oakland city limits, they are blocked by about 400 Oakland police in riot gear, brandishing weapons. Marchers stop less than a hundred yards from the police line, spectators and a group of about a hundred right-wing counterdemonstrators filling the gap between them and the police. A previously agreed-to subcommittee holds a swirling, confused discussion on what to do and eventually the marchers turn and head down Prince Street, on the Oakland-Berkeley line, to Shattuck Avenue. Some want to keep on toward the Oakland induction center but, due to the presence of families and children, "cooler heads prevail" and the march winds up at the Berkeley Civic Center where the teach-in continues in the park.

October 16, 1965. VDC marchers convene at the park, where a group of about a hundred protesters spent the night, and several thousand marchers head down Shattuck and Adeline to the Oakland City line, where they are met by the police, and by members of a right-wing group of Hell's Angels. The marchers sit down on the street, and Allen Ginsberg chants "Hare Krishna" at the front of the crowd. Before the police can act, Hell's Angels motorcycle gang members rip down banners and begin attacking protestors, yelling, "Go back to Russia, you fucking Communists!" creating an opening for the Oakland police to move in. Suddenly the Berkeley police arrive on the scene and charge in between, arrest a couple of Hell's Angels, thus preventing the Oakland police cops from charging in. The march does not go past the Oakland line. [In response to Angels' threat to attack the next planned peace march, Allen Ginsberg, along with Ken Kesey and a few of his Merry Pranksters, visits the home of Hell's Angels president Sonny Barger to discuss the situation. They bring along some LSD to share with Barger and his friends, and by dawn the two groups are chanting together.[75]]

---

74 Source for this paragraph and the next is Pacifica Radio/UC Berkeley Social Activism Sound Recording Project: *Anti-Vietnam War Protests in the San Francisco Bay Area & Beyond;* http://www.lib.berkeley.edu/MRC/pacificaviet.html.

75 "Hells Angels Attack Peace March at UC," *Los Angeles Times,* October 17, 1965.

Growing Domestic Resistance

November 6, 1965. Tom Cornell, Marc Paul Edelman, Roy Lisker, David McReynolds, and Jim Wilson burn their draft cards at a noon rally, before 1,500 people in Union Square in New York.[76]

November 12, 1965. In *LIFE* magazine, Loudon Wainwright writes about the self-immolation of Norman Morrison. In the same issue, two pages later, a photo of US pilots standing in prayer, is captioned, "A Prayer, a Take-off and the B-52 Strike Is On: A Job to Do. After final briefing in the theater of Anderson Air Force Base on Guam, B-52 crews bow their heads as they listen to the chaplain's prayer for the success of their mission." On subsequent pages, a series of photos is titled, "Mission Accomplished: Smoke and flames rise from Iron Triangle target plastered by 229 tons of bombs." Other text explains that the "main purpose of these air raids is to deny the Vietcong the safety of sanctuaries and bases hitherto used with impunity."[77]

November 27, 1965. In Washington, DC, an estimated 35,000 antiwar protesters encircle the White House, then march to the Washington Monument for a rally.[78] The march garners a long list of celebrity sponsors: novelists Saul Bellow and John Hersey; playwright Arthur Miller; artist Alexander Calder; actors Ossie Davis, Ruby Dee, and Tony Randall; and doctors Benjamin Spock and Albert Sabin (developer of the oral polio vaccine). During the march, Spock, Martin Luther King, Jr., and others hold formal discussions with three administration officials to discuss their concerns about the war.[79] SDS leader Carl Oglesby gives a speech in which he calls the US political system "corporate liberalism."[80] It will be eight more years before the last US troops leave Viet Nam.

Christmastime, 1965. Herbert Aptheker, an old leftist leader of the US Communist Party, Staughton Lynd, a socialist, pacifist, New Left history professor at Yale University, and Tom Hayden, founding president of SDS, travel together to North Viet Nam during a pause in US bombing. The three leave the US for Hanoi on December 19, 1965. Visiting with officials in European and Asian capitals en route, they finally arrive in North Viet Nam on December 28. They meet with various Vietnamese officials and villagers and inspect damage caused by US bombing. During their week in country, they visit with a US aircrew member imprisoned after being downed by anti-aircraft fire. Aptheker, Lynd, and Hayden return home with personal

---

76 Cooney and Michalowski, 186–187; R. N. Williams, 1971, 17.

77 "The fiery pangs of conscience," *LIFE*, Nov. 12, 1965, 34–38. Author's Note: Guam, the location of the photos in the *LIFE* magazine spread, is 2,800 miles east of Viet Nam. The Viet Cong "sanctuary" was in their own country, including areas along their border with neutral Cambodia also under attack from the US.

78 Bowman, 129.

79 "Demonstrators Decorous: 3 White House Aides Meet With Leaders; Thousands join antiwar march," *New York Times*, Nov. 28, 1965; Zaroulis and Sullivan, 64.

80 Berger, 321.

testimony of the brutality of the war; they readily describe the huge number of civilian casualties and the desire of the NLF to negotiate a truly just peace.[81]

January 21, 1966. SDS releases the first issue of their weekly, *New Left Notes*.[82]

February 1966. Highly decorated former US Army Green Beret Master Sergeant Donald Duncan fiercely condemns US conduct in Viet Nam in the February 1966 issue of *Ramparts*: "I had seen the effect of the bombing at close range. Those bombs would land and go for about 15 yards and tear off a lot of foliage from the trees, but that was it. Unless you drop those things in somebody's hip pocket, they don't do any good. . . . It would only work if aimed at concentrated targets such as villages." He describes how the US frequently tortured and murdered captured Viet Cong and others suspects, and how the US planned illegal assassination teams to murder leaders in North Viet Nam and neutral Cambodia. He asserts that many white GIs possessed racist contempt for both the South Vietnamese soldiers and Black US soldiers.[83]

February 5, 1966. The White House rebuffs a group of about a hundred war veterans and former military soldiers who travel from New York to return their medals along with honorable discharge and separation papers in protest of the Viet Nam war.[84]

February 16, 1966. The Central Committee of the World Council of Churches (WCC) adopts a resolution proposing an immediate cease-fire in Viet Nam.[85]

March 25, 1966. In his acceptance speech upon receiving an honorary degree from UC Berkeley at the campus' annual Charter Day, US Ambassador to the United Nations Arthur Goldberg delivers a defense of the Johnson Administration's Viet Nam policies. Many in the crowd of perhaps 14,000 display antiwar placards bearing slogans such as "Arthur Goldberg, Doctor of War." After the ceremonies, about half the audience moves to Harmon Gymnasium where Goldberg has agreed to discuss the issues with the Faculty Peace Committee. When a vote is called on the Johnson Administration's handling of the war, only about one hundred attendees vote for approval, while seven thousand stand in disapproval.[86]

Spring 1966. Barry Bondhus, a draft-eligible Minnesotan from rural Big Lake, breaks into the local draft board office and destroys hundreds of 1-A draft records using his own family's collected human manure. This action, which becomes known as "Big Lake One," is later celebrated as "the movement that

---

81 Herbert Aptheker, *Mission to Hanoi* (New York: International Publishers, 1966; Staughton Lynd and Thomas Hayden, *The Other Side* (New York: The New American Library, 1966).
82 Berger, 321.
83 Armstrong, 101–102.
84 "Veterans Rebuffed; Official Cold Shoulder," *New York Times*, February 6, 1966.
85 Bowman, 135.
86 Halstead, 142; "Antiwar Protest Set at UC; Antiwar Units Set to Disrupt Goldberg's Visit to UC Today," *Los Angeles Times*, March 25, 1966; "Berkeley Hears Goldberg," *New York Times*, March 26, 1966.

started the Movement," and is followed by dozens of civil disobedience actions targeting local draft boards, beginning with the high-profile "Baltimore Four" in 1967 (see p. 217).[87]

Spring 1966. A majority of UC Berkeley students vote for immediate US withdrawal from Viet Nam in a campus-wide VDC-initiated referendum. Graduate student teaching assistants used discussion sections to talk about the war in one-third of classes.[88]

April 9, 1966. A bomb explodes in the Berkeley office of the VDC, slightly injuring four people. The incident is the second bombing of a Bay Area activist organization in two months. A militant faction within the VDC responds by mounting a street demonstration on Telegraph Avenue, which is forcibly broken up by Berkeley police. Several protesters are injured, and later, when VDC spokesperson Jerry Rubin is criticized for putting people at risk by urging militancy, a split develops within the organization.[89]

April 10, 1966. At a National Council meeting, SDS devises a "counter-examination"—a "National Vietnam Exam"—to be circulated in an effort to reach nearly a half-million college students expected to take the first Selective Service deferment test on May 14. The Exam is designed to publicize SDS's opposition to the war. About 350,000 copies of the exam are distributed across 820 campuses.[90]

Mid-April 1966. A six-man pacifist delegation, sponsored by the Committee for Nonviolent Action, travels to Saigon under the leadership of A. J. Muste. The group includes Catholic Karl Meyer and pacifist Brad Lyttle. Muste concludes that "in the opinion of many responsible Vietnamese, if US support were withdrawn, the Ky regime would be replaced by a civilian regime composed of Buddhists, Roman Catholics, intellectuals, peasant representatives.... Such a civilian set-up—again according to our contacts—would favor a cease-fire ... and be ready to sit down to talk with the NLF and the Vietcong."[91]

May 1966. Stokely Carmichael is elected president of SNCC and popularizes the concept of Black Power, which will be taken up by the Black Panther organization later that year.[92]

---

87 Zaroulis and Sullivan, 82.
88 "People's History of Berkeley," Barrington Collective, March 24, 2005.
89 "Blast Rocks Coast Headquarters Of Group Opposing Vietnam War," *New York Times*, April 10, 1966; "Viet Group Splits on Berkeley Clash; Crowd of 2,000 Hears Criticism of Militants at UC Campus Rally," *Los Angeles Times*, Apr 14, 1966; "Bomb Rips VDC Building," *Fresno Bee*, April 9, 1966.
90 G. Louis Heath, ed., *Vandals in the Bomb Factory: The History and Literature of the Students for a Democratic Society* (Metuchen, NJ: Scarecrow Press, 1976), 52–53.
91 Lynd and Hayden, 124–125.
92 Miller, 1987, 273; Halstead, 310; S. Carmichael and C. Hamilton, *Black Power: The Politics of Liberation in America* (New York: Vintage, 1967), 42.

June 1966. A Gallup Poll reveals that public support for the handling of the US war in Viet Nam has dipped to forty-one percent. Thirty-seven percent express disapproval; the balance of those polled say they have no opinion.[93]

June 20, 1966. US Senate Internal Security subcommittee charges that Communists play a key role in antiwar demonstrations.[94]

July 4, 1966. The national convention of the Congress of Racial Equality (CORE) adopts two resolutions; one calls for withdrawal of US troops, the other attacks the draft as placing a "heavy discriminatory burden on minority groups and the poor."[95]

July 8, 1966. SNCC and SDS issue a joint statement condemning the US war and urging evasion of military service, especially for Blacks. Stokely Carmichael declares the military draft as nothing more than "White people sending Black people to make war on Yellow people in order to defend the land they stole from Red people." Earlier in the year, a press release issued from the Atlanta office of SNCC denounced the US role in Viet Nam while declaring support for men who refused conscription.[96]

August 7, 1966. The Port Chicago Vigil and demonstrations begin.

August 14, 1966. VDC is banned from organizing on the UC Berkeley campus.[97]

November 30, 1966. Between fifty and a hundred students stage a sit-down protest around a Navy recruiter table in the UC Berkeley Student Union after the VDC, SDS, and other radical student groups are prohibited by the Berkeley Associated Students of University of California (ASUC) from setting up tables in the union. Six protestors, including ex-students Mario Savio and Jerry Rubin, are arrested.[98]

February 20, 1967. The *Congressional Record* prints remarks made by Congressional Medal of Honor recipient General David M. Shoup, US Marine Corps, retired. Originally made on May 14, 1966, before Pierce Community College students in Los Angeles, Shoup's remarks echo the declaration made by Retired Marine General Smedley Butler in 1934 that war was a racket for capitalism.[99]

---

93 "Vietnam Support Slumps," *Los Angeles Times*, June 8, 1966.
94 "Campus Protests Are Tied to Reds By Senate Panel," *New York Times*, June 20, 1966.
95 Bowman, 143.
96 DeBenedetti, 158.
97 "Vietnam Day Group Banned In Berkeley Campus Dispute," *New York Times*, August 15, 1966.
98 "Classroom Strike; Berkeley Vote Follows Savio Speech Navy Recruiting on Campus Stirs New Student Turmoil," *Los Angeles Times*, December 1, 1966; "Students and Policemen Clash At Berkeley Antimilitary Sit-In; Officers Use Nightsticks," *New York Times*, December 1, 1966.
99 Greene, 1970, 109–110.

> *I believe that if we had and would keep our dirty, bloody, dollar-soaked fingers out of the business of these nations so full of depressed, exploited people, they will arrive at a solution of their own, one they design and want. That they fight and work for. And if unfortunately their revolution must be of the violent type because the 'haves' refuse to share with the 'have-nots' by any peaceful method, at least what they get will be their own, and not the American style, which they don't want and above all don't want crammed down their throats by Americans.*

March 25, 1967. Dr. Martin Luther King, Jr. leads 5,000 people down State Street in Chicago to protest the war in Viet Nam. This is King's first antiwar march.[100]

April 4, 1967. King delivers his historic address, "A Time to Break Silence," at a meeting of Clergy and Laity Concerned at the Riverside Church in New York City, exactly one year to the day before his assassination. This is his first direct attack on the Johnson Administration's war policy and the first time he links opposition to the war to the civil rights movement. He proclaims the US government "the greatest purveyor of violence in the world," and describes it as being under a spell of "madness" of "deadly Western arrogance." He states, "if we are to get on the right side of the world revolution, we as a nation must undergo a radical revolution of values," and begin a rapid "shift from a thing-oriented society to a person-oriented society." He concludes that "a nation that continues year after year to spend more money on military defense than on programs of social uplift is approaching spiritual death" and pleads with his fellow citizens to "rededicate ourselves to the long and bitter—but beautiful—struggle for a new world," saying "our brothers wait eagerly for our response." He urges US Americans to radically counter the "forces of the American life [that] militate against their arrival as full men."[101]

April 15, 1967. In a spring mobilization, massive antiwar marches are held in protest of US policy in Viet Nam in New York (400,000),[102] San Francisco (100,000),[103] and Los Angeles. A band of seven Viet Nam veterans, among them Jan Barry Crumb, Mark Donnelly, and David Bruam, march in New York City with a quickly put-together banner reading "Vietnam Veterans against the War," and is recognized as the origin of the organization of the same name, which becomes popularly known by the initials VVAW.[104]

---

100 Bowman, 164.

101 James Melvin Washington, *A Testament of Hope: The Essential Writings of Martin Luther King, Jr.* (San Francisco: Harper & Row Publishers, 1986), "A Time to Break Silence," 231–244.

102 "100,000 Rally at U.N. Against Vietnam War; Many Draft Cards Burned: Eggs Tossed at Parade," *New York Times*, April 16, 1967; Halstead, 307

103 "40,000 Parade in San Francisco for Viet Peace; 40,000 Protest War in San Francisco March," *Los Angeles Times*, April 15, 1967.

104 Nicosia, 16; Richard Stacewicz, *Winter Soldiers: An Oral History of the Vietnam Veterans against the War* (New York: Twayne, 1997), 195–197.

Seventy young men burned their draft cards at Central Park as part of the New York protest that day.[105]

April 24, 1967. Abbie Hoffman leads a group in a guerrilla theater gesture against capitalism and the war at the New York Stock Exchange. The pranksters throw fistfuls of real and fake dollars onto the trading floor, causing complete chaos as the traders scramble to scoop up the bills.[106]

April 28, 1967. Boxing champion Muhammad Ali (Cassius Clay) refuses induction into the armed forces, citing religious reasons. He tells reporters, "I ain't got no quarrel with them Vietcong." His comments (see p. 185, n. 2) lead the World Boxing Association to revoke his title and license,[107] but the five-year prison sentence Ali receives for his war refusal is eventually reversed by the Supreme Court in June 1971.[108]

June 1967. Vietnam Veterans Against the War (VVAW) holds its first formal organizational meeting, and begins with a membership of about two dozen.[109]

Early July 1967. A group of five nonviolent protestors including three members of Women for Peace go to a military port in California's East Bay to greet the battleship *Enterprise* upon its return from Viet Nam. To the protestors' amazement, the returning sailors rush toward them and, rather than attack them, take their leaflets, generally agree with them, etc.

September 19, 1967. In a letter addressed to President Johnson, 49 International Voluntary Services (IVS) members working in Viet Nam write, "Perhaps if you accept the war, all can be justified—the free strike zones, the refugees, the spraying of herbicide on crops, the napalm. But the Viet Nam war is in itself an overwhelming atrocity. Its every victim—the dead, the bereaved, the deprived—is a victim of this atrocity."[110]

September 20, 1967. An underway FBI investigation probes VVAW to determine if the organization is directed or controlled by the Communist Party.[111] The early probe is closed down after investigations of several chapters fail to turn up any "Marxist-Leninist" influence in the organization. [A fuller investigation of VVAW will be launched in 1971 after their April Dewey Canyon III action and continued until 1974.][112]

---

105 Zaroulis and Sullivan, 112.
106 "Hippies Shower, $1 Bills on Stock Exchange Floor; 'It's Death of Money,' Says One Leader Guards Hustle Group Out," *New York Times*, August 25, 1967.
107 "Clay Refuses Army Oath; Stripped of Boxing Crown," *New York Times*, April 29, 1967.
108 "Ali Wins in Draft Case Appeal; Calling Up of Boxer Ruled Improper Court Upholds Him on Religion, 8-0," *New York Times*, June 29, 1971.
109 Stacewicz, 196.
110 Luce and Sommer, 315–321.
111 Stacewicz, 318; Wells, 141.
112 Gentry, 602.

October 3, 1967. In the first large, decentralized, coordinated draft-card turn-in action, more than 1,500 would-be draftees return their cards to local draft board offices around the country.[113]

October 15–16, 1967. Antiwar resisters organize another round of mass turn-ins of draft cards across the country as part of Stop the Draft Week. Over a thousand cards are rejected in Washington, DC, and some 300 at the federal building in San Francisco.[114]

October 16, 1967. Over 5,000 mostly young people rally on the Boston Common, holding signs with slogans such as "Don't Dodge the Draft: Oppose It." Local clergymen urge that "the moral conscience of America . . . not submit to national policies that violate honor, decency, human compassion." Boston University professor Howard Zinn is the final speaker: "We owe it to our conscience, to the people of this county, to the principle of American democracy," he said, "to declare our independence of this war, to resist it in every way we can, until it comes to an end. . . ." Participants march quietly from the Common to the Arlington Street Church (Unitarian), where they fill the sanctuary, and an overflow crowd of 3,000 listens to the sermons over loudspeakers. At the end of the service, over 280 men come forward; 67 of them burn their draft cards while 214 others turn in theirs. The government chooses to respond not by going after the hundreds of resisters, whose numbers could easily overwhelm the courts, but instead focusing on a group of older, established men identified as ringleaders.[115]

October 16–20, 1967. On the first day of an organized action in Oakland, California, Stop the Draft Week organizers lead 3,000 marchers to the Oakland Army Induction Center, where they sit down in front of the building, forcing draftees to climb over them in order to get inside. As inductees enter, protesters hand them leaflets and ask them to change their minds, to refuse induction and join the protest. The police order the demonstrators to leave, and when they refuse they are attacked with nightsticks. Twenty are injured and forty are arrested, including folksinger Joan Baez.[116] On the second day, demonstrators return to the induction center and 97 more are arrested. On the third day, 10,000 protesters arrive, and when the police order them to leave, they retreat in an orderly fashion, but successfully block streets as they depart. On Friday, October 20, protesters organize into "affinity groups" and use "mobile tactics" in large-scale confrontations with police. [Following the demonstrations, seven activists, later referred to as the Oakland Seven—

---

113 Cooney and Michalowski, 194.

114 Halstead, 402–403.

115 "Spock and Coffin Indicted for Activity against Draft," *New York Times*, January 6, 1968, http://www.nytimes.com/books/98/05/17/specials/spock-indicted.html; Zaroulis and Sullivan, 133–134.

116 "Antiwar Demonstrations Held Outside Draft Boards Across US; 119 Persons Arrested on Coast," *New York Times*, Oct 17, 1967.

Reese Ehrlich, Terence Cannon, Mike Smith, Steve Hamilton, Bob Mandel, Jeff Segal, and Frank Bardacke—will be charged with conspiracy, but eventually acquitted on March 28, 1969.][117]

October 21–22, 1967. Up to 150,000 participants show up for an antiwar march in Washington, DC, initiated and organized by the National Mobilization Committee to End the War in Vietnam, a loose coalition of 150 activist groups. Jerry Rubin serves as project director for the march at the request of mobilization coordinator David Dellinger, and novelist Norman Mailer is among the 686 demonstrators arrested during the action.[118] The two-day demonstration includes numerous speeches, as well as folk music performed by Peter, Paul and Mary, and Phil Ochs, among others. A group of hippies led by Abbie Hoffman encircle the Pentagon in an exorcism attempt: The plan is for people to sing and chant until the building levitates and turns orange, driving out the evil spirits and ending the war in Viet Nam. At a large confrontation with MPs at the Pentagon, a group of protestors offer flowers to the soldiers, inspiring the antiwar slogan, "flower power."[119]

November 11, 1967. The Vietnamese National Liberation Front (Viet Cong) hands over three US war prisoners to a delegation headed by antiwar activist Tom Hayden in Phnom Penh, Cambodia.[120] Lacking US State Department approval,[121] the trip is subsequently criticized by SDS as a "frivolous" junket.[122]

November 30, 1967. US Senator Eugene McCarthy officially entered the race for the Democratic presidential nomination, running on an antiwar platform.

Late 1967. Stokely Carmichael travels to North Viet Nam, infuriating the Johnson administration.[123]

December 4–8, 1967. A coalition of about forty antiwar organizations stages more Stop the Draft Week demonstrations across the country.[124] Among 264 people arrested at New York's Whitehall induction center are Allen Ginsberg and Dr. Benjamin Spock. Draft cards are returned to the Justice Department

---

117 "Police Rout 3,000 At Oakland Protest; 3,000 Routed in Coast Antiwar Protest," *New York Times*, October 18, 1967; "Demonstration Fails to Close Oakland Army Induction Post," *Los Angeles Times*, October 21, 1967; Rorabaugh, 116–120.

118 Bishop, 92.

119 "Thousands Reach Capital To Protest Vietnam War," *New York Times*, October 21, 1967; Cooney and Michalowksi, 194.

120 "Reds Release 3 US Prisoners; Vietcong Release Three US Prisoners of War in Cambodia," *Los Angeles Times*, November 11, 1967.

121 Bowman, 188; "Three Leftist Leaders in Hanoi; Visit Has No Government Authorization, Could Subject Trio to Severe Penalties," *Los Angeles Times*, December 28, 1965.

122 "Student Antiwar Leader Calls Peace Drive 'Sham'; Head of 3,000-Member Group Also Sees Little Value in Trio's Mission to Hanoi," *Los Angeles Times*, January 2,1966.

123 Mary Hershberger, *Traveling to Vietnam: American Peace Activists and the War* (Syracuse, NY: Syracuse University Press, 1998), 97.

124 Bowman, 190.

from more than thirty different cities.[125] An estimated 500 people gather at the San Francisco Federal Building to protest the draft; 88 draft cards are collected and destroyed.

December 18, 1967. Pacifists block the Oakland Induction Center.[126]

BERTRAND RUSSELL INTERNATIONAL WAR CRIMES TRIBUNAL

The first Bertrand Russell International War Crimes Tribunal was held in Stockholm, Sweden, May 2–10, 1967, with Jean-Paul Sartre serving as executive president. Composed of 25 members from 18 countries who heard testimony from more than 30 witnesses, the Tribunal concluded that US American forces were engaged in the *massive extermination* of the people of South Viet Nam, and were committing "genocide in the strictest sense." Witnesses reported that US bombings in North Viet Nam between February 1965 and December 1966 had destroyed 80 Catholic churches and 30 Buddhist pagodas.[127]

November 20–December 1, 1967. At the Second Bertrand Russell International War Crimes Tribunal held in Roskilde, near Copenhagen, Denmark, three Viet Nam veterans testified: former Green Beret Sergeant Donald Duncan, Peter Martinsen, and David Tuck. Duncan had just published his book, *The New Legions*.[128] Testimony revealed that in the first 10 months of US bombing in 1967, 227 additional Catholic churches and 86 Buddhist pagodas had been destroyed. Thus, testimony given during the two tribunals, pointed to at least 307 Catholic churches and 116 Buddhist pagodas having been destroyed by US bombs by October 1967.

The hearings revealed the USAF pattern of *psychosocial targeting*. The USAF manual, *Fundamentals of Aerospace Weapons*, stated that the purpose of "attacking a nation's psychosocial structure" was "to create unrest, . . . to cause strikes, sabotage, riots, fear, panic, hunger and passive resistance to the government and to create a general feeling that the war should be terminated."[129] Classified USAF manuals defined hospitals, schools, and churches as psychosocial targets intended to destroy civilian allegiance and morale and Army intelligence admitted that hospitals had been routinely listed as targets: "The bigger the hospital the better it was."[130]

Frank Harvey, who was not a witness at the tribunals but a specialist who wrote a report on the air war,[131] described the early orientation of young pilots getting their first taste of combat with direction of a forward air controller (FAC). They were instructed to bomb over flat country during sunny days when there were no air defenses. "He learns how it feels to drop bombs on human beings and watch huts go up in a boil of orange flame when his aluminum napalm tanks tumble into them. He gets hardened to pressing the

---

125 R. N. Williams, 1971, 31.
126 Cooney and Michalowski, 196–197.
127 Zaroulis and Sullivan, 350–352.
128 Donald Duncan, *The New Legions* (New York: Random House, 1967).
129 Dave Dellinger, "Unmasking Genocide," *Liberation*, December 1967/January 1968, 4.
130 Gettleman, et al., 1995, 464, citing *San Francisco Chronicle*, August 9, 1973.
131 Frank Harvey, *The Air War: Vietnam* (New York: Bantam, 1966).

fire button and *cutting people down like little cloth dummies*, as they sprint frantically under him. He gets his sword bloodied [in the South] for the rougher things to come [in the North, where there are antiaircraft defenses].[132]

On the last day of the tribunals there was testimony from Erich Wulff, a West German doctor who had served on the faculty of medicine in the hospitals of Hue for six years from 1961-1967. He had first gone to Viet Nam to support US humanitarian efforts against the Communists. He testified that, step-by-step, the war had become a war against the whole population, and argued that the average US official in Viet Nam was able to shield himself from perceiving the reality of this total war. He asserted that, in fact, the less sophisticated Marine who had been conditioned to kill every *gook* came closer to the actuality of the present US policy than the rationalization of the officials.[133]

The complete proceedings of the two Russell tribunals were published in 1969, with the title, *Against the Crime of Silence*. The Russell tribunals accused the US of violating numerous international treaties in its conduct of the war, including the 1907 Hague Convention, the 1928 Kellogg-Briand Pact, the 1949 Geneva Convention, the United Nations Charter, and the Nuremberg Principles.[134]

About the same time, Clergy and Laymen Concerned About Vietnam (CALCAV) published a 420-page report that documented the US military conduct in Viet Nam as shown by published reports and compared it to the binding domestic and international laws of war.[135] It found massive, systematic lawless conduct. It cited the following International Legal Conventions relating to the conduct of war:

- Hague Convention No. IV, Annex; Regulations Respecting the Laws and Customs of War on Land, October 18, 1907;
- Hague Convention No. IX Concerning Bombardment by Naval Forces in Time of War, October 18, 1907;
- Geneva Convention Relative to the Protection of Civilian Persons in Time of War, August 12, 1949;
- Geneva Convention Relative to the Treatment of Prisoners of War, August 12, 1949;
- Geneva Convention for the Amelioration of the Condition of the Wounded and Sick in Armed Forces in the Field, August 12, 1949;
- The Nuremberg Principles of International Law, 1946/1950; and
- The US Government on the Law of Land Warfare—Excerpts from Department of the Army Field Manual 27-10, July 1956.

---

132 Dellinger, 4.
133 Dellinger, 8-9.
134 Duffett; the special double issue of *Liberation*, Dec. 1967-Jan. 1968, is devoted to the "War Crimes Tribunal: Testimony, Reports, Findings."
135 Clergy and Laymen Concerned about Viet Nam, *In the Name of America* (Annandale, VA: The Turnpike Press, 1968).

A CAUTIONARY NOTE ABOUT TREATIES | World history is littered with attempts to outlaw wars through treaty making, and for good reason. There have been 14,600 major wars documented over the past 5,600 years, proving perhaps the original "sin" of humanity.[136]

Historical Russian sociologist Jacques Novicow catalogued more than 8,000 treaties that sought to establish permanent peace between 1500 BCE and 1860 CE, an average of nearly 2.4 treaties per year over this 3,360-year period.[137] Between 1861 and 2013, at least 400 more such treaties were made,[138] an average of 2.6 treaties per year over this 153-year period. Thus there have been more than 8,400 treaties striving to mandate peace since 1500 BCE. This does not count the 400-plus treaties made between the US Government and various Indigenous tribes/nations.

In analyzing the futile efforts of treaty making, British historian and sociologist F. J. P. Veale cites the highly touted Kellogg-Briand Pact, which was broken at least ten times in its first two decades by a number of the 63 nations who had signed it in 1928. He noted that the Nuremberg Principles derived from the 1945–46 Nuremberg Trials, an earnest effort to restrain vertical power, managed to be ignored, as power continued to justify exemptions/exceptions to the rule of law to preserve its position. Nuremberg established the dangerous precedent of victors' justice in which all restraints on horrific future warfare were removed, as it *exempted* the war crimes of the US and its allies, notably the intentional bombings of civilian targets, and worse, the US atomic bombings of Hiroshima and Nagasaki.

Our challenge, once we honestly understand the inherent destructiveness of our vertical economic-political power structure, is to not only resist and subvert our top-down, profit-driven capitalist system, which is on a speedy collision course with life itself, but also withdraw our complicit support by dramatically changing our consumer habits. Climate disruption, a direct consequence of the Industrial Revolution, is perpetuated by the capitalist profits energized by our modern consumptive way of life, which is dependent exclusively on the burning of carbon. Each burned carbon molecule is a particle of mass destruction.

---

136 Edward Tick, *War and the Soul* (Wheaton, IL: Quest Books, 2005), 42; James Hillman, *A Terrible Love of War* (New York: Penguin Press, 2004), 17–18, identifying "decisive wars, not counting thousands of indecisive ones."

137 F. J. P. Veale, *Advance to Barbarism: How the Reversion to Barbarism in Warfare and War Trials Menaces Our Future* (Appleton, WI: C.C. Nelson, 1953), 8.

138 Wikipedia, List of Treaties: http://en.wikipedia.org/wiki/List_of_treaties

> While treaties may not guarantee peace, they still provide internationally accepted markers of illegitimate conduct which provide effective tools for peace activism. We will never put an end to war without addressing the inherent plundering corruption that is built into vertical economic-political power. Seeking to end war through the rule of law merely distracts and delays the radical exercise of people power. Ironically, it is vertical power's political structure that writes and adopts the treaties. Horizontal power is about exercising our freedom as individuals to recover our ancient human consciousness and reclaim a way of life that respects the sacredness and interconnectedness of all life, and seeks human relationships rooted in empathy, mutual respect, equity, and cooperation. The challenge is to withdraw our support from capitalism as swiftly as possible, while seeking to create local human communities that recognize the limits of the local carrying capacity of each natural bioregion.

The Baltimore Four

On October 27, 1967, priest Philip Berrigan, artist Tom Lewis, and writer Dave Eberhardt poured blood on Selective Service files at the Baltimore, Maryland Custom House. United Church of Christ (UCC) Pastor James L. Mengel donated blood in advance and distributed a version of the New Testament while the others destroyed the records. They methodically poured a mixture of human and duck blood over draft files and waited 30 minutes until embarrassed FBI agents arrested them on federal property.[139] None of the four attempted to avoid arrest. The four faced federal charges of destroying government property and interfering with the Selective Service system's operation, fairly standard wherever federal prosecution of draft board raids was undertaken. In their Baltimore trial, all four participants were convicted: Philip and Tom were sentenced to 6 years in prison; David to 2 years; and Jim Mengel to probation and mandatory psychiatric counseling. Before their sentencing, Berrigan and Lewis broke the law again when they burned draft files in Catonsville, Maryland, on May 17, 1968, with seven other Catholic activists.

The "Baltimore Four" action would be followed by more than 100 draft board actions across the country between 1967 and 1972.[140] In 1969, the floodgates would open and nine separate actions, including a raid conducted entirely by women (Women against Daddy Warbucks in Manhattan), would destroy hundreds of thousands of draft board records.[141]

---

139 Zaroulis and Sullivan, 230.
140 http://www.jonahhouse.org/archive/pics67-73.htm.
141 Zaroulis and Sullivan, 235.

GI Coffeehouses

In December 1967, the first GI Coffeehouse, the UFO, was set up by Fred Gardner and Donna Mickleson near Fort Jackson in Columbia, South Carolina.[142] By 1968, as many as 26 off-base antiwar coffee houses had sprung up in the US and Europe to support questioning GIs.[143] As the coffeehouse movement spread, and antiwar sentiment began infecting the military, President Johnson and US Army Chief of Staff William Westmoreland became sufficiently alarmed to assemble an Army task force to "analyze continuously all available information" on the coffeehouse movement and to "maintain close and coordinated surveillance of all aspects of antiwar-motivated actions adverse to Army morale and discipline. We intend . . . to detect any outside-induced problems . . . to prevent any real damage to military effectiveness."[144] Existence of the emerging coffeehouses became so politically and emotionally provocative that few of them lasted more than a few months. The majority were driven out of town by sabotage, shootings, and firebombings by angry townspeople or unknown persons, or closed down by local law enforcement due to "ordinance" violations.[145]

The Boston Five

On January 5, 1968, five activists known as the Boston Five were indicted for advocating draft resistance—i.e., conspiring to "counsel, aid, and abet Selective Service registrants to evade military service and refuse to carry draft cards." In addition to the Rev. William Sloane Coffin, chaplain at Yale University, and Dr. Benjamin Spock, a famous pediatrician, were Marcus Raskin of the Institute for Policy Studies, teacher Mitchell Goodman, and Harvard seminary student Michael Ferber. Only Ferber was an actual draft resister. The government focused on the older activists, thinking of them as leaders.[146]

> **RACISM ACKNOWLEDGED AS CAUSE OF DOMESTIC STRIFE** | On July 27, 1967, while riots raged in Detroit, President Johnson formed an eleven-member National Advisory Commission on Civil Disorders, alternately referred to as the Kerner Commission (after its chair, Governor Otto Kerner, Jr., of Illinois), the Riot Commission, or the Race Commission. The Detroit riots had followed on the heels of riots in L.A., Chicago, Newark, and elsewhere. The commission represented the political and economic establishment; composed of moderate liberals who shared wide reputations for successful action, realism, and sober judgment, its intention was not revolution but stability and progress.

---

142 Halstead, 495; Lewes, 154.
143 Gettleman et al, 1995, 331.
144 Wells, 282.
145 Lewes, 152.
146 Wells, 229–233; "Anti-war Activists Sentenced to Prison July 10, 1968: On this day . . . ," *Mass Moments* (Massachusetts Foundation for the Humanities): http://www.massmoments.org/moment.cfm?mid=201.

After seven months of investigating the causes of the 1967 race riots in the United States, the Kerner Commission issued a 426-page report of its findings on February 29, 1968.[147] The Kerner Report concluded that the US was "moving towards two societies, one Black, one White, separate and unequal. . . ." White racism and limited opportunities for black people were identified as major causes of the strife and rioting in urban ghettos. It spoke of the danger of large-scale violence, white retaliation, and ultimately of "the separation of the two communities in a garrison state," if drastic steps were not taken to improve employment, housing, education, and welfare—steps that would require greatly increased taxes and expenditures.

One of the first witnesses invited to appear before the Kerner Commission was Dr. Kenneth B. Clark, a distinguished and perceptive African-American scholar. Referring to the reports of earlier riot commissions, he said: *I read that report . . . of the 1919 riot in Chicago, and it is as if I were reading the report of the investigating committee of the Harlem riot of '35, the report of the investigating committee on the Harlem riot of '43, the report of the McCone Commission on the Watts riot. I must again in candor say to you members of this commission—it is a kind of Alice in Wonderland—with the same analysis, the same recommendations, and the same inaction.*[148]

The decade of the 1960s saw the worst race riots in the US (Black rage) since the years following WWI (White rage). From 1964 to 1971, in more than 750 riots, 228 were killed and 12,741 others injured. After more than 15,000 separate incidents of arson, many Black urban neighborhoods were in ruins.[149]

The Kerner Commission appealed to the long-range self-interest of a society it presumed would want to preserve itself and develop in continuity with the moral values and social institutions of its past. It spoke to the reason and conscience of the American people, confident that by these faculties the people would be moved.

---

147 *Report of the National Advisory Commission on Civil Disorders* (New York: Bantam Books, 1968).
148 *Report of the National Advisory Commission on Civil Disorders,* Clark Testimony, 1–29.
149 Virginia Postrel, "The Consequences of the 1960's Race Riots Come into View," *New York Times,* December 30, 2004; Jonathan White, "Fifty years since the Rochester, New York riots," *World Socialist Web Site,* http://www.wsws.org/en/articles/2014/09/05/roch-s05.html, September 5, 2014.

Politics of War at Home and in Southeast Asia

January 30, 1968. Vietnamese National Liberation forces launch the TET Offensive. This decisive battle will lead to a dramatic increase in US popular sentiment against the US war in Viet Nam.

March 4, 1968. New US Secretary of Defense/War Vance Clark Clifford recommends that Operation Phoenix, a plan to target the Viet Cong, be pursued more vigorously.[150]

March 16, 1968. Robert F. Kennedy, US Senator from New York since 1965, announces his Democratic candidacy for president with a strong anti–Viet Nam war message. The announcement coincides with the massacre of 504 Vietnamese villagers at My Lai by US Army soldiers (see pp. 137–141). Though it will be twenty months before the incident is reported in the US press, My Lai closes a circle begun in 1965, when US Americans first learned of the bombings, torture, murder, and mayhem being inflicted on countless civilians, from eye witnesses such as Australian journalist Wilfred Burchett and US Special Forces Master Sergeant Donald Duncan.

March 31, 1968. President Johnson announces on national TV that he will not "seek, nor accept," nomination as Democratic candidate for president in the November 1968 election.

April 4, 1968. Martin Luther King, Jr., is assassinated in Memphis, Tennessee.

April 4–11, 1968. King's murder provokes rebellions in 125 US cities and towns that is quelled by use of nearly 69,000 US troops. At least forty-six people are killed in the violence, all but five African Americans, and over twenty thousand arrests are made. An estimated forty-five million dollars of property loss results from widespread fires and looting.[151]

April 6, 1968. The Committee for Nonviolent Action demonstrators Dan Baty and Bob Greene attempt to block the battleship *USS New Jersey* with their canoe after its commissioning at the Philadelphia Navy Yard.[152]

April 6, 1968. Sixteen-year-old Bobby Hutton is shot by the Oakland Police. He is the first and youngest member of the Black Panther Party to be murdered by police.[153] (From 1968 into the 1970s, hundreds of Panthers will be arrested and dozens murdered; 749 arrested and 27 killed in 1969 alone.[154])

April 19, 1968. The *Los Angeles Free Press* prophetically suggests that Robert F. Kennedy, now ardently anti–Viet Nam war, might be the next target for assassination by his brother's murderer(s). Kennedy had remained silent

---

150 Chomsky and Herman, p. 323, citing *Pentagon Papers*, Gravel edition.
151 Bergman, 609; Trager, 1015.
152 Cooney and Michalowski, Philadelphia Enquirer photo, 207.
153 Berger, 323.
154 Max Elbaum, *Revolution in the Air* (London: Verso, 2002), 66.

about his brother's assassination, likely because of CIA involvement, but indicated he would reopen the investigation if elected president.[155]

April 23–30, 1968. In the largest campus rebellion since Berkeley's 1964 Free Speech Movement, more than a thousand students occupy five buildings at Columbia University in New York City. Led by SDS and its campus president Mark Rudd, students protest the university's plans to build a new gymnasium on adjoining property, because the project will cause displacement of many long-time African-American inhabitants. In a separate demonstration, students demand an end to the university's ties to the Institute for Defense Analysis (IDA), known to be involved in research supporting the Viet Nam war.[156]

April 27, 1968. Antiwar demonstrations take place across the country. The numbers are mostly small, except in New York City, where 200,000 turn out to protest the war.[157]

April 30, 1968. A thousand New York City police attack the Columbia University campus, injuring at least 148 students while arresting 712 of them.

May 3, 1968. With Ralph Abernathy replacing Martin Luther King, Jr. as head of a Poor People's Campaign, the group acts on King's vision of a tent city of 500,000 poor (Resurrection City) in Washington, DC, to be erected following a series of major antiwar demonstrations. The actual encampment begins on a designated 15-acre site in West Potomac Park on the Washington Mall, which is very muddy after a rainy spring. Hundreds, but not thousands, camp on the mall in May and June; the number never exceeds 2,600.

June 24, 1968. Heavily penetrated and infiltrated by the 109th, 111th, and 116th Military Intelligence Brigades of the US Army, the Poor People's Campaign encampment on the Washington Mall is finally shut down.[158]

May 13, 1968. The first formal "peace" talks commence between the US and (North) Vietnamese governments at the Majestic Hotel in Paris (site of the 1946 talks between France and Vietnamese nationalists led by Ho Chi Minh). The US team is led by W. Averell Harriman and Cyrus Vance; the Vietnamese by Xuan Thuy and Le Duc Tho.[159]

May 16, 1968. Exactly two months after the horrific events at My Lai, details of the massacre are published in France. The story appears in the French-language publication *Sud Vietnam en Lutte*, and in the *Bulletin du Vietnam*

---

155 "Mark Lane Asks: Is Bobby Silent Because Central Intelligence Agency Killed His Brother?" *Los Angeles Free Press*, April 19, 1968.
156 Elbaum, 25; Rudd, 319.
157 Halstead, 454.
158 *A Report of the Subcommittee on Constitutional Rights, Committee on the Judiciary, United States Senate: Military Surveillance of Civilian Politics* (1972), 21;
159 Lloyd C. Gardner, *The Search For Peace in Vietnam, 1964–1968* (College Station: Texas A&M University Press, 2004), 335.

published by the North Vietnamese delegation to the Paris Peace Talks. The story is not picked up in the US press.[160]

May 17, 1968. Parallel with Columbia University actions, Harlem community activists join forces with SDS members to seize a nearby tenement building in Morningside Heights and hold it until police move in and arrest 61 African Americans and 56 Columbia students.[161]

May 21, 1968. In response to the administration's attempt to expel SDS members, including Mark Rudd, Columbia students reoccupy Hamilton Hall and declare a strike. Some students enter into open combat with the police, and a number are injured. About 140 students are arrested and 66 are suspended.

August 8, 1968. Six African Americans are killed in disturbances outside the Republican National Convention in Miami, Florida, as Richard Nixon is nominated for the presidency.[162]

August 22–29, 1968. At the Democratic National Convention in Chicago, presidential candidate Hubert Humphrey runs against Richard Nixon, defending Johnson's Viet Nam war with his famous statement, "And I think that withdrawal would be totally unrealistic and would be a catastrophe." Chicago police are prepared for massive demonstrations, and when 10,000 antiwar protesters gather in downtown streets, they are met with brutal violence unleashed by more than twice as many police and national guardsmen. About 6,000 Illinois National Guard troops are activated to assist the twelve-thousand-member Chicago Police Force, and six thousand Regular Army troops in full field gear, equipped with rifles, flamethrowers, and bazookas, are airlifted to Chicago on Monday, August 26. At least eight hundred demonstrators are injured in the brutal crackdown, which is covered live on network TV.[163]

Domestic Spying

Carried on separately by the Department of Defense/War (DOD) Directorate for Civil Disturbance Planning and Operations (now known as the Division of Military Services), the Department of Army Intelligence Command for the Continental United States, and the Army's Civil Disturbance Plan Operations, increased domestic surveillance was carried out on thousands of US citizens. Throughout the 1960s, more than 1,500 army plainclothes intelligence agents, working out of 350 separate Civil Disturbance offices and record centers, spied on ordinary US residents. The intelligence operation was conducted without authority from Congress, the President, or even the Secretary of the Army. Data banks were kept on as many as 100,000 individuals, focusing first on the

---

160 Hersh, 1970, 104.
161 Churchill and Vander Wall, 373, n73.
162 Berger, 324.
163 Zaroulis and Sullivan, 175–208; Halstead, 473–493.

feared Civil Rights movement, then on the New Left, anti-Viet Nam war movement. These surveillance campaigns assumed there was foreign influence within the civil rights and antiwar movements.[164]

A May 9, 1968 FBI memo explains the bureau's intentions in regard to the New Left: "Counterinsurgence Program—Internal Security—Disruption of the New Left: The purpose of this program is to expose, disrupt and otherwise neutralize the activities of this group and the persons connected with it."[165] By this point in time, the FBI had already been sending routine, detailed reports to the White House and President Johnson warning of New Left demonstrations and demonstrators.[166]

American Indian Movement

The American Indian Movement (AIM) was formed in Minneapolis, Minnesota on July 28, 1968, in an effort to address Indian sovereignty, treaty issues, spirituality, and leadership, while at the same time confronting police harassment and racism against Native Americans who had been forced to move off reservations away from tribal culture.[167] It wasn't long before AIM's members became a target of FBI counterinsurgency repression.

An FBI memorandum dated April 24, 1975 describes "use of Special Agents of the FBI in a Paramilitary Law Enforcement Operation in the Indian Country," and admits conduction of "extremist and criminal investigations pertaining to AIM" since at least 1972. On May 4, 1975, according to FBI teletypes, the bureau initiated a nationwide "forceful and penetrative interview program" of all individual AIM activists in an effort to identify "extremists" and, separately, to deny funding from entertainer Sammy Davis, Jr. that investigators imagined was being used to purchase arms.[168] The FBI kept detailed profiles on many Native Americans identified as AIM leaders,[169] and by 1976, at least sixty-nine AIM members had been killed at Pine Ridge, South Dakota, alone, by FBI-supported Indian GOON squads and Bureau of Indian Affairs (BIA) police. More than 300 other American Indians were physically assaulted in this same time period.[170]

---

164 Ervin Hearings," officially the US Senate Committee on the Judiciary, Subcommittee on Constitutional Rights, hearings on Federal Data Banks, Computers, and the Bill of Rights, Part I, 92nd Cong., 1st Sess., 1971; Frank J. Donner, *The Age of Surveillance: The Aims and Methods of America's political Intelligence System* (New York: Vintage Books, 1981), 293–309; Christopher H. Pyle, "CONUS Intelligence: The Army Watches Civilian Politics," *Washington Monthly*, January 1970.

165 FBI Memorandum reproduced in Churchill & Vander Wall, 177; US Senate, *Supplementary Detailed Staff Reports on Intelligence Activities and the Rights of Americans Intelligence Activities and the Rights of Americans, Book III* (Washington: US GPO, 1976), 515–517.

166 Churchill and Vander Wall, 175.

167 *Wikipedia*, American Indian Movement, http://en.wikipedia.org/wiki/American_Indian_Movement.

168 Churchill, 1990, 250–261.

169 Churchill, 1990, 234–238.

170 Churchill and Vander Wall, 175.

Antiwar Movement: More Draft Board Actions

The Catonsville Nine

When Daniel Berrigan and eight other Catholic activists burned draft board files in the Baltimore suburb of Catonsville, Maryland on May 17, 1968,[171] they became known as the Catonsville Nine. In this case, Philip Berrigan and Tom Lewis, both out on bond from the Baltimore Four case, were joined by Phil's brother, Jesuit priest Daniel Berrigan, Tom and Marjorie Melville, John Hogan (the latter three Maryknoll Missioners recently returned from Guatemala), Mary Moylan, George Mische, and Brother David Darst, a Christian brother from St. Louis, Missouri. The nine walked into a Catonsville draft board office in the Knights of Columbus hall, and managed to carry about 600 1–A files in wire baskets out to the parking lot, where they proceeded to burn them with homemade napalm. They were prosecuted on federal and state charges, including arson. Most of the state charges eventually were dropped, but the federal charges stuck, and they were convicted and did prison time for their civil disobedience action. The incident garnered national attention and even became the subject of a Broadway play called *The Trial of the Catonsville Nine*.

The Milwaukee Fourteen

September 24, 1968. The Milwaukee Fourteen, all men including five priests and a minister,[172] removed approximately 10,000 1–A draft files from the Milwaukee, Wisconsin, Selective Service boards and burned them with home-made napalm in a nearby square dedicated to America's war dead.[173] After being arrested, they spent a month in prison, unable to raise the unusually harsh bail, set at $415,000. Trial was set for the following year, and most members served jail time. Protesters marched on every court date. Milwaukee Roman Catholic Father James Groppi came to the aid of the Milwaukee Fourteen, and agreed to co-chair their Defense Committee. Their actions, along with those of the Chicago Seven, the Catonsville Nine led by Daniel Berrigan, and other contemporaries, became legendary.

Violence and Repression at Home

Robert Kennedy was assassinated just after midnight on June 5, 1968, at a special appearance celebrating his having won the Democratic nomination for president the day before. Thus, the 1960s saw the assassination of four men, all of whom had a role in provoking radical shifts taking place in US American politics during that decade. John F. Kennedy was planning a pullout from Viet Nam; Malcolm X possessed the credibility and intellectual honesty to organize a radical Black uprising; Martin Luther King, Jr., was planning a major occupation of poor people in Washington, DC, that would demand an end to the Viet Nam war and redirection of war spending to social programs; and Robert F. Kennedy had become a serious anti–Viet Nam war presidential candidate. Late in the spring of 1968, the nation found itself in a collective emotional meltdown—from which,

---

171 Cooney and Michalowski, p. 206
172 One of these men, lay Catholic theologian Frank Kroncke, later became a personal friend of mine.
173 Zaroulis and Sullivan, 235.

it can be argued, the US has never recovered—brought on by the assassinations of four major leaders advocating a radically different direction for the country. The depression intensified with the TET offensive and Johnson's abdication, among other events.[174] As the war dragged on, amidst intensifying repression at home, Mark Rudd, a founding member of the Weathermen, described the grief and frustration he felt as the mass murder continued unabated in Southeast Asia, and business-as-usual continued in the USA. "What have we become as a people?" he asked.[175]

> **CAUSES AND PREVENTION OF VIOLENCE** | On June 10, 1968, following the assassinations of MLK and RFK, President Johnson established the National Commission on the Causes and Prevention of Violence and appointed Milton Eisenhower to head it up (often referred to as the Eisenhower Commission, or the Violence Commission). On September 4, 1968, Eisenhower announced the commission would investigate the violence at the Chicago Democratic convention and report its findings to President Johnson. Chicago lawyer Daniel Walker headed the team of 200-plus investigators who interviewed hundreds of witnesses and studied FBI reports and films of the confrontations.
>
> After reviewing over 20,000 pages of statements collected from 3,437 eyewitnesses and participants, 180 hours of film, and over 12,000 still photographs, *The Walker Report* was finally released on December 1, 1968 (coinciding with the launch of the bloody Operation Speedy Express in the Mekong Delta). The report revealed brutal government violence being used against US American protestors at home (while the US government used grotesque violence in Viet Nam against people resisting the illegal war waged against them in their own homeland). It characterized the convention violence in Chicago's parks and streets as a "police riot" and recommended prosecution of police who used indiscriminate violence.[176]
>
> > *The report prepared by an inspector from the Los Angeles Police Department, present as an official observer, while generally praising the police restraint he had observed in the parks during the week, had this to say about the events . . . :* "There is no question but that many officers acted without restraint and exerted force beyond that necessary under

---

174 Rudd, 314

175 Rudd, 312.

176 *Rights in Conflict. Convention Week in Chicago, August 25–29, 1968.* A Report submitted by Daniel Walker, Director of the Chicago Study Team, to the National Commission on the Causes and Prevention of Violence, with introduction by Max Frankel (New York: E.P. Dutton, 1968); Daniel Walker, *Rights in Conflict: The Violent Confrontation of Demonstrators and Police in the Parks and Streets of Chicago during the Week of the Democratic Convention of 1968* (New York: Bantam, 1968); Bowman, 216.

the circumstances. The leadership at the point of conflict did little to prevent such conduct and the direct control of officers by first line supervisors was virtually non-existent."[177]

The report essentially concluded that disorders resulted *primarily from refusal of authorities to grant permits* and from the subsequent brutal and indiscriminate attacks by Chicago police on demonstrators, most of whom were peaceful. The report cited "ferocious, malicious and mindless violence" and "gratuitous beating."[178] Years later, in 1978, a CBS broadcast would cite US Army sources admitting that "about one demonstrator in six was an undercover agent."[179]

December 10, 1969. In its final report, submitted under President Richard Nixon, the Commission identified the roots of violence as lack of employment and educational opportunity in inner city neighborhoods—set within a larger American culture of material success and a tradition of violence that the media transmitted particularly well.

> *To be a young, poor male; to be undereducated and without means of escape from an oppressive urban environment; to want what the society claims is available (but mostly to others); to see around oneself illegitimate and often violent methods being used to achieve material success; and to observe others using these means with impunity—all this is to be burdened with an enormous set of influences that pull many toward crime and delinquency. To be also a Black, Mexican or Puerto Rican American and subject to discrimination adds considerably to the pull.*

Violence in America, concluded the Commission, could be reduced by "nothing less than progress in reconstructing urban life. . . ." This was a *moral* vision, identifying with the earlier Kerner Commission's recommendation that there could be "no higher claim on the nation's conscience" than urban reconstruction. It reminded the reader that the US Constitution framed the Commission's vision: "The Preamble of the Constitution does not speak merely of justice or merely of order; it embraces both. Two of the six purposes set forth in the Preamble are to 'Establish justice' and to 'insure domestic tranquility.' If we are to succeed in preventing and controlling violence, we must achieve both of these goals."[180]

---

177 *Rights in Conflict*, 13.

178 In addition to Walker's *Rights in Conflict*, good accounts of the 1968 convention are found in Zaroulis and Sullivan, 175–208; Halstead, 473–493.

179 Myra MacPherson, *All Governments Lie: The Life and Times of Rebel Journalist I. F. Stone* (New York: Scribner, 2006), 421.

180 National Commission on the Causes and Prevention of Violence, *To Establish Justice, To Insure Domestic Tranquility: The Final Report of the National Commission on the Causes and Prevention of Violence* (Washington, DC: US Government Printing Office, 1969).

> The disconnect between our national rhetoric about wanting to understand causes of domestic violence, and our national policy of committing genocidal and systematic Nuremberg crimes abroad is nothing short of staggering. This unbelievable, moral blind spot suggests a lack of serious attention to the deeper causes of violence.
>
> On the home front, Congress passed The Omnibus Crime Control and Safe Streets Act of 1968 (P.L. 90-351) on June 19, 1968, and in its Title I established the Law Enforcement Assistance Administration (LEAA), ostensibly to help state and municipal governments' crime-control efforts, rehabilitate offenders, recruit and train corrections officers and police, and improve correctional facilities. The functions of the 1965-created Office of Law Enforcement Assistance (OLEA) were transferred to the LEAA. This act led to a massive expansion of the crime control complex.

1969: Wars Continue at Home and Abroad

February 16, 1969. Two hundred Black students at the University of Wisconsin lead a march of 4,500 civilians, demanding an immediate halt to the war. Two thousand National Guard troops are dispatched in response.[181]

February 22, 1969. Sweden grants asylum to more than 200 draft evaders and military deserters from the US military.[182]

March 22, 1969. A Gallup Poll shows 32 percent of US Americans support escalation of war or "going all-out," 26 percent are for pulling out, 19 percent favor continuation of the status quo, and 21 percent express no opinion.

March 29, 1969. More than a year after the My Lai massacre, 22-year-old Ronald Ridenhour, a former combat infantryman, who learned of the massacre from other eyewitness soldiers, writes a letter about his findings of the massacre to President Richard Nixon, several congressmembers, and the Department of the Army, triggering a government investigation of the incident.[183]

April 5–6, 1969. Nationwide antiwar protests take place in the USA.

May 9, 1969. William Beecher, military correspondent for the *New York Times*, publishes a one-page dispatch, "Raids in Cambodia by US Unprotested," that accurately describes secret US bombings in Cambodia. Within hours, a furious President Nixon orders his national security advisor Henry Kissinger to call Hoover and unleash the FBI to find the leakers of the story, in the name of national security. This order initiates a series of illegal wiretaps.[184]

---

181 "200 Servicemen Lead Seattle Antiwar March," *The Militant*, Vol. 33, No. 9, Feb. 28, 1969.
182 Bowman, 221.
183 Summers, 1999, 257.
184 Bowman, 226.

May 15, 1969. A daily presence of peace and civil liberties activists at the Presidio Army Base in San Francisco swells to 5,000 as GIs, discharged veterans, and civilians gather to protest unfair sentencing of the Presidio Twenty-seven.

June 18-22, 1969. SDS holds its ninth annual (and, as it turns out, its last) convention in Chicago. (SDS had grown from 30,000 members and 250 chapters in the fall of 1967 to a loose federation of 400 chapters around the country with 100,000 members in November 1968. Representatives of chapters convened four times a year in national council meetings.[185]) During this convention, an internal split erupts that will lead to the organization's demise within less than a year. A strong Progressive Labor Party (PLP) Maoist faction is pitted against the "regulars," led by a radical wing of SDS going by a new name, Revolutionary Youth Movement (RYM). The RYM in turn splits into the RYM II and the Weathermen faction, the name taken from a line in the Bob Dylan song, "Subterranean Homesick Blues": *"You don't need a weatherman to know which way the wind blows."*[186] Convention participants decide to organize a multi-day protest in Chicago in October, which they call "Days of Rage."

June 27, 1969. A *LIFE* magazine cover story, "The Faces of the American Dead in Vietnam: One Week's Toll," identifies in ten dramatic and devastating pages, photo after photo, name after name, 242 young US male soldiers killed over the course of seven days, May 28–June 3, including Memorial Day. This is the average death toll for every seven-day stretch during spring-summer 1969.[187] A total of 11,527 US soldiers would be killed in Viet Nam in 1969—an average of 222 per week.[188]

September 25, 1969. US Senator Charles Goodell (R-NY) proposes legislation requiring withdrawal of US troops by the end of 1970 and barring use of Congressionally appropriated funds for maintaining US military personnel in Viet Nam after December 1, 1970.[189]

October 5, 1969. The original Weathermen faction is responsible for planting a bomb that blows up a police memorial statue in Haymarket Square, Chicago.[190]

October 8-11, 1969. The SDS Days of Rage protest riot in Chicago is timed to coincide with the trial of the Chicago Eight, which commenced in September and is expected to last several months. With the tagline, "Bring the War Home," Days of Rage organizers anticipate 15,000 to 20,000, but in the end

---

185 Elbaum, 69–72; Rudd, 141–154.

186 Rudd, 146. The Weatherman faction morphed into the Weather Underground Organization by the end of 1969, and became generically known as "the Weathermen."

187 "The Faces of the American Dead in Vietnam—One Week's toll", *LIFE* magazine, June 27, 1969: http://life.time.com/history/faces-of-the-american-dead-in-vietnam-life-magazine-june-1969/#1

188 Dunnigan and Nofi, 244.

189 Bowman, 239.

190 Dan Berger, *Outlaws of America* (Oakland: AK Press, 2006), 325.

only a few hundred show up, mostly young people, and 250 are arrested in confrontations with the police. The Black Panthers, held up by SDS as a revolutionary movement of tremendous significance, denounce the Days of Rage as "foolish, non-revolutionary and Custeristic."[191] With SDS on its last legs, this failure will stimulate the emergence of a small number of radical "Weathermen," who will go underground to launch armed struggle.

December 26-31, 1969. Between three and four hundred people attend SDS's last National Council meeting, convened in Flint, Michigan. Calling themselves the "War Council" in front of the assembled group, the emerging radical Weathermen make two important decisions—to go underground and begin violent armed struggle against the state, and to dissolve SDS into clandestine cells.[192]

Targeting of the Black Panthers

Panther headquarters were continually raided by police, often multiple times, in cities such as San Francisco, Chicago, Salt Lake City, Indianapolis, Denver, Philadelphia, Omaha, San Diego, Sacramento, and Los Angeles. The offices and their contents were usually destroyed in the process. By 1970, the Black Panther Party had been severely damaged by arrests, trials, shootouts, and police-FBI harassment, all of which had led to the jailing, murder, or exile of most of the leadership of the party, with dozens more killed or injured in gunfights.[193]

Of 295 distinct operations conducted by the FBI against Black liberation/nationalist movements, 233 targeted the Black Panther Party. Panther membership peaked in 1969 at about 5,000 before the repression took its toll.[194] A 1970s poll indicated 800 hard-core members remained at that time, and that approximately 25 percent of the Black population possessed a great amount of respect for the Black Panthers.[195] By 1970, the newspaper, *The Black Panther*, had a circulation of anywhere from 100,000 to 139,000 to 250,000.[196]

---

191 Elbaum, 71; Rudd, 188.

192 Wells, 401-402; Rudd, 189-190; Elbaum, 70-72; *Wikipedia*, Weather Underground, http://en.wikipedia.org/wiki/Weather_Underground.

193 Churchill, 1990, 142-148; Robert Justin Goldstein, *Political Repression in Modern America: 1870 to the Present* (Cambridge, NY: Schenkman, 1978), 523-530.

194 Goldstein, 1978, 524.

195 Nelson Blackstock, *COINTELPRO: The FBI's Secret War on Political Freedom* (New York: Vintage Books, 1976), 14.

196 Differing numbers sourced (in order) from: Goldstein, 524; Churchill, 1990, 159; *Wikipedia*, "Black Panther Party" (accessed 2015).

Police and FBI Operations Targeting Black Panthers

April 2, 1969. Fifteen members of the New York City Black Panthers are arrested on charges of conspiring to blow up several landmarks, including the Statue of Liberty and the Botanical Gardens, and six others are indicted. This case, which comes to be known as the Panther 21, is part of the FBI's efforts to destroy the Black Panthers.[197] On May 13, 1971, the Panther 21 would be acquitted of all charges in less than one hour of jury deliberations, following the longest trial in New York City history up to that time.

December 4, 1969. Chicago police assassinate Black Panthers Fred Hampton and Mark Clark in a pre-dawn raid. The FBI had been monitoring Hampton on a daily basis and provided a detailed floor plan of the Hampton residence to Chicago police. The targeted assassination is a collaboration between the police and Hoover's FBI, which has been open about its intent to "to destroy, disrupt, and neutralize" the entire Black movement.[198]

December 8, 1969. Another pre-dawn raid, closely coordinated and enacted by a Panther-focused LAPD "subversives unit" and the local COINTELPRO section, targets Viet Nam–veteran Panther member Elmer "Geronimo" Pratt. In the first major challenge to the special police tactical teams created in Los Angeles in 1967, a firefight erupts after search warrants for illegal weapons are served at the Black Panther Headquarters in inner city Los Angeles. The Black Panthers resist the forty-member tactical unit in a four-hour siege, during which thousands of rounds of ammunition are fired. Six Panthers are wounded before they all surrender in front of the press and public witnesses, and thirteen are arrested. Miraculously, none are killed.[199]

ORIGIN OF SWAT TEAMS | Police tactical teams began to be used on a full-time basis around 1971 in response to perceived subversive groups. Adopting the acronym SWAT, for Special Weapons and Tactics, over the years, SWAT Teams would become the sexy addition to virtually every police department in the US, leading to ever more repressive and military approaches to domestic social problems. Such responses have only intensified[200] since the "war *of* global terror" was instituted by the US after September 11, 2001, which some US political and military officials have referred to as the "long war."[201]

---

197 Berger, 324.
198 Wise, 217, 176–177.
199 Churchill and Vander Wall, 1990, 142.
200 S. Brian Willson, "Domestic Counterterrorist Trainings: A Dangerous Trend," January 1, 1999: http://www.brianwillson.com/domestic-counterterrorist-trainings-a-dangerous-trend/; Jeffrey St. Clair, "A Short History of Escalating Police Violence: The Big Heat," *CounterPunch*, October 10–12, 2014: http://www.counterpunch.org/2014/10/10/the-big-heat-2/.
201 Josh White and Ann Scott Tyson, "Rumsfeld Offers Strategies for Current War Pentagon to Release 20-Year Plan Today," *The Washington Post*, February 3, 2006: http://www.washingtonpost.com/wp-dyn/content/

Spring Madness, 1970

The year 1970 delivered a frenzy of bombings and threats of bombings. In the first ten months, the New York City police recorded more than 8,700 telephone calls warning of bombs, though police believed the majority of these callers to be cranks, mentally ill persons, and pranksters, rather than political radicals.[202] As the Weathermen protested the grotesque violence being waged mercilessly by the US military machine against the people of Southeast Asia, their violent tactics seemed to motivate many other imitators and provocateurs to also promote the use of force. This obsession with violence began to undermine the potential and power of an authentically nonviolent antiwar movement.[203]

Days of Madness

January 18, 1970. An attempted bombing of the University of Washington ROTC building by two Seattle Weathermen is thwarted by their arrests.[204]

February 21, 1970. A Weathermen cell detonates three gasoline bombs outside the Manhattan home of Judge John Murtagh, the judge presiding over the trial of the Panther 21.[205]

March 6, 1970. Three Weathermen are killed when one of the nail (shrapnel) bombs they are making accidentally explodes. (The intended target for the bombs is a noncommissioned officers dance held that evening at Fort Dix, New Jersey.) Three huge blasts rip apart their Greenwich Village townhouse and shake a whole city block. After the three are killed, remaining Weathermen members immediately go underground, and become known as the Weather Underground. Their dwindling numbers are estimated to be 300 or fewer.[206]

March 9, 1970. A car bomb kills two SNCC activists, Ralph Featherstone and William "Che" Payne, in Maryland.[207]

March 11, 1970. When another bomb blows out the side of a Maryland courthouse in the early morning hours,[208] no one is present.

March 12, 1970. Multiple bombs rock three Manhattan skyscrapers housing the corporate offices of Socony Mobil, IBM, and General Telephone and Electronics.[209] On the same day, some 300 bomb threats delivered by anonymous phone calls force massive numbers of people into the streets

---

article/2006/02/02/AR2006020202296.html
  202 Zaroulis and Sullivan, 313.
  203 Zaroulis and Sullivan, 314.
  204 Jacobs, 197.
  205 Wells, 406–407.
  206 Zaroulis and Sullivan, 313, 314; Rudd, 193; Wells, 407–408.
  207 Berger, 326.
  208 Wells, 406–407.
  209 Wells, 406–407.

of Manhattan. Among the targets of the threats are ROTC buildings, draft board offices, police stations, and police cars.[210]

April 2, 1970. A federal indictment is issued against 12 Weather Underground members for actions at the October 1969 Chicago Days of Rage.[211]

April 30, 1970. President Richard Nixon's announcement of the US invasion of Cambodia provokes countless demonstrations on college campus and many other locations around the country.[212]

May 4, 1970. In a horrendous case of excessive force, four Kent State University students are murdered when Ohio National Guardsmen take aim and fire during an intensive student protest that erupts with Nixon's invasion of Cambodia. J. Edgar Hoover's response to the violence is to blame it on the victims, going so far as to call one of the four slain Kent students a "slut."

May 10, 1970. Weathermen bomb the National Guard Headquarters in DC.[213]

May 11, 1970. Police kill six African-Americans at an anti-police brutality demonstration in Augusta, Georgia.[214]

May 14, 1970. When a student demonstration erupts at Jackson State University in Mississippi in response to Nixon's expanded war and the drafting of Black students, Mississippi State Police arrive on campus to quell the disturbance. In a 28-second barrage of more than 400 bullets from shotguns, rifles, and a submachine gun aimed at a girls' dormitory windows, two students are killed and fourteen others are wounded, prompting one mother to cry, "They are killing our babies in Viet Nam and in our own backyard!"[215]

May 21, 1970. The Weather Underground issues its first communiqué, a Declaration of a State of War, in which it formally declares war on the US Government.[216]

June 10, 1970. A bomb explodes in New York City Police headquarters.[217]

July 25, 1970. The Weather Underground bombs the Presidio Army Base and Military Police Station in San Francisco, the explosions timed to coincide with the eleventh anniversary of the Cuban Revolution.[218]

July 28, 1970. A bomb rocks the entrance of a Manhattan Bank of America building. Soon after, on subsequent days, additional bombs target a

---

210 Wells, 406–407.
211 Berger, 326.
212 Jacobs, 105.
213 Berger, 327.
214 Berger, 327.
215 Zinn, 1980, 454; Halsted, 646–647.
216 DeBenedetti, 281; Jacobs, 108; *Wikipedia*, Bernadine Dorhn, http://en.wikipedia.org/wiki/Bernardine_Dohrn.
217 Wells, 452; Berger, 327.
218 Berger, 327.

Long Island courthouse, Capitol buildings, the Pentagon, and the State Department.[219]

August 24, 1970. Post-doctoral physicist Robert Fassnacht is killed and four others injured when a bomb explodes at 3:42 am on the Madison campus of the University of Wisconsin. The explosion emanates from a van loaded with 2,000 pounds of explosives parked just outside Sterling Hall Mathematics Building. Intended to destroy the Army Mathematics Research Center, an Army think tank housed on floors 2–4, the explosion destroys the lower floor physics department and damages 26 nearby buildings as well. The crime, committed by a group calling themselves "The New Year's Gang," is timed to avoid human casualties, but Fassnacht, a 33-year-old father of three, happened to be working late in the basement physics lab, finishing up a research project before leaving on a family vacation. The bombing is meant to obstruct on-campus military research related to the Viet Nam war, but neither Fassnacht or the physics department have anything to do with the Army Mathematics Research Center. Three of the four bombers will be arrested, convicted, and serve prison time, while the fourth suspect will escape and never be found.[220]

October 3, 1970. Three buildings are bombed on the West Coast.[221]

Kent State Massacre

In the fall of 1969, in shock from my recent Viet Nam tour, I myself was experiencing a heightened sense of unrest while completing my final year in the US air force at a base in very racist central Louisiana. Revelations in November 1969 of the My Lai Massacre, which had been kept quiet from the US American people for eighteen months, seemed to have launched a new cascade of seething reactionary rage against antiwar activists, at the same time that current developments in the war were serving to intensify nationwide protests. On April 7, 1970, less than a month before the Kent State massacre, California Governor Ronald Reagan declared that "if it takes a bloodbath to silence the demonstrators, let's get it over with."[222]

But when Ohio National Guardsmen opened fire on the unarmed students demonstrating at Kent State at 12:24 in the afternoon that fateful Monday, May 4, 1970, I felt the world had gone completely mad. I was driving from my office at England Air Force Base in Louisiana to the base gym to play a little basketball when I heard about the shootings

---

219 Wells, 453.

220 Betty Medsger, *The Burglary: The Discovery of J. Edgar Hoover's Secret FBI* (New York: Alfred A. Knopf, 2014), 24–27; Berger, 327–328; *Wikipedia*, Sterling Hall Bombing, http://en.wikipedia.org/wiki/Sterling_Hall_bombing. This University of Wisconsin bombing incident is covered in the 1979 documentary, "The War at Home." The film culminates with a riveting account of the fatal campus bombing and an interview with one of the convicted bombers, Karlton Armstrong, who explains his motive. In further riveting dialogue, Armstrong's father acknowledges how successful antiwar activists were in bringing ugly realities to light. "They were telling the truth," the father says. "We weren't listening."

221 Wells, 462.

222 *Lodi News-Standard*, Lodi, CA, Wednesday, April 8, 1970. Note: After Reagan was elected US President in 1981, he oversaw lots of bloodbaths in Central America.

on my car radio, and the shock nearly numbed me. I stopped my car and just started weeping.

Hundreds of guardsmen, under command of Governor Rhodes, had opened fire with a volley of 67 bullets in 13 seconds on the gathered students, and when the shooting was over, four had been murdered and nine wounded. Rhodes claimed his need to "preserve order," and some of the guardsmen said they had fired in self-defense, but of the thirteen people shot, only two were hit frontally. Seven had bullets in their sides and four in their backs. Thus, most of the students were fleeing when they were hit, not advancing.[223]

The four murdered: Jeffrey G. Miller, 20, transfer student, 265 feet away from the Guardsmen, shot in the mouth; Allison B. Krause, 19, honor student, 343 feet away, shot in the left side of her body causing massive internal injuries; William K. Schroeder, 19, a ROTC military-science student, 383 feet, shot in the left side of his back; and Sandra L. Scheuer, 20, honors student in speech therapy, 390 feet, shot in the left side of her neck, severing her jugular vein. The nine wounded were hit at distances varying from 71 to 730 feet away from the shooters.[224]

At the time these tragic events unfolded, the dean of Kent State Honors College, Myron J. Lunine, articulated four heavy psychological blows that had served to enrage young people at Kent State and other campuses around the country: (1) President Nixon's criminal invasion of the sovereign country of Cambodia even as troops were being withdrawn from Viet Nam; (2) the president's labeling of dissenting students as *bums*; (3) the occupation of Kent State campus by heavily armed US military troops; and (4) Ohio State Governor Rhodes' comment painting the student protesters a "worse than brown shirts . . . the worst kind of people we harbor in America."[225]

After May 4, outrage at the Cambodian invasion, combined with the Kent State shootings, prompted demonstrations to erupt nationwide, involving over 4 million students at 1,350 campuses—more than 50 percent of the nation's campuses—and resulting in 536 schools being completely shut down for at least a short period, 51 for the remainder of the academic year. It was the first general student strike in US history.[226] That first week of May 1970, no less than 30 on-campus ROTC buildings were burned or bombed.[227]

Society largely blamed student protesters for the excessive violence of the police and military, and a general "blame the victim" mood invited further violent backlash. The Friday immediately after the Kent State shootings, hundreds of students protesting in New York's financial district were bludgeoned by pro-war construction workers, who rampaged through the streets attacking students with crowbars and other tools wrapped in US American flags. Financial district workers showed their support for the violence

---

[223] Jules Archer, *The Incredible Sixties: The Stormy Years That Changed America* (San Diego, CA: Harcourt Brace Jovanovich, 1986), 1–9.
[224] Davies, 52–55; Halstead, 625.
[225] Peter Davies, *The Truth about Kent State: A Challenge to the American Conscience* (New York: Farrar Straus Giroux, 1973), 22.
[226] Zinn, 1980, 481.
[227] Zaroulis and Sullivan, 320; Wells, 425.

in the streets below by throwing streams of ticker tape out their windows. Twenty-two of those New York construction workers were later honored at the White House by President Nixon for their violent deeds, and an official letter signed by Vice President Spiro Agnew thanked the union official for organizing "the impressive display of patriotism" on the day of the attacks.

When two students were killed in a barrage of police bullets at Jackson State University in Mississippi ten days after the Kent State incident, a local grand jury found the attack "justified," and US District Court Judge Harold Cox, a Kennedy appointee, concluded that students who engage in civil disorders "must expect to be injured or killed."[228] Many Americans, including myself, were dismayed by the war at home, and saw the indiscriminate violence directed at students engaged in civil disobedience as sheer madness. The USA appeared to be coming apart at its very seams. Without a moral compass, it was irredeemably lost. As I witnessed all that was taking place, I wondered if, as Malcolm X had earlier said, the chickens were finally coming home to roost, as I tried to come to terms with the immensity of the lies behind the grandiose US American mythology that had led us to Viet Nam in the first place.

President's Commission on Campus Unrest (The Scranton Report)

The President's Commission on Campus Unrest, established on June 13, 1970 by President Nixon, issued what is known as the *Scranton Report* on October 4, 1970. The report's conclusions: "The actions of some students were violent and criminal and some others were dangerous, reckless, and irresponsible." The Kent State shootings were branded as "unnecessary, unwarranted, and inexcusable."[229] "Actions—and inactions—of government at all levels have contributed to campus unrest. The words of some political leaders have helped to inflame it." One of the politicians to whom the report refers is likely Vice-President Agnew, who was famous—or infamous—for his extreme rightwing opinions. In a February 1970 political banquet speech, for example, he denounced SDS and associated radicals, saying, "I would swap the whole damn zoo for a single platoon of the kind of young Americans I saw in Vietnam."[230] Agnew's remarks reveal the extent of contempt the Nixon government held for US citizens upholding their constitutional rights of free speech, while applauding the soldiers who were part of the killing machine in Viet Nam overseen by Nixon and Agnew themselves. Ironically, a section of recommendations in the Scranton Report, "For the President," begins: "We urge that the President exercise his reconciling moral leadership as the first step to prevent violence and create understanding."

---

228 Zinn, 1980, 454; Halsted, 646–647.
229 *The Report of the President's Commission on Campus Unrest* (New York: Arno Press, 1970).
230 *Newsweek,* February 23, 1970, 24.

The Weather Underground

By the end of 1976, the Weather Underground Organization had essentially ended as an entity. Because of the unstructured nature of the group, it is hard to know how many members there were after the Weathermen went underground; some speculate no more than three hundred, thought to be a high estimate.[231] By the mid-1970s, the Weather Underground had taken credit for at least 24 bombings[232] targeting government buildings, military installations, and banks, most of which were preceded by telephone warnings so that no persons were injured in the blasts. The timing of the targeted bombings was pointed. Weather Underground members bombed the US Capitol on March 1, 1971, in protest of the recent invasion of Laos. They bombed the Pentagon on May 19, 1972, in protest of continued bombing of Hanoi. They bombed the State Department on January 29, 1975, in response to feared escalation in Viet Nam, two years after the peace accord was signed in Paris, even as some US troops remained in country until April 30, 1975.[233]

Over the duration of the war, media covered at least 40 bombings, starting with the bombing of the Haymarket Police Statue in Chicago on October 6, 1969, and ending with the September 4, 1975, bombing of the Kennecott Corporation for its alleged role in the Chilean coup of September 1973 two years earlier.[234] The same bombings are identified, give or take one or two, in several sources.[235] In a political statement authored by four of its members, the Weather Underground took credit for over twenty bombings carried out between 1969 and 1974.[236]

There were at least half a dozen radical underground organizations at war with the US government in the 1970s and early 1980s, furious with the US barbaric war against the Vietnamese and with domestic repression of dissenters. The Weather Underground was merely the most significant. Over an eighteen-month period in 1971–72 the FBI reported more than 2,500 bombings inside the US; 1,900 of them in 1972 alone, more than five per day. Another violent revolutionary group, the United Federated Forces of the Symbionese Liberation Army, or SLA, became famous after abducting heiress Patty Hearst. The SLA carried out a number of bank robberies, two murders, and other acts of violence between 1973 and 1975.[237] The George Jackson Brigade robbed at least seven banks and detonated twenty pipe bombs in the Pacific Northwest between March and December 1977.[238]

---

231 Zaroulis and Sullivan, 314.
232 Rudd, 278.
233 *Wikipedia*, Weather Underground, http://en.wikipedia.org/wiki/Weather_Underground.
234 *Wikipedia*, List of Weatherman Actions: http://en.wikipedia.org/wiki/List_of_Weatherman_actions
235 Dan Berger, *Outlaws of America* (Oakland: AK Press, 2006), 327–334; Ron Jacobs, *The Way the Wind Blew* (London: Verso, 1997), 196–201.
236 Bernardine Dohrn, Billy Ayers, Jeff Jones, and Celia Sojourn, *Prairie Fire: The Politics of Revolutionary Anti-Imperialism* (Bay Area Prairie Fire Organizing Committee/Communications Co., 1974), 4–5.
237 *Wikipedia*, Symbionese Liberation Army, https://en.wikipedia.org/wiki/Symbionese_Liberation_Army accessed July 9, 2016.
238 Bryan Burrough, *Days of Rage: America's Radical Underground, The FBI, and the Forgotten Age of Revolutionary Violence* (New York: Penguin Press, 2015), 4–5.

High-profile Activist Trials

The Chicago Eight

Known as the Chicago Eight, on March 29, 1969, David Dellinger, Tom Hayden, Rennie Davis, Abbie Hoffman, Jerry Rubin, John Froines, Lee Weiner, and Bobby Seale were indicted for conspiracy and for traveling across state lines to "incite a riot" at the August 1968 Democratic Convention in Chicago. Alhough charges were contrived in order to stereotype and demonize antiwar activists, the case served as a major rallying event for peace and antiwar movements.[239] Eight Chicago policemen were indicted separately for their part in the melee; seven of them charged for assaulting demonstrators.[240]

The trial of the Chicago Eight began on September 24, 1969 and lasted for five months. On October 29, Black Panther Bobby Seale, whose courtroom theater allegedly displayed contempt for the repressive, 73-year-old judge, Julius Hoffman, was separated from the others, gagged, shackled, and chained to a courtroom chair. He was subsequently found guilty of contempt of court and sentenced to four years in prison. From the beginning, Seale, the only black defendant, had been denied a lawyer of his own choice and disallowed to speak for himself. He was released from prison in 1972.

In November, when the decision was made to try Seale separately, the remaining defendants became known as the Chicago Seven.[241] On February 18, 1970, all seven were acquitted of conspiracy; Froines and Weiner were acquitted of all charges, while the others were found guilty of crossing state lines with intent to incite a riot and sentenced to five years in prison. The case was overturned on appeal in 1972.[242]

The DC Nine

On March 22, 1969, nine antiwar protestors were arrested for breaking into and ransacking the Dow Chemical Company office in Washington, DC, in protest of its support of the war in Viet Nam with production of Agent Orange and napalm. The nine, eight of which were priests and nuns,[243] clandestinely entered the Dow office lobby, hung photos on the wall of napalmed Vietnamese victims, including children, splattered blood on the floors, smashed office equipment, and threw documents from fourth-story windows to the street below. Some of the documents revealed Dow's relationship during World War II with I. G. Farben, the German company that had manufactured the concentration camp gas chambers used for exterminating Jews and others during the Holocaust.

The nine were charged and convicted of three felony counts of burglary and two counts of property destruction in federal court in the District of Columbia in January 1970. On May 5, 1970, one day after the Kent State massacre, they were sentenced to federal prison.[244]

---

239 Berger, 324; Halstead, 522.
240 Bowman, 223.
241 Bowman, 241.
242 Bowman, 239; Zaroulis and Sullivan, 302–303; DeBenedetti, 246, 452 n101; Elbaum, 66.
243 Author's note: One of the clergy was Joe O'Rourke, a Jesuit priest with whom I worked in the mid-to-late 1970s organizing for a prison moratorium in New York State.
244 Bernie Meyer, *The American Gandhi* (Bloomington, IN: iUniverse, 2008), xiv-xv, 17.

Antiwar Movement and Government Repression, 1969–70

May 1969. Protestors in Chicago and Pasadena, California, burn more than 20,000 Selective Service records while people read names of the war dead at post offices and federal buildings all over the country.[245]

May 25, 1969. A group later known as the Chicago 15, including two Catholic priests and a seminarian named Joe Mulligan, enter the Selective Service office at 2:00 a.m. and burn draft records affecting 50,000 men in predominantly African-American and Spanish-American Southside Chicago. At the trial in spring 1970, only half the bailed defendants show up, but all are found guilty and sentenced to long prison terms.[246]

June 13, 1969. The Nixon government declares through Attorney General John N. Mitchell that the president has the power to wiretap *without* court order or supervision, notwithstanding the Fourth Amendment, and discloses its use of wiretapping to eavesdrop on the Chicago Eight antiwar activists. Mitchell contends the government has the right to eavesdrop without court order on members of any domestic group "which seeks to attack and subvert the government by unlawful means."[247]

July 9, 1969. David Dellinger, one of the Chicago Eight and chair of the National Mobilization Committee to End the War in Vietnam, arrives in Paris, at the invitation of the North Vietnamese, to arrange release of three US POWS with the blessing of the US State Department.[248]

August 15–17, 1969. The huge, historic Woodstock Music Festival takes place at Bethel in New York State's Catskill Mountains.[249]

October 9, 1969. The National Guard is called out as demonstrators in Chicago continue to protest the trial of the Chicago Eight.[250]

October 12, 1969. Five hundred active-duty GIs march in San Francisco in protest of the war.[251]

October 15, 1969. Coordinated "Viet Nam Memorial Day Moratorium" antiwar demonstrations take place throughout the US. For the first time, numbers reflect a full-fledged mass movement: 100,000 in New York; 100,000 in

---

245 Wells, 296.

246 R. N. Williams, 1971, 37–38; "Political Trials and the Social Construction of Deviance" by Paul G. Schervish, *Qualitative Sociology*, Vol. 7, No. 3, Fall 1984, 195–216.

247 Gerald Gold, ed., *The White House Transcripts: Submission of recorded Presidential conversations to the Committee on the Judiciary of the House of Representatives by President Richard Nixon* (New York: The Viking Press, 1974), 813. Note: Mitchell's argument is part of a pattern of those in power ignoring the Constitution. Both President Gerald Ford in 1975–76 and President George W. Bush in 2003–2006 rationalized using wiretapping without warrants.

248 Bowman, 231. Author's Note: Dave Dellinger later became one of my mentors.

249 Author's Note: Ironically, I was on post–Viet Nam leave with my wife Julie in Woodstock, Vermont when I learned about the event from a newspaper report.

250 Bowman, 241.

251 Halstead, photo, between 576–577.

Boston; 50,000 in Washington, DC; 25,000 in Ann Arbor, MI; 25,000 in Madison, WI; 20,000 in Minneapolis; 20,000 in Philadelphia; 20,000 in Detroit; 11,000 in Austin, TX; 5,000 in Salt Lake City, among others.[252] The remarkable shift toward anti–Viet Nam war sentiment is illustrated by the numbers; for example, 100,000 assembled in Boston Common for this 1969 action compared to 100 gathered there in early 1965.[253]

November 12, 1969. Reporter Seymour Hersh reveals the My Lai Massacre in a press release (known as "Pinkville"), a story that has been kept from the public for twenty months.[254]

November 12, 1969. The federal government, at the request of the Justice Department, assembles 9,000 troops in the Washington area in anticipation of massive antiwar protests and demonstrations planned for November 14–15. The federal troops augment a 1,200-man National Guard and a 3,700-man DC police force.[255]

November 13, 1969. The second moratorium on the war within a month begins, with nearly 50,000 participating in a March Against Death headed by relatives and friends of military personnel killed in Viet Nam.[256]

November 15, 1969. The New Mobilization Committee to End the War sees 250,000 protesters in San Francisco and 750,000 in Washington, DC, during the second national moratorium against the Viet Nam war in a month, the largest such gatherings to date.[257] In DC, the moratorium begins with a march down Pennsylvania Avenue in front of the White House (while President Nixon watches the Purdue-Ohio State football game on TV) to the Washington Monument, where a mass rally is held. Pete Seeger, Arlo Guthrie, Peter, Paul, and Mary, and four different touring casts of the musical *Hair* entertain the demonstrators.[258] Speakers include US Senators Charles Goodell (R-NY) and George McGovern (D-SD). The rally concludes with nearly 40 hours of continuous reading of known US deaths (to that date) in the Viet Nam war.[259]

---

252 Halstead, 565–566.

253 Zinn, 1980, 477.

254 Bowman, 242. Author's note: The government was secretive about domestic matters, too. The day after the My Lai Massacre story finally went public in the USA, President Nixon transmitted a memorandum to Mitchell to prepare a ten-year federal corrections system "reform" plan that included construction of a number of new federal prisons. In May 1970, the Federal Bureau of Prisons (BOP) quietly developed their first *Long Range Master Plan*, but it was not made public until 1972.

255 Bowman, 242; Wells, 388.

256 DeBenedetti, 261–262.

257 Halstead, photo, 576–577.

258 Wells, 392–393.

259 Zaroulis and Sullivan, 275–300; Halstead, 578–579.

November 15, 1969. For the first time, the US Army publicly discusses events surrounding the My Lai massacre. Survivors of My Lai interviewed by reporters assert a total of 567 Vietnamese men, women, and children were massacred by US troops on March 16, 1968.[260]

January 1970. A Citizens Commission of Inquiry on US War Crimes in Vietnam (CCI) is established to conduct a series of war crimes hearings in 14 cities.

February 3–5 and March 16, 1970. Congressional Hearings are held on *Vietnam Policy Proposals*, nine items of legislation proposed to end the US war in Viet Nam.[261]

February 6, 1970. Eleven members of the East Coast Conspiracy to Save Lives, ranging in age from 18 to 39, destroy draft files in Philadelphia. The next day the same group enters General Electric offices in Washington, DC, and reveals to the public files that exposed collusion between Congress and GE officials, GE being the second largest war contractor at the time.

June 1970. John Kerry joins Vietnam Veterans Against the War (VVAW) and subsequently becomes one of its unofficial spokespersons.[262]

June 5, 1970. At a meeting at the White House, the FBI's J. Edgar Hoover is appointed head of an interagency committee to formulate plans for domestic intelligence operations. Also present at the meeting: Richard Helms (CIA), Lt. General Donald V. Bennett, Defense Intelligence Agency (DIA), and Vice-Admiral Noel Gayler, National Security Agency (NSA).[263]

June 24, 1970. The US Senate votes overwhelmingly to repeal the 1964 Gulf of Tonkin Resolution.

June 25, 1970. Hoover's interagency committee submits its 43-page report (*The Huston Plan*) to President Nixon, in which it recommends surreptitious entry, covert mail coverage, and other activities it warns are "clearly illegal." The recommendations were authored by Tom Charles Huston, a young, conservative White House aide charged with designing an intelligence-gathering plan through illegal and unconstitutional searches and buggings to get whatever evidence the paranoid Nixon wanted. Hoover surprises his colleagues when he balks at the plan, calling Huston a "hippie intellectual."

July 14, 1970. Nixon approves Huston's top-secret dirty tricks plan, but Hoover later nixes it, forcing Nixon to revoke his approval.[264]

---

260 Bowman, 244; per AP story, November 19, 1969, "DOD: Incidents Seem Exaggerated" with "published reports that as many as 567 South Vietnamese civilians were killed at My Lai."

261 US Congress, 91-2, Senate Committee on Foreign Relations, Hearings, February 3, 4, 5, and March 16, 1970, 5+405 pages). SuDoc: Y 4.F 76/2:V 67/16, CIS: 71 S381-7, LCCN: 74606991, DL, WorldCat.

262 Nicosia, 72.

263 Marvin Miller, *The Breaking of a President: The Nixon Connection* (City of Industry, CA: Therapy Productions, 1975), 16–17; Gentry, 652–658; Gold, 813.

264 Gentry, 652–659; Hersh, 1983, 209; Zaroulis and Sullivan, 409.

Mid-1970. The Selective Service System (SSS) reports 271 destructive attacks (bombing, arson, destruction of records) have been made on draft boards in the past two years.[265]

November 6, 1970. The trial of the Seattle Seven begins for Seattle Liberation Front (SLF) antiwar protesters charged on February 17, 1970 with inciting a riot and conspiracy to damage the Seattle Federal Building. The defendants will ultimately serve three months in prison for contempt, despite unsuccessful prosecution of the original charges.[266]

THE HARRISBURG EIGHT

When FBI Director Hoover appeared before an appropriations subcommittee of the US Senate on November 27, 1970 to request $14.1 million to hire 1,000 additional agents and 702 clerks, he used the occasion to announce "an incipient plot on the part of an anarchist group ... the so-called East Coast Conspiracy to Save Lives ... a militant group, self-described as being composed of Catholic priests and nuns, teachers, students, and former students. ... The principal leaders were ... Catholic priests Philip and Daniel Berrigan...." According to Hoover, they were "concocting a scheme to kidnap a highly placed government official [Henry Kissinger]" and also "to blow up underground heating conduits and steam tunnels serving the Washington, DC area in order to disrupt federal governmental operations." Hoover claimed the group's goal was to force the end of US bombings in Southeast Asia and the release of all America's political prisoners.

On January 12, 1971, Dr. Eqbal Ahmad, Father Philip Berrigan, Sister Elizabeth McAlister, Father Neil McLaughlin, Anthony Scoblick (a married priest), and Father Joseph Wenderoth of the Harrisburg Eight were indicted on federal charges of conspiring to kidnap Kissinger and blow up the heating systems of federal buildings in Washington, DC. The government also cited as co-conspirators Father Daniel Berrigan, Sister Beverly Bell, Marjorie Shuman, married priest Paul Mayer, Sister Jogues Egan, Thomas Davidson, and William Davidon, a university physicist and mathematician. The defendants were arrested and jailed (the Berrigans were already in Danbury prison for their earlier antiwar protests). Many of these defendants were clergy and laypeople of what later came to be called the "Catholic Left"—some of the most radical activists in the 1960s Viet Nam war resistance movement.

At a hearing February 8, 1971, each defendant pled "not guilty." In a second indictment handed down on April 30, 1971, the name of John Theodore (Ted) Glick (draft resister) was added to those charged (the defendants thereafter known as the Harrisburg Eight), and the charges were expanded to include destroying files and property of the federal government and conspiracy to possess illegal explosives. On the same day, in a demonstration of 2,000 people at the Justice Department in Washington, DC, organized

---

265 R. N. Williams, 1971, 44.

266 *Wikipedia*, Seattle Liberation Front (Seattle 7), http://en.wikipedia.org/wiki/Seattle_Liberation_Front; "Looking Back on the Seattle Conspiracy Trial," December 1990, http://terrasol.home.igc.org/trial.htm, accessed October 24, 2014. Author's Note: Interestingly, defendant Michael Lerner later became a rabbi and the editor of the liberal *Tikkun* Magazine.

by the Harrisburg Defense Committee in conjunction with other defense groups representing victims of political repression, over 350 people were arrested for blocking the entrances to the Justice Department.

By the time of their trial in early 1972 at the federal courthouse in Harrisburg, Pennsylvania, the Harrisburg Eight had again become the Harrisburg Seven, as Ted Glick was severed from the group because of his petition to defend himself rather than have a lawyer act of his behalf. The trial continued for several months and received widespread attention. The defense team included former US Attorney General Ramsey Clark, Jesuit priest and lawyer William Cunningham, Leonard Boudin, and Paul O'Dwyer, who conducted a fierce cross-examination of the government's key witness, FBI informant and conman Boyd Douglas, who had been a fellow federal prisoner of Philip Berrigan's.

Finally, in April 5, 1972, the jury returned its verdict: Ten of the twelve jurors voted for acquittal and the judge declared a mistrial, a personal humiliation for Hoover. The government dropped the case. Glick was never tried. Although Berrigan and McAlister were separately found guilty on seven counts dealing with the smuggling of letters in and out of Lewisburg prison, these charges against them also were later dismissed. It was a costly victory for the defendants, however. The strain of the trial divided them, and several did not talk with Liz and Phil afterward. The Catholic Left was in disarray.[267] Interestingly, in York, Pennsylvania, not far from Harrisburg, the American Machine and Foundry Company, which produced 500-pound bombs, announced on March 27, 1972 that sabotage had recently occurred in its factory. A group called Citizens Committee to Demilitarize Industry took credit for disarming the munitions.[268]

The Camden Twenty-eight

The Camden Twenty-eight, a group of Catholic Left anti-Viet Nam war activists, executed a break-in at the Camden, New Jersey draft board in the early morning hours of August 22, 1971. Hoover and Mitchell announced that FBI agents had arrested 20 antiwar activists in and near the Camden draft board office in the act of destroying records. There had been an informant among their group. The major charges against the group were conspiracy to remove and destroy files from the draft board, the FBI office, and the Army Intelligence office, destruction of government property, and interfering with the Selective Service System. The men and women arrested that summer in Camden called themselves *America's conscience*. Included among them were four Catholic priests and one Lutheran minister. All but one of the remaining 23 were Catholic laypeople. The trial of the Camden 28 lasted sixty-three days, from February 5 to May 20, 1973. The defendants were acquitted on all charges due to the extent of FBI facilitation of the break-in. They were unified in refusing any plea deal, and put the war on trial, even as they faced more than forty years in federal prison for seven felony counts. The FBI hoped to uncover whether members of the Camden 28 had been involved in the unsolved case of the March 8, 1971 Media, Pennsylvania FBI office break-in, but they never did.

---

267 William O'Rourke, *The Trial of the Harrisburg 7 and the New Catholic Left* (Notre Dame, IN: Notre Dame University Press, 2012), review by Jim Forest.
268 Wells, 536.

Veterans Activate at Home

Vietnam Veterans Against the War: 1970-72

Mar. 1970–Dec. 1970. Citizens Commission of Inquiry (CCI) on US War Crimes in Vietnam conducts hearings in 12 cities in the US, utilizing the testimony primarily of Viet Nam veterans. The first hearing is held in Annapolis, Maryland, March 11-12, 1970. Subsequent hearings are held in Toronto, Canada (for deserters); Philadelphia; Springfield, Massachusetts; New York City; Los Angeles; Boston; Baltimore; Buffalo; Minneapolis; and Portland, Oregon. The final hearing is in Washington, DC, Dec. 1-3, 1970.

Hundreds of testimonies of Viet Nam veterans at all these inquiries/hearings covered activities of virtually every major unit and military operation in Viet Nam from 1965 to 1970. The Citizens' Commission of Inquiry requested a Congressional investigation into the Viet Nam war and the violations of international law by US soldiers, sailors, airmen, and marines. There was no Congressional interest. However, freshman Congressman from Oakland, Calif., Ron Dellums, just elected in November 1970 and yet to be seated, became interested (see April 26-27, below).

September 4-7, 1970. In a creative Labor Day holiday action orchestrated from the VVAW office in New York City, over 200 well-screened Viet Nam Veterans perform continuous guerrilla theater along 100 miles of the public road, from Morristown, New Jersey, to Valley Forge, Pennsylvania. Code-named Operation RAW (Rapid American Withdrawal), the action is designed to simulate public exposure to actual combat conditions in order to educate ordinary US Americans and challenge their ignorance about the war. Notables present for the final rally at Valley Forge, which attracts over 1,000 civilians, include Jane Fonda, Donald Sutherland, and an emerging John Kerry.[269]

December 1-3, 1970. A National Veterans Inquiry on US War Crimes in Vietnam sponsored by the Citizens Commission of Inquiry on US War Crimes (CCI) is held in Washington, DC.[270] Twenty-nine of the 32 people who testify are veterans.[271] At least ten CCI hearings had been held prior, the first in February 1970 in Toronto, Canada and Annapolis, Maryland. Subsequent others are held in Springfield, Massachusetts; Richmond, Virginia; New York

---

269 Nicosia, 56-73.

270 Transcript, 117 *Congressional Record* 4238-4271 (US Congress 92-1, March 1 1971), Permanent Edition.

271 Witnesses were: Robert Bowie Johnson Jr., Mike McCusker, Daniel K. Wilson Amigone, Greg Motoka, Kenneth Barton Osborn, Norman Kiger, Gail Graham, Steve Noetzel, Edward Murphy, Daniel Alfiero, Louis Paul Font, Robert Master, Peter Norman Martinsen, T. Griffiths Ellison, Ed Melton, Chuck Hamilton, Lee Meyrowitz, Gordon S. Livingston, Greg Turgeon, Richard Altenberger, Bob Connelly, Robert J. Lifton, Chaim Shatan, Donald Engel, Gary Thamer, Steven Hassett, Kenneth Campbell, Sam Rankin, Phillip Wingenbach, Tod Ensign, Larry Rottmann, and Robert Osman.

City; Buffalo, New York; Boston, Massachusetts; Minneapolis, Minnesota; Los Angeles, California; and Portland, Oregon. (CCI eventually becomes the veterans advocacy and antiwar group, Citizen Soldier, based in New York City and directed by Tod Ensign until his death in May 2014.)

January 12, 1971. President Nixon signs repeal of the 1964 Gulf of Tonkin Resolution.

January 31–February 2, 1971. Vietnam Veterans Against the War (VVAW) convene and coordinate public hearings, "The Winter Soldier Investigation: An Inquiry into American War Crimes," an opportunity for veterans to testify about US war crimes. During three days of hearings held at a Holiday Inn in Detroit, Michigan, 117 veterans testify about war crimes and atrocities they committed or witnessed in Viet Nam, Laos, and Cambodia; John Kerry helps interview the vets before they testify. Each veteran's authenticity and story are checked by organizers beforehand. (Who better to authenticate Viet Nam service than other Viet Nam vets?)

April 12, 1971. The FBI informs the White House about VVAW actions in Washington planned to begin on April 18. The information was to be disseminated locally to the 108th Military Intelligence Group, Naval Investigations Services Office, USAF's Office of Special Investigations (OSI), Secret Service, and the like.[272]

April 18, 1971. As many as 2,000 veterans and friends converge for Dewey Canyon III, a nonviolent invasion of Washington, DC organized by VVAW with the tagline, "a limited incursion into the country of Congress." At least 1,000 veterans set up camp on the Washington, DC Mall near the Capitol and engage in a variety of actions from guerrilla theater to conventional lobbying, generally focused on the need to end the war. Fifty veterans attempt to turn themselves in at the Pentagon as war criminals.

April 20, 1971. Threatened with forcible removal from the mall for lack of a permit, members of the 82nd Airborne Brigade (many combat returnees) tell the veterans they will refuse orders to arrest or interfere in any way with their brothers. The veterans remain on the mall despite being ordered by the US Government to move. No arrests are made.

April 22, 1971. John Kerry, one of the veterans' chief spokesmen, made his famous antiwar speech before Senator J. William Fulbright's Foreign Relations Committee.

April 23, 1971. On the last day of Dewey Canyon III, nearly 800 veterans return their war medals in a ceremony held on the steps of the Capitol, many calling the war immoral and illegal.

---

272 Stacewicz, 447n15.

April 26–29, 1971. Three years after the My Lai massacre, freshman US Congressperson Ron Dellums (D-Oakland) presides over the *Ad Hoc Congressional Hearings on War Crimes in Vietnam: An Inquiry into Command Responsibility in Southeast Asia,* taking testimony from members of the US Armed Services who had participated in the war in Viet Nam. The ad hoc panel of 22 congresspersons is denied official committee status, but Dellums provides space in his congressional office for the exhibition of evidence of US war crimes in Viet Nam, and the hearings are held in the US House of Representatives Caucus Room, Cannon House Office Building.[273] The committee inquires into vivid details of the war crimes issue, with Viet Nam veterans providing most of the testimony on what they had committed or witnessed in Viet Nam. [No other congressional committee, official or unofficial, has ever examined the war crimes or violations of international law by US forces in Viet Nam.]

December 27, 1971. A small number of VVAW members enters the Statue of Liberty, climbed to the top, and flew the US flag upside down as an international symbol of distress, demanding US withdrawal from Southeast Asia.[274]

April–June, 1972. Eight members of VVAW based in Gainesville, Florida begin planning nonviolent demonstrations for the July Democratic Presidential Convention, and, more importantly, the August Republican Presidential Convention, both to be held in Miami.[275]

---

273 Citizens Commission of Inquiry, ed., *The Dellums Committee Hearings on War Crimes in Vietnam* (New York: Vintage Books, 1972): 26 testified, of whom 24 were veterans. Witnesses:
• April 26: Five West Point graduates—Captain Fred Laughlin, Major Dr. Gordon Livingston, Captain Robert B. Johnson, Captain Greg Hayward, Captain Ron Bartek, and Captain Michael O'Mera. Captain Greg Hayward, US Army West Point, Class of 1964—stated, among other comments, *"General Ewell was promoted above several officers to the job of Field Force commander, and he used the term, not an Indian hunt, but he used the term killing fish in a barrel, and that is how he described several operations, and I personally heard him talk about 'killing fish in a barrel.' We put great emphasis on this body count. It seems ironic that General Ewell is our military representative to the Paris Peace Talks. It is hard to understand that he can deal in good faith across a bargaining table now when he made his reputation as an American in Viet Nam killing Vietnamese; that he can in good faith bargain. I don't think he is that sort of diplomat that we should have"* (63–64).
• April 27: Five former military intelligence special agents and POW interrogators: Nathan Hale, 1st Lieutenant Michael Uhl, Kenneth Osborn, Steve Noetzel, Peter Martinsen.
• April 28: Ten former Americal Division members: Gary Battles, Daniel S. Notley, John Beitzel, Guadalupe G. Villarreal, Daniel Barnes, Charles David Locke, William Toffling, Thomas Cole, Terry Mullen, Steve Padoris.
• April 29: Six regarding overview of air war, pacification and forced urbanization: John Sack, Kenneth Campbell, David Bresum, Captain Randy Floyd, IVS Staff Fred Branfman, Elliot L Meyrowitz.
274 Cooney and Michalowski, 209.
275 Nicosia, 247–254.

Summer 1972. VVAW members appear, many in wheelchairs, at the Republican National Convention in Miami, calling for an end to the war, and are forcibly removed from the convention, including Viet Nam veteran Ron Kovic, who upon being removed to a spot outside the convention floor, makes a passionate statement against the Viet Nam war. Journalists present, including Hunter S. Thompson, say that if Kovic's comments had aired on national television, the war would have ended at that moment.

Winter Soldier

The Winter Soldier hearings were held in response to the My Lai massacre. VVAW intended to convey the notion that such practices were not unique but rather an inevitable result of US policy. One soldier who testified was former Fifth Special Forces Master Sergeant Donald Duncan, who had served in Viet Nam in 1964–65, and who had already published an autobiographical critique of the war.[276] Duncan concluded, "the fact that so much can be done to so many men by so few people is the greatest testament to the fact that our colleges, our high schools, our everyday life is nothing but pre-basic training. . . . The idea that the United States has a God-given right to go into any country and take out its raw materials at an advantage to ourselves is not something that they learned in Viet Nam. They learned it in our schools. They learned it from their mothers, fathers, their sisters and their brothers, their uncles. They learned it from all of us."[277] This statement particularly resonated with me because I had been such a "good Christian boy," a good student from elementary to graduate school. I had virtually no critical thinking skills, having grown up in "America."

The hearings of course infuriated the Nixon administration.[278] Special Counsel to Nixon, hatchet-man Charles Colson, had arranged infiltration of VVAW soon after Nixon took office in January 1969, with the intention of destroying the organization's credibility.[279] One Nixon team memo says about VVAW, "Several of their regional coordinators are former Kennedy supporters."[280] In response to Winter Soldier, Colson's crew was tasked with investigating each veteran's authenticity and testimony. In a confidential *Plan to Counteract Viet Nam Veterans against the War*, Colson wrote, "The men that participated in the pseudo-atrocity hearings in Detroit will be checked to ascertain if they are genuine combat veterans."

---

276 Don Duncan, *The New Legions* (New York: Random House, 1967).

277 Vietnam Veterans against the War, 167–168.

278 Vietnam Veterans against the War; transcript, 117 *Congressional Record* 9947-10055 (US Congress 92-1, April 6 1971, Permanent Edition/red bound–SuDoc: X.92/1:117/PT.8, ISSN: 0883-1947, LCCN: 12036438.

279 Nicosia, 252.

280 Doug Brinkley, *Tour of Duty: John Kerry and the Vietnam War* (William Morrow, 2004), 349, 356–357; Wells, 489–490.

Dewey Canyon III: Veterans Incursion into Congress

The name of the April 18–23, 1971 VVAW action, Dewey Canyon III, mocked the US invasions of Laos in 1969 and the subsequent invasion of Laos in February 1971, which were code-named Dewey Canyon I and Dewey Canyon II, respectively.

Learning of VVAW's Dewey Canyon III plans a few days in advance, the Justice Department worked with the Secretary of the Interior to seek an injunction in US District Court to prevent the veterans from camping on the Mall. The judge ruled in the government's favor. The vets camped in defiance. Former Attorney General Ramsey Clark represented the veterans in appealing the ruling. The Court of Appeals overturned the lower court, thus allowing the encampment. Desperate to get the raw antiwar veterans out of the public eye, President Nixon submitted an emergency petition to the Supreme Court to overturn the Court of Appeals ruling. Almost immediately, the highest court reversed the ruling and reinstated the earlier injunction, giving the vets until 4:30 pm on April 21 to vacate the Mall. Many Congresspersons and Senators publicly supported the veterans, though traditional veterans groups like the American Legion and the Veterans of Foreign Wars harshly condemned them. However, despite assertions that these veterans did not represent most of their peers, a number of active-duty troops from local bases stated publicly they would not participate in riot control against the vets if so ordered.

The deadline came and went, as Ramsey Clark appeared before the Supreme Court in emergency session. In the early evening, Clark came to the campsite and announced that the Court had compromised and agreed to let the vets stay on the Mall as long as they didn't sleep there. If the vets decided to continue sleeping there, they would be subject to arrest. John Kerry spoke in favor of abiding by the Court. However, there was much resistance to leaving the Mall, and many announced their intention to stay overnight again. In a democratic process, the 900 or so vets met in home state caucuses to decide what course to take. The final vote of the encamped vets was 480 to 400 to sleep on the Mall and risk arrest. The gathered vets then voted to make their defiance unanimous. Someone raised the question of whether the US military would storm this gathering of restive vets, as had happened in 1932 when General Douglas MacArthur's armed troops burned down the Bonus Marchers' twenty-seven encampments in Washington, DC, including on the Mall, on the Capitol grounds, and in Anacostia Flats across the Anacostia River.[281] Before the vets dug in under ponchos and makeshift shelters that night, they erected a perimeter of their own sentries in anticipation of a police visit. A 10:00 pm newscast reported the police did not plan any arrests that night; that no action was expected until Thursday morning. A Thursday morning newspaper headline read, "Vets Overrule Supreme Court." And so it was. No arrests were made. It was that day that Kerry spoke before US Senator Fulbright's Foreign Relations Committee. The momentum was now with the weary vets. The next day, hundreds of the veterans threw their medals over a hastily erected fence near the west steps of the US Capitol building, where they directed angry words against the policy makers, declaring in effect that the medals were drenched in the blood of the

---

281 Donald J. Lisio, *The President and Protest: Hoover, Conspiracy, and the Bonus Riot* (Columbia, Missouri: University of Missouri Press, 1974), 76–77; Lucy G. Barber, *Marching on Washington: The Forging of an American Political Tradition* (Berkeley: University of California Press, 2002), 75–107.

The poster advertising Dewey Canyon III, the April 18–23, 1971 nonviolent invasion of Washington, DC, by more than a thousand Viet Nam veterans, organized by Vietnam Veterans Against the War (VVAW).

The Dewey Canyon III encampment established on the Washington Mall near the Capitol building was not far from the author's office at the DC Public Defender Service, enabling him to visit regularly. The goal of VVAW's "limited incursion into the country of Congress" was to stop funding for the war using a variety of actions, from guerrilla theater, to conventional lobbying, to veterans attempting to turn themselves in as war criminals, to the Friday, April 23 ceremony where many of the veterans returned their war medals over a hastily erected fence near the west steps of the Capitol building. As a result of this week of actions, VVAW soon became a target of the FBI as a "subversive" group.

innocent Vietnamese. The vets indeed managed to demonstrate a moral superiority over the highest law of the land while defying their commander-in-chief.

I was living in Washington, DC, at the time, working at the nearby office of the DC Public Defender Service, so I had the pleasure of walking to the encampment after work and observing some of the on-site activities, and I remember being in total sympathy with the encamped veterans. Most Dewey Canyon III participants had either supported the war at first, as I had, or had no opinion about the war before going to Viet Nam. However, more than half of these veterans (62 percent) reported undergoing "a drastic change in their views about US involvement in Vietnam" while serving there.[282] That was my case as well.

Nixon was even more furious with Dewey Canyon III than he had been when he learned of the Winter Soldier hearings held in Detroit earlier that year. He used Colson to discredit and disempower VVAW however he could, and Colson's efforts included an attempt to revoke the VVAW's IRS tax status.[283] Soon, the VVAW became a target of the FBI as a "subversive group." On April 29, 1971, only six days after conclusion of the veterans' actions, the FBI sent an informational memo to various agencies and field offices describing in detail the six days of Dewey Canyon III activities and events. The FBI sent a letter to all its offices on August 3, 1971, with instructions "to initiate a survey to determine existence of VVAW." The letter claimed "increasing indication that the VVAW may be a target for infiltration by subversive groups such as the Communist Party USA and the Socialist Workers Party and their respective youth groups." Other reports said VVAW was involved in "aiding and financing US deserters, including false identity papers and reportedly in one area has a cache of arms. VVAW has become increasingly active in the antiwar field and must be considered a prime target for infiltration."[284] FBI files on VVAW later obtained through the Freedom of Information Act numbered 19,978 pages.[285]

Ironically, by the end of the Viet Nam war, VVAW was the most successful antiwar protest group in the country. It was a long, strange war where the men who had fought in it became the most effective protesters against it.[286]

---

282 Lewes, 54; David Thorne and George Butler, eds., *The New Soldier* (New York: Collier Books, 1971), 174.

283 Nicosia, 155, 200.

284 Inspection Report of Domestic Intelligence Division, August 17–September 9, 1971, p. 111, as cited in *Supplementary Detailed Staff Reports on Intelligence Activities and the Rights of Americans, Book III, Final Report of the Select Committee to Study Governmental Operations with Respect to Intelligence Activities*, United States Senate, April 23, 1976, p. 534 (also known as the Church Committee Report).

285 Medsger, 274.

286 O'Rourke.

Bombs and Threats of Bombs

In 1970, 32 bombings or attempted bombings of federal buildings continued to frustrate the FBI. They had neither developed good leads on the perpetrators nor discovered the whereabouts of suspected members of the Weather Underground.[287]

The academic year 1969–70 witnessed nearly 500 terrorist and arson bombings, both on and off campuses, with six people killed. Making matters even tenser, in the first ten months of 1970, New York City police received more than 8,700 bomb warnings, though not all from political radicals, and the majority false alarms, but nonetheless building hostility toward an antiwar movement that appeared to be mindlessly violent.[288]

On March 1, 1971, at 1:32 am, a powerful bomb explosion ripped through a men's restroom on the ground floor of the US Capitol. Credit for the blast was claimed by the Weather Underground, the bombing being their response to Nixon's February 8 illegal invasion of Laos.[289]

Media, Pennsylvania FBI Office Break-in

On the evening of March 8, 1971, a small group of activists calling themselves the *Citizens Commission to Investigate the FBI* broke into a small, two-man FBI field office in the borough of Media, Pennsylvania, and removed over 1,000 classified documents. One of the key instigators was William Davidon, a suspected co-conspirator in the Harrisburg Eight case (see p. 241). Among the files discovered was a routing slip entitled "COINTELPRO-NEW LEFT," a term and program unknown outside the Bureau until that time.[290]

COINTELPRO was Hoover's long-standing secret dirty tricks campaign (since 1955) within the FBI to investigate and disrupt virtually any and all dissident political groups in the country. The break-in was timed to coincide with the celebrated "fight of the century" boxing match between Nixon friend and war supporter Joe Frazier and antiwar Muhammad Ali at Madison Square Garden in New York.

The Citizens Commission soon began disseminating the file's contents to the press, some of which was published as early as April 6. Hoover, now 76, was furious, and his frustration at being unable to identify the burglars is speculated to have sped up his death, which occurred just over a year later on May 2, 1972.[291] The burglars were never caught.

May Day 1971

A crowd of 50,000 turned out for a rock concert on Saturday, May 1 at the Lincoln Memorial, and on Sunday and Monday, when tens of thousands protesters engaged in nonviolent disobedience in a number of locations in Washington, DC, more than 12,000

---

287 Wise, 368.
288 Zaroulis and Sullivan, 301, 313.
289 Wells, 477–478.
290 Medsger, 271.
291 Medsger, 282.

were arrested. Washington's 5,000-person-strong police force was supplemented by 2,000 National Guardsmen, 8,000 army and marine soldiers, and an unknown number of federal marshals. The maximum estimate of the number of demonstrators on the streets was 15,000, meaning that the majority were arrested by the approximately similar force of 15,000 police and soldiers.[292]

> **HISTORY OF GOVERNMENT REPRESSION** | Sophisticated surveillance was conducted on US Americans as early as 1934 when President Franklin Roosevelt instituted a long-standing, joint FBI-military domestic intelligence program that had broad investigative scope using the "fundamental tool" of paid informants to exact "an adverse impact on the rights of individuals." The program included spying on the nation's college campuses. An alliance with the American Legion allowed recruitment of volunteer informants in the quest to identify suspected domestic subversives. In May 1940, Roosevelt authorized Attorney General Robert H. Jackson to "secure information by listening devices of persons suspected of 'subversive activities' in 'grave matters involving the defense of the nation.'" In June 1940, Hoover asked Jackson for assistance in establishing "a suspect list of individuals whose arrest might be considered necessary in the event of war." In 1947, the Justice Department began checking with the IRS the charitable status of any organization on the growing list of identified subversive organizations. In 1948, Attorney General Tom Clark asked Hoover to start an emergency detention program.[293] Already open about the need to detain domestic persons deemed a threat to national security, the US embarked on the single worst wholesale violation of civil rights of US Americans in our history (not counting the centuries of repression of African and native Americans) when, on February 19, 1942, President Roosevelt authorized the military to forcefully intern more than 110,000 Japanese Americans, of whom 70,000 were full-fledged US citizens, mostly school-age children. Japanese Americans were rounded up and moved into a variety of assembly and relocation centers, and Justice Department and Citizen Isolation Internment Camps scattered in 21 states.[294]

---

292 Zaroulis and Sullivan, 361; Halstead, 714–722. Author's note: Two of my sisters-in-law were among those arrested; one was detained in Robert F. Kennedy Stadium along with several thousand others, while the other was held several days at an overflow federal prison in Occoquan, Virginia.

293 Senate Select Committee to Study Governmental Operations with Respect to Intelligence Activities, *Supplementary Detailed Staff Reports on Intelligence Activities and the Rights of Americans*, Book III, Final Report, 94th Cong., 2nd sess., April 23 (Washington, DC: GPO, 1976), 377, 392; Roy Talbert, Jr., *Negative Intelligence: The Army and the American Left, 1917–1941* (Jackson, MS: University Press of Mississippi, 1991), 253–255; Nathan Miller, *Spying for America: The Hidden History of US Intelligence* (New York: Paragon House, 1989), 220, 229, 237; Gentry, 206–207, 225; Fred J. Cook, *The FBI Nobody Knows* (New York: Pyramid Books, 1965), 231–232; Robert Ellis Smith, Deborah Caulfield, David Crook, and Michael Gersham, *The Big Brother Book of Lists* (Los Angeles: Price/Stern/Sloan, 1984), 58, 233; Wise, 98, 151.

294 Michi Weglyn, *Years of Infamy: The Untold Story of America's Concentration Camps* (New York: William Morrow and Company, 1976), 6, 176–177; Goldstein, 262–268.

The Pentagon Papers and Watergate

RELEASE OF THE PENTAGON PAPERS

October 1, 1969. Daniel Ellsberg, aided by Rand colleague Anthony Russo, begins the monumental task of copying the secret history of the war commissioned by Secretary of Defense/War Robert McNamara. The copying is done on a primitive Xerox machine in the office of Russo's friend Lynda Sinay, owner of a small advertising agency. Working through the night, they copy 3,000 pages of historical analysis and 4,000 pages of original documents contained in 47 volumes known as the *Pentagon Papers*. They cut off the "Top Secret" on each page in order to make additional copies in commercial copy shops.

June 13, 1971. The *Pentagon Papers*, entitled *United States-Vietnam Relations 1945–1967*, were first published in the *New York Times*. This inside, secret history of the US war ordered by the Pentagon revealed the total deception of the US American people from the very beginning in the mid-1940s with lies masking the US Government's criminal intentions to prevent an independent Viet Nam. With the public release of this secret history, suddenly all could see how the US had deliberately violated the Geneva Accords that ended the French-Indochina war in 1954, conducted clandestine destabilizing operations against the temporarily divided Viet Nam early in 1954 even before the Peace Accords were signed, and begun a military buildup in the South to assure the undermining of the mandated 1956 elections for unifying the country. The criminal intent to destroy a people's independence movement was carried out by one of the most barbaric wars in history.[295]

June 28, 1971. Ellsberg was indicted on two counts for releasing the secret Pentagon Papers to the media, in violation of the 1917 Espionage Act.[296]

July 1, 1971. A transcript of a telephone call between Charles Colson and E. Howard Hunt, an ex-CIA operative for 23 years and a Colson protégé, reveals that Hunt replied affirmatively when Colson asked whether "we should go down the line to nail the guy [Ellsberg] cold."[297]

December 29, 1971. Ellsberg and co-worker Anthony Russo were indicted on 12 criminal charges for espionage and conspiracy in the *Pentagon Papers* case.[298]

---

[295] There are three versions of *The Pentagon Papers* with the following citations: (1) Neil Sheehan, Hedrick Smith, E.W. Kenworthy, and Fox Butterfield, *The Pentagon Papers as Published by the New York Times* (New York: Bantam Books, Inc., 1971), 677 pages; (2) *The Pentagon Papers: The Defense Department History of United States Decision-Making on Vietnam: The Senator Gravel Edition* (Boston: Beacon Press, 1971), 2,899 pages; (3) *United States-Vietnam Relations, 1945–1967: Study Prepared by the Department of Defense*, 12 vols. printed for the use of the House Committee on Armed Services (Washington: US Government Printing Office, 1971), sometimes referred to as the Hebert edition.

[296] Gold, 814.

[297] Gold, 814.

[298] Trager, 1033.

Nixon's Dirty Tricks; Enemies List; "The Plumbers"

January 25, 1971. Nixon's speechwriter and Chief of Staff H. R. Haldeman's aide, Tom Huston, establishes the President's enemies list. By July, Colson and White House Counsel, John Dean, expand the list of suspects to include hundreds of people Nixon simply hated.[299]

Ongoing, 1971. Nixon directs Colson to discredit antiwar veterans groups including VVAW by digging up dirt on their members and planting letters to newspapers exposing leaders such as John Kerry as frauds.[300] President Nixon uses Colson in the summer and fall of 1971 to stage-manage events to discredit VVAW's popular antiwar message.[301]

July 24, 1971. President Nixon orders his Chief Domestic Adviser John Ehrlichman to form a top-secret White House Special Investigations Unit which comes to be called *the Plumbers* due to its direction to discover and stop the "leaks." In doing their job, the plumbers follow a resurrected Huston Plan prompted by Ellsberg's leaking of the *Pentagon Papers*. G. Gordon Liddy, an ex-FBI agent who served as Mitchell's action man, and E. Howard Hunt are hired to create the dirty tricks plan. (No stranger to dirty tricks; Hunt had been involved in organizing both the CIA overthrow of democratically elected Guatemalan President Jacobo Arbenz in 1954 and the illegal Bay of Pigs invasion of Cuba in 1961.)[302]

August 1971. VVAW Executive Committee member Joe Urgo travels with other antiwar leaders to North Viet Nam, where they meet with Prime Minister Pham Van Dong and others. Urgo, believed to be the first Viet Nam veteran to visit Hanoi,[303] proposes to the Communist leaders that the VVAW make tapes to be broadcast over Radio Hanoi to urge US troops to stop fighting.[304] The US American delegation also includes David McReynolds of the People's Coalition for Peace and Justice and War Resisters League, and Socialist Party member Judy Learner of Women's Strike for Peace, an old SDSer from the West Coast.

September 4, 1971. Nixon's Plumbers, led by Liddy and Hunt, used three Bay of Pigs Cuban exiles, including Bernard Barker, to burglarize Ellsberg's psychiatrist's office in Santa Monica, California.[305]

September 9, 1971. Colson sends Dean a "Priority List of 20 political enemies."[306]

---

299 Evans, 571.
300 Wells, 489–491.
301 Stacewicz, 317.
302 Zaroulis, 368; Evans, 571–575.
303 Wells, 524; Stacewicz, 288–290; Nicosia, 213.
304 http://www.wintersoldier.com/index.php?topic=Timeline
305 Evans, 575.
306 Gold, 815.

October 1, 1971. James McCord begins work on the Committee for Re-election of the President (CREEP), headed by Mitchell. On December 1, Liddy becomes counsel for CREEP.[307] McCord orders Alfred C. Baldwin, a former FBI agent, to act on behalf of CREEP to infiltrate VVAW.[308]

January 27, 1972. Mitchell unveils the plan for a law-breaking enterprise on behalf of CREEP to be formulated by Liddy. Subsequently proved in April 1972, the plan includes kidnappings, buggings, break-ins, sabotages of infrastructure, electronic surveillance, and assaults.[309]

May 4, 1972. Liddy and Colson order an assault on Ellsberg at an antiwar demonstration, six weeks before the foiled Watergate break-in on June 17.[310]

May 28, 1972. In a successful break-in at the Democratic National Convention offices in the Watergate Hotel, key documents are photographed and phones are wiretapped.[311]

June 17, 1972. At 2:30 a.m., a burglary at the Democratic National Headquarters in the Watergate Complex Washington, DC is interrupted in process by a 24-year-old security guard named Frank Wills. The apprehended burglars, including anti-Castro Cubans, all have CIA connections: Bernard Barker, Frank A. Sturgis, Virgilio R. Gonzalez, Eugenio R. Martinez and CREEP representative and ex-FBI agent McCord.

June 23, 1972. Nixon and Haldeman agreed on the pretext of national security to thwart any FBI investigation of Watergate, and asked the CIA to intervene with new FBI Director Patrick Gray to call off his agents.[312] The CIA cover-up of its connection to Watergate was extensive: (1) it cooperated with Nixon in helping stop the FBI investigation; (2) it concealed from prosecution its assistance to Hunt; and (3) it hid its participation in Nixon's cover up.[313]

INTERSECTION OF US CRIMINAL POLICY AND VIET NAM VETERANS

The Cubans involved in the break-in at Democratic National Headquarters at the Watergate Hotel had been hired by the FBI and Miami police prior to the Republican Convention to infiltrate, disrupt and expose VVAW's organizing activities, on Nixon's orders "to nail the leaders of VVAW."[314] Nixon had hoped to connect VVAW with, and subsequently embarrass, selected Democratic nominee George McGovern, whose antiwar position was perceived as threatening to the Nixon Administration.[315]

---

307 Gold, 816.
308 Carl Bernstein and Bob Woodward, *All the President's Men* (New York: Warner, 1975), 108–109, 11.
309 Evans, 577–578.
310 Hersh, 1983, 520–521.
311 Miller, 1975, 27–28.
312 Glennon, 539.
313 Wise, 257.
314 Nicosia, 266.
315 Stacewicz, 447–448, n24.

The Watergate burglars were arrested with cameras, electronic surveillance equipment, and numerically sequenced $100 bills from Barker's bank. Soon it became clear that E. Howard Hunt and Gordon Liddy were in fact the overseers of the burglary. McCord later testified under oath that the Watergate break-in, as well as plans to burglarize McGovern's offices, was justified by the plausible threat of collusion between the Democratic Party and VVAW members to violently obstruct the re-election of Richard Nixon.[316] The plot to gather information on the Democrats had, in part, been aimed at discovering such a link.[317] Nixon was eager to label VVAW as a "terrorist" group with ties to the Democratic Party, as the subsequent Gainesville Eight prosecution later alleged, in efforts to neutralize the antiwar movement.[318]

The Watergate scandal dominated the US political scene for the next two years. In fact, Watergate derailed Nixon's plans to use the ongoing Paris Peace Talks as a convenient cover to continue bombing Viet Nam. His war momentum was lost due to his conniving, deceitful response to the scandal.[319] Watergate unfolded primarily because of Nixon's twisted paranoia, more than from any rational political calculation.[320]

NIXON, WATERGATE, AND THE GAINESVILLE EIGHT

July 7, 1972. Gainesville's VVAW organizers are first interviewed by the FBI three weeks after the Watergate break-in.

July 10, 1972. On the first day of the Democratic Convention in Miami Beach, a grand jury is convened in Tallahassee, Florida, in front of which 23 members of the VVAW have been subpoenaed to appear.

July 14, 1972. VVAW members from Gainesville are secretly indicted for planning to incite a riot at the August Republican Convention. McCord would later testify that prior to these indictments, he received reports from the Department of Justice's Internal Security Division about VVAW materials, plans, etc., much of it the result of bugging. The government's ardent denials of any link between Watergate espionage and its conduct in the Gainesville Eight case collapses when Palo Fernandez, who had offered weapons to the Gainesville defendants, is shown to be directly connected to Watergate burglar Bernard Barker. The link between Watergate and Gainesville is again confirmed when another associate of Barker's, Vincent Hanard, admits to being offered money by Hunt to infiltrate VVAW.[321]

September 15, 1972. The US Grand Jury indicts the five Watergate burglars along with their bosses, Hunt and Liddy.

---

316 Nicosia, 264.
317 Stacewicz, 344–345.
318 Stacewicz, 344–345.
319 Berman, 265–273.
320 Evans, 571.
321 Nicosia, 267.

October 1972. A superseding Grand Jury indictment of Gainesville VVAW members is filed for conspiracy "to organize numerous 'fire teams' to attack with automatic weapons fire and incendiary devices, police stations, police cars and stores in Miami Beach," using "lead weights, 'fried' marbles, ball bearings, 'cherry' and smoke bombs by means of wrist rocket slingshots and cross bows."

December 8, 1972. A mistrial is declared in the government prosecution of Daniel Ellsberg for leaking the *Pentagon Papers*.

January 27, 1973. US and Vietnamese representatives sign the war-ending peace treaty in Paris.

February 7, 1973. A Senate committee votes to investigate the Watergate break-in.

April 1973. A pre-trial hearing is conducted for Gainesville VVAW defendants.

May 11, 1973. A second trial against Ellsberg is dismissed due to illegal US government complicity in the break-in at Ellsberg's psychiatrist's office.

June 25, 1973. Existence of Nixon's "Enemies List" is publicly revealed by John Dean during Senate hearings. Among the listed enemies: Edward Kennedy, Walter Mondale, John Lindsay, John Kenneth Galbraith, Theodore Sorenson, Jane Fonda, Ramsey Clark, Dick Gregory, and Leonard Woodcock.[322]

August 31, 1973. The Gainesville Eight are all acquitted after a highly publicized jury trial reveals the group's infiltration by FBI undercover agents.[323]

August 8, 1974. Nixon resigns rather than face formal impeachment.

April 30, 1975. All remaining US military forces and civilian personnel are forced to evacuate Viet Nam as the North Vietnamese troops entered Saigon to reunite their country, thus ending the 30-year criminal and immoral US war waged against the Vietnamese, Cambodians, and Laotians.

The Heinous Crime Behind Watergate[324]

The following comments were published by investigate journalist Robert Parry in response to media reports on the Watergate break-in and its coverup on the fortieth anniversary of Nixon's resignation in 2014.

> [T]he mistaken lesson that the US mainstream media derived from the scandal was that "the cover-up is always worse than the crime," a silly saying that reflected the media's ignorance about what the underlying crime was. In this case, the historical record now shows that Nixon set the Watergate scandal in motion in 1971 out of fear that perhaps his greatest

---

322 Evans, 571.

323 http://my.firedoglake.com/davidswanson/2013/08/23/the-gainesville-8-and-a-nixonized-world/

324 Robert Parry, *Consortium News*, August 9, 2014: https://consortiumnews.com/2014/08/09/the-heinous-crime-behind-watergate/

crime would be exposed—how he sabotaged Viet Nam peace talks to gain a political edge in an election. . . .

To fully understand the Watergate scandal, which led to President Richard Nixon's resignation 40 years ago, you have to know the back story starting in 1968 when candidate Nixon took part in a secret maneuver to scuttle the Viet Nam peace talks to salvage a narrow victory over Vice President Hubert Humphrey.[325]

In essence, what Nixon and his campaign team did was to contact South Vietnamese leaders behind President Lyndon Johnson's back and promise them a better deal if they stayed away from Johnson's Paris peace talks, which President Nguyen van Thieu agreed to do. So, with Johnson's peace talks stymied as Nixon suggested that he had a secret plan to end the war, Nixon edged out Humphrey.

After his election, Nixon learned from FBI Director J. Edgar Hoover that President Johnson had amassed a detailed file on what Johnson called Nixon's "treason," but Nixon couldn't locate the file once he took office and ordered an intensive search for the material that explained why the Paris peace talks had failed. But the material stayed missing.

Nixon's worries grew more acute in mid-June 1971 when the New York Times and other major US newspapers began publishing the Pentagon Papers leaked by former Defense Department official Daniel Ellsberg. Though the Pentagon Papers—covering the years 1945 through 1967—exposed mostly Democratic deceptions, Nixon knew something that few others did, that there was a potential sequel that could be even more explosive than the original.

...

In June, the Pentagon Papers further fueled antiwar fury by revealing many of the lies that had led the nation into the bloody Viet Nam quagmire. So, Nixon recognized the political danger if someone revealed how Nixon's pre-election maneuvers in 1968 had prevented President Johnson from bringing the war to an end. Nixon became desperate to get his hands on the missing report (or file) about the failed peace talks.

...

There was even talk about fire-bombing the centrist Washington think tank [the Brookings Institution], but the break-in never apparently happened, although Brookings' historians say there was an attempted break-in during that time frame. The historians also say that Brookings never possessed the missing file or report. . . .

---

325 Christopher Hitchens describes Kissinger's key role in sabotaging the 1968 peace negotiations: Christopher Hitchens, *The Trial of Henry Kissinger* (London, UK: Verso, 2001), 6–13.

Though his questioning may have begun during his ten-and-a-half months flying F-8 jets in Viet Nam (right), John David Borgman was not one of those who vocally protested the war while active duty in the Marine Corps. But thirteen years later, a broken veteran, he made a powerful public confession of his complicity in supporting the wrongful use of state power (below), and burned his Marine Captain's uniform, a moment of anguish captured in the cover photo of this book.

---

i am john david borgman (usmcr 069559 inactive). i am the seventh son in a family of ten. i served for 10½ months in vietnam in 1967 and flew 181 missions as a pilot of an f-8 with the rank of captain. my father's death of a heart attack brought me home early.
when i was an officer in the marines, i believed in what i was doing and gave myself to my responsibilities with all my body, mind, and spirit. i come to the pentagon today as the culmination of thirteen years of deep soul searching which ends in my public act of repentance today. i have come to see that i violated God's law to "love God with all your heart and soul and love your neighbor as yourself." i am forgiven by God's grace through Jesus when he said "Father, forgive them, for they know not what they are doing."

i have come today to break my thirteen years of silence. i have come for public confession and repentance. i am burning my captain's uniform as a visible end to the john david borgman of this uniform. God's call to this government and military is to an act of repentance. from the beginning as a nation, we have, in the name of God, killed native americans, enslaved african people, exploited the peoples of the third world countries to satisfy our greed and our lust for power. as a nation we remain unrepentant for sins in vietnam, our sins in iran, the philippines, and wherever we have served economic power rather than serving fellow human beings. we have the material desires of our hearts, but our souls are lean.
my act of today is to break with this system which pertetuates fear and violence. i do not act out of hatred for individuals in the military, government, or big business. i act out of a deep love for my beautiful wife and our two children and for the future generation of human beings. i am proclaiming an end to my allegiance to this particular government and announcing my place in the kingdom of God. i aspire to be a non-violent citizen of this planet. all people are my sisters and my brothers (including those who could arrest me). i am a child of God with allegiance to him alone. thanks be to God. all glory and honor to him.

28 april 1980   john david borgman

Chapter Seven
Upheaval and Resistance among Active Duty Military

"General, your tank is a powerful vehicle.
It smashes down forests, and crushes a hundred men.
But it has one defect: it needs a driver."

—Bertolt Brecht[1]

Introduction

What if the government called a war and the soldiers refused to fight? There is a tradition of resistance that arises when soldiers discover they are simply serving as cannon fodder for the rich and powerful, rather than, as they'd been told, for noble purposes of freedom and justice.

Approximately 26.8 million men came of draft age between August 10, 1964, the date the Gulf of Tonkin Resolution was signed, and March 28, 1973, when the last US American troops left Viet Nam.[2] This was the pool of men available for Viet Nam.

Nearly 16 million, or 60 percent of these potential troops, did not serve, due to deferments given for critical occupations such as agriculture, for qualified students, and in cases of family hardship. Other exemptions were granted for physical and/or mental factors, for age, or for other disqualifications. But 2.2 million men were drafted, while another 8.7 million men (and women) enlisted, many because they knew they would otherwise be drafted.[3] Of this 10.9 million total, slightly more than 8.6 million served during what is formally defined as the Viet Nam Era (VNE).[4]

Because of the growing unpopularity of the war, and its immorality that became increasingly clear to service members as it wore on, many active-duty military personnel directly resisted, sabotaged or refused particular missions, were indifferent, or performed

---

1 "General, Your Tank Is a Powerful Vehicle," published in *From a German War Primer*, part of the Svendborg Poems (1939); as translated by Lee Baxandall in *Poems, 1913–1956*, p. 289.

2 Lawrence M. Baskir and William A. Strauss, *Chance and Circumstance: The Draft, the War and the Vietnam Generation* (New York: Vintage Books, 1978), 3; Appy, 1993, 28.

3 Appy, 1993, 28. The first Congressionally legislated forced conscription occurred during the Civil War in order to fill the ranks of the Union Army. It was used during World Wars I and II, then reinstituted again in 1948. It was suspended in 1973 with advent of the volunteer army though a registration requirement remains.

4 Baskir and Strauss, 5. For those who served in country, the VNE began February 28, 1961 and ended May 7, 1975; for those other veterans who did not serve in-country, the VNE began August 5, 1964 and ended May 7, 1975.

their duties unenthusiastically. There were numerous incidents of sabotage and rebellion throughout Germany and other US military base locations in Europe and Asia, as well as in the US and Viet Nam.

Levels of prosecutions for resistance activities dramatically increased during the Viet Nam war (450 courts-martial involving serious resistance in 1971 alone).

A minimum of 1.1 million soldiers received less than honorable discharges or participated in desertion incidents.[5] A higher estimate indicates nearly 800,000 received less than honorable discharges.[6] In addition, there were over 560,000 desertions[7] and as many as 1.5 million recorded incidents of AWOL.[8]

Therefore, of the original pool of 8,600,000 men, the data suggests as many as 30 percent were unreliable as fighting soldiers. Other information indicates that more than half of all VNE soldiers became involved in some form of resistance activity.[9] Of those who actually served in Viet Nam, official military commissions reveal that the number of soldiers who participated in disobedience, dissidence, or frequent drug use approached 55 percent, and that this type of oppositional behavior was more common among volunteers than among draftees.[10] Additionally, as many as 200,000 soldiers were granted Conscientious Objector (CO) status before or during their military service.[11]

The record of GI resistance during the Viet Nam era is worth remembering as an important part of our nation's history. It provides a clue to the kind of opposition that is possible for US soldiers who may find themselves dispatched to the Middle East or other "Third World" countries, purportedly to fight for things like freedom and democracy. In fact, in a capitalist society, corporations and government act in tandem to send US soldiers off to kill and be killed, so that both corporations and politicians can profit from war making. It is not surprising that some of the soldiers placed in the middle of armed conflict are the first to question the stated mission of the conflict, and often the first to resist.

The upshot is that personal conscience is the ultimate legal and moral authority in a truly democratic society, and soldiers are no exception to this principle. As Vietnamese Buddhist monk Thich Nhat Hanh has observed, "Veterans are the light at the tip of the candle, illuminating the way for the whole nation." They are able to stop wars even if the politicians authorize and fund them.

---

5 Baskir and Strauss, 115, 285n2; Horne, 13.
6 Nicosia, 358; Moser, 81.
7 Baskir and Strauss, 122; Appy, 1993, 95.
8 Baskir and Strauss, 122.
9 Lewes, 4.
10 Cortright, 270.
11 Estimates of Center on Conscience & War, 1830 Connecticut Ave., NW, Washington, DC 20009: http://www.centeronconscience.org/; Peter Karsten, ed., *Encyclopedia of War and American Society* (Thousand Oaks, CA: Sage Publications, 2005), 184; Gabriel Packard/Inter Press Service/IPS, "Iraq: Hundreds of US Soldiers Emerge as Conscientious Objectors," New York, April 15, 2003; Ann Fagan Ginger, ed., *Meiklejohn Civil Liberties Institute: Challenging U. S. Human Rights Violations Since 9/11* (Amherst, NY: Prometheus Books, 2005), 262; Bob Aldridge, ed., *Conscription, Conscience, & War: Conscription of Conscience—You have a Choice* (Santa Clara, CA: Pacific Life Research Center/PLRC #050227, Updated 27 February 2005), 8: http://www.plrc.org/docs/050227.pdf.

How many soldiers actually served in Viet Nam?

The Veterans Administration (VA) has traditionally reported 32 percent of VNE veterans served in the Viet Nam theater (2,752,000), but a July 1980 survey by Louis Harris and Associates on behalf of the VA, submitted to Congress, concluded that 43 percent served in Viet Nam proper (3,700,000) and 48 percent served in the Viet Nam "theater" (4,128,000).[12] The discrepancy is partially explained by the fact that at any one time there were thousands of US military in the Viet Nam theater on a temporary duty status of 179 days or less (TDY), or in covert operations not officially "in country," and therefore not counted as part of the in-country "permanent" troops. This enabled the Pentagon to appear in compliance with the congressionally mandated cap of 543,400 troops in Southeast Asia on permanent change-of-station (PCS) status.

For example, I was part of a 559-man US Air Force Safeside squadron, one of three such USAF combat security police squadrons that served in-country from 1967 to 1969. All were TDY, therefore not officially in country. Originally we were to serve two consecutive TDY assignments, separated by a 30-day leave in the US, meaning we would effectively serve a full year in Viet Nam, but never be statistically counted as being in-country.

A Broken Army

As the war dragged on, there was a dramatic increase in applications and in ultimate granting of Conscientious Objector (CO) requests; 145,000 successful claims were granted in the last three years of the war, alone.[13] In 1971 there was a record total of over 61,000 CO registrations. In 1972 there were more COs than draftees.

There was also a dramatic increase in draft resisters. The National Council for Universal and Unconditional Amnesty (NCUUA) estimated that more than a million men illegally failed to register for the draft at all.[14]

There was a reduction in enlistments and in re-enlistments, and a dramatic increase in desertions. There was a dramatic increase in administrative discharges for "misconduct," "unfitness," or "unsuitability": 700,000 received less than honorable discharge.

For the entire Viet Nam era, the US Government reported 206,000 persons as delinquent. However, it appears, from examination of other statistics, that another 300,000 to 400,000 draft violators were never accused or convicted. Thus, the total number of draft resisters may have been as high as 500,000 to 600,000.

- In 1970, the Army reported 65,643 deserters.
- Between 1967 and 1971, the number of deserters doubled from 47,000 to 89,000.
- The DOD reported 503,926 "incidents of desertion" from July 1, 1966, to Dec. 31, 1973.

---

12 "Myths and Realities: A Study of Attitudes toward Vietnam Era Veterans," submitted by the Veterans Administration to the Committee On Veterans' Affairs, US House of Representatives, July 1980.
13 Cortright, 5.
14 Nicosia, 358.

- The use of early-outs and punitive discharges to Viet Nam veterans in 1971 substantially reduced the AWOL (and desertion) rates.
- Army desertion and AWOL rates in 1971 were the highest in modern history: 17 AWOLs + 7 deserters + 2 disciplinary discharges + 18 non-judicial punishments + 12 complaints to Congress for every 100 soldiers. And there were 24 soldiers AWOL or deserters for every 100 soldiers (24 percent). Thus, 56 of every 100 soldiers in 1971 had serious problems with the military.
- In 1971, registered complaints from military service members to Congress numbered over 250,000—a quantity unheard of in the history of the US military, especially during a war.

The more than 1,500,000 incidents of soldiers being away without leave (AWOL) represent one million man-years of service lost.[15] The rate of soldiers intentionally going missing in 1971—170 AWOL and 70 desertions per thousand, equaling one in four—was the highest in modern history.[16]

The American Deserters Committee and more than 20 other organizations helped the thousands of military deserters and exiles who sought refuge in Canada.[17] To illustrate how the trend grew as the war dragged on: the desertion rate in 1966 was 14.9 per 1000 soldiers; by 1971, it was 73.4 per 1000, (an increase of more than 400 percent).[18] By 1969, the desertion rate had already increased fourfold, significantly escalating after TET 1968. An underground movement of deserters spread to Sweden, Germany, Canada, Japan, and the Soviet Union, and the establishment of an antiwar infrastructure, or RITA (resistance inside the army), organized demonstrations, including one that drew 1,000 active-duty servicemen in London, England.[19]

The number of US soldiers who achieved exile in other countries is unclear. The number of soldiers who ended up in nearby Canada, the primary desertion destination, ranges from 50,000 to 100,000 as estimated by a variety of sources.[20] Canadian immigration data reflects that a minimum of 30,000 went to Canada. Estimated numbers of deserters who fled to other countries: 1,000 went to Sweden, 1,000 to Mexico, and 8,000 distributed themselves among several other countries. It is estimated that at least 10,000 lived underground in the USA. Many observers agreed that 100,000 was a credible figure for the number of deserters who went into exile, many of whom rightfully considered that they were not draft dodgers but modern runaway slaves.[21] According to *The Nation* magazine, desertions in the early 1970s had reached 250,000 annually.[22]

---

15 Baskir and Strauss, 115; Moser, 80.
16 Moser, 80; Cortright, 11.
17 Moser, 80.
18 Cortright, 10.
19 "1,000 GIs in Britain Stage Vietnam Protest," *San Francisco Chronicle*, June 1, 1971.
20 Zinn, 1980, 484; R. N. Williams, 1971, 84–85, quoting sources such as the *New York Times* (60,000), the Canadian Press (80,000), members of the Canadian Parliament (100,000), and Canadian psychologists (100,000).
21 Baskir and Strauss, 169, 180, 185.
22 Armstrong, 112.

Draft dodgers numbered as many as 570,000, and nearly 210,000 were formally reported to the Justice Department.[23] Only 8,700 of those soldiers were indicted, and fewer than 5,000 actually served prison time;[24] the majority of charges were dropped and many defendants were pardoned under the 1974–75 clemency program.[25]

In September 1974, President Gerald Ford announced his clemency program for draft evaders and military deserters, convicted or not, to be applied to all those men who had evaded the draft or deserted the military between August 4, 1968, and March 28, 1973. A nine-man clemency board was created with former US Senator from New York Charles Goodell named as its head. Ramsey Clark, former attorney general under President Lyndon B. Johnson, who later renounced the war, declared that the ACLU's estimate of 750,000 personnel in need of universal and unconditional amnesty under Ford's plan was way too low. Instead, Clark provided evidence that close to 2,000,000 US American men were in legal jeopardy because of their resistance to the war.[26]

> **CONSCIENTIOUS OBJECTION** | The choice by military personnel to disobey orders in deference to conscience and/or international law is a time-honored tradition. The first mutinies were reported during the Revolutionary War in the Continental Army; soldiers refused re-enlistment in the Mexican War; and there were draft riots during the Civil War. There were conscientious objectors during World Wars I and II as well as many deserters. In 1914, an amazing outbreak of peace, though brief, occurred when as many as 100,000 or 10 percent of the millions stationed along the 500-mile Western Front in World War I, mutually, and spontaneously, stopped fighting for 24–36 hours, December 24–26. This outbreak of fraternization became known as the Christmas Truce.[27] Korea did not escape GI dissent, and in that war too, some men left the country rather than agreeing to become soldiers. But the Viet Nam war was unique in the level of opposition it provoked among soldiers, prospective soldiers, and war veterans; opposition on a scale and with a fervor that had never been seen before.[28]

Indeed, the morale, discipline, and combat readiness of US military forces were lower than at any time in the twentieth century, and possibly in the history of the United States. Colonel Robert D. Heinl, Jr., wrote in 1971:

---

23 Baskir and Strauss, 69.
24 Karsten, 231.
25 Baskir and Strauss, 5.
26 Emerson, 132–134.
27 S. Brian Willson, "The Importance of the December 1914 Christmas Truce," published on S. Brian Willson's blog, December 2, 2014: http://www.brianwillson.com/the-importance-of-the-december-1914-christmas-truce/.
28 Richard Severo and Lewis Milford, *The Wages of War: When America's Soldiers Came Home—From Valley Forge to Vietnam* (New York: Simon and Schuster, 1989; Zinn, 1980, 483).

> "By every conceivable indicator, our army that now remains in Viet Nam is in a state approaching collapse, with individual units avoiding or having refused combat, murdering their officers and noncommissioned officers, drug-ridden, and dispirited where not near-mutinous.... Nowhere... in the history of the Armed Forces have comparable past troubles presented themselves in such general magnitude, acuteness, or concentrated focus as today."[29]

Widespread Resistance of GIs in Viet Nam

Hundreds of thousands of VNE soldiers, perhaps more than half, became involved in some form of resistance activity.[30] By fall 1969, every major US military base in the world had a group of active-duty soldier activists who courageously engaged in publishing antiwar journals, organizing rallies, establishing peace centers, and otherwise countering the war effort, despite severe attempts by the authorities to repress such activity.[31] Resistance was common among US troops stationed in Europe (especially England and Germany), Japan, and the Philippines. Among these outposts could be found dozens of GI organizations and at least ten underground newspapers.

A conservative estimate claimed up to a quarter of military personnel actively worked against the war over a period of months or years, articulating the sentiment of *half* of all soldiers and veterans during the period.[32]

Drug Use

Official military commissions revealed that the number of soldiers who participated in dissidence or frequent drug use approached 55 percent, with more disaffection evident among volunteers than draftees.[33]

Use of heroin and marijuana was rampant in Viet Nam. Overall, heroin use in Viet Nam is estimated at ten percent; in some units and areas in Viet Nam, the percentage was much higher. A 1973 study showed that thirty-five percent of all Army enlisted men who served in Viet Nam had used heroin; twenty percent had become addicted. Some estimates of the drug's regular use among soldiers were much higher.[34]

Probably fifty percent of all soldiers engaged in regular pot smoking. Incidence of drug use in the US military worldwide in 1970 was estimated at thirty percent, while incidence of marijuana use among troops in Viet Nam and elsewhere was estimated to be thirty to fifty percent.

Predictably, drug use escalated as the war wore on. For example, the number of discharges of Naval personnel for drug offenses grew from 170 in 1966 to 5,000 in 1970.

---

29 Robert D. Heinl, Jr., "The Collapse of the Armed Forces," 1971, reprinted in Gettleman et al., 1995, 327.
30 Lewes, 4.
31 Lewes, 61.
32 Moser, 132.
33 Cortright, 270.
34 Kolko, 1985, 363.

Fraggings

Between 1969 and 1971, the Army officially reported 730 incidents of fragging of officers and NCOs by enlisted personnel.[35] Fragging is any action by a military member intended to murder a superior in their command structure. The term comes from fragmentation grenade, the weapon of choice in many such incidents. Fragging occurred in Viet Nam in much larger proportions than took place in WWI, WWII, or Korea.

By 1972, the Army had confirmed 788 fragging incidents, resulting in 86 deaths and 702 wounded from explosive devices alone. The number killed or wounded by firearms is unknown.[36] From January 1970 to January 1972, 363 fragging cases were tried in court-martial proceedings.[37] Other reports raise the number of documented killings or attempted killings of officers and NCOs in Viet Nam to 1,013,[38] or 1,016,[39] with some estimates being twice that. A Pentagon study by Colonel David Hackworth found a staggering fifteen to twenty percent of all US casualties in Viet Nam were caused by friendly fire (not specifically fragging), due to poor training.[40] Another source cites an estimate that twenty percent of the approximately 5,000 US American officers and high-ranking NCOs who died in Viet Nam were assassinated by their own men.[41] Only a tenth of the attempted fragging cases ended up in court.

Acts of mutiny, insubordination, and disobedience to orders grew from 252 in 1968 to about twice that in 1971.[42] There were at least thirty riots by soldiers languishing in prisons in Viet Nam, the US, or Germany, and there were countless cases of "combat refusals" starting as early as February 1968.[43]

Notes on Fragging:

- Fraggings were rooted in the growing disgust for the war, low morale, reaction to flagrant racism, and earned disrespect for authority.
- The Department of Defense/War (DOD) reported 69 fragging incidents in 1969, 209 in 1970.

---

35 Appy, 1993, 245–246.
36 Dunnigan and Nofi, 221–222; Moser, 48; Cortright, 43–44.
37 Moser, 48.
38 Jonathan Shay, *Achilles in Vietnam: Combat Trauma and the Undoing of Character* (New York: Touchstone, 1994, 127, citing Richard A. Gabriel, *No More Heroes: Madness and Psychiatry in War* (New York: Hill and Wang, 1987), 55–56.
39 Kolko, 1985, 364.
40 David H. Hackworth, *About Face: The Odyssey of an American Warrior* (New York: Simon and Schuster, 1989), 594.
41 Richard Holmes, *Acts of War: The Behavior of Men in Battle* (Glencoe, IL: Free Press, 1985), 329; Dunnigan and Nofi, 243].
42 Kolko, 1985, 364.
43 Lewes, 154–164.

- According to the DOD Report, *Assaults with Explosive Devices* (omitting shootings with firearms): By end of 1970, there had been 300 reported fragging incidents leading to 73 deaths and over 500 injured. By July 1972, there had been over 550 reported fragging incidents leading to 86 deaths and over 700 injured.
- "Bounties" began appearing in GI underground newspapers in Viet Nam of from $50 to $10,000 for murder of specified military "leaders."
- Army lawyers disclosed that they believed fraggings were daily occurrences in 1970 and 1971.
- The number of assaults carried out against commanders (eighty percent reportedly officers and senior NCOs) by their own troops reached into the thousands during the course of the war.
- Thousands of threats and intimidations were reported throughout the war. However, there do not seem to be statistics on the number of intentional shootings during the war.

Racial Tension

Army prison population tripled during the course of the Viet Nam war. By the end of 1969, the Army had 7,000 prisoners, the majority non-White. Racism and racial tension was a chronic problem in all branches of the service during the Viet Nam war, and as many as twenty percent of all fraggings may have been racially motivated.

Many Black study groups were convened in Viet Nam, the US, and Europe to deal with the racial tension and antiwar feelings. These groups shared ideas and engaged in activities to oppose both racism and the war.

Sabotage

The Navy experienced *many* cases of ship sabotage (see pp. 276–277 for examples). Massive covert obstructions short of overt acts of sabotage occurred in the Navy, Army, and Air Force.

Private Ceasefires: Echoes of the 1914 Christmas Truce

Soldiers' combat refusals, the euphemism for mutinies, became so intense by 1970 and later, that there were reports of units initiating their own private ceasefires with the NVA and the Viet Cong. On October 10, 1971, the soldiers of Bravo Company of the First Cavalry Division openly declared their own ceasefire with the North Vietnamese. The soldiers had figured out that it wasn't the Vietnamese who were their enemies, but the lifers (those who were making the military a career).[44] The June 1971 issue of the GI paper, *People's Press*, ran an article reporting that NLF and NVA were ordered not to conduct hostilities against US troops who displayed red bandanas or flashed peace signs,

---

44 Boyle, 235–236.

unless fired upon first.[45] Former USAF security policeman Joe Urgo, a survivor of the TET 1968 Viet Cong overrun at Tan Son Nhut Air Base, in 1971, became the first US American veteran to visit Hanoi. While there, he was shown a copy of the orders given to North Vietnamese troops not to shoot US soldiers who were wearing antiwar symbols or carrying their rifles pointed down to the ground.[46] The Viet Cong delegation to the Paris Peace Talks also issued a statement that their units in Viet Nam had been ordered not to engage US units that had obviously chosen not to attack or fire upon them.[47]

Underground Newspapers

The first issue of *The Bond*, the first and possibly the most important of underground GI newspapers, was published by the American Servicemen's Union (ASU) in Berkeley, California on June 23, 1967. The next year, *The Bond* publishers relocated to New York. Distributed internationally on military bases and ships, and in Viet Nam, *The Bond* claimed a circulation of 100,000 by 1971,[48] but it was just one of hundreds of underground newspapers that proliferated beginning in the Summer of Love (1967) through the end of the war. By the summer of 1969 thirty-five papers were in publication; by 1970 there were fifty. In a count done in 1972, the Pentagon reported 245 GI newspapers, but Viet Nam veteran Dave Cortright, in his book, *Soldiers in Revolt*, estimates there were 300 GI newspapers created by the end of the war. Published in Viet Nam, the United States, and Europe,[49] the underground newspaper movement succeeded in getting hundreds of antiwar articles into the hands of thousands of soldiers.[50]

Mutinies (Combat Refusals)

In 1968 a rapid increase in combat refusals began. By 1972, at least 10 were considered major mutinies, with the likelihood of hundreds of minor ones that mostly went unreported.[51] In 1968 the first mutinies occurred at unit- and platoon-level through rejections of an order to fight. The army recorded 68 such mutinies that year.[52] Rumors of troops quitting in combat areas were commonplace.[53] Refusals of orders, mutinies, and fraggings had become so common by 1970–71 that ground operations became virtually impossible to conduct as "search and evade" or "search and avoid" replaced "search and destroy" missions, to the chagrin of superior officers.[54] Serving in the 1st Infantry Division

---

45 Moser, 132.
46 Wells, 525–526.
47 Gettleman et al., 1995, 329.
48 Armstrong, 112.
49 Cortright, 55; Moser, 96.
50 Lewes, 154.
51 Zaroulis and Sullivan, 365–66; Moser, 45; Cincinnatus, 154.
52 Joel Grier, "Vietnam: The Soldier's Revolt," *International Socialist Review*, 9, Aug–Sep 2000; Moser, 45; Matthew Rinaldi, "The Olive Drab Rebels: Military Organizing during the Vietnam War," *Radical America* (May–June 1974, 17–51, especially 29; Gettleman et al., 1995, 329.
53 Boyle, 85.
54 Grier.

from August 1967 to August 1968, Guillermo Alvidrez remembers, "We had a barracks full of guys waiting for courts-martial for refusing to fight. They felt it wasn't worth it."[55] August 24, 1969, the first recorded incident in Viet Nam of *mass* mutiny occurred in A Company of 3rd Battalion/196th Infantry in Songchang Valley south of Da Nang.[56]

Historian Christian G. Appy revealed that by 1969 combat avoidance increasingly developed into direct refusal. Though official statistics on soldier disobedience are very incomplete and predictably on the low side, the official numbers of soldiers convicted of "insubordination, mutiny, or other acts involving the willful refusal to perform a lawful order" rose from 94 in 1968 to 152 in 1970. The 1st Air Cavalry Division downplayed their *unit* refusals, but it admitted 35 *individual* refusals in 1970 alone, and there is evidence of at least 245 mutinies that year among all US troops.[57] On October 26, 1970, a soldier stationed at Cu Chi wrote to a friend that separate companies had been created for men refusing to go into the field to fight. "It's no big thing here anymore to refuse to go," he explained. The French newspaper *Le Monde* reported that over a four-month stretch, 109 soldiers of the First Air Cavalry Division were charged with refusal to fight.[58]

The March 1971 invasion of Laos by South Vietnamese forces, with substantial fire support by the US, witnessed Troop B of the 1st squadron, 1st Cavalry, refusing to move into combat positions. During the same invasion, an entire platoon of the 1st Brigade, 5th Mechanized Division, also refused to participate in combat.[59]

The Presidio Twenty-Seven

On October 14, 1968, twenty-seven inmates of the stockade at the Army's Presidio, at the tip of the San Francisco peninsula, conducted a nonviolent sit-down strike three days after a guard killed mentally ill inmate Private Richard Bunch with a shotgun at close range. Bunch, denied the psychiatric aid that the Army had promised his mother in writing, had already left two suicide notes under his mattress, and had asked a guard to aim at his head. He subsequently ran from a work detail and was killed at 10 paces.[60]

Singing "We shall overcome" while flashing peace signs, the striking inmates were charged with mutiny. Terrence Hallinan, son of prominent San Francisco attorney Vincent Hallinan and a lawyer himself, represented some of the GIs in this case.[61]

Conditions at the stockade were deplorable. The Presido imprisoned 140 prisoners in a brig designed for 88. Rations for 115 were stretched to feed the 140 prisoners, nine guards, and three cooks. The guards and cooks got what they needed and then the prisoners got the less than seventy-five percent of rations leftover, in complete violation of Army

---

55 Charley Trujillo, *Soldados: Chicanos in Viet Nam* (San Jose, CA: Chusma House, 1990), 64).
56 Cortright, 35; Boyle, 85.
57 Appy, 1993, 245.
58 Zinn, 1980, 485.
59 Cortright, 37–38.
60 Halstead, 505; Fred Gardner, *The Unlawful Concert: An Account of the Presidio Mutiny Case* (New York: The Viking Press, 1970).
61 Halsted, 579.

regulations. Men in need of medical and psychiatric care were denied it, in violation of Army regulations. Sanitary facilities were such that both prisoners and guards testified about human excrement sloshing on the shower room floor for days on end, another violation of Army regulations. Guard brutality was rampant, and 21 prisoners reportedly made 33 suicide attempts in six months.

Bunch's death and the giant GI-led peace march in San Francisco the next day aroused the inmates to mass protest.[62] One of the march participants was a GI who went AWOL for eight hours in order to take part, and then landed in the stockade. Another stockade prisoner, an ordinary AWOL case, had been driven by nervous guards through streets thronged with marchers after coincidentally turning himself in on October 12.

Within a week, the Presidio 27 were court-martialed for mutiny. They subsequently received sentences of 14, 15, and 16 years.[63] On appeal in June 1970, the sentences for mutiny were voided by the Court of Military Review[64] and reduced to short sentences for willful disobedience of a superior officer.[65]

On December 24, 1968, Presidio 27 GI Keith Mather and fellow prisoner Walter Pawlowski escaped from the Presidio stockade in San Francisco and traveled to Vancouver, British Columbia, Canada.[66]

The Presidio 27 case provoked demonstrations and protests across the country after the first trial and sentencing in February 1969, at which Private Nesrey D. Sood, a 26-year-old father of three from Oakland, California, was found guilty and given 15 years of hard labor, forfeiture of all pay and allowances, and an eventual dishonorable discharge. (His sentence was later reduced to two years.) Eight hundred clergy, law students and seminarians protested in Boston. Mrs. Helen Osczepinski, whose poor, white, small-town background was typical of the victims, led a demonstration before the Florida, New York post office in support of her son and his buddies. Similar actions were staged in small California communities as well as in New York, Chicago, and dozens of other cities. Senators Alan Cranston (D-CA) and Charles Goodell (R-NY) and Congressmen Don Claussen, Philip Burton, Jerome Waldie, Jeffrey Cohelan and Don Edwards of California, as well as Mayor Joseph Alieto of San Francisco, joined in the protests.[67]

---

62 Gardner; http://www.sirnosir.com/archives_and_resources/library/articles/vssp_05.html, Sir, No SiR! Library-Reading Room.

63 Daniel Hallock, *Hell, Healing and Resistance* (Farmington, PA: Plough Publishing House, 1998), 259.

64 Walt Crowley, *Rites of Passage: A Memoir of the Sixties in Seattle* (Univ. of Washington Press, 1997), 287.

65 Erwin N. Thompson, *Defender of the Gate: The Presidio of San Francisco: A History from 1946 to 1995* (Washington, DC: National Park Service), Chapter XXI: Sixth US Army, 1946–1980.

66 Keith Mather, http://www.sfgate.com/news/article/Summer-of-Love-40-Years-Later-Keith-Mather-2559482.php: "Summer of Love: 40 Years Later," *SFGate*, May 20, 2007.

67 http://www.sirnosir.com/archives_and_resources/library/articles/vssp_05.html; *Sir! No Sir! Library-Reading Room*.

Innate Resistance to Killing

Retired Lt. Colonel Dave Grossman, former infantry commander, US Army Ranger, and West Point psychology professor, is the founder of a new field, *killology*, formed to develop insights into our understanding of killing in war, the physiological and psychological costs of war, and the root causes of violence.[68] In his book, *On Killing*,[69] Grossman analyzes the physiological and psychological processes involved with killing another human being. He discloses evidence that the vast majority of people have a deep phobia-level revulsion to violence, which is why soldiers need to be specifically trained to kill. He details the physical effects that violent stresses produce on human beings, including tunnel vision, alterations of sonic perception, and post-traumatic stress disorder. Even for those who are well trained and compliant with orders to target others for killing, the subsequent psychic damage to the killer is very debilitating, often leading to suicide.

This helps explain why resistance to being ordered to kill for the state is so strong. About a quarter of all those eligible to serve during the Viet Nam war, in one way or another, either resisted totally or were so unreliable as to be kicked out of the military.[70] Of those who fought in Viet Nam, over half were unreliable, even among enlistees.[71] Grossman's thesis is that people have a strong, innate resistance to killing others, requiring the state and its military to develop specially developed training techniques and to exert fierce, authoritative enforcement mechanisms to ensure follow-through. But even with those things in place, once the belief in the *reason* for the killing evaporates, people will find ways to avoid obeying orders.

Grossman assembles overwhelming evidence that, as a species, we cannot continue to kill for the state or an ideology without destroying what makes us human—the moral conscience resting innately within our ancient soul that knows everything is interconnected in a sacred weave. In the words of Martin Luther King, Jr., "We are caught in an inescapable network of mutuality, tied in a single garment of destiny." Being part of an undivided whole means the bayonet thrust into another ultimately comes back into our own gut.

Cultural historian Andrew Bard Schmookler has described how the emergence of vertical power (what some call "civilization") some 5,500 to 6,000 years ago created a corresponding rise in warfare. The trauma of imperial colonialism separated people from their locally self-reliant tribes and fractured traditional societies. Schmookler asked whether as a species we might viscerally discover our interconnected consciousness and thereby come to realize the need to contain the rule of vertical power; he described the remarkably peaceful early Neolithic societies as models of horizontal organization. But as Schmookler describes, one aggressive society can quickly ruin the peace of all the remainder, no matter how peaceful the others are. He called this dilemma the parable of

---

68 Killology Research Group, Mascoutah, Illinois: http://www.killology.com/.
69 Dave Grossman, *On Killing: The Psychological Cost of Learning to Kill in War and Society* (New York: Back Bay Books, 1996).
70 Baskir and Strauss, 115; Moser, 80.
71 Lewes, 4.

the tribes.[72] And this is, I believe, the challenge to the human condition in the twenty-first century. Martin Luther King, Jr., prophetically proclaimed that an "Injustice anywhere is a threat to justice everywhere. We are caught in an inescapable network of mutuality," he said, "tied in a single garment of destiny."[73] In a later sermon, King declared: "We must all learn to live together as brothers. Or we will all perish together as fools. . . . It is no longer a choice . . . between violence and nonviolence. It is either nonviolence or nonexistence."[74]

Resistance Among Pilots

In May 1969, I met a pilot at Binh Thuy Airbase who refused to fly any further missions. As a result, he was being sent back to the US. We eagerly shared perspectives during the few days he was around. I thought of him when I realized how pilots' resistance during one of the last phases of the US war in Viet Nam helped bring the war to a close.

Throughout 1972, demonstrations were taking place on most US air bases in Japan, Germany, and the US. One military man on Guam wrote to Congress: "Ground crews no longer care whether or not their planes are safe and operational. Flight crews do not wish to fly wasted missions and consequently abort when given the opportunity." Another airman wrote, "I for one, sir, do not wish to die as a mercenary for a foreign dictator" [i.e., Thieu].[75]

Resistance and demoralization were rampant throughout the Air Force near the end of that year. Hundreds and perhaps thousands of airmen in Thailand, Guam, and elsewhere were escalating their resistance to the barbaric bombing orders, and acts of sabotage and insubordination were becoming more and more frequent.

Resistance to Cambodian air raids undermined US Air Force military operations, leading to a crisis among pilots, and especially crews of B-52s. Making matters worse, as most B-52s were flying their missions from Guam, twenty-five hundred miles to the east, North Viet Nam's excellent air defenses were beginning to take their toll on morale. In November, some pilots began diverting their missions.

Resistance in the Air Force also became a major restraint in the bombing of North Viet Nam which contributed to a severe limitation on air operations during the final stages of US intervention. During the final act of the war, tactical aircraft failed to show up to target antiaircraft defenses for Nixon's *Linebacker II*, the planned around-the-clock 24-hour Christmas bombings, and fifteen B-52s were shot down. At least two pilots refused to participate in the bombings, as well: Phantom fighter pilot Captain Dwight Evans refused to fly over North Viet Nam from his base in Thailand, and, even though B-52

---

72 Andrew Bard Schmookler, *The Parable of the Tribes: The Problem of Power in Social Evolution* (Albany, NY: State University of New York Press, 1995), 40, 77, 331, 18–19.

73 From King's "Letter from Birmingham City Jail," April 16, 1963.

74 From King's last Sunday sermon, March 31, 1968, at the National (Episcopal) Cathedral, Washington, DC, "Remaining Awake Through a Great Revolution."

75 Neale, 2003, 179–180.

pilot Captain Michael Heck had flown over two hundred combat missions, on December 26, he refused to fly over North Viet Nam, saying, "A man has to answer to himself first."[76]

The crisis represented by a near mutiny among B-52 crews was averted only by the signing of the Paris Peace Accords in late January 1973.

Resistance Among Sailors

In 1971, the breakdown of the Army in Viet Nam forced the Pentagon to accelerate naval and air bombing to pick up the slack. Just as in the Air Force, active resistance to the war flared up in the Navy as the war became more and more unpopular.

Over the course of the war, major disruptions were reported on at least fifteen navy ships. During the air war of the 1970s, sabotage became an increasingly severe problem, and the Navy reported 488 sabotage incidents in 1971 alone. In their investigation of these "incidents causing damage," the Navy attributed 191 to sabotage, 135 to arson, and 162 to wanton destruction.

As bombing escalated in 1972, unrest grew on all the aircraft carriers involved.[77] There was an antiwar movement on almost every US naval base of any size all over the world.[78] In the fall of 1972, sabotage and resistance by active duty African Americans combined to physically impede the Navy's ability to carry out its mission in the air war. December 1972 saw a mass discharge of enlisted Navy men.

GI Movement and Culture Change

In 1965, Reserve Officer Training Corps (ROTC) programs were located on 268 campuses across the United States, and boasted 231,000 cadet participants. By 1972, participation in ROTC had declined dramatically, with less than 73,000 cadets.[79] Some of the decline can be attributed to ROTCs being targeted by antiwar student activists as a symbol of the military. During the 1968–69 academic year, Army ROTC units sustained 23 serious attacks; during the 1969–70 year, ROTC units sustained 323 assaults. But dissent was also felt within the ranks: By 1970, nearly forty percent of ROTC participants were opposed to US troops being in Viet Nam, and sixty percent made it known they did not intend to volunteer to serve there.[80]

At least fourteen active-duty dissent organizations existed during the Viet Nam era, including the Concerned Officers Movement (COM).[81] The first formal organization was the American Servicemen's Union (ASU).

---

76 Kolko, 1985, 365; Jonathan Neale, *A People's History of the Vietnam War* (New York: The New Press, 2003), 180; Cortright, 135.
77 Neale, 2003, 178–179.
78 Neale, 2003, 158.
79 Cortright, 6.
80 Kolko, 1985, 360.
81 Gettleman et al., 1995, 330.

In Viet Nam, regular flashing of the "V," signifying peace, not victory, was common among antiwar troops. Black armbands and peace symbols were seen regularly on soldiers' clothing and helmets.

In addition, groups sprang up in support of GI resisters and would-be resisters, including a documented twenty-six off-base antiwar coffeehouses.[82] At least twenty-six coffeehouses were opened during the course of the war around the US, Europe, and Asia. The first, the UFO, opened in 1967 near Fort Jackson, South Carolina, and after it became established, an average of 600 GIs visited every week.

Pacific Counseling Service, which provided counseling services for veterans at eight different locations in the US and Asia, was funded by Unitarian and other church groups.

Three well-established lawyers groups assisted with protecting rights and dissent activities of GIs during the Viet Nam war: the GI Civil Liberties Defense Committee, the New York Draft and Military Law Panel; and a semi-underground network of lawyers contacted through the GI Alliance in Washington.[83] The Lawyers Military Defense Committee maintained a small office in Saigon, Viet Nam.

As many as twenty-two antiwar veterans groups emerged out of the Viet Nam war era, including Vietnam Veterans Against the War, National Association of Black Veterans, National Veterans Inquiry into US War Crimes, GIs and Veterans for Peace, Ad Hoc Committee of Veterans for Peace in Vietnam (which became an early version of today's Veterans For Peace), GI Press Service (GIPS), and Veterans and Reservists to End the War in Vietnam.[84] At least six veterans' antiwar organizations actively strived to influence GIs during the Viet Nam war. The largest of these, Vietnam Veterans Against the War (VVAW), began in 1967 in New York City and continues to this day.

"GIs and Vets March for Peace" was the headline when 500 active-duty service members and some 15,000 civilians came together for an antiwar demonstration in San Francisco on October 12, 1968. The activity originated with groups of GIs from Hamilton Air Force Base and Fort Ord who had also attended the April 27, 1968, demonstrations.[85]

---

82 Gettleman et al., 1995, 331.

83 Gettleman et al., 1995, 330.

84 B. Franklin, 2000, 105–76; Moser, 102–129; Jerry Lembcke, *The Spitting Image: Myth, Memory, and the Legacy of Vietnam* (New York: New York University Press, 1998), 27–28, 190n3.

85 Halstead, 504.

Active-Duty Resistance to the War

GROUND COMBAT TROOPS	
June 1965	Combat refusal—Richard Steinke, West Point graduate, while in Viet Nam, refused to board an aircraft destined for a remote Vietnamese village. He said, "This war is not worth a single American life." He was subsequently court-martialed and dismissed from the Army.
Sept. 30, 1965	Letter—The Associated Press (AP) quoted a letter from a soldier in Viet Nam to his mother in Kansas: "Mom, I had to kill a woman and a baby. I swear to God this place is worse than hell. Why must I kill women and kids?"
Feb. 20, 1968	Combat refusal—9th Infantry Division at Me Tho
June 12, 1968	Combat refusal—Seventy soldiers at Lai Khe
Aug. 1968	Riot—Two hundred Marine prisoners at Danang Brig
Aug. 16–18, 1968	Riot—Long Binh Jail
Aug. 16, 1968	Prison riot occurred over racist attitudes at DaNang, Viet Nam prison brig.
Aug. 29, 1968	Riot—In a prison riot at Long Binh brig, 63 are injured, 1 Black was killed, and the brig was destroyed.
Nov. 27, 1968	Antiwar demonstration—Three thousand soldiers in Twenty-Fifth Division at Cu Chi
Jan. 1969	Combat refusal—9th Infantry Division
Feb. 23, 1969	Riot—Duc Hoa
Mar. 18, 1969	Combat refusal—Son Phu
Apr. 1, 1969	Combat refusal and riot—9th Infantry Division at Binh Duc
May 1969	Solidarity action—Eighteen soldiers in 101st Airborne at Phu Bai issued a statement in support of the Presidio 27.
June 1969	Insubordination—101st Airborne soldiers offered $10,000 reward for assassinating their commanding officer
July 30, 1969	Antiwar demonstration—One hundred soldiers at Qui Nhon
Aug. 24, 1969	Combat refusal—A Company, 101st Airborne
Aug. 26, 1969	Combat refusal—196th Light Infantry Brigade (the entire company) publicly refused to follow patrol orders in the first reported incident of mass mutiny in Viet Nam.

Sept. 1969	Combat refusal—Alpha Company of Americal Division at Que Son
Sept. 1969	Riot—Prisoners destroy the prison at Camp Pendleton, California.
Nov. 1969	Solidarity action—Capt. Al Goldstein and others at Long Binh collected 136 names on a petition supporting the aims of the Viet Nam Moratorium demonstrations in the US.
Nov. 15, 1969	Solidarity action—Many soldiers wore armbands in support of the Viet Nam Moratorium marches.
Thanksgiving Day, 1969	Solidarity action at Pleiku—133 of 141 enlisted men from 71st evacuation hospital and 44th medical detachment abstained (fasted) from traditional turkey dinner and wore black armbands in solidarity with moratorium mobilizations in the US. They also wrote a letter to President Nixon opposing the war.
Nov. 1969	Combat refusal—First Platoon, B Company of Second Battalion/Twenty-seventh Infantry Patrol refused to advance near Cu Chi.
Late 1969	Combat refusal—Rifle Company from First Air Cavalry Division refused to go on patrol.
Late 1969	Solidarity action—Fifteen soldiers on patrol near Danang wore black armbands in solidarity with the moratorium demonstrations.
Late 1969	Teach-In—Soldiers at Quang Tri conducted a seminar about the immorality of the war.
Christmas Eve 1969	Demonstration—Fifty soldiers gathered in JFK Square in Saigon and distributed leaflets urging fellow GIs to stop all fighting and to declare a ceasefire.
April 1970	Combat refusal—Seventh Cavalry refused to follow orders to go on patrol while being filmed by CBS TV.
Dec. 1970	Combat refusal—Enlisted men and their field commanders disobeyed higher command orders to advance on patrol and ambush mission.
Dec. 1970	Riot—Prisoners destroy the prison at Fort Hood, Texas.
July 4, 1971	Pot party and peace talks—1,000 soldiers at Chu Lai

Fall 1971	Antiwar petition—Vietnam Veterans against the War (VVAW) in Saigon circulated a petition to Congress expressing opposition to further military involvement in Southeast Asia. This action spread to soldiers and airmen at other locations, including Pleiku and Cam Ranh Bay. Thousands of signatures were gathered until most petitions were confiscated by the US Military Police and the leaders were arrested and/or discharged.
Oct. 10, 1971	Combat refusal—Bravo Company, First Cavalry Division refused patrol at Firebase Pace, 1.2 miles from the border with Cambodia. In a mini-mutiny, they declared their own private ceasefire with the North Vietnamese, assuring it was all quiet on the Cambodian front.
1971	Riot—Major race riot occurred at the DaNang marine base.
Apr. 1972	Combat refusal—One hundred GIs refused to advance at Phu Bai.

Navy

Oct. 23, 1967	Desertion—In the first known antiwar incident to take place in the Navy during Viet Nam, four sailors deserted from the carrier *USS Intrepid* while on leave in Japan and went to Sweden.
Nov. 15, 1967	Order refusal—Pfc. Dennis Cisielski refused orders to sail with the *USS Dewey* to Viet Nam from Norfolk, Virginia. He was sentenced to one year in prison.
1970	Organizing—Sailors in Southern California founded Movement for a Democratic Military (MDM), a militant anti-racist organization supporting Third World struggles.
Spring 1970	Organizing—Concerned Officers Movement (COM) was formed. It had 3,000 members by 1971, especially Navy and Marine officers. In COM's campaign to stop war crimes, its members spoke of the applicability of the Nuremberg Principles to the Armed Forces.
May 26, 1970	Sabotage—Destroyer *USS Anderson,* leaving for Viet Nam from San Diego, suffered a major breakdown and over two hundred thousand dollars in property damage causing several weeks delay. Investigation revealed sabotage by persons aboard ship.
Spring 1971	Onboard resistance—The Seventh Naval Fleet experienced a surge of resistance from sailors aboard ships and the Save Our Sailors (SOS) movement began.

Nov. 1971	Sabotage—One hundred thousand dollars in damage suffered by *USS Chilton*.
Late 1971	Refusal to sail—The *USS Kitty Hawk* crew began to resist. Nine sailors refused to sail and took refuge in San Diego churches. An onboard, underground newspaper, Kitty Litter, was published.
Oct. 1972	Revolt and riot—Black sailors revolt on the *Kitty Hawk*. Forty Whites and six Blacks injured during an October 13 riot.
Apr. 1972	Various—Five major aircraft carriers dispatched to the South China Sea encountered some form of opposition from crew members and local civilian activists:
	USS Midway (left Alameda)—Petition against the war signed by sixteen sailors.
	USS Ticonderoga (left San Diego)—Three sailors refused to go; seventy-five sailors organized antiwar meetings onboard ship.
	USS Oriskany (left Alameda)—Twenty-five sailors refused to sail.
	USS America (left Norfolk, Virginia)—A large number of sailors expressed antiwar sentiment.
	USS Enterprise—Much dissent on board; underground newspaper, SOS Enterprise Ledger; petition against the war signed by 100 sailors; many incidents of sabotage.
April 24, 1972	Blockade—As the *USS Nitro* left Leonardo, New Jersey for Viet Nam, numerous canoes attempted to block the ship's departure and seven sailors jumped overboard into the ocean to join the people's blockade.
July 1972	Sabotage—Carrier *USS Forrestal*, sailing out of Norfolk, Virginia, suffered a massive fire, causing seven million dollars in damage and a two-month delay in its mission. This fire remains the largest single act of sabotage in Naval history.
July 1972	Sabotage—Carrier *USS Ranger*, sailing out of Alameda, California, suffered one million dollars damage to its engines due to intentional acts that introduced foreign metal parts into the engines. This caused a three-and-a-half-month delay in mission. At least twenty-four other sabotage incidents occurred aboard *USS Ranger* in May and June of that same year.
Nov. 1972	Strike—The first mass mutiny in Navy history occurred on the *USS Constellation* when over 100 sailors participated in a sit-down strike demanding that their commander hear grievances. This led to a dockside strike by 130 sailors in San Diego, California.

Air Force	
1969	Underground papers—First known resistance in the Air Force included the publication of *Aerospaced* at Grissom AFB, Indiana; *United Servicemen's Action for Freedom* or *USAF* at Wright-Patterson AFB, Ohio; and *Harass the Brass,* a one-issue paper published at Chanute AFB, Illinois.
1969	Coffeehouse—Airmen joined with students of the University of Illinois at Champaign-Urbana to found the first coffeehouse for airmen, the Red Herring.
Aug. 1969	Organizing—The first overseas organization in the Air Force was Human Activities in Retrospect (HAIR), formed at Misawa AFB in northern Japan.
March 4, 1970	Organizing—About thirty-five airmen from Grissom AFB, Indiana met to discuss plans for forming a chapter of GIs United against the War.
Summer 1970	Organizing—Coordinated antiwar rallies and underground newspapers at eight US air bases in England, the first sign of mass political movement within the Air Force.
1970	Coffeehouse—The Owl, the first GI coffeehouse located in Asia, opens in Japan with the support of the Japanese activist group, *Beheiren* (Citizen's League for Peace in Vietnam).
May 1971	Petition—Three hundred airmen presented an antiwar petition to the US Embassy in London, England.
1971	Organizing—A discussion group was organized by Black airmen at Plattsburg AFB in New York.
May 1971	Riot—Six hundred airmen got in a brawl over prison conditions and other issues at Travis AFB, California, the primary Viet Nam transfer point, leading to the burning to the ground of the officers club. Many were injured and 135 Black airmen were arrested in the largest mass rebellion in Air Force history.
Early 1971	Underground papers—Ten underground papers were published by airmen on various airbases.
Spring 1972	Underground papers—Over thirty underground papers were published by airmen and circulated at various airbases.
Spring 1972	Coffeehouses and demonstrations—The Air Force experienced a surge of coffeehouses and demonstrations at or near a number of airbases. An Easter bombing campaign sparked waves of protests at dozens of bases around the world.

Dec. 18, 1972	Combat refusal—Captain Dwight Evans, an F-4 Phantom pilot based in Thailand, refused to bomb North Viet Nam in opposition to US policy that targeted civilians.
Dec. 27, 1972	Combat refusal—Captain Michael Heck, a B-52 bomber pilot based in Thailand, with a record of over 200 previous completed missions, refused to bomb targets in North Viet Nam—at that time, hospitals and civilian neighborhoods. Heck stated he was in "moral shock" and invoked the Nuremberg Principles, declaring he had an obligation to disobey orders that are conscientiously objectionable.
May 1973	Political Action—Four pilots from Guam wrote US Senators and Congresspersons to protest the war and then joined with Congresswoman Elizabeth Holtzman (D-NY) in a legal suit challenging the Constitutionality of the Cambodian bombing. The four pilots were: Captain James Strain, B-52 pilot with 230 missions; Capt. Michael Flugger, co-pilot; Lieutenant Arthur Watson, electronic warfare crewman; and Captain Donald E. Dawson, a B-52 pilot. Dawson confessed, "I began to think of what had happened on the ground after a mission."

Active Duty Military in the US

Nov. 6, 1965	Demonstration—While stationed at Fort Bliss near El Paso, Texas, Army Lieutenant Henry Howe participated in a small civilian peace demonstration at Texas Western College in downtown Fort Bliss by carrying a sign reading "End Johnson's Fascist Aggression." He was court-martialed and was sentenced to two years in prison, of which he served one.
Nov. 12, 1965	Order refusal/CO—Felix Chavez, who had become a Jehovah's Witness while a soldier, was court-martialed for refusing to wear his uniform.
Feb. 1966	Publication—Master Sergeant Donald Duncan, retired, wrote an essay, "The Whole Thing Was a Lie," published in *Ramparts* magazine.
June 12, 1966	Combat refusal/CO—Private Adam R. Weber, Jr., of the Twenty-fifth Infantry Division, was sentenced to a year in prison for his refusal to bear arms in Vietnam.
August 17, 1966	Organizing—GIs for Peace formed at Fort Bliss, Texas.

Oct. 1966	Conscientious objection—Captain Howard Levy, an Army doctor at Fort Jackson, South Carolina, refused to teach Green Berets medical procedures on their way to Viet Nam duty. He declared Green Berets to be "murderers of women and children" and the "killers of peasants." At his court-martial, he argued a Nuremberg defense (personal obligation to disobey orders to participate in war crimes, crimes against humanity, and crimes against peace). He was convicted and sentenced to three years in prison, of which he served 26 months.
1967	Combat refusal/CO—A Black private in Oakland, California who refused to board a troop plane to Viet Nam was court-martialed and received a sentence of eleven years in prison.
Feb. 23, 1967	Order refusal/CO—Spec 4 J. Harry Muir III, a conscientious objector who said he could not serve in Vietnam because he loved peace more than America, was sentenced to two years at hard labor for the kind of conduct that "loses wars and countries."
May 1, 1967	Desertion—Private Philip Wagner publicly deserted in opposition to the war.
June 1967	Solidarity action—Private Andy Stapp and five other GIs at Fort Sill, Oklahoma, sent a telegram in support of Howard Levy.
June 23, 1967	Publication—The first issue of the first known underground GI newspaper, *The Bond*, was published by the American Servicemen's Union (ASU) in Berkeley, California.
July 1967	Organizing—The Committee for GI Rights was founded.
July 1967	Insubordination—Two Black marines at Camp Pendleton, CA, Pfc George Daniels and Cpl William Harvey, convened an on-base meeting to discuss whether Blacks should have to serve in the military and serve a White man's war in Viet Nam. They were arrested and charged with insubordination and disloyalty. They were convicted and given prison terms of six and ten years, respectively.
July 4, 1967	Demonstration—Three hundred veterans held an antiwar rally opposite Independence Hall in Philadelphia, Pennsylvania.
July 27, 1967	Publication—Private Richard Perrin published an antiwar statement in issue number 3 of *The Bond*.
Oct. 3, 1967	Riot—Fort Hood, Texas
Nov. 1967	Organizing—American Servicemen's Union (ASU) was founded.

G.I. Resistance

Nov. 1967	Order refusal—Fred Chard refused to obey orders to Viet Nam; Pvt. Ronald Lockman refused to obey orders to Viet Nam; Steve Masono at Fort Benning, Georgia went publicly AWOL to avoid shipment to Viet Nam.
Jan. 1967	Coffeehouse—Harvard grad and Viet Nam reservist veteran Fred Gardner opened the UFO, the first GI coffeehouse, in Columbia, South Carolina.
Jan. 19, 1968	Leafletting—Soldiers distributed antiwar pamphlets at Fort Sam Houston in Texas.
Jan. 24, 1968	Desertion—Pfc. Terry Wilsono publicly deserted in opposition to the war.
Feb. 13, 1968	Pray-in—Twenty-five GIs at Fort Jackson, South Carolina held a pray-in against the war. At least two were arrested.
Feb. 21, 1968	Leafletting—Pvt. Ken Stolte and Pfc. Dick Amick distributed antiwar leaflets at Fort Ord, California.
1968	Order refusal/CO—A sailor refused to train fighter pilots at Norfolk, Virginia because he said the war was "immoral."
March 10, 1968	Protest—Army Lt. Dennis Mottiseau was arrested in Washington, DC for picketing the White House with a sign reading "120,000 American Casualties: Why?"
March 8, 1968	Order refusal/CO—Air Force Capt. Dan Noyd refused to train Vietnamese pilots in New Mexico. Noyd, an Air Force Academy graduate with nearly a dozen years service, was court-martialed and imprisoned.
April 1968	CO—Judge Weigel ordered the military to allow David Crane's resignation as a Conscientious objector in Santa Cruz, California.
April 1968	Desertion—E. Arnet, P. Callicote, C. Kennette, J. Knetz, M. Shapiro, and T. Whitmore deserted the Marine Corps in opposition to the war.
Apr. 11–12, 1968	Riot—Fort Campbell, Kentucky.
Apr. 27, 1968	Demonstration—Forty GIs from California bases at Hamilton AFB, Fort Ord Army base, and Travis AFB, marched at the head of an antiwar demonstration in San Francisco.
May 1968	Order refusal—Army Private John Perry refused to obey orders to Viet Nam at Oakland, California.
May 1968	Political asylum—Ten American GIs were granted asylum in Sweden.

May 10, 1968	Desertion—Private Richard Decker publicly went AWOL to avoid inoculations.
May 20, 1968	Sanctuary movement—Spec 4 William Chase from Boston was granted sanctuary at Arlington Unitarian Church.
June 1968	Order refusal—Navy sailor Fred Patrick returned to Naval Air Facility El Centro, California after being AWOL but refused all duty.
June 23, 1968	Sanctuary movement—Sailor Allen Loehmer from Providence, Rhode Island was granted sanctuary.
July 4, 1968	Riot—Presidio Stockade, San Francisco.
July 5, 1968	Demonstration—The first significant large-scale GI action in the US at Fort Hood in Kileen, Texas, saw participation in a love-in with antiwar speeches.
July 15, 1968	Sanctuary movement—Nine enlisted men gone AWOL took sanctuary at Howard Presbyterian Church in San Francisco, California. They were arrested by Military Police after 48 hours.
July 23, 1968	Riot—238 inmates at the Fort Bragg Stockade, North Carolina.
July 26, 1968	Resignation/CO—Lieutenant Corporal Barry Laing from Camp Pendleton, California sent a public letter of resignation from US Marine Corps in which he cited moral and religious opposition to the Viet Nam war.
Aug. 1968	Order refusal—One hundred fifty GIs stationed at Fort Carson, Colorado, refused Chicago Democratic Convention duty.
	Lawsuit—113 Army reservists in Cleveland filed suit to block their recall; 1,113 Army reservists from Baltimore filed suit to block their recall.
	Sanctuary movement—Private Griswold Wilson from Berkeley was offered sanctuary at Quaker Meeting House; Private Michael Locianto from New York was offered sanctuary in Greenwich Village Church; Allan Wakoski from Seattle was offered sanctuary.
	Teach-In—A GI teach-in was organized at Provo Park in Berkeley, California.
Aug. 23, 1968	Order refusal—Sixty-four GIs from Ft Hood, TX demonstrated against riot control duty at the Democratic Convention in Chicago.
Aug. 25, 1968	Order refusal—Forty-three GIs at Fort Hood, Texas refused Chicago Convention duty.

G.I. Resistance

Sept. 1968	Resignation/CO—Private Gerald Condon at Fort Bragg, North Carolina, resigned from the Green Berets in opposition to the war.
Sept. 2, 1968	Lawsuit—206 reservists filed suit to declare their recall illegal.
Oct. 1968	Resignation—Major Lewis Olive resigned his commission because of limitations on his right to speak out to preserve civil rights.
	Organizing—GI Civilian Alliance was formed.
Oct. 10, 1968	Leafletting—Navy Lt. Susan Schnall bombed the aircraft carrier USS Ranger and 5 naval installations in the San Francisco Bay area with leaflets announcing an antiwar march on October 12 in San Francisco.
Oct. 12, 1968	Demonstration—Between 450 and 500 GIs converged at a large antiwar rally and march with fifteen thousand civilians in San Francisco. Navy Lieutenant Susan Schnall marched in uniform and was subsequently court-martialed and dismissed from the Navy.
Oct. 12, 1968	Solidarity action—A GI solidarity picnic held in Austin, Texas drew three hundred people, half GIs and half civilians.
Oct. 14, 1968	Prison strike—The Presidio 27, military prisoners at the Presidio, San Francisco stockade, participated in a sit-down strike to protest the shooting death by a military police guard of a fellow emotionally disturbed prisoner Richard Bunch, who walked away from a work detail.
Oct. 26–27, 1968	Demonstrations—GIs turned out for antiwar rallies in: Chicago, Illiinois (30–40 GIs, 1,200 civilians); Atlanta, Georgia (50 GIs; 600 civilians); Austin, Texas (50 GIs, 1500 civilians; and Seattle, Washington (200 GIs; 100 civilians).
Oct. 29, 1968	Sanctuary movement—Pvt. John Michael O'Connor was offered sanctuary at the Massachusetts Institute of Technology.
Nov. 1968	Political asylum—Four American GIs were granted political asylum in France.
Nov. 1968	Lawsuit—In San Francisco, 116 GIs filed suit on behalf of the soldier killed by a guard at the Presidio.
Nov. 7, 1968	Riot—Camp Pendleton Brig, California.
Nov. 7, 1968	GI Teach-In—Organized by New Jersey Free Speech Movement at the University of Pennsylvania.
Nov. 8, 1968	Sanctuary movement—Pvt. W. Brakefield and Airman D. Copp were offered sanctuary at New York University.

Nov. 27–29, 1968	Student movement—A GI-civilian conference was organized in Chicago.
Nov. 29, 1968	Petition—Sixty-seven men of Company B, Sixth Battalion, Second Basic Combat Training Brigade at Fort Jackson, South Carolina signed an antiwar letter addressed to President Nixon.
Jan. 6, 1969	Riot—Camp Pendleton Brig, California.
Jan. 19, 1969	Demonstration—GIs participated in an anti–Nixon Inauguration event in Washington, DC.
Jan. 21, 1969	Organizing—A chapter of GIs United was formed at Fort Jackson, South Carolina.
Feb. 2, 1969	Riot—Fort Hood Stockade, Texas.
Feb. 16, 1969	Demonstration—Two-hundred GIs and forty-five hundred civilians came together for an antiwar march in Seattle.
Feb. 26, 1969	Organizing—GIs United petitioned for the right to convene a meeting at Fort Jackson, South Carolina.
Mar. 1969	Riot—One hundred GIs at Fort Bliss, Texas.
Mar. 1969	Student movement—GI Day was held at the University of Pennsylvania.
Mar. 1969	Order refusal—Henry Mills refused orders to South Viet Nam from Fort Dix, New Jersey.
Mar. 2, 1969	Student movement—A GI-civilian Conference was held at Wright State University in Ohio.
Mar. 20, 1969	Organizing—One hundred GIs attended an antiwar meeting held at Fort Jackson, South Carolina.
Apr. 1969	Order refusal—Fifteen GIs refused orders to South Viet Nam from Fort Sill, Oklahoma.
Apr. 5, 1969	Demonstration—Two hundred GIs and somewhere between 75 and 100 thousand civilians attended a GI-civilian march in New York City.
Apr. 5, 1969	Demonstration—Thirty GIs and thirty thousand civilians attend a GI–Civilian march in Chicago.
Apr. 6, 1969	Demonstrations—Fifty GIs and six thousand civilians attended a Free the Presidio 27 march in Los Angeles; fifty GIs and four thousand civilians attended a GI–Civilian march in Atlanta.
Apr. 6, 1969	Riot—Fort Riley Stockade, Kansas.
Apr. 10, 1969	Trial—US Army officials admitted that Pvt. John Huffman, one of the Fort Jackson 8 in South Carolina, was an agent provocateur.

Apr. 12, 1969	Demonstration—One hundred GIs and twelve hundred civilians jointly marched in Austin, Texas against the war.
Apr. 19, 1969	Riot—Camp Pendleton Brig, California.
Apr. 21, 1969	Publication—Soldiers at Fort Eustis, Virginia, formally sought permission to distribute the GI newspaper, *Rough Draft*.
Apr. 24, 1969	Publication—Spec 4 Allan Myers, editor of the GI newspaper, *The Ultimate Weapon*, formally applied for permission to distribute the paper at Fort Dix, New Jersey.
May 1969	Trial—Charges were dropped against the Fort Jackson 8; on May 21 they were released from the stockade.
May 7, 1969	Protest and Riot—In support of the Presidio 27 at Fort Ord Stockade, California.
May 13, 1969	Riot—Fort Carson, Colorado.
May 18, 1969	Publication—Dennis Ciesielski, editor of the GI paper, *Rough Draft*, requested permission to distribute the paper at Fort Eustis, Virginia.
May 20, 1969	Boycott—Five hundred inmates at Ft Ord Stockade in California boycotted the mess hall.
May 24, 1969	Demonstration—GIs and Vietnam Veterans against the War (VVAW) organized an antiwar picnic at Riverside.
June 1969	Riot—Fort Leonard Wood Stockade, Missouri
June 5, 1969	Riot—Two hundred inmates at Fort Dix Stockade, New Jersey.
June 11, 1969	Publication—Eleven Gs requested permission to distribute the GI paper, *The Ultimate Weapon*, at Fort Dix, New Jersey.
June 14, 1969	Demonstration—One hundred and fifty inmates held a sit-in at Fort Jackson Stockade, South Carolina.
June 20, 1969	Leafletting—Antiwar leaflets distributed at Fort Meade, Maryland.
June 22, 1969	Riot—Camp Pendleton Brig, California, and Fort Riley Stockade, Kansas.
June 30, 1969	Organizing—CO committee was formed Fort Jackson, South Carolina.
July 1969	Demonstration—Pvt. Benny Amos immolated himself in protest of the war at Fort Ord, California, but was not seriously hurt.
July 1969	Publication—In an antiwar letter published in Playboy, Pfc. Michael Madler claimed seventy-five percent of GIs opposed the war.

July 4–5, 1969	Conference—First national antiwar conference involving GIs was convened in Cleveland.
July 11, 1969	Riot—Camp Lejeune Stockade, North Carolina.
July 20, 1969	Riot—Camp Lejeune Stockade, North Carolina.
July 21, 1969	Riot—Naval Air Station in Memphis
	Riot—Two hundred inmates at Fort Riley Stockade, Kansas.
July 26, 1969	Riot—Fort Hood, Texas.
July 30, 1969	Riot—Fort Carson, Colorado
Aug. 1969	Sanctuary movement—At least 35 GIs were granted sanctuary for a month in Hawaii.
Aug. 1969	Organizing—GIs for Peace was founded at Fort Bliss, TX.
Aug. 11, 1969	Riot—Fort Bragg, North Carolina.
Aug. 16, 1969	Leafletting—GIs for Peace distributed antiwar leaflets at Fort Bliss, Texas.
Aug. 17, 1969	Riot—Camp Pendleton Brig, California.
Sept. 7, 1969	Organizing—GIs from four posts in Washington, DC, formed a GI mobilization committee.
Oct. 11, 1969	Demonstration—One hundred Fort Bragg, North Carolina soldiers, mostly returned combat veterans from Viet Nam, marched in a Viet Nam Moratorium against the War demonstration in Fayetteville, North Carolina.
Oct.–Nov. 1969	Demonstrations—Many GI demonstrations occurred in solidarity with moratorium demonstrations.
Nov. 9, 1969	Publication—A total of 1,365 active duty GIs signed a full-page ad in the *New York Times* asking for an end to the war.
Nov. 11, 1969	Demonstration—One hundred GIs held a Veteran's Day antiwar demonstration in El Paso, Texas.
November 13–14, 1969	Conference—National Conference on GI Rights, organized by the GI Defense Organization in Washington, DC.
Nov. 15, 1969	Demonstration—One hundred sixty GIs and four hundred forty civilians attended an antiwar demonstration in El Paso, Texas.
Nov. 16, 1969	Organizing—Soldier's Liberation Front was formed at Fort Dix, New Jersey.
Nov. 16, 1969	Demonstration—GI demonstration was held in Washington, DC.

Dec. 14, 1969	Demonstration—One thousand GIs joined four thousand civilians in Oceanside, California in an antiwar march and rally near Camp Pendleton, California.
Jan. 5, 1970	Demonstration—Eighty GIs joined GIs for Peace in picketing General Westmoreland at Fort Bliss, Texas.
Feb. 1970	Organizing—A chapter of GIs United was formed in Baltimore, Maryland.
Feb. 27, 1970	Conscientious objection—First Lieutenant Louis P. Font, a West Point graduate, asked to be released from the military because US actions in Viet Nam countered his religious beliefs.
Mar. 15, 1970	Demonstration—GI peace rally was held in El Paso, Texas.
May 1970	Demonstrations—GI movement called for national demonstrations against the war to celebrate Armed Forces Day (third Saturday in May).
May 2, 1970	Petition/Publication—Four hundred and seventy reservists signed an antiwar petition published in the *New Republic*.
May 16, 1970	Demonstrations—In its first effective national action, the GI movement called for national demonstrations against the war to celebrate Armed Forces Day (third Saturday in May). Demonstrations were held at twelve Army and Marine Corps installations and at five Air Force and Navy bases (seventeen total) with thousands of GIs participating.
May 29, 1970	Organizing—National GI Alliance was formed.
June 1970	Demonstration—Antiwar reservists picketed the annual convention of the Reserve Officers Association in Philadelphia.
June 26, 1970	Conscientious objection—Six non-combatant conscientious objectors publicly refused orders to go to Viet Nam at Fort Lewis, Washington.
June 30, 1970	Organizing—The call was put out for a national GI strike.
July 1970	Organizing—A chapter of GIs United was formed at Fort Hamilton, New York.
July 26, 1970	Sabotage—Three soldiers from Fort Carson, Colorado, were indicted for dynamiting the telephone exchange, power plant, and water works of another military installation at Camp McCoy, Wisconsin.
Aug. 15, 1970	Petition—At least one thousand national guardsmen and reservists signed a petition calling for immediate, total withdrawal from Viet Nam.

Nov. 1970	The Arts—GI band members, held a series of peace concerts in the New York City area.
Apr. 1972	Petition—Twelve hundred GIs signed a petition demanding the end of the Viet Nam war.
June 1973	Insubordination—A large number of West Point Cadets dropped out of the academy in protest of the military and the Viet Nam war.

Draft Resistance	
May 1964	First refusals to register for draft and public burning of draft cards
Mid-1965	First prosecutions against men refusing to be inducted (380)
Mid-1968	3,305 prosecutions against men refusing to be inducted into military
End of 1969	US Government reported 33,905 delinquents nationwide.
May 1969	At the Oakland, CA induction center (which served all of Northern California), of 4,400 men ordered to report for induction, 2,400 did not show up.
Sept. 1969	By this time, 65 of the 4,000 local draft boards in US had been reportedly attacked or harassed; 11 incidents involved burning or mutilation of records.
March 1970	At Oakland, California, for the six-month period October-March 1970, fifty percent of those called failed to report and eleven percent of those who did show up refused induction.
Early 1971	Chicago Area Draft Resisters (CADRE) estimated that by early 1971, total induction refusals exceeded 15,000 and the number of men failing to report approached 100,000.
Jan. 1971–March 1972	In a year and a quarter as the war wound down, no less than 196 acts of disruption directed against the draft were reported in the US.
Sept. 19, 1974	As of this date, 9,118 draft evaders and resisters had been convicted and 4,400 were still "at large." The admitted total of deserters still at large at that point was reported as 28,661.

Sources for GI and Veterans' Resistance

Baskir, Lawrence M., and William A. Strauss. *Chance and Circumstance: The Draft, the War and the Vietnam Generation.* New York: Vintage Books, 1978.

Boyle, Richard. *Flower of the Dragon: The Breakdown of the US Army in Vietnam.* San Francisco: Ramparts Press, 1973.

The Citizens Commission Inquiry (Ed.). *The Dellums Committee Hearings on War Crimes in Vietnam.* New York: Vintage Books, 1972.

Clergy and Laymen Concerned About Vietnam. *In the Name of America.* New York: Clergy and Laymen Concerned About Vietnam, 1968. [This is an excellent and comprehensive description of the actual criminal conduct by the armed forces of the US in Viet Nam as revealed in published reports, compared with the Laws of War binding on the US government and on its citizens.]

Cincinnatus. *Self-Destruction: The Disintegration and Decay of the United States Army During the Vietnam Era.* New York: W.W. Norton & Co., 1981.

Cortright, David. *Soldiers in Revolt: The American Military Today.* Garden City, NY: Doubleday, 1975/ Chicago: Haymarket, 2005.

Franklin, H. Bruce. *Back Where You Came From.* New York: Harper's Magazine Press, 1975.

French, Peter (Ed.). *Individual and Collective Responsibility: Massacre at My Lai.* Cambridge, MA: Schenkman Publishing Co., 1972.

Gettleman, Marvin E., Jane Franklin, Marilyn Young, and Bruce H. Franklin. *Vietnam and America: A Documented History.* New York: Grove Press, 1985. [Note: In this author's opinion, this is the single best general resource book available on the Viet Nam war.]

Grier, Joel. "Vietnam: The Soldier's Revolt." *International Socialist Review* (Aug.-Sept. 2000, No. 9).

Heinl, Colonel Robert D., Jr. "The Collapse of the Armed Forces." *Armed Forces Journal* (June 7, 1971), 30–37.

Horne, A.D., ed. *The Wounded Generation: America After Vietnam.* Englewood Cliffs, NJ: Prentice-Hall, 1981.

Knoll, Erwin and Judith Nies McFadden (Eds.). *War Crimes and the American Conscience.* New York: Holt, Rinehart & Winston, 1970.

Lewes, James. *Protest and Survive: Underground GI Newspapers During the Vietnam War.* Westport, CT: Praeger, 2003.

Moser, Richard. *The New Winter Soldiers.* New Brunswick, NJ: Rutgers University Press, 1996.

Neale, Jonathan. *A People's History of the Vietnam War.* New York: The New Press, 2003.

Nicosia, Gerald. *Home to War: A History of the Vietnam Veterans' Movement.* New York: Crown, 2001.

Rinaldi, Mathew. "The Olive-Drab Rebels: Military Organizing During the Vietnam Era." *Radical America,* 8 (1974), No. 3, 17–52.

Stacewicz, Richard. *Winter Soldiers: An Oral History of the Vietnam Veterans Against the War.* New York: Twayne Publishers, 1997.

Taylor, Telford. *Nuremberg and Vietnam: An American Tragedy.* Chicago: Quadrangle Books, 1970.

Vietnam Veterans Against the War. *The New Soldier.* New York: Collier Books, 1971.

Vietnam Veterans Against the War. *The Winter Soldier Investigation: An Inquiry into American War Crimes.* Boston: Beacon Press, 1972.

Waterhouse, Larry G., and Mariann G. Wizard. *Turning the Guns Around: Notes on the GI Movement.* New York: Delta Books, 1971.

Wells, Tom. *The War Within: America's Battle Over Vietnam.* New York: Henry Holt and Co., 1994.

Zaroulis, Nancy, and Gerald Sullivan. *Who Spoke Up? American Protest Against the War in Vietnam, 1963–1975.* New York: Holt, Rinehart and Winston, 1984.

Zinn, Howard. *A People's History of the United States.* New York: Harper Colophon Books, 1980.

Left to right: George Mizo, S. Brian Willson, Duncan Murphy, Charles Liteky (all Vietnam veterans except Murphy, who served as an ambulance driver in World War II). Like John David Borgman, the author's military experience in Viet Nam led him to engage in public protests against war and imperialism a dozen years later. In September–October 1986, the four veterans pictured above staged a high-profile, water-only, open-ended Veterans Fast for Life on the east steps of the US Capitol in Washington, DC, to protest US policies bent on overthrowing the sovereign government of Nicaragua and preserving the oppressive government of El Salvador—policies directly causing thousands of civilian deaths in both countries.

Chapter Eight
The Lasting Toll of War

*"The roots of war are in the way we live our
daily lives—the way we develop our industries,
build up our society, and consume goods."*
—Thich Nhat Hanh[1]

Introduction

Just as the American war in Southeast Asia can be seen as an extension of the Cold War, the ripple effects of the US invasion of Viet Nam, and our subsequent defeat, are devastating in both ecological and human terms.

The American war caused tragic, long-term severe damage to Viet Nam, Cambodia, and Laos, including horrendous destruction of ancient cultural, village, and family life. Postwar economic woes required the people to often look desperately to the West for financial help, and to adopt western capitalist values. The US "loss" was in many ways a *victory for capitalism* ("normalization"). Globalized supermarket economics serves as a "nonviolent" instrument of recolonization and impoverishment. But in fact it is insidiously violent.

Domestically, the emergence of attempts at popular democracy in the US in the 1960s was seen as a severe threat to the status quo (indeed, a "crisis in democracy"), leading to a systematic reactionary counter-revolution launched by the US oligarchy, especially those on the far right of the religious and political spectrum. This reaction continues today as the structural politics move further to the right.

The fallout from this reactionary pushback has been severe curtailment of popular social programs. In recent decades, the main focus of education has gradually shifted from the humanities to business. Free or low-cost tuition that once existed at such institutions as the University of California and at City University of New York (CUNY) has been terminated. Tax cuts for the wealthy have dramatically reduced social spending, directly causing increases in homelessness and the deterioration of health care. Simultaneously, the formal "wars" on crime and drugs initiated in the 1960s and '70s (wars on the poor) have led to *massive* prison construction and consequent dramatic increase of incarceration of *millions*, especially of African American males: Incarceration increased from 415,000 total prisoners in 1974 to a figure approaching 2.5 million in the 2000s. Per capita detention *rates* per 100,000 population accelerated from 195 prisoners in 1974 to near 800 today!

---

1 "Peace Is Every Step—Mindfulness and the Roots of War," *Parabola*, Vol. 16:4, Winter 1991.

The US American public's distaste for war, referred to by politicians as our "Viet Nam Syndrome," directly led to rapid expansion of counterinsurgency (COIN) and *low-intensity* warfare, whereby Special Forces, created under a Special Operations Unified Command, participated in skyrocketing numbers of covert operations and rollbacks of movements seeking self-determination, often with no public knowledge whatsoever. Initially, this secret operation model was used to counter popular liberation struggles in Central America, in an application of old Monroe Doctrine/Roosevelt Corollary policies, as the US sought to repair an ego severely damaged by its humiliating defeat by the Vietnamese.[2]

After the fall of the Soviet Union in 1991, this pattern of US aggression morphed into global PAX Americana. In the early 2000s the US had a military presence in 153 nations, with 725 major bases in 38 countries. The Pentagon operates 150 different military educational institutions in the US and other countries, and regularly sends Special Forces trainers to 133 countries to train local militaries in "foreign internal defense."[3] The US is also the leading arms exporter to some 140 countries, 90 percent of which are repressive, abusive, and anti-democratic.[4] Special Forces conduct covert aggressive operations in at least 150 countries, including death squads, in order to ensure preservation of US geostrategic/financial interests.[5]

GI resistance during the Viet Nam era is one of the main factors that finally brought the war to an end, leading to the preference among the power elite for a volunteer army. A permanent back draft was created, an insidious form of economic conscription, in effect producing a publicly-funded mercenary ("volunteer") military force designed to protect corporate globalization everywhere under PAX Americana. The continual undermining of social services for the poor and the ever-increasing economic gap between the haves and have-nots reliably funnels a steady stream of volunteers seeking the only available jobs program entirely subsidized by the government—thereby ensuring an imperial military force.

Finally, the US defeat by the Vietnamese, perceived as "gooks," led to a severe entrenchment of US narcissism as the culture desperately sought to deny the shameful humiliation of its defeat. Its bubble of invincibility, and delusion of exceptionalism, had been painfully pierced. Historically spoiled by the forceful dispossession of millions of Indigenous of their lands, lives, and cultures with impunity, and a similarly unpunished forceful dispossession of millions of Africans of their lives, culture, and labor, US Americans never developed a culture of responsible accountability. Rather than embrace the horrible Viet Nam experience as an historical opportunity for deep healing, the US chose to retreat to a morbid, pathological adolescence. Our national narcissism provides

---

2 Gandin.

3 Chalmers Johnson, *The Sorrows of Empire: Militarism, Secrecy and the End of the Republic* (New York: Metropolitan Books, 2004), 154, 132, 124.

4 Johnson, 2000, 88.

5 Nick Turse, "A Shadow War in 150 Countries", *Tomgram*, January 20, 2015 (accessed October 27, 2015); http://www.tomdispatch.com/blog/175945/.

a lethal distraction, preventing us from normalization as a nation among many, authentic and mutually respectful, requiring instead that we engage in ever more arrogant and dangerous behavior in order to demonstrate our stated "superiority."

The Spread of Violence in Southeast Asia

After the US began bombing Cambodia in March 1969, followed by invasion of that country in spring 1970, much of its countryside increasingly became a free-fire zone for US and Vietnamese air forces. Rural Cambodia was flattened and decimated, with 61,000 sorties in 1971 alone. The majority of the Cambodian people became radicalized as their lives were increasingly destabilized from the intensity of the US military firepower. A report by the Defense Intelligence Agency (DIA) speculated that the main reason for the strong emergence of rebellious Khmer Rouge forces in the 1970s was because of this alienation of most of the rural population.

Post-war reconstruction of Viet Nam's civilian economy was further obstructed by the consequent growing Cambodian-Vietnamese Civil War, 1975-1979. The next-door Khmer Rouge forces, formed in 1968 under the leadership of Pol Pot, attacked ethnic Vietnamese in eastern Cambodia while also going across the border to attack Vietnamese villages, especially after Khmer Rouge forces captured the capitol in Phnom Penh in 1975. The Khmer Rouge ruled Cambodia until 1979 when they were forced out by the Vietnamese.[6]

The extensive US bombing of Cambodia indeed had helped create conditions that brought Pol Pot's Khmer Rouge to power in 1975. Ironically, the US subsequently became an important political *defender* and financial supporter of Pol Pot after his government and forces were ousted during the 1979 Vietnamese invasion. As genocidal as they were, the US considered the Vietnamese Communists more evil than the Khmer Rouge.[7]

The January 1979 Vietnamese invasion succeeded not only in overthrowing the Pol Pot government, but in installing a government friendly to Viet Nam. The US condemned the Vietnamese action as "illegal." Fifty CIA operatives coordinated support for Pol Pot's exiled forces, which had been pushed to western Cambodia and into Thailand. More difficulty was faced by the Vietnamese in February 1979 when the Chinese Army invaded northern Viet Nam with 600,000 troops in a limited but destructive strike, in retaliation for Vietnam's action against China's ally, Cambodia.[8]

---

6 Gibson, 409–410, 418; John Pilger, "The Long Secret Alliance: Uncle Sam and Pol Pot," *Covert Action Quarterly*, 62, 1997.

7 Blum, 87–90; Pilger, 1997.

8 Blum, 87–89; Pilger, 1997; Henry Kamm, *Cambodia: Report from a Stricken Land* (New York: Arcade Publishing, 1998), xix-xxi. [Note: After Pol Pot was removed in 1979, his seat representing Cambodia at the United Nations was continued largely because it was defended by the US under President Carter as part of the continuing Cold War against Communism as well as to exact revenge against Viet Nam and to foster the emerging alliance between the US and China, the latter being Pol Pot's principal underwriter. Carter's national security adviser, Zbigniew Brzezinski, acknowledged that he had "encouraged the Chinese to support Pal Pot" and acquiesced to China sending arms to the Khmer Rouge forces in eastern Cambodia through Thailand.]

Same War, Different Tactics

BROKEN PROMISES

The Paris Peace Accords, in effect what the Nixon administration would term an agreement "to end the war and bring peace with honor in Vietnam and Southeast Asia," included a pledge from President Nixon of postwar aid amounting to over $4 billion. The US subsequently denied this aid promise had been part of the agreement. However, the text of the letter released on May 19, 1977, more than four years after it was written, mentions a "range of $3.25 billion" over five years, and one of the two addenda mentions an additional $1 billion to $1.5 billion in *other* forms of aid, amounting to well over $4 billion total. Despite the fact that Kissinger and Le Duc Tho had negotiated the terms of the letter during the peace talks, the promise of aid was never honored.[9]

This refusal by the US to honor its agreement to pay post-war aid to help repair Viet Nam's war-ruined economy is consistent with our history of exacting revenge, begun with the practice of eliminating Indigenous nations who rightfully resisted European invasion of their lands.[10] Furthermore, on the day the war officially ended, April 30, 1975, the US Treasury Department froze $70 million of Vietnamese assets. By mid-May 1975, the US Commerce Department required all exports to Viet Nam to be approved by the State Department. This was applied to foreign subsidiaries of US companies as well.[11]

---

9 Gettleman et al., 471–488.

10 There is a famous American Indian quote that the "White man speaks with forked tongue." The POW/MIA concocted issue was a major rationalization for not signing a peace treaty several years earlier, and then reneging on promised post-war aid for the needlessly prolonged war.

The Indian saying is often attributed to Chief Joseph (1840-1904), leader of the Wallowa band of the Nez Perce Indian tribe, as the US Army was attempting to force the tribe's removal to reservations far away from their ancestral lands in the Columbia River Plateau of the Pacific Northwest, which had been granted to them in earlier treaties with the US government. Land was "needed" for more White settlers in the rush for gold. About 650 Nez Perce fled north toward the safety of Canada pursued by 1,900 soldiers. Four months later, after traversing 1,700 circuitous miles of mountains, canyons, plains, and rivers, the tired and freezing survivors, including many women and children, surrendered on October 5, 1877, not far from the border. Chief Joseph famously said, "The little children are freezing to death. My people, some of them, have run away to the hills, and have no blankets, no food. No one knows where they are–perhaps freezing to death. . . . Hear, my chiefs. I am tired. My heart is sick and sad. From where the sun now stands, I will fight no more forever." [Alan Axelrod, *Chronicle of the Indian Wars From Colonial Times to Wounded Knee* (New York: Prentice Hall General Reference, 1993), 235; Hirschfelder, 114–115.

Some were sent by train to prison at Ft. Leavenworth before they were subsequently settled on a reservation in Colville, Washington. Chief Joseph's father had told him, "Stop your ears whenever you are asked to sign a treaty selling your home." [Chief Joseph, Wikipedia, http://en.wikipedia.org/wiki/Chief_Joseph; Peter Cozzens, *Eyewitnesses to the Indian Wars, 1865-1890: The Wars for the Pacific Northwest* (Mechnicsburg, PA: Stackpole Books, 2001), 304]. Chief Joseph had not agreed to sell but like so many others on the Continent and later around the world, he had been forced at gunpoint to leave his lands in deference to the plunder of the Whites. Chief Joseph painfully experienced what the Vietnamese would suffer 75 years later at the hands of the US. Like Chief Joseph, I too am tired, and my heart is sick and sad.

11 Pilger, *Hidden Agendas* (New York: The New Press, 1998), 321–324.

The Economic War

Grinding down Viet Nam even further, in 1979 the US convinced the European community to halt its regular shipments of milk to Vietnamese children. This move directly contributed to a third of all Vietnamese children under 5 experiencing stunted growth, and many going blind due to Vitamin A deficiency. In 1981, the US very selectively chose to enforce the 1917 Trading with the Enemy Act to deny voluntary agencies export licenses for humanitarian aid intended for all of Indochina. Not even Cuba was subjected to such a complete embargo. By 1986, the Communist leadership in Hanoi faced harsh criticism both from within and outside the party due to shortage of food and basic goods and rising prices. There was mass party resignation. The new leadership in December 1986 announced major economic and social changes as they embraced the neoliberal ideology of the free market to confront the Western/US-led embargo. At the time, it was touted as a new economic strategy of "socialism" (*Doi Moi*).[12]

Eventually, as Viet Nam's attitudes came to be more in line to the US version of so-called democratic corporate capitalism, President Bill Clinton lifted the thirty-year embargo on Viet Nam in February 1994. However, even though Viet Nam had never received the US promised war reparations, a condition of normalization and lifting of the embargo was that Viet Nam make good on undisclosed massive multilateral debts incurred by the former US-backed Saigon regime prior to 1975. Reimbursement of arrears of $140 million owed to the IMF by the former US government-propped Thieu dictatorship was an additional condition for receiving new credit. From the US, a total of nearly $2 billion in aid and loans was pledged in support of Viet Nam's "market reforms."[13]

The tragedy was complete. Viet Nam was granted membership into the "international community" as long as it accepted globalization and the consequent *de facto* economic recolonization with its extreme divisions between new wealth and major impoverishment. In Viet Nam—a small country with about 1.3% of the world's population, situated 9,000 miles west of my rural home town farming village in upstate New York—the US had finally achieved, with money and market expansion, the victory that had eluded it through years and years of incredible military savagery, firepower, chemical warfare, and bombings.[14]

The Propaganda War

At the conclusion of the Paris Peace Accords in January 1973, the US promised more than $4 billion to Viet Nam for reconstruction costs. Having no intention of honoring that pledge, Nixon used the MIA accounting as an excuse for reneging. With overwhelming popular and Congressional support, the POW/MIA issue managed to stalemate the Paris Peace talks for nearly four years.[15] Subsequent administrations continued to use

---

12 Michel Chossudovsky, *The Globalization of Poverty* (Penang, Malaysia: Third World Network, 1997), 148–150.

13 Chossudovsky, 148–150; Pilger, 1997, 321–324.

14 S. Brian Willson, "The Columbus Enterprise Prevails in Vietnam: The US Finally Enjoys a Long Eluded Victory," March 1, 1994, http://www.brianwillson.com/the-columbus-enterprise-prevails-in-vietnam-the-u-s-finally-enjoys-a-long-eluded-victory/.

15 B. Franklin, 2000, 173–184.

the possibility that Vietnam continued to hold US solders in captivity to feed hostility toward the newly independent Vietnamese government that emerged after the US quick withdrawal in April 1975.[16]

Whenever there have been wars, there have been MIAs. Missing In Action means either a person unaccounted for or a body not recovered (BNR). Nearly 79,000 are still unaccounted for in WWII, another 8,100 in Korea.[17] Texan billionaire Ross Perot helped launch an organization called the National League of Families (of American Prisoners in Southeast Asia) in 1969, headed up by Sybil Stockdale, spouse of the highest ranking naval officer imprisoned in Viet Nam. The league's first goal was to deadlock the Paris Peace talks over the issue of missing US prisoners.

By the 1980s, Ann Mills Griffiths, whose pilot brother had been shot down in North Viet Nam, became the executive director of the National League of Families. Griffiths also served as official liaison between the Pentagon and the US public, and helped design the POW/MIA flag, which is sold at a profit to the US government, the 50 state governments, local governments, and private organizations and citizens.

The flag to this day remains a divisive symbol for veterans and others, but most people don't know its deceitful history, and just assume it is a symbol of solidarity for Viet Nam veterans. However, it is, in fact, a war flag, a symbol that gives people permission to continue to hate the Vietnamese, rather than admit that our intervention was criminal in the first place, and acknowledge the war's grotesque destruction of much of Vietnamese society and village structure.

Lasting Toll on US Veterans

Veteran Suicides: Moral Injury to the Soul

In Viet Nam I was staggered at how terribly dumbed-down I was as I turned 28. Because of historical ignorance, I had thoughtlessly become part of a brutal killing machine that was murdering countless innocents, though I never pulled a trigger or dropped a bomb. This has caused me serious moral and soul injuries, a dis-ease much deeper and very different from and, I believe, more uncomfortable than anxiety. This may explain the high suicide rate among veterans who have experienced serious, deep cognitive dissonance that challenges the essence of the right and wrong innately known by the soul.[18] And, it explains the suicidal thoughts that came in and out of my head while experiencing the Fellini movie–like experience called Viet Nam.

Afghanistan veteran Jacob George (who did three tours in the Army between 2001–2004) described how basic training itself weaponizes the soul, as military training is intentionally designed to dehumanize the enemy. This invariably leads to the dehumanization of oneself, which causes deep moral injury.

---

16 B. Franklin, 2000, 187–188.

17 B. Franklin, 2000, 175.

18 Alice Lynd with Staughton Lynd, *Moral Injury and Conscientious Objection: Saying No to Military Service* (Fayetteville, NC: Quaker House, 2015).

The banjo-playing George clearly recognized and understood his own post-traumatic stress disorder (PTSD) and moral injury, though he felt the World War I term used for PTSD, "Soldier's Heart," more accurately described his wounds and experiences, and thus chose it for the title of a song and of his 2013 album. The chorus of this song speaks to the soldier's deep feelings of betrayal by the nation that sent him to war:

> *now i can't have a relationship, i can't hold down a job*
> *some may say i'm broken, i call it soldier's heart*
> *every time i go outside, i gotta look her in the eyes*
> *knowing that she broke my heart, and turned around and lied*
>
> *red, white, and blue, i trusted you*
> *   and you never even told me why*

Jacob George was provoked to new angst when, on September 10, 2014, he heard that President Obama had ordered a new war against Syria and ISIS. One week later, at age 32, George committed suicide in his Arkansas home. Fortunately, he left a beautiful legacy: his songs, recorded for *Soldier's Heart* and published in a companion songbook, which reveal such profound wisdom about moral injury and PTSD that it behooves a serious read (and listen) for anyone interested in treating and/or healing from these injuries.[19]

Nonetheless, honestly addressing moral injuries by honoring one's innate empathy, rather than just prescribing pharmaceuticals designed for more standard anxiety disorders, offers fertile ground for huge consciousness shifts, as well as a deep transformation of a veteran's values and perceptions. For me, personal transformation has been accompanied by serious study of the historical patterns of US interventionism, which turned out to be gruesome imperialism as with previous empires. This, along with reflection on painful experiences in Viet Nam and a study of Jungian psychology, have guided me in a long process of recovering my own humanity.

In 1981 I came across an article by psychologist Peter Marin titled "Living in Moral Pain."[20] It started me thinking that what I had been experiencing—a marked alienation for a decade—was a moral dis-ease. One symptom was, I often felt alone even when around lots of acquaintances, friends and family.[21]

Then I read a book by William P. Mahedy, *Out of the Night: The Spiritual Journey of Vietnam Vets*[22] in which he concludes that healing from the wounds of Viet Nam is fundamentally

---

19 Jacob George, *Soldier's Heart*, with lyrics/commentary with assistance from April Helen, Fayetteville, AR, 2012, http://www.operationawareness.org/.

20 Peter Marin, "Living in Moral Pain," *Psychology Today*, November 1981.

21 Carl Jung said that "loneliness does not come from having no people about one, but from being unable to communicate the things that seem important to oneself, or from holding certain views which others find inadmissible." [Carl Jung, *Memories Dreams and Reflections* (New York: Random House, 1965, 356]. In other words loneliness is the feeling of not being known. War experiences are so far removed from normal ranges of experiences that what is known to the veteran is often not possible to communicate to the non-veteran.

22 William P. Mahedy, *Out of the Night: The Spiritual Journey of Vietnam Vets* (New York: Ballantine Books, 1986).

a religious, spiritual, and theological issue, best understood in a holistic community context. Clinical psychiatrist Jonathan Shay, in *Achilles in Vietnam: Combat Trauma and the Undoing of Character*,[23] compares combat soldiers in Viet Nam with those in the nearly 3,000-year-old Greek poem, "The Iliad." He reveals how betrayal undermines our basic humanity and character, often producing bestial behavior, making moral recovery extremely challenging and sometimes seemingly impossible. Shay originally coined the term, "moral injury."

Psychotherapist Edward Tick, in *War and the Soul*,[24] explains that PTSD is an identity, rather than an anxiety disorder. In other words, it is primarily a moral, spiritual, and soul disorder. Where a deep transformation of the soldier occurs, nourishment and validation are required for the new identity to flourish. But what the soldier gets more often is belittlement of difficult feelings. Cases of moral injury are commonly mis-diagnosed as anxiety and the main objective of treatment, primarily with pharmaceuticals, is to enable the soldier's re-adjustment to conventional society.

No matter how well trained we might be to prepare us to overcome our innate revulsion to killing, once we participate in the act, there is a breach of our primordial glue. PTSD afflicts thousands of veterans often manifesting in suicide. Our soul is screaming at us, "Please stop assaulting the very moral fabric of your being!"

In the early 2000s, while writing my psychohistorical memoir,[25] I attempted to track down the five officer friends from the 823rd Combat Security Police Squadron who served with me in Viet Nam. I was shocked to discover that three of them had since died of Agent Orange–related diseases, including my immediate superior. A fourth had committed suicide after murdering his wife of 37 years. The fifth's whereabouts or existence was unknown at the time, but we have subsequently reconnected and resumed our friendshiop. The war had obviously taken a tremendous toll on us. I was diagnosed in 1997 by the VA as being totally and permanently disabled due to PTSD. Indeed, the war affected the entire society, especially psychically.

Once one begins to see outside the fog of the Cold War, it becomes clear that the people of Viet Nam, as with most people everywhere, possessed a most natural and understandable desire for self-determination and independence from Western control. But to the US (and France before that), this earnest striving by the Vietnamese was deemed a serious threat to US plans for global hegemony on our selfish terms, i.e., obedience to corporate, exploitive capitalism. In the geostrategic minds of the West and the United States, Viet Nam was an empowering example, a dangerous threat that had to be crushed at any cost, to prevent its infective virus from igniting the hearts and minds of the other 80 percent of the world's peoples who yearn for liberation from 500 years of brutal slavery and impoverishment by Eurocentric powers. Viet Nam was no aberration, as I had initially assumed, but in

---

23 New York: Atheneum, 1994.

24 Edward Tick, *War and the Soul* (Wheaton, IL: Quest Books, 2005).

25 S. Brian Willson, *Blood on the Tracks: The Life and Times of S. Brian Willson* (Oakland: PM Press, 2011); S. Brian Willson, *My Country Is the World: Photo Journey of a Stumbling Western Satyagrahi* (Portland, OR: B&B Books, 2012, updated 2015), 34–35, photos and brief bios of the five officer friends: http://www.amazon.com/My-Country-World-Stumbling-Satyagrahi/dp/1456414968.

fact one of hundreds of countries where people and their resources were being brutally exploited to assure US prosperity. The US demands that everyone "cry uncle," i.e., be at our mercy, do as we say. The American Way of Life—AWOL—means Empire as a way of life.[26] We might ask, if we dare, how many dead human beings in the developing world does it take to extract one barrel of oil?

Asking questions like this for more than four decades now, has led to the articulation of my own mantra, "We are not worth more; they are not worth less."

Please, do not thank me for my service. If you feel compelled to make any comment, then thank me for striving to tell the truth about the American war in Viet Nam and the history of US criminality behind it. Ask yourself what is your own truth about living in the selfish, materialist world of Disney America dependent upon destroying others and the precious ecosystem of the Earth.

How Many Suicides?

Estimates of the number of suicides among US Viet Nam veterans are wide ranging, but no authentic empirical evidence is conclusive of total numbers, showing only that the rates are elevated. Some estimates place the figure at 100,000 or more,[27] and others at 150,000[28] or even 200,000,[29] the latter suggested by several authors, one of whom cites Joel Brende, a retired VA doctor, who explains the high number due primarily to large numbers of single-car drunk-driving accidents and self-inflicted gunshot wounds not accompanied by a suicide note.

I became deeply sensitized to the extent of suicide among veterans when in the early 1980s I served as director of a storefront Viet Nam veterans center in Western Massachusetts. I was devastated during that time by the suicides of no less than a dozen local Viet Nam veterans. The burden of becoming a trained killer is heavy indeed.

While I was director of that veterans center, the office of the Massachusetts Commissioner of Veterans Services conducted a Viet Nam veteran mortality study. It concluded that deaths due to suicide and motor vehicle accidents of Viet Nam veterans were "significantly elevated," as much as 40 to 65 percent over Massachusetts non-veterans in the same period.[30] Shortly afterwards, the *New England Journal of Medicine* issued a report on effects of conscription on mortality and found that, among veterans studied in California and Pennsylvania, Viet Nam veterans were 86 percent more likely than non-veterans to

---

26 William Appleman Williams, *Empire as a Way of Life* (New York: Oxford University Press, 1980).

27 Edward Tick, *War and the Soul* (Wheaton, Illinois: Quest Books, 2005), 165, citing Daniel Hallock, *Hell Healing and Resistance* (Farmington, PA: Pough Publishing House, 1998), 106.

28 Chuck Dean, Nam Vet (Portland: Multnomah Press, 1990).

29 Alexander Paul, *Suicide Wall* (Portland: PakDonald Publishing, 1996), suicide statistics: http://www.suicidewall.com/suicides-statistics/; C.D.B. Bryan, *Friendly Fire* (New York: Putnam, 1976), 380, quotes Alexander Paul's figure of 200,000; Normal L. Russell, *Suicide Charlie: A Vietnam War Story* (New York: Preager, 1993), estimates 200,000.

30 M.D. Kogan and R.W. Clapp, *Mortality among Vietnam Veterans in Massachusetts, 1972–1983* (Boston: Massachusetts Office of the Commissioner of Veterans Services, Agent Orange Program, 1985): http://www.nal.usda.gov/exhibits/speccoll/items/show/3278?tags=ao_seriesIII.

commit suicide, and 53 percent more likely to die in traffic accidents.[31] I was struck by how these two studies, published within a few months of each other, were corroborative. Many other studies as well as anecdotal evidence have suggested a high rate of suicides among veterans of wars.

In 2000, the Vietnam Veterans Association of Australia discovered that the families of veterans also psychically suffer. It found that the children of Viet Nam veterans had three times the suicide rate of the general community.[32]

An Associated Press story in 2007 reported that veterans returning from Afghanistan and Iraq already had exhibited increased risks for suicide, and that one-third already had been diagnosed with post-traumatic stress disorder (PTSD). The story also reported that 5,000 veterans in general commit suicide every year.[33]

Six months later a report published by CBS News found at least 120 veterans on average commit suicide every week (over 17 per day), more than double the rate for non-veterans.[34] And in February 2008, CNN reported that, in 2007, an average of five soldiers per day tried to commit suicide, a rate six times that of 2002, before the start of our current wars.[35]

In 2010, Veterans Administration figures revealed that 22 veterans commit suicide each day.[36] Suicides committed by active-duty soldiers are occurring at record rates. The US Department of Defense reported that in 2012, during the Iraq and Afghanistan occupations, a record 349 active-duty service members committed suicide. That is one every 25 hours, exceeding the 311 killed in combat that year, and this record figure does not include 110 "pending" reported suicides.[37]

Thus, we have substantial evidence that being trained to kill, and participating in combat, tears at the soul of humans, in effect revealing that participants in such activity ultimately turn their own weapon back onto themselves. Retired Lt. Colonel Dave Grossman, founder of a new field called "killology,"[38] in his book, *On Killing*, shows that the vast majority of people have a deep phobia-level revulsion to violence, and thus soldiers need

---

[31] Norman Hearst, Thomas B. Newton, and Stephen B. Hulley, "Delayed Effects of the Military Draft on Mortality," *New England Journal of Medicine*, March 6, 1986: http://www.nejm.org/doi/full/10.1056/NEJM198603063141005.

[32] Vietnam Veterans Association of Australia, "Massive Suicide Rate For Vietnam Veterans' Children," August 7, 2000: http://www.vvaa.org.au/media12.htm.

[33] Alfonso Serrano/AP, "Report: Veterans Have Greater Suicide Risk," May 10, 2007: http://www.cbsnews.com/news/report-veterans-have-greater-suicide-risk/.

[34] Armen Keteyian/CBS, "Suicide Epidemic Among Veterans," November 13, 2007: http://www.cbsnews.com/news/suicide-epidemic-among-veterans-13-11-2007/.

[35] CNN, Concern Mounts Over Rising Troop Suicides, February 3, 2008: http://www.cnn.com/2008/US/02/01/military.suicides/index.html?iref=topnews

[36] Kevin Freking, "Veteran Suicide Rate at 22 Each Day, Department of Veterans Affairs Report Finds," February 1, 2013, reported in Huff Post Politics; http://www.huffingtonpost.com/2013/02/01/veteran-suicide-rate_n_2599019.html.

[37] "US Military Suicides Exceed Combat Deaths," CBS News, January 14, 2013; "US Military Suicides in Charts: How They Overtook Combat Deaths," *The Guardian* DataBlog; http://www.theguardian.com/news/datablog/2013/feb/01/us-military-suicides-trend-charts].

[38] Killology Research Group: http://killology.com.

to be specifically trained to kill. One of the consequences of killing in combat is this severe pattern of PTSD that too often leads to suicide.[39]

Conclusion

The Weight of it All: We are Responsible for Millions of Casualties

On July 3, 1979, US President Jimmy Carter, upon advice from eminent Jewish Middle East and Muslim historian, Bernard Lewis, and his own National Security Advisor, Zbigniew Brzezinski, initially authorized $500,000 to fund thousands of Mujahideen fundamentalist Islamic fighters to overthrow a popular reformist Afghanistan government allied with the Soviet Union, for the purpose of inducing a Soviet invasion that would become their version of a Viet Nam quagmire.[40] By 1992, the US had provided as much as $5 billion to the Mujahideen in a CIA operation even larger than its 1980s efforts to overthrow Nicaragua's Sandinista revolutionary government. Saudi Arabia and other European and Islamic countries worked with the CIA to fund an additional $5 billion for the Islamic fighters. These decisions led directly to 1.5 million deaths in the decade-long war against the Soviets which, in turn, directly led in 1990 to emergence of the Taliban as a second-generation Mujahideen.[41]

There is a direct timeline from Carter's July 1979 decision to the attacks on September 11, 2001 in New York and Washington, DC, the most significant instance of blowback in the history of the CIA.[42] The blowback continues with escalating out-of-control turmoil in

---

39 Lt. Colonel Dave Grossman, *On Killing: The Psychological Cost of Learning to Kill in War and Society* (New York: Back Bay Books, 1996).

40 Steve Coll, *Ghost Wars: The Secret History of the CIA, Afghanistan, and Bin Laden, From the Soviet Invasion to September 10, 2001* (New York: The Penguin Press, 2004), 45–46; Robert M. Gates, *From the Shadows* (New York: Touchstone, 1996), 143–149; Jeffrey St. Clair and Alexander Cockburn, "How Jimmy Carter and I [Brzezinski] Started the Mujahideen," *Counterpunch*, January 15, 1998, http://www.counterpunch.org/1998/01/15/how-jimmy-carter-and-i-started-the-mujahideen/. Brzezinski: "According to the official version of history, CIA aid to the Mujahadeen began during 1980, that is to say, after the Soviet army invaded Afghanistan, 24 Dec 1979. But the reality, secretly guarded until now, is completely otherwise: Indeed, it was July 3, 1979 that President Carter signed the first directive for secret aid to the opponents of the pro-Soviet regime in Kabul. And that very day, I wrote a note to the president in which I explained to him that in my opinion this aid was going to induce a Soviet military intervention."

41 Ahmed Rashid, *Taliban: Militant Islam, Oil and Fundamentalism in Central Asia* (New Haven: Yale University Press, 2001), 13, 18.

42 "Chalmers Johnson on the CIA and a blowback world", *Tomgram*, November 5, 2004, http://www.tomdispatch.com/post/1984/chalmers_johnson_on_the_cia_and_a_blowback_world. "Blowback" first appeared in CIA reports when it overthrew the Iranian government in 1953 with aid of and on behalf of British Petroleum. On June 18, 2000, James Risen of the *New York Times* ["WORD FOR WORD/ABC'S OF COUPS; Oh, What a Fine Plot We Hatched (And Here's What to Do the Next Time)"], explained: "When the Central Intelligence Agency helped overthrow Muhammad Mossadegh as Iran's prime minister in 1953, ensuring another 25 years of rule for Shah Muhammad Reza Pahlavi, the CIA was already figuring that its first effort to topple a foreign government would not be its last. The CIA, then just six years old and deeply committed to winning the Cold War, viewed its covert action in Iran as a blueprint for coup plots elsewhere around the world, and commissioned a secret history to detail for future generations of CIA operatives how it had been done ... Amid the sometimes curious argot of the spy world—'safebases' and 'assets' and the like—the CIA warns of the possibilities of "blowback".

the Middle East region, and the increased numbers of retail[43] terrorist attacks in Europe and elsewhere, fueled by years of US military interventions.

In 1990–91, accompanying the sending of military forces to the Gulf in preparation for invading oil-rich Iraq, the US immediately orchestrated UN-imposed sanctions in August 1990, such that no raw materials or modular system parts, including those necessary to treat water and sewage, and supply critical medical equipment, could be received by Iraq. Once the 43-day incessant bombing began on January 17, 1991, the sanctions devastated reconstruction efforts, while accelerating hunger and malnutrition that led to hundreds of thousands of children dying. The 20 years of sanctions, 1990–2010, are estimated to have directly caused between 670,000 and 880,000 excess child deaths.[44]

When I visited Iraq with other veterans in October 1991, seven months after termination of the bombings, but fourteen months after imposition of the harsh sanctions, dying children could be seen everywhere with their desperate mothers—in hospitals if they were lucky to get a bed to wait out the death process, or lying hopelessly along the streets. This tragedy, and egregious crime, was highlighted in the media when on May 12, 1996, Lesley Stahl of CBS 60 Minutes, asked President Bill Clinton's Secretary of State Madeleine Albright: "We have heard that a half million children have died. I mean, that's more children than died in Hiroshima. And, you know, is the price worth it?" Albright responded: *I think this is a very hard choice, but the price—we think the price is worth it.*[45]

A March 20, 1991 United Nations Report found that approximately 9,000 Iraqi homes were destroyed or damaged beyond repair by the bombing in Gulf War I. The report cites destruction of Iraq's infrastructure: (1) The sole vaccine producing laboratory; (2) All vaccines; (3) Virtually all electrical power plants; (4) Virtually all oil refineries; (5) Virtually all oil storage facilities; (6) Virtually all electrically operated installations; (7) Virtually all plants manufacturing water treatment chemicals; (8) Virtually all telephone and communications systems; (9) All ports; and (10) Eighty-three bridges.[46] The U.N. Report used the terms, "near apocalyptic results," "relegated to a pre-industrial age," "imminent catastrophe," "calamitous consequences," "devastation," and "grave deficiencies" of food.

---

43 US aggressive foreign policy, along with its sponsored, funded, armed and/or trained "authoritarian" and "democratic" states, comprise the real terror network, i.e., the network of "wholesale" terrorists using bombs, jet fighters, drones, and unlimited military technology. The increasingly sophisticated, nearly unchecked propaganda machinery of the "democratic" West has successfully censored this demonic history of the real terror network. Substituted in its place is an often desperate, frequently concocted network of the voiceless that includes, by careful selective definition, only those "terrorists" who challenge important Western "neoliberal" economic interests, or who can be linked in some way, no matter how remotely, to the "enemies" of these interests. This substituted group of individuals and smaller groups of relatively poor people, in fact, become the network of "retail" terrorists who serve to distract attention from the more substantial and systemic destructive behavior of the "wholesale" terrorists.

44 "Lessons We Should Have Learned From the Iraqi Sanctions," *Foreign Policy*, January 4, 2012.

45 FAIR, 'We Think the Price Is Worth It', November 1, 2001; http://fair.org/extra/we-think-the-price-is-worth-it/

46 UN Document S/22366, *Report on Humanitarian Needs in Iraq*, of March 20, 1991, http://www.un.org/Depts/oip/background/reports/s22366.pdf

The *New York Times* (June 5, 1991) estimated 100,000 Iraqi military killed, and 300,000 wounded, citing DOD "tentative" figures. Other estimates suggest 200,000 Iraqi soldiers killed (*London Times*, March 3, 1991), with many more maimed. Civilian dead directly from bombings and immediate after effects are in the 25,000 to 50,000 range, with as many as 100,000 post-war adult deaths as of 1992, for a total of 150,000 civilian deaths.[47] A US Census Bureau demographer estimated 158,000 Iraqis killed in the war and its aftermath.[48] Thus, as many as 350,000 adult Iraqis, both military and civilian, were killed directly from the war and its immediate aftermath. When added to the estimated 670,000 to 880,000 children who died over twenty years as a direct result of the sanctions,[49] a total of 1,020,000 to 1,230,000 Iraqis were killed, or nearly 7 percent of that country's 1990 population of 17.5 million, directly attributable to the US-led war and its accompanying sanctions. To grasp the gravity of these casualties, they would be equivalent to 17 million US dead of its 1990 250 million population.

Two other Western Christian leaders—Tony Blair and George W. Bush—adding to Carter's July 1979 decision to intervene into Afghanistan, conspired in the early 2000s to launch military campaigns to achieve regime changes that devastated geostrategically-located Afghanistan and Iraq. From October 2001, when the US and its UK junior partner led the invasion of Afghanistan (code-named "Operation Enduring Freedom") to today, there have been as many as 116,000 civilian deaths.[50] Thousands of US forces remain in Afghanistan today.

From the March 2003 US-led invasion of Iraq (code-named "Operation Iraqi Freedom") to its official conclusion in December 2011, as many as one million Iraqis were killed.[51] Nonetheless, as of Summer 2016, the US still had as many as 4,000 troops in Iraq. These criminal invasions of Afghanistan and Iraq carried out by the US and the UK have caused egregious destabilization of neighboring countries in West Asia and the Middle East.

When the figure of as many as 1,230,000 Iraqis killed in the first Gulf massacre (see above) is added to the one million killed in Afghanistan and Iraq in the 2000s during the second Gulf War, it is likely that more than two million Iraqis were murdered. In addition 600,000 orphans were created, 1.3 million Iraqi citizens were internally displaced, and twice that many went into exile.[52]

---

47 Ramsey Clark, *The Fire This Time: US War Crimes in the Gulf* (New York: Thunder Mouth's Press, 1992), 83–84, 130, 209.

48 Geoff Simons, *Iraq: From Sumer to Post-Saddam* (New York: Palgrave, 2004), 6, citing Simon Jones, "US Demographer Sacked For Exposing Iraqi Civilian Deaths," *The Independent*, London, April 23, 1992.

49 Jonathan Marcus, "Analysis: Do economic sanctions work?", *BBC News*, July 26, 2010; http://www.bbc.com/news/world-middle-east-10742109.

50 Physicians For Social Responsibility, Body Count, "Casualty Figures After 10 Years of the 'War on Terror,'" http://www.psr.org/assets/pdfs/body-count.pdf.

51 Nicolas J. S. Davies, *Blood on our Hands: the American Invasion and Destruction of Iraq* (Ann Arbor, MI: Nimble Books, 2010); "Over One Million Iraqi Deaths Caused by US Occupation," *Project Censored*, April 10, 2010, http://www.projectcensored.org/1-over-one-million-iraqi-deaths-caused-by-us-occupation/.

52 Stephen Zunes, "Iraq: Remembering Those Responsible", *Truthout*, January 1, 2012; http://www.truthout.org/iraq-remember-those-responsible/1325433300.

Ironically, without the US American- and UK-led crimes of lawless wars, there would be no Jihadist retail terrorist group—ISIS (Islamic State in Iraq and Syria)/ISIL (Islamic State in Iraq and the Levant), and no Al Qaeda. Geographical Levant comprises western Syria, Lebanon, western Jordan, Palestine, Israel, Egyptian Sinai and parts of Turkey.

And without US ally Saudi and Western arming of Sunni extremist groups throughout the Middle East used as proxies to defeat Iran, Syria, and their respective allies, there would be no effective ISIS/ISIL. And, due to the extensive recruiting of a global movement of armed Sunni extremists—during both Carter and Reagan presidencies—we are saddled with an endless "War on Terror," now provoking in retaliation a number of retail terrorist attacks, such as in Paris in November 2015, etc. This is severe Blowback![53]

Efforts to defeat ISIS/ISIL have led to a general war in the Middle East. Syria has become at least the 14th country in the Islamic world where US military forces have invaded, occupied, and bombed in which US American soldiers have killed, or been killed, since 1980: Iran (1980, 1987–1988), Libya (1981, 1986, 1989, 2011), Lebanon (1983), Kuwait (1991), Iraq (1991–2011, 2014–), Somalia (1992–1993, 2007–), Bosnia (1995), Saudi Arabia (1991, 1996), Afghanistan (1998, 2001–), Sudan (1998), Kosovo (1999), Yemen (2000, 2002–), Pakistan (2004–), now Syria[54]. Violence breeds violence, a lesson not heeded for most of recorded history.

This wholesale terror war waged by the US and the UK now includes armed drones, an ultimate terror weapon from the sky of the most egregious kind. The US has been employing armed drones since the early 2000s, now joined by UK, in the firing of hundreds of Reaper drone attacks in the Middle East and West Asia, including Iraq, Syria and Afghanistan.[55] Since 2002, the US, and more recently supplemented by UK air forces, has flown thousands of armed drone sorties, carrying out nearly 1,200 drone strikes against Pakistan, Yemen, Somalia, Afghanistan, Libya, and Iraq, killing as many as 6,600, while injuring as many as 2200.[56]

Additionally, the US terrorizes people virtually everywhere with secret "Special Operations" boots on the ground functioning as death squads. US Special Forces operatives, comprised of 70,000 soldiers, have set foot in 150 countries from 2011–2014 (three fourths of the planet's 196 nations), tracking and killing suspected "terrorists." In the process, they torture, destroy homes and families, and kill and wound many innocent. The Special Forces also provide names and cell phone numbers of those they have supposedly identified as targets for guiding drone strikes.[57]

---

53 Chris Floyd, "The Age of Despair: Reaping the Whirlwind of Western Support for Extremist Violence", *CounterPunch*, November 13, 2015.

54 Andrew Bacevich, "Even If We Defeat the Islamic State, We'll Still Lose the Bigger War," *Washington Post*, October 3, 2014.

55 Chris Cole, "500 days of British drone operations in Iraq and Syria", Drone Wars UK, April 3, 2016; https://dronewars.net/2016/03/04/500-days-of-british-drone-operations-in-iraq-and-syria/

56 "Get the data: Drone wars," The Bureau of Investigative Journalism - https://www.thebureauinvestigates.com/category/projects/drones/drones-graphs/.

57 Nick Turse, "A Shadow War in 150 Countries", *Tomgram*, January 20, 2015 (accessed October 27, 2015): http://www.tomdispatch.com/blog/175945/.

All of the young men and women who obey, and have obeyed, military orders from above to "serve" their supposed nation's interests to invade and occupy these countries must face their own responsibility for having been complicit in carrying out death and destruction, their souls now suffering from painful moral injury.

This premeditated Western murdering plunder has been committed with virtual impunity. This means that for those citizens in the West whose governments carried out these egregious crimes, historic memory of the diabolical carnage is virtually erased, and there is little feeling of the need to take responsibility for it—it never really happened. It is therefore incumbent upon participating soldiers who viscerally experienced an awakening to ensure that the historic memory of these awful crimes shall not be forgotten in hope they shall never be repeated.

British Playwright Harold Pinter has argued that the United States supported and often encouraged every rightwing military dictatorship in the world after World War II. Citing many examples, Pinter concludes with biting irony, "It never happened. Nothing ever happened. Even while it was happening, it wasn't happening. It didn't matter. It was of no interest."[58]

No wool blanket is needed to cover US American eyes—they are made of wool, resting in the bliss of pathological historical amnesia. We learned nothing from Viet Nam, because we learned nothing from our original crime of forceful dispossession through genocide of hundreds of Indigenous nations, stealing their land with virtual impunity. Our cultural DNA is rooted in extreme denial. Deeper yet, we have not overcome millennia of tyrannical patriarchy.

So, it is up to we the people to recover our right minds and to practice disobedience to centralized power and its militarism. Then we would have an opportunity for discovering a capacity to reconfigure ourselves into hundreds of cooperative bioregional communities where there remain chances of sustainability, withdrawing our support from the political economy that we have heretofore been conditioned to obey, even if reluctantly, to our detriment.

---

58 Michael Billington, "Passionate Pinter's Devastating Assault on US Foreign Policy Shades of Beckett as Ailing Playwright Delivers Powerful Nobel Lecture", *The Guardian UK*, December 8, 2005.

The author (number 34, center left) was one of the star players on the 1958–59 Chautauqua (New York) Central High School "Indians" varsity basketball team.

Chapter Nine
My Story

"Please, don't thank me for my service."
—S. Brian Willson

Introduction

Although I possessed a II-S (school) deferment, I was conscripted into the military in March 1966 at age 24. I was in my fourth semester of study in a joint law-master's degree program at the Washington College of Law, American University, Washington, DC. President Johnson was rapidly escalating US involvement in Viet Nam, and monthly draft calls had jumped from 10,000 to 30,000 a month, leading to a shortage of the most eligible registrants, those categorized as I-A.[1]

At the time, my residence was an old jail cell in the terribly overcrowded, 100-year-old Washington, DC, jail (1,400 prisoners in a jail designed for 700). I had been living there since October 1965 as part of a law school internship program. I was responsible for interviewing prisoners received each day from the courts, gathering basic intake information for the jail's classification office. I ate my meals with inmates and my clothes were regularly washed in the jail laundry. During the ten-plus months I lived at the jail, I was the only white man who attended weekly Black Muslim meetings. At the time I was reading *The Autobiography of Malcolm X*.[2] Living at the DC jail provided me with a crash course exposing me to the extent and toxic nature of both racism and classism before I ever set foot in Viet Nam.

Thinking my draft must be a mistake, I traveled from Washington to personally meet with my Selective Service Board in Fredonia, NY, one of 4,000 local draft boards that were located in every county in the US. The three elderly men sitting at the table explained that I had slipped through a loophole in the draft deferment law. In my rural, agricultural county there were fewer eligible young men because II-C farming deferments were absolute, whereas a II-S school deferment was preferential.

In 1966, only two out of every hundred draftees were college graduates, and I was one of them. Graduate school II-S deferments were abolished altogether in 1967. And despite my academic pursuits, my humble origins worked against me. Statistically, young men from low-income backgrounds like myself were three times as likely to die in Viet Nam as youths from high-income neighborhoods.[3]

---

1 Baskir and Strauss, 22.
2 Malcolm X, with Alex Haley, *The Autobiography of Malcolm X* (New York: Grove Press, 1965).
3 Baskir and Strauss, 6–10.

I was not an eager conscript even though I possessed no philosophical or political opposition to war. In fact, I was a strong supporter, but I was a "chicken hawk"—I preferred that others fight the advance of Communism while I cheered them on from my comfortable place at a university. Coming from a very conservative, lower working-class Republican family, I grew up amidst the Cold War passions of the McCarthy era. Among the first TV shows I watched as a young teenager was, *I Led Three Lives*, about FBI counterspy Herbert Philbrick. As a senior in high school, I was enamored with the immensely popular 1958 book by J. Edgar Hoover, *Masters of Deceit: The Story of Communism in America and How to Fight It*.[4]

During Spring 1964, as a pre-ministerial student at Eastern Baptist College (now Eastern University), during the Q&A portion of a chapel service where the guest speaker had announced that four US advisers had recently been killed in Viet Nam, I made a comment that the US should bomb the godless Communists in Viet Nam into oblivion to destroy communism once and for all, similar to what General Curtis LeMay, as well as presidential candidate Barry Goldwater, were saying at the time. I could not have known then that exactly five years later I would be an eyewitness to the bombing of inhabited, undefended villages.

I even applied for a position as a junior FBI Agent. Despite my identity as a patriotic American, I had expected to be able to pursue my graduate education while happily missing military service. However, as it turned out, I would not get away with being a chicken hawk. Little did I know that the education I was about to receive from my military experiences would dwarf anything I might learn in graduate school.

My Selective Service Board apparently felt sorry for me because they did agree to defer my draft for three months, enabling me to complete the semester, which ended in June. I enlisted in the Air Force in the meantime and was locked into a September 1966 entrance date for Officer Training School, when I would be 25.

I was in the US Air Force from September 14, 1966 to August 30, 1970, primarily as a security and law enforcement officer. I was commissioned a 2nd Lieutenant on November 25, 1966. Because my first two years were spent in a white-collar assignment at headquarters USAF in Washington, DC, my psychological, mental, and cultural life continued relatively similar to what I had experienced prior. I was the lowest ranking officer in a white-collar assignment with 33 officers and civilians. Because I was in Washington, DC, I was amazingly able to continue attending graduate classes in the evenings at the very same university from where I had been drafted. In 1968, I completed the master's portion of my joint corrections/law degree.

My next military order, however, thrust me into a surreal world that dramatically changed my life. In November 1968 I reported to the 823rd Combat Security Police Squadron (823rd CSPS) stationed at England Air Force Base in Alexandria, Louisiana. This immediately required my being a student at the 12-week USAF Combat Security Police Training School at Fort Campbell, Kentucky, patterned after the Army's ranger school at

---

4 J. Edgar Hoover, *Masters of Deceit: The Story of Communism in America and How to Fight It* (New York: Henry Holt and Company, 1958).

Fort Benning, Georgia, in preparation for Viet Nam. I did not know that the USAF had a combat security unit and certainly was not interested in being part of it. One of the superior officers in my job at headquarters Air Force Systems Command had formerly been part of this combat group. He shared with me that it required highly motivated volunteers and he was surprised that I would be tapped for such an assignment as he knew my lack of enthusiasm. He even made a call to headquarters Air Force questioning the orders. Nonetheless, orders were orders.

My Viet Nam experience I am sure was relatively tame compared to duty in the Army or Marines. Nonetheless, similar to what many other soldiers, perhaps most, experienced from their time in Viet Nam, nothing has been the same since. Like soldier Paul Baumer (Lew Ayres) said in the classic 1930 anti-war film about World War I, based on the book by Erich Maria Remarque, *All Quiet on the Western Front*: "I'm no good for back there any more.... None of us are. We've been in this too long.... It's not home back there anymore."

I have had it pretty good, all in all. Professionally educated before and since the military, older than most other non-lifers when in Viet Nam, I have generally been engaged in various meaningful endeavors promoting healing and justice. I have never been without a warm home, have not been an abuser of drugs or alcohol, etc., but nonetheless have struggled with feeling that I do not belong, certainly not in my home country, perhaps nowhere. Forever working on healing my own soul has itself proved to be an extraordinarily worthwhile endeavor.

Inside "Operation Safeside": Diary of an Air Force Security Officer

Many of my memories blur due both to the long time that has elapsed since, and because of interruptive moments of disturbing trauma. Nevertheless, the following section is my sincere attempt to reconstruct some important events that occurred while in Viet Nam. I consulted historical accounts and a perpetual calendar in addition to my own memory, in efforts to reconstruct my activities as accurately as possible. The days between an April 10–11 attack on Vinh Long City, and April 19, when I traveled to consult with 7th Air Force intelligence personnel at Tan Son Nhut, are especially difficult. The experience still seems surreal to me to this day.

Fort Campbell, Kentucky

December 16, 1968. I report to Fort Campbell to begin my new assignment—a 12-week touted as ranger-type training as a section leader in the 559-man 823rd CSPS. Our section will join "Operation Safeside" in Viet Nam, an Air Force version of "rangers" patterned after the Army's ranger school at Fort Benning, Georgia. In fact, some of our Air Force instructors are graduates of the US Army's ranger training school. Interestingly, we are briefed that there is an outside possibility of being deployed to Korea, or even Guatemala, but I know nothing of the circumstances in Guatemala. In fact what we experienced was more like advanced infantry training, than Army ranger training.

Things get off to a tense start when I share with my 823rd commander, a Lieutenant Colonel, that I had not volunteered for ranger-style training, and furthermore did not feel I was a good fit for a ranger-type unit that required a high degree of motivation. He responds angrily that he didn't want to hear that kind of talk. The two of us maintained an acrimonious relationship throughout the 12-week training and beyond.

January 10, 1969. During a typical military training bayonet drill, I feel an automatic revulsion at hearing orders to plunge the blade into a dummy while screaming "Kill!" a hundred times. I pause anxiously, attempting to muster the motivation to carry out the order but the trainer's repeated screams directed at my hesitation only fed my reluctance. I didn't know in advance I would have such strong feelings and I am stunned by my refusal. I share with my immediate superior, a Captain commander of our Flight B, my distress over this assignment.

January 13. My flight commander arranges a meeting with our 823rd CSPS operations officer, a Major, who counsels me that responsibilities to my men and country require important training, and stresses the need to become professionally prepared to secure air bases from Communists in hostile Viet Nam.

January 14. Our operations officer arranges a meeting with our squadron commander, a Lieutenant Colonel, with the operations officer sitting in. The commander fears that my refusal to comply with the bayonet drill is having a deleterious effect on the morale of other members of the squadron. He literally screams at me. With arms flailing, he threatens that my behavior could lead to 20 years at Leavenworth Penitentiary. However, the operations officer corrected him, reading from the Uniform Code of Military Justice (UCMJ) that the penalty is only 5 years. I do not know what the specific charge is. My commander tells me I am "as good as a VC," and that he will do anything to keep me from becoming a Captain. In post-meeting counseling, the commander writes about me: "he is dissatisfied with his present assignment and has a complete lack of desire for a military life. Further counselling is believe [sic] to be fruitless."

He then orders me to see the squadron chaplain, a Major, a Southern Baptist. After saying a short prayer as I sit nervously next to his desk, he shows me DOD photos of what appear to be atrocities in Viet Nam, telling me I have an obligation to stop these crimes against the Vietnamese. He shames me over and over for being disloyal to god and country while turning a deaf ear to my concerns and feelings. Instead, he angrily judges me "disturbed" and orders an immediate assessment by an Air Force psychiatrist.

Soon thereafter, I am driven in a USAF vehicle to Sewart Air Force Base near Nashville, Tennessee, to be assessed by a USAF psychiatrist, a Captain. A very kind man, he met with me for several hours during which we enjoy lunch. He listens attentively to my concerns and makes me feel validated. He concludes that I am of sound mind and recommends reassignment to duty that will not conflict with my ethical and dispositional concerns about being a combat "ranger officer." Upon receipt of the psychiatrist's report, however, my commander proclaims that since I am of sound mind, I must comply with the orders as they stand. This, of course, depresses me. I feel like a character in Joseph Heller's novel, *Catch 22*. What will I do on the day I am ordered to board the plane? *Goddamn it!*

January 20, 1969. During our training, Richard Nixon was inaugurated, becoming the fifth president within 20 years, (along with Truman, Eisenhower, Kennedy, and Johnson) to oversee US American military and CIA intervention in Southeast Asia. I wonder whether his election might shorten the war and perhaps make my deployment unnecessary? After all, he has promised during his campaign to "end the war and win the peace" in Viet Nam.

On January 27, my commander places me on the "Officer Control Roster," ordering me to be "under special observation for a period of 180 days" due to "self-admitted failure to accept the responsibilities commensurate with your grade." Furthermore, his order acknowledged that I "do not agree with certain concepts and policies of the 82nd Combat Security Police Wing" and that I "cannot, in good conscience, support the Wing mission." I have never heard of the "Officer Control Roster," but here I am, on it. I feel emotionally shaky as I find my conscience in direct conflict with my ego, which clamors for acceptance and respect. But I also continue to wonder why my superiors would even want me in this squadron. It seems foolish on their part, not in the best interests for achieving a motivated fighting force.

The officers of the 823rd receive a closed briefing that our specific squadron organizational structure, its distribution of personnel, and the dates of our expected movement to Viet Nam, are classified. With a total of 559 personnel in the squadron, we are to be moved on four different dates, beginning with command and intelligence functions sometime in early February, and three combat groups following in a staggered fashion—one later in February, one in early March, the other in late March. Our specific locational assignments will not be known until the moment we arrive in Viet Nam.

On February 8, the 82nd Combat Security Police Wing commander, a full Colonel, orders me to his office at Fort Campbell for a consult. He is kind enough to acknowledge my concerns, and wrote in his report of our meeting, "I respected his ethics and appreciated the difficult position that he was facing." At the same time, he makes it clear that if I refuse a direct order to deploy, he "would then be forced to initiate court-martial action for failure to obey," which is understandable. At least he is respectful.

The colonel further informs me that he is in contact with Tactical Air Command (TAC) headquarters in Virginia (823rd CSPS is part of TAC) and "the Judge Advocate would come to Fort Campbell if necessary" to avoid any situation that could embarrass TAC commander, General William Momyer, former commander of 7th Air Force in Viet Nam. Three days after our meeting, the Wing commander shares with me a three-page typed summary of our meeting, which remains in my personal files today.

February 19. The Wing Commander orders my removal from the Officer Control Roster, saying, "it is inappropriate to place an officer on the Control Roster while he is attending a formal school. Any failure to meet training standards should be noted by the school commandant and faculty board action taken as deemed necessary."

February 22–23. The 1969 TET offensive in Viet Nam begins with rocket and mortar attacks that hit at least 71 cities and military targets, and cause several hundred US

American casualties.[5] This information is shared with us during our training, presumably to keep us psyched up. At this point we are only two weeks away from our "graduation" and shipment to Viet Nam.

During our last week of ranger training (in effect, light infantry training) in early March, we learn that nearly 500 US soldiers have been killed with nearly 3,000 wounded by the end of the first week of TET 1969.[6] Knowing our squadron is about to be dispatched to Viet Nam raises my anxiety to new levels as I nervously wonder whether I will be able to follow orders to deploy.

Friday morning, March 7, 1969. I graduate with 558 others in this "Operation Safeside" unit. As one of 21 officers, a lowly first lieutenant serving as a section leader, I had received separate training in leadership skills—how to utilize air base defense planning, command and control techniques in ground combat situations, tactics, intrusion detection, and tactical communications with a special emphasis on combat security intelligence. Although I refused to participate in the bayonet drill, and became hopelessly lost with one other officer buddy during a two-day (and night) compass-directed hike through the wilds of Ft. Campbell, my certificate nonetheless proclaims my successful completion of the twelve-week training. No matter. The military needs bodies in Viet Nam, including Air Force lightweights like me. Some in our squadron were excited to hear we had been promised blue berets, but the formal authorization for the berets never came, much to my pleasure.

Our flight to Viet Nam has been scheduled to leave immediately on the evening of graduation day. As the time draws near, I wonder if I might possibly be able to muster enough courage to refuse when the impending orders to board the plane are given. Am I up for facing a court-martial, I wondered? What is my conscience worth? I consider what others might think of me, including my family. If I refuse, I figure I would be judged a coward and any chance for a professional career ruined. By this time I was experiencing serious doubts about the war in addition to doubt and anxiety about my ability to lead men into a combat situation. Finally, allegiance to my conscience collapses in the face of court-martial and likely imprisonment, and all thought of refusing to board the plane was dissolved by my fear of being disgraced.

I am depressed by my own timidity. However, somehow I hope for the best even as my stomach cramps up. With a dry mouth, I board the windowless C-141 plane with the rest of my men. Almost immediately we are in the air, settled in for the nearly 9,000-air mile journey to Viet Nam.

---

5 Bowman, 221.
6 Bowman, 222.

Arrival in Country

Saturday, March 8. After a full day of travel that includes refueling stops at Elmendorf Air Force Base in Alaska, and Yokota Air Force Base in Japan, we land in Viet Nam at Cam Ranh Bay airbase on the South China Sea in the early evening of March 8. We are quickly transferred to a waiting C-123 plane for the short 35-mile flight south to the large Phan Rang airbase where our USAF 823rd Combat Security Police Squadron (CSPS), the in-country location of "Operation Safeside," is headquartered. At the entrance to the compound a large-lettered sign proclaims: "Welcome to Ranger Country."[7]

As a First Lieutenant, I am the Combat Security Leader of Section 6, "B" Flight, 823rd CSPS, a section that will fluctuate anywhere from 34 to 44 men. I listen with heightened anxiety as our 823rd squadron commander outlines our orders. My unit is to be immediately flown to Binh Thuy airbase, 250 miles further southwest in the Mekong Delta, to supplement its regular security police squadron. An experienced in-country airman in the room chuckles as he informs me that Binh Thuy is nicknamed "mortar alley" because, up to that point in the war, it had been the most attacked of all ten 7th Air Force bases in Viet Nam.[8] During the February 1969 TET Offensive alone, it had been hit with 11 mortars. Hearing this brings a lump to my throat and a heavy knot in my stomach. What fucking luck, I thought! My insecurity and anxiety are only increased by the fact that I do not have an experienced NCO, only a staff sergeant who has no more interest in being in the 823rd than I.

Binh Thuy

It is late in the evening. With no time to waste, two "deuce and a half" (2-1/2-ton) trucks transfer us with our gear to the awaiting C-123. Near midnight, our plane sets down on the runway at Binh Thuy airbase. As the pilot nervously observes flashes in the distance, he screams at us to exit as fast as possible so he can rapidly become airborne to avoid incoming mortars. We hear explosions in the distance but nothing seems to be hitting close to the base as we grab our gear and scramble off via the large rear drop-down loading door. The base personnel who are there to greet us escort us with small flashlights into a nearby bunker as a precaution, due to incoming mortar warnings. When they deem all is clear, we are guided to our respective quarters for the night. Later we learned that 50 military targets were hit last night in Viet Nam, but Binh Thuy air base is spared.

Sunday, March 9. I am provided an air-conditioned trailer, and am issued a US Government Viet Nam vehicle driver's license authorizing my use as needed of M-151 jeeps, V-100 Armored Personnel Carriers (APCs), deuce-and-a-half cargo trucks, and station wagon passenger vehicles.

---

[7] At the time of our arrival, Secretary of Defense/War Melvin Laird and Chair of the Joint Chief of Staff General Earle Wheeler are in South Viet Nam discussing vietnamizing the war. On March 19, Laird asks Congress for $156,000,000 to increase capabilites of the South Vietnamese military [Bowman, 222-223].

[8] Roger P. Fox, *Air Base Defense in the Republic of Vietnam, 1961-1973* (Wash., DC: Office of Air Force History, USAF, 1979), 172-184. The chronology of attacks listed in Appendix 1 reveals Biny Thuy had been hit 45 times as of March 8, 1969.

I meet with the Major who is in charge of the regular base security police, and his operations officer, a Captain. The Captain shares with me that he is a friend of my 823rd squadron commander. He also tells me something that surprises me—that he had eagerly sought the very position I held and that he knew from my commander that I did not want the assignment. I wonder out loud if perhaps we might be able to swap assignments, even though I have been told it is not possible at this stage. What luck, I thought! Now I have to work closely with a guy who clearly resents me.

Since 7th Air Force has assigned our Safeside section to augment Binh Thuy's regular security police, I am to work in close cooperation with the host security squadron. The Major assigns me to serve as the night security commander for all Operation Safeside and regular security personnel, about 130 in all, from 8:30 pm to 6:00 am, seven days a week. Each member of my six, six-man fire teams is issued 270 rounds of M-16 ammo. In addition my unit is assigned five strategically positioned machineguns. We also have several electronic Starlight Scopes, which greatly aid in picking up faint light at night magnifying it 40,000–50,000 times, producing visible images in a yellow-green hue. My equipment manifest lists an ungodly arsenal of M-16s, 81mm mortars, two kinds of machine guns, M-72 rocket launchers, 90 mm recoilless rifles, parachute pop flares, hand grenades, portable anti-personnel radar units, several Smith and Wesson .38 revolvers, shotguns, ammunition for each type of firearm, and three jeeps! *Yikes!*

Located in Phong Dinh Province in IV Corps, 90 miles southwest of Saigon, Binh Thuy is the smallest of the ten 7th Air Force bases in country. Just over a half-mile wide and almost a mile and a half long—less than a square mile—its size is sufficient for securing the longest jet-capable runway in the Mekong Delta at over 6,000 feet. Situated seven feet above sea level with no landing or runway lights, its very low buildings, including an extremely short 15-foot control tower, make it difficult to be targeted by mortars and recoilless rifles. The base was built in 1964–1965 for the US by RMK-BRJ (Raymond International, Morrison-Knudsen, Brown & Root, and J.A. Jones Construction), a US consortium of private builders.[9]

At the time Binh Thuy housed a US Air Force combat support group of about 900 personnel, plus Vietnamese military. A very important facility located in a far corner of the base—the 22nd Tactical Air Support Squadron (22nd TASS)—is responsible for directing and controlling air strikes, including B-52 bombings, over a vast area of southern Viet Nam. Housed in a giant windowless building protected by extremely thick concrete walls, the 22nd TASS was one of five such centers in Southeast Asia. Laserbeam tracking viewed

---

9 Binh Thuy was constructed in 1964–65 by the huge Raymond International, Morrison-Knudsen, Brown and Root, and J.A. Jones Construction Consortium (RMK-BRJ). RMK-BRJ, "The Vietnam Builders," was a consortium of private corporations that turned South Viet Nam into a modern, integrated military installation comprised of a system of national communications, roads and highways, bridges, canals, airfields, army bases, ports, police stations, jails and prisons. They profited immensely from exclusive "no bid" contracts. This consortium later manifested in an altered form in Iraq, Houston-based KBR (Kellogg Brown & Root), a spin off from energy giant Halliburton whose CEO had been Richard Cheney, that acquired billions in US funds through no bid contracts to build the elaborate military infrastructure in Iraq. [James M. Carter, "The Merchants of Blood: War Profiteering from Vietnam to Iraq," *Counterpunch*, December 11, 2003: http://www.counterpunch.org/2003/12/11/war-profiteering-from-vietnam-to-iraq/].

on a large floor-to-ceiling plotting screen is used to guide precision bombing, while also supporting visual reconnaissance and convoy escort missions. Lieutenants sit in front of each of about two-dozen computers monitoring particular flights that are cumulatively visible on the huge screen, revealing numerous bombing flights in process, day and night. It is overwhelming to see the technology behind the massive amount of bombings being conducted.[10]

As I settle into my daily routine, I have a hard time getting used to the loud roar of helicopters and fixed-wing aircraft taking off and landing all day long. I soon learn to plug my ears with cotton to lessen the deadening noise, and mitigate potential damage to my ear-drums. Corresponding with all that flightline activity is the constant smell of diesel fumes. I wonder what breathing the toxic fumes might do to my health over the long haul, but there is no getting away from them.

As night security commander, I become acquainted with all present facilities, aircraft, and personnel that loom as targets for attacks. There are a variety of both SVNAF and USAF aircraft housed at Binh Thuy.[11]

Rumbling of the earth accompanied by what felt like mild earthquake tremors, I learn, is caused by B-52 bombings in the region. It is common to see clouds of dark smoke rising in every direction—a daily sight so routine it can hardly be called memorable. From studying regular intelligence reports in the command bunker I digest the pervasiveness of the bombings that support ground operations. Day after day, they are creating staggering cumulative body counts, virtually all of which are labeled Viet Cong (VC).

I am informed that on the day of our arrival, the nearby Can Tho Army Military Police (MP) commander was seriously injured in a fragging that left two dead and eleven wounded. The information put me a little on edge. Over time, the Can Tho MP station becomes a place I will regularly check when any of my troops get in trouble in Can Tho City, about five miles away.

Next to the Can Tho MP compound I discover a fenced-in area that contains hundreds of freshly imported Japanese Honda and Yamaha motorcycles. The MPs tell me they are used as "recruitment bait" to encourage young Vietnamese men to join the military.[12]

---

10 Years later, I resonated with veteran Eric Herter when he testified about high-altitude B-52 bombings guided by electronic targeting, that "the people of villages have gone from being human beings or even *gooks* and *dinks* to being grid-coordinates, blips on radar screens, dots of light on infrared film. They are never seen, never known, never even hated. The machine functions. The radar blip disappears. No village is destroyed. No humans die. For none existed" [Kim McQuaid, *The Anxious Years: America in the Vietnam-Watergate Era* (New York: Basic Books, 1989), 77].

11 Douglas Skyraider A-1 fighters bombers, A-37s and soon improved A-37B light attack planes, Sikorki helicopters, FAC (Forward Air Controller) planes, two Spooky aircraft C-47s gunships, Helio Couriers used in counterinsurgency operations, two Air America/CIA Douglas CH 47s used in counterinsurgency, F-5 fighter jets, T-28 propellor-driven small fighter-bombers/trainers, usually a number of C-130s and C-123s, and a variety of helicopters.

12 Bernard B. Fall, *Last Reflections On a War: Bernard B. Fall's Last Comments on Vietnam* (Garden City, NY: Double Day & Company, 1967), 47: US soldiers had nicknamed Saigon "Hondaville" due to the incredible traffic jams caused by thousands of military vehicles exacerbated by motorcycles.

Newly elected President Nixon has immediately launched his plan to end the war, or more accurately to end direct US troop involvement, by declaring increased support for South Vietnamese military forces. This process later would come to be called "Vietnamization"[13]—indeed, a strange term considering the Vietnamese had been killing and dying in large numbers under US direction for a number of years. But what it certainly meant was that South Vietnamese military officials and their air force and army units are expected to produce, and prove, dramatically increased body counts. Vietnamization would demand increased bombings in greatly expanded free-fire zones, euphemistically called *specified strike zones*.

We are briefed that US military forces would begin to be withdrawn in June or July. As ARVN forces are readied to begin their takeover from US personnel, SVNAF bombing becomes ever more important, especially as it is increasingly obvious to US peers and superiors that the ARVN lack enthusiasm and purpose for conducting ground actions[14] and they have astoundingly high desertion rates.[15]

I am briefed about the significantly expanded free-fire zones, which only make it more difficult to keep track of total areas encompassed within them, as if it matters at all.[16] I begin to sense, from reading various reports and from conversations with airmen who have been in country for awhile, that there is little that is off limits in terms of routine killing. Any Vietnamese can be tabbed as another VC in the quest for body counts. Official policy seems to be, "A dead Vietnamese is a VC, period!"

Early Acrimony

Shortly after my arrival at Binh Thuy, I am tested by the base security police operations officer, the captain who resents not having my job, in an encounter along the perimeter road during early evening hours, just as I am coming on night duty. We argue about the enforcement of the "free-fire zone" after he orders me to fire at a couple of fisherman

---

13 Interestingly, President Nixon did not internationally declare his Vietnamization policy until Friday, July 25, 1969, when he announced it at a press conference in Guam. Nixon stated that the United States henceforth expected its Asian allies to take care of their own military defense. Nixon had by this time already announced on June 8 the first installment of troop withdrawals. This came to be known as the Nixon Doctrine—to pursue peace through a partnership with American allies.

14 Fitzgerald, 2601, 307–308.

15 Greene, 1966, 148: Secretary "Mcnamara was forced to admit on May 11, 1966, that 12,000 were deserting every month." In 1968, the ARVN net desertion rate was equivalent to losing one division per month [Dougan and Weiss, 184]. Similarly high rates continued into 1970 when inside the US's Saigon government itself, there were some 30,000 people cooperating with the NLF (National Liberation Front), often identified as the Viet Cong/VC [FitzGerald, 418; McGehee, 156–157]. The reputation of the US-recruited, -trained, and -armed ARVN had become very tarnished early in the US war because of ARVN's chronic abuse of villagers while exhibiting corruption among their upper echelon [Appy, 1993, 158]. In cities like Vinh Long north of Can Tho, ARVN troops backed up trucks to store fronts and stole mass merchandise for their own profits [Luce and Sommer, 272]. By 1965, Vietnamese military officers were known to have ordered hamlets and villages "blown off the map" by airpower in order to cover-up their grotesque expropriation of local tax monies when the graft was threatened with exposure [Malcolm Browne, *The New Face of War* (Indianapolis, IN: Bobbs-Merrill, 1965), 210]. The incredible pattern of corruption was consistently exposed over the war years [David Halberstam, "Return to Vietnam," *Harper's*, December 1967, 47–58].

16 Sheehan, 617–618.

in a small boat. It is dusk, and they are barely visible, several hundred meters out in the waterway. I refuse. He sternly asks me if I am refusing his direct order? I respond, "I refuse your order." This leads to a physical tussle during which he threatens to charge me with failure to comply with a lawful order. I tell him, "Fuck you," and repeat that I am not going to fire on the fishermen or order my men to do so. Finally, he fumes off. I didn't know what he might do, but I am prepared to face the consequences, whatever they might be.

Body Bags

A little less than two weeks after arriving in Viet Nam, I am jolted when I observe a pile of body bags on a pallet on the Binh Thuy flightline, presumably awaiting a flight to a morgue in Saigon. They sit there for an hour or so before being loaded on a plane. One bag is ripped and I could see an arm partly hanging out—my first glimpse of a dead US soldier since arriving in country.[17]

Congressional Correspondence

Already pretty pissed off about the war soon after my arrival, I write letters to my New York US Senators, Jacob Javits and Charlie E. Goodell, both Republicans. I described the illegality and barbarity of the war and ask that they demand immediate and unconditional US withdrawal. I actually receive sympathetic responses, including this from Goodell: *"Thank you [f]or bringing to my attention your concern with the progress in peaceful settlement of the fighting in Vietnam and your suggestion for an immediate cease fire and withdrawal of troops."*[18]

March 27. Admiral Elmo Zumwalt, commander of all naval forces in Viet Nam, paid a visit to Binh Thuy air base to formally welcome a new squadron of OV-10 Bronco light attack, observation and forward air control (FAC) aircraft. We are all alerted of his presence, which is mildly intriguing at the time. Although I am not on duty during his visit, I do manage to catch a glimpse of the admiral from a distance.

---

17 Later, my 823rd Operation Safeside lieutenant counterpart at Pleiku airbase, who also served as its night security commander, told me he observed, almost nightly, pallets loaded with body bags arriving *and* departing within the same nighttime hours so that few US personnel ever got to see these fatalities, a concerted effort to prevent demoralization of the troops. In the Central Highlands, 250 miles north of Saigon, about 45 miles east of the Cambodian border/Ho Chi Minh Trail, Pleiku airbase housed numerous forward air controller missions, provided close air support for numerous ground troop operations, and was a major center of air commando and counterinsurgency operations. This combat context was far different than what I experienced at Binh Thuy, no matter how hostile I found conditions there. The closest US Army combat operations were 40 miles to the north, and fatalities from those operations likely were flown directly north to the morgue in Saigon before departing on planes for the US.
  The June 27, 1969 issue of *LIFE* magazine revealed the photos of 242 soldiers killed from May 28 through June 3. A number of these fatalities were likely inside those body bags my counterpart witnessed night after night on the Pleiku flightline. Over the course of 1969, there were 11,527 US fatal casualties in Viet Nam, or an average of 222 killed per week.
  18 Charles Goodell had been my US Congressional Representative (May 26, 1959–September 10, 1968) before being appointed to the US Senate by New York Governor Rockefeller to replace Robert F. Kennedy's unexpired term after the latter's assassination on June 5, 1968. Goodell was from the same Jamestown region of southwestern New York in Chautauqua County.

Pilot Killed

April 2, in the afternoon. During a routine roam in my jeep along the flightline, I receive word that an incoming flight has been hit and is requesting an emergency landing. The base fire truck races to the flightline along with a medic crew. The fuselage of the T-28 propeller-driven fighter-bomber-trainer is visibly riddled with bullet holes but lands safely with a Vietnamese co-pilot at the controls in the rear seat. The US pilot in the forward seat is slumped, with a single stream of blood cascading down his cheek from one bullet hole in his left temple. This is the second dead US soldier I have witnessed since my arrival in country, and I am sickened and depressed by the sight. *Oh my God, what a mess,* I think, *and I am right in it.*

April, first week. We receive intelligence reports showing that the nearby hamlet of My Thuan in the District of Binh Minh in southeastern Vinh Long Province has been hard hit by the NLF, and suffered a number of casualties. Binh Minh, just across the Bassac River from Can Tho City, is considered a strategic location due to its proximity to Highway 4, the main route between Can Tho and Saigon, and the attack signified that VC are very active in our area. It appears that Phong Dinh Province and Can Tho City have become more vulnerable since the number of friendly ground forces have been reduced in our immediate area.

New South Vietnamese Pilots; New A-37Bs

April, first week. South Vietnamese pilots newly trained by the US arrive. Simultaneously, improved US A-37B jet fighter bombers are transferred to the SVNAF. The SVNAF pilots at Binh Thuy are critical to supplement the unreliable ARVN ground forces operating in and around the small cities to our north. Many of the ARVN are clearing populations in concert with US Army's 9th Infantry Division operations further north in Kien Hoa Province. Expanded free-fire zones facilitate Vietnamization "pacification" operations.

Scary Moment

April 6, Sunday morning. I accompany the operations officer of the regular base security squadron on a routine reconnaissance mission in a Hughes OH6 "Loach" helicopter to observe areas surrounding our air base in both Phong Dinh and southern Vinh Long Provinces. I have been doing this with him for the last two weeks, despite the acrimony between us. However, on this particular morning, we experience a scary moment when our helicopter suddenly experiences difficulty staying in the air over southern Vinh Long. The pilot tells us he thinks the rotor blade is malfunctioning, perhaps from groundfire. The helicopter ride becomes turbulent and choppy as the pilot quickly drops altitude. When we land with a jolt in a rice paddy I am thrown out of the open door into the wet paddy. Though I experience some bruising, I am relieved to be able to quickly stand upright, only to immediately drop down again as groundfire seems to be coming from our right flank. After a brief, cautious assessment, we determine that the popping noises are not groundfire after all, and I breathe another sigh of relief. With the help of an ARVN NCO from a nearby kitchen unit, our pilot earnestly works on fixing the rotor blade, and within an hour we are able to take off again, fingers crossed. We return safely to Binh Thuy by midday, but after this anxiety-producing flight, I decide to discontinue any further recon flights. I am not convinced they are accomplishing anything anyway, since the VC are unlikely to make any obvious movements during daytime in the primarily treeless delta. Although the flights have served as good time-killers, and the base security operations officer and I were reasonably amicable with each other during these morning missions, enough is enough. As a side note, the pilot subsequently learns that the Loach helicopter model we have been flying has a record of chronic problems with tail rotor blades. The average life of these blades turns out to be 105 hours, just a fraction of their programmed life expectancy. Oh well; just a minor detail.

April 10-11 Attacks

April 11, Friday morning. Fresh intelligence reveals nearly four dozen coordinated mortar- and-rocket attacks throughout South Viet Nam last night. Thankfully, though our base siren warned us of incoming, no mortars struck inside our base perimeter, but a nearby Buddhist temple was hit resulting in several casualties. This round of attacks of course make us all anxious. More significant from a military and political perspective, the large city of Vinh Long, a Provincial capital of 100,000 people, located less than twenty miles northeast of our base, is hit with dozens of mortars, causing many casualties, including a number of deaths.[19] This news causes increased panic in the command bunker.

Binh Thuy Vietnamese base commander Colonel Anh is furious about the April 10-11 attacks, especially the devastation in Vinh Long City. It is a compelling moment to unleash his newly US-trained SVNAF pilots and their newly US-supplied A-37B fighter-bombers to begin systematic bombing of numerous "targets" in the region around Binh Thuy, especially in the provinces of Phong Dinh to the south and west, and Vinh Long to the north. He is under intense pressure to impress his US military masters, both politicians and generals, with increased body counts to prove the initial success of Vietnamization. Except for the cities of Sa Dec and Vinh Long, the entire Vinh Long Province is considered a free-fire zone. The thirty villages in the southernmost section of the province closest to Binh Thuy are all within free-fire zones and therefore easy bombing targets. I have only met base commander Colonel Anh in passing and did not really know him. In fact, I have never met and only rarely seen his US Colonel counterpart.

Though the city of My Tho is 25 miles northeast of Vinh Long, it is the family home of both South Viet Nam's First Lady (President Thieu's wife), and respected General Nguyen Khanh, the former South Vietnamese general who became prime minister after Diem's coup. Colonel Anh feels this latest Viet Cong activity is getting too close to My Tho for comfort and he apparently has been in contact with President Nguyen Van Thieu.

---

19 Later it was revealed that the city, which prior to TET 1968 had been considered relatively safe, was struck by more than 100 mortars injuring 103, killing 15, indicating that it was still unsafe from large scale VC attacks despite US intelligence saying otherwise. [Bowman, 225].

A Serious but Strange Request

April 13, Sunday evening. I am in the command bunker examining new intelligence data when Anh approaches me with a surprising question. Speaking quite good English, he asks if I might do him a favor. Though outside my chain of command, he nonetheless asks if I would be willing to help him assess whether the new pilots were in fact hitting their designated targets. I find his request so strangely inappropriate I have a hard time taking it serioiusly. I tell him I am not interested. Then he explains that there are no trustworthy ARVN units available to conduct post-bombing ground assessments since they are busy augmenting the intense campaign of the US Army 9th Infantry Division forty miles further north in Kien Hoa Province called Speedy Express.

Why the fuck does he want me to make assessments? He prefers, he said, that a US officer make some initial assessments. I presume that in his mind the presence of a US officer might provide added validity to any report on the success (or failure) of the bombings. However, I tell him, there are other officers or NCOs with more experience who would be much more competent and reliable than me. He tells me recent intelligence information gathered from VC prisoners at the nearby Can Tho CIA interrogation center suggests that one or more of the new pilots are VC infiltrators who intend to sabotage missions or defect.[20] This seems far-fetched to me. If any of the pilots are suspected of being VC they will not survive more than a day. They would be tortured and killed.[21] Since I am relatively

---

20 There were a number of incidents in the 1960s of SVNAF pilots defecting with their planes to Cambodia. During a 1962 coup attempt two VNAF pilots bombed and napalmed Diem's Presidential palace in Saigon, though Diem and his family survived [John S. Bowman, ed., *The Vietnam War: An Almanac* (New York: World Almanac Publications, 1985), 55]. One was shot down by anti-aircraft fire while the other escaped to Cambodia [John Morrocco, ed., *The Vietnam Experience: Thunder from Above, Air War, 1941–1968* (Boston: Boston Publishing Co., 1984), 14]. In 1963, a Royal Lao Air Force T-28 piloted by Lieutenant Chert Saibory defected to North Vietnam and it became the first fighter aircraft in the North Vietnamese Air Force [IstvanToperczer, *MiG-17 and MiG-19 Units of the Vietnam War* (London: Osprey Publishing Ltd., 2001), 8–9.]. In 1964, a SVNAF pilot flew to Cambodia in protest of Diem's persecution of Buddhists [Albert Grandolini, Tom Cooper, and Troung, "Indochina Database, Cambodia, 1954–1999, Part 1," *ACIG Journal*, Jan. 25, 2004: http://www.acig.org/artman/publish/article_410.shtml.]; In 1966 two SVNAF pilots defected with planes to Cambodia [http://www.aeroflight.co.uk/waf/aa-eastasia/cambodia/cam-af1-aircraft.htm].

On April 8, 1975, near the end of the war, Nguyen Thanh Trung, a 26-year-old SVNAF pilot who had been a US trained fighter pilot took off from Bien Hoa airbase and dropped four 500-pound bombs on Thieu's presidential palace in Saigon. He had become sympathetic with the Viet Cong after his father was murdered by South Vietnamese troops. After Trung dropped the bombs, he flew to a runway prepared by the Viet Cong 125 miles north of Saigon. On April 28, 1975, he led a small squadron of planes bombing Saigon's Tan Son Nhut airbase, as US Americans began fleeing Saigon [www.vnaf.net/april75/palace_bomb.html].

President Johnson's Rolling Thunder bombing campaign, initiated in 1965, was a joint operation with the South Vietnamese Air Force (SVNAF). But because rival factions competed for power in Saigon, with Nguyen Cao Ky holding the balance, SVNAF pilots were often grounded because of fears of coup plots and defections. Thus, Rolling Thunder operations were often unable to meet scheduled strike dates, causing serious delays [John Morrocco, ed., *The Vietnam Experience: Thunder from Above, Air War, 1941–1968* (Boston: Boston Publishing Co., 1984), 54].

21 Many prisoners are warehoused in the grotesquely hot, overcrowded Can Tho Provincial jail built to house 500 but which then held 2,000, where nude detainees literally had no room to sit [Luce and Sommer, 157]. It was one of more than 80 built by the French after 60 years of colonial government [Greene, 1965, 15]. By 1970 there were an estimated minimum of 200,000 political prisoners held in squalid conditions in Thieu's 42 provincial jails and four national prisons [Joseph Buttinger, "Thieu's Prisoners," *The New York Review of Books*, June 14, 1973].

new to Viet Nam and Binh Thuy, I suppose anything is conceivable, but I already feel over my head in responsibilities, and I am very naïve.

I speculate that he chose me to ask because I spend a lot of time in the command bunker studying various intelligence reports. I find that applying study habits I had formed in graduate school tended to relieve my acute anxiety, though such study isn't necessarily helpful in carrying out my nightly security duties. Another factor in Anh's decision to approach me may have been my notably consistent sobriety.

Serving as the base night security commander, I use my daytime free time to get away on solo trips into Can Tho City, an almost daily routine. I feel increasingly distant from many of the other military personnel after constant exposure to their racist and callous attitudes. I brought with me to Viet Nam two books my wife had given me before I left—one by Black Panther Eldridge Cleaver and a book of poetry by African-American Langston Hughes.[22] Reading these books contributed to my heightened sensitivity to the toxic racism of my culture, so viscerally present at Binh Thuy. When I am in Can Tho I get a little break from base culture, and also find some relief from the loud flight-line noise and the ever-present diesel fumes that so irritated me.

The fourth largest city in South Viet Nam, Can Tho has any number of cafés and restaurants catering to GIs. I can hang out in any one of the many *mamasan* bars, occasionally engaging in conversations with US army personnel, just to kill some time. Sometimes I run across members of the US Army's 9th Infantry Division, who tell me they are "kicking ass" in provinces to the north, especially Kien Hoa. [At the time, I had no idea just how incredibly bloody this campaign was (see pp. 144–145). Perhaps the helicopter I saw at the Can Tho Army airfield had been involved in this ass-kicking operation. Its front was painted with snarling teeth of a dragon with the words, *Death is our business, and business is good.*]

Anh assures me that this proposed extra-duty assignment will occur during safe daytime hours. He tells me a scattering of ARVN troops on logistical missions will be around to provide additional "comfort." I begin considering this assignment as just another way to kill time. A trusted Vietnamese lieutenant will accompany me, directing my driving to the target locations. Anh suggests that a half dozen or so of such assessments would be sufficient to give him the confidence to determine if there are, or are not, bad apples in the new pilot group. The first mission is to begin tomorrow morning. *What?! Fuck! Jesus Christ, tomorrow?* He assures me that each assessment is not likely to take more than two or three hours. Finally, with some anxiety, I reluctantly agree to do it. I wonder if I will feel the same in the morning.

Little did I know, the traumatic events of Monday, April 14, 1969, would change me forever. They are described in my introduction to this book, in the section titled "A Snapshot of Viet Nam 'Service'" (pp. xiii–xvi). I returned to my duty as night security commander at Binh Thuy Air Base emotionally shaken, feeling weak physically, and entertaining suicidal thoughts as I struggled to come to grips with what I'd just experienced.

---

22 Eldridge Cleaver, *Soul On Ice* (New York: A Delta Book, 1968) and Langston Hughes, *The Panther and the Lash: Poems of Our Times* (Alfred A. Knopf, Inc., 1967).

During the night after this traumatic experience, I choose to walk rather than drive my jeep along the Binh Thuy perimeter. I still can't fathom what I saw and smelled in that bombed village. Usually I drive the perimeter road in my jeep with lights out, slowly moving from security post to security post, checking on the alertness of my men. I carry water, coffee, and snacks. Smoking is absolutely prohibited so as to avoid targeting triggered by the glow of a cigarette or flames of a match. Sometimes during my rounds I find men dosing off, a no-no that only makes me more anxious. When this happens, I of course wake them up, even though every position has a minimum of two men present, ensuring at least one is awake and alert. I am so disturbed and distracted by what I witnessed earlier in the day, that walking helps me achieve a semblance of calm reflection, even for a moment. I consciously take deep breaths in an effort to relax, breaking the practice of shallow breathing I have developed to enable acute hearing to pick up the slightest noise off the perimeter during the darkness of night. The slightest splash of water or rustling of tall grass off the perimeter can signify nearby enemy movement.

I replay in my mind the brusque manner in which Bo had asked me why I was crying, the way he had smirked when I responded that I had discovered my "family." I still feel the shock I experienced at his response and his callused reaction to the suffering of the bombing victims. I struggle desperately to believe that what I witnessed was an egregious, horrendous mistake, rather than an intentional crime. After all, why would we target a small fishing and rice farming community? Jesus Christ! What were those pilots thinking? It occurs to me that there must—*there must*—be a good explanation for targeting that village. Maybe I had jumped too quickly to the conclusion that the murderous bombing was intended to create body counts. Surely my country and its political and military leaders would not conceive of such a criminal policy, let alone carry it out.

Initially I decide not to participate anymore in these assessments. But after mulling it over, I reason that there must be some rational military or moral explanation for such bombings, and it would be a great relief to learn what they are. I conclude that I need more information to acquire a better foundation for making any judgment. To do this, I will need to conduct a couple more assessments. Okay, I say to myself, I'll go out again later this morning (it is now after midnight on Tuesday morning), and perhaps several other mornings later this week. It depends on what I find. I urgently need relief from the devastation I feel, otherwise, my thoughts easily turn to suicide. I so want to believe we Americans are the good guys. But what if we aren't? It is a troubling idea that I am not yet quite ready to entertain. It is easier to think something is wrong with me. *What a fucking mess, I am,* I think. *Jesus Christ, I need help!*

I continue to walk along Binh Thuy's perimeter road. At a post on the far northwest corner of the base, one of my men thinks he hears water rustling, though he didn't see any human movement through his starlight scope. One challenge is the grass surrounding the base, which had grown to six feet, even ten feet in places, making it more difficult to detect any approaching humans with the starlight scope. The potential threat momentarily distracts me from my distress. Taking no chances, I pop one of the several parachute flares strapped to my fatigues. The flare shoots up into the sky like a rocket and then its parachute opens, and it floats slowly back down to the ground while brilliantly illuminating the area below as in broad daylight. If something is detected, I always have the option of calling for an AC 47 "Spooky" gunship, which will arrive within a couple of minutes to provide ever more brilliant illumination, plus dramatic firepower if needed. In this case, seeing nothing, I feel relief. No call needed. At about 6:00 am, my men's day-shift replacements arrive and my night shift is over. Exhausted, I walk to my trailer quarters to catch a few hours of sleep.

At about 11:00 am I am awakened to go on another assessment mission. Here is another chance to refuse to go. Should I or not? I decide that I do desperately need to find an explanation. I get dressed and walk to my jeep, parked just outside my trailer. I drove again to the ferry crossing in Can Tho with Bo as my guiding passenger. After we cross the Bassac River, Bo directs me on a similar route into Vinh Long, and then left onto another narrow dirt track....

A Traumatic Week

Friday afternoon, April 18. The past week feels like a blurry, surreal nightmare after having visited five "targets" in southern Vinh Long Province. I have not seen Colonel Anh this entire time, but I presume Bo kept him abreast of what we have seen. Bo knows how upset I am, but he also knows I am earnest in seeking to understand the official bombing policy. By now it is clear to both of us that I will not be going on any more assessment missions, because quite simply they are no longer necessary. We have seen no evidence of sabotaged missions. There are no VC pilot infiltrators.

I estimate I have witnessed somewhere between 700 and 900 total Vietnamese civilians killed or mortally wounded in the five bombed villages we visited this week. I believe that murder is the correct term, since the bombing of those civilian villages was intentional, and no effort was made to provide medical assistance for those not killed instantly. My extreme naivete has rapidly evaporated. It is now incontrovertible that *all* the targets we investigated are undefended, *inhabited* fishing/farming villages. All of the homes and outbuildings are so completely destroyed, it is as if they never existed; just charred remains, barely identifiable. If any of those villagers survived the initial round of bombs, they were certainly finished off with the rolling and roaring flames of napalm bombs that follow. Napalm not only burns through flesh, but causes quick asphyxiation.

Is the US a lawless invader and occupier like it seems? I am 27, and still somewhat insecure. My brain is just starting to think critically. Here I am, participating in the destruction of small farming villages located 9,000 miles from my own hometown farming village in upstate New York. I know that under international law a people may rightfully defend their villages from outside attackers by any means possible. But these people didn't appear to have any means of defense. And I am their enemy.[23] *Fuck! Fuck! Fuck!*

---

[23] A great number of veterans like me witnessed atrocities rather than actively participating in them. We were complicit nevertheless. A terrible plight—for life! But I have to believe it was worse for those on the ground who directly participated in the direct murders of villagers. These experiences of course are a major contributor to PTSD. Often soldiers who complained or lodged complaints about commission of atrocities, which I did but regrettably only mildly, were isolated or punished, so the larger context of the war of atrocities, and US brutal policy in general, remained and remains unchallenged. No US court

Once again I entertain suicidal thoughts. In order to survive psychologically, I have to make one last effort to discover an explanation. I decide that tomorrow morning, Saturday, after getting off night duty and taking a nap, I will catch a plane to Tan Son Nhut and consult with our squadron intelligence office at 7th Air Force headquarters. Perhaps they will be able to provide a broader and more conclusive perspective.

Consult With Squadron Intelligence at Tan Son Nhut

Saturday morning, April 19, 1969. I hop a C-123 flight to Tan Son Nhut Air Base in Saigon in order to meet with our 823rd Combat Security Police Squadron's three-man intelligence section. There I spend time with one of the intelligence officers, Captain Paul, examining the week's bombings. We use grid coordinates within Vinh Long Province to look up reported bombings by date, and read the brief assessment of each bombing. What we determine from studying the data is that in all cases, bombing casualties are identified as Viet Cong (VC), with no mention of civilian inhabitants. It seems to me that some of the grid coordinates roughly correspond to areas I assessed. Paul admits he has been mystified by reports consistently indicating entire VC units being wiped out in US bombings, including B-52 strikes, only to discover these same units reappearing elsewhere a few days later. This was an "aha!" experience for both Captain Paul and me. Together we realize the fraud of the body counts. I have to confront the fact that bombing civilians is deliberate and intentional. Counting the dead as "enemy VC" is an effective way to meet the demand for increased body counts. The official policy seems to be, "A dead Vietnamese is VC, period!"

Though depressed, I also feel a strange sense of relief at now discovering a clear explanation for what I have witnessed. I am now confident in my conclusion of the official policy and unafraid to call it what it is: premeditated mass murder. Paul thanks me for sharing my observations and helping him confirm his suspicions that we aren't killing VC, especially in the Delta region. From this point on, I become expressly antiwar, and begin describing the war's lawlessness to my superiors every chance I get, virtually every day.

Still, there are unanswered questions. It is not clear to me how coordinated the various bombings are, or how complete the bombing reports, especially because of the expanding role of South Vietnamese pilots. I wonder how much Colonel Anh is coordinating his directed bombings from Binh Thuy with 7th Air Force? The extent and use of bombings is still allegedly controlled by 7th Air Force. But in the Delta region, bombings seem to be planned quite independent of Saigon/MACV/7th Air Force. Having come into full swing

---

ever entertained adjudging the legality of air strikes in populated areas as being in violation of the rules of engagement. No court ever examined the legality of counting dead civilians as part of enemy body counts [Chris Appy, *Working-Class War* (Chapel Hill, NC: University of North Carolina Press, 1993), 273].

Throughout the war, including at My Lai where many officers had knowledge of massacres or were eyewitnesses to them, the higher command levels remained nearly exempt from accountability and legal scrutiny. Thus, the policy of genocide with impunity continues according to historical pattern—precisely the unwritten policy of erasing memory upon which the United States of America is founded and has been maintained all along.

that spring, Vietnamization brought a dramatic increase in South Viet Nam Air Force bombings.[24]

I fear that this obsession with body counts will drive me insane.[25]

My ultimate superior, 7th Air Force Commander General George S. Brown, is in fact lying about who is being murdered in these villages.

While at Tan Son Nhut I enjoy a conversation with my B Flight Commander, Captain Joel, a six-foot-five African-American career officer from Louisiana. Joel listens patiently as I describe my distress about the bombings, and share my firm conclusion that it is deliberate policy to murder civilians for the sake of achieving high body counts. To my great relief, Joel not only affirms my earnest search to get to the bottom of my dilemma, he actually commends my efforts. He encourages me to tell it like I am seeing it, while at the same time he cautions me to continue to conscientiously carry out all my assigned duties as Binh Thuy's night security commander

Relating to security responsibilities, I share with him another problem I face. Several of my men have already received "Dear John" letters from girlfriends or wives, and this is contributing to declining morale that impacts their capacity to be fully focused during all-night security duty. Captain Joel encourages me to spend as much personal time as necessary with these men, to serve as a sort of father figure for them, even though some are only a few years younger than me. I decide to let it be known that I will make a greater effort to talk with them during daylight hours if they are open.

---

24 SVNAF bombings increased 28.5 percent between April and May, with much greater increases throughout the remainder of 1969 and 1970 [Littauer and Uphoff (eds.), *The Air War in Indochina* (Boston: Beacon Press, 1972), 276].

25 Anthony Herbert, *Soldier* (New York: Dell, 1973), 402: A professional soldier with much combat experience, Colonel Anthony Herbert described the US sickness with body counts: *If anything has happened to our country as a result of the Vietnam War, it is our national infection with the sickness of the numbers game. We reduced the blood and suffering and the death and destruction to mere ciphers, and in so doing we reduced our own souls. Numbers don't die; people do. Columns of figures don't disintegrate in the explosion of a bomb; human beings do. Statistics don't bleed, and if you can make your war a war of numbers, you have no trouble sleeping. Most generals and presidents sleep well.*

RE controversy of estimating enemy numbers: Sam Adams, *War of Numbers: An Intelligence Memoir* (South Royalton, VT: Steerforth Press, 1994); Harold P. Ford, *CIA and the Vietnam Policymakers: Three Episodes 1962–1968* (Wash., DC: Center for the Study of Intelligence, Central Intelligence Agency, 1998), 89–90, 93, 100, 103; Valentine, 272. In a January 23, 1982 CBS documentary, *The Uncounted Enemy: A Vietnam Deception*, former prodigious CIA researcher Sam Adams, a descendent of the celebrated Adams family of Massachusetts, accused General William Westmoreland of a deliberate cover-up in *under*estimating enemy forces. General Westmoreland, commander of all military operations in Viet Nam, 1964–1968, with the encouragement of his civilian "pacification" advisor, had issued 1967 instructions that effectively directed an order that VC strength would not exceed a 300,000 ceiling. But after four research trips to Viet Nam, Adams concluded that senior military and intelligence officers were underestimating the strength of the Viet Cong and North Vietnamese forces *by half*. He concluded that total enemy forces in South Viet Nam numbered 600,000. Despite Adams' research, by late 1967 military and CIA reports continued to issue reports using the much lower numbers. Adams responded, proclaiming the estimates were ill informed and incoherent, less than candid and amounted to unwise "self-delusion." TET 1968 changed all that. Westmoreland's insistence on the 300,000 figure indeed was an artificial position dictated by political considerations in Washington. Westmoreland subsequently sued Adams and CBS for libel but the case was settled with a mere apology. Westmoreland's lawyers concluded he would lose the case if it went to trial.

Joel tells me officials at 7th Air Force are impressed with my regular situation reports helpful in evaluating regional security conditions in and around the hostile environment of Binh Thuy and Can Tho. Gosh! Up until that moment, I had no idea my reports were even being read. Was he telling the truth I wonder? I often feel I am still functioning like a graduate student, processing and reporting information that comes to my attention. I certainly appreciate hearing that someone somewhere is not only reading my reports, but finding them useful.

Before parting, Joel calls over another airman and asks him to take a photo of the two of us with an instant Polaroid camera. When the camera spits out the developed photo a couple minutes later, Joel grabs it and writes on the back: "Tan Son Nhut AB, RVN, 19 April 69, Pacifist and Warrior" and then signs his name. I think he recognizes the radical transformation that has taken place in me, before I fully realize it myself.

April 20, Sunday. I return to Binh Thuy wearing a broken peace sign about my neck along with my dogtags. I possess a renewed confidence that my observations revealed, beyond a reasonable doubt, an intentional policy of turkey-shoot bombings of inhabited villages.

While I was in Saigon on Saturday, the remainder of my troops had arrived at Binh Thuy Air Base. They include an experienced NCO, Tech Sgt Jim, plus a three-man counter mortar radar unit, a medic, and three administrative support personnel, making a total of 44 men in my Section, including myself. Jim, a real lifer, is one of the original 18 USAF security personnel who graduated from the Army's Ranger School at Fort Benning, Georgia, and is on his third tour in Viet Nam. He has a shaved head. His demeanor is calm, somewhat quiet, but very personable. He seems extremely competent, and his presence greatly eases my regular anxiety. The two of us get along all right, and I enjoy conversing with him about politics. We both detest President Nixon. I laugh when he tells me he favors famous Teamster official, Jimmy Hoffa, for US President, despite the fact Hoffa is currently doing time in federal prison for bribery and fraud. The medic also has a great sense of humor and adds much needed moments of comic relief.

With an experienced NCO present, my nighttime security duties will be more equitably shared, and I don't feel it is all on me. We decide that, on some nights, only one of us needs to be on the perimeter, unless intelligence reports or warning sirens indicate an imminent threat.

Confrontation in the Binh Thuy Command Bunker

Monday, April 21. I meander into our BT command bunker to examine the latest intelligence reports. I take special note of the wall maps with pins indicating the latest VC sightings in our area. Virtually all are in free-fire zones in Vinh Long and Phong Dinh Provinces, which suggests imminent bombings in numbered grid coordinates, each pin likely representing one or more inhabited "targets."

I examine a 1965 census of South Viet Nam conducted by the US Mission in Saigon. It reported populations for all 45 provinces, showing Vinh Long's population at nearly 600,000 inhabitants distributed among 81 villages. Each village usually contains five to ten smaller hamlets, and each hamlet is typically further a grouping of "settlements," or clusters of extended families. The census lists the Vinh Long population density as 810 persons per square mile with average family size of 6.3 persons. Phong Dinh Province, within which Binh Thuy and Can Tho city are located, has another 40 villages.

I deduce there must be thousands of "settlements" recognizable from the air, located within officially designated free-fire zones (which I now think of as genocide zones), each considered an "enemy target." I calculate that each target community might represent 100 and 200 human beings to be annihilated. Though not guided by electronic sensors like so many pilots operating in other parts of the country, the pilots of the low-flying bombers over southern Vinh Long Province can easily see the villagers below—perhaps instructed to consider them non-human—and watch villages disappear, instantly incinerated in flames fed by napalm. It is as if the village never existed. It is just a horrible fucking game.

I feel rage building up inside of me as I walk to the large map on the wall and begin pulling out pins, angrily proclaiming that these are all villages—undefended, inhabited villages. A major I have never seen before, about six-foot-five and broad-shouldered, suddenly appears, grabs my arm and shoves me out of the bunker. Nearly six-foot-three myself, I am taken by surprise, and perhaps in a bit of shock, as I slowly walk away from the command bunker. I ponder the reality that US policy amounts to genocide, that nobody seems to give a shit, and that a strange officer has just assaulted me. Trembling and near tears, I am grief-stricken, dejected and depressed.

April 21. On this same Monday, the USAF conducts routine aerial spraying of chemical herbicides around our base perimeter. Necessary for Binh Thuy's security, the herbicides destroy the tall elephant grass and other vegetation that furnish concealment for potential sapper attacks. I am fully supportive of the periodic spraying. Though my thoughts are more and more that I am on the wrong side in this war, I nonetheless want base personnel and myself to be safe from dangerous attacks.[26]

Late this evening, I wander over to the Binh Thuy officer's club, a hangout for both US American and South Vietnamese pilots. What I hear certainly doesn't settle me down any. Vietnamese people are often referred to as *gooks*, by both US and South Vietnamese pilots and air crew. They proudly describe the success of their daily bombings of targets. As long as they are thought of as "communist" targets, the pilots can just consider them easy and nameless "VC." Some of the pilots are watching a pornographic movie on the patio while enjoying steaks and beer with Vietnamese "girlfriends" (prostitutes) when an incoming siren suddenly sounds, warning of potential incoming. I scramble with everyone else into the club's bunker. The explosions remain distant, and fortunately none seem close enough

---

26 In the more specific areas in the Mekong Delta where I served in 1969, chemical spraying occurred between December 14, 1965 and June 27, 1970 at Can Tho, Binh Thuy, Sa Dec, Long Xuyen, Cao Lanh and Vinh Long. Official data revealed there were (1) 70,550 gallons sprayed of Agent Orange, contaminated with a lethal variation of dioxin, a mix of 2-4-5-trichlorophenoxyacetic acid (2-4-5-T) and 2-4-dichloro-phenoxyacetic acid (2-4-D), used as a defoliant (51.3%); (2) 53,504 gallons of Agent White containing Picloram and 2,4-D, aka Tordon/hexachlorobenzene used as a defoliant (38.9 %); and (3) 13,525 gallons of Agent Blue containing arsenic/cacodylic acid intended to destroy rice crops (9.8%); for a total of 137,579 gallons (100%).

to hit on base. From inside the bunker I hear the clicking sound of the outdoor movie projector as the film continued to roll. At the "all clear" signal, couples resume their seats in front of the flick or move into nearby "fucking hooches" as if nothing has happened. The scene is so surreal I feel like I am in a Fellini movie but unable to leave the theater. Feeling my rage building, I race to the perimeter to focus on my nighttime security duties before I explode. But it is an appropriate time to get to the perimeter since the warning siren suggests possible mortars.

April 21, later that week. I notice a report in *Stars and Stripes* (an independent newspaper for soldiers) of the arrest and jailing of a young man for burning a US flag at an anti-war rally in the US. It discussed a new US Supreme Court ruling protecting desecration of the flag as free speech, which spelled exoneration for the young man. What a mind fuck, I think. Pilots who bomb and burn human beings in Vietnamese villages are seen as heroes and promoted, while people of conscience who burn the US flag—to me a symbol of the policy of burning human beings—are jailed. I sit on my bunk, head in my hands, too depressed to grasp this insanity. It all seems so evil and immoral. What distinguishes our armed forces from mercenaries, I wonder? Later I remember Thomas Jefferson's reference, in penning our nation's Declaration of Independence, to the "merciless Indian Savages."[27] I had recently been struck by those words while in law school. It was startling to realize how precisely the words "merciless savages" describe our behavior against the Vietnamese.

April, late in the month. The regular base security police First Sergeant asks to borrow a jeep for a daytime run into Can Tho. The 632nd (regular base security police squadron) is chronically short of jeeps due to mechanical failures and previous destructions from mortars. I have a third 823rd jeep that is normally unused, so I consent. That evening the First Sergeant got drunk in Can Tho, and on his drive back to Binh Thuy hit a deuce-and-a-half troop truck in a head-on collision, doing serious damage to the jeep and breaking one of his legs. His boss, the commander of the regular security police squadron, assures me I will get the jeep back, whether the same one fixed, or another similar one. When I finally receive a replacement in early July, I never think about matching its serial number with the equipment manifest list that I am responsible for. Later I am shocked to be charged with theft of my own jeep, since the jeep I received was a replacement, not the original one. This ultimately is one of the court-martial charges read to me upon leaving the country in August.

Resisting Pilot

May, first week. I am thrilled to meet a lieutenant pilot who has been grounded, first for refusing to fly bombing missions, and subsequently for refusing to fly psyop missions dropping anti-Communist propaganda leaflets on Vietnamese villages. He tells me that Vietnamese language leaflets announce to villagers that they are in free-fire zones and

---

27 The full phrase in the Declaration of Independence relates to King George III who *has excited domestic insurrections amongst us, and has endeavoured to bring on the inhabitants of our frontiers, the merciless Indian Savages, whose known rule of warfare, is an undistinguished destruction of all ages, sexes and conditions.* This seems to describe precisely the behavior and intent of the US war against the peoples of Southeast Asia.

warned to flee within a couple of days to designated safe areas to avoid being bombed. But, he shares with me, the leaflets are not clearly worded, and there really are no safe areas to which to flee. There are real reasons the vast majority of villagers do not leave, even at the risk of being bombed. They refuse to leave their farm animals, their sacred ancestral burial grounds, and their spiritual connection to the land. I imagine their experience is similar to that of the Indigenous in the New World in the 1600s when Europeans arrived and began forcing them off their lands. This pilot who is moved in a few days, presumably to the US for punishment, is the only other person I met while in country who is explicitly and passionately antiwar.

What I Learn at the Binh Thuy Library

Early May. The day after the lieutenant is sent back to the US for what I presume is a likely court-martial, I become ever more angry about the war, and am inspired to actually learn Vietnamese history. I venture into the small library at Binh Thuy, which consists largely of taped music on large reels. Many GIs copy songs onto other tapes using reel-to-reel taping machines, for their personal listening pleasure or to send home. But on this particular day, I want to read any history about Viet Nam I can get my hands on, since I know virtually nothing about the country. I initiate conversations with the base librarian, a US-hired English-speaking, young Chinese-Vietnamese woman named Anh Ly (nicknamed "Annie"). She had earned her degree in Library Science at Can Tho University before the battle of TET 1968 destroyed it. She leads me to a small history section on a back shelf of the library, and there I find several books of great interest. I immediately begin to read them and take notes as if I'm in graduate school preparing for an exam.

In a book by French journalist Bernard Fall, *Hell in a Very Small Place*, I learn that the French Indochina War dragged on from December 19, 1946 to May 7, 1954 (2,695 days) and cost France $10 billion, in addition to $954 million of US aid expended prior to July 1954.[28] I had no idea! Another book of Fall's, *Last Reflections on a War*,[29] shocks me again with the figure of one million Vietnamese having already died in the nearly eight-year war with the French. *Jesus, Christ, what are we doing here? Who do we Westerners think we are, anyway?*

But it is a book by two Cornell Professors that rocks my mind, *The United States in Vietnam*.[30] It explains, in very historical terms, the chicanery the US had instituted in 1945, and that continues up to the time of the book's publication in 1967, to assure destruction of the Vietnamese independence movement. I am outraged to discover that the US had sabotaged the Geneva Accords mandating the 1956 unifying elections. It seems strange that this book is offering me my first critical history lesson on Viet Nam, and the US involvement since 1945, and the French before. Why haven't I been briefed about this ugly history? Am I the only one that doesn't know this? It seems so critical for understanding

---

28 Bernard B. Fall, *Hell in a Very Small Place* (Philadelphia: J.B. Lippincott Company, 1967), vii-viii.

29 Bernard B. Fall, *Last Reflections ona War: Bernard B. Fall's Last Comments on Vietnam* (Garden City, NY: Doubleday & Co., Inc., 1967), 224.

30 George McTurnan Kahin and John W. Lewis, *The United States in Vietnam* (New York: The Dial Press, 1967).

the war. Even though they are in the base library, I doubt anybody else on Binh Thuy Air Base has read these books let alone studied them as I have, taking notes with pen and paper. The librarian seems surprised at my intense curiosity about Vietnamese history and the origins of the US war, and I wonder where her private sympathies lie.

Binh Thuy Attacked

On Sunday, May 11, shortly after midnight. Binh Thuy is hit with eleven mortars. My NCO is somewhere along the perimeter, but in the case of attack we work together to coordinate support for the security posts. When the warning siren sounds, I rush to my jeep, only to find it is not parked where I left it immediately outside my quarters. I am pissed. I am mystified as to what happened to it, but I have no time to puzzle over it at this moment. I immediately run to the perimeter road and walk briskly down it, looking for the first security post. Mortars are exploding inside the base and I just hope I don't take a direct hit. Two hours after walking back and forth on the dark perimeter road, I finally discover my jeep being driven by my nemesis, the Captain who serves as the regular security police operations officer. Though we have experienced acrimony there is no excuse for this and I let him know it. "You Shit! You're driving my jeep, you bastard. What the fuck!?" Without his own jeep, I figure he is probably jealous that I have three jeeps when I only need two, and simply got into my jeep and drove to the perimeter. I remind him that my third jeep is inoperable because his First Sergeant had borrowed it and then wrecked it in a serious drunk-driving accident.

Furious, I tell him that I am going to write him up in a formal serious incident report, that I will submit to 7th Air Force, for interfering with my command responsibilities by stealing my jeep during an attack. I spend a couple of hours handwriting my account of this breach using carbon paper in order to retain a copy for myself. The captain is startled at the intensity of my response, even though he himself had earlier threatened to file an Article 15 nonjudicial punishment against one of my men for not wearing a hat, an absurd charge. But he is a career officer and does not want any complaint in his record. He agrees that from here on out he will leave me and my men alone, and I will sit on my written report until I leave Viet Nam, at which time I will destroy it. We actually shake hands.

When I arrive with my jeep back at my quarters at about 6:30 am, I discover a mortar round has hit very near my trailer, and shrapnel has destroyed my window air conditioner. It never gets fixed, but I don't pursue it. I feel almost embarrassed to have air conditioning when none of my men have such privilege.

An Unusual, Surprising Invitation

Saturday, May 24. After a number of days spent in the library reading these books, the librarian asks me if I am interested in having dinner at her family's home in Can Tho. The invitation surprises me at first, and I am reluctant to agree. Then I speculate that the librarian is fascinated because I am the only officer on the base who is openly expressing my feelings about the war. My antiwar expressions to other NCOs and officers are becoming daily, increasingly irritating them.

I wonder if she is sympathetic to the Vietnamese revolution even though she has been hired to work as a librarian at this US air base. The question intrigues me.

Her invitation is unusual enough that I think perhaps it might be some kind of setup. Our quadron intelligence officer Captain Paul, who has shared several meetings with me at both Binh Thuy and Tan Son Nhut, has warned me that our squadron commander really has it in for me, which I am aware of. I don't want to be paranoid, but her unsusual request causes me a fair amount of anxiety. Is this perhaps some plan to undermine me? Or is it purely a social invitation? Dare I take a chance?

Another Dead Pilot

Sunday, May 25, 1969. The co-pilot lands a damaged OV-10 Bronco on Binh Thuy's runway with the pilot mortally shot in the head. I am not far away in my jeep at the moment and rush to the flightline along with an ambulance. This is only the third dead US military person I have personally seen. The OV-10 Bronco is a light attack, observation and forward air control aircraft designed for counter-insurgency combat.

Saint Norman

Sunday, June 1. I agree to dinner with the librarian's family. I follow a hand-drawn map she has provided with directions for driving to her family home in Can Tho City. I take a bit of a circuitous route and check several times to see if I am being followed. I finally find the home in a nice section of Can Tho. I enjoy a wonderful Vietnamese meal with polite, but rather lively conversation as some in her family speak good English. It both startles me and makes me a little anxious when the family starts discussing the history of people's revolutions, a conversation I have never had, nor considered having until that moment. How do they know they can trust me, a complete stranger? Or am I about to be arrested in a trap?

After dinner the family softly sings a special ode to Norman Morrison, the young man who had immolated himself in November 1965 outside Secretary of War/Defense Robert McNamara's office at the Pentagon. Morrison, a Quaker from Baltimore, Maryland acted in protest of the bombings of Vietnamese villages. When I suddenly understand that her family is singing about Norman Morrison, and that Morrison was a hero to them, I start crying.

This has special significance for me, because Norman Morrison and I happened to have graduated from the same small rural high school in western New York State. We were seven years apart in age, but he was the first Eagle Scout I ever knew and had made a big impression on me. When I first heard of his immolation while living in Washington, DC (see p. 198), I thought Morrison must have gone off his rocker. Now, I see it from a different perspective, directly the opposite. This family has no idea, of course, of the personal, historical connection I share with Norman, but they are moved by my show of emotion. It is an incredible moment, another of those surreal experiences.

Visits By Military Heavies

Thursday, May 22. US Secretary of the Navy John Chaffee arrives on a routine visit to Binh Thuy airbase and nearby Binh Thuy navy base.

Thursday, June 5, 1969. Vice-Admiral Elmo Zumwalt, Commander of Naval Forces in Viet Nam, makes a return visit to Binh Thuy.

A Light Basketball Moment amid Insanity

First week in June. In contrast with the heaviness of the war and the serious dinner conversation with the librarian's family in Can Tho, Binh Thuy is visited by Wes Unseld, the six-foot-seven, 250-pound NBA Rookie of the Year for 1968–69 as well as Most Valuable Player, playing for the Baltimore Bullets, and by Jon McGlocklin, a six-foot-five guard playing for the Milwaukee Bucks. They are on a goodwill tour to entertain US troops, and we briefly play a three-on-three basketball game on our one hot cement court. Unseld and McGlocklin split their time between the two teams. It is thrilling to be able to say I played with them, and to shake each of their hands.

Binh Thuy Attacked, Then I am Dispatched to Phan Rang

Friday, June 6, near 2 am. Binh Thuy is attacked with 11 mortars, destroying the mess hall, but creating no casualties.

Saturday, June 7. I am surprised when my unit without warning is ordered immediately dispatched to rocket-besieged Phan Rang Air Base some 250 miles further northeast, to provide extra security. Phan Rang is the in-country headquarters for our 823rd Combat Security Police Squadron, composed of 10 combat sections located at different air bases similar to the one I command, plus a weapons section and a separate intelligence section. I quickly find myself in another tense conversation with our 823rd commander. He again tells me I am "as good as a VC," slipping at one point in calling me like "vermin." I have no respect for the man. I tell him how Thomas Jefferson described Native Americans "merciless savages" in our Declaration of Independence, but that Jefferson had it backwards, that *we* are the savages—not the Indians, and not the Vietnamese. He simply walks away with a smirk, shaking his head. He likely does not take anything I say with any seriousness, just thinking that I am a loser, and a traitor for being so outspoken against the war. I wonder again why he even wants to keep me in the squadron.

Rocket Attack

Saturday, June 7, Phan Rang. A little before 4:30 pm in the afternoon, I and an Aussie officer I have just met at the officer's club over a beer are headed to our respective living quarters. We are walking down a slight grade when all of a sudden, with no warning, the Aussie threw me to the ground and jumps on top of me. There is a huge explosion. The first of three 107mm rockets explode within fifty or sixty yards of us, throwing litter and shrapnel in every direction. I hear debris hitting the ground around me. After the all-clear signal, we get up and the Aussie explains that he heard the eerie sound of an incoming rocket—something that usually didn't occur during daylight hours. A Camberra bomber pilot with the Royal Australian Air Force, he has been at the base for a number of months and is familiar with rocket attacks. His quick action likely saved my life and his. I am not used to the more powerful rockets, because at Binh Thuy we are only shelled by lighter mortars and recoilless rifles and they don't have the immediate air sound of approaching rockets.

We resume walking and find the remains of a totally destroyed structure nearby. I am shaken at what appears to be a severed head lying not far away. We learn that two airmen have been killed in the attack, along with a K-9 dog, and that eight people have been wounded. The first rocket has hit close to the post office damaging some living quarters, another hit near the BX, the third near the base theater. The emaciated severed head I glimpse is a horrible mess, and I wonder, does it belong to one of the airmen or to the dog?

Our primary daytime duty at Phan Rang throughout June is to construct a number of new bunkers. In addition, we alternately take turns with other forces to provide night perimeter security. We have not been provided any of the materials or equipment to build the bunkers. In order to fulfill the orders, we are forced to steal the necessary materials. Shit, I don't know how or where to acquire the necessary sand, bags, PCP steel plates and tools. The difficulty of carrying out orders causes extra anxiety. To construct the bunkers we need to fill hundreds, if not thousands of bags with sand.

Fortunately, Jim, my calm, experienced NCO, has a plan. "Don't worry, lieutenant. I got it covered," he tells me. He discovers where to get bags (or steal them perhaps), confiscates an "idle" military dump truck, and finds a nearby Vietnamese sandpit operator with a power shovel that can load our truck, multiple times and trips. True to his word, Jim drops off numerous loads of sand for our work projects. He also finds plates of PCP steel as well as shovels. We pay out of our own pockets for the labor of the Vietnamese power shovel operator, and for the sand. *Jesus Christ, what an amazing operation the US military is,* I think.

Wednesday, June 11, just after midnight. Phan Rang is targeted and hit with 17 rockets. This attack causes no casualties or serious damages, just anxiety. The next day, we learn that three US combat units are about to be withdrawn from Viet Nam—two Brigades of the 9th Infantry Division and a team from the 3rd Marine Division.

June 18, Wednesday, just before midnight. Phan Rang is attacked by 14 rockets, wounding one, but causing much anxiety and sleeplessness.

June 20, Friday, at almost 7:30 pm. Phan Rang is attacked by 4 rockets, damaging one aircraft.

Return to Binh Thuy

July 3, Thursday. My 823 CSPS Section 6 is flown back to Binh Thuy from Phan Rang. During the time of our stay in Phan Rang, it has been hit with 4 rocket attacks, but since March 1968, Phan Rang has been hit 27 times.[31]

July 4, Friday. My twenty-eighth birthday slips by quietly. I don't bother to tell anyone it is my birthday.

July 10, Thursday, a little before 9 pm. Binh Thuy is attacked by mortars, only one of which explodes inside our perimeter.

July 11, Friday. Binh Thuy is probed by two sapper units but both are repelled. Almost simultaneously, a satchel charge explodes in Ben Xe Moi red light district, four miles east of the base on the western edge of Can Tho City.

July 12, Saturday. An OV-10 Bronco from Binh Thuy is shot down, both air crew are presumed dead.

Sunday, July 13. Three probing sapper attacks are made but repelled along the Binh Thuy perimeter, while several satchel charges are once again set off in nearby Ben Xe Moi, killing four and wounding a large number.

July, final week. Two US helicopters and 1 SVNAF A-37 from Binh Thuy are shot down, all crew presumed killed. Three next door Navy PBRs (Patrol Boats, River) are destroyed during the same time frame, all crew presumed killed.

Wednesday, July 30. President Nixon makes an unscheduled five-and-a-half hour visit to US troops of the 1st Infantry Division at Dian, 12 miles south of Saigon, while also consulting with President Thieu and US commanders. This is Nixon's only trip to Viet Nam during his presidency.

I am elated to learn that the July 1969 issue of *Playboy* has published an antiwar letter written by a Pfc. Michael Madler, claiming that three-quarters of veterans oppose the war.[32]

Orders Home

August 2, Saturday afternoon. I receive a special telegram hand-delivered by courier from my commander at Phan Rang ordering me to immediately return to the States on the first available aircraft. Earlier in the morning, I receive a visit from an Army Judge Advocate General officer, a Captain from nearby Can Tho Army airfield, who informs me that I face three pages worth of court-martial charges upon my return to the US. My superiors,

---

31 Fox, 172–184.

32 Lewes, 162; In February 1971, an advertisement for Vietnam Veterans Against the War is published in *Playboy*, that includes the words, *We have seen the Vietnam War for ourselves. And from what we have seen, we believe that it is wrong, unjustifiable and contrary to the principle of self-determination on which our nation was founded.* The ad produces thousands of new VVAW membership applications.

of course, have been angered by my regularly expressed views about the immoral and lawless nature of the war. I have no idea what might happen, and feel another surge of anxiety, but at the same time I am greatly relieved to be leaving Viet Nam. I say goodbye to all my men and my NCO. I will never see any of them again.

In my officer evaluation report (OER, dated October 9, 1969), my reporting officer, Captain Joel, 823rd Flight B Commander, wrote:

> Lt. Willson expended considerable additional effort to expedite his section's adjustment to the extremely hostile environment at Binh Thuy AB, RVN . . . (and) devoted additional effort to become thoroughly familiar with the peculiarities not only of the security posts to which his men were assigned but, also, those positions manned by Vietnamese. His knowledge of associated functions such as the fire support furnished by Army Aviation Units was extensive.... Despite an inadequate communications system, Lt. Willson reliably kept his superiors well informed with accurate situation reports which generally aided higher headquarters in the evaluation of security conditions in the Binh Thuy AB area. His ability to communicate well with subordinates and to quickly obtain their respect and trust is remarkable. The period . . . was exceptionally well performed in a combat area of Southeast Asia.

However, the next highest superior in my chain of command, our 823rd squadron operations officer, Major Maynard, the "endorsing official," wrote an entire page rebutting the captain's evaluation. He berated me in several areas of performance. He understandably condemned the fact that my "personal views on the Vietnam War, which were expressed on a number of occasions, tended to create friction in certain quarters." He continued, "The Lieutenant's readiness to express them in a combat zone did not always reflect the best of tact." But, he concludes, "I have no doubt that in another career field, given a challenge compatible with his personal feelings, he could perform outstandingly." Of course, this is precisely what I had tried to explain to our commander when I first reported to 823rd ranger-type training at Fort Campbell, Kentucky, in December 1968.

Special note: The 823rd CSPS Intelligence officer, Captain Paul, visited me at Binh Thuy Air Base on two occasions, and I visited him at his Tan Son Nhut office on April 19, 1969, as discussed above, and again in early May. I was pleasantly surprised to receive an email from him in October 2003, long after his retirement, in which he reminded me of our visit at Tan Son Nhut in April 1969 some 34 years earlier where we discussed the "mystery" of the body counts and that our 823rd commander was out to get me killed:

> You told me everything. I knew why you were given that duty by our commander. He was trying to get both Captain Joel and I killed also. Joel fraternized with his troops also. The intel I was getting from the field made no sense to me so I went out on my own to see what was going on. Especially IV Corps area because I would get reports of dozens of VC KIA in a particular unit being wiped out in an ARC Light strike and

then a week later after the unit was supposedly vaporized there would be another firefight with that unit. I'd get reports like 24 VC KIA and two pistols captured. Never made sense until I started talking to people like you. You came to Tan Son Nhut and I showed you one of the after action reports of a hundred VC killed. You confirmed my suspicions that we weren't killing VC.

Captain Paul subsequently died of an Agent Orange–connected illness.

Epilogue: Viet Nam Nightmare Ends

August 5, Tuesday. I arrive back in the US at England Air Force Base in Alexandria, Louisiana, after having been in Viet Nam 151 days. I report to the personnel office to learn of my new assignment, but surprisingly they have no information about me, though there is more than a year left of my four-year Air Force tour. They tell me to take leave and return in a month. And, they know nothing about any court-martial charges. I wonder what the hell is going to happen to me?

In mid-August, I finally am able to relax a little bit while on a vacation with my wife at a B&B in Woodstock, Vermont. At breakfast on Saturday morning, August 16, we read in the morning newspaper about an incredible music gathering happening in a small town in upstate New York by the same name—Woodstock! I know nothing, but I am ecstatic to learn about it, thinking perhaps it signifies a radical shift in our cultural consciousness, a turn away from war and capitalist economics. Sitting next to us at breakfast is a couple from Connecticut, who, it turns out, are on a healing vacation after having lost their son, their only child, just a month earlier in Viet Nam. He had been a draftee, reluctantly serving his conscriptive combat assignment, hoping to return home and start a career in a healing profession.

As many as five hundred thousand people were celebrating at Woodstock. As a fresh war returnee, I was excited to detect a new spirit in the wind as I sat next to the couple grieving over their son's needless death. Suddenly I am overcome with emotion and begin sobbing. The mourning parents gently reach over, and for a few moments we clasp hands and cry together. I share their sadness, even as I am also flooded with joy that the eight-month living nightmare that began on December 16, 1968, the day I started USAF "ranger training," is finally over! Such relief! Thank the Great Spirit.

Final Duty Station: England Air Force Base, Alexandria, Louisiana

September 1969–August 1970. I am buried in a rather benign assignment as the executive support officer for the commander of the 250-man England AFB Supply Squadron in Alexandria, Louisiana. I am a conspicuous antiwar voice on the base, and drive a Volkswagon bug plastered with flower decals to work every day from my Alexandria home five miles away. On four separate occasions that year I was ordered into the base Wing Commander's office for some allegation or other of behavioral "indiscretions," all ridiculous, of course. This superior is a career combat pilot who had been a POW in a

German prison camp for nearly three years during WWII. I am sure he thinks I am a flake.

The informal charges the commander confronts me with in his office:

1. Conduct unbecoming an officer for participating in a local "civil disobedience" action/picket on a Saturday afternoon relating to racial discrimination at a local department store;
2. Defying the chain of command for seeking assistance from the base chaplain, instead of base housing office, for addressing local housing racial discrimination against African American airmen;
3. Communicating with my lawyer wife about so-called "confidential" issues of racism that exist on the base that she in turn mentioned while teaching her Louisana State University Extension sociology class on England AFB; and
4. Conduct unbecoming an officer for conducting a series of Sunday lectures at the local Alexandria Unitarian Fellowship on the history of US illegal and criminal intervention in Southeast Asia.

The book I used as the basis for my Sunday lecture series is none other than the one that rocked my mind from the Binh Thuy library, *The United States in Vietnam*, by the two Cornell University professors, Kahin and Lewis. I purchased the book shortly after my return to the US and I have already extensively underlined it.

Major Eng, my immediate commander at England Air Force Base is Chinese (from Formosa); he had formerly served as a pilot in Viet Nam. He politely accommodates my contentious attitude throughout the year. As his executive officer, I hear complaints from local merchants about supply airmen not keeping up with debt payments. He graciously wrote in my final officer evaluation report that "on his replies to civilian creditors, Captain Willson[33] was tactful but firm on protecting the individual right of the airmen concerned." He also commends me for conducting lots of counseling sessions with airmen experiencing various family, drug/alcohol, and financial problems. He concluded by saying that I was "an active participant in squadron athletics" and "encouraged other airmen to support the squadron athletic program." In one final supportive statement, he concluded, "This has undoubtedly contributed to the Squadron winning the Wing Commander's Trophy in base support competition." Interestingly, this is the same base wing commander who had admonished me on four different occasions in his office. But I was done with the USAF. As a former jock I love the fact that his very last words in my four years worth of officer evaluations lauded me for my athletic participation.

On August 30, 1970. I am formally separated from the US Air Force at the rank of Captain, after enduring 3 years, 11 months, 17 days in it. I happily receive a 13-day early out, which allows me to return to law school. Thankfully, despite earlier threats, I face no charges. Is

---

[33] Note: In November 1969, I was promoted to rank of captain. Such promotion was virtually automatic three years after commissioning, unless the candidate had received a court martial conviction.

it really true, I wonder, that I am separated with no discussion of any court-martial? Wow, I can't believe I am free! Soon, I will burn my military uniforms.

Civvy Return to Law School

I immediately resume study at the Washington College of Law at American University in Washington, DC, from where I had been drafted in 1966. At that earlier time, university dress code required a coat and tie. But when I arrive on campus in September 1970, most of the men have long hair and are dressed much more casually, wearing sandals and even beads around their neck. Pleasantly surprised by this huge change, I also make the acquaintance of several male students who are angry antiwar Viet Nam veterans like me. I had missed an entire radical cultural revolution.

One of the students mentions that he is attending meetings of the Weather Underground in the basement of a bookstore. I am fascinated with the Weather Underground's intense passion to end the mass murders by the US in Viet Nam and I accompany him one evening. I find the participants to be very colorful and theatrical with their antiwar expressions, but their reliance on rhetorical and strategic violence as a tool for change turns me off. Still, they possess a deep commitment to justice that few others can match. I relate very much to their stated desire to stop the human suffering caused by patriarchal structures. I tried the Communist Party, too, but I find their meetings to be too rigid and fundamentalist. I felt like I was back in Baptist church. My wife and I did attend the Unitarian church in Washington, DC, and there I find wonderful people who oppose the war, but seem to lack the intensity I crave. I have a hard time finding a group I can be comfortable with that shares my rage and passion, even though most people I am meeting at the time are very antiwar. I am still searching to this day.

Law: A Tool for the Powerful

I graduated from American University in 1972 with a Juris Doctor degree, passed the Washington, DC bar exam, and was soon admitted to the practice of law. But by the time I made it into the courtroom, I had apparently become far too sensitized—or perhaps radicalized—to obey the protocol of the court. I found I had a very strong visceral resistance to automatically standing up for the judge as he/she entered the courtroom. I think there were two things at play: an aversion to authority bred of my several years in the military, plus a change in consciousness that recognized the judge's role in overseeing what I was beginning to see as a fundamentally class- and race-based system—an understanding gleaned during my time living at the DC jail as well as my time in Viet Nam. To my own surprise, I could not agree to stand. Nor could I any longer follow the rote order to take an oath to uphold the Constitution, the purpose of which was to protect the powerful. I also found it impossible to respect the conspicuously displayed US American flag. I still, to this day, consider our flag the most violent symbol on Planet Earth.[34]

---

[34] From my Viet Nam experience I understand in a new way that being born a white male citizen of the US indoctrinated me with unearned and undeserved privilege. This had made me stupid. And this in turn tends to motivate one to remain stupid about the nature of the system that brought on this privilege. To emerge from stupidity I am finding takes courage, and a careful listening to my heart. Following courtroom protocol

I had personally participated in grotesque US criminality conducted with total impunity against the Vietnamese people even though I did not pull a trigger or drop a bomb. *The Pentagon Papers,* released in 1971, confirmed the criminal intentions of the US from the beginning to destroy an entire people's aspirations for freedom. The US government did not confine its grotesque illegal acts to other countries. At home, too, the government regularly suppressed dissent with illegal monitoring, prosecution, and imprisonment of those who were seriously critiquing its policies both at home and abroad. I watched military troops repress and corral thousands of protesters, including in Washington, DC, in 1971, one of my own relatives (by marriage) demonstrating against the US criminal war in Southeast Asia.

Years later I learned that in July 1969, while I was still at Binh Thuy, Nixon had developed contingency military plans under the codename Duck Hook that considered using some kind of nuclear weapons, e.g., nuclear "air bursts," against the North Vietnamese if they did not agree to a "compromise." Nixon's national security adviser, Henry Kissinger, set up a planning committee, called the September group, to "examine the option of a savage, decisive blow against North Vietnam," directing the group to start "without any preconceptions at all." Furious at the Vietnamese, Kissinger declared, "I refuse to believe that a little fourth-rate power like North Vietnam does not have a breaking point."[35]

By 1972, Nixon's Watergate scandal revealed the existence of an insidious network of domestic surveillance far beyond Nixon's earlier 1970 illegal Huston Plan—an episode of lawlessness and criminality within the highest levels of government. Eventually, I learned of the FBI's COINTELPRO program, in which more than 2,000 illegal actions were conducted against US citizens between 1956 and 1971; the CIA's Operation CHAOS, which kept tabs on 300,000 US citizens suspected of being opposed to the country's policies; and the National Security Agency's 30-year Operation Shamrock, which kept a massive watch list of people and analyzed 150,000 overseas telegraphic and telephone communications per month.[36] As stated earlier, sophisticated intelligence on US Americans began at least

---

of automatic deference to authority while looking at the US flag when knowing what it truly represents, suggested I had no choice but to embark on an experimental journey of rediscovering my moral universe and pathway forward with little guidance for taking next steps. But because the nation has never been held to account for its pattern of genocides we suffer from a national stupidity which is extremely dangerous.

35 Tuchman, 361; National Security Archive Briefing Book No. 195, "Nixon White House Considered Nuclear Options against North Vietnam, Declassified Documents Reveal—Nuclear Weapons, the Vietnam War, and the 'Nuclear Taboo,'" July 31, 2006.

36 In 1967 the CIA initiated "Operation CHAOS," exceeding its statutory authority in response to a presidential request that the agency unearth any ties between US anti-war groups and foreign interests. The operation indexed 300,000 names, kept 13,000 subject files, and intercepted large numbers of letters and cables to compile information on the domestic activities of US citizens [James Trager, *The People's Chronology* (New York: Henry Holt and Company, 1992), 1008]. The other major CIA domestic spying programs that involved collection of information about US Americans were CHAOS, MERRIMAC, and RESISTANCE [*Supplementary Detailed Staff Reports On Intelligence Activities and the Rights of Americans, Final Report of the Select Committee To Study Governmental Operations With Respect to Intelligence Activities, United States Senate* {"The Church Committee Report"} (Washington, D.C.: US Government Printing Office, 1976), 681–732]; Ward Churchill, *On the Justice of Roosting Chickens* (Oakland: AK Press, 2003), 71. However there is evidence that Operation Chaos actually began much earlier—in 1959. [Verne Lyon, "CUBA—Domestic Surveillance: The History of Operation CHAOS," *Covert Action Information Bulletin,* Summer 1990. Verne Lyon is a former CIA undercover operative].

as early as 1934 when President Roosevelt instituted a long-standing joint FBI-military program to conduct domestic intelligence with broad investigative scope.

Why on earth would I have any respect for the US judicial system or its agents, such as judges, no matter how well intentioned they might be? Why would I take an oath to uphold a paper document called the Constitution, which had long been demonstrated as intended to preserve property and elite political power over human liberty? And why would I honor the flag symbolizing a nation that had long patterns of ruthless intervention into other countries while preserving a class- and race-based system at home?

Though I dropped out of the law profession, I eventually am able to apply what I'd learned in law school in my work as an activist for justice issues at home. I took a reprieve to work first as a dairy farmer, then as director of a veterans outreach center, before turning my attention to the lawless behavior of my own country around the world, about which, of course, I had learned so personally and so viscerally in Viet Nam.

Serving as director of a storefront Viet Nam veterans outreach center in Western Massachusetts, 1983 to 1985, I became aware in a deeper way of the price soldiers pay for becoming trained killers and then applying that training in real-life war settings. A dozen local veterans committed suicide in that time. What a heavy burden the war exacted on their souls, on my soul, on all our souls!

Please, don't thank me for my service. If you want to thank me, thank me for my effort to tell the truth about the US war against Southeast Asia, if you want. But, do not thank me for my (dis)service.

340

Appendix I
Overt and Covert US Interventions Around the World, by the Numbers

560 Overt Interventions Since 1798

Drawing on the following three references, we can identify 330 (Congressional Research Service or CRS), plus 196 (Blechman minus overlap with CRS), plus 34 (Collins minus overlap with CRS and Blechman), for a total 560 US overt military interventions between 1798 and 2008.

• 330 Interventions

A report prepared for Congress by Richard Grimmett, *Instances of Use of United States Armed Forces Abroad, 1798-2008* (Washington, DC: Congressional Research Service, February 2, 2009), lists 167 interventions from 1798 (undeclared naval war with France, 1798-1800) to 1945 (WWII, 1941-45), plus 163 interventions from 1945 (China) to 2008 (Kosovo/Afghanistan).

• 196 Additional Interventions

In a study titled *Force Without War: US Armed Forces as a Political Instrument,* Appendix B (Washington, DC: The Brookings Institution, 1978), authors B. M. Blechman and S. S. Kaplan list 218 occasions on which the US used its armed forces "as a political instrument" from January 1, 1946 through December 31, 1975. Of these 218 occasions, 22 are included in the CRS report cited above, leaving 196 additional distinct interventions.

• 34 Other Interventions

Figure 4 on page 14 of J. M. Collins' *America's Small Wars: Lessons for the Future* (Washington, DC: Brassey's, 1991) lists 60 "foremost" US low intensity conflicts (LICs) from 1899 to 1990. Of these 60, 37 are *not* included in the CRS report, and of those, three are included in *Force Without War*.

Bombings of 30 Countries since WWII

The full listing of US interventions is even worse. The US military has conventionally bombed 30 countries since the end of World War II.[1]

---

[1] William Blum, *Rogue State* (Monroe, ME: Common Courage Press, 2000), 92–95; information updated by William Blum, *The Anti-Empire Report #132*, September 16, 2014: http://williamblum.org/aer/read/132.

1,240 Army Battles against Native Americans

Between 1775 and 1902, US Continental and Regular Army units engaged in over 9,000 distinct battles and skirmishes.[2] In 3,195 of these battles, regular army units incurred serious casualties (wounded/killed), and 1,240 of the battles were waged against Native Americans.[3]

Claiming 94 Islands in the Pacific and Caribbean

During the latter half of the Nineteenth Century, the US conquered over 100 islands in the Pacific and Caribbean, claiming 94 of them.[4] The 1856 Guano Island Acts (under President Franklin Pierce) authorized expeditions of US citizens that had occurred long before 1856, and for 50 years thereafter, engaged in the guano trade (seeking rich fertilizer from bird droppings on many Pacific Islands). This was commercially important and financially lucrative due to the rapid depletion of soil nutrients in the United States. Industrialized capitalist agriculture was increasingly robbing soil fertility without returning it to the land. Under authority of the Guano Acts, the US sent out ships searching for guano deposits. Between 1856 and 1903, US American entrepreneurs explored 103 locations, of which 94 islands, rocks, and keys were claimed/seized. Of these, 66 in the Caribbean and Pacific Ocean were at least temporarily recognized by the US State Department as legal US properties. However, fewer than two dozen were ever mined. Today, nine of these locations remain US possessions: Navassa Island, 1857; Baker Island, 1857; Howland Island, 1857; Jarvis Island, 1858; Johnston Atoll, 1858; Palmyra Atoll, 1859; Kingman Reef, 1860; Midway Atoll Islands, 1867; Wake Island, 1899 (US Cable Station). US began planning a route for a trans-oceanic cable in the late 1890s.

Global Imperialism Established

By the mid-nineteenth century, with finishing touches extending into the early twentieth century, the US military had conquered all continental lands and their original inhabitants, stolen half of Mexico, invaded Korea, annexed Hawaii, and conquered the Philippines, Puerto Rico, and Cuba. In its push south, by 1930, Washington had sent military gunboats into Latin American ports over 6,000 times, in addition to having invaded Cuba and Mexico once again, as well as Guatemala and Honduras, *and* taken Panama from Columbia. These aggressions, in addition to protracted wars fought in the Dominican Republic, Nicaragua, and Haiti, all enabled US corporations and financial houses to dominate the economies of most of Mexico, the Caribbean, Central America, and much of South America.

---

2 Quincy Wright, *A Study of War,* Vol II (Chicago: University of Chicago Press, 1942), 687; Francis B. Heitman, *Historical Register and Dictionary of the United States Army, 1789–1903*, Vol II (Washington, DC: GPO, 1903), 301–474.

3 Heitman, 295.

4 Jimmy M. Skaggs, *The Great Guano Rush: Entrepreneurs and American Overseas Expansion* (New York: St. Martin's Griffin, 1994), 115, 133, 200–236; John Bellamy Foster, "The Ecology of Destruction," Monthly Review, 58(9), 2007, 9–10.

Thousands of Covert Interventions since 1947

Covert operations were specifically, and broadly, defined in National Security Directive 10/2 (NSC 10/2), signed on June 18, 1948 by President Truman. In this directive, the Central Intelligence Agency (CIA), created less than a year earlier and directly answerable to the president through the newly established National Security Council (NSC), was given primary responsibility for carrying out covert actions as the NSC might from "time to time direct." There was an important stipulation, however, that "the US government can plausibly disclaim any responsibility for them."

This vaguely worded authority has been utilized thousands of times to carry out covert actions including assassination attempts, government overthrows, paramilitary operations, concerted propaganda efforts, interference in free elections, economic destabilization campaigns, and "secret" rendition, torture and murder of countless people in every corner of the world. The first indication of numbers of operations was revealed in 1976 when the Church Committee Report on CIA activities was published, and its chair, US Senator Frank Church (D-ID), stated that from 1961 to 1974 he had identified 900 major and 3,000 minor operations.[5] Former CIA officer John Stockwell extrapolated in 1990 that the CIA likely had initiated and overseen about 3,000 major and over 10,000 minor covert operations up to that time.[6]

According to historian William Blum, since the end of World War II the US has attempted to overthrow more than 50 foreign governments, attempted to assassinate more than 50 foreign leaders, attempted to suppress populist or nationalist movements in 20 countries, and seriously interfered in democratic elections in at least 30 countries.[7]

---

5 John Prados, *President's Secret Wars: CIA and Pentagon Covert Operations from World War II through the Persian Gulf* (Chicago: Elephant/Ivan R. Dee, 1996), 336.

6 John Stockwell, *The Praetorian Guard: The US Role in the New World Order* (Cambridge, MA: South End Press, 1991), 70; 1976 Church Committee: The Central Intelligence Agency: History and Documents; Final Report of the Select Committee to Study Governmental Operations with Respect to Intelligence Activities, United States Senate, Book I, Foreign and Military Intelligence (Washington: GPO, 1976).

7 William Blum, *The Anti-Empire Report #132*, September 16, 2014: http://williamblum.org/aer/read/132.

Appendix II
Casualties and Destruction in Southeast Asia

First Indochina War, 1946–1954

By 1954, the French Union Forces had some 100,000 troops, and over 200,000 Indochinese troops, some of whom later became the core of the US-financed and US-armed South Vietnamese Army. Fatalities for French Union Forces at the end of the nine-year war totaled nearly 95,000 (French, Algerians, Moroccans, Senegalese, Vietnamese, Laotians, and Cambodians), with an additional 78,000 wounded, total casualties numbering 173,000, out of more than 325,000 total troops (53 percent).[8] The Viet Minh casualties probably ran three times higher than the 173,000 of the French Union forces (i.e., over 500,000), and perhaps another 250,000 Vietnamese civilians were killed.[9] Thus, grand total casualties of the First French Indochina War likely exceeded 900,000.

Second Indochina War, 1954–1975

Human fatalities: There has long been a controversy over the number of Southeast Asians killed during the active period of US covert and overt combat operations. The Vietnamese government figures reported 2 million civilians killed in the north and 2 million civilians killed in the south for a total of 4 million civilians killed. In addition, there were 1.1 million military fatalities. Thus, 5.1 million Vietnamese were killed, not counting South Vietnamese soldiers, from 1954 to 1975.[10] When South Viet Nam disintegrated in 1975, it counted 223,748 of its fighters dead.[11] Adding this figure brings the total of Vietnamese fatalities to more than 5.3 million.

- Edward S. Herman and Noam Chomsky concluded that 4 million or more were killed in Viet Nam, 350,000 in Laos, and 600,000 in Cambodia (1969–1975), for a total of 4.95 million Southeast Asians killed.[12] Thus, combining Viet Nam with Cambodia and Laos, Herman and Chomsky estimated 4,950,000 were killed. The Cambodian figure represented 8.5 percent of a population of 7 million. For comparison, 8.5 percent of the United States population at that time (204 million in 1970) would have been 17.3 million.

---

8 James William Gibson, *The Perfect War: The War We Couldn't Lose and How We Did* (New York: Vintage Books, 1986), 67; James F. Dunnigan & Albert A. Nofi, *Dirty Little Secrets of the Vietnam War* (New York: Thomas Dunne Books, 1999), 37.

9 Horst Faas and Tim Page, *REQUIEM By the Photographers Who Died in Vietnam and Indochina* (New York: Random House, 1997), 34.

10 *Agence France*, April 4, 1995; BBC News Vietnam War History archives.

11 Faas and Page, 36.

12 Herman and Chomsky, *Manufacturing Consent* (New York: Pantheon Books, 1988), 184, 260, 263.

Appendix

- *Encyclopedia Britannica, Vietnam War, 1954–1975* reports Vietnamese official estimates of 4 million Vietnamese civilians killed, 1.1 million North Vietnamese and Viet Cong fighters killed, as many as 250,000 South Vietnamese soldiers killed, along with over 63,000 soldiers from the US, South Korea, Australia, Thailand, and New Zealand.[13] Thus, as many as 5.4 million people died in the Viet Nam war, exclusive of Laos and Cambodia. When using Herman and Chomsky's figures (above) for 350,000 killed in Laos, and 600,000 in Cambodia, the total casualties would be nearly 6.4 million.

- Robert McNamara, Secretary of War/Defense under President Johnson, reported that 3.8 million Vietnamese, North and South, military and civilians, were killed. Shocked at these numbers, he calculated that "had the United States lost in proportion to its population the same percentage as Vietnam, 27 million Americans would have been killed."[14]

- I offer another perspective. There are 58,272 US soldiers' names inscribed on the 493.5-foot-long Vietnam Veterans Memorial wall in Washington. If we use the base figure of 5 million Southeast Asians killed during the US war, a wall inscribed with that many names would be 8 *miles* long, stretching from the Lincoln Memorial to Falls Church, Virginia. A wall representing 6 million Southeast Asian dead would be 9.6 miles long, stretching from the Lincoln Memorial to Chevy Chase, Maryland.

Summary of War Dead in Vietnam

Two million civilians killed/murdered in North Viet Nam; 2 million civilians killed/murdered in South Viet Nam (out of 17 million population in the South, or 12 percent); 1.1 million North Vietnamese fighters killed, plus 223,748 South Vietnamese fighters killed. Total Vietnamese killed: over 5.32 million. Total Southeast Asians killed: 5.32 million Vietnamese, plus 600,000 Cambodians, plus 350,000 Laotians equals 6.27 million.

When adding the 58,272 US killed and the 6,155 soldiers killed from four countries allied with the US (Australia 496; New Zealand 37; South Korea 5,083; and Thailand 539),[15] the war's grand total reaches 6,334,427 dead. Most of these fatalities occurred in the 10-year active combat operations period, 1964–1973. Thus, during this period, more than 1,700 soldiers and civilians were killed on average every day.

Other Casualty Figures in Viet Nam

Air Crew Deaths. The number of US helicopter pilots and crew killed is 3,534; fixed-wing pilots and crew killed, 1,084; total air crew killed, 4,618.[16]

---

13 Encyclopedia Britannica, Vietnam War, 1954–1975, http://www.britannica.com/EBchecked/topic/628478/Vietnam-War.

14 Robert McNamara, *Argument Without End: In Search of Answers to the Vietnam Tragedy* (New York: Public Affairs, 2000), 1.

15 Faas and Page, 36.

16 Summers, 1999, 190.

Friendly Fire. An extraordinary number of US Americans were killed by friendly fire. A Pentagon study in early 1968 concluded that 15 to 20 percent of all US casualties were from friendly fire: misdirected bombs, artillery, strafing fire, and accidental discharges. In the confusion of battle, some men were shot by their own units. The intentional murder, i.e., fragging, of US officers and noncommissioned officers may have accounted for as much as 10 percent of friendly fire deaths. Since more than 58,000 US soldiers were killed in Viet Nam, as many as 11,600 could have been from friendly fire, with more than 1,100 of those from fraggings.[17]

Prostitution. After Saigon fell in 1975, the Democratic Republic of Viet Nam estimated that 200,000 Vietnamese women had become prostitutes during the war. In the mid-1960s, prostitutes earned about $700 a month, twice as much as was paid to the country's new premier.[18]

Missing Soldiers. As of May 2014, 1,642 US soldiers remain missing in Viet Nam. In historical perspective, 83,282 US Americans remain missing from all wars combined: World War II (73,624), Korean War (7,884), Cold War (126), Viet Nam war (1,642), and Iraq and other conflicts (6).[19] In contrast, 250,000[20] to 300,000[21] North Vietnamese soldiers remain missing.

Destruction Wrought by the War

First, a note regarding Viet Nam's political categories: Bombed population centers are often reported as *communities*, but in Viet Nam they are categorized as villages, hamlets, or settlements (usually of extended families). In Western reporting, "village" is the generic term used in reference to civilian population targets.

- Provinces were composed of numerous districts.
- Districts were composed of numerous villages.
- Villages were composed of a number of hamlets, usually 4–10.
- Hamlets were composed of a group of settlements.
- Settlements were clusters of families, usually 10–20.
- Average household had 6.3 persons (1965 census).

Details of Destruction in the South[22]

- Hamlets/communities damaged or destroyed: 9,000 out of 15,000
- Cattle killed: 1.5 million
- Widows: one million
- Orphans: 800,000

---

17 Appy, 1993, 185.
18 Gibson, 262–263.
19 Department of Defense, DPMO/Defense Prisoners of War, Missing Personnel Office, May 7, 2014.
20 Edward Tick, *War and the Soul* (Wheaton, IL: Quest Books, 2005), 72.
21 Haas and Page, 35.
22 Herman and Chomsky, 239.

- Farmland destroyed: 25 million acres
- Forest destroyed: 12 million acres

Details of Destruction in the North[23]

- Hamlets/communities damaged or destroyed: 4,000 out of 5,800
- Industrial cities damaged/destroyed: all 6; 3 razed to the ground)
- Provincial towns damaged or destroyed: 28 out of 30; 12 razed to the ground
- District towns damages or destroyed: 96 out of 116
- Cattle killed: 400,000
- Farmland damaged: over 1 million acres

Civilian Targets of Air War and Artillery in Southeast Asia

Of the nearly 21,000 communities that existed in all of Viet Nam prior to the war:

- 13,000 (62 percent) were severely damaged or destroyed.[24]
- In the south, 9,000 of 15,000 (60 percent) were destroyed or severely damaged.
- In the north, 4,000 of 5,800 (70 percent) were destroyed or severely damaged.
- In January 1969, over 4 million South Vietnamese, nearly a quarter of the population, experienced one or more air strikes within 1.8 miles of their hamlet.[25]

Civilian casualties by category[26]

- Refugees: 10,270,000
- Amputees: 83,000
- Paraplegics: 8,000
- Blind: 30,000
- Deaf: 10,000
- Other categories: 50,000

Destroyed Vietnamese Infrastructure (other than villages)[27]

- Dikes: 10 million cubic meters
- Hydroelectric works: 815
- Lake embankments: 1,100
- Agricultural research centers: 48 (includes destruction of 6,000 agricultural machines and 46,000 water buffalo)
- Factories: 400

---

23 Herman and Chomsky, 239.
24 Herman and Chomsky, 239.
25 Gabriel Kolko, *Anatomy of a War* (New York: The New Press, 1994), 200.
26 Gloria Emerson, *Winners & Losers* (New York: Harcourt Brace Jovanovich, 1972/1976), 357, citing data prepared by Le Anh Tu, National Action Research on the Military Industrial Complex (NARMIC), a project of American Friends Service Committee (AFSC).
27 Tick, 72–73.

- Power plants: 18
- Boats: 13,000
- Bridges: 15,100
- High schools and universities: 2,923
- Hospitals: 350
- Maternity wards: 1,500
- Churches: 484
- Pagodas: 465
- Thatched homes: 240,540

Dikes and Dams Bombed

On October 9, 1965, in the *National Guardian*, Wilfred Burchett wrote, "during August and September there has been systematic bombing of irrigation dams and flood control dikes in an attempt to produce famine and even disastrous flooding of the Red River, which could cost literally millions of lives."[28] Ten millon cubic meters of dikes were destroyed.[29]

Munitions Expended

Note: Various sources reveal different numbers.

- Eight million tons dropped by air in SEA; 7 million tons of munitions fired by ground troops.[30]
- 6,162,000 tons by USAF; 1,500,000 tons by US Navy and Marine air.[31]
- The North Vietnamese Minister of Health in 1976 told officials of the World Health Organization (WHO) that the US dropped 7.6 million tons on North Viet Nam alone, estimating total aerial tonnage dropped in SEA as 15 million tons. The Health Minister also reported 500,000 tons of toxic chemicals were dropped on North Viet Nam and seven tons of toxic gas.[32]
- 7.8 million tons were dropped by USAF on all of Southeast Asia; 7.5 million tons of munitions were fired by ground troops; 200,000 tons artillery were fired by naval forces off ships for a total of 15.5 million tons of munitions.[33]
- 13 million tons were dropped from all aircraft.[34]

---

28 *A Trumpet to Arms*, 99; Stockholm International Peace Research Institute (SIPRI), *Ecological Consequences of the Second Indochina War* (Stockholm, Sweden: SIPRI, 1976), 57–58.

29 Tick, 72–73.

30 Barry Leonard, ed., *Iraq and Vietnam: Differences, Similarities, and Insights* (Darby, PA: Diane Publishing, 2004), 10.

31 Kausik Basu, *Beyond the Invisible Hand* (Princeton, NJ: Princeton University Press, 2010), 180; Summers 199, 100.

32 Vietnam Agent Orange Relief & Responsibility Campaign, "Costs of the Vietnam War"; Emerson, 358; Gibson, 319, 495n1.

33 Vietnam Agent Orange Relief & Responsibility Campaign, "Costs of the Vietnam War"; Gibson, 495n1.

34 Dunnigan, 130.

- 7 million tons were from artillery strikes alone.[35]
- Tonnage of high explosives and shrapnel detonating from howitzers and mortars was roughly equivalent to that of all the bombs dropped.[36]
- 8 million tons of bombs were dropped in Southeast Asia.[37]
- 2.5 million tons of bombs were dropped over Laos.[38]
- Total of 13 million tons of bombs were dropped during the war, six times the total the US dropped in World War II. The total explosive force was sufficient to displace 3.4 billion tons of earth that created an estimated 26 million craters, flattening 20,000 square kilometers (7800 square miles/5 million acres) of forest, an area nearly the size of the state of Massachusetts.[39]
- B-52s alone dropped 3.5 million tons of bombs over Viet Nam.[40]
- 2.8 million tons were dropped over Cambodia.[41]
- US expended 30 billion pounds (15 tons) of munitions.[42]
- USAF dropped 7.35 million tons of bombs, a total of 15 million tons of munitions expended.[43]

Summary of Reported Tonnage Expended

The highest tonnage estimate, when adding USAF aerial bombing (7.6 million tons in North plus 7.4 million in South plus 2.8 million in Cambodia plus 2.5 million in Laos) plus Marine air (1.5 million) and Naval bombing (200,000), total artillery (7 million), and ground combat firepower (7 million), amounts to 36 million total tons. The general consensus has been 8 million tons of aerial bombs in all of Southeast Asia and about the same amount in other ordnance, for a total of 16 million tons. It is not clear whether this number takes into consideration aerial bombing in four countries, naval and ground-based artillery, and ground combat tonnage expended.

Seventy-five percent of South Viet Nam was ultimately considered a free-fire zone.[44]

---

35 Gettleman, 5.
36 Sheehan, 619.
37 Lindqvist, 163.
38 H. F. Bhojani, "Watch the US Drop 2.5 Million Tons of Bombs on Laos," *Mother Jones*, March 26, 2014.
39 Dunnigan, 131.
40 Dunnigan, 130.
41 Taylor Owen, "Bombs Over Cambodia," September 19, 2006, http://taylorowen.com/bombs-over-cambodia.
42 Tom Engelhardt, "Seeing the Reality of the Vietnam War, 50 Years Late," January 17, 2013, http://original.antiwar.com.
43 Van Nguyen Duong, The Tragedy of the Vietnam War (Jefferson, NC: McFarland, 2008), 223.
44 SIPRI, 13.

Sorties

- 3.4 million total aircraft sorties[45]
- 3.124 million fixed-wing sorties during war[46]
- 36,125,000 helicopter sorties[47]
- 127,000 B-52 sorties[48]
- 550,000 sorties by the USAF alone[49]
- 230,515 USAF sorties over Cambodia, targeting 113,716 sites[50]

B-52s

Between 1965 and 1973, US Strategic Air Command (SAC) devoted more than 200 B-52s to Southeast Asia.[51] It flew nearly 127,000 B-52 sorties, 55 percent against targets in South Viet Nam, 27 percent against targets in Laos, 12 percent in Cambodia, and 6 percent in North Viet Nam, each with a crew of six to ten with a range of more than 7,500 miles unrefueled[52] or 12,500 miles if fueled in the air.[53] B-52s alone averaged 42 sorties per day throughout the war, releasing a daily average of nearly 3,900 bombs somewhere over Indochina.[54]

Each B-52, powered by 8-engine jets, could carry 20–30 tons of bombs—as many as 84 500-pound bombs internally, plus 24 750-pound bombs on wing racks,[55] releasing them from 30,000 feet.[56] By the end of the war, 29 had been lost.[57] Each B-52 sortie cost $30,000 in bombs alone.[58] A six-plane mission could take out everything within a rectangular box approximately five-eighths of a mile wide and two miles long. It would be equivalent of taking out everything from the Lincoln Memorial to the west steps of the US Capitol building in Washington, DC, and wiping out the Departments of State, Interior, Commerce, Justice, Internal Revenue Service, the FBI, and the National Archives, among other government buildings.[59] Each B-52 damaged a strike zone of 160 acres per mission/sortie. There were an average of 4.6 B-52s per mission with an average strike zone of just under 300 acres. The total area carpeted by B-52s was just over 11 percent of the total area

---

45 Engelhardt.
46 Dunnigan, 107–108.
47 Summers, 1999, 190.
48 Summers, 1999, 321.
49 Leonard, 10.
50 Taylor Owen and Ben Kiernan, "Bombs over Cambodia: New Light on US Air War" http://japanfocus.org/products/details/2420.
51 Prados, 2009, 512.
52 Summers, 1999, 99, 321.
53 James F. Dunnigan and Albert A. Nofi, *Dirty Little Secrets of the Vietnam War* (New York: Thomas Dunne Books, 1999), 127.
54 SIPRI, 16.
55 Gibson, 229; Dunnigan, 126–130; Summers, 86.
56 Summers, 1999, 86.
57 Summers, 1999, 86.
58 Bowman, 358.
59 Neil Sheehan, *A Bright Shining Lie* (New York: Random House, 1988), 618.

of Indochina. It is estimated that 26% of South Viet Nam's area was carpeted with B-52 bombs.[60]

Craters

Twenty-six million craters flattened 4,992,000 acres of forest (7,800 square miles/20,000 square kilometers).[61] Thus, over the 13 years of bombing (1961–1973), 5,480 craters per day (228 per hour) were being created. A B-52 bomb crater could be 20 feet deep and 40 feet across.[62]

Land Impacted by Bombs/Shells

Thirty-nine million *acres* of land in Indochina were infected with fragments of bombs and shells (60,938 square miles/157,828 square kilometers).[63] This is the equivalent of 91% of the land area of South Viet Nam, or nearly 244,000 (160-acre) farms, or an area equivalent in size to all the states of New England except Connecticut. Over the 13 years of bombing, an average of 8,220 acres of land per day was severely impacted.

Artillery

Through most of the 1960s US and South Vietnamese forces possessed about 1,000 artillery pieces, mostly 105 mm and 155 mm. A single gun could fire over 100 shells a day.[64] The US deployed some 65 artillery battalions, about the same number as operated by the South Vietnamese.[65] On an average day, US artillery expended 10,000 or so rounds. At about $100 per shell, this represents $1 million per day.[66]

Chemical Warfare

- 21 million gallons of extremely poisonous chemicals (herbicides) were applied in 20,000 chemical spraying missions between 1961 and 1970, with anywhere from 2.1 million to 4.8 million Vietnamese living in 3,181 villages directly sprayed by the chemicals.[67] Agent Orange destroyed 60 percent of tropical forests.
- Agent Blue destroyed 8 percent of cultivated food crops, especially rice.
- Agent White destroyed 18 percent of inland forests.
- Over 500,000 children have already died from birth defects with an estimated 650,000 still suffering from chronic conditions;[68] 24 percent of South Viet Nam was sprayed, or

---

60 SIPRI, 16, 38.
61 Dunnigan, 131
62 Doyle and Weiss, 141.
63 Emerson, 314.
64 Dunnigan, 70.
65 Summers, 1999, 88–89.
66 Bowman, 358.
67 "Scientists Boost Estimate of Agent Orange Used in Vietnam," *USA Today*, April 16, 2003.
68 Cathy Scott-Clark and Adrian Levy, "Spectre Orange," *Guardian Unlimited,* Saturday March 29 2003: http://www.theguardian.com/world/2003/mar/29/usa.adrianlevy; Robert Dreyfuss. "Apocalypse Still,"

16,100 square miles, an area larger than the states of Connecticut, Vermont, and Rhode Island combined.
- Nearly 375,000 tons of napalm was dropped on villages.
- 1,000 square miles of South Viet Nam was leveled by incendiary bombs

Clearing by Rome Plows

Rome Plows were huge 20-ton earthmoving D7E Caterpillar tractors, fitted with a nearly 2.5-ton curved 11-foot wide attached blade protected by 14 additional tons of armor plate. Nicknamed "hog jaws," Rome Plows could splinter tree trunks 3 feet in diameter.[69] It was estimated that an average team of 25 tractors operating at any one time could clear 400 to 600 acres a day of light jungle, whereas heavy jungle clearing was limited to 100 acres a day.[70] The name Rome Plow came from Rome, Georgia, the location of the company that manufactured the huge tree-cutting blade. Over the course of the war, these machines scraped clean between 700,000 and 750,000 acres (1,200 square miles), an area equivalent to Rhode Island, leaving bare earth, rocks, and smashed trees. Each Rome Plow consumed 600 gallons of fuel per day.[71]

Unexploded Ordnance (UXO)

- 150,00–300,000 tons of UXO remain scattered around Southeast Asia.[72]
- 40,000 have been killed in Viet Nam since the end of the war in 1975, and 66,000 injured, per Viet Nam's Ministry of Labor, Invalids and Social Affairs.[73]
- 20,000 Laotians have been killed or injured since the end of the war.[74]

War Costs in Dollars

The total cost of the American war in Viet Nam for the United States, in 2013 dollars, is estimated at nearly $800 billion. Here is a sampling of the war materiel paid for by all those dollars:
- Between 1966–1972, about 13.7 billion gallons of fuel were consumed by US forces in the war.[75]

Mother Jones, January-February 2000: http://www.motherjones.com/politics/2000/01/apocalypse-still.
69 *The Vietnam Experience: A Collision of Cultures,* 141; Caputo, 42.
70 SIPRI, 49, 50.
71 Bernard William Rogers, *Vietnam Studies: Cedar Falls-Junction City: A Turning Point* (Washington, DC: Department of the Army, 1989), 64.
72 Agent Orange Relief and Responsibility Campaign,
73 Wyatt Olson, "A New Approach to Ridding Vietnam of Unexploded Ordnance," *Stars and Stripes,* May 6, 2012.
74 "Young Laotians Highlight Legacy of Unexploded Bombs," *Radio Free Asia,* April 23, 2013.
75 Agent Orange Relief and Responsibility Campaign, "Costs of the Vietnam War."

Appendix

- The US paid for 25,000 thousand barrels of fuel *each day* during the war. A barrel contained 42 gallons, meaning that a million gallons of fuel a day was expended in Viet Nam, or 365 million gallons a year.[76]
- Varied estimates of fixed-wing airplanes lost: 3,338,[77] or 3,689,[78] or 3,720.[79]
- Varied estimates of helicopters lost: 4,643,[80] or 4,857,[81] or 4865.[82] (Another 6,000 were severely damaged.) Thus, about 10,500 helicopters were destroyed or severely damaged.
- Each average helicopter cost about $250,000.[83] But, each Huey cost $300,000, each Cobra gunship cost $500,000, CH 47 Chinook cost $1,500,000, and a CH 54 Flying Crane cost $2,000,000.[84]
- Each B-52 cost nearly $8 million.[85]
- The US spent $110 billion over and above normal defense/war costs.[86]
- $168.1 billion in direct costs to US; final cost as much as $900 billion.[87] Total cost of munitions expended is estimated at $30–35 billion.[88]

---

[76] Emerson, 355; Duong, 223.
[77] Dunnigan, 107–108.
[78] Kolko, 190,
[79] Bowman, 358.
[80] Dunnigan, 109.
[81] Kolko, 190.
[82] Bowman, 358.
[83] Agent Orange Relief and Responsibility Campaign, "Costs of the Vietnam War"; Maclear, 234; Bowman, 358.
[84] Emerson, 263.
[85] Maclear, 422.
[86] Maclear, 234.
[87] Agent Orange Relief and Responsibility Campaign, "Costs of the Vietnam War."
[88] Duong, 223.

Acknowledgments

Once I began drafting the manuscript that became this book, it languished on my desk for more than a year. I sent it to a couple publishers with no response. Some may have considered it a bit unwieldy, with more than 1,400 footnotes, and difficult to categorize for marketing purposes, because it includes a combination of personal experiences while at the same time presenting those experiences in a radical, historical context. I nearly convinced myself to just forget the idea of publishing another book. However, a good friend who read the manuscript felt it was an important work, worthy of a wider audience, and was adamant that a publisher be found, sooner or later. That friend—David Hartsough, himself the author of a fine book, *Waging Peace: Global Adventures of a Lifelong Activist*—started sharing the manuscript with his friends as well as sending it to other publishers. His enthusiasm encouraged me to persevere.

Another wonderful friend, Frank Dorrel, publisher of the incredible political comic book, *Addicted to War*, which pulls no punches in its description of US history, and producer of the popular video compilation, *What I've Learned About US Foreign Policy*, liked the manuscript and began to enthusiastically share it with his contacts and successfully seeking endorsements for the book.

Michel Chossudovsky, professor of economics and director of the Centre for Research on Globalization in Canada, suggested I contact Diana Collier at Clarity Press in Georgia about publishing my manuscript. Diana was receptive, then enthusiastic, and she became a wonderful final editor in this long process. Thank you Diana.

Early in my writing process, I received invaluable guidance and feedback from professional editor Jill Kelly, and as the book took shape, I received additional professional assistance from editor Paula Friedman. I am very grateful for the involvement of my long-time friend and ex-partner, Becky Luening, in this project. Becky contributed additional copy-editing and editorial suggestions that further improved the readability of the manuscript. More, she formatted the entire book, and took on the tedious job of creating the index.

Finally, I want to express my appreciation for the people of Viet Nam, to whom I was involuntarily exposed while my country, the United States, was brutalizing them, simply because of their earnestness in fighting for, and finally achieving, self-determination. Later, I chose to voluntarily expose myself to the people of Nicaragua and El Salvador in order to better understand their efforts to achieve justice and liberation from long-time US-supported dictators. These experiences significantly contributed to my liberation from traditional Eurocentric, patriarchal conditioning, and for that I am forever grateful.

About the Author

S. Brian Willson was born to a conservative religious family in rural New York State, on Independence Day 1941. He was conscripted into the military from graduate school in 1966, and by 1969 he was commander of a USAF combat security unit in Viet Nam. Subsequently he became a trained lawyer and criminologist. Sparked by his war experiences, Willson became a student of patterns of US lawlessness in its domestic criminal injustice system as well as its foreign policy. He has been an advocate for prisoners, Viet Nam veterans, and impoverished people around the world striving for justice. As an anti-war activist, he has been a conscientious tax refuser, has participated in water-only fasts and various civil (dis)obedience actions, and has led delegations to a number of countries to document the effects of US aggression.

For participation in a lengthy, water-only "Veterans Fast for Life" on the steps of the Capitol in Washington, DC, in 1986, in protest of President Ronald Reagan's terrorist policies in Central America, Willson and three other veterans were identified by the FBI as domestic terrorist suspects. One year later, on September 1, 1987, Willson and two other vets commenced another fast, on tracks used by the Navy to move shipments of munitions by train to be loaded on a ship; weapons they believed were destined to kill innocent *campesinos* in El Salvador and Nicaragua. Willson was nearly killed on the first day of the well publicized nonviolent blocking action when, instead of following routine protocol and stopping to arrest blockers, the train crew followed orders not to stop, and sped up to over three times the 5 mph speed limit, striking Willson head on as he struggled to rise from his position sitting on the tracks. He lost both his legs below the knee and sustained a severe skull fracture and brain injury as a result of the assault. Almost thirty years later, Willson continues to walk his talk, striving for right livelihood and pursuing a simpler lifestyle within local community while speaking out against his country's unjust domestic and foreign policies. An avid cyclist, he averages 4,000 miles a year, alternating between arm-powered and leg-powered recumbent tricycles.

S. Brian Willson is the author of *Blood On The Tracks: The Life and Times of S. Brian Willson* (PM Press, 2011), and the subject of a 2016 documentary film, *Paying the Price for Peace: The Story of S. Brian Willson*. His essays and blog can be found at *brianwillson.com* and *bloodonthetracks.info*. Willson possesses a Juris Doctor degree and is a past member of the Washington, DC, Bar. He has been granted honorary doctorates in law and humanities, and has received more than two dozen awards for his peace and justice work, including Nicaragua's highest honor, the Order of Augusto Cesar Sandino, in 1988.

September 1, 1987, Concord, California Naval Weapons Station. Left to right: Michael Kroll, Felix Khatzianov, Duncan Murphy, the author, Bob Lassalle, Marilyn Coffey, and David Duncombe stand in front of the Nuremberg Actions banner. On this day, Duncan Murphy, the author, and David Duncombe, began a 40-day fasting blockade of munitions trains carrying weapons destined for Central America.

The blockers took their positions as the first train began rolling just before noon. Established protocol dictated the Navy make arrests before moving the train when demonstrators were present.

[Photos: Andy Peri]

Right: On this day, the train accelerated to more than three times the 5-mph legal speed limit, catching the blockers by surprise. As a result, the author was run over and nearly killed. It was later learned the train crew that day was ordered not to stop the train

[Photo: John Skerce]

INDEX

7th Air Force xiv, 105, 148, 309, 311, 313–314, 324–326, 330
22nd Tactical Air Support Squadron (22nd TASS) 314
823rd Combat Security Police Squadron (823rd CSPS) 308

A

A-37Bs 318–319
Abernathy, Ralph 221
Abrams, Creighton 140, 147
Acheson, Dean 29, 48, 54, 85, 87–88
Active-Duty Resistance to the War—CHART 274–288
Ad Hoc Committee of Veterans for Peace in Vietnam 273
Ad Hoc Congressional Hearings on War Crimes in Vietnam 245
Afghanistan 28, 34, 113, 165, 300–301, 303–304, 341
Agent Orange
  in Korea 184
  in Okinawa, Japan 179
  manufacturers of
    Diamond Alkali 170–171
    Dow Chemical 170, 237
    Hercules 170–171
    Hooker Chemical 171
    Monsanto 170–171
    Thompson Chemical 170
    Thompson-Hayward Agriculture and Nutrition 170
    Uniroyal 170
  US veterans' lawsuit 173–175
  Vietnamese victims' lawsuit 176
  Vietnam Map Book, The 176
Air America 109, 113–114, 146, 315
Alamogordo Test Range 34, 44
Albright, Madeleine
  interviewed by Lesley Stahl of *60 Minutes* 302
Ali, Muhammad 211, 250
All Quiet on the Western Front 309
Al Qaeda 303
American Century 22, 55, 77
American Deserters Committee 262
American Exceptionalism 3, 6, 24, 28
American Indian Movement (AIM) 223
American Legion National Americanism Committee
  Summary of Trends and Developments Exposing the Communist Conspiracy 62
American Servicemen's Union (ASU) 267, 272, 280

American Way of Life 1–2, 13, 46, 57, 78, 299
Anderson, William 161
Andreotta, Glenn 141
Anglo-Iranian Oil Company 64
Anglo-Persian Company. *See* Anglo-Iranian Oil Company
Angola 22
Anh, Colonel 319, 323–324
Appy, Christian G. 165, 268
Aptheker, Herbert 206
Arbenz, Jacabo 63–64, 68, 253
Archangel 38
Arendt, Hannah
  Eichmann in Jerusalem 155
Atlantic Charter 81–84
atomic bombings 34–35, 43–45, 58, 67, 115, 127, 216
Autobiography of Malcolm X 307

B

B-52s 129–130, 350–351
Balaguer, Joaquin 123
Ball, George 102, 134
Bao Dai 84, 86, 88, 91–94
Barger, Sonny 205
Barker, Bernard 254
Barker, Frank 139
Battle of Ap Bac 106
Bay of Pigs 68, 71, 101, 253
Beard, Charles A. 10
Beaumont, Florence 199
Beckwith, Byron de la 193
Berkeley Barb, The 204
Bernays, Edward 31
  Crystallizing Public Opinion 31
  Propaganda 31
Bernique, Roger P. 84
Berrigan, Daniel 185, 224, 241
Berrigan, Philip 217, 224, 241–242
Bertrand Russell International War Crimes Tribunal 214–215
Bill of Rights 11
Binh Thuy 313–319, 321–335
Birmingham church bombing 193–194
Black Panthers 195–196, 208, 220, 229–230, 237, 321
Blair, Tony 303
Bloody Sunday 200–201
Bolshevism 38–39, 41, 61
bombing targets, invention of 105
Bondhus, Barry 207
Borgman, John David 258, 290
Bosch, Juan 123

Brecht, Bertolt 259
British M16 intelligence 64
British Petroleum (BP) 65
Brown, Chester L. 136
Brown, George S. 148, 325
Brzezinski, Zbigniew 293, 301
  The Grand Chessboard 15
Bunch, Richard 268
Bundy, McGeorge 69, 116, 122, 134
Burchett, Wilfred 127, 134–136, 220, 348
Bush, George H. W. 183
Bush, George W. 28, 141, 238, 303
Butler, Smedley 209

C

Calley, William 140–141, 143
Cambodia 37, 52, 62, 79, 89, 94, 99, 103, 107,
    109, 127, 131, 148, 153–157, 206–207,
    213, 227, 232, 234, 244, 276, 291, 293,
    320, 344–345, 349–350
  Cambodian-Vietnamese Civil War, 1975–1979
    293
  ground invasion of 1970 157
  secret "Menu" bombings 154–155
Can Tho 84, 160, 170, 176, 315–316, 318,
    320–322, 326–334
Carmichael, Stokely 208–209, 213
Carter, Jimmy 15, 141, 301, 303–304
Castro, Fidel 68–69, 71, 112, 254
Casualties and Destruction in Southeast Asia
    Appendix II 344–352
Central Intelligence Agency (CIA) 22, 36, 41,
    43, 46, 51, 54–58, 60, 63–65, 67–71, 80,
    90, 92, 96, 98–99, 101, 105, 107–109,
    112–114, 116, 118–119, 125, 132–133,
    144, 146–148, 150, 159–162, 181–183,
    202, 221, 240, 252–254, 293, 301–302,
    311, 315, 320, 325–326, 339, 343
  National Security Act, July 26, 1947 56
  Office of Policy Coordination (OPC) 56
Central Intelligence Organization (CIO) 160
Chaffee, John 332
Chambliss, Robert Edward 193
Chaney, James Earl 194–195
chemical and germ warfare, US use of ix, 46,
    99–101, 130, 167–184, 197, 295, 351–352
  early use in Indian Wars 180
  in China 180
  in Cuba 183
  in Korea 179–184
Chiang Kai-shek 59
Chicago Eight 228, 237–238
China 13, 43, 48–49, 51, 59, 61–62, 65, 67, 74–75,
    77–80, 82–83, 85–86, 88, 94–95, 102, 115,
    136, 142, 144, 156, 158, 161, 179–183,
    277, 293, 313, 329, 337, 341
Chinese Communist Revolution 59
Chomsky, Noam 1, 66, 83, 344–345

Fifth Freedom 1, 66
Church Committee 22, 249, 339, 343
Church, Frank 22, 343
Churchill, Winston 38, 43, 52, 81
  Iron Curtain Speech 52–53
  "to strangle at its birth" (the Bolshevik state) 38
Citizens Commission of Inquiry on US War Crimes
    in Vietnam (CCI) 240, 243
Citizens Commission to Investigate the FBI 250
Citizen Soldier 244
Civil Air Transport 96
Civil Operations and Revolutionary Development
    Support (CORDS 132, 149–150, 161
Clark, Jim 200
Clark, Ramsey 242, 247, 256, 263
Clay, Cassius. *See* Muhammad Ali
Clay, Lucius 44
Clergy and Laymen Concerned About Vietnam
    (CALCAV) / Clergy and Laity Concerned
    (CALC) 146, 210, 215
Clifford, Vance Clark 137, 220
cluster bombs 159
COINTELPRO 229–230, 250, 339
Colburn, Lawrence 141
Colby, William 133, 149, 162
Cold War 29–72
Collins, Addie Mae 193
Colson, Charles 246, 249, 252–254
Columbus, Christopher 4, 5, 14, 17, 75, 295
combat refusals / mutinies / private ceasefires
    263–269, 272, 274–277, 279–280
Committee for Nonviolent Action 220
Committee for Re-election of the President
    (CREEP) 254
Committee for the Preparation of Korean Independence (CKPI) 47
Committee on Public Information (CPI) 31–33
"Communist beachhead" 63
Concerned Officers Movement (COM) 272, 276
Congress of Racial Equality (CORE) 209
Conrad, Joseph
  Heart of Darkness 36
Conscientious Objection / COs 260–261, 279–283,
    285, 287
  tradition of 263
Con Son Island prison 160–163
Constitutional Convention 8
Continental Congress 8, 25, 27
*Convention on the Prevention and Punishment of
    the Crime of Genocide* 165
Copping, J. D. 199
corporate personhood 11–12
cost of war in dollars 356
Council on Foreign Relations 77, 82
counterinsurgency (COIN) 292
counter-terror (CT) teams 132, 150–151, 159–160.
  See also provincial reconnaissance units
    (PRUs)

358

Creel, George 31–33, 42
Crimea 38
Cronkite, Walter 126, 136–137
Crumb, Jan Barry 210
CS Gas 101
Cuba 13, 27, 67–71, 76, 98, 101, 165, 183, 253, 295, 342
Cuban Missile Crisis, Psychological Impact of 71–72
Cuban Revolution 67, 232
Custer, General 15

D

Davis, Rennie 237
DC Nine 237
Dean, John 253, 256
Declaration of Independence 25, 328, 332
Defense Intelligence Agency (DIA) 293
de Gaulle, Charles 99
Dellinger, David 123, 213, 237, 238
Dellums, Ron 243, 245
  ad hoc committee hearings on war crimes in Vietnam 245, 289
Democratic Republic of Viet Nam (DRV) 83, 86, 95
desertion 114, 128, 146, 157, 160, 227, 243, 249, 260–263, 276, 280–282, 288, 316
DESOTO 114, 117
Dewey, A. Peter 84
Dewey Canyon III: Veterans Incursion into Congress 211, 244, 245, 247–249
Dewey Canyon II, secret invasion of Laos 130, 153, 157, 158, 247
Dewey Canyon I, secret invasion of Laos 153–154, 247
Dien Bien Phu 90–92, 95
Dies Committee 43
Dobrynin, Anatoly F. 71
Doctrine of Christian Discovery 4
Doi Moi 295
domestic bombings 231–233, 236, 250
domestic spying 218, 222–223, 251, 254–255, 339
Dominican Republic 13, 27, 123–124, 165, 191, 202, 342
Donovan, William "Wild Bill" 41, 63–64
draft resistance actions 202, 204, 206, 211–214, 218, 288
  Baltimore Four 217
  Big Lake One 208
  Boston Five 218
  Camden Twenty-eight 242–243
  Catonsville Nine 224
  East Coast Conspiracy to Save Lives 240
  Milwaukee Fourteen 224
drug use among US soldiers 264
Duck Hook 339
Dukakis, Michael 174–175

Dulles, Allen 55, 63–64, 90, 181
Dulles, John Foster 44, 55, 63–64, 89–93, 96
Duncan, Donald 207, 214, 220, 246, 279
  Ramparts article, Feb. 1966 207
DuPuy, William 131
Dylan, Bob
  "Subterranean Homesick Blues" 228

E

Eastern Baptist College (now Eastern University) 308
Economic Research and Action Project (ERAP) 185
economic war against Viet Nam 295
Ehrlichman, John 253
Eisenhower, Dwight 40, 63–64, 66–68
Ellsberg, Daniel 252–254, 256–257
empire as a way of life 24
England Air Force Base, Alexandria, Louisiana 233, 308, 336–337
Ensign, Tod 244
Equiano, Oloudah 17
European Recovery Program (ERP). *See* Marshall Plan
Evers, Medgar 192–193
Ewell, Julian 144–145
Executive Order 9066 35

F

Falk, Richard 146
Fall, Bernard B. 121, 166
  Hell in a Very Small Place 329
  Last Reflections on a War 329
Federal Bureau of Investigation (FBI) 20–21, 30, 36, 41, 119, 124, 137, 193–196, 201, 211, 217, 223, 225, 227, 229–230, 233, 236, 240–244, 248–257, 308, 339, 350, 355
  anti-radical division 39
Federal Employee Loyalty Program 53–54
Federalist Papers 11
Fish Committee 43
Fleming, D. F. 57
Fonda, Jane 243, 256
Ford, Gerald 238, 263
Fort Campbell, Kentucky 309, 311, 335
Founding Fathers 8–12
Four Freedoms 66
Four Minute Men 32
fragging 265–267, 315, 346
Frankfurter, Felix 40
Franklin, Benjamin 8
free-fire zones 97, 143, 153, 154, 196, 293, 316, 318–319, 326, 328, 349
French Indochina War (1946–1954) 344
  US Support of 83–92
French troops and Foreign Legionnaires
  US transport from France to Viet Nam 85

359

Freud, Sigmund 3, 31
friendly fire 265, 299, 345
Froines, John 237
Fulbright, J. William 119, 244, 247
   Foreign Relations Committee 244, 247
Fulbright University Vietnam 144
full-spectrum dominance 24

G

Gainesville Eight 246, 255–256
Galbraith, John Kenneth 256
General Electric
   war contractor 240
Geneva Agreements 92–96, 103, 109
George, Jacob 296
   Soldier's Heart 297
Ghost Dance 15
GI Alliance 273
GI Civil Liberties Defense Committee 273
GI coffeehouses 218, 273, 278, 281
Ginsberg, Allen 205
GI Press Service (GIPS) 273
GI resistance 185, 259–289, 292
GIs and Veterans for Peace 273
Glen, Tom 140
global plunder 21–23
Goebbels, Joseph 31, 33, 42
Goldberg, Arthur 207
Goldwater, Barry 115, 119–120, 308
Gonzalez, Virgilio R. 254
Goodell, Charles 228, 317
Goodman, Andrew 194–195
government repression, history of 251
Grand Area 77
Gray, Patrick 254
Green Berets 99, 101, 107, 109, 114, 160, 207, 214, 280, 283
Gregory, Dick 256
Grelecki, Ramon 84
Griffiths, Ann Mills 296
Grossman, Dave
   On Killing 270, 300
Gruening, Ernest 118
Guatemala 13, 27, 63–65, 68, 125, 224, 309, 342
Gulf of Tonkin 113–119
Gulf of Tonkin Resolution 114, 116, 118–119, 190, 240, 244, 259
Gulf War 22, 32, 302, 303

H

Hackworth, David 142, 265
Haiphong 86, 91, 158–159
Halberstam, David 190
Haldeman, H. R. 253–254
Hallinan, Terrence 268
Hamilton, Alexander 11, 31
Harkins, Paul 104, 116

Harkin, Tom 161
Harriman, W. Averell 35, 150, 152, 221
Harrisburg Eight 241–242
Hausman, James H. 47
Hawkins, Augustus 161
Hayden, Tom 189, 206, 213, 237
Heinl, Robert D., Jr. 263, 289
Heller, Joseph
   Catch 22 310
Hell's Angels 205
Helms, Richard 240
Henderson, Gregory 48
Henderson, Oran 139–140
Henry, Patrick 8
HERBS Tapes 175–176
Herman, Edward S. 146, 347
heroin 108, 146, 157, 264
Hersh, Seymour
   The Price of Power (biography of Henry Kissinger) 150
Herz, Alice 197, 199–200
Hilsman, Roger 103
Hiroshima 34, 44–45, 127, 164, 216, 302
Hitchens, Christopher
   The Trial of Henry Kissinger 150
Ho Chi Minh 47, 79–80, 83–84, 86, 91–92, 94, 99, 114, 129–130, 147–148, 154, 167, 169, 178, 221, 317
   messages to Truman 84
Ho Chi Minh Trail 114, 129–130, 154, 169, 317
Hoffa, Jimmy 326
Hoffman, Abbie 211, 213, 237
Hoffman, Julius 237
Hollywood Ten 61
Hoover, J. Edgar 30, 39–41, 119, 193–196, 201, 227, 230, 232, 240–242, 250–251, 257, 308
   Masters of Deceit: The Story of Communism in America and How to Fight It 308
House Un-American Activities Committee (HUAC) 43, 61–62
Hull, Cordell 82
Humphrey, Hubert 149–150, 222, 257
Hunt, E. Howard 252–255
Huntington, Samuel
   "The Bases of Accommodation" 148
Huston Plan 240, 253, 339
Huston, Tom Charles 240–241, 253
Hutton, Bobby 220

I

I. G. Farben 237
II-S deferment 307
impunity x, 1, 3, 4, 7, 14, 17, 20, 22, 28, 206, 226, 292, 305, 324, 339
incarceration 19–20, 35, 291
Indian schools 15–16
indigenous genocide 13–17

Indonesia 52, 87, 90–91, 94, 124–125, 132, 159
    massacre 125
insubordination 15, 265, 268, 271, 280
Intelligence Coordination and Exploitation (ICEX) 132–133
International Legal Conventions relating to conduct of war, 1907–1956 (CALCAV list) 215
International Military Tribunal (IMT) 44–45
International Volunteer Services (IVS) 161, 211
Iran 64–65, 152, 301, 304
Iraq 28, 32, 34, 163, 260, 300, 302–304, 314, 346, 348
Iron Triangle 131–132, 206
Iroquois 25, 27
ISIS / ISIL 297, 304

J

Jackson, Jimmy Lee 195, 200
Jackson, Robert H. 44–45
Javits, Jacob 317
Jay, John 9, 11
Jefferson, Thomas 8, 9, 25, 328, 332
Jeju Island 49
Jim Crow 19–21, 185, 187, 193
Johnson, Louis 87
Johnson, Lyndon B. 58, 76, 113–124, 126, 130–132, 134–135, 137, 149–150, 152, 170–171, 186, 190, 201–202, 204, 207, 210–211, 213, 218, 220, 222–223, 225, 257, 263, 279, 307, 311, 345
    announcement re November 1968 election 220
    doubts about Viet Nam, 1964 115
    reversal of Kennedy's plans 113
Jung, Carl 2, 3, 54, 119

K

Kahin and Lewis
    The United States in Vietnam 329
Keegan, John 23
Kennan, George 48, 54–55, 57–58, 61
Kennedy, Edward 256
Kennedy, Jacqueline 70
Kennedy, John F. 68–71, 76, 98–104, 107, 111–113, 119, 192, 194, 246, 311
Kennedy, Robert F. 69, 71, 119–120, 220, 224–225
Kent State Massacre 233–235
Kerner Commission 218
Kerner, Otto, Jr. 218
Kerrey, Bob
    massacre at Thang Phong Village 142–144
Kerry, John 240, 243–247, 253
Kesey, Ken 205
Khmer Rouge 293
Khrushchev, Nikita 66–67, 71, 99, 112–113
Kien Hoa Province 80, 97, 136, 142, 144, 318, 320–321
Kim Il Sung 47

King, Martin Luther, Jr. 137, 194, 196, 200–201, 203, 206, 210, 220, 221, 224, 270–271
Knapp, Robert H. 84
Kolko, Gabriel 146
Komer, Robert 132–135, 149–150
Koning, Hans 2
Korea 14, 26–27, 29, 43–44, 46–52, 54, 59, 62, 64–66, 83, 88, 89, 96, 101, 116, 128, 131, 142, 165, 179–184, 263, 265, 296, 309, 342, 345
    UN Security Council resolution to defend South Korea, June 27, 1950 49
Korean People's Republic (KPR) 47
Korea Truth Commission 49
Ku Klux Klan (KKK) 124, 193, 195, 200–201
Kuomintang 59

L

Laird, Melvin 152
Lakota (Sioux) 15, 75
Lansdale, Edward 69–70, 90, 93, 95, 99
Laos 58, 62–65, 79, 89, 94, 98–99, 101, 103, 107–110, 113–114, 122, 129–130, 148, 153–159, 169, 236, 244, 247, 250, 268, 291, 344–345, 349–350
LaPorte, Roger 199
Las Casas, Bartolomé de 4, 17
Lawyers Military Defense Committee 273
Leahy, William D. 44
Learner, Judy 253
Le Duc Tho 163, 221, 294
LeMay, Curtis 51, 121, 149, 308
Lemnitzer, Lyman 69–70, 102
levitation of the Pentagon 213
Lewis, Bernard 301
Lewis, John 186, 200–201
Liddy, G. Gordon 253–255
Lifton, Robert Jay 146
Lindsay, John 256
Linebacker 158, 271
Linebacker I and II, bombings of North Viet Nam 158
Lippman, Walter 30–31
    Public Opinion 30
Liteky, Charles 290
Little Big Horn 15
Liuzzo, Viola 200–201
Locke, John 23
Lodge, Henry Cabot 76
Lodge, Henry Cabot, Jr. 76, 112, 126, 152
London Agreement and Charter 44
Lon Nol 52
low-intensity warfare 292
LSD 205
Luce, Don 161–162
Luce, Henry 55
lynching 19, 21, 187

361

Lynd, Staughton 206
Lyttle, Brad 208

M

MacArthur, Douglas 47, 49–50, 247
Madame Nhu 111
Madison, James 8–11
Mahedy, William P.
   Out of the Night: The Spiritual Journey of Vietnam Vets 297
Mailer, Norman 213
Malcolm X 195, 224, 235, 307
Manifest Destiny 13, 23, 25, 57, 74–75
manufacture of consent 30, 31
Mao Tse-Tung 59
Marcos, Ferdinand 52
Marin, Peter
   "Living in Moral Pain" 297
Marshall, George E. 54–55
Marshall Plan 54–55
Martinez, Eugenio R. 254
Martin, Graham 163
Marx, Karl 73
Massachusetts Commissioner of Veterans Services Vietnam veteran mortality study 299–300
Mather, Cotton
   "Army of Devils" 59
Mather, Keith 269
McAlister, Elizabeth 241
McCarthy, Eugene 213
McCarthy, Joseph 59, 308
McComb Mississippi Vietnam Position 203
McCord, James 254–255
McDermott, Jim 167
McGehee, Ralph 148–149
McGovern, George 116, 240, 254–255
McGrath, J. Howard 48
McKinley, William 22, 76–77
McNair, Denise 193
McNamara, Robert 70, 73–74, 111, 117–118, 121, 126, 128, 130–131, 133, 134, 151, 168, 189, 198, 252, 331, 345
   Argument Without End 73
   In Retrospect 73
McNaughton, John 128
McReynolds, David 206, 253
Media, Pennsylvania FBI Office Break-in 250
Mee, Charles L., Jr. 35
Merry Pranksters 205
Meyer, Karl 208
Middle East 37, 64–65, 260, 301–304
Military Assistance Command Viet Nam (MACV) 104, 106, 113, 116, 132, 149, 160, 175, 324
Military Intelligence Division (MID) 41
Miller, Orloff 200
Min Ki Sik 48
Mississippi Freedom Democratic Party 203

Mitchell, John N. 238, 242, 253, 254
Mizo, George 177, 290
Mondale, Walter 256
Monroe Doctrine 23, 41, 61, 292
Montagnards 78, 102
Montagu, Ashley 18
moral injury 296–299
Morrison, Norman 198, 199, 206, 331
Morse, Wayne 118–119
Mossadegh, Mohammad 64–65
Moyers, Bill 134
Mujahideen 301
Mulligan, Joe 238
Mumford, Lewis 2, 7, 37
Murphy, Duncan 290
Muste, A. J. 208
My Lai massacre 137–141, 143, 166, 196, 220–221, 227, 233, 239–240, 245–246

N

NAACP 19, 187, 192
Nagasaki 34, 44–45, 164, 216
napalm xv–xvi, 49–51, 100–101, 109–110, 124, 130, 145, 197, 204, 211, 214, 224, 237, 323, 327, 352
National Advisory Commission on Civil Disorders (a.k.a. Kerner Commission, Riot Commission, Race Commission) 218
National Association of Black Veterans 273
National Council for Universal and Unconditional Amnesty (NCUUA) 261
National Interrogation Center (NIC) 160
National League of Families 296
National Liberation Front (NLF) 97, 104, 106, 122, 133–136, 144, 149, 156, 207–208, 213, 266, 316, 318
National Mobilization Committee to End the War in Vietnam 213, 238
National Security Action Memoranda
   NSAM 239 111
   NSAM 263 112
   NSAM 273 113–114
National Security Agency (NSA) 240, 339
National Security Council (NSC) 56–60, 69, 86, 90–91, 93, 102, 152, 168, 344
   NSC 10/2 56, 343
   NSC 20/4, "US Objectives with Respect to the USSR to Counter Soviet Threats to US Security" 58
   NSC 64 86–87
      original basis for "domino theory" 86
   NSC 68 59–60, 69, 87
   NSC 5405, "US Objectives and Courses of Action with Respect to Southeast Asia" 90
   NSC 5492/2 93–95
National Veterans Inquiry into US War Crimes 273
Navarre, Henri 89

Navarre Plan 89
New Deal 42, 46, 52, 54
New England Journal of Medicine
   report on effects of conscription on mortality 299
New Mobilization Committee to End the War 239
Newton, Huey 195
New York Draft and Military Law Panel 273
Ngo Dinh Diem 52, 94–97, 99, 105–107, 111–112,
   114, 189, 197, 319
Ngo Dinh Nhu 111–112, 147
Nguyen Ai Quoc. *See* Ho Chi Minh
Nguyen Cao Ky 52, 98, 103, 116, 124, 126,
   147–148, 159, 199, 208, 320
Nguyen Dinh Thuan 99
Nguyen Khanh 116, 319
Nguyen Thi Dinh 97
Nguyen Van Thieu 52, 150, 319
Nicaragua 13, 26–27, 41, 63, 103, 165, 290, 301,
   342, 355
Nixon, Richard 89–90, 119–120, 125, 127, 140,
   144, 148–150, 152–154, 156–158, 183,
   222, 226–227, 232, 234–235, 238–241,
   244, 246–247, 249–250, 253–257, 271,
   275, 284, 294–295, 311, 316, 326, 334, 339
   Enemies List 256
North Carolina A&T College 188
North Vietnamese People's Army (NVPA) 94
Northwest Ordinance 8
Nuremberg Principles 45–46, 215–216, 276, 279

O

Oakland Seven 212
Ochs, Phil 213
Office of Naval Intelligence (ONI) 41
Office of Strategic Services (OSS) 41, 43, 46,
   55–56, 58, 63
Office of the Coordinator of Information (COI)
   41–42
Office of War Information (OWI) 42
Officer Control Roster 311
Olsen, Clark 200
Open Door Policy 77
Operation Ajax 64–65
Operation Cedar Falls 131–132
Operation CHAOS 339
Operation Chopper 103
Operation Enduring Freedom 303
Operation Farm Gate 102–104
Operation Flaming Dart 122
Operation Gladio 56
Operation Iraqi Freedom 303
Operation Mongoose 69–71
Operation Northwoods. 70
Operation Ranch Hand 99–100, 167–175
Operation Rolling Thunder 120–122, 149, 151
Operation Safeside 309
Operation Sealord 148

Operation Shamrock 339
Operation Speedy Express 143–145, 225, 320
OPLAN 34A 113–114, 117
Orwell, George, *1984* ix–x, 30, 61
O'Sullivan, John L. 23
Overman Committee 43

P

Pacific Counseling Service 273
Palmer, Alexander Mitchell 39–40
Paris Peace Accords 163, 272, 294–295
   failed promise of 294
Paris Peace Talks, 1968 221
Parry, Robert 256
Pathet Lao 107–110, 114
Patti, Archimedes L. A. 80, 84
Patton, George S., III 152
Pawlowski, Walter 269
PAX Americana 292
Pearl Harbor 33, 35, 41, 82
Peers, W. R. 139
Pentagon Papers, The i, 34, 73–74, 90, 95, 97–98,
   102–103, 113, 121, 128, 135, 137, 220,
   252–253, 256–257, 339
People's Coalition for Peace and Justice 253
People's Liberation Armed Forces (PLAF) 106
Perot, Ross 156, 296
Peter, Paul and Mary 213
Peurifoy, John 63–64
Pham Van Dong 79, 253
Phan Rang xiv, 142, 313, 332–334
Philbrick, Herbert
   I Led Three Lives 308
Philippines 14, 27, 52, 76–77, 87, 90–91, 94, 264,
   342
Phoenix Program 88, 132–133, 160
Phong Dinh Province 176, 314, 318–319, 327
Pilgrims 5
Pine Ridge 15–16, 223
Pinter, Harold 1, 4, 305
Pleiku 122, 275–276, 317
Plumbers 253
Pol Pot 293
Poor People's Campaign 221
Post-Traumatic Stress Disorder (PTSD) ix, 270,
   297–298, 300–301, 324
Potsdam Conference 44, 83
Pound, Roscoe 40
Powell, Colin 140
Powers, Gary 66
POW/MIA 156, 294–296
Pratt, Richard 16
President's Commission on Campus Unrest
   The Scranton Report 235
Presidio Twenty-Seven 228, 268–269, 274,
   283–284
prisons and incarceration, US 291

Progressive Labor Party (PLP) 228
Project Success 64
Project Tiger 98
propaganda 29–36, 41–43, 55–57, 61, 63, 70, 124, 295–296, 328, 343
provincial interrogation center (PIC) 160, 162
provincial reconnaissance unit (PRU) 132, 150, 160
Putin, Vladimir 24, 72

Q

Quoc Dan Dang (VNQDD/Vietnamese Nationalist Party) 79

R

racism i–ii, 20, 35, 146, 165, 185, 202, 223, 265–266, 307, 321, 337
  acknowledged as cause of domestic strife 218–219
Rand, Ayn 62
Raymond, Morrison, Knudson-Brown, Root and Jones (RMK-BRJ) 162
Reagan, Ronald 63, 120, 141, 152, 183, 202, 233, 304, 355
Red Channels: The Report of Communist Influence in Radio and Television 62
Red Scare 39–40, 53–54
Reeb, James 200–201
Report upon the Illegal Practices of the United States Department of Justice 40
Reserve Officer Training Corps (ROTC) 199, 231–232, 234, 272
resistance among pilots 271–272
resistance among sailors 272
Revolutionary Youth Movement (RYM) 228
Rhee, Syngman 47, 51–52, 54, 99, 116
Ridenhour, Ron 138, 227
riots by troops 265, 274–278, 280–286
Robertson, Carole 193
Roberts, William L. 47
Robinson, Johnny 193
Rogers, William P. 152
Rome Plows 131, 352
Roosevelt Corollary 23, 292
Roosevelt Corollary of 1904 23
Roosevelt, Franklin D. 33, 35, 41–43, 64, 66, 81–82, 84–85, 251, 340
Roosevelt, Kermit "Kim" Jr. 64
Roosevelt, Theodore 23, 64
Rostow, Walt 102, 114, 116, 132
Rubin, Jerry 208–209, 213, 237
Rudd, Mark 221–222, 225
Rusk, Dean 68
Russell, Bertrand 190, 214–215
Russell, Richard 115
Russia 13, 24, 34–35, 38–39, 41, 46–47, 52, 60–61, 66, 75, 205

Russian civil war 1918–1920 38
Russian Revolution 29, 39–40
Russo, Anthony 252

S

sabotage 41, 46, 68, 70–71, 93, 95, 105, 114, 116, 150, 181, 214, 218, 242, 260, 266, 271–272, 276–277, 320
Sa Dec 176, 319
Safer, Morley 126
Saigon Military Mission (SMM) 90, 93
Santayana, George 2
Sartre, Jean-Paul 214
Saudi Arabia 301, 304
Saul, John Ralston 23
Savio, Mario 190, 209
Scherr, Max 204
Schmookler, Andrew Bard 36, 270
Schwerner, Michael Mickey 194–195
Seale, Bobby 195, 237
search and evade 267
Secord, Richard 103
Selective Service 208, 217–218, 224, 238, 241–242, 307–308
Selma-to-Montgomery march 186, 195, 200–201
Seneca 27
Shay, Jonathan
  Achilles in Vietnam: Combat Trauma and the Undoing of Character 298
Sheldrake, Rupert 2
Shoup, David M. 209
Six Nations 26
slavery of Africans 16–21
Smith, Walter Bedell 92
Son My Village. *See* My Lai massacre
Sorenson, Theodore 256
Southeast Asia
  colonial context, cultural history 78
  historical interest in 74
  strategic importance 82, 90
Southeast Asia Treaty Organization (SEATO) 93–94
Southern Christian Leadership Conference (SCLC) 189, 195
South Korean Army (ROK) 47
South Korean Marine Corps (ROKMC) 142
South Korean massacres 142
South Korean Security Forces (SKSF) 47
South Vietnamese Air Force (SVNAF) 97, 100, 102–103, 105, 116, 153, 168, 315–316, 318–319, 334
Soviet losses, WWII 60–61
Special Operations Group (SOG). *See* Studies and Operations Group (SOG)
Special Operations Unified Command 292
Spellman, Francis Joseph 94
Spock, Benjamin 213

Stars and Stripes 184, 328, 352
Steinke, Richard 274
Stimson, Henry L. 35, 43, 82
Stockwell, John 22
Stone, I. F. 54, 198
Strategic Air Command (SAC) 51, 108, 350
strategic hamlets 106, 112
Student Nonviolent Coordinating Committee (SNCC) 189, 191–192, 195, 201–202, 208–209, 231
Students for a Democratic Society (SDS) 185, 188–190, 201–202, 206–209, 213, 221–222, 228–229, 235, 253
  Days of Rage protest 228
Studies and Operations Group (SOG) 113–114, 117
Sturgis, Frank A. 254
Suharto 52
Sullivan, John 25–27
Supreme Court rulings
  and Fourteenth Amendment 6–7
  Dartmouth College Case 12
  flag burning as free speech 330
  Muhammad Ali reversal 211
  Santa Clara County v. Southern Pacific Railroad 12
  VVAW Dewey Canyon III injunction 247
Sutherland, Donald 243
SWAT Teams
  origin of 230
Syngman Rhee 26, 47, 51–52, 54, 99, 116

T

Taiwan 49, 52, 114
Tan Son Nhut Air Base xiv, 98, 105, 148, 267, 309, 324–326, 331, 335
Tarde, Gabriel 31
Taylor, Maxwell 69, 102, 126
Taylor, Telford 146, 164
teach-ins 202–203, 205, 282
Tet Offensive 135–136, 137, 150, 154
Thailand 52, 63–65, 91, 94, 96, 105, 107–109, 128, 148, 155, 271, 279, 293, 345
Thich Nhat Hanh 260, 291
Thich Quang Duc 111
Thoen, Erik 199
Thompson, Hugh 141
Three Genocides 13–24
Thurmond, Strom 128
Tick, Edward
  War and the Soul 298
tiger cages, Con Son Island 161–163
Tiger Force 142, 144
torture 5, 49, 65, 133, 149–150, 159–163, 165, 220, 304, 343
Trading with the Enemy Act 295
treaties, a cautionary note about 216–217

Truman Doctrine 37, 53–55
Truman, Harry 34, 37, 40, 42–48, 52–56, 59, 83–86, 88, 152, 311, 343
Trumbo, Dalton 61
Truong Chinh 79

U

U-2 Affair 66–67, 71
underground newspapers 264, 266, 267, 277–278, 280, 285, 289
unexploded ordnance (UXO) 352
Uniform Code of Military Justice (UCMJ) 310
United Fruit Company 63–64
United Nations 45, 49, 70, 83, 93, 95, 112, 128, 164, 181, 190, 207, 215, 293, 302
  Freedom from Hunger Campaign 172
  Resolution to defend South Korea, 1950 49
  UN Charter 83, 95, 128
United States Relations 1945–1967.
  See Pentagon Papers, The
Urgo, Joe 253, 267
US Agency for International Development (USAID) 109, 159–163
  Office of Public Safety (OPS) 159, 161
USA, legal origins of 6–13
US Army 9th Infantry Division 274, 318, 320–321, 333
US Army 29th Evacuation Hospital xvi, 324
US criminal policy and Viet Nam veterans, intersection of 254–255
US intervention, overt and covert 1, 4, 15, 22–23, 25, 27–28, 34, 38, 48, 54, 56, 65–66, 70, 73–74, 76–77, 90–91, 95, 124, 128, 164, 190, 271, 296–297, 302, 311, 337, 340
  Appendix I 341–343
US Military Assistance Advisory Group (MAAG) 88, 104
US Military Government Korea 47
US military operating principles 26
US State Department
  white paper, "A Threat to the Peace: North Vietnam's Effort to Conquer South Vietnam" 102
USS Maddox 114, 117–118
USS Ticonderoga 117, 277
USS Turner Joy 117–118

V

Vance, Cyrus 221
Vang Pao 109
Versailles Treaty 38
Veterans Administration (VA) 173, 175, 177, 184, 261, 298–300
Veterans and Reservists to End the War in Vietnam 273
veteran suicides 296–301
  exceed combat deaths 300

365

Viet Cong 102, 104–106, 115, 121
    pejorative 97
Viet Cong Infrastructure (VCI) 132–133, 150,
    160–162
Viet Minh 80–81, 83–84, 86, 88–89, 91–94,
    97–98, 344
Vietnam Agent Orange Relief and Responsibility
    Campaign (VAORRC) 177–178
Vietnam Day Committee (VDC) 204–205,
    208–209
Viet Nam Era (VNE) 259–261, 264
Vietnamese resistance 78–80
Vietnamization 144, 148–149, 152–153, 157–158,
    316, 318–319, 325
Viet Nam Moratorium protests 239, 275, 286
Vietnam Veterans Against the War (VVAW) 154,
    210–211, 240, 243–249, 248, 253–256,
    273, 276, 285, 334
Vietnam Veterans Association of Australia 300
Vinh Long City 309, 319, 323
Vinh Long Province 145, 170, 176, 318–319,
    324–325, 327
Vladivostok 38
Vo Nguyen Giap 79–80, 92

W

Walker, Daniel 225
Walker Report 225
Wallace, George 149, 186
Wallace, Henry 42, 52, 54
War Resisters League 253
Washington College of Law, American University
    307, 338
Washington, DC, jail 307
Washington, George 8, 10, 25–26
Watergate 155, 252, 254–257, 315, 339
    Robert Parry commentary on crime behind
        256–257
Watts riots 195, 219
Weathermen / Weather Underground 195, 225,
    228–229, 231–232, 236, 250
Weinberg, Albert K. 13
Weiner, Lee 237
Weinstein, Jack B. 174, 176
Welles, Sumner 82
Wesley, Cynthia 193
Westmoreland, William 28, 116, 132–135,
    145–146
Williams, Hosea 200
Williams, William Appleman 9
Wilson's Fourteen Points 81, 84
Wilson, Woodrow 12–13, 30–32, 38, 81, 84
Winne, George, Jr. 199
Winter Soldier Investigation: An Inquiry into
    American War Crimes 154, 176, 244, 246,
    249, 289
Winthrop, John 6, 13, 25, 55

Wisner, Frank 56
Women's Strike for Peace 253
Woodcock, Leonard 256
Woodstock Music Festival 238, 336
Wounded Knee 14–15, 75–76, 294

X

Xuan Thuy 221

Y

Yalta Conference 43–44

Z

Zablocki, Clement 128
Zimbardo, Philip
    The Lucifer Effect 187
Zumwalt, Elmo 172–173, 317, 332